The Contemporary Novel

A Checklist of Critical Literature
on the British and American Novel
Since 1945

by
IRVING ADELMAN

and
RITA DWORKIN

The Scarecrow Press, Inc.
Metuchen, N.J.   1972

Library of Congress Cataloging in Publication Data

Adelman, Irving.
   The contemporary novel.

    1. American fiction--20th century--History and
criticism--Bibliography. 2. English fiction--20th
century--History and criticism--Bibliography.
I. Dworkin, Rita, joint author. II. Title.
Z1231.F4A34   016.823'03   72-4451
ISBN 0-8108-0517-0

To our young
in heart--
two steve's,
a marc,
a betsey,
and a tom
again.

PREFACE

We have attempted to survey, selectively, the critical literature on contemporary British and American novels. Generally, selections are from journals and books representing literary scholarship rather than from book reviews. There are exceptions, however, because of our own judgment of the unusual quality of a review, the similar judgment of an authority on an individual writer, or, simply, a lack of other critical material.

Novelists are included if they wrote after 1945 (such as Joseph Heller), if they wrote before 1945 but achieved their most significant recognition after 1945 (such as Henry Roth and William Faulkner), or if they wrote before 1945 but continued with major publications after 1945. This last criterion includes writers such as Hemingway and excludes such as Maugham. Once a writer qualified, all his or her work (before and after 1945) for which critiques could be found was included. Some anthologies analyzed included essays or articles originally written before 1945. These have been accepted when the book fell within our period of concern.

The cut-off date on material examined is 1968 for periodicals and 1969 for books. The time lag to publication is accounted for by the fact that every article was examined, except those obviously discussing a specific novel or those few cited as "Not seen." Those pages of articles or books dealing with a specific novel were then listed under that novel. For this reason page references herein are often to a portion of a book chapter or to part of an article rather than to the chapter or article in its entirety.

At the back of this work on p. 585 is a list of Books Analyzed. This provides complete bibliographical data to works cited only briefly here and there throughout the book.

ABBREVIATIONS

AAAPSS	American Academy of Political and Social Science. Annals
A&S	Arts and Sciences (New York Univ.)
ABC	American Book Collector (Chicago)
ABR	American Benedictine Review (Atchison, Kan.)
AH	American Heritage (New York)
AI	American Imago (New York)
AIR	Adam International Review (Univ. of Rochester)
AJP	American Journal of Psychoanalysis (New York)
AL	American Literature (Duke Univ. Press)
AlaR	Alabama Review (Auburn Univ.)
ALitASH	Acta Litteraria Academiae Scientiarum Hungaricae (Budapest)
ALS	Australian Literary Studies (Univ. of Tasmania)
AmMerc	American Mercury
AmOx	American Oxonian (Philadelphia)
AN&Q	American Notes and Queries (New Haven, Conn.)
AQ	American Quarterly (Univ. of Penn. Trustees)
AR	Antioch Review
ArQ	Arizona Quarterly (Univ. of Ariz.)
AS	American Speech (Columbia Univ. Press)
ASch	American Scholar (Washington, D.C.)
AUMLA	Australasian Universities Language and Literature Association. Journal (Christ Church, N.Z.)
AusL	Australian Letters (Adelaide)
AusQ	Australian Quarterly (Sydney)
AWR	Anglo-Welsh Review (Pembroke Dock, Wales)
BA	Books Abroad (Univ. of Okla. Press)
BAASB	British Association for American Studies. Bulletin (now called: Journal of Amer. Studies; *also JAMS)
Balcony	Balcony: The Sydney Review (Univ. of Sydney)

BB	Bulletin of Bibliography and Magazine Notes (Westwood, Mass.)
BBr	Books at Brown (Brown Univ.)
BC	Book Collector (London)
BCLQ	British Columbia Library Quarterly (Victoria)
BDEC	Calcutta Univ. Dept. of English. Bulletin
BI	Books at Iowa (Univ. of Iowa)
BJA	British Journal of Aesthetics (London)
BNYPL	New York Public Library. Bulletin
BRMMLA	Rocky Mountain Modern Language Association Bulletin (Univ. of Colo.)
BSTCF	Ball State Teachers College Forum (now called: Ball State University Forum; *also BSUF)
BSUF	Ball State University Forum (*also BSTCF)
BuR	Bucknell Review
BUSE	Boston University. Studies in English
BYUS	Brigham Young University Studies
CamQ	Cambridge Quarterly (Cambridge, England)
CamR	Cambridge Review (London)
CanF	The Canadian Forum (Toronto)
CanL	Canadian Literature/ Littérature Canadienne (Vancouver)
CarQ	Carolina Quarterly (Chapel Hill, N.C.)
Carrell	The Carrell (Friends of Univ. of Miami, Fla., Library)
CaSE	Carnegie Series in English (Carnegie Inst. of Tech.)
CathW	Catholic World (New York)
CC	Cross Currents (West Nyack, N.Y.)
CCTE	Conference of College Teachers of English of Texas. Proceedings
CE	College English (Champaign, Ill.)
CEA	CEA Critic (College English Association)
CEJ	California English Journal (Auburn, Cal.)
CEMW	Columbia Essays on Modern Writers (Pamphlet series. Columbia Univ.)
CenR	Centennial Review (Mich. St. Univ.; *also CentR)
CentR	Centennial Review (Mich. St. Univ.; *also CenR)
ChC	Christian Century (Chicago)
ChiR	Chicago Review (Univ. of Chicago)
Chr&Cr	Christianity and Crisis (New York)
ChrPer	Christian Perspectives (Toronto)
ChS	Christian Scholar (New Haven, Conn.; now

	called: Soundings)
CimR	Cimarron Review (Okla. St. Univ.)
CJF	Chicago Jewish Forum (now suspended)
CL	Comparative Literature (Univ. of Oregon)
CLAJ	College Language Association Journal (Morgan St. College, Baltimore)
ClareQ	Claremont Quarterly (Claremont, Cal.)
CLQ	Colby Library Quarterly (Waterville, Me.)
CLS	Comparative Literature Studies (Univ. of Ill.)
CM	Cornhill Magazine (London)
ColQ	Colorado Quarterly (Univ. of Colo.)
Comment	Wayne State University Graduate Comment
ConnR	Connecticut Review (Hartford)
ConR	Contemporary Review (London)
CQ	Classical Quarterly (London)
CRAS	Centennial Review of Arts and Sciences (Michigan St. Univ.)
Crit	Critique: Studies in Modern Fiction (Minneapolis)
CritQ	Critical Quarterly (Manchester)
CritR	Critical Review (Univ. of Melbourne)
CS	Cahiers du Sud (Marseilles)
Ctary	Commentary (New York)
CUF	Columbia University Forum
CW	Classical World (Lehigh Univ.)
CWCP	Contemporary Writers in Christian Perspective (Grand Rapids, Mich.)
Cweal	Commonweal (New York)
DA	Dissertation Abstracts International (Ann Arbor, Mich.)
Delta	Delta: The Cambridge Literary Review (Cambridge, England)
DenverQ	Denver Quarterly (Univ. of Denver)
DESB	Delta Epsilon Sigma Bulletin (Loras College, Dubuque)
DilimanR	Diliman Review (Univ. of the Philippines)
DM	Dublin Magazine
DownR	Downside Review (Bath, England)
DR	Dalhousie Review (Halifax, N.S.)
DubR	Dublin Review (London; now called Wiseman Review [*WiseR])
DUJ	Durham University Journal (England)
DWB	Dietsche Warande en Belfort (Antwerp)
EA	Etudes Anglaises (Vanves, France; and Philadelphia)

E&S	Essays and Studies by Members of the English Association (Oxford Univ.)
ECr	L'Esprit Createur (Lawrence, Kan.)
EDH	Essays by Divers Hands (Royal Soc. of Lit., London)
EdL	Educational Leadership (Washington, D.C.)
EFT	English Fiction in Transition (1880-1920) (Purdue Univ.)
EIC	Essays in Criticism (Bucks, England)
EJ	English Journal (Nat. Council of Teachers of Eng.)
EL	Educational Leader (Pittsburg, Kansas St. College)
ELH	ELH: Journal of English Literary History (Johns Hopkins)
ELN	English Language Notes (Univ. of Colorado)
EM	English Miscellany (Rome)
EMD	An English Miscellany (St. Stephen's College, Delhi)
English	English (English Association, London)
EngR	English Record (N.Y. State English Council)
ES	English Studies (Netherlands)
ESA	English Studies in Africa (Johannesburg)
ESELL	Essays and Studies in English Language and Literature (Sendai, Japan)
ESQ	Emerson Society Quarterly (Hartford)
ESRS	Emporia State Research Studies (Kansas St. Teachers College of Emporia)
ET	Expository Times (Edinburgh)
EUQ	Emory University Quarterly
EvR	Evergreen Review (New York)
EWN	Evelyn Waugh Newsletter (Nassau Comm. College, Garden City, N.Y.)
EWR	East-West Review (Doshisha Univ., Kyoto, Japan)
Expl	Explicator (Va. Commonwealth Univ.)
Explor	Explorations (Univ. of Toronto)
FitzN	Fitzgerald Newsletter (Charlottesville, Va.)
FloQ	Florida Quarterly (Univ. of Fla.)
ForumH	Forum (Univ. of Houston; now called Forum of Texas)
FP	Filoloski Pregled (Belgrade)
FQ	Four Quarters (La Salle College)
FR	French Review (Amer. Assoc. of Teachers of French)
FurmS	Furman Studies (Furman Univ.)

GaR	Georgia Review (Univ. of Ga.)
GHQ	Georgia Historical Quarterly (Savannah)
HAB	Humanities Association Bulletin (Univ. of New Brunswick, Canada)
HarvardA	Harvard Advocate (Cambridge, Mass.)
HC	The Hollins Critic (Hollins College, Va.)
HINL	History of Ideas Newsletter (New York)
HJ	Hibbert Journal (London)
HJAS	Hitotsubashi Journal of Arts and Sciences (Tokyo)
HLQ	Huntington Library Quarterly (San Marino, Cal.)
HPR	The Homiletic and Pastoral Review (New York)
HudR	Hudson Review (New York)
IEY	Iowa English Yearbook (Iowa State Univ.)
IHML	International Henry Miller Letter (Nijmegen, Netherlands)
IJES	Indian Journal of English Studies (Calcutta)
ILA	International Literary Annual (London)
IrEccRec	Irish Ecclesiastical Record (Dublin)
IrM	Irish Monthly (Dublin)
ISB	Independent School Bulletin (Nat'l. Assoc. of Indep. Schools, Boston)
Ital	Italica (Amer. Assoc. of Teachers of Italian)
JA	Jahrbuch für Amerikastudien (West Berlin)
JAAC	Journal of Aesthetics and Art Criticism (Wayne St. Univ.)
JAF	Journal of American Folklore (Univ. of Texas Press)
JAmS	Journal of American Studies (London; *also BAASB)
JCL	Journal of Commonwealth Literature (Univ. of Leeds)
JCMVASA	Central Mississippi Valley American Studies Association. Journal (Lawrence, Kan.)
JEGP	Journal of English and Germanic Philology (Univ. of Ill.)
JGE	Journal of General Education (Penn. St. Univ.)
JIAS	Journal of Inter-American Studies (Univ. of Miami, Fla.)

JJQ	James Joyce Quarterly (Univ. of Tulsa)
JNH	Journal of Negro History (Washington, D.C.)
JP	Journal of Philosophy (Columbia Univ.)
JPC	Journal of Popular Culture (Bowling Green, Ohio, Univ.)
KAL	Kyusha American Literature (Fukuoka, Japan)
KFQ	Keystone Folklore Quarterly (Point Park College, Pittsburgh)
KM	Kansas Magazine (Kansas St. Univ.; now called Kansas Quarterly)
KN	Kwartalnik Neofilologiczny (Warsaw)
KR	Kenyon Review (suspended pub. in 1970)
KSJ	Keats-Shelley Journal (Harvard Univ., Cambridge, Mass.)
KyR	The Kentucky Review (Univ. of Kentucky)
LaH	Louisiana History (Baton Rouge)
L&P	Literature and Psychology (Fairleigh Dickinson Univ.)
LauR	Laurel Review (W. Va. Wesleyan College)
LC	Library Chronicle (Univ. of Pennsylvania)
LCrit	Literary Criterion (Univ. of Mysore, India)
LCUT	Library Chronicle (Univ. of Texas)
LE&W	Literature East and West (Modern Lang. Assoc. of Amer.)
LetN	Lettres Nouvelles (Paris)
LHR	Lock Haven Review (Lock Haven St. College, Penn.)
LHY	Literary Half-Yearly (Mysore, India)
LitR	Literary Review (Fairleigh Dickinson Univ.)
LonM	London Magazine
LS	Spectator (London)
LSUSHS	Louisiana State University Studies. Humanities Series
LWU	Literatur in Wissenschaft und Unterricht (Kiel, Germany)
M&M	Masses and Mainstream (New York)
MAQR	Michigan Alumnus Quarterly Review (Ann Arbor: now called: Mich. Quarterly Review)
MASJ	Midcontinent American Studies Journal (Lawrence, Kansas; now called: American Studies)

McNR	McNeese Review (McNeese State College, Lake Charles, La.)
MCR	Critical Review: Melbourne (Univ. of Melbourne)
MF	Midwest Folklore (Indiana Univ.)
MFS	Modern Fiction Studies (Purdue Univ.)
MGW	Manchester Guardian Weekly
MidR	Midwest Review (Nebraska St. Teachers College, Wayne)
MinnR	Minnesota Review (St. Paul)
MissQ	Mississippi Quarterly (Miss. St. Univ.)
MJ	Midwest Journal (Lincoln Univ., Jefferson City, Mo.)
MLN	Modern Language Notes (Johns Hopkins Press)
MLQ	Modern Language Quarterly (Univ. of Washington)
MM	Maclean's Magazine (Toronto)
ModA	Modern Age (Chicago)
MP	Modern Philology (Univ. of Chicago)
MQ	Midwest Quarterly (Kansas St. College of Pittsburg)
MR	Massachusetts Review (Univ. of Mass.)
MRR	Mad River Review (Dayton, Ohio)
MS	Moderna Sprak (Modern Lang. Teachers Assoc. of Sweden; *also MSpr)
MSCS	Mankato State College Studies (Minn.)
MSE	Massachusetts Studies in English (Amherst)
MSpr	Moderna Sprak (Sweden; *also MS)
MTJ	Mark Twain Journal (Kirkwood, Mo.)
NALF	Negro American Literature Forum (Ind. St. Univ.)
N&Q	Notes and Queries (London)
NatR	National Review (New York)
NDQ	North Dakota Quarterly (Univ. of N. Dak.)
NEQ	New England Quarterly (Bowdoin College)
NFS	Nottingham French Studies (Univ. of Nottingham, England)
NM	Neuphilologische Mitteilungen (Helsinki)
NMQ	New Mexico Quarterly (Univ. of New Mexico; *also NMQR)
NMQR	New Mexico Quarterly Review (Univ. of New Mexico; *also NMQ)
NMW	Notes on Mississippi Writers (Univ. of So. Miss.)
NOQ	Northwest Ohio Quarterly (Maumee, Ohio)
NoR	Northern Review (Montreal)

NRep	New Republic (Washington, D.C.)
NRF	Nouvelle Revue Française (Paris)
NS	Die Neuren Sprachen (Frankfurt)
NSammlung	Neue Sammlung (Göttingen, W. Germany)
NS&N	New Statesman and Nation (London; *also NS&Nation)
NS&Nation	New Statesman and Nation (London; *also NS&N)
NStat	New Statesman (London)
NWR	Northwest Review (Univ. of Oregon)
NY	New Yorker
NyA	Nya Argus (Helsingfors [i.e., Helsinki])
NYHTBR	New York Herald Tribune Book Review (ceased publication)
NYHTBW	New York Herald Tribune Book Week (ceased publication)
NYRB	New York Review of Books
NYTBR	New York Times Book Review
NYTMag	New York Times Magazine
OJES	Osmania Journal of English Studies (Osmania Univ., Hyderabad)
OL	Orbis Litterarum (Copenhagen)
OR	Oxford Review (Cleveland)
OUR	Ohio University Review
OW	Orient/West (Tokyo)
PacSp	Pacific Spectator (Stanford, Cal.)
P&L	Politics and Letters (London)
P&PR	Psychoanalysis and the Psychoanalytic Review (New York; now called: Psychoanalytic Review; *also PsyR)
Par	Paragone (Florence, Italy)
ParisR	Paris Review (Flushing, N.Y.)
PBSA	Bibliographical Society of America. Papers
PCTEB	Pennsylvania Council of Teacher of English Bulletin
PELL	Papers on English Language and Literature (So. Ill. Univ.; now called: Papers on Language and Literature; *also PLL)
Per	Perspective (Washington Univ.)
Person	Personalist (Univ. of So. Cal.)
PhoenixC	Phoenix (College of Charleston, S.C.)
PhoenixK	Phoenix (Korea Univ.)
PLL	Papers on Language and Literature (So. Ill. Univ.)

PMASAL	Michigan Academy of Science, Arts, and Letters. Papers (now called: Michigan Academician)
PMLA	Publications of the Modern Language Association of America (New York)
PolQ	Political Quarterly (London)
PolR	Polish Review (New York)
PQ	Philological Quarterly (Univ. of Iowa)
PR	Partisan Review (New Brunswick, N.J.)
Prov	Provincial (Indianapolis)
PrS	Prairie Schooner (Univ. of Nebr.)
PSQ	Political Science Quarterly (Columbia Univ.)
PsyR	Psychoanalytic Review (New York; formerly P&PR)
PUASAL	Proceedings of the Utah Academy of Sciences, Arts, and Letters (Salt Lake City)
PULC	Princeton University Library Chronicle
PUSA	Perspectives U.S.A. (New York)
QJS	Quarterly Journal of Speech (New York)
QQ	Queen's Quarterly (Kingston, Ont.)
QRL	Quarterly Review of Literature (Princeton, N.J.)
RdP	Revue de Paris (Paris)
REL	Review of English Literature (Leeds)
Ren	Renascence (Viterbo College, La Crosse, Wis.)
RevN	La Revue Nouvelle (Paris)
RIB	Revista Interamericana de Bibliografía/Inter-American Review of Bibliography (OAS, Washington, D.C.)
RIP	Rice Institute Pamphlets (Houston; now called: Rice Univ. Studies)
RLC	Revue de Littérature Comparée (Paris)
RLM	La Revue des Lettres Modernes (Paris)
RLV	Revue des Langues Vivantes (Brussells)
RomN	Romance Notes (Univ. of N.C.)
RPol	Review of Politics (Notre Dame, Ind.)
RQ	Riverside Quarterly (Univ. of Saskatchewan)
RS	Research Studies (Washington St. Univ.)
RSSCW	Washington State (Univ.). Research Studies
RUO	Revue de l'Université d'Ottawa (Canada)
RusR	Russian Review (Hoover Inst., Stanford, Cal.)

SA	Studi Americani (Rome)
SAB	South Atlantic Bulletin (Chapel Hill, N.C.)
Salmagundi	Salmagundi (Skidmore College)
S&S	Science and Society (New York; *also Sci&Soc)
SAQ	South Atlantic Quarterly (Duke Univ.)
SatR	Saturday Review (New York; *also SRL)
SB	Studies in Bibliography (Univ. of Va. Bibliographical society)
SCB	South Central Bulletin (South Central Modern Lang. Assoc., Houston; *also SoCB)
Sci&Soc	Science and Society (New York; *also S&S)
SDD-UW	Summaries of Doctoral Dissertations, Univ. of Wis.
SDR	South Dakota Review (South Dakota Univ.)
SEEJ	Slavic and East European Journal (Univ. of Wis. Press)
SEER	Slavonic and East European Review (Cambridge Univ. Press)
SEL	Studies in English Literature/Sibungaku Kinkyu (English Literary Soc. of Japan, Tokyo; *also SELit)
SELit	Studies in English Literature (*also SEL)
SELL	Studies in English Language and Literature (Tokyo)
SFQ	Southern Folklore Quarterly (Univ. of Fla.)
SG	Studium Generale (W. Berlin)
SGG	Studia Germanica Gandensia (Ghent)
ShawR	Shaw Review (Penn. St. Univ. Press)
Shen	Shenandoah (Washington and Lee Univ.)
SHR	Southern Humanities Review (Auburn Univ.)
SLitI	Studies in the Literary Imagination (Georgia St. Univ.)
SNL	Satire Newsletter (State Univ. College, Oneonta, N.Y.)
SoCB	South Central Bulletin (South Central Modern Lang. Assoc., Houston; *also SCB)
SoQ	The Southern Quarterly (Univ. of So. Miss.)
SoR	Southern Review (Louisiana St. Univ.)
SoRA	Southern Review (Univ. of Adelaide)
Soviet Lit	Soviet Literature (Moscow)
SovietR	Soviet Review (White Plains, N.Y.)
SR	Sewanee Review (Univ. of the South)
SRA	Studia Romanica et Anglica-Zagrebiensia (Zagreb, Yugoslavia)
SRL	Saturday Review of Literature (*also SatR)
SS	Scandinavian Studies (Lawrence, Kan.)
SSF	Studies in Short Fiction (Newberry College, S.C.)

SSJ	Southern Speech Journal (Univ. of Ga.)
SSL	Studies in Scottish Literature (Univ. of S.C. Press)
StL	Studies on the Left (New York; ceased publication 1967)
Studies	Studies: An Irish Quarterly (Dublin)
SUS	Susquehanna University Studies (Selingsgrove, Pa.)
SWR	Southwest Review (So. Methodist Univ. Press)
SWS	Southwest Writers Series (Steck-Vaughn, Austin)
Sym	Symposium (Syracuse Univ. Press)
TamR	Tamarack Review (Toronto)
T&T	Time and Tide (London)
TC	Twentieth Century (London)
TCL	Twentieth Century Literature (Los Angeles)
TCM	Twentieth Century (Victoria, Australia)
TEAS	Twayne's English Author Series
TFSB	Tennessee Folklore Society Bulletin (Middle Tenn. St. Univ.)
Thoth	Thoth (Syracuse Univ.)
THQ	Tennessee Historical Quarterly (Nashville)
Tirade	Tirade (Antwerp)
TJ	Tolkien Journal (Belknap College, N.H.)
TLS	Times Literary Supplement (London)
TP	Terzo Programma (Rome)
TPRSL	Royal Society of Literature. Transactions and Proceedings (London)
TQ	Texas Quarterly (Univ. of Texas)
TriQ	Tri-Quarterly (Northwestern Univ.)
TSE	Tulane Studies in English
TSL	Tennessee Studies in Literature (Knoxville)
TSLL	Texas Studies in Literature and Language (Univ. of Texas; *formerly TxSE)
TUSAS	Twayne's United States Authors Series
TWA	Wisconsin Academy of Science, Arts, and Letters. Transactions
TWAS	Twayne's World Authors Series
TxSE	Texas Studies in English (Univ. of Texas; now called Texas Studies in Literature and Language [*TSLL])
UA	United Asia (Bombay)
UCQ	University College Quarterly (Mich. St. Univ.)

UCSSLL	University of Colorado Studies. Series in Language and Literature
UDQ	University of Denver Quarterly
UES	UNISA English Studies (Univ. of S. Africa)
UHQ	Utah Historical Quarterly (Salt Lake City)
UKCR	University of Kansas City Review (now called: University Review [*UR])
UMPAL	University of Minnesota. Pamphlets on American Literature
UMPAW	University of Minnesota. Pamphlets on American Writers
UMPEAL	University of Miami. Publications in English and American Literature
UMSE	University of Mississippi Studies in English
UR	University Review (Kansas City; *formerly UKCR)
USCAD	University of Southern California. Abstracts of Dissertations
USFLQ	USF Language Quarterly (Univ. of S. Fla.)
UTQ	University of Toronto Quarterly
UTSH	University of Tennessee (Nashville). Studies in the Humanities
UVM	University of Virginia Magazine (*also UVMag)
UVMag	University of Virginia Magazine (*also UVM)
UWR	University of Windsor Review (Ontario)
VN	Victorian Newsletter (New York Univ.)
VQR	Virginia Quarterly Review (Univ. of Va.)
WAL	Western American Literature (Colo. St. Univ.)
WascanaR	Wascana Review (Regina, Sask.)
WCR	West Coast Review (Simon Fraser Univ., B.C.)
WF	Western Folklore (Univ. of Cal. Press)
WHR	Western Humanities Review (Univ. of Utah)
WiseR	Wiseman Review (London; *formerly DubR)
WisSL	Wisconsin Studies in Literature (Wisc. Council of Teachers, Oshkosh)
WoR	World Review (Univ. of Queensland, Australia)
WR	Western Review (West. New Mexico Univ.)
WSCL	Wisconsin Studies in Contemporary Literature (Univ. of Wis.; now called: Contemporary Literature)
WTW	Writers and Their Work(British Council, London)

WVUPP	West Virginia University Philological Papers
WWR	Walt Whitman Review (Wayne St. Univ. Press)
XR	X, A Quarterly Review (London)
XUS	Xavier University Studies
YCGL	Yearbook of Comparative and General Literature (Univ. of N.C. Studies in Comparative Literature)
YFS	Yale French Studies
YLM	Yale Literary Magazine
YR	Yale Review
YULG	Yale University Library Gazette
ZAA	Zeitschrift für Anglistik und Amerikanistik (Leipzig)

A CHECKLIST OF CRITICAL LITERATURE
ON THE BRITISH AND AMERICAN NOVEL SINCE 1945

AGEE, JAMES, 1909-1955.

GENERAL

Behar, Jack, "James Agee: The World of His Work," DA, XXIV (1964), 4690 (Ohio State).

Burger, Nash K., "A Story to Tell: Agee, Wolfe, Faulkner," SAQ, LXIII (1964), 32-43.

Fitzgerald, Robert, "James Agee: A Memoir," KR, XXX (1968), 587-624. Also (expanded) in Fitzgerald, R., "Introduction," Collected Short Prose of James Agee, Boston: Houghton, 1969.

Frohock, W.M., "James Agee: The Question of Unkept Promise," SWR, XLII (Summer, 1957), 221-9. Also in Frohock, W.M., "James Agee: The Question of Wasted Talent," in Novel of Violence in America, 212-230.

Hayes, Richard, "Rhetoric of Splendor," Cweal, LXVIII (September 12, 1959), 591-2.

MacDonald, Dwight, "James Agee," Encounter, XIX (December, 1962), 73-84.

Ohlin, P.H., Agee.

Perry, J. Douglas, Jr., "James Agee and the American Romantic Tradition," DA, XXIX (1968), 1233A (Temple).

da Ponte, Durant, "James Agee: The Quest for Identity," TSL, VIII (Winter, 1963), 25-37.

Seib, K., James Agee.

A DEATH IN THE FAMILY

Dupee, F.W., "The Prodigious James Agee," New Leader, XL (December 9, 1957), 20-1. Also in Dupee, F.W., King of the Cats, 80-4.

Fiedler, Leslie, "Encounter With Death," NRep, CXXXVII (December 9, 1957), 25.

Frohock, W.M., Novel of Violence in America, 225-9.

Hayes, Richard, "Rhetoric of Splendor," Cweal, LXVIII (September 12, 1958), 591-2.

Hoffman, F.J., Art of Southern Fiction, 75-7.

Kazin, A., Contemporaries, 185-7. Also in Kostelanetz,
  R., ed., On Contemporary Literature, 223-4.
MacDonald, Dwight, "Death of a Poet," NY, XXXIII (No-
  vember 16, 1957), 224-41.
Ohlin, P.H., Agee, 194-214.
Roe, Michael M., Jr., "A Point of Focus in James Agee's
  A DEATH IN THE FAMILY," TCL, XII (October, 1966),
  149-53.
Ruhe, Edward, Epoch, VIII (Winter, 1958), 247-51.
Seib, K., James Agee, 73-96.
Sosnoski, James J., "Craft and Intention in James Agee's
  A DEATH IN THE FAMILY," JGE, XX (1968), 170-83.
Stuckey, W.J., Pulitzer Prize Novels, 181-4.
Sullivan, Walter, in Rubin, L.D., Jr., and R.D. Jacobs,
  eds., South, 387-8.
Trilling, Lionel, "The Story and the Novel," The Griffin,
  VII (January, 1958), 4-12.

THE MORNING WATCH

Chase, Richard, "Sense and Sensibility," KR, XIII (Autumn,
  1951), 688-91.
Frohock, W.M., "James Agee: The Question of Unkept
  Promise," SWR, XLII (1957), 228. Also in Frohock,
  W.M., Novel of Violence in America, 224-5.
Hoffman, F.J., Art of Southern Fiction, 77-81.
Ohlin, P.H., Agee, 182-94.
Phillipson, John S., "Character, Theme, and Symbol in
  THE MORNING WATCH," WHR, XV (Autumn, 1961),
  359-67.
Pryce-Jones, Alan, "Preface" to THE MORNING WATCH,
  N.Y.: Ballantine Books, 1966.
Seib, K., James Agee, 69-73.

BIBLIOGRAPHY

Ohlin, P.H., Agee, 239-47.
Seib, K., James Agee, 153-72.

ALGREN, NELSON, 1909-

GENERAL

Allen, W., Modern Novel, 154-5.
Anderson, Alston, and Terry Southern, "Nelson Algren,"
  in Writers at Work, 1st Series, 231-49.

Bluestone, George, "Nelson Algren," WR, XXII (Autumn, 1957), 27-44.
Donohue, H.E.F., Conversations with Nelson Algren, N.Y.: Hill and Wang, 1964.
Eisinger, C.E., Fiction of the Forties, 73-85.
Geismar, Maxwell, "Nelson Algren: The Iron Sanctuary," CE, XIV (March, 1953), 311-15. Also in EJ, XLII (March, 1953), 121-5. Also (expanded) in American Moderns, 187-94.
Grebstein, Sheldon N., "Nelson Algren and the Whole Truth," in French, W., ed., Forties, 298-309.
Lipton, Lawrence, "A Voyeur's View of the Wild Side: Nelson Algren and His Critics," ChiR, X (Winter, 1957), 4-14. Also in Ray, David, ed., Chicago Review Anthology, Chicago: Un. of Chicago Pr., 1951, 31-41.
Miyamoto, Youkichi, "Chicago Naturalism-Nelson Algren," SEL, XXXVI (1959), 177-8. (not seen)
O'Connor, W.V., Grotesque, 9-11.
Omick, Robert E., "Compassion in the Novels of Nelson Algren," DA, XXVIII (1968), 3194A (Iowa).
Perlongo, Robert A., "Interview with Nelson Algren," ChiR, XI (Autumn, 1957), 92-8.
Walcutt, C.C., American Literary Naturalism, 299-300.

THE MAN WITH THE GOLDEN ARM

Bluestone, George, "Nelson Algren," WR, XXII (1957), 35-9.
Eisinger, C.E., Fiction of the Forties, 81-5.
Geismar, Maxwell, "Nelson Algren: The Iron Sanctuary," CE, XIV (1953), 311-15. Also in EJ, XLII (1953), 123-4. Also in Geismar, M., American Moderns, 191-2.
Gelfant, B., American City Novel, 252-7.
Grebstein, Sheldon N., in French, W., ed., Forties, 305-9.
Veler, Richard P., "THE MAN WITH THE GOLDEN ARM: A Genetic Study," DA, XXV (1965), 7281 (Ohio State).

NEVER COME MORNING

Bluestone, George, "Nelson Algren," WR, XXII (1947), 30-3.
Eisinger, C.E., Fiction of the Forties, 77-80.
Geismar, Maxwell, "Nelson Algren: The Iron Sanctuary," CE, XIV (1953), 312-13. Also in EJ, XLII (1953), 122-3. Also in Geismar, M., American Moderns, 189-90.
Grebstein, Sheldon N., in French, W., ed., Forties, 302-5.

SOMEBODY IN BOOTS

Bluestone, George, "Nelson Algren," WR, XXII (1957), 27-30.
Eisinger, C. E. , Fiction of the Forties, 76-7.
Grebstein, Sheldon N. , in French, W. , ed. , Forties, 301-2.
Green, Gerald, in Madden, D. , ed. , Proletarian Writers of
    the Thirties, 27-8.

A WALK ON THE WILD SIDE

Bluestone, George, "Nelson Algren," WR, XXII (1957), 40-3.
Widmer, L. , "Contemporary American Outcasts," in Liter-
    ary Rebel, 130-1.

AMIS, KINGSLEY, 1922-

GENERAL

Amis, Kingsley, "My Kind of Comedy," TC, CLXX (July,
    1961), 46-50.
Bergonzi, Bernard, "Kingsley Amis," LonM, N.S. III (Janu-
    ary, 1964), 50-65.
Caplan, Ralph, in Shapiro, C. , ed. , Contemporary British
    Novelists, 3-15.
Chase, Richard, "Middlebrow England. The Novels of Kings-
    ley Amis," Ctary, XXII (September, 1956), 263-9.
Colville, Derek, "The Sane New World of Kingsley Amis,"
    BuR, IX (March, 1960), 46-57.
Gindin, J. , "Kingsley Amis' Funny Novels," in Postwar
    British Fiction, 34-50.
Green, Martin, "Amis and Salinger: The Latitude of Private
    Conscience," ChiR, XI, iv (Winter, 1958), 20-5.
Hamilton, Kenneth, "Kingsley Amis, Moralist," DR, XLIV
    (Autumn, 1964), 339-47.
Harkness, Bruce, "The Lucky Crowd- Contemporary British
    Fiction, EJ, XLVII (October, 1958), 392-4.
Heppenstall, R. , Fourfold Tradition, 213-25.
Hilty, Peter, "Kingsley Amis and Mid-Century Humor,"
    Discourse, III (January, 1960), 26-8.
Hurrell, John D. , "Class and Consciousness in John Braine
    and Kingsley Amis," Crit, II, i (1958), 39-53.
Lebowitz, Naomi, "Kingsley Amis: The Penitent Hero," Per,
    X (Summer-Autumn, 1958), 129-36.
Lodge, David, "The Modern, the Contemporary, and the Im-
    portance of Being Amis," CritQ, V, iv (Winter, 1963),
    335-54. Also in Language of Fiction: Essays in Criti-

cism and Verbal Analysis of the English Novel, London: Routledge and Kegan Paul; N. Y.: Columbia Un. Pr., 1966, 249-67.

Moberg, George, "Structure and Theme in Amis's Novels," CEA, XXV, vi (March, 1963), 7, 10.

O'Connor, W. V., "Kingsley Amis: That Uncertain Feeling," in New University Wits, 75-102.

Rabinovitz, R., Reaction Against Experiment in the English Novel, 38-63.

Smith, Robert B., "An Analysis of the Novels of Kingsley Amis," DA, XXVI (1965), 2762 (Un. of Washington).

THE ANTI-DEATH LEAGUE

Anon., in TLS (March 17, 1966). Also Anon., "Novels of 1966. Kingsley Amis: THE ANTI-DEATH LEAGUE" in T. L. S. Essays and Reviews, 1966, 29-31.

Byatt, A. S., "Mess and Mystery," Encounter, XXVII (July, 1966), 59-62.

I LIKE IT HERE

Allsop, K., Angry Decade, 55-7.

Hopkins, Robert H., "The Satire of Kingsley Amis's I LIKE IT HERE," Crit, VIII, ii (1966), 62-70.

Hurrell, John D., "Class and Consciousness in John Braine and Kingsley Amis," Crit, II, i (1958), 50-2.

Lodge, David, "The Modern, the Contemporary, and the Importance of Being Amis," CritQ, V, iv (Winter, 1963), 349-54. Also in Language of Fiction: Essays in Criticism and Verbal Analysis of the English Novel, London: Routledge and Kegan Paul; N. Y.: Columbia Un. Pr., 1966, 261-67.

O'Connor, W. V., New University Wits, 94-6.

Smith, Robert B., "An Analysis of the Novels of Kingsley Amis," DA, XXVI (1965), 2762 (Un. of Washington).

I WANT IT NOW

Anon., in TLS (October 10, 1968). Also Anon., "Fiction of 1968. Kingsley Amis: I WANT IT NOW," in T. L. S. Essays and Reviews from the Times Literary Supplement, 1968, 186-8.

Bradbury, Malcolm, "Delayed Orgasm," NStat (October 11, 1968), 464, 466.

LUCKY JIM

Allen, Walter, Modern Novel, 279-81.
_____, Reading a Novel, 58-61.
_____, in NStat & Nation, XLVII (January 30, 1954). Also
  in Feldman, Gene, and Max Gartenberg, eds., The Beat
  Generation and the Angry Young Men, N.Y.: Citadel,
  1958, 339-41.
Allsop, K., Angry Decade, 43-52.
Boyle, Ted E., and Terence Brown, "The Serious Side of
  Kingsley Amis's LUCKY JIM," Crit, IX, i (1967), 100-7.
Brophy, B., in Sunday Times Magazine Colour Supplement
  (London) (January 26, 1964), 11, 13. Also in Don't Never
  Forget, 217-22.
Conquest, Robert, "Christian Symbolism in LUCKY JIM,"
  CritQ, VII (Spring, 1965), 87-92.
Hurrell, John D., "Class and Consciousness in John Braine
  and Kingsley Amis," Crit, II, i (1958), 43-8.
Karl, F.R., "The Angries: Is There a Protestant in the
  House?" in Contemporary English Novel, 220-9.
Lodge, David, "The Modern, the Contemporary, and the Im-
  portance of Being Amis," CritQ, V, iv (Winter, 1963),
  341-5. Also in Language of Fiction: Essays in Criticism
  and Verbal Analysis of the English Novel, London: Rout-
  ledge and Kegan Paul; N.Y.: Columbia Un. Pr., 1966,
  250-5.
Mehoke, James S., "Sartre's Theory of Emotion and Three
  English Novelists: Waugh, Green, and Amis," Wisconsin
  Studies in Literature, No. 3 (1966), 110-11.
Noon, William T., S.J., "Satire: Poison and the Profes-
  sor," EngR, XI (Fall, 1960), 56.
O'Connor, W.V., New University Wits, 85-90, passim.
Proctor, Mortimer R., English University Novel, Berkeley
  and Los Angeles: Un. of California, 1957, 175-6.
Rippier, J.S., Some Postwar English Novelists, 140-9.
Smith, Robert B., "An Analysis of the Novels of Kingsley
  Amis," DA, XXVI (1965), 2762 (Un. of Washington).

ONE FAT ENGLISHMAN

Anon., in TLS (November 14, 1963). Also, Anon., "Novels
  of 1963. Kingsley Amis: ONE FAT ENGLISHMAN," in
  T.L.S.: Essays and Reviews from the Times Literary
  Supplement, 1963, 107-9.
Furbank, P.N., Encounter, XXII (January, 1964), 76-7.
Hamilton, Kenneth, "Kingsley Amis, Moralist," DR, XLIV
  (Autumn, 1964), 345-7.

Kuehn, Robert E. , "Fiction Chronicle," WSCL, VI (1965), 138-9.
Smith, Robert B. , "An Analysis of the Novels of Kingsley Amis," DA, XXVI (1965), 2762 (Un. of Washington).
Soule, George, "The High Cost of Plunging," Carleton Miscellany, V (Fall, 1964), 106-11.

TAKE A GIRL LIKE YOU

Coleman, John, "King of Shaft," Spectator, No. 6900 (September 23, 1960), 445-6.
Lodge, David, "The Modern, the Contemporary, and the Importance of Being Amis," CritQ, V, iv (Winter, 1963), 346-9. Also in Language of Fiction: Essays in Criticism and Verbal Analysis of the English Novel, London: Routledge and Kegan Paul; N.Y.: Columbia Un. Pr. , 1966, 257-9.
O'Connor, W.V. , New University Wits, 96-8.
Parker, R.B. , "Farce and Society: The Range of Kingsley Amis," WSCL, II, iii (Fall, 1961), 27-38.
Rippier, J.S. , Some Postwar English Novelists, 154-8.
Ross, T.J. , "Lucky Jenny, or Affluent Times," NRep, CXLIV (March 27, 1961), 21-2.
Smith, Robert B. , "An Analysis of the Novels of Kingsley Amis," DA, XXVI (1965), 2762 (Un. of Washington).
Urwin, G.G. , ed. , Taste for Living, 145-8.

THAT UNCERTAIN FEELING

Allsop, K. , Angry Decade, 52-5.
Chase, Richard, "Middlebrow England: The Novels of Kingsley Amis," Ctary, XXII (September, 1956), 264-7.
Hurrell, John D. , "Class and Consciousness in John Braine and Kingsley Amis," Crit, II, i (1958), 49-50.
O'Connor, W.V. , New University Wits, 90-4.
Rees, David, "That Petrine Cock," Spectator (August 27, 1965), 268-9.
Rippier, J.S. , Some Postwar English Novelists, 149-53.
Smith, Robert B. , "An Analysis of the Novels of Kingsley Amis," DA, XXVI (1965), 2762 (Un. of Washington).
Wilson, Edmund, "Is It Possible to Pat Kingsley Amis?" NY (March 24, 1956), 140-2. Also in Wilson, E. , The Bit Between My Teeth, N.Y.: Farrar, Straus & Giroux, 1965, 274-81.

ASHTON-WARNER, SYLVIA

INCENSE TO IDOLS

Stevens, J., New Zealand Novel, 106-8.

SPINSTER

Bettelheim, Bruno, "Violence: A Neglected Mode of Behav-
ior," AAAPSS, CCCLXIV (March, 1966), 57-9.
Stevens, J., New Zealand Novel, 103-6; 127-8.

AUCHINCLOSS, LOUIS, 1917-

GENERAL

Kane, Patricia, "Lawyers at the Top: The Fiction of Louis
Auchincloss," Crit, VII, ii (Winter, 1964-65), 36-46.
Milne, W. Gordon, "Auchincloss and the Novel of Manners,"
UKCR, XXIX (March, 1963), 177-85.

THE HOUSE OF FIVE TALENTS

Macauley, Robie, "Let Me Tell You About the Rich...," KR,
XXVII (Autumn, 1965), 653-5.

THE RECTOR OF JUSTIN

Auchincloss, L., "Writing THE RECTOR OF JUSTIN" in
McCormack, T., ed., Afterwords, 3-9.
Spender, Stephen, "Traditional vs. Underground Novels," in
Encyclopedia Britannica, Great Ideas Today, 1965, 186-7.

VENUS IN SPARTA

Allen, W., Modern Novel, 313-14.

BAKER, ELLIOTT

A FINE MADNESS

Noland, Richard W., "Lunacy and Poetry: Elliott Baker's
A FINE MADNESS," Crit, VIII, iii (Spring-Summer, 1966),
71-8.

BALDWIN, JAMES, 1924-

GENERAL

Alexander, Charlotte, "The 'Stink' of Reality: Mothers and
Whores in James Baldwin's Fiction," L&P, XVIII (1968),
9-26.

Anon., in TLS (September 6, 1963). Also, Anon., "Black
Man's Burden: James Baldwin as Man and Writer," in
T.L.S.: Essays and Reviews from The Times Literary
Supplement, 1963, 16-21.

Arana, Gregorio, "The Baffling Creator--A Study of the
Writing of James Baldwin," Caribbean Qtly, XII (1966),
3-23. (Not seen.)

Bhattacharya, Lokenath, "James Baldwin," Quest (India),
No. 44 (Winter, 1965), 78-83.

Bone, Robert A., Negro Novel in America, 215-18.
_____, "The Novels of James Baldwin," TriQ, No. 2
(Winter, 1965), 3-20. Also in Gross, S.L., and J.E.
Hardy, eds., Images of the Negro in American Literature,
265-88.

Boyle, Kay, "Introducing James Baldwin," in Moore, H.T.,
ed., Contemporary American Novelists, 155-7.

Bradford, Melvin E., "Faulkner, James Baldwin and the
South," GaR, XX (Winter, 1966), 431-43.

Breit, Harvey, in Balakian, N., and C. Simmons, eds.,
Creative Present, 5-18.

Britt, David D., "The Image of the White Man in the Fiction
of Langston Hughes, Richard Wright, James Baldwin and
Ralph Ellison," DA, XIX (1968), 1532A (Emory).

Charney, Maurice, "James Baldwin's Quarrel with Richard
Wright," AQ, XV (Spring, 1963), 65-75.

Cleaver, Eldridge, "Notes on a Native Son," Ramparts, V
(June, 1966), 51-6.

Coles, Robert, "Baldwin's Burden," PR, XXXI (Summer,
1964), 409-16.

Eckman, Fern M., The Furious Passage of James Baldwin,
N.Y.: M. Evans, 1966.

Elkoff, Marvin, "Everybody Knows His Name," Esquire,
LXII, ii (August, 1964), 59-64+.

English, Charles, "Another Viewpoint," Jubilee, XI (August,
1963), 43-6.

Finkelstein, S., Existentialism and Alienation in American
Literature, 276-84.

Finn, James, "The Identity of James Baldwin," Cweal,
LXXVII (October 26, 1962), 113-16.

Gayle, Addison, Jr., "A Defense of James Baldwin," CLAJ,
    X (March, 1967), 201-8.
Gray, Simon, "Whose Little Boy?" Delta (Cambridge, Eng-
    land), No. 35 (Spring, 1965), 2-8.
Gross, Theodore, "The World of James Baldwin," Crit, VII,
    ii (Winter, 1964-65), 139-49.
Harper, H. M., Jr., "James Baldwin--Art or Propaganda?"
    in Desperate Faith, 137-61.
Howe, I., "Black Boys and Native Sons," in A World More
    Attractive, 98-122.
Isaacs, Harold R., "Five Writers and their African Ances-
    tors," Phylon, XXI (1960), 322-9.
Jones, B. F., "James Baldwin: The Struggle for Identity,"
    Brit Jnl of Soc, XVII (June, 1966), 107-21.
Kent, George E., "Baldwin and the Problem of Being,"
    CLAJ, VII (March, 1964), 202-14.
Langer, Lawrence, "To Make Freedom Real: James Baldwin
    and the Conscience of America," in Lanzinger, Klaus, ed.,
    Americana-Austriaca, 217-28.
Lash, John S., "Baldwin Beside Himself: A Study in Modern
    Phallicism," CLAJ, VIII (December, 1964), 132-40.
Lee, Brian, "James Baldwin: Caliban to Prospero," in
    Bigsby, C. W. E., ed., Black American Writer, Vol. I,
    169-79.
MacInnes, Colin, "Dark Angel: The Writings of James Bald-
    win," Encounter, XXI, ii (August, 1963), 22-33.
Margolies, E., "The Negro Church: James Baldwin and the
    Christian Vision," in Native Sons, 102-26.
Mergen, Bernard, "James Baldwin and the American Conun-
    drum," MSpr, LVII (1963), 397-406.
Noble, D. W., Eternal Adam and the New World Garden,
    215-16.
O'Brien, C. C., "White Gods and Black Americans," NStat
    (May, 1964). Also in Writers and Politics, N. Y.:
    Pantheon, 1964, 17-22.
O'Daniel, Therman B., "James Baldwin: An Interpretive
    Study," CLAJ, VII (September, 1963), 37-47.
Sayre, Robert F., "James Baldwin's Other Country," in
    Moore,* H. T., ed., Contemporary American Novelists,
    158-69.
Schroth, Raymond A., S. J., "James Baldwin's Search,"
    CathW, CXCVIII (February, 1964), 288-94.
Standley, Fred L., "James Baldwin: The Crucial Situation,"
    SAQ, LXV (Summer, 1966), 371-81.
Van Sickle, Milton, "James Baldwin in Black and White,"
    Trace, No. 54 (Autumn, 1964), 222-5.
Watson, Edward A., "The Novels of James Baldwin: Case-

Book of a 'Lover's War' with the United States," QQ, LXXII (1965), 385-402.

Zietlow, Edward R., "Wright to Hansberry: The Evolution of Outlook in Four Negro Writers," DA, XXVIII (1967), 701A (Un. of Washington).

ANOTHER COUNTRY

Alexander, Charlotte, "The 'Stink' of Reality: Mothers and Whores in James Baldwin's Fiction," L&P, XVIII (1968), 15-21.

Auchincloss, Eve, and Nancy Lynch, "Disturber of the Peace: James Baldwin, An Interview," in Bigsby, C. W. E., ed., Black American Writer, Vol. I, 199-215.

Ayman, S. E., "No Country of Young Men," in Standards, 78-82.

Beja, Morris, "It Must Be Important: Negroes in Contemporary American Fiction," AR, XXIV (Fall, 1964), 333-6.

Berry, Boyd M., "Another Man Done Gone: Self Pity in Baldwin's ANOTHER COUNTRY," Mich Qtly Rev, V (Fall, 1966), 285-90.

Blount, Trevor, "A Slight Error in Continuity in James Baldwin's ANOTHER COUNTRY," N&Q, XIII (March, 1966), 102-3.

Bone, Robert A., Negro Novel in America, 228-39.
_____, "The Novels of James Baldwin," TriQ, No. 2 (Winter, 1965), 12-20. Also in Gross, S. L., and J. E. Hardy, eds., Images of the Negro in American Literature, 278-88.

Collier, Eugenia W., "The Phrase Unbearably Repeated," Phylon, XXV (Fall, 1964), 288-96.

Cox, C. B., and A. R. Jones, "After the Tranquilized Fifties: Notes on Sylvia Plath and James Baldwin," CritQ, VI (Summer, 1964), 115-19.

Dane, Peter, "Baldwin's Other Country," Transition, V (1966), 38-40.

Finkelstein, S., Existentialism and Alienation in American Literature, 280-4.

Finn, James, "The Identity of James Baldwin," Cweal, LXXVII (October 26, 1962), 114-16.

Glazier, Lyle, "Suffering Doesn't Have a Color," Litera, VIII (1965), 91-8.

Gross, Theodore, "The World of James Baldwin," Crit, VII, ii (1965), 142-6.

Harper, H. M., Jr., in Desperate Faith, 151-9.

Hentoff, Nat, in Midstream, VIII (December, 1962), 103-6.

Klein, M., in After Alienation, 188-95.

Lee, Brian, "James Baldwin: Caliban to Prospero," in
    Bigsby, C. W. E. , ed. , Black American Writer, Vol. I,
    173-6.
Littlejohn, D. , Black on White, 125-33.
MacInnes, Colin, "Dark Angel: The Writings of James Bald-
    win," Encounter, XXI, ii (August, 1963), 28-31.
Margolies, E. , "The Negro Church: James Baldwin and the
    Christian Vision," in Native Sons, 118-22.
Newman, Charles, "The Lesson of the Master: Henry James
    and James Baldwin," YR, LVI (Autumn, 1966), 45-59.
Podhoretz, Norman, "In Defense of a Maltreated Best Seller,"
    Show, II (October 1962), 91-2. Also in Kostelanetz, R. ,
    ed. , On Contemporary Literature, 232-7. Also in Pod-
    horetz, N. , Doings and Undoings, 244-50.
Sayre, Robert F. , in Moore, H. T. , ed. , Contemporary Am-
    erican Novelists, 165-9.
Thelwell, Mike, "ANOTHER COUNTRY: Baldwin's New York
    Novel," in Bigsby, C. W. E. , ed. , Black American Writer,
    Vol. I, 181-98.
Watson, Edward A. , "The Novels and Essays of James Bald-
    win," QQ, LXXII (Summer, 1965), 305-7.

GIOVANNI'S ROOM

Alexander, Charlotte, "The 'Stink' of Reality: Mothers and
    Whores in James Baldwin's Fiction," L&P, XVIII (1968),
    9-15.
Bone, Robert A. , Negro Novel in America, 226-8.
_____, "The Novels of James Baldwin," TriQ, No. 2
    (Winter, 1965), 10-12. Also in Gross, S. L. , and J. E.
    Hardy, eds. , Images of the Negro in American Literature,
    275-8.
Harper, H. M. , Jr. , Desperate Faith, 147-51.
Hoffman, Stanton, "The Cities of Night: John Rechy's CITY
    OF NIGHT and the American Literature of Homosexuality,"
    ChiR, XVII, ii-iii (1964-65), 198-200.
Klein, M. , After Alienation, 184-8.
Littlejohn, D. , Black on White, 124-5.
MacInnes, Colin, "Dark Angel: The Writings of James Bald-
    win," Encounter, XXI, ii (August, 1963), 25-8.
Margolies, E. , "The Negro Church: James Baldwin and the
    Christian Vision," in Native Sons, 114-18.
Noble, D. W. , Eternal Adam and the New World Garden,
    212-15.
Sayre, Robert F. , in Moore, H. T. , ed. , Contemporary
    American Novelists, 163-5.
Straumann, H. , American Literature in the Twentieth

Century, 40-1.
Watson, Edward, "The Novels and Essays of James Baldwin," QQ, LXXII (Summer, 1965), 391-2.

GO TELL IT ON THE MOUNTAIN

Alexander, Charlotte, "The 'Stink' of Reality: Mothers and Whores in James Baldwin's Fiction," L&P, XVIII (1968), 21-3.
Allen, W., Modern Novel, 320-1.
Bloomfield, Caroline, "Religion and Alienation in James Baldwin, Bernard Malamud, and James F. Powers," Religious Education, LVII (March-April, 1962), 100-1.
Bone, Robert A., Negro Novel in America, 218-25.
_____, "The Novels of James Baldwin," TriQ, No. 2 (Winter, 1965), 5-10. Also in Gross, S. L., and J. E. Hardy, eds., Images of the Negro in American Literature, 268-75.
Cartey, Wilfred, "The Realities of Four Negro Writers," CUF, IX (Summer, 1966), 34-42.
Gérard, Albert, "Humanism and Negritude: Notes on the Contemporary Afro-American Novel," Diogenes, No. 37 (Spring, 1962), 127-32.
Graves, Wallace, "The Question of Moral Energy in James Baldwin's GO TELL IT ON THE MOUNTAIN," CLAJ, VII (March, 1964), 215-23.
Gross, John, "Day of Wrath," NStat (July 19, 1963), 79-80.
Harper, H. M., Jr., Desperate Faith, 142-7.
Hassan, I., Radical Innocence, 81-3.
Kent, George E., "Baldwin and the Problem of Being," CLAJ, VII (March, 1964), 204-7.
Klein, M., After Alienation, 178-84.
Lee, Brian, "James Baldwin: Caliban to Prospero," in Bigsby, C. W. E., ed., Black American Writer, Vol. I, 172-3.
Littlejohn, D., Black on White, 121-4.
MacInnes, Colin, "Dark Angel: The Writings of James Baldwin," Encounter, XXI, ii (August, 1963), 23-5.
Marcus, Steven, "The American Negro in Search of Identity," Ctary, XVI (November, 1953), 459-63.
Margolies, E., "The Negro Church: James Baldwin and the Christian Vision," in Native Sons, 109-14.
Noble, D. W., Eternal Adam and the New World Garden, 209-12.
Sayre, Robert F., in Moore, H. T., ed., Contemporary American Novelists, 161-3.
Scott, Nathan A., Jr., "Judgment Marked by a Cellar: The

American Negro Writer and the Dialectic of Despair,"
UDQ, II, ii (1967), 26-9. Also in Mooney, H. J., and
T. F. Staley, eds., Shapeless God, 159-61.
Watson, Edward, "The Novels and Essays of James Baldwin,"
QQ, LXXII (Summer, 1965), 386-8.

TELL ME HOW LONG THE TRAIN'S BEEN GONE

Howe, Irving, "James Baldwin: At Ease in Apocalypse,"
Harper, CCXXXVII (September, 1968), 92-5.
Lee, Brian, "James Baldwin: Caliban to Prospero," in
Bigsby, C. W. E., ed., Black American Writer, Vol. I,
177-9.
Thompson, John, "Baldwin: The Prophet as Artist," Ctary,
XLV (June, 1968), 67-9.

BIBLIOGRAPHY

Fischer, Russell, "James Baldwin: a bibliography, 1947-
1962," BB, XXIV (January-April, 1965), 127-30.
Gross, S. L., and J. E. Hardy, eds., Images of the Negro in
American Literature, 301-2.
Kindt, Kathleen A., "James Baldwin, A Checklist: 1947-
1962," BB, XXIV (January-April, 1965), 123-6.
Standley, F. L., "James Baldwin: a checklist, 1963-1967,"
BB, XXV (May-August, 1968), 135-7, 160.

BARTH, JOHN, 1930-

GENERAL

Bluestone, George, "John Wain and John Barth: The Angry
and the Accurate," MR, I (May, 1960), 582-9.
Enck, John, "John Barth: An Interview," WSCL, VI (Winter-
Spring, 1965), 3-14.
Garis, Robert, "What Happened to John Barth?" Ctary, XLII
(October, 1966), 89-95.
Gross, Beverly, "The Anti-Novels of John Barth," ChiR,
XX (November, 1968), 95-109.
Kostelanetz, Richard, "The New American Fiction," Ram-
parts, III (January-February, 1965), 57-60. Also in
New American Arts, 203-10.
Noland, Richard W., "John Barth and the Novel of Comic
Nihilism," WSCL, VII (Autumn, 1966), 239-57.
Samuels, Charles T., "John Barth: A Buoyant Denial of
Relevance," Cweal, LXXXV (October 21, 1966), 80-2.

Stubbs, John C., "John Barth as a Novelist of Ideas: The
  Themes of Value and Identity," Crit, VIII, ii (Winter,
  1965-66), 101-16.
Tanner, Tony, "The Hoax That Joke Bilked," PR, XXXIV
  (Winter, 1967), 102-9.
Trachtenberg, Alan, "Barth and Hawkes: Two Fabulists,"
  Crit, VI, ii (1963), 4-18.

THE END OF THE ROAD

Boyers, Robert, "Attitudes Toward Sex in American 'High
  Culture'," AAAPS, CCCLXXVI (March, 1968), 47-9.
Kerner, David, "Psychodrama in Eden," ChiR, XIII (Winter-
  Spring, 1959), 59-67.
Noland, Richard, "John Barth and the Novel of Comic Real-
  ism," WSCL, VII (Autumn, 1964), 244-7.
Raban, J., "Narrative: Cause and Contingency," in Tech-
  nique of Modern Fiction, 76-8.
Smith, Herbert F., "Barth's Endless Road," Crit, VI (Fall,
  1963), 68-76.
Stubbs, John C., "John Barth as a Novelist of Ideas: The
  Themes of Value and Identity," Crit, VIII, ii (Winter,
  1965-66), 105-8.
Trachtenberg, Alan, "Barth and Hawkes: Two Fabulists,"
  Crit, VI (Fall, 1963), 11-15.

THE FLOATING OPERA

Hyman, Stanley E., "John Barth's First Novel," New Leader,
  XLVIII (April 12, 1965), 20-1.
Kostelanetz, Richard, "The New American Fiction," Ram-
  parts, III (January-February, 1965), 58-9. Also in New
  American Arts, 209-10.
Noland, Richard, "John Barth and the Novel of Comic Real-
  ism," WSCL, VII (Autumn, 1966), 239-44.
Schickel, Richard, "THE FLOATING OPERA," Crit, VI (Fall,
  1963), 53-67.
Stubbs, John C., "John Barth as Novelist of Ideas: The
  Themes of Value and Identity," Crit, VIII, ii (Winter,
  1965-66), 102-5.

GILES GOAT-BOY

Byrd, Scott, "GILES GOAT-BOY Visited," Crit IX, i (1967),
  108-12.
Kiely, Benedict, "Ripeness Was Not All: John Barth's
  GILES GOAT-BOY," HC, III (December, 1966), 1-12.

McColm, Pearlmarie, "The Revised New Syllabus and the Unrevised Old," DenverQ, I (Autumn, 1966), 136-8.

Samuels, Charles T., "John Barth: A Buoyant Denial of Relevance," Cweal, LXXXV (October 21, 1966), 80-2.

Scholes, R., Fabulators, 135-73.

Tanner, Tony, "The Hoax That Joke Bilked," PR, XXXIV (Winter, 1967), 102-9.

LOST IN THE FUNHOUSE

Knapp, Edgar H., "Found in the Barthhouse: Novelist as Savior," MFS, XIV (Winter, 1968-69), 446-51.

THE SOT-WEED FACTOR

Diser, Philip E., "The Historical Ebenezer Cooke," Crit, X, iii (1968), 48-59.

Fiedler, Leslie A., "John Barth, an Eccentric Genius," New Leader, XLIV (February 13, 1961), 22. Also in Kostelanetz, R., ed., Contemporary Literature, 238-43.

Holder, Alan, "What Marvelous Plot... Was Afoot? History in Barth's THE SOT-WEED FACTOR," AQ, XX (1968), 596-604.

Hyman, S. E., "The American Adam," in Standards, 204-8.

Kostelanetz, Richard, "The New American Fiction," Ramparts, III (January-February, 1965), 57-8. Also in New American Arts, 203-9.

Lee, L. L., "Some Uses of FINNEGANS WAKE in John Barth's the Sot-Weed," JJQ, V (Winter, 1968), 177-8.

Lewis, R. W. B., "Days of Wrath and Laughter," in Trials of the Word, 220-6.

Miller, Russell H., "THE SOT-WEED FACTOR: A Contemporary Mock-Epic," Crit, VIII, ii (Winter, 1965-66), 88-100.

Noland, Richard, "John Barth and the Novel of Comic Realism," WSCL, VII (Autumn, 1966), 247-56.

Rovit, Earl, "The Novel as Parody: John Barth," Crit, VI (Fall, 1963), 77-85.

Stubbs, John C., "John Barth as a Novelist of Ideas: The Themes of Value and Identity," Crit, VIII, ii (Winter, 1965-66), 108-13.

Sutcliffe, Denham, "Worth a Guilty Conscience," KR, XXIII (Winter, 1961), 181-6.

Trachtenberg, Alan, "Barth and Hawkes: Two Fabulists," Crit, VI (Fall, 1963), 15-18.

BIBLIOGRAPHY

Bryer, Jackson R. , "John Barth," Crit, VI (Fall, 1963),
86-9.

BASSO, HAMILTON, 1904-

GENERAL

Cowley, Malcolm, "The Writer as Craftsman: The Literary
Heroism of Hamilton Basso," SatR, XLVII (June 27, 1964),
17-18.

IN THEIR OWN IMAGE

Bishop, J. P. , "Vanity Fair," NRep (May 29, 1938).   Also
in Collected Essays, 254-5.

SUN IN CAPRICORN

Milne, G. , American Political Novel, 132-4.
Rubin, Louis D. , Jr. , "All the King's Meanings," GaR, VII
(1954), 422-3.   Also in Rubin, L. D. , Curious Death of
the Novel, 222-5.

THE VIEW FROM POMPEY'S HEAD

Hoffman, F. J.   Art of Southern Fiction, 25-6.

BECKETT, SAMUEL, 1906-

GENERAL

Allsop, K. , Angry Decade, 37-40.
Anon. , "Paradise of Indignity," TLS (March 28, 1958), 168.
Beckett at 60: A Festschrift, London: Calder and Boyars,
1967.
Bersani, Leo, "No Exit for Beckett," PR, XXXIII (Spring,
1966), 261-8.
Brooke-Rose, Christine, "Samuel Becket and the Anti-Novel,"
LonM, V, xii (December, 1958), 38-46.
Chambers, Ross, "Beckett's Brinkmanship," AUMLA, No.
19 (May, 1963), 57-75.
Coe, Richard N. , Beckett.
_____ , "God and Samuel Beckett," Meanjin, XXIV (March,

1965), 66-85.

Cohn, Ruby, "The Comedy of Samuel Beckett: 'Something old, something new---'," YFS, no. 23 (Summer, 1959), 11-17.

_____, "Philosophical Fragments in the Works of Samuel Beckett," Criticism, VI (1964), 33-43. Also in Esslin, M., ed., Samuel Beckett, 169-77.

_____, "Preliminary Observations," Per, XI (Autumn, 1959), 119-31.

_____, Samuel Beckett.

_____, "Samuel Beckett Self-Translater," PMLA, LXXVI (1961), 613-21.

_____, "Still Novel," YFS, No. 24 (1959), 48-53.

Cronin, Anthony, "Molloy Becomes Unnamable," Question of Modernity, London: Secker & Warburg, 1966, 97-110.

Erickson, John D., "Objects and Systems in the Novels of Samuel Beckett," ECr, VII (Summer, 1967), 113-22.

Esslin, Martin, ed., Samuel Beckett.

_____, "Samuel Beckett," in Cruickshank, J., ed., Novelist as Philosopher, 128-46.

Evers, Francis, "Samuel Beckett: The Incurious Seeker," DM, VII, i (Spring, 1968), 84-8.

Federman, Raymond, Journey to Chaos.

Finch, Roy, "The Reality of the Nothing: the Importance of Samuel Beckett," Lugano Rev, I, iii-iv (Summer, 1965), 211-22.

Fletcher, John, "Beckett and the Fictional Tradition," Caliban (Annales pub. par la Faculté des Lettres et Sciences Humaines de Toulouse), N.S., I, i (1965), 147-58.

_____, "Beckett's Debt to Dante," NFS, IV (May, 1965), 41-52.

_____, Novels of Samuel Beckett.

_____, "Samuel Beckett and the Philosophers," CL, XVII (Winter, 1965), 43-56.

_____, "Samuel Beckett; or, the Morbid Dread of Sphinxes," New Durham (June, 1965), 5-9. (Not seen.)

_____, Samuel Beckett's Art, N.Y.: Barnes & Noble, 1967.

Friedman, Melvin J., "The Creative Writer as Polyglot: Valery Larbaud and Samuel Beckett," TWA, XLIX (1960), 229-36.

_____, "A Note on Leibniz and Samuel Beckett," RomN, IV (Spring, 1963), 93-6.

_____, "The Novels of Samuel Beckett: An Amalgam of Joyce and Proust," CL, XII (Winter, 1960), 47-58.

_____, "Samuel Beckett and the Nouveau Roman," WSCL, I, ii (Spring-Summer, 1960), 22-36.

Furbank, P. N. , "Beckett's Purgatory," Encounter, XXII, vi (June, 1964), 69-72.

Glicksberg, Charles I. , "Samuel Beckett's World of Fiction," ArQ, XVIII (Spring, 1962), 32-47.

Greenberg, Alvin, "The Novel of Disintegration: Paradoxical Impossibility in Contemporary Literature," WSCL, VII (Winter-Spring, 1966), 109-12.

Hamilton, Kenneth, "Negative Salvation in Samuel Beckett," QQ, LXIX (Spring, 1962), 102-11.

Harvey, Lawrence E. , "Samuel Beckett on Life, Art and Criticism," MLN, LXXX (December, 1965), 545-62.

Hassan, Ihab, Literature of Silence.

_____, "The Literature of Silence: From Henry Miller to Beckett and Burroughs," Encounter, XXVIII (January, 1967), 74-82.

Heppenstall, R. , Fourfold Tradition, 254-66.

Hicks, Granville, "Beckett's World," SatR, XLI (October 4, 1958), 14.

Hoffman, F. J. , Samuel Beckett.

Jacobsen, Josephine, and William R. Mueller, "Beckett as Poet," PrS, XXXVII (Fall, 1963), 196-216. Also in Jacobsen, J. , and W. R. Mueller, Testament of Samuel Beckett.

Karl, Frederick R. , "Waiting for Beckett: Quest and Re-Quest," SR, LXIX (Autumn, 1961), 661-76. Also in Karl, F. R. , Contemporary English Novel, 19-39.

Kenner, Hugh, "The Beckett Landscape," Spectrum, II (Winter, 1958), 8-24.

_____, "Beckett: The Rational Domain," ForumH, III, iv (Summer, 1960), 39-47.

_____, "The Cartesian Centaur," Per, XI (Autumn, 1959), 132-41.

_____, "Samuel Beckett: Comedian of the Impasse," Flaubert, Joyce and Beckett: The Stoic Comedians, Boston: Beacon Pr. , 1962, 67-107.

_____, Samuel Beckett: A Critical Study, N. Y. : Grove, 1961; London: Calder, 1962.

_____, "Voices in the Night," Spectrum, V (Spring, 1961), 3-20. Also in Kenner, H. , Samuel Beckett: A Critical Study, 1961.

Kermode, Frank, "Beckett, Snow, and Pure Poverty," Encounter, XV (July, 1960), 73-7. Also in Kermode, F. , Puzzles and Epiphanies, 155-61.

Klawitter, Robert L. , "Being and Time in Samuel Beckett's Novels," DA, XXVI (1966), 7320 (Yale).

Leventhal, A. J. , "The Beckett Hero," Crit, VII, ii (Winter,

1965), 18-35.   Also in Esslin, M. , ed. , Samuel Beckett,
  37-51.
Matthews, H. , Hard Journey, 139-68.
Mauriac, Claude, The New Literature, N. Y. :   Braziller,
  1959, 75-90.
Mayoux, Jean-Jacques, "Samuel Beckett and Universal Par-
  ody," in Esslin, M. , ed. , Samuel Beckett, 77-91.
Montgomery, Niall, "No Symbols Where None Intended,"
  New World Writing, Fifth Mentor Selection, N. Y. :   New
  American Library, 1954.
Morse, J. Mitchell, "The Contemplative Life According to
  Samuel Beckett," HudR, XV (Winter, 1962-63), 512-24.
O'Neill, Joseph P. , "The Absurd in Samuel Beckett," Person,
  XLVIII (Winter, 1967), 56-76.
Radke, Judith J. , "Doubt and the Disintegration of Form in
  the French Novels and Drama of Samuel Beckett," DA,
  XXII (1962), 3205-6 (Colorado).
Rexroth, Kenneth, "The Point is Irrelevance," Nation,
  CLXXXII (April 14, 1956), 325-8.   Also in Kostelanetz, R. ,
  ed. , On Contemporary Literature, 244-8.
_____, "Samuel Beckett and the Importance of Waiting,"
  Bird in the Bush; Obvious Essays, N. Y. :   New Directions,
  1954, 75-85.
Ricks, Christopher, "The Roots of Samuel Beckett," Listen-
  er, LXXII (December 17, 1964), 963-4.
Scott, Nathan A. , Jr. , "The Recent Journey into the Zone of
  Zero: The Example of Beckett and His Despair of Litera-
  ture," CRAS, VI (Spring, 1962), 144-81.   Also (slightly
  revised) in Scott, N. A. , Jr. , Craters of the Spirit, 157-
  200.
_____, Samuel Beckett.
Stamirowska, Krystyna, "The Conception of a Character in
  the Works of Joyce and Beckett," KN, XIV (1967), 443-7.
Steiner, George, "Of Nuance and Scruple," NY, XLIV (April
  27, 1968), 164-74.
Strauss, Walter, "Dante's Belacqua and Beckett's Tramps,"
  CL, XI (Summer, 1959), 250-61.
Sypher, Wylie, "The Anonymous Self: A Defensive Human-
  ism," Loss of the Self in Modern Literature and Art,
  N. Y. :   Random House, 1962, 147-54.
Tindall, William Y. , "Beckett's Bums," Crit, II, i (Spring-
  Summer, 1958), 3-15.
_____, Samuel Beckett.
Wellershoff, Dieter, "Failure of an Attempt at De-Mythologi-
  zation: Samuel Beckett's Novels," in Esslin, M. , ed. ,
  Samuel Beckett, 92-107.
Wells, Charles M. , "The Transcendence of Life: The Posi- ·

tive Dimension in Samuel Beckett," DA, XXIX (1968), 619A
(New Mexico).
Wellwarth, G. E. , "Life in the Void: Samuel Beckett,"
UKCR, XXVIII (October, 1961), 25-33.
Wendler, Herbert W. , "Graveyard Humanism," SWR, XLIX
(Winter, 1964), 44-52.

DREAM OF FAIR TO MIDDLING WOMEN (Unpublished)

Fletcher, J. , Novels of Samuel Beckett, Chapter 1, passim.

HOW IT IS

Esslin, Martin, "Samuel Beckett," in Cruickshank, J. , ed. ,
Novelist as Philosopher, 143-4.
Federman, Raymond, "Beckett and the Fiction of Mud," in
Kostelanetz, R. , ed. , On Contemporary Literature, 255-
61.
_____, "HOW IT IS: With Beckett's Fiction," FR,
XXXVIII (February, 1965), 459-68.
Furbank, P. N. , "Beckett's Purgatory," Encounter, XXII, vi
(June, 1964), 69-72.
Hassan, I. , Literature of Silence, 168-73.
Kermode, Frank, NYRB, XI (March 19, 1964), 9-11. Also
in Kermode, F. , Continuities, 169-72.
"Novels of 1964. Samuel Beckett: HOW IT IS," TLS (May
21, 1964). Also in T. L. S.: Essays and Reviews from
The Times Literary Supplement, 1964, 45-7.
Scott, N. A. , Jr. , "Beckett's Journey into the Zone of Zero,"
Craters of the Spirit, 193-4.
Tindall, William Y. , Samuel Beckett, 37-9.

MALONE DIES (See also TRILOGY)

Cmarada, Geraldine, "MALONE DIES: A Round of Con-
sciousness," Sym, XIV (Fall, 1960), 199-212.
Coe, R. N. , Beckett, 62-8.
Fletcher, J. , Novels of Samuel Beckett, 151-76.
Glicksberg, Charles I. , "Samuel Beckett's World of Fiction,"
ArQ, XVIII (Spring, 1962), 39-41.
_____, Self in Modern Literature, 127-9.
Hassan, I. , Literature of Silence, 158-62.
Hoffman, F. J. , Samuel Beckett, 127-32.
Karl, F. R. , "Waiting for Beckett: Quest and Re-Quest,"
Contemporary English Novel, 35-7.
MacNeice, Louis, Varieties of Parable, London: Cambridge
Un. Pr. , 1965, 141-6.

Tindall, William Y., "Beckett's Bums," Crit, II, i (Spring-
Summer, 1958), 11-13.
_____, Samuel Beckett, 26-9.
Walcutt, C. C., Man's Changing Mask, 339-42.

MOLLOY (See also TRILOGY)

Bowles, Patrick, "How Beckett Sees the Universe: MOL-
LOY," Listener, LIX, no. 1525 (June 19, 1958), 1011-12.
Boyle, Kevin, "Molloy: Icon of the Negative," Westwind, V,
no. 1 (Fall, 1961).
Coe, R. N., Beckett, 54-62.
Davies, R., Voice from the Attic, 232-4.
Esslin, Martin, "Samuel Beckett," in Cruickshank, J., ed.,
Novelist as Philosopher, 135-8.
Fletcher, J., Novels of Samuel Beckett, 119-50.
Friedman, Melvin J., "Molloy's 'Sacred' Stones," RomN, IX
(Autumn, 1967), 8-11.
Glicksberg, Charles I., "Samuel Beckett's World of Fiction,"
ArQ, XVIII (Spring, 1962), 35-9.
_____, Self in Modern Literature, 124-7.
Hassan, I., Literature of Silence, 151-8.
Hayman, David, "Quest for Meaninglessness: The Boundless
Poverty of MOLLOY," in Sutherland, W. O. S., ed., Six
Contemporary Novels, 90-112.
Hoffman, F. J., Samuel Beckett, 120-7.
Karl, F. R., "Waiting for Beckett: Quest and Re-Quest,"
Contemporary English Novel, 31-5.
Kermode, F., Puzzles and Epiphanies, 158-60.
Kern, Edith M., "Moran-Molloy: The Hero as Author,"
Per, XI (Autumn, 1959), 183-93.
_____, "Samuel Beckett--Dionysian Poet," Descant, III
(Fall, 1958), 33-6.
Lee, Warren, "The Bitter Pill of Samuel Beckett," ChiR,
X (Winter, 1957), 84-7.
Matthews, H., Hard Journey, 151-66.
Nadeau, Maurice, "Samuel Beckett: Humor and the Void,"
in Esslin, M., ed., Samuel Beckett, 33-6.
Solomon, Philip H., "The Imagery of MOLLOY and It's Ex-
tension into Beckett's Other Fiction," DA, XXVIII (1968),
3198A-9A (Wisc.).
_____, "Samuel Beckett's MOLLOY: A Dog's Life," FR,
XLI (1967), 84-91.
Tindall, William Y., "Beckett's Bums," Crit, II, i (Spring-
Summer, 1958), 7-11.
_____, Samuel Beckett, 21-6.
Wellershoff, Dieter, "Failure of an Attempt at De-Mythologi-

zation: Samuel Beckett's Novels," in Esslin, M., ed.,
Samuel Beckett, 93-104.

MURPHY

Chambers, Ross, "Samuel Beckett and the Padded Cell,"
  Meanjin, XXI (1962), 451-62.
Coe, R. N., Beckett, 20-34.
Cohn, R., Samuel Beckett, 45-64.
Cooney, Séamus, "Beckett's MURPHY," Expl, XXV (September, 1966), item 3.
Esslin, Martin, "Samuel Beckett," in Cruickshank, J., ed.,
  Novelist as Philosopher, 131-3.
Federman, R., Journey to Chaos, 56-93.
Fletcher, J., Novels of Samuel Beckett, 38-55.
Glicksberg, Charles I., "Samuel Beckett's World of Fiction,"
  ArQ, XVIII (Spring, 1962), 33-5.
_____, Self in Modern Literature, 122-4.
Harrison, Robert, Samuel Beckett's MURPHY: A Critical
  Excursion (Un. of Georgia Monographs, No. 15), Athens:
  Un. of Georgia Pr., 1968.
Hassan, I., Literature of Silence, 140-5.
Hoffman, F. J., Samuel Beckett, 105-14.
Jacobsen, J., and W. R. Mueller, Testament of Samuel Beckett, 25-30; 67-72.
Karl, F. R., "Waiting for Beckett: Quest and Re-Quest,"
  Contemporary English Novel, 20-1; 27-9.
Mintz, Samuel, "Beckett's MURPHY: A 'Cartesian' Novel,"
  Per, XI (Autumn, 1959), 156-65.
Scott, N. A., Jr., "Beckett's Journey into the Zone of Zero,"
  Craters of the Spirit, 178-80. Also in CRAS, VI (1962),
  162-4.
_____, Samuel Beckett, 41-6.
Tindall, William Y., "Beckett's Bums," Crit, II, i (Spring-Summer, 1958), 5-6.
_____, Samuel Beckett, 13-17.
Wells, Charles M., "The Transcendence of Life: The Positive Dimension in Samuel Beckett," DA, XXIX (1968),
  619A (New Mexico).

TRILOGY

Barrett, William, "How I understand less and less every
  year...," CUF, II (Winter, 1959), 44-8.
Blanchot, Maurice, "Where Now? Who Now?" EvR, II
  (Winter, 1959), 222-9.
Chambers, Ross, "Samuel Beckett and the Padded Cell,"

Meanjin, XXI (1962), 451-62.
Cohn, Ruby, Samuel Beckett, 114-68.
_____, "Still Novel," YFS, No. 24 (Summer, 1959), 48-
    53.
Friedman, Melvin J., "The Novels of Samuel Beckett: An
    Amalgam of Joyce and Proust," CL, XII (1960), 53-6.
Frye, Northrop, "The Nightmare Life in Death," HudR, XIII
    (Autumn, 1960), 442-9.
Gerard, Martin, "Molloy Becomes Unnamable," XR, I (Oc-
    tober, 1960), 314-19.
Goldberg, Gerald J., "The Search for the Artist in Some Re-
    cent British Fiction," SAQ, LXII (Summer, 1963), 396-
    401.
Hamilton, Carol, "Portrait in Old Age: The Image of Man
    in Beckett's Trilogy," WHR, XVI (Spring, 1962), 157-65.
Hamilton, Kenneth, "Boon or Thorn? Joyce Cary and Samuel
    Beckett on Human Life," DR, XXXVIII (1959), 433-42.
Kenner, Hugh, "The Absurdity of Fiction," Griffin, VIII
    (November, 1959), 13-16.
Oates, J. C., "The Trilogy of Samuel Beckett," Ren, XIV
    (Spring, 1962), 160-5.
Pritchett, V. S., "An Irish Oblomov," NS & Nation, LIX
    (April 2, 1960), 489. Also in Working Novelist, 25-9.
Scott, N. A., Jr., "Beckett's Journey into the Zone of Zero,"
    CRAS, VI (1962), 169-75. Also in Craters of the Spirit,
    185-92.
_____, Samuel Beckett, 60-74.
Unterecker, John, "Samuel Beckett's No-Man's Land," New
    Leader, XLII (May 18, 1959), 24-5.
Webb, E., III, "Samuel Beckett, Novelist: A Study of His
    Trilogy," DA, XXVIII (1968), 4191A.

THE UNNAMABLE (See also TRILOGY)

Blanchot, Maurice, "Where Now? Who Now?" EvR, II
    (Winter, 1959), 224-9. Also (abridged) in Kostelanetz,
    R., ed., On Contemporary Literature, 249-54.
Coe, R. N., Beckett, 69-79.
Esslin, Martin, in Cruickshank, J., ed., Novelist as Phi-
    losopher, 139-43.
Fletcher, J., Novels of Samuel Beckett, 179-94.
Glicksberg, Charles I., "Samuel Beckett's World of Fiction,"
    ArQ, XVIII (Spring, 1962), 41-7.
_____, Self in Modern Literature, 129-33.
Hassan, I., Literature of Silence, 162-8.
Hoffman, F. J., Samuel Beckett, 132-7.
Karl, F. R., "Waiting for Beckett: Quest and Re-Quest,"

Contemporary English Novel, 37-9.
Rickels, Milton, "Existential Themes in Beckett's UNNAM-
    ABLE," Criticism, IV (Spring, 1962), 134-47.
Tindall, William Y., "Beckett's Bums," Crit, II (Spring-
    Summer, 1958), 13-14.
_____, Samuel Beckett, 29-32.

WATT

Abbey, Edward, NMQ, XXIX (1959), 381-3.
Brée, Germaine, "Beckett's Abstractors of Quintessence,"
    FR, XXXVI (May, 1963), 567-76.
Brick, Allan, "The Madman in His Cell: Joyce, Beckett,
    Nabakov, and the Stereotypes," MR, I (1959), 45-9.
Brooke-Rose, Christine, "Samuel Beckett and the Anti-Novel,"
    LonM, V, xii (December, 1958), 38-43.
Coe, R.N., Beckett, 36-53.
Cohn, R., Samuel Beckett, 65-94.
_____, "WATT in the Light of THE CASTLE," CL, XIII
    (Spring, 1961), 154-66.
Esslin, Martin, "Samuel Beckett," in Cruickshank, J., ed.,
    Novelist as Philosopher, 133-5.
Federman, R., Journey to Chaos, 94-132.
Fletcher, J., Novels of Samuel Beckett, 59-89.
Greenberg, Alvin, "The Death of the Psyche: A Way to the
    Self in the Contemporary Novel," Criticism, VIII (Winter,
    1966), 1-18.
Hassan, I., Literature of Silence, 145-51.
Hesla, David H., "The Shape of Chaos: A Reading of Beck-
    ett's WATT," Crit, VI, i (Spring, 1963), 85-105.
Hoefer, Jacqueline, "Watt," Per, XI, No. 3 (Autumn, 1959),
    166-82.
Hoffman, F.J., Samuel Beckett, 114-19.
Jacobsen, J., and W.R. Mueller, Testament of Samuel Beck-
    ett, 73-7.
Karl, F.R., "Waiting for Beckett: Quest and Re-Quest,"
    Contemporary English Novel, 27-9.
Lombardi, Thomas W., "Who Tells Who WATT?" Chelsea,
    22/23 (June, 1968), 170-9.
Scott, N.A., Jr., "Beckett's Journey into the Zone of Zero,"
    CRAS, VI (1962), 164-9. Also in Craters of the Spirit,
    180-5.
_____, Samuel Beckett, 48-58.
Senneff, Susan F., "Song and Music in Samuel Beckett's
    WATT," MFS, X (Summer, 1964), 137-49.
Tindall, William Y., "Beckett's Bums," Crit, II, i (Spring-
    Summer, 1958), 6-7.

_____, Samuel Beckett, 17-21.
Warhaft, Sidney, "Threne and Theme in WATT," WSCL, IV,
iii (Autumn, 1963), 261-78.

BIBLIOGRAPHY

Cohn, R. , Samuel Beckett, 328-40.
Federman, R. , Journey to Chaos, 224-35.
Tanner, James T. F. , and J. Don Vann, Samuel Beckett; A
    Checklist of Criticism, Kent, Ohio: Kent St. Un. Pr. ,
    1969.

BELLOW, SAUL, 1915-

GENERAL

Allen, Michael, "Idiomatic Language in Two Novels by Saul
    Bellow," JAmS, I (October, 1967), 275-80.
Alter, Robert, "The Stature of Saul Bellow," Midstream, X
    (December, 1964), 3-15.   Also (revised) as "Saul Bellow:
    A Dissent from Modernism," After the Tradition, 95-115.
Baker, Sheridan, "Saul Bellow's Bout with Chivalry," Criti-
    cism, IX (Spring, 1967), 109-22.
Bradbury, Malcolm, "Saul Bellow and the Naturalist Tradi-
    tion," REL, IV, iv (October, 1963), 80-92.
Burgess, Anthony, "The Jew as American," Spectator (Oc-
    tober 7, 1966), 455-6.
Chapman, Abraham, "The Image of Man as Portrayed by
    Saul Bellow," CLAJ, X (June, 1967), 285-98.
Chase, Richard, "The Adventures of Saul Bellow: Progress
    of a Novelist," Ctary, XXVII (April, 1959), 323-30.   Also
    in Malin, I. , ed. , Saul Bellow and the Critics, 25-38.
Clayton, J. J. , Saul Bellow.
Craig, Harry E. , "The Affirmation of the Heroes in the
    Novels of Saul Bellow," DA, XXVIII (1968), 5012A (Pitts-
    burgh).
Detweiler, Robert, Saul Bellow: A Critical Essay (CWCP),
    Grand Rapids, Mich.:   Eerdmans, 1967.
Dickstein, Morris, "For Art's Sake," PR, XXXIII (Fall,
    1966), 617-21.
Donoghue, Denis "Commitment and the Dangling Man,"
    Studies, LIII (Summer, 1964), 174-87.
_____, The Ordinary Universe: Soundings in Modern Lit-
    erature, N. Y.: Macmillan, 1968, 194-203.
Dutton, Robert R. , "The Subangelic Vision of Saul Bellow:
    A Study of His First Six Novels, 1944-1964," DA, XXVII

(1966), 1363A (Un. of the Pacific).

Eisinger, Chester E., Fiction of the Forties, 341-62.

_____, "Saul Bellow: Love and Identity," Accent, XVIII (Summer, 1958), 179-203.

Fiedler, Leslie, "Saul Bellow," PrS, XXXI (Summer, 1957), 103-10.   Also in Goldberg, Gerald J., and Nancy M. Goldberg, eds., The Modern Critical Spectrum, N.Y.: Prentice-Hall, 1962, 155-61.   Also in Kostelanetz, R., ed., On Contemporary Literature, 286-95.   Also in Malin, I., ed. Saul Bellow and the Critics, 1-11.

Finkelstein, S., Existentialism and Alienation in American Literature, 263-8.

Fossum, Robert H., "The Devil and Saul Bellow," CLS, III (1966), 197-206.   Also in Panichas, G.A., ed., Mansions of the Spirit, 345-55.

Frank, Rueben, "Saul Bellow: The Evolution of a Contemporary Novelist," WR, XVIII (Winter, 1954), 101-12.

Freedman, Ralph, "Saul Bellow: The Illusion of Environment," WSCL, I, i (Winter, 1960), 50-65.

Galloway, David D., "The Absurd Man as Picaro: The Novels of Saul Bellow," TSLL, VI (Summer, 1964), 226-54.   Also in Absurd Hero, 82-139.

Geismar, M., "Saul Bellow: Novelist of the Intellectuals," American Moderns, 210-24.   Also in Malin, I., ed., Saul Bellow and the Critics, 10-24.

Hall, J., Lunatic Giant in the Drawing Room, 127-80.

Harper, Gordon L., "The Art of Fiction: Saul Bellow, An Interview," ParisR, No. 36 (Winter, 1966), 48-73.   Also in Writers at Work, 3rd series, 175-96.

Harper, H.M., Jr., "Saul Bellow: The Heart's Ultimate Need," Desperate Faith, 7-64.

Hartman, Hugh C., "Character, Theme and Tradition in the Novels of Saul Bellow," DA, XXIX (1968), 898A-9A (Un. of Washington).

Hassan, Ihab H., Radical Innocence, 290-4.

_____, "Saul Bellow: Five Faces of a Hero," Crit, III, iii (Summer, 1960), 28-36.

Hoffman, Frederick J., "The Fool of Experience: Saul Bellow's Fiction," in Moore, H.T., ed., Contemporary American Novelists, 80-94.

Hux, Samuel H., "American Myth and Existentialism of Mailer, Bellow, Styron, and Ellison," DA, XXVI (1966), 5437 (Conn.)

Kazin, Alfred, "Bellow's Purgatory," NYRB (March 28, 1968), 32-6.

_____, "My Friend Saul Bellow," Atlantic, CCXV (January, 1965), 51-4.

_____, "The World of Saul Bellow," Contemporaries, 217-25.

_____, "The World of Saul Bellow," Griffin, VIII (June, 1959), 4-9.

Klein, Marcus, "Saul Bellow: A Discipline of Nobility," KR, XXIV (Spring, 1962), 203-26. Also (expanded) in After Alienation, 33-70. Also in Malin, I., ed., Saul Bellow and the Critics, 92-113. Also in Waldmeir, J. J., ed., Recent American Fiction, 121-38.

Kramer, Maurice, "The Secular Mode of Jewishness," Works, I (Autumn, 1967), 110-16.

Levenson, J. C., "Bellow's Dangling Men," Crit, III, iii (Summer, 1960), 3-14. Also in Malin, I., ed., Saul Bellow and the Critics, 39-50.

Levine, Paul, "Saul Bellow: The Affirmation of the Philosophical Fool," Per, X (Winter, 1959), 163-76.

Lewin, Lois S., "The Theme of Suffering in the Work of Bernard Malamud and Saul Bellow," DA, XXVIII (1968), 5021A (Pittsburgh).

Ludwig, Jack, Recent American Novelists (UMPAW, No. 22), 1962, 7-18.

Malin, Irving, in Jewish Heritage Reader, 257-63.

_____, Jews and Americans.

_____, "Reputations- XIV: Saul Bellow," LonM, IV (January, 1965), 43-54.

_____, ed., Saul Bellow and the Critics.

_____, Saul Bellow's Fiction.

_____, "Seven Images," in Malin, I., ed., Saul Bellow and the Critics, 142-76.

Markos, Donald W., "The Humanism of Saul Bellow," DA, XXVII (1966), 3875A (Illinois).

Morrow, Patrick, "Threat and Accommodation: The Novels of Saul Bellow," MQ, VIII (Summer, 1967), 389-411.

Mudrick, Marvin, "Who Killed Herzog? or, Three American Novelists," UDQ, I, i (Spring, 1966), 61-97.

Mukherji, N., "The Bellow Hero," IJES, IX (1968), 74-86. (Not seen.)

Noble, D. W., Eternal Adam and the New World Garden, 216-33.

Opdahl, K. M., Novels of Saul Bellow.

Pinsker, Sanford S., "The Schlemiel as Metaphor: Studies in the Yiddish and American Jewish Novel," DA, XXVIII (1968), 3679A-80A (Un. of Washington).

Podhoretz, N., "The Adventures of Saul Bellow," Doings and Undoings, 205-27.

Raider, Ruth, "Saul Bellow," CamQ, II (Spring, 1967), 172-
83.
Rans, Geoffrey, "The Novels of Saul Bellow," REL, IV, iv
(October, 1963), 18-30.
Ross, Theodore J., "Notes on Saul Bellow," CJF, XVIII
(Fall, 1959), 21-7.
Rovit, E., Saul Bellow.
Schulz, M. F., "Saul Bellow and the Burden of Selfhood,"
Radical Sophistication, 110-52.
Scott, Nathan A., Jr., "Sola Gratia- The Principle of Saul
Bellow's Fiction," in Scott, N. A., Jr., ed., Adversity
and Grace, 27-57. Also in Scott, N. A., Jr., Craters of
the Spirit, 233-65.
Shaw, Peter, "The Tough Guy Intellectual," CritQ, VIII
(Spring, 1966), 23-7.
Stock, Irvin, "The Novels of Saul Bellow," SoR, III (Winter,
1967), 13-42.
Swados, H., "Certain Jewish Writers," A Radical's America,
164-76.
Tajuddin, Mohammad, "The Tragicomic Novel: Camus, Mala-
mud, Hawkes, Bellow," DA, XXVIII (1968), 2698A-99A
(Indiana).
Tanner, Tony, Saul Bellow.
_____, "Saul Bellow: The Flight from Monologue," En-
counter, XXIV (February, 1965), 58-70.
Trachtenberg, Stanley, "Saul Bellow's Luftmenschen: The
Compromise with Reality," Crit, IX, iii (1967), 37-61.

THE ADVENTURES OF AUGIE MARCH

Aldridge, J. R., In Search of Heresy, 131-9.
Allen, Michael, "Idiomatic Language in Two Novels by Saul
Bellow," JAmS, I (October, 1967), 275-80.
Allen, W., Modern Novel, 325-7.
Alter, Robert, Rogue's Progress, 121-5.
_____, "The Stature of Saul Bellow," Midstream, X (De-
cember, 1964), 8-9.
Bellow, Saul, "How I Wrote Augie March's Story," NYTBR
(January 31, 1954), 3+.
Bergler, Edmund, M. D., "Writers of Half-Talent," AI (Sum-
mer, 1957), 156-9.
Chase, Richard, Ctary, XXVII (April, 1959). Also in Malin,
I., ed., Saul Bellow and the Critics, 27-30.
Clayton, J. J., Saul Bellow, 26-8; 60-1; 74-6; 83-92; 106-12;
122-8; 241-7.
Cowley, Malcolm, "Naturalism: No Teacup Tragedies," The
Literary Situation, N. Y.: Viking, 1954, 91-3.

Crozier, Robert D., "Theme in AUGIE MARCH," Crit, VII
    (Spring-Summer, 1965), 18-32.
Davis, Robert G., in Balakian, N., and C. Simmons, eds.,
    Creative Present, 120-4.
_____, NYTBR (September 20, 1953), 1+.
Eisinger, Chester E., Fiction of the Forties, 354-62.
_____, "Saul Bellow: Love and Identity," Accent, XVIII
    (Summer, 1958), 192-9.
Finn, James, ChiR, VIII (Spring-Summer, 1954), 104-11.
Frank, Reuben, "Saul Bellow: The Evolution of a Contempo-
    rary Novelist," WR, XVIII (Winter, 1954), 108-12.
Freedman, Ralph, "Saul Bellow: The Illusion of Environ-
    ment," WSCL, I, i (Winter, 1960), 57-61. Also in Malin,
    I., ed., Saul Bellow and the Critics, 59-64.
Frohock, W.M., "Saul Bellow and His Penitant Hero," SWR,
    LIII (Winter, 1968), 36-44.
Galloway, David D., Absurd Hero, 94-104.
_____, "The Absurd Man as Picaro: The Novels of Saul
    Bellow," TSLL, VI (Summer, 1964), 234-41.
Geismar, Maxwell, Nation, CLXXVII (November 14, 1953),
    404.
_____, "Saul Bellow: Novelist of the Intellectuals,"
    American Moderns, 216-18. Also in Malin, I., ed.,
    Saul Bellow and the Critics, 16-19.
Goldberg, Gerald J., "Life's Customer: Augie March,"
    Crit, III, iii (Summer, 1960), 15-27.
Guerard, Albert J., "Saul Bellow and the Activists: On
    THE ADVENTURES OF AUGIE MARCH," SoR, III (July,
    1967), 582-96.
Hall, James, Lunatic Giant in the Drawing Room, 149-60.
_____, "Play, the Training Camp, and American Angry
    Comedy," HAB, XV (Spring, 1964), 11-16.
Harper, H.M., Jr., Desperate Faith, 23-32.
Harwell, Meade, SWR, XXXIX (Summer, 1954), 273-6.
Hassan, I., Radical Innocence, 303-11.
Hoffman, Frederick J., in Moore, H.T., ed., Contemporary
    American Novelists, 88-93.
Levine, Paul, "Saul Bellow: The Affirmation of the Philo-
    sophical Fool," Per, X (Winter, 1959), 167-72.
Ludwig, J., Recent American Novelists, 10-15.
Malin, Irving, in Jewish Heritage Reader, 260-1.
Mizener, Arthur, NYHTBR (September 20, 1953), 2.
Morrow, Patrick, "Threat and Accommodation: The Novels
    of Saul Bellow," MQ, VIII (Summer, 1967), 401-3.
Opdahl, K.M., Novels of Saul Bellow, 70-95.
Overbeck, Pat T., "The Women in 'Augie March'," TSLL,
    X (Fall, 1968), 471-84.

Podhoretz, N., "The Adventures of Saul Bellow," <u>Doings and Undoings,</u> 215-19.
Priestley, J. B., <u>Sunday Times</u> (London) (May 9, 1954), 5.
Pritchett, V. S., <u>NS & Nation,</u> n. s. XLVII (June 19, 1954), 803.
Rans, Geoffrey, "The Novels of Saul Bellow," <u>REL,</u> IV, iv (October, 1963), 22-6.
Rovit, E., <u>Saul Bellow,</u> 20-2.
Schorer, Mark, "A Book of Yes and No," <u>HudR,</u> VII (Spring, 1954), 134-41.
Scott, Nathan A., Jr., "Sole Gratia- The Principle of Saul Bellow's Fiction," in Scott, N. A., Jr., ed., <u>Adversity and Grace,</u> 43-5. Also in Scott, N. A., Jr., <u>Craters of the Spirit,</u> 250-2.
Sherman, B., <u>Invention of the Jew,</u> 132-45.
Shulman, Robert, "The Style of Bellow's Comedy," <u>PMLA,</u> LXXXIII (March, 1968), 109-17.
Stock, Irvin, "The Novels of Saul Bellow," <u>SoR,</u> III (Winter, 1967), 23-7.
Tanner, T., <u>Saul Bellow,</u> 41-56.
Trachtenberg, Stanley, "Saul Bellow's <u>Luftmenschen:</u> The Compromise with Reality," <u>Crit,</u> IX, iii (1967), 43-9.
Warren, Robert Penn, "Man with no Commitments," <u>NRep,</u> CXXIX (November 2, 1953), 22-3.
Way, Brian, "Character and Society in THE ADVENTURES OF AUGIE MARCH," <u>BAASB,</u> No. 8 (June, 1964), 36-44.
Webster, Harvey C., <u>SatR,</u> XXXVI (September 19, 1953), 13-14.
West, Anthony, <u>NY,</u> XXIX (September 26, 1953), 140+.
West, Ray B., <u>Shen,</u> V (Winter, 1953), 85-90.

DANGLING MAN

Allen, W., <u>Modern Novel,</u> 322-5.
Alter, Robert, "The Stature of Saul Bellow," <u>Midstream,</u> X (December, 1964), 5-7.
Baumbach, J., <u>Landscape of Nightmare,</u> 35-9.
Clayton, J. J., <u>Saul Bellow,</u> 24-6; 56-9; 61-9; 77-83; 97-105; 114-22; 238-40.
Davis, Robert G., in Balakian, N., and C. Simmons, eds., <u>Creative Present,</u> 112-16.
Donoghue, Denis, "Commitment and the Dangling Man," <u>Studies,</u> LIII (Summer, 1964), 174-87.
Eisinger, Chester E., <u>Fiction of the Forties,</u> 345-9.
_____, "Saul Bellow: Love and Identity," <u>Accent,</u> XVIII (Summer, 1968), 183-8.
Frank, Reuben, "Saul Bellow: The Evolution of a Contempo-

rary Novelist," WR, XVIII (Winter, 1954), 102-5.
Galloway, David D., Absurd Hero, 82-9.
_____, "The Absurd Man as Picaro: The Novels of Saul
    Bellow," TSLL, VI (Summer, 1964), 226-31.
Geismar, M., "Saul Bellow: Novelist of the Intellectuals,"
    American Moderns, 210-13. Also in Malin, I., ed.,
    Saul Bellow and the Critics, 10-13.
Hall, J., Lunatic Giant in the Drawing Room, 134-8.
Harper, H.M., Jr., Desperate Faith, 8-16.
Hassan, I., Radical Innocence, 294-9.
Hoffman, Frederick J., in Moore, H.T., ed., Contemporary
    American Novelists, 83-5.
Lehan, Richard, "Existentialism in Recent American Fiction:
    The Demonic Quest," TSLL, I (Summer, 1959), 187-92.
Levenson, J.C., "Bellow's Dangling Men," Crit, III, iii
    (1960), 4-7.
Levine, Paul, "Saul Bellow: The Affirmation of the Philo-
    sophical Fool," Per, X (Winter, 1959), 164-5.
Malin, Irving, in Jewish Heritage Reader, 258-60.
_____, Saul Bellow's Fiction, 71-6; 139-40.
Morrow, Patrick, "Threat and Accommodation: The Novels
    of Saul Bellow," MQ, VIII (Summer, 1967), 397-401.
O'Brien, Kate, Spectator (January 3, 1947), 26.
Opdahl, K.M., Novels of Saul Bellow, 28-50.
Podhoretz, N., "The Adventures of Saul Bellow," Doings
    and Undoings, 206-11.
Rans, Geoffrey, "The Novels of Saul Bellow," REL, IV, iv
    (October, 1963), 18-20.
Rovit, E., Saul Bellow, 17-18.
Scott, Nathan A., Jr., "Solia Gratia- The Principle of Bel-
    low's Fiction," in Scott, N.A., Jr., ed., Adversity and
    Grace, 37-40. Also in Scott, N.A., Jr., Craters of the
    Spirit, 245-6.
Stock, Irvin, "The Novels of Saul Bellow," SoR, III (Winter,
    1967), 17-19.
Tanner, T., Saul Bellow, 18-25.
Trachtenberg, Stanley, "Saul Bellow's Luftmenschen: The
    Compromise with Reality," Crit, IX, iii (1967), 39-41.

                    HENDERSON THE RAIN KING

Allen, Michael, "Idiomatic Language in Two Novels by Saul
    Bellow," JAmS, I (October, 1967), 275-80.
Allen, W., Modern Novel, 327-8.
Alter, Robert, "The Stature of Saul Bellow," Midstream, X
    (December, 1964), 10-11.
Anon., TLS (June 12, 1959), 352.

Baker, Carlos, NYTBR (February 22, 1959), 4-5.

Baumbach, J., Landscape of Nightmare, 52-4.

Bradbury, Malcolm, "Saul Bellow's HENDERSON THE RAIN
  KING," Listener, LXXI (January 30, 1964), 187-8.

Chase, Richard, "The Adventures of Saul Bellow: Progress
  of a Novelist," Ctary, XXVII (April, 1959), 323-30. Also
  in Malin, I., ed., Saul Bellow and the Critics, 25-6; 33-8.

Clayton, J.J., Saul Bellow, 166-85; 251-2.

Davis, Robert G., in Balakian, N. and C. Simmons, eds.,
  Creative Present, 127-30+.

_____, "Salvation in Lions?" Midstream, V (Spring,
  1959), 101-4.

Detweiler, Robert, "Patterns of Rebirth in HENDERSON THE
  RAIN KING," MFS, XII (Winter, 1966-67), 405-14.

Freedman, Ralph, "Saul Bellow: The Illusion of Environment," WSCL, I, i (Winter, 1960), 61-5. Also in Malin,
  I., ed., Saul Bellow and the Critics, 64-8.

Galloway, David D., Absurd Hero, 110-23.

_____, "The Absurd Man as Picaro: The Novels of Saul
  Bellow," TSLL, VI (Summer, 1964), 244-53.

_____, "Clown and Saint: The Hero in Current American
  Fiction," Crit, VII (Spring-Summer, 1965), 52-3.

Gold, Herbert, Nation, CLXXXVIII (February 21, 1959), 169-
  70.

Goldfinch, Michael A., "A Journey to the Interior," ES,
  XLIII (October, 1962), 439-43.

Greenberg, Alvin, "The Death of the Psyche: A Way to the
  Self in the Contemporary Novel," Criticism, VIII (Winter,
  1966), 11-14.

Guttmann, Allen, "Bellow's Henderson," Crit, VII (Spring-
  Summer, 1965), 33-42.

Harper, H.M., Jr., Desperate Faith, 39-50.

Hassan, I., Radical Innocence, 316-21. Also in Westbrook,
  M., ed., Modern American Fiction, 223-9.

Hicks, Granville, SatR, XLII (February 21, 1959), 20.

Hoffman, Frederick J., in Moore, H.T., ed., Contemporary
  American Novelists, 92-3.

Hughes, Daniel J., "Reality and the Hero: LOLITA and
  HENDERSON THE RAIN KING," MFS, VI (Winter, 1960-
  61), 345-64. Also in Malin, I., ed., Saul Bellow and the
  Critics, 69-91.

Jacobson, Dan, "The Solitariness of Saul Bellow," Spectator
  (May 22, 1959), 735.

Leach, Elsie, "From Ritual to Romance Again: HENDERSON
  THE RAIN KING," WHR, XIV (Spring, 1961), 223-4.

Ludwig, J., Recent American Novelists, 16-18. Also in
  Kostelanetz, R., ed., On Contemporary Literature, 297-9.

Morrow, Patrick, "Threat and Accommodation: The Novels of Saul Bellow," MQ, VIII (Summer, 1967), 403-6.

Noble, D. W., Eternal Adam and the New World Garden, 219-21.

Opdahl, K. M., Novels of Saul Bellow, 118-39.

Podhoretz, N., "The Adventures of Saul Bellow," Doings and Undoings, 224-7.

_____, NYHTBR (February 22, 1959), 3.

Price, Martin, YR, n. s. XLVIII (March, 1959), 453-6.

Quinton, Anthony, "The Adventures of Saul Bellow," LonM, VI, xii (December, 1959), 55-9.

Rans, Geoffrey, "The Novels of Saul Bellow," REL, IV, iv (October, 1963), 27-30.

Scott, Nathan A., Jr., "Sola Gratia- The Principle of Saul Bellow's Fiction," in Scott, N. A., Jr., ed., Adversity and Grace, 50-2. Also in Scott, N. A., Jr., Craters of the Spirit, 257-60.

Stern, Richard G., "Henderson's Bellow," KR, XXI (Autumn, 1959), 655-6; 658-61.

Stock, Irvin, "The Novels of Saul Bellow," SoR, III (Winter, 1967), 31-6.

Swados, Harvey, "Bellow's Adventures in Africa," New Leader (March 23, 1959), 23-4.

Symons, J., "Bellow Before Herzog," Critical Occasions, 112-18.

Tanner, T., Saul Bellow, 71-86.

Trachtenberg, Stanley, "Saul Bellow's Luftmenschen: The Compromise with Reality," Crit, IX, iii (1967), 52-5.

Waterhouse, Keith, NS & Nation, n. s. LVII (June 6, 1959). 805-6.

Whittemore, Reed, NRep, CXL (March 16, 1959), 17-18.

HERZOG

Aldridge, J. W., "The Complacency of Herzog," Time to Murder and Create, 133-8. Also in Malin, I., Saul Bellow and the Critics, 207-10.

Alter, Robert, "The Stature of Saul Bellow," Midstream, X (December, 1964), 11-15. Also (revised) in Alter, R., After the Tradition, 95-114.

Anon., TLS (February 4, 1965). Also as "Novels of 1965. Saul Bellow: HERZOG," in T. L. S., Essays and Reviews from The Times Literary Review, 1965, 31-4.

Axthelm, P. M., Modern Confessional Novel, 128-77.

Baruch, Franklin R., "Bellow and Milton: Professor Herzog in His Garden," Crit, IX, iii (1967), 74-83.

Bradbury, Malcolm, "Saul Bellow's HERZOG," CritQ, VII

(Autumn, 1965), 269-78.

Clayton, J. J. , Saul Bellow, 186-229; 252-3.

Donoghue, Denis, The Ordinary Universe: Soundings in Modern Literature, N. Y. : Macmillan, 1968, 199-203.

Finkelstein, S. , Existentialism and Alienation in American Literature, 264-6.

Fisch, Harold, "The Hero as Jew: Reflections on HERZOG," Judaism, XVII (1968), 42-54.

Galloway, David D. , "Moses-Bloom-Herzog: Bellow's Everyman," SoR, II (Winter, 1966), 61-76. Also in Galloway, D. D. , Absurd Hero, 123-39.

Gard, Roger, "Saul Bellow," Delta (Cambridge, Eng.), No. 36 (Summer, 1965), 27-30.

Garrett, George, "To Do Right in a Bad World: Saul Bellow's HERZOG," HC, II, ii (April, 1965), 1-12.

Gill, Brendan, "Surprised by Joy," NY, XL (October 3, 1964), 218-22.

Gross, Beverly, "Bellow's Herzog," ChiR, XVII, ii-iii (1964-65), 217-21.

Hall, J. , Lunatic Giant in the Drawing Room, 163-79.

Harper, H. M. , Jr. , Desperate Faith, 51-62.

Howe, Irving, "Odysseus, Flat on His Back," NRep (September 19, 1964), 21-4, 26.

Kazin, Alfred, "My Friend Saul Bellow," Atlantic, CCXV (January, 1965), 53-4.

Kermode, F. , NStat, LXIX (February 5, 1965), 200-1. Also in Kermode, F. , Continuities, 221-7.

Kuehn, Robert E. , "Fiction Chronicle," WSCL, VI (1965), 132-3.

Ludwig, Jack, "The Wayward Reader," Holiday, XXXVII (February, 1965), 16-19.

Malin, I. , Saul Bellow's Fiction, 145-62.

Morrow, Patrick, "Threat and Accommodation: The Novels of Saul Bellow," MQ, VIII (Summer, 1967), 406-10.

Noble, D. W. , Eternal Adam and the New World Garden, 221-3.

Opdahl, K. M. , Novels of Saul Bellow, 140-66.

Poirier, Richard, "Bellows to Herzog," PR, XXXII (Spring, 1965), 264-71.

Raban, J. , "Narrative: Dramatized Consciousness," Technique of Modern Fiction, 53-5.

Rahv, P. , "Saul Bellow's Progress," Myth and the Powerhouse, 218-24. Also in Rahv, P. , Literature and the Sixth Sense, 392-7.

Read, Forrest, "HERZOG: A Review," Epoch, XIV (Fall, 1964), 81-96. Also in Malin, I. , ed. , Saul Bellow and the Critics, 184-206.

Rovit, Earl, "Bellow in Occupancy," ASch, XXXIV (Spring,
    1965), 292-8. Also in Malin, I., ed., Saul Bellow and
    the Critics, 177-83.
Rubin, Louis D., "Southerners and Jews," SoR, II (1966),
    705-8. Also in Rubin, L. D., Jr., Curious Death of the
    Novel, 271-5.
Samuel Maurice, "My Friend, the Late Moses Herzog,"
    Midstream, XII (April, 1966), 3-25.
Schulz, M. F., "Saul Bellow and the Burden of Selfhood,"
    Radical Sophistication, 131-44.
Scott, Nathan A., Jr., "Sola Gratia- The Principle of Saul
    Bellow's Fiction," in Scott, N. A., Jr., ed., Adversity
    and Grace, 52-6. Also in Scott, N. A., Jr., Craters of
    the Spirit, 260-3.
Spender, Stephen, "Bellow in Search of Himself," in Encyclo-
    paedia Britannica, Great Ideas Today, 1965, 170-3.
Stock, Irvin, "The Novels of Saul Bellow," SoR, III (Winter,
    1967), 36-42.
Tanner, Tony, Saul Bellow, 87-102.
_____, "Saul Bellow: The Flight from Monologue," En-
    counter, XXIV (February, 1965), 61-6.
Trachtenberg, Stanley, "Saul Bellow's Luftmenschen: The
    Compromise with Reality," Crit, IX, iii (1967), 55-8.
Uphaus, Suzanne H., "From Innocence to Experience: A
    Study of HERZOG," DR, XLVI (Spring, 1966), 67-78.
Van Egmond, Peter, "Herzog's Quotation of Walt Whitman,"
    WWR, XIII (June, 1967), 54-6.
Walcutt, C. C., Man's Changing Mask, 352-5.
Weber, Ronald, "Bellow's Thinkers," WHR, XXII (Autumn,
    1968), 305-13.
Young, James D., "Bellow's View of the Heart," Crit, VII
    iii (1965), 5-17.

                          SEIZE THE DAY

Alter, Robert, "The Stature of Saul Bellow," Midstream,
    X (December, 1964), 9-10.
Baker, Robert, ChiR, II (Spring, 1957), 107-10.
Bowen, Robert O., NWR, I (Spring, 1957), 52-6.
Chase, Richard, Ctary, XXVII (April, 1959). Also in Malin,
    I., ed., Saul Bellow and the Critics, 30-2.
Ciancio, Ralph, "The Achievement of Saul Bellow's SEIZE
    THE DAY," in Staley, Thomas F., and L. F. Zimmerman,
    eds., Literature and Theology, Tulsa, Okla.: Un. of Tul-
    sa, 1969, 49-80.
Clayton, J. J., Saul Bellow, 28-9; 59-60; 69-74; 92-6; 105-6;
    128-34; 247-51.

Davis, Robert G., in Balakian, N., and C. Simmons, eds.,
    Creative Present, 124-7.
Eisinger, Chester E., "Saul Bellow: Love and Identity,"
    Accent, XVIII (Summer, 1958), 199-203.
Fossum, Robert R., "The Devil and Saul Bellow," CLS, III
    (1966), 200-4. Also in Panichas, G.A., ed., Mansions of
    the Spirit, 349-53.
Freedman, Ralph, "Saul Bellow: The Illusion of Environ-
    ment," WSCL, I, i (Winter, 1960), 55-7. Also in Malin,
    I., ed., Saul Bellow and the Critics, 57-9.
Galloway, David D., Absurd Hero, 104-10.
_____, "The Absurd Man as Picaro: The Novels of Saul
    Bellow," TSLL, VI (Summer, 1964), 241-4.
Geismar, M., "Saul Bellow: Novelist of the Intellectuals,"
    American Moderns, 218-24. Also in Malin, I., ed.,
    Saul Bellow and the Critics, 19-24.
Gill, Brendan, NY, XXXII (January 5, 1957), 69-70.
Gold, Herbert, "The Discovered Self," Nation, CLXXXIII
    (November 17, 1956), 435-6.
Hall, J., Lunatic Giant in the Drawing Room, 159-62.
Handy, William J., "Saul Bellow and the Naturalistic Hero,"
    TSLL, V (Winter, 1964), 538-45.
Harper, H.M., Jr., Desperate Faith, 32-9.
Hassan, I., Radical Innocence, 311-16.
Hoffman, Frederick J., in Moore, H.T., ed., Contemporary
    American Novelists, 93-4.
Kazin, Alfred, NYTBR (November 18, 1956), 5+.
_____, "Bellow's Purgatory," NYRB (March 28, 1968),
    34-6.
Levine, Paul, "Saul Bellow: The Affirmation of the Philo-
    sophical Fool," Per, X (Winter, 1959), 172-6.
Ludwig, J., Recent American Novelists, 15-16. Also in
    Kostelanetz, R., ed., On Contemporary Literature, 296-7.
Malin, Irving, in Jewish Heritage Reader, 261-3.
_____, Saul Bellow's Fiction, 66-8.
Mathis, James C., "The Theme of SEIZE THE DAY," Crit,
    VII (Spring-Summer, 1965), 43-5.
Morrow, Patrick, "Threat and Accommodation: The Novels
    of Saul Bellow," MQ, VIII (Summer, 1967), 391-4.
Opdahl, K.M., Novels of Saul Bellow, 96-117.
Podhoretz, N., "The Adventures of Saul Bellow," Doings and
    Undoings, 219-24.
Rans, Geoffrey, "The Novels of Saul Bellow," REL, IV, iv
    (October, 1963), 26-7.
Rugoff, Milton, NYTBR (November 18, 1956), 3.
Schwartz, Edward, "Chronicles of the City," NRep, CXXXV
    (December 3, 1956), 20-1.

Scott, Nathan A., Jr., "Sola Gratia- The Principle of Saul
    Bellow's Fiction," in Scott, N.A., Jr., ed., Adversity
    and Grace, 48-50. Also in Scott, N.A., Jr., Craters of
    the Spirit, 255-7.
Stern, Richard G., KR, XXI (Autumn, 1959), 655-61.
Stock, Irvin, "The Novels of Saul Bellow," SoR, III (Winter,
    1967), 27-31.
Swados, Harvey, NY Post Week-End Mag (November 18,
    1956), 11.
Tanner, T., Saul Bellow, 58-70.
Trachtenberg, Stanley, "Saul Bellow's Luftmenschen: The
    Compromise with Reality," Crit, IX, iii (1967), 49-52.
Trowbridge, Clinton W., "Water Imagery in SEIZE THE
    DAY," Crit, IX, iii (1967), 62-73.
Weiss, Daniel, "Caliban on Prospero: A Psychoanalytic
    Study on the Novel SEIZE THE DAY, by Saul Bellow," AI,
    XIX (Fall, 1962), 277-306. Also in Malin, I., ed., Psy-
    choanalysis and American Fiction, 279-307. Also in Ma-
    lin, I., ed., Saul Bellow and the Critics, 114-41.
West, Ray B., Jr., SR, LXIV (Summer, 1957), 498-508.

THE VICTIM

Allen, W., Modern Novel, 324-5.
Baumbach, J., "The Double Vision: THE VICTIM," Land-
    scape of Nightmare, 35-54.
Bradbury, Malcolm, "Saul Bellow's THE VICTIM," CritQ,
    V (Summer, 1963), 119-28.
Clayton, J.J., Saul Bellow, 139-65; 240-1.
Davis, Robert G., in Balakian, N., and C. Simmons, eds.,
    Creative Present, 116-20.
Eisinger, Chester E., Fiction of the Forties, 340-54.
_____, "Saul Bellow: Love and Identity," Accent, XVIII
    (Summer, 1958), 188-92.
Farrelly, John, NRep, CXVII (December 8, 1947), 27-8.
Fiedler, L., Love and Death in the American Novel, 360-1.
Frank, Reuben, "Saul Bellow: The Evolution of a Contempo-
    rary Novelist," WR, XVIII (Winter, 1954), 105-8.
Freedman, Ralph, "Saul Bellow: The Illusion of Environment,
    WSCL, I, i (Winter, 1960), 52-5. Also in Malin, I., ed.,
    Saul Bellow and the Critics, 53-7.
Galloway, David D., Absurd Hero, 89-94.
_____, "The Absurd Man as Picaro: The Novels of Saul
    Bellow," TSLL, VI (Summer, 1964), 231-4.
Geismar, M., "Saul Bellow: Novelist of the Intellectuals,"
    American Moderns, 213-16. Also in Malin, I., ed.,
    Saul Bellow and the Critics, 13-16.

Hall, J., Lunatic Giant in the Drawing Room, 138-49.
Harper, H. M., Jr., Desperate Faith, 16-23.
Hassan, I., Radical Innocence, 299-303.
Hoffman, Frederick J., in Moore, H. T., ed., Contemporary American Novelists, 85-8.
Jensen, Emily, "Saul Bellow's THE VICTIM: A View of Modern Man," Literature, No. 4 (1963), 38-44.
Levine, Paul, "Saul Bellow: The Affirmation of the Philosophical Fool," Per, X (Winter, 1959), 165-7.
Malin, Irving, in Jewish Heritage Reader, 259-60.
_____, Saul Bellow's Fiction, 59-63.
Miller, Karl, "Leventhal," NStat (September 10, 1965), 360-1.
Morrow, Patrick, "Threat and Accommodation: The Novels of Saul Bellow," MQ, VIII (Summer, 1967), 395-7.
Opdahl, K. M., Novels of Saul Bellow, 51-69.
Podhoretz, N., "The Adventures of Saul Bellow," Doings and Undoings, 211-15.
Rans, Geoffrey, "The Novels of Saul Bellow," REL, IV, iv (October, 1963), 20-2.
Scott, Nathan A., "Sola Gratia- The Principle of Saul Bellow's Fiction," in Scott, N. A., Jr., ed., Adversity and Grace, 40-3. Also in Scott, N. A., Jr., Craters of the Spirit, 246-9.
Stock, Irvin, "The Novels of Saul Bellow," SoR, III (Winter, 1967), 19-23.
Tanner, T., Saul Bellow, 26-37.
Trachtenberg, Stanley, "Saul Bellow's Luftmenschen: The Compromise with Reality," Crit, IX, iii (1967), 41-3.
Trilling, Diana, Nation, CLXVI (January 3, 1948), 24-5.

BIBLIOGRAPHY

Galloway, D. D., Absurd Hero, 220-6.
Opdahl, K. M., Novels of Saul Bellow, 181-93.
Schneider, Harold W., "Two Bibliographies: Saul Bellow, William Styron," Crit, III, iii (1960), 71-91.

BOURJAILY, VANCE, 1922-

GENERAL

Dienstfrey, Harris, "The Novels of Vance Bourjaily," Ctary, XXXI (April, 1961), 360-3.
Galligan, Edward L., "Hemingway's Staying Power," MR, VIII (Summer, 1967), 435-7.

CONFESSIONS OF A SPENT YOUTH

Bourjaily, Vance, "A Certain Kind of Work," in McCormack,
T., ed., Afterwords, 177-91.
Dienstfrey, Harris, "The Novels of Vance Bourjaily," Ctary,
XXXI (April, 1961), 360-3.

THE END OF MY LIFE

Aldridge, J. W., After the Lost Generation, 121-32.
Bourjaily, Vance, in Madden, C. F., ed., Talks with Authors,
201-14.
DeLancey, Robert W., "Man and Mankind in the Novels of
Vance Bourjaily," EngR, X (Winter, 1959), 3-4.
Waldmeir, J. J., American Novels of the Second World War,
20-3.

THE HOUND OF EARTH

DeLancey, Robert W., "Man and Mankind in the Novels of
Vance Bourjaily," EngR, X (Winter, 1959), 5-6.

THE VIOLATED

Hicks, Granville, "The Maturity of Vance Bourjaily," SatR
(August 23, 1958), 13.

BOWEN, ELIZABETH, 1899-

GENERAL

Brooke, J., Elizabeth Bowen.
Daiches, David, "The Novels of Elizabeth Bowen," EJ,
XXXVIII (June, 1949), 305-13.
Dostal, Sister Rose Margaret, O. S. U., "Innocence and Knowl-
edge in the Novels of Elizabeth Bowen," DA, XXV (1964),
2509-10 (Notre Dame).
Greene, George, "Elizabeth Bowen: Imagination as Therapy,"
Per, XIV (Spring, 1965), 42-52.
Hall, J., Lunatic Giant in the Drawing Room, 17-55.
Hanna, John G., "Elizabeth Bowen and the Art of Fiction: A
Study of Her Theory and Practice," DA, XXII (1961), 1175-
6 (Boston Univ.).
Hardwick, Elizabeth, "Elizabeth Bowen's Fiction," PR, XVI
(November, 1949), 1114-21.
Harkness, Bruce, "The Fiction of Elizabeth Bowen," EJ,

XLIV (December, 1955), 499-506.

Heath, W. , <u>Elizabeth Bowen</u>.

Karl, F. R. , "The World of Elizabeth Bowen," <u>Contemporary English Novel,</u> 107-30.

Kendris, Thomas, "The Novels of Elizabeth Bowen," <u>DA,</u> XXVI (1965), 1648 (Columbia).

Kirkpatrick, Larry J. , "Elizabeth Bowen and Company: A Comparative Essay in Literary Judgment," <u>DA,</u> XXVI (1966), 6044 (Duke).

Miller, Donald W. , "Scene and Image in Three Novels by Elizabeth Bowen," <u>DA,</u> XXVIII (1967), 637A-8A (Columbia).

O'Faolain, S. , <u>Vanishing Hero,</u> 146-69.

Pendry, E. D. , <u>New Feminism of English Fiction,</u> 120-52.

Rupp, Richard H. , "The Achievement of Elizabeth Bowen: A Study of Her Fiction and Criticism," <u>DA,</u> XXV (1965), 5286 (Ind.).

_____ , "The Post-War Fiction of Elizabeth Bowen," <u>XUS,</u> IV (1965), 55-67.

Sackville-West, Edward, "Ladies whose bright Pens...," <u>Inclinations</u>, London: Secker and Warburg, 1949, 78-103. Port Washington, N. Y. : Kennikat Pr. , 1967, 78-103.

Seward, Barbara, "Elizabeth Bowen's World of Impoverished Love," <u>CE,</u> XVIII (October, 1956), 30-7.

Sharp, Sister M. Corona, O. S. U. , "The House as Setting and Symbol in Three Novels by Elizabeth Bowen," <u>XUS,</u> II (December, 1963), 93-103.

Snow, Lotus, "The Uncertain 'I': A Study of Elizabeth Bowen's Fiction," <u>WHR,</u> IV (Autumn, 1950), 299-310.

Stokes, Edward, "Elizabeth Bowen- Pre-Assumptions or Moral Angle?" <u>AUMLA,</u> No. 11 (September, 1959), 35-47.

Strong, Leonard A. G. , <u>Personal Remarks,</u> N. Y. : Liveright, 1953, 132-45.

Wagner, Geoffrey, "Elizabeth Bowen and the Artificial Novel," <u>EIC,</u> XIII (April, 1963), 155-63.

THE DEATH OF THE HEART

Allen, W. , <u>Modern Novel,</u> 192-4.

Bogan, Louise, "The Pure in Heart," <u>Nation,</u> CXLVIII (January 28, 1939), 123+. Also in <u>Selected Criticism: Prose, Poetry,</u> N. Y. : Noonday Pr. , 1955, 125-8.

Brooke, J. , <u>Elizabeth Bowen,</u> 21-4.

Daiches, David, "The Novels of Elizabeth Bowen," <u>EJ,</u> XXXVIII (June, 1949), 310-11.

Fraser, G. S. , "Muffled Poetry," <u>NS & Nation</u> (October 13, 1961), 520-1.

Hall, J., Lunatic Giant in the Drawing Room, 32-50.
Harkness, Bruce, "The Fiction of Elizabeth Bowen," EJ,
    XLIV (December, 1955), 501-4.
Heath, W., Elizabeth Bowen, 83-102.
Heinemann, Alison, "The Indoor Landscape in Bowen's THE
    DEATH OF THE HEART," Crit, X, iii (1968), 5-12.
Karl, F.R., "The World of Elizabeth Bowen," Contemporary
    English Novel, 118-26.
Miller, Donald W., "Scene and Image in Three Novels by
    Elizabeth Bowen," DA, XXVIII (1967), 637A-8A (Columbia).
O'Faolain, S., Vanishing Hero, 161-4.
Sharp, Sister M. Corona, O.S.U., "The House as Setting
    and Symbol in Three Novels by Elizabeth Bowen," XUS, II
    (December, 1963), 99-102.
Snow, Lotus, "The Uncertain 'I': A Study of Elizabeth
    Bowen's Fiction," WHR, IV (1950), 306-8.
Strong, Leonard A.G., Personal Remarks, N.Y.: Liveright,
    1953, 140-4.
Van Duyn, Mona, "Pattern and Pilgrimage: A Reading of
    THE DEATH OF THE HEART," Crit, IV, ii (1961), 52-66.

EVA TROUT

Moss, H., "The Heiress Is an Outsider," NYTBR (October
    13, 1968), 1, 28, 30. Also as "Elizabeth Bowen: Intelli-
    gence at War," Writing Against Time, 214-19.

FRIENDS AND RELATIONS

Brooke, J., Elizabeth Bowen, 14-17.
Daiches, David, "The Novels of Elizabeth Bowen," EJ,
    XXXVIII (June, 1949), 306-7.
Heath, W., Elizabeth Bowen, 51-8.
Pendry, E.D., New Feminism of English Fiction, 125-8.

THE HEAT OF THE DAY

Allen, W., Modern Novel, 194-5.
Brooke, J., Elizabeth Bowen, 24-8.
Daiches, David, "The Novels of Elizabeth Bowen," EJ,
    XXXVIII (June, 1949), 311-12.
Dorenkamp, Angela G., "'Fall or Leap': Bowen's THE
    HEAT OF THE DAY," Crit, X, iii (1968), 13-21.
Hall, J., Lunatic Giant in the Drawing Room, 50-5.
Hardwick, Elizabeth, "Elizabeth Bowen's Fiction," PR, XVI
    (1949), 1116-18.
Heath, W., Elizabeth Bowen, 108-24.

Karl, F. R. , "The World of Elizabeth Bowen," Contemporary
English Novel, 126-9.
Prescott, O. , In My Opinion, 102-4.
Rupp, Richard H. , "The Post-War Fiction of Elizabeth
Bowen," XUS, IV (1965), 56-9.

THE HOTEL

Heath, W. , Elizabeth Bowen, 21-33.
Karl, F. R. , "The World of Elizabeth Bowen," Contemporary
English Novel, 111-12.

THE HOUSE IN PARIS

Brooke, J. , Elizabeth Bowen, 20-1.
Daiches, David, "The Novels of Elizabeth Bowen," EJ,
XXXVIII (June, 1949), 308-10.
Hall, J. , Lunatic Giant in the Drawing Room, 20-32.
Hardwick, Elizabeth, "Elizabeth Bowen's Fiction," PR, XVI
(1949), 1118-19.
Heath, W. , Elizabeth Bowen, 72-83.
Karl, F. R. , "The World of Elizabeth Bowen," Contemporary
English Novel, 114-18.
Miller, Donald W. , "Scene and Image in Three Novels by
Elizabeth Bowen," DA, XXVIII (1967), 637A-8A (Colum-
bia).
Sharp, Sister M. Corona, O. S. U. , "The House as Setting
and Symbol in Three Novels by Elizabeth Bowen," XUS,
II (December, 1963), 95-8.

THE LAST SEPTEMBER

Bowen, E. , Preface to THE LAST SEPTEMBER, N. Y. :
Knopf, 1952. Also in Bowen, E. , Seven Winters and
Afterthoughts, 197-204.
Brooke, J. , Elizabeth Bowen, 13-14.
Heath, W. , Elizabeth Bowen, 32-46.
O'Faolain, S. , Vanishing Hero, 151-6.
Sharp, Sister M. Corona, O. S. U. , "The House as Setting
and Symbol in Three Novels by Elizabeth Bowen," XUS,
II (December, 1963), 93-5.

THE LITTLE GIRLS

Burgess, A. , Urgent Copy, 149-53.
Greene, George, "Elizabeth Bowen: Imagination as Therapy,"
Per, XIV (Spring, 1965), 48-52.

McDowell, Frederick P.W., "Elizabeth Bowen's THE LITTLE
  GIRLS," Crit, VII (Spring, 1964), 139-43.
Rupp, Richard H., "The Post-War Fiction of Elizabeth Bow-
  en," XUS, IV (1965), 64-6.

TO THE NORTH

Brooke, J. Elizabeth Bowen, 17-18.
Heath, W., Elizabeth Bowen, 58-70.
Karl, F.R., "The World of Elizabeth Bowen," Contemporary
  English Novel, 113-14.

A WORLD OF LOVE

Baker, Carlos, "Death of a Ghost," Nation, CLXX (Febru-
  ary 21, 1955), 123.
Heath, W., Elizabeth Bowen, 130-44.
Miller, Donald W., "Scene and Image in Three Novels by
  Elizabeth Bowen," DA, XXVIII (1967), 637A-8A (Colum-
  bia).
Rupp, Richard H., "The Post-War Fiction of Elizabeth
  Bowen," XUS, IV (1965), 59-64.
Wagner, Geoffrey, "Elizabeth Bowen and the Artificial Novel,"
  EIC, XIII (April, 1963), 156-63.
Wyndham, Francis, LonM, II (June, 1955), 86-9.

BIBLIOGRAPHY

Heath, W., Elizabeth Bowen, 170-6.

BOWEN, JOHN, 1924-

GENERAL

Gindin, J., "Creeping Americanism," Postwar British Fiction, 114-27.

STORYBOARD

Urwin, G.G., ed., Taste for Living, 186-9.

BOWLES, PAUL, 1911-

GENERAL

Eisinger, C. E. , Fiction of the Forties, 283-8.
Evans, Oliver, "Paul Bowles and the 'Natural' Man," Crit,
    III, i (1959), 43-59. Also in Waldmeir, J. J. , ed. , Re-
    cent American Fiction, 139-52.
Fytton, Francis, "The Pipe Dreams of Paul Bowles," LonM,
    n. s. VI (February 1967), 102-9.
Hassan, Ihab H. , "The Pilgrim as Prey: A Note on Paul
    Bowles," WR, XIX (Autumn, 1954), 23-36.
O'Connor, W. V. , Grotesque, 11-12.

LET IT COME DOWN

Evans, Oliver, "Paul Bowles and the 'Natural' Man," Crit,
    III, i (1959), 50-3. Also in Waldmeir, J. J. , ed. , Recent
    American Fiction, 145-8.
Glicksberg, Charles I. , "The Literary Struggle for Selfhood,"
    Person, XLII (January, 1961), 62-3.
_____, "Literature and the Meaning of Life," SAQ, LV
    (April, 1956), 157-8.
Hassan, Ihab H. , "The Pilgrim as Prey: A Note on Paul
    Bowles, WR, XIX (Autumn, 1954), 28-30.
_____, Radical Innocence, 87-8.
Lehan, Richard, "Existentialism in Recent American Fiction:
    The Demonic Quest," TSLL, I (Summer, 1959), 185-6.

THE SHELTERING SKY

Aldridge, J. W. , After the Lost Generation, 186-93.
Allen, W. , Modern Novel, 300 -1.
Eisinger, C. E. , Fiction of the Forties, 285-7.
Evans, Oliver, "Paul Bowles and the 'Natural' Man," Crit,
    III, i (1959), 45-8. Also in Waldmeir, J. J. , ed. , Recent
    American Fiction, 141-3.
Glicksberg, Charles I. , Literature and Religion: A Study in
    Conflict, Dallas: Southern Methodist Un. Pr. , 1960, 183-4.
Hassan, Ihab H. , "The Pilgrim as Prey: A Note on Paul
    Bowles," WR, XIX (Autumn, 1954), 25-7.
_____, Radical Innocence, 86-7.
Joost, Nicholas, in Gardiner, H. C. , Fifty Years of the Amer-
    ican Novel, 286-7.
Lehan, Richard, "Existentialism in Recent American Fiction:
    The Demonic Quest," TSLL, I (Summer, 1959), 184-5.
Prescott, O. , In My Opinion, 116-17.

Straumann, H., American Literature in the Twentieth Century, 79-80.

THE SPIDER'S HOUSE

Evans, Oliver, "Paul Bowles and the 'Natural' Man," Crit,
   III, i (1959), 53-7. Also in Waldmeir, J. J., ed., Re-
   cent American Fiction, 148-51.
Lehan, Richard, "Existentialism in Recent American Fiction:
   The Demonic Quest," TSLL, I (Summer, 1959), 186-7.

BOYLE, KAY, 1903-

GENERAL

Carpenter, Richard C., "Kay Boyle," CE, XV (1953), 81-7.
   Also in EJ, XLII (1953), 425-30.
Jackson, Byron K., "The Achievement of Kay Boyle," DA,
   XXIX (1968), 899A (Florida).
Van Gelder, Robert, Writers on Writing, 193-6.

AVALANCHE

Wilson, E., NY (January 15, 1944). Also in Classics and
   Commercials, 128-32.

BRACE, GERALD WARNER, 1901-

GENERAL

Harris, Arthur S., Jr., "Gerald Warner Brace: Teacher-
   Novelist," CE, XVIII (1956), 157-60.
Wagenknecht, E., Cavalcade of the American Novel, 458-60.

THE SPIRE

Lyons, J. O., College Novel in America, 127-9.

BRAINE, JOHN, 1922-

GENERAL

Lee, J. W., John Braine.
Lockwood, Bernard, "Four Contemporary British Working-

Class Novelists: A Thematic and Critical Approach to the
Fiction of Raymond Williams, John Braine, David Storey
and Alan Sillitoe," DA, XXVIII (1967), 1081A (Wisconsin).
Shestakov, Dmitri, "John Braine Facing His Fourth Novel,"
Soviet Lit, No. 8 (1964), 178-81.

THE CRYING GAME

Anon., "Fiction of 1968. John Braine: THE CRYING
GAME," TLS (August 29, 1968). Also in T.L.S. Essays
and Reviews from The Times Literary Supplement, 1968,
73-5.

THE JEALOUS GOD

Lee, J.W., John Braine, 95-107.
Spender, Stephen, "Must There Always be a Red Brick England?" in Encyclopaedia Britannica, Great Ideas Today,
1965, 181-3.

LIFE AT THE TOP

Lee, J.W., John Braine, 82-94.
McDowell, Frederick P.W., " 'The Devious Involutions of
Human Character and Emotions' : Reflections on Some
Recent British Novels," WSCL, IV, iii (Autumn, 1963),
344-6
Rippier, J.S., Some Postwar English Novelists, 188-92.

ROOM AT THE TOP

Allsop, K., Angry Decade, 78-85.
Fraser, G.S., Modern Writer and His World, 181-2.
Hurrell, John, "Class and Consciousness in John Braine and
Kingsley Amis," Crit, II, i (1958), 39-53.
Karl, F.R., "The Angries: Is There a Protestant in the
House?" Contemporary English Novel, 229-30.
Lee, J.W., John Braine, 52-68
Rippier, J.S., Some Postwar English Novelists, 178-85.

THE VODI (FROM THE HAND OF THE HUNTER)

Jelly, Oliver, "Fiction and Illness," REL, III (January,
1962), 80-9.
Karl, F.R., "The Angries: Is There a Protestant in the
House?" Contemporary English Novel, 230-1.
Lee, J.W., John Braine, 69-81.

Rippier, J. S. , Some Postwar English Novelists, 185-8.
Urwin, G. G. , ed. , Taste for Living, 44-7.

BUCK, PEARL S. , 1892-

GENERAL

Buck, Pearl S. , My Several Worlds: A Personal Record,
    N. Y. : Day, 1954.
Cevasco, George A. , "Pearl Buck and the Chinese Novel, "
    Asian Studies, V (December, 1967), 437-50.
Doàn-Cao-Lý, Image of the Chinese Family in Pearl Buck's
    Novels.
Doyle, P. A. , Pearl S. Buck.
Gray, J. , On Second Thought, 28-35.
Thompson, Dody W. , in French, W. G. , and Kidd, W. E. ,
    eds. , American Winners of the Nobel Literary Prize, 85-
    110.
Van Gelder, R. , Writers on Writing, 26-8.

COMMAND THE MORNING

Doyle, P. A. , Pearl S. Buck, 137-40.

DRAGON SEED

Doàn-Cao-Lý, Image of the Chinese Family in Pearl Buck's
    Novels, 109-22.
Doyle, P. A. , Pearl S. Buck, 117-21.

EAST WIND: WEST WIND

Doàn-Cao-Lý, Image of the Chinese Family in Pearl Buck's
    Novels, 31-66.
Doyle, P. A. , Pearl S. Buck, 29-35.

THE GOOD EARTH (See also HOUSE OF EARTH Trilogy)

Cevasco, George A. , "Pearl Buck and the Chinese Novel, "
    Asian Studies, V (December, 1967), 444-9.
Doyle, P. A. , Pearl S. Buck, 36-54.
Gray, J. , On Second Thought, 30-2.
Langlois, Walter G. , "THE DREAM OF THE RED CHAM-
    BER, THE GOOD EARTH, and MAN'S FATE: Chronicles
    of Social Change in China, " LE&W, XI (March, 1967), 1-
    10.

Shimizu, Mamoru, "On Some Stylistic Features, Chiefly Biblical, of THE GOOD EARTH," SELit, Engl. No. (1964), 117-34.

Stuckey, W. J., Pulitzer Prize Novels, 90-3.

A HOUSE DIVIDED (See also HOUSE OF EARTH Trilogy)

Cowley, M., "The Good Earthling," NRep (January 23, 1935). Also in Think Back on Us, 251-4.

Doyle, P. A., Pearl S. Buck, 64-70.

HOUSE OF EARTH Trilogy

Doàn-Cao-Lý, Image of the Chinese Family in Pearl Buck's Novels, 67-94.

Doyle, P. A., Pearl S. Buck, 57-70.

KINFOLK

Doyle, P. A., Pearl S. Buck, 134-7.

THE MOTHER

Doàn-Cao-Lý, Image of the Chinese Family in Pearl Buck's Novels, 128-31.

Doyle, P. A., Pearl S. Buck, 70-5.

OTHER GODS

Doyle, P. A., Pearl S. Buck, 108-12.

THE PATRIOT

Doàn-Cao-Lý, Image of the Chinese Family in Pearl Buck's Novels, 95-108.

Doyle, P. A., Pearl S. Buck, 104-8.

PAVILION OF WOMEN

Doàn-Cao-Lý, Image of the Chinese Family in Pearl Buck's Novels, 131-40.

Doyle, P. A., Pearl S. Buck, 130-4.

Vollmershausen, Joseph, "PAVILION OF WOMEN. A Psychoanalytic Interpretation," AJP, X (1950), 53-60.

THE PROMISE

Doyle, P. A. , <u>Pearl S. Buck,</u> 121-4.

SONS (See also HOUSE OF EARTH Trilogy)

Doyle, P. A. , <u>Pearl S. Buck,</u> 58-64.

THIS PROUD HEART

Doyle, P. A. , <u>Pearl S. Buck,</u> 87-91.

THE TOWNSMAN (Under pseudonym, John Sedges)

Doyle, P. A. , <u>Pearl S. Buck,</u> 125-30.

BIBLIOGRAPHY

Brenni, Vito, "Pearl Buck: A Selected Bibliography," <u>BB,</u>
XXII (May-August, 1957), 65-9; (September-December,
1957), 94-6.

BUECHNER, FREDERICK, 1926-

A LONG DAY'S DYING

Aldridge, J. W. , <u>After the Lost Generation,</u> 219-30.
Allen, W. , <u>Modern Novel,</u> 303-5.
Hassan, I. , <u>Radical Innocence,</u> 153-61.

THE RETURN OF ANSEL GIBBS

Blotner, J. , <u>Modern American Political Novel,</u> 331-3.
Podhoretz, N. , "The New Nihilism and the Novel," <u>PR,</u> XXV
(Fall, 1958), 580-1. Also in Podhoretz, N. , <u>Doings and
Undoings,</u> 164-6.

BURGESS, ANTHONY, 1917-

GENERAL

Davis, Earle, " 'Laugh Now--Think Later!' : The Genius of
Anthony Burgess," <u>KM</u> (1968), 7-12.
Hyman, Stanley E. , Afterword to Burgess, A. , A CLOCK-
WORK ORANGE, N. Y. : Norton, 1963. Also in Kostel-

anetz, R., ed., <u>Contemporary Literature,</u> 300-5.

Mitchell, Julian, "Anthony Burgess," <u>LonM</u>, n. s. III (February, 1964), 48-54.

Pritchard, William H., "The Novels of Anthony Burgess," <u>MR</u>, VII (Summer, 1966), 525-39.

A CLOCKWORK ORANGE

Pritchard, William H., "The Novels of Anthony Burgess," <u>MR</u>, VII (Summer, 1966), 532-4.

HONEY FOR THE BEARS

Pritchard, William H., "The Novels of Anthony Burgess," <u>MR</u>, VII (Summer, 1966), 536-9.

THE LONG DAY WANES Trilogy

Pritchard, William H., "The Novels of Anthony Burgess," <u>MR</u>, VII (Summer, 1966), 526-9.

NOTHING LIKE THE SUN

Burgess, Anthony, "Genesis and Headache," in McCormack, T., ed., <u>Afterwords,</u> 29-47.

THE RIGHT TO AN ANSWER

Pritchard, William H., "The Novels of Anthony Burgess," <u>MR</u>, VII (Summer, 1966), 529-32.

THE WANTING SEED

Pritchard, William H., "The Novels of Anthony Burgess," <u>MR</u>, VII (Summer, 1966), 534-6.

BURNS, JOHN HORNE, 1916-1953

GENERAL

Brophy, Brigid, in (London) <u>Sunday Times Magazine</u> (October, 1964). Also in Brophy, B., <u>Don't Never Forget,</u> 192-202.

A CRY OF CHILDREN

Brophy, B., Don't Never Forget, 198-9.

THE GALLERY

Aldridge, J.W., After the Lost Generation, 140-6.
Allen, W., Modern Novel, 294-6.
Brophy, B., Don't Never Forget, 192-8.
Eisinger, C.E., Fiction of the Forties, 40-1.
French, Warren, in French, W., ed., Forties, 27-32.
Healey, Robert C., in Gardiner, H.C., ed., Fifty Years of
the American Novel, 265-6.
Valk, E.M., "Baraka: A Reminiscence in Memory of John
Horne Burns," LitR, III (1959), 280-6.
Waldmeir, J.J., American Novels of the Second World War,
81; 103-7.

BURROUGHS, WILLIAM, 1914-

GENERAL

Anon., "The Novels of William Burroughs," TLS (November
14, 1963). Also in T.L.S.: Essays and Reviews from
The Times Literary Supplement, 1963, 221-5.
Ansen, Alan, "Anyone Who Can Pick Up a Frying Pan Owns
Death," Big Table #2, I (Summer, 1959), 32-41. Also in
Parkinson, T., ed., Casebook on the Beat, 107-13.
Fiedler, L.A., Waiting for the End, 163-71.
Hassan, Ihab, "The Literature of Silence: From Henry Mil-
ler to Beckett and Burroughs," Encounter, XXVIII (Janu-
ary, 1967), 74-82.
_____, "The Subtracting Machine: The Work of William
Burroughs," Crit, VI, i (Spring, 1963), 4-23.
Knickerbocker, Conrad, "William Burroughs," Paris Rev,
No. 35 (Fall, 1965), 13-49. Also in Writers at Work,
3rd ser., 141-74.
Tanner, Tony, "The New Demonology," PR, XXXIII (Fall,
1966), 547-72.
Weston, Donald, "William Burroughs, High Priest of Hipster-
ism," Fact, II (November-December, 1965), 11-17.

THE NAKED LUNCH

Abel, Lionel, "Beyond the Fringe," PR, XXX (Spring, 1963),
109-12.

Adam, Ian W., "Society as Novelist," JAAC, XXV (Summer, 1967), 375-86.
"The Boston Trial of NAKED LUNCH," EvR, IX (June, 1965), 40-9, 87-8.
Bradbury, Malcolm, "Saul Bellow's HERZOG," CritQ, VII (1965), 269-78.
Hassan, Ihab, "The Subtracting Machine: The Work of William Burroughs," Crit, VI, i (Spring, 1963), 11-14.
Hoffman, F. J., Mortal No, 486-8.
Kostelanetz, Richard, "From Nightmare to Seredipity (sic); A Retrospective Look at William Burroughs," TCL, XI (October, 1965), 123-30. Also (much abridged) as "The New American Fiction," in Kostelanetz, R., ed., New American Arts, 229-31.
Lodge, David, "Objections to William Burroughs," CritQ, VIII (Autumn, 1966), 203-12.
McCarthy, Mary, "Burroughs' NAKED LUNCH," Encounter, XX (April, 1963), 92-8.
_____, "Dejeuner sur l'Herbe," NYRB, I, i (1963), 4-5.
McConnell, Frank, "William Burroughs and the Literature of Addiction," MR, VIII (Autumn, 1967), 665-80. Also in Plimpton, George, and Peter Ardery, eds., The American Literary Anthology /2, N.Y.: Random House, 1969, 367-81.
Malcolm, Donald, "The Heroin of Our Times," NY, XXXVIII (February 2, 1963), 114-21.
Michelson, Peter, "Beardsley, Burroughs, Decadence, and the Poetics of Obscenity," TriQ, XII (Spring, 1968), 148-55.
Peterson, R. G., "A Picture is a Fact: Wittgenstein and THE NAKED LUNCH," TCL, XII (July, 1966), 78-86.
Selden, E. S., "On NAKED LUNCH," EvR, No. 22 (January-February, 1962), 110-13. Also in Seaver, Richard, Terry Southern, and Alexander Trocchi, eds., Writers in Revolt: An Anthology, N.Y.: Frederick Fell, 1963, 323-7.
Widmer, L., "Rebellion Against Rebellion?" Literary Rebel, 155-8.

NOVA EXPRESS

Bernard, Sidney, "Literati: William Burroughs," Ramparts, V (August, 1966), 51-2.
Lodge, David, "Objections to William Burroughs," CritQ, VIII (Autumn, 1966), 203-12.
Phillips, William, "The New Immoralists," Ctary, XXXIX (April, 1965), 66-9.

THE SOFT MACHINE

Hassan, Ihab, "The Subtracting Machine: The Work of William Burroughs," Crit, VI, i (Spring, 1963), 15-18.

THE TICKET THAT EXPLODED

Hassan, Ihab, "The Subtracting Machine: The Work of William Burroughs," Crit, VI, i (Spring, 1963), 18-21.
Solotaroff, Theodore, "The Algebra Need," NRep (August 5, 1967), 29-34.

CALDWELL, ERSKINE, 1903-

GENERAL

Beach, J. W., American Fiction, 219-49.
Benedict, Stewart H., "Gallic Light on Erskine Caldwell," SAQ, LX (Autumn, 1961), 390-7.
Bode, Carl, "Erskine Caldwell: A Note for the Negative," CE, XVII (1956), 357-9. Also in Bode, Carl, The Half-World of American Culture; A Miscellany, Carbondale: So. Ill. Un. Pr., 1965, 170-4.
Burke, Kenneth, "Caldwell: Maker of Grotesques," The Philosophy of Literary Form, 2nd ed., Baton Rouge: La. State Un. Pr., 1967, 350-60. Also in Howe, I., ed., Modern Literary Criticism: An Anthology, N. Y.: Grove, 1961 (c. 1958, Beacon), 291-8. Also in Malin, I., ed., Psychoanalysis and American Fiction, 245-54.
Caldwell, Erskine, "The Art, Craft, and Personality of Writing," TQ, VII, i (Spring, 1964), 37-43.
Cantwell, Robert, "Caldwell's Characters: Why Don't They Leave," GaR, XI (Fall, 1957), 252-64.
Collins, Carvel, "Erskine Caldwell at Work," Atlantic, CCII (July, 1958), 21-7.
Cross, Carlyle, "Erskine Caldwell as a Southern Writer," DA, XXIV (1964), 4696-7 (Georgia).
Frohock, W. M., "Erskine Caldwell: Sentimental Gentleman from Georgia," SWR, XXXI (Autumn, 1946), 351-9. Also as "Erskine Caldwell: The Dangers of Ambiguity," Novel of Violence in America, 106-23.
Gossett, L. Y., Violence in Recent Southern Fiction, 16-29.
Gurko, L., Angry Decade, 137-9.
Hazel, Robert, in Rubin, L. D., Jr., and R. D. Jacobs, eds., Southern Renascence, 316-24. Also in Rubin, L. D., Jr., and R. D. Jacobs, eds., South, 323-33.

Korges, J., Erskine Caldwell.
Lelchuk, Alan, and Robin White, "Erskine Caldwell," Per/
Se, II, i (Spring, 1967), 11-20.
Maclachlan, John M., "Folk and Culture in the Novels of
Erskine Caldwell," SFQ, IX (June, 1945), 93-101.
Snell, G., Shapers of American Fiction, 263-76.
Thorp, W., American Writing in the Twentieth Century,
261-2.
Van Gelder, Robert, Writers on Writing, 34-7.
Wagenknecht, E., Cavalcade of the American Novel, 415-17.

THE BASTARD

Korges, J., Erskine Caldwell, 12-13.

EPISODE IN PALMETTO

Korges, J., Erskine Caldwell, 40-1.

GEORGIA BOY

Frohock, W.M., "Erskine Caldwell: Sentimental Gentleman
from Georgia," SWR, XXXI (Autumn, 1946), 351-2. Also
in Novel of Violence in America, 106-8.
Korges, J., Erskine Caldwell, 37-9.

GOD'S LITTLE ACRE

Allen, W., Modern Novel, 119-20.
Beach, J.W., American Fiction, 240-5.
Itofuji, Horomi, "An Aspect of Erskine Caldwell in GOD'S
LITTLE ACRE," KAL, No. 2 (May, 1959), 17-22.
Korges, J., Erskine Caldwell, 25-32.
Kubie, Lawrence S., M.D., "GOD'S LITTLE ACRE," SatR
(November 24, 1934). Also in Saturday Review, The
Saturday Review Treasury, N.Y.: Simon & Schuster,
1957, 89-97.

GRETTA

Korges, J., Erskine Caldwell, 30-2.

JOURNEYMAN

Beach, J.W., American Fiction, 235-8.
Frohock, W.M., "Erskine Caldwell: Sentimental Gentleman
from Georgia," SWR, XXXI (Autumn, 1946), 356-7. Also

in Frohock, W. M. , Novel of Violence in America, 118-19.
Korges, J. , Erskine Caldwell, 32-5.

MISS MAMMA AIMEE

Korges, J. , Erskine Caldwell, 43-4.

THE SACRILEGE OF ALAN KENT

Korges, J. , Erskine Caldwell, 10-12.

SUMMERTIME ISLAND

Korges, J. , Erskine Caldwell, 42-3.

TOBACCO ROAD

Beach, J. W. , American Fiction, 225-31.
Gray, J. , On Second Thought, 119-23.
Korges, J. , Erskine Caldwell, 22-4.
Snell, G. , Shapers of American Fiction, 272-4.

TRAGIC GROUND

Frohock, W. M. , "Erskine Caldwell: Sentimental Gentleman
    from Georgia," SWR, XXXI (Autumn, 1946), 354-6.   Also
    in Frohock, W. M. , Novel of Violence in America, 112-
    16.
Gray, J. , On Second Thought, 125-6.

TROUBLE IN JULY

Beach, J. W. , American Fiction, 238-40.
Frohock, W. M. , "Erskine Caldwell: Sentimental Gentleman
    from Georgia," SWR, XXXI (Autumn, 1946), 352-4.   Also
    in Frohock, W. M. , Novel of Violence in America, 108-
    10.

BIBLIOGRAPHY

Korges, J. , Erskine Caldwell, 47-8.

CALISHER, HORTENSE, 1911-

GENERAL

Hahn, Emily, "In Appreciation of Hortense Calisher," WSCL,

VI (Summer, 1965), 243-9.

TEXTURES OF LIFE

Brophy, Brigid, in NStat (September 13, 1963), 326. Also in Brophy, B., Don't Never Forget, 160-2.

CALLAGHAN, MORLEY, 1903-

GENERAL

Conron, B., Morley Callaghan.
Fajardo, Salvador, "Morley Callaghan's Novels and Short Stories," Dissertation, Un. of Montreal, 1962.
Heaton, Cherrill P., "The Great Sin: A Critical Study of Morley Callaghan's Novels," DA, XXVII (1966), 1056A-7A (Florida St. Un.).
Klinck, C. F., ed., Literary History of Canada, Toronto: Un. of Toronto Pr., 1965, 688-93.
McPherson, Hugo, "The Two Worlds of Morley Callaghan: Man's Earthly Quest," QQ, LXIV (Autumn, 1957), 350-65.
Moon, Barbara, "The Second Coming of Morley Callaghan," MM, LXXIII (December 3, 1960), 62-4.
Pacey, D., Creative Writing in Canada, 209-14.
Ripley, J. D., "A Critical Study of Morley Callaghan," Unpublished M. A. thesis, Un. of New Brunswick, 1959.
Watt, F. W., "Morley Callaghan as Thinker," DR, XXXIX (Autumn, 1959), 305-13. Also in Smith, A. J. M., ed., Masks of Fiction, 116-27.
Weaver, Robert L., "A Talk with Morley Callaghan," TamR, VII (Spring, 1958), 3-29.
Wilson, Edmund, "Morley Callaghan of Toronto," NY, XXXVI (November 26, 1960), 224-37. Also in Wilson, E., O Canada, 9-21. In addition, 22-31.
_____, "That Summer in Paris," NY, XXXIX (February 23, 1963), 139-48.
Woodcock, George, "Lost Eurydice: The Novels of Morley Callaghan," CanL, No. 21 (Summer, 1964), 21-35. Also in Canadian Literature. A Choice of Critics, 185-202.

A BROKEN JOURNEY

Conron, B., Morley Callaghan, 70-8.

IT'S NEVER OVER

Conron, B., Morley Callaghan, 59-65.
Wilson, Edmund, "Morley Callaghan of Toronto," O Canada,
   24-6.

THE LOVED AND THE LOST

Conron, B., Morley Callaghan, 128-35.
McPherson, Hugo, "The Two Worlds of Morley Callaghan:
   Man's Earthly Quest," QQ, LXIV (Autumn, 1957), 362-5.
Phelps, Arthur L., Canadian Writers, 10-18.
Wilson, Edmund, "Morley Callaghan of Toronto," NY,
   XXXVI (November 26, 1960), 226-30. Also in Wilson,
   E., O Canada, 12-15.

THE MANY COLORED COAT

Conron, B., Morley Callaghan, 135-47.
McPherson, Hugo, "A Tale Retold," CanL, No. 7 (Winter,
   1961), 59-61.
Watt, F.W., "Fiction," in "Letters in Canada: 1960," UTQ,
   XXX (July, 1961), 402-4.
Wilson, Edmund, "Morley Callaghan of Toronto," NY, XXXVI
   (November 26, 1960), 230-3. Also in Wilson, E., O Can-
   ada, 15-18.

MORE JOY IN HEAVEN

Conron, B., Morley Callaghan, 108-18.
McPherson, Hugo, "The Two Worlds of Morley Callaghan:
   Man's Earthly Quest," QQ, LXIV (Autumn, 1957), 360-2.

NO MAN'S MEAT

Conron, B., Morley Callaghan, 65-9.

A PASSION IN ROME

Conron, B., Morley Callaghan, 155-67.
Woodcock, George, "The Callaghan Case," CanL, No. 12
   (Spring, 1962), 60-4.

STRANGE FUGITIVE

Conron, B., Morley Callaghan, 23-8
McPherson, Hugo, "The Two Worlds of Morley Callaghan:

Man's Earthly Quest," QQ, LXIV (Autumn, 1957), 352-6.
Wilson, E., O Canada, 22-3.

SUCH IS MY BELOVED

Conron, B., Morley Callaghan, 78-86.
McPherson, Hugo, "The Two Worlds of Morley Callaghan:
Man's Earthly Quest," QQ, LXIV (Autumn, 1957), 357-9.

THEY SHALL INHERIT THE EARTH

Conron, B., Morley Callaghan, 86-96.

THE VARSITY STORY

Conron, B., Morley Callaghan, 124-6.
Wilson, E., O Canada, 26-8.

BIBLIOGRAPHY

Conron, B., Morley Callaghan, 181-4.

CAPOTE, TRUMAN, 1924-

GENERAL

Aldridge, J. W., After the Lost Generation, 196-219.
Allen, W., Modern Novel, 301-3.
Baldanza, Frank, "Plato in Dixie," GaR, XII (Summer, 1958),
162-5.
Bucco, Martin, "Truman Capote and the Country Below the
Surface," Four Quarters, VII, i (November, 1957), 22-5.
Friedman, Melvin J., in Malin, I., ed., Truman Capote's
IN COLD BLOOD, 163-76.
Goad, Craig M., "Daylight and Darkness, Dream and Delu-
sion: The Works of Truman Capote," ESRS, XVI (Sep-
tember, 1967), 5-57.
Gossett, L. Y., "Violence in a Private World: Truman Ca-
pote," Violence in Recent Southern Fiction, 145-58.
Hassan, Ihab H., "The Daydream and Nightmare of Narcis-
sus," WSCL, I, ii (Spring-Summer, 1960), 5-21. Also,
slightly altered, in Radical Innocence, 230-5.
Hill, Pati, "Truman Capote Interview," in Cowley, M., ed.,
Writers at Work, 1st ser., 283-9. Also in Malin, I.,
ed., Truman Capote's IN COLD BLOOD, 131-41.
Levine, Paul, "Truman Capote: The Revelation of the Broken

Image," VQR, XXXIV (Autumn, 1958), 600-17. Also in Mal-
in, I., ed., Truman Capote's IN COLD BLOOD, 141-53. Al-
so in Waldmeir J. J., ed., Recent American Fiction, 153-66.
Littlejohn, David, "Capote Collected," Cweal, LXXVIII (May
10, 1963), 187-8.
Ludwig, J., Recent American Novelists, 33-6.
Meeker, Richard K., in Simonini, R. C., Jr., ed., Southern
Writers, 181-4.
Moravia, Alberto, "Two American Writers (1949)," SR,
LXVIII (Summer, 1960), 477-81.
Norden, Eric, "Playboy Interview: Truman Capote," Play-
boy (March, 1968), 51-3; 56; 58-62; 160-2; 164-70.
Schorer, Mark, Introduction to Selected Writings of Truman
Capote, N. Y.: Random House, 1963, vii-xii.
_____, "McCullers and Capote: Basic Patterns," in Bala-
kian, N., and C. Simmons, eds., Creative Present, 96-
107. Also in Schorer, M., World We Imagine, 285-96.

BREAKFAST AT TIFFANY'S

Goad, Craig M., "Daylight and Darkness, Dream and Delu-
sion: The Works of Truman Capote," ESRS, XVI (Sep-
tember, 1967), 39-41.
Hassan, Ihab H., "Birth of a Heroine," PrS, XXXIV (Spring,
1960), 78-83.
_____, "The Daydream and Nightmare of Narcissus,"
WSCL, I, ii (Spring-Summer, 1960), 16-21. Also, slight-
ly altered, in Hassan, I., Radical Innocence, 250-5.
Hyman, S. E., "Fruitcake at Tiffany's," Standards, 149-50.
Kazin, Alfred, "Truman Capote and the Army of Wrongness,"
Reporter, XIX (November 13, 1958), 40-1. Also in Kaz-
in, A., Contemporaries, 250-4.
Levine, Paul, GaR, XIII (Fall, 1959), 350-2.
Ludwig, J., Recent American Novelists, 34-6.
Mayhew, Alice E., "Familiar Phantoms in the Country of
Capote," Cweal, LXIX (November 28, 1958), 236-7.
Merrick, Gordon, "How to Write Lying Down," NRep,
CXXXIX (December 8, 1958), 23-4.

THE GRASS HARP

Eisinger, C. E., Fiction of the Forties, 241-2.
Goad, Craig M., "Daylight and Darkness, Dream and Delusion: The Works of Truman Capote," ESRS, XVI (September, 1967), 33-5.
Hassan, Ihab H., "The Daydream and Nightmare of Narcissus," WSCL, I, ii (Spring-Summer, 1960), 13-16. Also,

slightly altered, in Radical Innocence, 245-50.
Hoffman, F. J., Art of Southern Fiction, 123-4.
Levine, Paul, "Truman Capote: The Revelation of the Broken
Image," VQR, XXXIV (Autumn, 1958), 615-17. Also in
Malin, I., ed., Truman Capote's IN COLD BLOOD, 152-
3. Also in Waldmeir, J. J., ed., Recent American Fic-
tion, 164-6.

IN COLD BLOOD

Anon., "A Machine and Sympathy," TLS (March 17, 1966),
223.
Dupee, F. W., "Truman Capote's Score," NYRB, VI (Febru-
ary 3, 1966), 3-5.
Eckstein, George, Dissent (July-August, 1966), 433-5.
Friedman, Melvin J., in Malin, I., ed., Truman Capote's
IN COLD BLOOD, 163-76.
Galloway, David, in Malin, I., ed., Truman Capote's IN
COLD BLOOD, 154-63.
Garrett, George, "Crime and Punishment in Kansas: Truman
Capote's IN COLD BLOOD," HC, III (February, 1966), 1-
12. Also in Malin, I., ed., Truman Capote's IN COLD
BLOOD, 81-91.
Goad, Craig M., "Daylight and Darkness, Dream and Delu-
sion: The Works of Truman Capote," ESRS, XVI (Sep-
tember, 1967), 42-55.
Kauffmann, Stanley, "Capote in Kansas," NRep, CLIV (Janu-
ary 22, 1966), 19-21+. Also in Malin, I., ed., Truman
Capote's IN COLD BLOOD, 60-4.
King, James, "Turning New Leaves," CanF, XLV (March,
1966), 281-2.
Kramer, Hilton, "Real Gardens with Real Toads," New
Leader, (January 31, 1966), 18-19. Also in Malin, I.,
ed., Truman Capote's IN COLD BLOOD, 65-8.
Langbaum, Robert, "Capote's Nonfiction Novel," ASch, XXXV
(Summer, 1966), 570-80. Also in Malin, I., ed., Tru-
man Capote's IN COLD BLOOD, 114-20.
Levine, Paul, "Reality and Fiction," HudR, XIX (Spring,
1966), 135-8.
Meacham, William S., "A Non-Fiction Study in Scarlet,"
VQR, XLII (Spring, 1966), 316-19.
Morris, Robert K., "Capote's Imagery," in Malin, I., ed.,
Truman Capote's IN COLD BLOOD, 176-86.
Phillips, William, "But Is It Good for Literature?" Ctary,
XLI (May, 1966), 77-80. Also in Malin, I., ed., Truman
Capote's IN COLD BLOOD, 102-6.
Plimpton, George, "The Story Behind a Nonfiction Novel,"

NYTBR (January 16, 1966), 2-3, 38-43. Also in Malin,
    I. , ed. , Truman Capote's IN COLD BLOOD, 25-43.
Tanner, Tony, "Death in Kansas," Spectator, CCVIII (March
    18, 1966), 331-2. Also in Malin, I. , ed. , Truman Ca-
    pote's IN COLD BLOOD, 98-102.
Tompkins, Phillip K. , "In Cold Fact," Esquire, LXV (June,
    1966), 125+. Also in Malin, I. , ed. , Truman Capote's
    IN COLD BLOOD, 44-58.
Trilling, Diana, "Capote's Crime and Punishment," PR,
    XXXIII (Spring, 1966), 252-9. Also in Malin, I. , ed. ,
    Truman Capote's IN COLD BLOOD, 107-13.
Walcutt, C. C. , Man's Changing Mask, 344-6.
West, Rebecca, "A Grave and Reverend Book," Harper's,
    CCXXXII (February, 1966), 108+. Also in Malin, I. ,
    ed. , Truman Capote's IN COLD BLOOD, 91-8.
Wiegand, William, "The 'Non-Fiction' Novel," NMQ, XXXVII
    (Autumn, 1967), 243-57.
Yurick, Sol, "Sob-Sister Gothic," Nation, CCII (February 7,
    1966), 158-60.
Zaslove, Jerald, "IN COLD BLOOD: More Cultural Cool-
    Aid," Paunch, No. 26 (April, 1966), 79-84.

OTHER VOICES, OTHER ROOMS

Aldridge, John W. , After the Lost Generation, 202-18.
_____ , "The Metaphorical World of Truman Capote," WR,
    XV (Summer, 1951), 250-60.
Baumbach, J. , Landscape of Nightmare, 7-8.
Capote, Truman, "Voice From a Cloud," in McCormack,
    T. , ed. , Afterwords, 139-45. Also in Capote, T. , OTH-
    ER VOICES, OTHER ROOMS (Twentieth Anniversary ed.),
    N. Y. : Random House, 1967.
Collins, Carvel, "Other Voices," ASch, XXV (Winter, 1955-
    56), 108-16.
Eisinger, C. E. , Fiction of the Forties, 237-40.
Goad, Craig M. , "Daylight and Darkness, Dream and Delu-
    sion: The Works of Truman Capote," ESRS, XVI (Sep-
    tember, 1967), 26-32.
Hassan, Ihab H. , "The Daydream and Nightmare of Narcis-
    sus," WSCL, I, ii (Spring-Summer, 1960), 9-13. Also in
    Hassan, I. H. , Radical Innocence, 239-45.
Hoffman, F. J. , Art of Southern Fiction, 118-22.
Levine, Paul, "Truman Capote: The Revelation of the Brok-
    en Image," VQR, XXXIV (Autumn, 1958), 610-15. Also
    in Malin, I. , ed. , Truman Capote's IN COLD BLOOD,
    149-52. Also in Waldmeir, J. J. , ed. , Recent American
    Fiction, 161-4.

Malin, Irving, "The Gothic Family," Psychoanalysis and
    American Fiction, 255-6. Also in Malin, I., New Amer-
    ican Gothic, 50-2.
Mengeling, Marvin E., "OTHER VOICES, OTHER ROOMS:
    Oedipus Between the Covers," AI, XIX (Winter, 1962),
    361-74.
Prescott, O., In My Opinion, 114-15.
Ruoff, Gene W., "Truman Capote: The Novelist as a Com-
    modity," in French, W., ed., Forties, 261-9.
Shrike, J. S., "Recent Phenomena," HudR, I (Spring, 1948),
    136-44.
Trilling, Diana, "Fiction in Review," Nation, CLXVI (Janu-
    ary 31, 1948), 133-4.
Young, Marguerite, "Tiger Lilies," KR, X (Summer, 1948),
    516-18.

BIBLIOGRAPHY

Bryer, Jackson R., "Truman Capote: A Bibliography," in
    Malin, I., ed., Truman Capote's IN COLD BLOOD, 239-
    69.

CARY, JOYCE, 1888-1957

GENERAL

Adam International Review, XVIII (November-December,
    1950). Cary Issue.
Adams, Hazard, "Introduction" to Joyce Cary's POWER IN
    MEN, Seattle: Un. of Wash. Pr., 1963, vii-xlvi.
_____, "Joyce Cary: Posthumous Volumes and Criticism
    to Date," TSLL, I (1959), 289-99.
_____, "Joyce Cary's Swimming Swan," ASch, XXIX
    (Spring, 1960), 235-9.
Allen, W., Joyce Cary.
_____, Modern Novel, 242-8.
Barba, Harry, "Image of the African in Transition," UKCR,
    XXIX (March, 1963), 215-21.
Bettman, Elizabeth R., "Joyce Cary and the Problem of Po-
    litical Morality," AR, XVII (Summer, 1957), 266-72.
Bloom, R., Indeterminate World.
Burrows, John, and Alex Hamilton, "The Art of Fiction,
    Joyce Cary," ParisR, No. 7 (Winter, 1954-55), 62-78.
    Also in Writers at Work, 1st ser., 51-67.
Cary, Joyce, "The Novelist at Work: A Conversation Be-
    tween Joyce Cary and Lord David Cecil," AIR, XVIII

(November-December, 1950), 15-25.

_____, "The Way a Novel Gets Written," AIR, XVIII
(November-December, 1950), 3-11.

Case, Edward, "The Free World of Joyce Cary," ModA, III
(Spring, 1959), 115-24.

Cohen, Nathan, "A Conversation with Joyce Cary," TamR,
No. 3 (Spring, 1957), 5-15.

Collins, Harold R., "Joyce Cary's Troublesome Africans,"
AR, XIII (September, 1953), 397-406.

Cosman, Max, "The Protean Joyce Cary," Cweal, LXIX
(March 6, 1959), 596-8.

Craig, David, "Idea and Imagination: A Study of Joyce
Cary," Fox (Aberdeen Un. Classical, Literary and Philosophical Societies), n.d. (c. 1954), 3-10. (Not seen.)

Dwyer, John T., "Joyce Cary's Critical Theory and Its Relationship to the Development of His Fiction," DA, XXIX
(1968), 258A (Un. of Pa.).

Echeruo, Michael J.K., "The Dimensions of Order: A Study
of Joyce Cary," DA, XXVI (1966), 5431 (Cornell).

Foster, Malcolm, "Fell of the Lion, Fleece of the Sheep,"
MFS, IX, iii (Autumn, 1963), 257-62.

_____, Joyce Cary.

Friedson, Anthony M., "The Novels of Joyce Cary," DA,
XXI (1961), 3781 (Iowa).

Galligan, Edward L., "Intuition and Concept: Joyce Cary and
the Critics," TSLL, VIII (Winter, 1967), 581-7.

Geering, R.G., "Joyce Cary: The Man and His Work,"
Quadrant, II (Winter, 1959), 45-51.

Hansen, Janis T., "The Novels of Joyce Cary: Uses of the
Picaresque," DA, XXVI (1966), 5435 (Oregon).

Hardy, Barbara, "Form in Joyce Cary's Novels," EIC, IV
(April, 1954), 180-90.

Hatfield, Glenn W., Jr., "Form and Character in the Sequence Novels of Joyce Cary," Thesis (Unpublished), Ohio
St. Un., 1956.

Hoffmann, Charles G., Joyce Cary.

_____, "Joyce Cary: Art and Reality. The Interaction of
Form and Narrator," UKCR, XXVI (June, 1960), 273-82.

_____, "Joyce Cary's African Novels: There's a War
On," SAQ, LXII (Spring, 1963), 229-43.

Holloway, John, "Joyce Cary's Fiction: Modernity and 'Sus-
taining Power'," TLS (August 7, 1959), 14-15.

Johnson, Pamela H., "Three Novelists and the Drawing of
Character: C.P. Snow, Joyce Cary and Ivy Compton-
Burnett," in English Association, Essays and Studies,
1950, 82-4; 89-94.

Karl, Frederick R., "Joyce Cary: The Moralist as Novelist," TCL, V (January, 1960), 183-96. Also in Contemporary English Novel, 131-47.

Kelleher, John J., "The Theme of Freedom in the Novels of Joyce Cary," DA, XXVI (1965), 369-70 (Pittsburgh).

Kennedy, Richard S., "Joyce Cary's Comic Affirmation of Life," PCTEB, No. 13 (May, 1966), 3-14. (Not seen.)

King, Carlyle, "Joyce Cary," CanF, XXXIII (March, 1954), 273-4.

_____, "Joyce Cary and the Creative Imagination," TamR, No. 10 (Winter, 1959), 39-51.

Kraus, Richard, "Archetypes and the Trilogy Structure--A Study of Joyce Cary's Fiction," DA, XXVII (1967), 3430A (Stanford).

Larsen, G. L., Dark Descent.

Lucchesi, Peter G., "The Charismatic as Center of Irony in the Novels of James (sic) Joyce Cary," DA, XXVIII (1967), 683A-4A (Wisconsin).

Mahood, M. M., Joyce Cary's Africa.

Moody, P. R., "Road and Bridge in Joyce Cary's African Novels," BRMMLA, XXI (December, 1967), 145-9. (Not seen.)

O'Connor, W. V., Joyce Cary.

Owen, B. Evan, "The Supremacy of the Individual in the Novels of Joyce Cary," AIR, XVIII (November-December, 1950), 25-9.

Prescott, O., In My Opinion, 191-9.

Ready, William B., "Joyce Cary," Critic, XVIII (June-July, 1960), 9-10, 59-60.

Rosenthal, Michael, "Comedy and Despair in Joyce Cary's Fiction," DA, XXVIII (1967), 693A (Columbia).

Salz, Paulina J., "The Novels of Joyce Cary in Relation to His Critical Writings," DA, XXII (1962), 3208-9. (So. Calif.).

_____, "The Philosophical Principles in Joyce Cary's Work," WHR, XX (Spring, 1966), 159-65.

Starkie, Enid, "Joyce Cary: A Personal Portrait," VQR, XXXVII (Winter, 1961), 110-34. Also in EDH, XXXII (1963), 125-44.

Steinbrecher, George, Jr., "Joyce Cary: Master Novelist," CE, XVIII (May, 1957), 387-95.

Stewart, Douglas, Ark of God, 129-58.

Teeling, John, "Joyce Cary's Moral World," MFS, IX, iii (Autumn, 1963), 276-83.

Van Horn, Ruth G., "Freedom and Imagination in the Novels of Joyce Cary," Midwest Jnl, V (Winter, 1952-53), 19-30.

Wolkenfeld, J., Joyce Cary.

Wright, Andrew, Joyce Cary.

_____, "Joyce Cary's Unpublished Work," LonM, V, i
(January, 1958), 35-42.
_____, "A Note on Joyce Cary's Reputation," MFS, IX,
iii (Autumn, 1963), 207-9.

THE AFRICAN WITCH

Barba, Harry, "Cary's Image of the African in Transition,"
UKCR, XXIX (June, 1963), 291-3.
Bloom, R., Indeterminate World, 52-4.
Foster, M., Joyce Cary, 321-4.
Hall, Alan, "The African Novels of Joyce Cary," Standpunte,
XII (March-April, 1958), 47-50.
Hoffmann, Charles G., Joyce Cary, 25-34.
_____, "Joyce Cary's African Novels: There's a War
On," SAQ, LXII (Spring, 1963), 236-40.
Larsen, G.L., Dark Descent, 36-45.
Mahood, M.M., Joyce Cary's Africa, 145-66.
O'Connor, W.V., Joyce Cary, 19-21.
Tucker, M., Africa in Modern Literature, 40-2.
Wiley, Paul, WSCL, IV, ii (Spring-Summer, 1963), 230-2.
Wolkenfeld, J., Joyce Cary, 3-20, 78-87, 116-20.
Wright, A., Joyce Cary, 60-2, 80-2, 101-3.

AISSA SAVED

Bloom, R., Indeterminate World, 46-8.
Cary, Joyce, "My First Novel," Listener, XLIX (April 16,
1953), 637.
Foster, M., Joyce Cary, 315-18.
Hall, A.D., "The African Novels of Joyce Cary," Standpunte,
X (June-July, 1956), 14-23.
Hoffmann, Charles G., Joyce Cary, 8-18.
_____, "Joyce Cary's African Novels: There's a War
On," SAQ, LXII (Spring, 1963), 229-33.
Larsen, G.L., Dark Descent, 22-7.
Mahood, M.M., Joyce Cary's Africa, 105-24.
O'Connor, W.V., Joyce Cary, 17-18.
Tucker, M., Africa in Modern Literature, 37-9.
Wolkenfeld, J., Joyce Cary, 56-69, 172-4.
Wright, A., Joyce Cary, 58-9, 77-9.

AN AMERICAN VISITOR

Bloom, R., Indeterminate World, 48-52.
Foster, M., Joyce Cary, 318-21.
French, Warren G., "Joyce Cary's American Rover Girl,"

TSLL, II (Autumn, 1960), 281-91.
Hall, Alan, "The African Novels of Joyce Cary," Standpunte,
    XII (March-April, 1958), 43-7.
Hoffmann, Charles G. , Joyce Cary, 18-25.
          , "Joyce Cary's African Novels: There's a War
    On," SAQ, LXII (Spring, 1963), 233-6.
Larsen, G. L. , Dark Descent, 27-36.
Mahood, M. M. , Joyce Cary's Africa, 125-44.
O'Connor, W. V. , Joyce Cary, 18-19.
Tucker, M. , Africa in Modern Literature, 39-40.
Wolkenfeld, J. , Joyce Cary, 69-78, 111-13.
Wright, A. , Joyce Cary, 59-60, 99-101.

ARABELLA (Unpublished)

Wright, A. , Joyce Cary, 51-2.

THE CAPTIVE AND THE FREE

Adams, Hazard, "Joyce Cary: Posthumous Volumes and
    Criticism to Date," TSLL, I (1959), 290-4.
Cecil, David, "Introduction," THE CAPTIVE AND THE FREE,
    N. Y. : Harper, 1959.
Foster, M. , Joyce Cary, 506-11.
Hoffmann, Charles G. , Joyce Cary, 99-107, 157-69.
          , "THE CAPTIVE AND THE FREE: Joyce Cary's
    Unfinished Trilogy," TSLL, V (1963), 17-24.
O'Connor, W. V. , Joyce Cary, 41-2.
Watson, Kenneth, "THE CAPTIVE AND THE FREE: Artist,
    Child, and Society in the World of Joyce Cary," English,
    XVI (Summer, 1966), 49-54.

CASTLE CORNER

Bloom, R. , Indeterminate World, 66-72.
Foster, M. , Joyce Cary, 352-7.
Hoffmann, Charles G. , Joyce Cary, 44-53.
          , " 'They Want To Be Happy': Joyce Cary's Unfin-
    ished CASTLE CORNER Series," MFS, IX, iii (Autumn,
    1963), 217-25.
Larsen, G. L. , Dark Descent, 45-8.
O'Connor, W. V. , Joyce Cary, 30-1.
Stevenson, Lionel, "Joyce Cary and the Anglo-Irish Tradi-
    tion," MFS, IX, iii (Autumn, 1963), 210-16.
Weintraub, Stanley, "CASTLE CORNER: Joyce Cary's BUD-
    DENBROOKS," WSCL, V, i (Winter-Spring, 1964), 54-63.
Wolkenfeld, J. , Joyce Cary, 87-9.

Woodcock, George, "Citizens of Babel: A Study of Joyce
    Cary," QQ, LXIII (Summer, 1956), 237-40.
Wright, A., Joyce Cary, 66-7, 82-4, 94-6.

CHARLEY IS MY DARLING

Bloom, R., Indeterminate World, 59-63.
Foster, M., Joyce Cary, 346-51.
Hoffmann, C. G., Joyce Cary, 54-66.
Kerr, Elizabeth M., WSCL, II, i (Winter, 1961), 102-6.
Larsen, G. L., Dark Descent, 79-82.
O'Connor, W. V., Joyce Cary, 23-4.
Wright, A., Joyce Cary, 62-5.

COCK JARVIS (Unpublished)

Foster, M., Joyce Cary, 246-58.
Mahood, M. M., Joyce Cary's Africa, 96-104.
Wright, A., Joyce Cary, 50-1.

DAVENTRY (Unpublished)

Mahood, M. M., Joyce Cary's Africa, 89-96.

EXCEPT THE LORD (See also SECOND TRILOGY)

Bellow, Saul, "A Personal Record," NRep (February 22,
    1954), 20-1.
Bettman, Elizabeth R., "Joyce Cary and the Problem of Po-
    litical Morality," AR, XVII (Summer, 1957), 270-1.
Bloom, R., Indeterminate World, 139-69.
Foster, M., Joyce Cary, 483-7.
Hoffmann, C. G., Joyce Cary, 139-47.
Wright, A., Joyce Cary, 142-8.

A FEARFUL JOY

Allen, W., Joyce Cary, 16-19.
Bloom, R., Indeterminate World, 77-83.
Eastman, Richard M., "Historical Grace in Cary's A FEAR-
    FUL JOY," Novel, I (Winter, 1968), 150-7.
Foster, M., Joyce Cary, 428-34.
Hall, J., Tragic Comedians, 84-5.
Hoffmann, C. G., Joyce Cary, 118-26.
McCormick, J., Catastrophe and Imagination, 151-4.
O'Connor, W. V., Joyce Cary, 33-6.
Pittock, Malcolm, "Joyce Cary: A FEARFUL JOY," EIC,

XIII (October, 1963), 428-32.
Wolkenfeld, J., Joyce Cary, 135-9.
Wright, A., Joyce Cary, 69-70.

FIRST TRILOGY

Adams, Hazard, "Blake and Gulley Jimson: English Symbol-
    ists," Crit, III, i (Spring-Fall, 1959), 3-14.
_____, "Joyce Cary's Three Speakers," MFS, V (Summer,
    1959), 108-20.
Allen, W., Joyce Cary, 19-27.
Averitt, Margie N.T., "And Three's A Crowd: A Study of
    Joyce Cary's FIRST TRILOGY," DA, XXIV (1964), 5404
    (Texas).
Bloom, R., Indeterminate World, 83-4.
Faber, Kathleen R., and M.D., "An Important Theme of
    Joyce Cary's Trilogy," Discourse, XI (Winter, 1968), 26-
    31.
Hall, J., Tragic Comedians, 82-98.
Hamilton, Kenneth, "Boon or Thorn? Joyce Cary and Sam-
    uel Beckett on Human Life," DR, XXXVIII (Winter, 1959),
    433-42.
Hoffmann, Charles G., "The Genesis and Development of
    Joyce Cary's FIRST TRILOGY," PMLA, LXXVIII (Septem-
    ber, 1963), 431-9.
_____, Joyce Cary, 67-70.
_____, "Joyce Cary and the Comic Mask," WHR, XIII
    (Spring, 1959), 135-42.
_____, "Joyce Cary: Art and Reality," UKCR, XXVI
    (June, 1960), 275-7.
Larsen, G.L., Dark Descent, 89-179.
McQuaid, Catherine F., "The Multiple Realities of Artistic
    Creation: Joyce Cary's 'Art and Reality' and His FIRST
    TRILOGY," DA, XXVIII (1967), 2154A-55A (Ohio).
Mitchell, Giles R., "The Art Theme in Joyce Cary's FIRST
    TRILOGY," DA, XXVI (1965), 1652 (Oklahoma).
Monas, Sidney, "What to Do with a Drunken Sailor," HudR,
    III (Autumn, 1950), 466-74.
O'Connor, W.V., Joyce Cary, 26-9.
Reed, Peter J., "Trial by Discard: Joyce Cary's FIRST
    TRILOGY," DA, XXVI (1966), 4672 (Un. of Washington).
Robertson, D., Voice From the Attic, 246-9.
Stockholder, Fred, "The Triple Vision in Joyce Cary's FIRST
    TRILOGY," MFS, IX, iii (Autumn, 1963), 231-44.
Wolkenfeld, J., Joyce Cary, 21-2, 38-45.

HERSELF SURPRISED (See also FIRST TRILOGY)

Hall, J. , Tragic Comedians, 86-7.
Bloom, R. , Indeterminate World, 84-90.
Cary, Joyce, "Three New Prefaces," AIR, XVIII (November-
    December, 1950), 11-12.
Foster, M. , Joyce Cary, 381-4.
Hoffmann, C. G. , Joyce Cary, 70-7.
Larsen, G. L. , Dark Descent, 102-25.
Wolkenfeld, J. , Joyce Cary, 22-3.
Wright, A. , Joyce Cary, 110-19.

THE HORSE'S MOUTH (See also FIRST TRILOGY)

Adams, Hazard, "Blake and Gulley Jimson: English Symbol-
    ists," Crit, III, i (Spring-Fall, 1959), 3-14.
Adams, Robert H. , "Freedom in THE HORSE'S MOUTH,"
    CE, XXVI (March, 1965), 451-4, 459-60.
Allen, W. , Reading a Novel, 50-4.
Alter, R. , Rogue's Progress, 129-32.
Barr, Donald, "A Careful and Profound Thinker," AIR,
    XVIII (November-December, 1950), 30-1.
Bloom, R. , Indeterminate World, 96-105.
Cary, Joyce, "Three New Prefaces," AIR, XVIII (November-
    December, 1950), 13-14.
Foster, M. , Joyce Cary, 389-93.
Garant, Jeanne, "Joyce Cary's Portrait of the Artist," RLV,
    No. 6 (1958), 476-86.
Hall, J. , Tragic Comedians, 87-97, passim.
Hoffmann, C. G. , Joyce Cary, 85-98.
Larsen, G. L. , Dark Descent, 156-79.
Mustanoja, Tauno F. , "Two Painters: Joyce Cary and Gul-
    ley Jimson," NM, LXI (1960), 221-44.
Ryan, Marjorie, "An Interpretation of Joyce Cary's THE
    HORSE'S MOUTH," Crit, II, i (Spring-Summer, 1958),
    29-38.
Salz, Paulina J. , "The Philosophical Principles in Joyce
    Cary's Work," WHR, XX (Spring, 1966), 164-5.
Shapiro, Stephen A. , "Leopold Bloom and Gulley Jimson:
    The Economics of Survival," TCL, X (April, 1964), 3-11.
Wolkenfeld, J. , Joyce Cary, 23-41.
Woodcock, George, "Citizens of Babel: A Study of Joyce
    Cary," QQ, LXIII (Summer, 1956), 242-4.
Wright, Andrew, "An Authoritative Text of THE HORSE'S
    MOUTH," PBSA, LXI (1967), 100-9.
Wright, A. , Joyce Cary, 124-37, 156-73.

A HOUSE OF CHILDREN

Bloom, R., Indeterminate World, 63-6.
Foster, M., Joyce Cary, 357-61.
Hoffmann, C. G., Joyce Cary, 54-66.
Larsen, G. L., Dark Descent, 82-8.
O'Connor, W. V., Joyce Cary, 24-6.
Stevenson, Lionel, "Joyce Cary and the Anglo-Irish Tradition," MFS, IX, iii (Autumn, 1963), 210-16.
Wright, A., Joyce Cary, 17-19, 62-5, 88-90.

MISTER JOHNSON

Barba, Harry, "Cary's Image of the African in Transition," UKCR, XXIX (June, 1963), 293-6.
Bloom, R., Indeterminate World, 54-9.
Foster, M., Joyce Cary, 324-9.
Fyfe, Christopher, "The Colonial Situation in MISTER JOHNSON," MFS, IX, iii (Autumn, 1963), 226-30.
Hall, Alan, "The African Novels of Joyce Cary," Standpunte, XII (March-April, 1958), 50-5.
Hoffmann, Charles G., Joyce Cary, 34-43.
_____, "Joyce Cary's African Novels: There's a War On," SAQ, LXII (Spring, 1963), 240-3.
Kettle, A., Introduction to the English Novel, 177-84.
Larsen, G. L., Dark Descent, 49-79.
Mahood, M. M., Joyce Cary's Africa, 169-86.
Moore, Gerald, "MISTER JOHNSON Reconsidered," Black Orpheus, No. 4 (October, 1958), 16-23.
O'Connor, W. V., Joyce Cary, 21-3.
Prescott, O., In My Opinion, 192-4.
Tucker, M., Africa in Modern Literature, 43-7.
Wolkenfeld, J., Joyce Cary, 94-103, 121-5.
Woodcock, George, "Citizens of Babel: A Study of Joyce Cary," QQ, LXIII (Summer, 1956), 240-2.
Wright, A., Joyce Cary, 84-7.

THE MOONLIGHT

Bloom, R., Indeterminate World, 72-7.
Foster, M., Joyce Cary, 425-8.
Hoffmann, C. G., Joyce Cary, 107-18.
Larsen, G. L., Dark Descent, 183-5.
O'Connor, W. V., Joyce Cary, 31-3.
Wolkenfeld, J., Joyce Cary, 129-35.
Wright, A., Joyce Cary, 67-9.

NOT HONOUR MORE (See also SECOND TRILOGY)

Battaglia, Francis J., "Spurious Armaggedon: Joyce Cary's
NOT HONOUR MORE," MFS, XIII (Winter, 1967-68), 479-
91.
Bettman, Elizabeth R., "Joyce Cary and the Problem of Po-
litical Morality," AR, XVII (Summer, 1957), 271-2.
Bloom, R., Indeterminate World, 170-200.
Foster, M., Joyce Cary, 487-92.
Hoffmann, C.G., Joyce Cary, 148-56.
Wolkenfeld, J., Joyce Cary, 178-81.
Wright, A., Joyce Cary, 148-53.

PRISONER OF GRACE (See also SECOND TRILOGY)

Bettman, Elizabeth R., "Joyce Cary and the Problem of Po-
litical Morality," AR, XVII (Summer, 1957), 267-70.
Bloom, R., Indeterminate World, 108-38.
Foster, M., Joyce Cary, 479-82.
Hoffmann, C.G., Joyce Cary, 133-9.
Mitchell, Giles, "Joyce Cary's PRISONER OF GRACE," MFS,
IX, iii (Autumn, 1963), 263-75.
Wolkenfeld, J., Joyce Cary, 183-7.
Woodcock, George, "Citizens of Babel: A Study of Joyce
Cary," QQ, LXIII (Summer, 1956), 244-6.
Wright, A., Joyce Cary, 137-42.

SECOND TRILOGY

Battaglia, Francis J., "The Problem of Reliability in Joyce
Cary's Political Trilogy," DA, XXVII (1967), 2522A-23A
(Calif.-Davis).
Hoffmann, Charles G., Joyce Cary, 127-33.
————, "Joyce Cary: Art and Reality," UKCR, XXVI
(June, 1960), 277-82.
Kerr, Elizabeth M., "Joyce Cary's SECOND TRILOGY,"
UTQ, XXIX (April, 1960), 310-25.
Larsen, G.L., Dark Descent, 187-92
Nyce, James M., "Joyce Cary as Political Novelist," DA,
XXIX (1968), 574A-5A (Claremont).
O'Connor, W.V., Joyce Cary, 36-41.
Teeling, John P., S.J., "British History in Joyce Cary's
SECOND TRILOGY," DA, XXVI (1965), 1655-56 (No.
Carolina).
————, "Joyce Cary's Moral World," MFS, IX, iii (Au-
tumn, 1963), 279-83.
Wolkenfeld, J., Joyce Cary, 46-7, 90-4, 178-87.

TO BE A PILGRIM (See also FIRST TRILOGY)

Bloom, R. , Indeterminate World, 90-6.
Cary, Joyce, "Three New Prefaces," AIR, XVIII (November-
    December, 1950), 12.
Foster, M. , Joyce Cary, 384-9.
Hoffmann, C. G. , Joyce Cary, 77-85.
Larsen, G. L. , Dark Descent, 125-56.
Lyons, Richard S. , "Narrative Method in Cary's TO BE A
    PILGRIM," TSLL, VI (1964), 269-79.
Shapiro, Stephen A. , "Joyce Cary's TO BE A PILGRIM: Mr.
    Facing-Both-Ways," TSLL, VIII (Spring, 1966), 81-91.
Wolkenfeld, J. , Joyce Cary, 139-42.
Wright, A. , Joyce Cary, 119-24.

BIBLIOGRAPHY

Beebe, Maurice, J. W. Lee, and S. Henderson, "Criticism
    of Joyce Cary: A Selected Checklist," MFS, IX, iii
    (Autumn, 1963), 284-8.
Bloom, R. , Indeterminate World, 201-8.
Hoffmann, C. G. , Joyce Cary, 199-202.
Larsen, G. L. , Dark Descent, 194-8.
Reed, Peter J. , "Joyce Cary: A Selected Checklist of Criti-
    cism," BB, XXV (May-August, 1968), 133-4, 151.
Wolkenfeld, J. , Joyce Cary, 193-6.

CHEEVER, JOHN, 1912-

GENERAL

Aldridge, J. W. , "John Cheever and the Soft Sell of Disaster,"
    Time to Murder and Create, 171-7.
Bracher, Frederick, "John Cheever: A Vision of the World,"
    ClareQ, XI, ii (Winter, 1964), 47-57.
_____ , "John Cheever and Comedy," Crit, VI, i (Spring,
    1963), 66-77.

THE WAPSHOT CHRONICLE

Bracher, Frederick, "John Cheever and Comedy," Crit, VI,
    i (Spring, 1963), 66-77.
Hassan, I. , Radical Innocence, 187-94.

THE WAPSHOT SCANDAL

Garrett, George, "John Cheever and the Charms of Innocence: The Craft of THE WAPSHOT SCANDAL," HC, I,
ii (April, 1964), 1-4, 6-12.
Hyman, S. E., "John Cheever's Golden Egg," Standards, 199-
203.

COHEN, LEONARD NORMAN, 1934-

GENERAL

Djwa, Sandra, "Leonard Cohen: Black Romantic," CanL,
No. 34 (Autumn, 1967), 32-42.
Pacey, Desmond, "The Phenomenon of Leonard Cohen,"
CanL, No. 34 (Autumn 1967), 5-23.

BEAUTIFUL LOSERS

Boyers, Robert, "Attitudes Toward Sex in American 'High
Culture'," AAAPSS, CCCLXXVI (March, 1968), 51-2.
Gose, E. B., "Of Beauty and Unmeaning," CanL, No. 29
(Summer, 1966), 61-3.
Pacey, Desmond, "The Phenomenon of Leonard Cohen,"
CanL, No. 34 (Autumn, 1967), 5-23.

THE FAVOURITE GAME

Pacey, Desmond, "The Phenomenon of Leonard Cohen,"
CanL, No. 34 (Autumn, 1967), 9-15.

COMPTON-BURNETT, IVY, 1892-1969

GENERAL

Allen, W., Modern Novel, 188-91.
Amis, Kingsley, "One World and Its Way," TC, CLVIII
(August, 1955), 168-75.
Anon., "Interview with Miss Compton-Burnett," REL, III,
iv (October, 1962), 96-112.
Baldanza, F., Ivy Compton-Burnett.
Bland, D.S., "T.S. Eliot's Case-Book," MLN, LXXV (Janu-
ary, 1960), 23-6.
Burkhart, C., I. Compton-Burnett.
Cottrell, Beekman W., "Conversation Piece: Four Twentieth

Century English Dialogue Novelists," DA, XVI (1956), 2159 (Columbia).

Curtis, Mary M., "The Moral Comedy of Miss Compton-Burnett," WSCL, V, iii (Autumn, 1964), 213-21.

Gold, Joseph, "Exit Everybody: The Novels of Ivy Compton-Burnett," DR, XLII (Summer, 1962), 227-38.

Jefferson, D.W., "A Note on Ivy Compton-Burnett," REL, I, ii (April, 1960), 19-24.

Johnson, Pamela H., I. Compton-Burnett.

_____, "Three Novelists and the Drawing of Character: C.P. Snow, Joyce Cary and Ivy Compton-Burnett," in English Association. Essays and Studies, 1950, 82-4, 94-9.

Karl, F.R., "The Intimate World of Ivy Compton-Burnett," Contemporary English Novel, 201-19.

Kermode, Frank, "The House of Fiction: Interviews with Seven English Novelists," PR, XXX (Spring, 1963), 71-4.

Liddell, Robert, The Novels of I. Compton-Burnett, London: Victor Gollancz, 1955.

_____, A Treatise on the Novel, London: Jonathan Cape, 1947; paperback ed., 1965, 146-63.

McCabe, Bernard, "Ivy Compton-Burnett: An English Eccentric," Crit, III, ii (Winter-Spring, 1960), 47-63.

McCarthy, Mary, "The Inventions of I. Compton-Burnett," Encounter, XXVII, v (November, 1966), 19-31.

Pendry, E.D., New Feminism of English Fiction, 90-119.

Preston, John, " 'The Matter in a Word'," EIC, X (July, 1960), 348-56.

Sackville-West, Edward, "Ladies whose bright Pens...," in Inclinations, London: Secker and Warburg, 1949, 78-103. Port Washington, N.Y.: Kennikat Pr., 1967, 78-103.

Snow, Lotus, " 'Good is Bad Condensed': Ivy Compton-Burnett's View of Human Nature," WHR, X (Summer, 1956), 271-6.

Wilson, Angus, "Ivy Compton-Burnett," LonM, II (July, 1955), 64-70.

BROTHERS AND SISTERS

Baldanza, F., Ivy Compton-Burnett, 43-6.

Burkhart, C., I. Compton-Burnett, 101-3.

Johnson, P.H., I. Compton-Burnett, 27.

May, James B., "Towards Print (Ivy Compton-Burnett; A Time Exposure)," Trace, No. 49 (Summer, 1963), 92-9.

BULLIVANT AND THE LAMBS
(MANSERVANT AND MAIDSERVANT)

Baldanza, F., Ivy Compton-Burnett, 72-6.
Burkhart, C., I. Compton-Burnett, 115-17.
Johnson, P. H., I. Compton-Burnett, 32-3.
Karl, F. R., "The Intimate World of Ivy Compton-Burnett,"
  Contemporary English Novel, 212-15.

DARKNESS AND DAY

Baldanza, F., Ivy Compton-Burnett, 83-6.
Bogan, Louise, Selected Criticism: Prose, Poetry, N.Y.:
  Noonday, 1955, 189-90.
Burkhart, C., I. Compton-Burnett, 54-5, 119-21.
Curtis, Mary M., "The Moral Comedy of Miss Compton-
  Burnett," WSCL, V, iii (Autumn, 1964), 216-18.
Johnson, P. H., I. Compton-Burnett, 34-5.

DAUGHTERS AND SONS

Baldanza, F., Ivy Compton-Burnett, 58-61.
Burkhart, C., I. Compton-Burnett, 108-10.
Johnson, P. H., I. Compton-Burnett, 30-1.

DOLORES

Baldanza, F., Ivy Compton-Burnett, 39-41.
Johnson, P. H., I. Compton-Burnett, 24-5.

ELDERS AND BETTERS

Baldanza, F., Ivy Compton-Burnett, 69-72.
Bowen, E., Collected Impressions, N.Y.: Knopf, 1950, 85-
  91.
Burkhart, C., I. Compton-Burnett, 113-15.
Johnson, P. H., I. Compton-Burnett, 11-13.

A FAMILY AND A FORTUNE

Baldanza, F., Ivy Compton-Burnett, 61-5.
Burkhart, C., I. Compton-Burnett, 110-11.
Johnson, P. H., I. Compton-Burnett, 14-17.
Kettle, A., Introduction to the English Novel, 184-90.

A FATHER AND HIS FATE

Baldanza, F., Ivy Compton-Burnett, 93-6.
Burkhart, C., I. Compton-Burnett, 124-5.

A GOD AND HIS GIFTS

Baldanza, F., Ivy Compton-Burnett, 102-5.
Brophy, Brigid, in NStat (December 6, 1963), 865. Also in
    Brophy, B., Don't Never Forget, 167-70.
Burkhart, C., I. Compton-Burnett, 56-7, 128-9.
"Novels of 1963. I. Compton-Burnett: A GOD AND HIS
    GIFTS," in T.L.S.: Essays and Reviews from The Times
    Literary Supplement, 1963, 178-80. Also in TLS (Novem-
    ber 21, 1963).
Prescott, O., In My Opinion, 98-100.

A HERITAGE AND ITS HISTORY

Baldanza, F., Ivy Compton-Burnett, 96-9.
Burkhart, C., I. Compton-Burnett, 125-7.
Preston, John, " 'The Matter in a Word'," EIC, X (July,
    1960), 348-56.

A HOUSE AND ITS HEAD

Burkhart, C., I. Compton-Burnett, 107-8.
Johnson, P.H., I. Compton-Burnett, 30.

MEN AND WIVES

Baldanza, F., Ivy Compton-Burnett, 46-9.
Burkhart, C., I. Compton-Burnett, 103-4.
Johnson, P.H., I. Compton-Burnett, 27-8.
Reaney, James, "Novels of Ivy Compton-Burnett," CanF,
    XXIX (April, 1949), 11-12.

THE MIGHTY AND THEIR FALL

Baldanza, F., Ivy Compton-Burnett, 99-102.
Burkhart, C., I. Compton-Burnett, 127-8.
Curtis, Mary M., "The Moral Comedy of Miss Compton-
    Burnett," WSCL, V, iii (Autumn, 1964), 214-16, 217-18.
Wiley, Paul, WSCL, IV, ii (Spring-Summer, 1963), 232-4.

MORE WOMEN THAN MEN

Baldanza, F., Ivy Compton-Burnett, 49-53.
Burkhart, C., I. Compton-Burnett, 104-6.
Johnson, P.H., I. Compton-Burnett, 28-9.

MOTHER AND SON

Amis, Kingsley, "One World and Its Way," TC, CLVIII
    (August, 1955), 168-75.
Baldanza, F., Ivy Compton-Burnett, 89-92.
Burkhart, C., I. Compton-Burnett, 122-4.
West, A., Principles and Persuasions, 225-32.

PARENTS AND CHILDREN

Baldanza, F., Ivy Compton-Burnett, 65-9.
Bowen, E., Collected Impressions, N.Y.: Knopf, 1950, 82-
    5.
Burkhart, C., I. Compton-Burnett, 111-13.
Johnson, P.H., I. Compton-Burnett, 31-2.

PASTORS AND MASTERS

Baldanza, F., Ivy Compton-Burnett, 41-3.
Burkhart, C., I. Compton-Burnett, 100-1.
Greenfield, Stanley B., "PASTORS AND MASTERS: The
    Spoils of Genius," Criticism, II (Winter, 1960), 66-80.
Johnson, P.H., I. Compton-Burnett, 26.

THE PRESENT AND THE PAST

Baldanza, F., Ivy Compton-Burnett, 86-9.
Burkhart, C., I. Compton-Burnett, 121-2.

TWO WORLDS AND THEIR WAYS

Baldanza, F., Ivy Compton-Burnett, 76-9.
Burkhart, C., I. Compton-Burnett, 118-19.
Johnson, P.H., I. Compton-Burnett, 33-4.
Karl, F.R., "The Intimate World of Ivy Compton-Burnett,"
    Contemporary English Novel, 215-18.

BIBLIOGRAPHY

Baldanza, F., Ivy Compton-Burnett, 135-8.
Burkhart, C., I. Compton-Burnett, 135-7.

CONNELL, EVAN S., JR., 1924-

GENERAL

Blaisdell, Gus, "After Ground Zero: The Writings of Evan
S. Connell, Jr.," NMQR, XXXVI (Summer, 1966), 181-
207.

THE DIARY OF A RAPIST

Blaisdell, Gus, "After Ground Zero: The Writings of Evan
S. Connell, Jr.," NMQR, XXXVI (Summer, 1966), 200-6.

MRS. BRIDGE

Blaisdell, Gus, "After Ground Zero: The Writings of Evan S.
Connell, Jr.," NMQR, XXXVI (Summer, 1966), 186-8.
Van Bark, Bella S., "The Alienated Person in Literature,"
AJP, XXI (1961), 189-91.

THE PATRIOT

Blaisdell, Gus, "After Ground Zero: The Writings of Evan
S. Connell, Jr.," NMQR, XXXVI (Summer, 1966), 188-
92.

COOPER, WILLIAM, PSEUD. (HOFF, HARRY SUMMER-
FIELD), 1910-

SCENES FROM MARRIED LIFE

Deakin, Nicholas, "An Appraisal of William Cooper: In
Search of Banality," T&T, XLII (January 27, 1961), 140-
1.
Enright, D.J., "The New Pastoral-Comical," Spectator, No.
6919 (February 3, 1961), 154-5.
Johnson, Pamela H., "Smart Chap Grows Up," Reporter,
XXIV (March 16, 1961), 55-6.

SCENES FROM PROVINCIAL LIFE

Allen, W., Modern Novel, 251-2.
Deakin, Nicholas, "An Appraisal of William Cooper: In
Search of Banality," T&T, XLII (January 27, 1961), 140-
1.

Enright, D. J., "The New Pastoral-Comical," Spectator, No.
    6919 (February 3, 1961), 154-5.
Fraser, G. S., Modern Writer and His World, 164-5.
Johnson, Pamela H., "Smart Chap Grows Up," Reporter,
    XXIV (March 16, 1961), 55-6.

YOUNG PEOPLE

Allen, W., Modern Novel, 252-3.
Fraser, G. S., Modern Writer and His World, 165-6.

COZZENS, JAMES GOULD, 1903-

GENERAL

Adams, R. P., "James Gould Cozzens: A Cultural Dilemma,"
    in Langford, R. E., ed., Essays in Modern American Lit-
    erature, 103-11.
Allen, W., Modern Novel, 185-7.
Anon., "The Hermit of Lambertville," Time, LXX (Septem-
    ber 2, 1957), 72-8.
Bracher, Frederick, "James Gould Cozzens: Humanist,"
    Crit, I, iii (Winter, 1958), 10-29.
Bracher, F., Novels of James Gould Cozzens.
_____, "Of Youth and Age: James Gould Cozzens,"
    PacSp, V (Winter, 1951), 48-62.
Coxe, Louis O., "Comments on Cozzens: A High Place,"
    Crit, I, iii (1958), 48-51.
_____, "The Complex World of James Gould Cozzens,"
    AL, XXVII (May, 1955), 157-71.
Duggan, Francis X, "Facts and All Man's Fictions," Thought,
    XXXIII (Winter, 1958-59), 604-16.
Eisinger, Chester E., "The Voice of Aggressive Aristocra-
    cy," Midway, No. 18 (Spring, 1964), 100-28. Also in
    Eisinger, C. E., Fiction of the Forties, 146-71.
Finn, James, "Cozzens Dispossessed," Cweal, LXVIII (Ap-
    ril 4, 1958), 11-13.
Frederick, John T., "Love By Adverse Possession: The
    Case of Mr. Cozzens," CE, XIX (April, 1958), 313-16.
Frohock, W. M., Strangers to this Ground, 63-83.
Galligan, Edward L., "Within Limits: The Novels of James
    Gould Cozzens," DA, XIX (1959), 2951-52 (Penn.).
Geismar, Maxwell, "Comments on Cozzens: By Cozzens
    Possessed," Crit, I, iii (Winter, 1958), 51-3.
Hamblen, Abigail A., "The Paradox of James Gould Coz-
    zens," WHR, XIX (Autumn, 1965), 355-61.

Harlan, Earl, "Somewhat by Love Possessed," English Record, X (Fall, 1959), 35-40.

Hicks, Granville, James Gould Cozzens.

_____, "The Reputation of James Gould Cozzens," EJ, XXXIX (January, 1950), 1-7. Also in CE, XI (January, 1950), 177-83.

Howe, Irving, "James Gould Cozzens: Novelist of the Republic," NRep, CXXXVIII (January 20, 1958), 15-19.

Hyman, Stanley E., "James Gould Cozzens and the Art of the Possible," NMQ, XIX (Winter, 1949), 476-98.

Janeway, Elizabeth, "Guardian of Middle-Class Honor," NYTBR (August 2, 1959), 1, 18.

Long, Richard A., "The Image of Man in James Gould Cozzens," CLAJ, X (June, 1967), 299-307.

Ludwig, Richard M., "A Reading of the James Gould Cozzens Manuscripts," PULC, XIX (Autumn, 1957), 1-14.

Lydenberg, John, "Cozzens and the Conservatives," Crit, I, iii (Winter, 1958), 3-9.

_____, "Cozzens and the Critics," CE, XIX (December, (1957), 99-104.

_____, "Cozzens' Man of Responsibility," Shen, X, ii (Winter, 1959), 11-18.

Marx, Leo, "Controversy," ASch, XXVII (Spring, 1958), 228-9.

Maxwell, D. E. S., Cozzens.

Michel, Pierre, "A Note on James Gould Cozzens," RLV, No. 3 (1960), 192-210.

Millgate, M., American Social Fiction, 181-94.

_____, "The Judgements of James Gould Cozzens," CritQ, IV (Spring, 1962), 87-91.

Mizener, A., "...Anthony Powell and James Gould Cozzens," Sense of Life in the Modern Novel, 85-9.

_____, Twelve Great American Novels, 160-4.

_____, "The Undistorting Mirror," KR, XXVIII (November, 1966), 595-611.

Mooney, H. J., Jr., James Gould Cozzens.

O'Connor, William V., "Comments on Cozzens: A Muted Violence," Crit, I, iii (1958), 54-5.

Parrish, James, "James Gould Cozzens: A Critical Analysis," DA, XV (1955), 1856-57 (Florida State).

_____, "James Gould Cozzens Fights a War," ArQ, XVIII (Winter, 1962), 335-40.

Prescott, O., In My Opinion, 182-91.

Rees, David, "Ministers of Fate," Spectator (May 21, 1965), 666-7.

Rideout, Walter B., "Comments on Cozzens: James Gould Cozzens," Crit, I, iii (Winter, 1958), 55-6.

Scholes, Robert E. , "The Commitment of James Gould Coz-
    zens," ArQ, XVI (Summer, 1960), 129-44.
Updike, John, "Indifference," NY, XLIV (November 2, 1968),
    197-201.
Ward, John W. , "James Gould Cozzens and the Condition of
    Modern Man," ASch, XXVII (Winter, 1957-58), 92-9.
Watts, Harold H. , "James Gould Cozzens and the Genteel
    Tradition," ColQ, VI (Winter, 1958), 257-73.
Weaver, Robert, "The World of the Just and the Unjust,"
    TamR, V (Autumn, 1957), 61-7.
Wiegand, William G. , "James Gould Cozzens and the Pro-
    fessional Man in American Fiction," DA, XXII (1960),
    266 (Stanford).

ASK ME TOMORROW

Eisinger, Chester E. , "The Voice of Aggressive Aristocra-
    cy," Midway, No. 18 (Spring, 1964), 111-14.   Also in
    Eisinger, C. E. , Fiction of the Forties, 158-60.
Hicks, G. , James Gould Cozzens, 19-23.
Maxwell, D. E. S. , Cozzens, 27-33, 69-71.
Mooney, H. J. , Jr. , James Gould Cozzens, 63-73.

BY LOVE POSSESSED

Adams, R. P. , "James Gould Cozzens: A Cultural Dilem-
    ma," in Langford, R. E. , ed. , Essays in Modern Ameri-
    can Literature, 106-9.
Anon. , "The Hermit of Lambertville," Time, LXX (Septem-
    ber 2, 1957), 72-3.
Bracher, F. , Novels of James Gould Cozzens, 49-51, 106-
    8, 155-8.
Burns, Wayne, "Cozzens vs. Life and Art," NWR, I (Sum-
    mer, 1958), 7-18.
_____, "Reiterations," NWR, II (Fall-Winter, 1958), 38-
    43.
Davies, H. , A Mirror of the Ministry in Modern Novels,
    162-4.
De Mott, Benjamin, "Cozzens and Others," HudR, X (Win-
    ter, 1957-58), 622-6.
Ellmann, Richard, Reporter, XVII (October 3, 1957), 42-3,
    44.
Finn, James, "Cozzens Dispossessed," Cweal, LXVIII
    (April 4, 1958), 11-13.
Frederick, John T. , "Love By Adverse Possession: The
    Case of Mr. Cozzens," CE, XIX (April, 1958), 313-16.
Frost, William, "Cozzens: Some Reservations about BLP,"

CE, XIX (April, 1958), 317-18.

Gardiner, H. C. , "Monument to Hollow Men," In All Conscience, 143-4.   Also in America, XCVIII (October 5,
1957), 20.

Garrett, George, "BY LOVE POSSESSED: The Pattern and
the Hero," Crit, I, iii (Winter, 1958), 41-7.

Geismar, Maxwell, "Comments on Cozzens: By Cozzens
Possessed," Crit, I, iii (1958), 51-3.

Gould, Edward J. , "BY LOVE POSSESSED: A Review from
the Legal Point of View," Am Bar Assn Jnl, XLIV (August, 1958), 731-4, 799-800.

Harding, D. W. , "The Limits of Conscience," LS (April 18,
1959), 451.

Hermann, John, "Cozzens and a Critic," CE, XIX (April,
1958), 316-17.

Hicks, G. , James Gould Cozzens, 31-5.

Howe, Irving, "James Gould Cozzens: Novelist of the Republic," NRep, CXXXVIII (January 20, 1958), 17-19.

Leopold, Robert E. , "The Contemporary Novel and Its Con-
densation," DA, XXV (1964), 1211-12 (Columbia).

Macdonald, Dwight, "By Cozzens Possessed: A Review of
Reviews," Ctary, XXV (January, 1958), 36-47.   Also in
Commentary.   Commentary Reader, 567-85.

McKernan, Louis, "Profile of an Aristocrat: James Gould
Cozzens," CathW, CLXXXVI (November, 1957), 114-19.

Maxwell, D. E. S. , Cozzens, 102-6.

Mazzara, Richard A. , " 'Misère et grandeur de l'homme':
Pascal's PENSÉES and Cozzens' BY LOVE POSSESSED,"
BSTCF, V, i (Winter, 1964), 17-20.

Michel, Pierre, "A Note on James Gould Cozzens," RLV,
No. 3 (1960), 205-8.

Millgate, Michael, "By Cozzens Unpossessed," NRep,
CXXXVIII (June 9, 1958), 21.

Mizener, Arthur, Twelve Great American Novels, 164-6.
_____, "The Undistorting Mirror," KR, XXVIII (Novem-
ber, 1966), 595-601.

Mooney, H. J. , Jr. , James Gould Cozzens, 125-56.

Nemerov, Howard, "The Discovery of Cozzens," Nation,
CLXXXV (November 2, 1957), 306-8.   Also in Nemerov,
H. , Poetry and Fiction, 270-6.

Noble, D. W. , Eternal Adam and the New World Garden,
186-93.

Powers, Richard S. , "Praise the Mighty: Cozzens and the
Critics," SWR, XLIII (Summer, 1958), 263-70.

Price, Martin, YaleR, XLVII (Autumn, 1957), 153-5.

Scholes, Robert E. , "The Commitment of James Gould Cozzens," ArQ, XVI (Summer, 1960), 141-4.

Sherwood, John C., "Burns vs. Cozzens: The Defense,"
   NWR, II (Fall-Winter, 1958), 33-7.
Stern, Richard G., "A Perverse Fiction," KR, I (Winter,
   1958), 140-4.
Straumann, Heinrich, American Literature in the Twentieth
   Century, 28-9.
_____, "The Quarrel About Cozzens or the Vagaries of
   Book Reviewing," English Studies, XL (August, 1959),
   251-69.
Walcutt, C. C., Man's Changing Mask, 281-6.
Watts, Harold H., "James Gould Cozzens and the genteel
   tradition," ColQ, VI (Winter, 1958), 263-73.

CASTAWAY

Bracher, F., Novels of James Gould Cozzens, 38-46.
Fiedler, Leslie, in Madden, D., ed., Proletarian Writers
   of the Thirties, 19-20.
Fowler, Alastair, "Isolation and Its Discontents," TCL, VI
   (July, 1960), 51-64.
Hicks, G., James Gould Cozzens, 14-15.
Hyman, Stanley E., "My Favorite Forgotten Book," Tomor-
   row, VII (May, 1957), 58-9.
Maxwell, D. E. S., American Fiction, 278-80.
_____, Cozzens, 58-61.
Mooney, H. J., Jr., James Gould Cozzens, 17-26.

COCK PIT

Maxwell, D. E. S., Cozzens, 35-8.

GUARD OF HONOR

Bracher, F., Novels of James Gould Cozzens, 69-76, 87-8,
   130-5, 165-8.
Eisinger, Chester E., Fiction of the Forties, 164-70.
_____, "The Voice of Aggressive Aristocracy," Midway,
   No. 18 (Spring, 1964), 119-27.
Fergusson, Francis, "Three Novels," Perspectives USA,
   No. 6 (Winter, 1954), 30-44.
French, Warren, in French, W., ed., Forties, 9-15.
Healey, Robert C., in Gardiner, H. C., ed., Fifty Years
   of the American Novel, 268-9.
Hicks, G., James Gould Cozzens, 28-31.
Maxwell, D. E. S., American Fiction, 284-7.
_____, Cozzens, 92-102.
Michel, Pierre, "A Note on James Gould Cozzens," RLV,

No. 3 (1960), 203-5.

Millgate, M. , Americana Social Fiction, 188-94.

Mizener, Arthur, Twelve Great American Novels, 166-76.

_____, "The Undistorting Mirror," KR, XXVIII (November, 1966), 601-11.

Mooney, H. J. , Jr. , James Gould Cozzens, 99-124.

Parrish, James A. , Jr. , "James Gould Cozzens Fights a War," ArQ, XVIII (Winter, 1962), 335-40.

Scholes, Robert E. , "The Commitment of James Gould Cozzens," ArQ, XVI (Summer, 1960), 138-41.

Stuckey, W. J. , Pulitzer Prize Novels, 143-51.

Waldmeir, J. J. , American Novels of the Second World War, 130-7.

THE JUST AND THE UNJUST

Eisinger, Chester E. , Fiction of the Forties, 160-4.

_____, "The Voice of Aggressive Aristocracy," Midway, No. 18 (Spring, 1964), 114-19.

Hicks, G. , James Gould Cozzens, 23-8.

Maxwell, D. E. S. , American Fiction, 280-4.

_____, Cozzens, 81-92.

Michel, Pierre, "A Note on James Gould Cozzens," RLV, No. 3 (1960), 200-3.

Mooney, H. J. , Jr. , James Gould Cozzens, 75-97.

Prescott, O. , In My Opinion, 186-8.

Watts, Harold H. , "James Gould Cozzens and the genteel tradition," ColQ, VI (Winter, 1958), 263-73.

Weimer, David R. , "The Breath of Chaos in THE JUST AND THE UNJUST," Crit, I, iii (Winter, 1958), 30-40.

THE LAST ADAM (A CURE OF FLESH)

Bracher, F. , Novels of James Gould Cozzens, 37-8.

Eisinger, Chester E. , "Class and American Fiction: The Aristocracy in Some Novels of the Thirties," in Lanzinger, K. , ed. , Americana-Austriaca, 141-3.

_____, Fiction of the Forties, 154-8.

_____, "The Voice of Aggressive Aristocracy," Midway, No. 18 (Spring, 1964), 106-11.

Hicks, G. , James Gould Cozzens, 12-14.

Lewis, R. W. , "The Conflicts of Reality: Cozzens' THE LAST ADAM," in Whitbread, T. B. , ed. , Seven Contemporary Authors, 3-22.

Maxwell, D. E. S. , Cozzens, 49-57.

Mooney, H. J. , Jr. , James Gould Cozzens, 27-46.

Ober, William B. , M. D. , Carleton Misc, IV (Fall, 1963), 101-6.

MEN AND BRETHREN

Bracher, F., Novels of James Gould Cozzens, 90-1, 99-100, 184-93, 198-9.
Davies, H., A Mirror of the Ministry in Modern Novels, 153-62.
Hicks, G., James Gould Cozzens, 15-19.
Maxwell, D. E. S., Cozzens, 61-9.
Mooney, H. J., Jr., James Gould Cozzens, 47-61.
Scholes, Robert E., "The Commitment of James Gould Cozzens," ArQ, XVI (Summer, 1960), 135-7.

S. S. SAN PEDRO

Bracher, F., Novels of James Gould Cozzens, 97-9.
Hicks, G., James Gould Cozzens, 9-12.
Maxwell, D. E. S., Cozzens, 38-43.
Mooney, H. J., Jr., James Gould Cozzens, 5-17.

THE SON OF PERDITION

Bracher, F., Novels of James Gould Cozzens, 31-4, 200-2.
Levenson, J. C., "Comments on Cozzens: Prudence and Perdition," Crit, I, iii (1958), 53-4.
Maxwell, D. E. S., Cozzens, 34-5.

BIBLIOGRAPHY

Ludwig, Richard M., "James Gould Cozzens: A Review of Research and Criticism," TSLL, I (Spring, 1959), 123-36.
Maxwell, D. E. S., Cozzens, 118-19.
Meriwether, James B., "A James Gould Cozzens Check List," Crit, I (Winter, 1958), 57-63.

CRONIN, (A)RCHIBALD (J)OSEPH, 1896-

GRAND CANARY

Davies, H., Mirror of the Ministry in Modern Fiction, 123-4.

THE KEYS OF THE KINGDOM

Davies, H., Mirror of the Ministry in Modern Fiction, 124-8.

DENNIS, NIGEL FORBES, 1912-

BOYS AND GIRLS COME OUT TO PLAY

Ewart, Gavin, "Nigel Dennis- Identity Man," LonM, n. s.,
III (November, 1963), 35-8.

CARDS OF IDENTITY

Allen, W., Modern Novel, 274-6.
Allsop, K., Angry Decade, 140-3.
Ewart, Gavin, "Nigel Dennis- Identity Man," LonM, III, n. s.,
(November, 1963), 39-46.
Gindin, J., "Identity and the Existential," Postwar British
Fiction, 227-9.
Karl, F. R., "Nigel Dennis's CARDS OF IDENTITY," Con-
temporary English Novel, 249-53.
Peake, Charles, "CARDS OF IDENTITY; An Intellectual Sat-
ire," LHY, I (July, 1960), 49-57.

A HOUSE IN ORDER

Dooley, D. J., in Crit, X, i (1967), 95-9.

DE VRIES, PETER, 1910-

GENERAL

Davis, Douglas M., "An Interview with Peter De Vries,"
CE, XXVIII (April, 1967), 524-8.
Hamblen, Abigail A., "Peter De Vries: Calvinist Gone Un-
derground," Trace, No. 48 (Spring, 1963), 20-4.
Jellema, Roderick, Peter De Vries.
_____, "Peter De Vries: The Decline and Fall of Moot
Point," The Reformed Journal, XIII (April, 1963), 9-15.
(Not seen.)
Ter Maat, Cornelius J., "Three Novelists and a Community:
A Study of American Novelists with Dutch Calvinist Ori-
gins," DA, XXIV (1963), 751 (Michigan).

THE BLOOD OF THE LAMB

Jellema, R., Peter De Vries, 36-40.

COMFORT ME WITH APPLES

Jellema, R., Peter De Vries, 18-20.

LET ME COUNT THE WAYS

Jellema, R., Peter De Vries, 40-3.

THE MACKEREL PLAZA

Davies, H., A Mirror of the Ministry in Modern Novels,
164-72.
Jellema, R., Peter De Vries, 32-5.

REUBEN, REUBEN

Jellema, R., Peter De Vries, 27-31.

THE TENTS OF WICKEDNESS

Jellema, R., Peter De Vries, 20-3.
Walcutt, C. C., Man's Changing Mask, 247-51.

THROUGH THE FIELDS OF CLOVER

Jellema, R., Peter De Vries, 24-7.
Wain, John, "Home Truths," NY, XXXVIII (February 25,
1961), 130-3.

THE TUNNEL OF LOVE

Jellema, R., Peter De Vries, 15-18.

THE VALE OF LAUGHTER

"Fiction of 1968. Peter De Vries: THE VALE OF LAUGH-
TER," in T. L. S. Essays and Reviews from The Times
Literary Supplement, 1968, 188-90. Also in TLS (March
7, 1968).

DONLEAVY, (J)AMES (P)ATRICK, 1926-

GENERAL

Sherman, William D., "J. P. Donleavy: Anarchic Man as
Dying Dionysian," TCL, XIII (January, 1968), 216-28.

THE GINGER MAN

Allsop, K., Angry Decade, 73-5.
Corrigan, Robert A., "The Artist as Censor: J. P. Donleavy
and THE GINGER MAN," MASJ, VIII, i (Spring, 1967),
60-72.
Hassan, I., Radical Innocence, 194-200.
Morris, William E., "J. P. Donleavy's Wild Gingerbread
Man: Antichrist and Crazy Cookie," USFLQ, VI (Spring-
Summer, 1968), 41-2.
"Novels of 1963. J. P. Donleavy: THE GINGER MAN," in
T. L. S. Essays and Reviews from The Times Literary
Supplement, 1963, 185-7. Also in TLS (July 26, 1963).
Podhoretz, N., "The New Nihilism and the Novel," Doings
and Undoings, 168-70.
Sherman, William D., "J. P. Donleavy: Anarchic Man as
Dying Dionysian," TCL, XIII (January, 1968), 216-21.
Weales, Gerald, in Moore, H. T., ed., Contemporary Amer-
ican Novelists, 149-53.
Widmer, L., "Contemporary American Outcasts," Literary
Rebel, 136-9.

THE SADDEST SUMMER OF SAMUEL S.

Moore, John R., "J. P. Donleavy's Season Discontent,"
Crit, IX, ii (1967), 95-9.
Sherman, William D., "J. P. Donleavy: Anarchic Man as
Dying Dionysian," TCL, XIII (January, 1968), 226-8.

A SINGULAR MAN

Moore, John R., "Hard Times and the Noble Savage: J. P.
Donleavy's A SINGULAR MAN," HC, I, i (February,
1964), 1-4, 6-11.
Sherman, William D., "J. P. Donleavy: Anarchic Man as
Dying Dionysian," TCL, XIII (January, 1968), 221-4.
Weales, Gerald, in Moore, H. T., ed., Contemporary Amer-
ican Novelists, 153-4.

DOS PASSOS, JOHN RODERIGO, 1896-1970

GENERAL

Aaron, Daniel, "The Adventures of John Dos Passos,"
Writers on the Left; Episodes in American Literary Communism, N. Y.: Harcourt, World & Brace, 1961, 343-53.

_____, "The Riddle of John Dos Passos," Harpers,
    CCXXIV (March, 1962), 55-60.
Aldridge, J. W. , After the Lost Generation, 59-81.
Beach, Joseph W. , "Dos Passos, 1947," SR, LV (July-Sep-
    tember, 1947), 406-18.
_____, "John Dos Passos: The Artist in Uniform,"
    American Fiction, 25-35.
Belkind, Allen J. , "Satirical Social Criticism in the Novels
    of John Dos Passos," DA, XXVII (1966), 1049A-50A (Un.
    of So. Calif.).
Bernardin, Charles W. , "The Development of John Dos Pas-
    sos," Unpub. Diss. (Un. of Wisconsin), 1949.
Blake, N. M. , Novelist's America, 163-8.
Blankenship, R. , American Literature, 759-61.
Borenstein, Walter, "The Failure of Nerve: The Impact of
    Pío Baroja's Spain on John Dos Passos" in Stanford, D.
    E. , ed. , Nine Essays in Modern Literature, 63-87.
Brantley, J. D. , Fiction of John Dos Passos.
Brown, Deming, "Dos Passos in Soviet Criticism," CL, V
    (1953), 332-50.
Canario, John W. , "A Study of the Artistic Development of
    John Dos Passos in His Novels from ONE MAN'S INITIA-
    TION-1917 Through U. S. A." DA, XXIV (1964), 4693-4
    (Un. of Wash.).
Chase, Richard, "The Chronicles of Dos Passos," Ctary,
    XXXI (May, 1961), 395-400.
Cowley, Malcolm, "Dos Passos and His Critics," NRep,
    CXX (February 25, 1949), 21-3.
Davis, R. G. , John Dos Passos.
Diggins, John P. , "Dos Passos and Veblen's Villains," AR,
    XXIII (Winter, 1963-64), 485-500.
Donnell, Richard S. , "John Dos Passos: Satirical Historian
    of American Morality," Unpub. Doct. Diss. , Harvard Un. ,
    1960.
Dos Passos, John, in Madden, C. F. , ed. , Talks with Au-
    thors, 3-11.
Eisinger, C. E. , Fiction of the Forties, 119-25.
Evans, William A. , "Influences on and Development of John
    Dos Passos' Collectivist Technique," DA, XXVII (1966),
    745A-6A (Un. of New Mexico).
Fitelson, David, "The Art of John Dos Passos: A Study of
    the Novels Through U. S. A. ," DA, XXV (1964), 2510
    (Emory).

Frohock, W. M., "John Dos Passos: Of Time and Frustration," SWR, XXXIII (Winter, 1948), 71-80; XXXIII (Spring,
1948), 170-9.   Also in Frohock, W. M., Novel of Violence in America, 23-51.

Geismar, M., Writers in Crisis, 89-139.

Gelfant, B. H., "The Novelist as Architect of History,"
American City Novel, 133-8.

_____, "The Search for Identity in the Novels of John Dos
Passos," PMLA, LXXVI (March, 1961), 133-49.

Gorman, Thomas R., "Words and Deeds: A Study of the
Political Attitudes of John Dos Passos," DA, XXI (1960),
893-4 (Pennsylvania).

Gray, J., On Second Thought, 67-9.

Hicks, Granville, "The Politics of John Dos Passos," AR,
X (March, 1950), 85-98.

Holditch, William K., "Literary Technique in the Novels of
John Dos Passos," DA, XXII (1961), 3184-5 (Miss.).

Horchler, Richard, "Prophet Without Hope," Cweal, LXXV
(September 29, 1961), 13-16.

Howe, Irving, "John Dos Passos: The Loss of Passion,"
Tomorrow, VIII (March, 1949), 54-7.

Kallich, Martin, "John Dos Passos Fellow Traveller: A
Dossier with Commentary," TCL, I (January, 1956), 173-
90.

_____, "John Dos Passos: Liberty and the Father-Image,"
AR, X (March, 1950), 99-106.

Knox, George, "Dos Passos and Painting," TSLL, VI (Spring,
1964), 22-38.

Landsberg, Melvin, "John R. Dos Passos: His Influence on
the Novelist's Early Political Development," AQ, XVI
(Fall, 1964), 473-85.

Ledbetter, Kenneth, "The Journey of John Dos Passos,"
HAB, XVIII, ii (Fall, 1967), 36-48.

Lowry, Edward D., " 'The Writer As Technician': The
Method of John Dos Passos, 1925-1936," DA, XXVII
(1966), 1374A (N. Y. U.).

Lydenberg, John, "Dos Passos and the Ruined Words,"
PacSp, V (Summer, 1951), 316-27.

Lynde, Lowell F., "John Dos Passos: The Theme is Freedom," DA, XXVIII (1967), 235A (La. State).

Lynn, Kenneth, "Dos Passos' Chosen Country," NRep (October 15, 1966), 15-20.

_____, Introduction to World in a Glass: A View of Our
Century Selected from the Novels of John Dos Passos,

Boston: Houghton, Mifflin, 1966, v-xv.

McHugh, Vincent, "Dos Passos and the Thirty Thousand Souls," in Fiskin, A. M. I. , ed. , Writers of Our Years, Denver, Colo.: Un. of Denver Pr. , 1950, 79-100.

McLuhan, Herbert Marshall, "John Dos Passos: Technique vs. Sensibility," in Gardiner, H. , ed. , Fifty Years of the American Novel, 151-64.   Also in Litz, A. W. , ed. , Modern American Fiction, 138-49.

Menton, Seymour, "Érico Veríssimo and John Dos Passos: Two Interpretations of the National Novel," RIB, XIV (January-March, 1964), 54-9.

Millgate, M. , American Social Fiction, 128-41.

Mizener, Arthur, "The Gullivers of Dos Passos," SatR (June 30, 1951), 6, 7, 34-6.

_____, Sense of Life in the Modern Novel, 148-60.

Poster, William, "The Progress of John Dos Passos," AmMerc, LXXIV (March, 1952), 115-18.

Rideout, W. B. , Radical Novel in the U. S. , 154-64.

Sanders, David, "The 'Anarchism' of John Dos Passos," SAQ, LX (Winter, 1961), 44-55.

_____, "Interview with John Dos Passos," ClareQ, XI, iii (Spring, 1964), 89-100.

Smith, James S. , "The Novelist of Discomfort: A Reconsideration of John Dos Passos," CE, XIX (May, 1958), 332-8.

Snell, G. , Shapers of American Fiction, 249-63.

Spiller, Robert E. , The Third Dimension: Studies in Literary History, N. Y.: Macmillan, 1965, 163-6.

Stoltzfus, Ben, "John Dos Passos and the French," CL, XV (Spring, 1963), 146-63.

Straumann, H. , American Literature in the Twentieth Century, 22-8.

Thorp, W. , "Class and Caste in the Novel, 1920-1950," American Writing in the Twentieth Century, 136-42.

Van Gelder, R. , Writers on Writing, 237-40.

Wagenknecht, E. , "John Dos Passos: The Collectivist Novel," Cavalcade of the American Novel, 382-9.

Wakefield, Dan, "Dos, Which Side Are You On?" Esquire, LIX, iv (April, 1963), 112-18.

West, T. R. , Flesh of Steel, 54-70.

Wilson, Edmund, "Dos Passos and the Social Revolution," The Shores of Light: A Literary Chronicle of the Twenties and Thirties, N. Y.: Farrar, Straus & Young, 1952, 432-4.   Also in Rubin, L. D. , and J. R. Moore, eds. , Idea of an American Novel, 331-2.

Winner, Anthony, "The Needs of a Man: A Study of the Formation of Themes, Characters and Style in the Work

of John Dos Passos," Unpub. Doct. Diss., Harvard Un.,
1962.
Wrenn, J. H., <u>John Dos Passos.</u>

ADVENTURES OF A YOUNG MAN
(See also DISTRICT OF COLUMBIA)

Aldridge, J. W., <u>After the Lost Generation,</u> 77-8.
Beach, J. W., <u>American Fiction,</u> 62-4.
Blake, N. M., <u>Novelist's America,</u> 183-93.
Blotner, J., <u>Modern American Political Novel,</u> 312-15.
Brantley, J. D., <u>Fiction of John Dos Passos,</u> 79-85.
Davis, R. G., <u>John Dos Passos,</u> 31-3.
Eisinger, C. E., <u>Fiction of the Forties,</u> 121-2.
Geismar, M., <u>Writers in Crisis,</u> 130-5.
Milne, G., <u>American Political Novel,</u> 137-8.
Slochower, H., <u>No Voice is Wholly Lost,</u> 74-5.
Snell, G., <u>Shapers of American Fiction,</u> 260-1.

THE BIG MONEY (See also U. S. A.)

Blake, N. M., <u>Novelist's America,</u> 174-5, 177-83.
Geismar, Maxwell, Introduction to THE BIG MONEY, N. Y.:
   Pocket Books, 1955. Also in Geismar, M., <u>American</u>
   <u>Moderns,</u> 72-6.
_____, <u>Writers in Crisis,</u> 123-7.
Mizener, A., <u>Twelve Great American Novels,</u> 92-103.

CHOSEN COUNTRY

Brantley, J. D., <u>Fiction of John Dos Passos,</u> 102-8.
Eisinger, C. E., <u>Fiction of the Forties,</u> 124-5.
Poster, William, "The Progress of John Dos Passos,"
   <u>AmMerc,</u> LXXIV (March, 1952), 115-18.

DISTRICT OF COLUMBIA

Brantley, J. D., <u>Fiction of John Dos Passos,</u> 99-101.
Davis, R. G., <u>John Dos Passos,</u> 34-6.
Lydenberg, John, "Dos Passos and the Ruined Words," <u>PacSp,</u>
   V (Summer, 1951), 316-27.

FIRST ENCOUNTER (See ONE MAN'S INITIATION-1917)

THE 42nd PARALLEL (See also U. S. A.)

Geismar, M., Introduction to THE 42nd PARALLEL, N. Y.:

Pocket Books, 1952. Also in Geismar, M., American
Moderns, 65-8.
_____, Introduction, in Dos Passos, John, THE 42nd
PARALLEL, N.Y.: Wash. Sq. Pr., 1961.
_____, Writers in Crisis, 109-14.
Gray, J., On Second Thought, 69-72.
Gurko, L., Angry Decade, 50-2.
Wilson, E., Shores of Light, 446-50.

THE GRAND DESIGN (See also DISTRICT OF COLUMBIA)

Aldridge, J.W., After the Lost Generation, 79-80.
Blotner, J., Modern American Political Novel, 312-15.
Brantley, J.D., Fiction of John Dos Passos, 89-98.
Davis, R.G., John Dos Passos, 34-5.
Diggins, John P., "Dos Passos and Veblen's Villains," AR,
XXIII (Winter, 1963-64), 490-2.
Eisinger, C.E., Fiction of the Forties, 123-4.
Geismar, Maxwell, in NYTBR (January 2, 1949), 4. Also
in Geismar, M., American Moderns, 76-9.
Hicks, Granville, "Dos Passos and His Critics," AmMerc,
LXVIII (May, 1949), 623-30.
Howe, Irving, "John Dos Passos: The Loss of Passion,"
Tomorrow, VIII (March, 1949), 56-7.

THE GREAT DAYS

Aaron, Daniel, "Dos Passos Obsessed," New Leader, XLI
(June 2, 1958), 24.
Brantley, J.D., Fiction of John Dos Passos, 114-22.
Farrell, James T., "How Should We Rate Dos Passos?"
NRep, CXXXVIII (April 28, 1958), 17-18.
Geismar, M., American Moderns, 84-90.

MANHATTAN TRANSFER

Aldridge, J.W., After the Lost Generation, 69-72.
Arden, Eugene, "MANHATTAN TRANSFER: An Experiment
in Technique," UKCR, XXII (Winter, 1955), 153-8.
Beach, J.W., American Fiction, 35-44, 47-52.
Davis, R.G., John Dos Passos, 18-20.
Friedman, M., Stream of Consciousness, 245-6.
Frohock, W.H., "John Dos Passos: Of Time and Frustra-
tion," SWR, XXXIII (Spring, 1948), 170-4.
_____, Novel of Violence in America, 36-43.
Geismar, M., Writers in Crisis, 102-4.
Gelfant, B.H., "Technique as Social Commentary in MAN-

HATTAN TRANSFER," American City Novel, 138-66.
Lowry, E. A., "MANHATTAN TRANSFER: Dos Passos'
Wasteland," UR, XXX (October, 1963), 47-52.
Lowry, Edward D., " 'The Writer as Technician': The
Method of John Dos Passos, 1925-1936," DA, XXVII
(1966), 1374A (N. Y. U.).
Mizener, A., Twelve Great American Novels, 91-2.
Ruoff, Gene W., "Social Mobility and the Artist in MAN-
HATTAN TRANSFER and the MUSIC OF TIME," WSCL,
V, i (Winter-Spring, 1964), 64-76.
Snell, G., Shapers of American Fiction, 252-5.
Walcutt, C. C., American Literary Naturalism, 280-3.
Wrenn, J. H., John Dos Passos, 121-31.

MIDCENTURY

Brantley, J. D., Fiction of John Dos Passos, 122-6.
Chase, Richard, "The Chronicles of Dos Passos," Ctary,
XXXI (May, 1961), 396-8.
Davis, R. G., John Dos Passos, 39-44.
Diggins, John P., "Dos Passos and Veblen's Villains," AR,
XXIII (Winter, 1963-64), 492-6.
Dos Passos, John, in Madden, C. F., ed., Talks with Au-
thors, 3-11.
Kilpatrick, James J., "Midnight at Midcentury," National
Rev, X (April 22, 1961), 252-3.
Sanders, David, WSCL, II, iii (Fall, 1961), 47-50.

MOST LIKELY TO SUCCEED

Brantley, J. D., Fiction of John Dos Passos, 108-14.

1919 (See also U. S. A.)

Blake, N. M., Novelist's America, 168-74, 176-7.
Cooperman, S., World War I and the American Novel, 141-
5.
Cowley, Malcolm, "The Poet and the World," in Zabel,
M. D., ed., Literary Opinion in America, 488-90. Also
in Cowley, M., ed., After the Genteel Tradition, 134-46.
Also in Cowley, M., Think Back On Us, 215-19.
Geismar, Maxwell, Introduction to 1919, N. Y.: Pocket
Books, 1954. Also in Geismar, M., American Moderns,
68-72.
_____, Introduction to 1919, N. Y.: Wash. Sq. Pr., 1961.
Sartre, J. P., Literary and Philosophical Essays, 88-96.

NUMBER ONE (See also DISTRICT OF COLUMBIA)

Aldridge, J.W., After the Lost Generation, 78-9.
Blotner, J., Modern American Political Novel, 215-17.
Brantley, J.D., Fiction of John Dos Passos, 85-9.
Davis, R.G., John Dos Passos, 33-4.
Eisinger, C.E., Fiction of the Forties, 122-3.
Gray, J., On Second Thought, 73-4.

ONE MAN'S INITIATION- 1917

Aldridge, J.W., After the Lost Generation, 59-66.
Brantley, J.D., Fiction of John Dos Passos, 13-21.
Davis, R.G., John Dos Passos, 8-10.
Geismar, M., Writers in Crisis, 92-3.
Holditch, Kenneth, "ONE MAN'S INITIATION: The Origin of
    Techniques in the Novels of John Dos Passos," in Reck,
    Rima D., ed., Explorations of Literature (LSUSHS, 18),
    Baton Rouge: La. St. Un. Pr., 1966, 115-23.
Sanders, David, " 'Lies' and the System: Enduring Themes
    from Dos Passos' Early Novels," SAQ, LXV (Spring,
    1966), 215-26.

STREETS OF NIGHT

Beach, J.W., American Fiction, 26-9.
Brantley, J.D., Fiction of John Dos Passos, 38-45.
Davis, R.G., John Dos Passos, 16-17.
Sanders, David, " 'Lies' and the System: Enduring Themes
    from Dos Passos' Early Novels," SAQ, LXV (Spring,
    1966), 226-8.
Wrenn, J.H., John Dos Passos, 116-21.

THREE SOLDIERS

Aldridge, J.W., After the Lost Generation, 66-8.
Allen, W., Modern Novel, 136.
Bishop, J.P., "Three Brilliant Young Novelists," Collected
    Essays, 232-3. Also in Vanity Fair (October, 1921).
Brantley, J.D., Fiction of John Dos Passos, 21-36.
Cooperman, S., World War I and the American Novel, 152-
    5, 175-81, passim.
Davis, R.G., John Dos Passos, 10-12.
Frohock, W.M., "John Dos Passos: Of Time and Frustra-
    tion," SWR, XXXIII (Winter, 1948), 77-80. Also in Fro-
    hock, W.M., Novel of Violence in America, 31-6.
Geismar, M., Writers in Crisis, 93-6.

Hoffman, F. J., "I Had Seen Nothing Sacred," Twenties, 57-61.

Mizener, A., Twelve Great American Novels, 89-90.

Ross, Frank, "The Assailant-Victim in Three War Protest Novels," Paunch, XXXII (August, 1968), 46-57.

Sanders, David, " 'Lies' and the System: Enduring Themes from Dos Passos' Early Novels," SAQ, LXV (Spring, 1966), 215-26.

Snell, G., Shapers of American Fiction, 250-2.

Wrenn, J. H., John Dos Passos, 108-17.

U. S. A.

Aldridge, J. W., After the Lost Generation, 71-7.

Allen, W., Modern Novel, 144-8.

_____, Urgent West, 208-10.

Anon., "Two American Novelists," TLS, No. 2543 (October 27, 1950), 669-70.

Beach, Joseph W., American Fiction, 52-66.

_____, "Dos Passos, 1947," SR, LV (July-September, 1947), 411-15.

Blake, N. M., Novelist's America, 168-83.

Brantley, J. D., Fiction of John Dos Passos, 55-78.

Chametzky, Jules, "Reflections on U. S. A. as a Novel and Play," MR, I (February, 1960), 391-9.

Cowley, Malcolm, "John Dos Passos: The Poet and the World," NRep, LXX (April 27, 1932), 303-5; LXXXVII (September 9, 1936), 34. Also in Zabel, M. D., ed., Literary Opinion in America, 485-93. Also in Cowley, M., ed., Think Back On Us, 212-19. Also revised as "The Poet Against the World," in Cowley, M., ed., After the Genteel Tradition, 134-46.

Davis, R. G., John Dos Passos, 21-31.

Diggins, John P., "Dos Passos and Veblen's Villains," AR, XXIII (Winter, 1963-64), 487-90.

Feied, F., No Pie in the Sky, 41-56.

Finkelstein, S., Existentialism and Alienation in American Literature, 198-203.

Geismar, M., Writers in Crisis, 109-20, 123-30.

Geist, Stanley, "Fictitious Americans," HudR, V (Summer, 1952), 206-11.

Gelfant, B. H., "The Fulfillment of Form in U. S. A.," American City Novel, 166-74.

Gurko, Leo, "John Dos Passos' U. S. A.: A 1930's Spectacular," in Madden, D., ed., Proletarian Writers of the Thirties, 46-63.

Hoffman, Arnold R., "An Element of Strcuture in U. S. A.,"

CEA, XXXI (October, 1968), 12-13.
Irwin, William R., "Dos Passos and Fitzgerald as Reviewers of the American Social Scene," NS (September, 1960), 417-22.
Knox, George, "Voice in the U.S.A. Biographies," TSLL, IV (1962), 109-16.
Lehan, Richard, "The Trilogies of Jean-Paul Sartre and John Dos Passos," IEY, No. 9 (1964), 60-4.
Lowry, Edward D., " 'The Writer as Technician': The Method of John Dos Passos, 1925-1936," DA, XXVII (1966), 1374A (N.Y.U.).
Lydenberg, John, "Dos Passos's U.S.A.: The Words of the Hollow Men," in Krause, S.J., ed., Essays on Determinism, 97-107.
Maxwell, D.E.S., American Fiction, 269-72.
Maynard, Reid, "John Dos Passos' One-Sided Panorama," Discourse, XI (Autumn, 1968), 468-74.
Millgate, M., American Social Fiction, 130-5.
Nelson, F. William, "An Analysis of John Dos Passos' U.S.A.," DA, XVII (1957), 1767 (Oklahoma).
Schwartz, Delmore, "John Dos Passos and the Whole Truth," SoR, IV (Autumn, 1938), 351-65. Also in Rubin, L.D., Jr., and J.R. Moore, eds., Idea of an American Novel, 332-9. Also in Aldridge, J.W., ed., Critiques and Essays on Modern Fiction, 176-89.
Slochower, H., No Voice is Wholly Lost, 70-4.
Smith, James S., "The Novelist of Discomfort: A Reconsideration of John Dos Passos," CE, XIX (May, 1958), 332-8.
Snell, G., Shapers of American Fiction, 255-60.
Walcutt, C.C., American Literary Naturalism, 283-9.
Ward, John W., "Lindbergh, Dos Passos and History," Carleton Miscellany, VI (Summer, 1965), 20-41.
Widmer, Eleanor, "The Lost Girls of U.S.A.: Dos Passos' 30's Movie," in French, Warren, ed., The Thirties: Fiction, Poetry, Drama, De Land, Fla.: Everett Edwards, Inc., 11-19.
Wrenn, J.H., John Dos Passos, 154-66.

BIBLIOGRAPHY

Potter, Jack, A Bibliography of John Dos Passos, Chicago: Normandie House, 1950.
Reinhart, Virginia S., "John Dos Passos Bibliography: 1950-1966," TCL, XIII (October, 1967), 167-78.
White, William, "More Dos Passos: Bibliographical Addenda," PBSA, XLV (1951), 156-8.
Wrenn, J.H., John Dos Passos, 198-205.

DURRELL, LAWRENCE, 1912-

GENERAL

Arthos, John, "Lawrence Durrell's Gnosticism," Person,
    XLIII (Summer, 1962), 360-73.
Flint, R. W. , "A Major Novelist," Ctary, XXVII (April,
    1959), 353-6.
Fraser, G. S. , Lawrence Durrell.
Friedman, Alan W. , "A 'Key' to Lawrence Durrell," WSCL,
    VIII (Winter, 1967), 31-42.
Glicksberg, Charles I. , "The Fictional World of Lawrence
    Durrell," BuR, XI, ii (March, 1963), 118-33.
Green, Martin, "Lawrence Durrell, II: A Minority Report,"
    YR, XLIX (Summer, 1960), 496-508.
Howarth, Herbert, "Lawrence Durrell and Some Early Mas-
    ters," BA, XXXVII (Winter, 1963), 5-11.
Kameyama, Masako, "Lawrence Durrell: A Sketch," in
    Collected Essays by the Members of the Faculty, No. 11,
    Kyoritsu, Japan: Kyoritsu Womens Junior College, 1968,
    32-49.
Kelly, John C. , "Lawrence Durrell's Style," Studies, LII
    (Summer, 1963), 199-204.
Leslie, Ann, "This Infuriating Man- Lawrence Durrell,"
    Irish Digest, LXXXII (February, 1965), 67-70. (Not seen.)
Lund, Mary G. , "Durrell: Soft Focus on Crime," PrS,
    XXXV (Winter, 1961), 339-44.
Mitchell, Julian, and Gene Andrewski, "Lawrence Durrell,"
    ParisR, No. 22 (Autumn-Winter, 1960), 32-61.   Also in
    Writers at Work, 2nd ser. , 257-82.
Moore, H. T. , ed. , World of Lawrence Durrell.
Sullivan, Nancy, "Lawrence Durrell's Epitaph for the Novel,"
    Person, XLIV (Winter, 1963), 79-88.
Unterecker, J. , Lawrence Durrell.
Weigel, J. A. , Lawrence Durrell.
Wickes, George, ed. , Lawrence Durrell, Henry Miller: A
    Private Correspondence, N. Y. :   Dutton, 1962.
Young, Kenneth, "A Dialogue with Durrell," Encounter, XIII
    (December, 1959), 61-2, 64-8.

THE ALEXANDRIA QUARTET

Aldington, Richard, in Moore, H. T. , ed. , World of Law-
    rence Durrell, 3-12.
Baldanza, Frank, "Lawrence Durrell's 'Word Continuum',"
    Crit, IV, ii (Spring-Summer, 1961), 3-17.

Bliven, Naomi, "Books: Alexandrine in Tetrameter," NY, XXXVI (August 13, 1960), 97-103.

Bode, Carl, "Durrell's Way to Alexandria," CE, XXII (May, 1961), 531-8. Also in Moore, H. T., ed., World of Lawrence Durrell, 205-21.

_____, "Lawrence Durrell," John O'London's, IV (February 16, 1961), 169.

Bork, Alfred M., "Durrell and Relativity," CRAS, VII (Spring, 1963), 191-203.

Brown, Sharon Lee, "Lawrence Durrell and Relativity," DA, XXVI (1966), 7310 (Oregon).

Burns, J. Christopher, "Durrell's Heraldic Universe," MFS, XIII (Autumn, 1967), 375-88.

Cate, Curtis, "Lawrence Durrell," Atlantic Monthly, CCVIII (December, 1961), 63-9.

Coleman, John, "Mr. Durrell's Dimensions," Spectator (February 19, 1960), 256-7.

Corke, Hilary, "Lawrence Durrell," LHY, II (January, 1961), 43-9.

_____, "Mr. Durrell and Brother Criticus," Encounter, XIV (May, 1960), 65-70.

Cortland, Peter, "Durrell's Sentimentalism," EngR, XIV (April, 1964), 15-19.

Cox, W. D. G., in Moore, H. T., ed., World of Lawrence Durrell, 112-16.

Crowder, Richard, "Durrell, Libido, and Eros," BSTCF, III, ii (Winter, 1962-63), 34-9.

Dare, H., "The Quest for Durrell's Scobie," MFS, X (Winter, 1964-65), 379-82.

Decancq, Roland, "What Lies Beyond? An Analysis of Darley's 'Quest' in Lawrence Durrell's ALEXANDRIA QUARTET," RLV, XXXIV (1968), 134-50.

De Mott, Benjamin, "Grading the Emanglons," HudR, XIII (Autumn, 1960), 457-64.

Dobrée, Bonamy, "Durrell's Alexandrian Series," SR, LXIX (Winter, 1961), 61-79. Also in Moore, H. T., ed., World of Lawrence Durrell, 184-204. Also in Dobrée, B., The Lamp and the Lute, London: Frank Cass & Co., 1964, 150-68.

Edel, Leon, The Modern Psychological Novel, N. Y.: Grosset & Dunlap, 1964, 185-91.

Elliott, George P., in Moore, H. T., ed., World of Lawrence Durrell, 87-94.

Enright, D. J., "Alexandrian Nights' Entertainments: Lawrence Durrell's QUARTET," ILA, III (1961), 30-9. Also in Enright, D. J., Conspirators and Poets, 111-20.

Eskin, Stanley G., "Durrell's Themes in THE ALEXANDRIA

QUARTET," TQ, V, iv (Winter, 1962), 43-60.

Fraiberg, Louis, "Durrell's Dissonant Quartet," in Shapiro, C., ed., Contemporary British Novelists, 16-35.

Fraser, G. S., Lawrence Durrell, 129-62.

Friedman, Alan W., "Art for Love's Sake: Lawrence Durrell and THE ALEXANDRIA QUARTET," DA, XXVII (1966), 1365A-6A (Rochester).

_____, "A 'Key' to Lawrence Durrell," WSCL, VIII (Winter, 1967), 36-42.

Gindin, J., Postwar British Fiction, 215-22.

Glicksberg, Charles I., "The Fictional World of Lawrence Durrell," BuR, XI, ii (March, 1963), 122-33.

_____, Self in Modern Literature, 90-4.

Godshalk, William L., "Some Sources of Durrell's ALEX-ANDRIA QUARTET," MFS, XIII (Autumn, 1967), 361-74.

Goldberg, Gerald J., "The Search for the Artist in Some Recent British Fiction," SAQ, LXII (Summer, 1963), 387-92.

Gordon, Ambrose, Jr., "Time, Space and Eros: THE ALEXANDRIA QUARTET Rehearsed," in Sutherland, W. O. S., ed., Six Contemporary Novels, 6-21.

Gossman, Ann, "Some Characters in Search of a Mirror," Crit, VIII, iii (Spring-Summer, 1966), 179-84.

Green, Martin, "Lawrence Durrell, II: A Minority Report," YR, XLIX (Summer, 1960), 498-500. Also in Moore, H. T., ed., World of Lawrence Durrell, 132-8.

Hagopian, John V., "The Resolution of the ALEXANDRIA QUARTET," Crit, VII (Spring, 1964), 97-106.

Hamard, Jean, "Lawrence Durrell: A European Writer," DUJ, XXIX (1968), 171-81.

Hartt, J. N., Lost Image of Man, 63-7.

Hawkins, Joanna L., "A Study of the Relationship of Point of View to the Structure of THE ALEXANDRIA QUARTET," DA, XXVI (1965), 3338-39 (Northwestern).

Highet, Gilbert, "The Alexandrians of Lawrence Durrell," Horizon, II (March, 1960), 113-18.

Howarth, Herbert, "A Segment of Durrell's QUARTET," UTQ, XXXII (April, 1963), 282-93.

Hutchens, Eleanor H., "The Heraldic Universe in THE ALEXANDRIA QUARTET," CE, XXIV (October, 1962), 56-61.

Johnson, Ann S., "Lawrence Durrell's 'Prism-Sightedness': The Structure of THE ALEXANDRIA QUARTET," DA, XXIX (1968), 264A (Un. of Pennsylvania).

Karl, F. R., "Lawrence Durrell: Physical and Metaphysical Love," Contemporary English Novel, 40-61.

Kazin, A., Contemporaries, 188-92.

Kelly, John C., "Lawrence Durrell: THE ALEXANDRIA
    QUARTET," Studies, LII (Spring, 1963), 52-68.
_____, "Lawrence Durrell's Style," Studies, LII (Summer,
    1963), 199-204.
Kermode, Frank, "Fourth Dimension," REL, I, ii (April,
    1960), 73-7.
_____, Puzzles and Epiphanies, 218-27.
"The Kneller Tape (Hamburg)," in Moore, H.T., ed., World
    of Lawrence Durrell, 161-8.
Kruppa, Joseph E., "Durrell's ALEXANDRIA QUARTET and
    the 'Implosion' of the Modern Consciousness," MFS, XIII
    (Autumn, 1967), 401-16.
"Lawrence Durrell Answers a Few Questions," in Moore, H.
    T., ed., World of Lawrence Durrell, 156-60.
Lemon, Lee T., "THE ALEXANDRIA QUARTET: Form and
    Fiction," WSCL, IV, iii (Autumn, 1963), 327-32.
Levidova, I., "A 'Four-Decker' in Stagnant Waters," Anglo-
    Soviet Jnl, XXIII (Summer, 1962), 39-41.
Levitt, Morton P., "Art and Correspondences: Durrell,
    Miller, and THE ALEXANDRIA QUARTET," MFS, XIII
    (Autumn, 1967), 299-313.
Littlejohn, David, "Lawrence Durrell: The Novelist as En-
    tertainer," Motive, XXIII (November, 1962), 14-16.
_____, "The Permanence of Lawrence Durrell," ColQ,
    XIV (Summer, 1965), 63-71.
Lund, Mary G., "The Alexandrian Projection," AR, XXI
    (Summer, 1961), 193-204.
_____, "The Big Rock Crystal Mountain," FQ, XI (May,
    1962), 15-18.
_____, "Eight Aspects of Melissa," ForumH, III ix
    (Winter, 1962), 18-22.
_____, "Submerge for Reality: The New Novel Form of
    Lawrence Durrell," SWR, LXIV (Summer, 1959), 229-35.
Mackworth, Cecily, "Lawrence Durrell and the New Ro-
    manticism," TC, CLXVII (March, 1960), 203-13. Also
    in Moore, H.T., ed., World of Lawrence Durrell, 24-37.
Manzalaoui, Mahmoud, "Curate's Egg; An Alexandrian Opin-
    ion of Durrell's QUARTET," EA, XV (July, 1962), 248-
    60.
Michot, Paulette, "Lawrence Durrell's ALEXANDRIA QUAR-
    TET," RLV, No. 5 (1960), 361-7.
Morcos, Mona L., "Elements of the Autobiographical in THE
    ALEXANDRIA QUARTET," MFS, XIII (Autumn, 1967),
    343-59.
Neifer, Leo J., "Durrell's Method and Purpose of Art,"
    WisSL, No. 3 (1966), 99-103.
O'Brien, R.A., "Time, Space and Language in Lawrence

Durrell," Waterloo Rev VI (Winter, 1961), 16-24.
Pritchett, V. S. , "Alexandrian Hothouse," Working Novelist,
    30-5.
Proser, Matthew N. , "Darley's Dilemma: The Problem of
    Structure in Durrell's ALEXANDRIA QUARTET," Crit,
    IV, ii (Spring-Summer, 1961), 18-28.
Read, Phyllis J. , "The Illusion of Personality: Cyclical
    Time in Durrell's ALEXANDRIA QUARTET," MFS, XIII
    (Autumn, 1967), 389-99.
Rippier, J. S. , Some Postwar English Novelists, 106-33.
Robinson, W. R. , "Intellect and Imagination in THE ALEX-
    ANDRIA QUARTET," Shen, XVIII (Summer, 1967), 55-68.
Scholes, Robert, "Return to Alexandria: Lawrence Durrell
    and the Western Narrative Tradition," VQR, XL (Summer,
    1964), 411-20.   Also in Scholes, R. , Fabulators, 17-31.
Steiner, George, "Lawrence Durrell, I: The Baroque Novel,"
    YR, XLIX (Summer, 1960), 488-95.   Also in Steiner, G. ,
    Language and Silence; Essays on Language, Literature
    and the Inhuman, N. Y. : Atheneum, 1967, 280-7.   Also in
    Moore, H. T. , ed. , World of Lawrence Durrell, 13-23.
Sullivan, Nancy, "Lawrence Durrell's Epitaph for the Novel,"
    Person, XLIV (Winter, 1963), 79-88.
Sykes, Gerald, in Moore, H. T. , ed. , World of Lawrence
    Durrell, 146-55.
Trilling, Lionel, in Moore, H. T. , ed. , World of Lawrence
    Durrell, 49-65.
Unterecker, John, Lawrence Durrell, 36-46.
_____, "The Protean World of Lawrence Durrell," in
    Kostelanetz, R. , ed. , On Contemporary Literature, 322-
    9.
Weatherhead, A. K. , "Romantic Anachronism in THE ALEX-
    ANDRIA QUARTET," MFS, X (Summer, 1964), 128-36.
Weigel, J. A. , Lawrence Durrell, 56-112.
Wotton, G. E. , in Moore, H. T. , ed. , World of Lawrence
    Durrell, 103-11.

THE BLACK BOOK

Allen, W. , Modern Novel, 284-8.
Brown, Sharon L. , "THE BLACK BOOK: A Search for
    Method," MFS, XIII (Autumn, 1967), 319-28.
_____, "Lawrence Durrell and Relativity," DA, XXVI
    (1966), 7310 (Oregon).
Fraser, G. S. , Lawrence Durrell, 61-83.
Glicksberg, Charles I. , "The Fictional World of Lawrence
    Durrell," BuR, XI, ii (March, 1963), 118-22.
_____, Self in Modern Literature, 89-90.

Moore, Harry T., in Moore, H.T., ed., World of Lawrence
  Durrell, 100-2.
Pritchett, V.S., "Alexandrian Hothouse," Living Novel, 303-
  9.
Rexroth, Kenneth, "The Artifice of Convincing Immodesty,"
  The Griffin, IX (September, 1960), 3-9. Also in Assays,
  N.Y.: New Directions, 1962, 125-30.
Unterecker, J., Lawrence Durrell, 11-12, 24-31.
Weigel, J.A., Lawrence Durrell, 43-8.

CLEA (See also THE ALEXANDRIA QUARTET)

Hagopian, John V., in Hagopian, J.V., and Dolch, M.,
  eds., Insight II, 95-103.
Weyergans, Franz, "CLEA, by Lawrence Durrell," Revue
  Nouvelle, XXXII (July 15, 1960), 94-8.

THE DARK LABYRINTH (CEFALÛ)

Fraser, G.S., Lawrence Durrell, 96-100.
Weigel, J.A., Lawrence Durrell, 48-54.

MOUNTOLIVE (See also THE ALEXANDRIA QUARTET)

Mullins, Edward, "On MOUNTOLIVE," Two Cities, I (April
  15, 1959), 21-4.

PANIC SPRING

Weigel, J.A., Lawrence Durrell, 41-3.

PIED PIPER OF LOVERS

Weigel, John A., "Lawrence Durrell's First Novel," TCL,
  XIV (July, 1968), 75-83.

TUNC

"Fiction of 1968. Lawrence Durrell: TUNC," in T.L.S.
  Essays and Reviews from The Times Literary Supplement,
  1968, 63-8. Also in TLS (April 25, 1968).
Fraser, G.S., Lawrence Durrell, 164-91.

WHITE EAGLES OVER SERBIA

Fraser, G.S., Lawrence Durrell, 127-8.
Weigel, J.A., Lawrence Durrell, 54-5.

BIBLIOGRAPHY

Beebe, Maurice, "Criticism of Lawrence Durrell: A Selected Checklist," MFS, XIII (Autumn, 1967), 417-21.
Thomas, Alan G., in Fraser, G. S., Lawrence Durrell, 200-
50.
Weigel, J. A., Lawrence Durrell, 163-70.

EASTLAKE, WILLIAM

GENERAL

Phelps, Donald, "The Land of Grace and Isolation," Nation,
CXCIX (October 12, 1964), 225-7.
Wylder, Delbert E., "The Novels of William Eastlake,"
NMQ, XXXIV (Summer, 1964), 188-203.

THE BRONC PEOPLE

Gold, Herbert, "Wit and Truth," Nation, CLXXXVII (Sep-
tember 20, 1968), 158-9.
Woolf, Douglas, "One of the Truly Good Men," EvR, II, No.
8 (Spring, 1959), 194-6.
Wylder, Delbert E., "The Novels of William Eastlake,"
NMQ, XXXIV (Summer, 1964), 190-7.

GO IN BEAUTY

Wylder, Delbert E., "The Novels of William Eastlake,"
NMQ, XXXIV (Summer, 1964), 189-90.

PORTRAIT OF AN ARTIST WITH TWENTY-SIX HORSES

Smith, William J., "An Original, Thus Disturbing, Talent,"
Cweal, LXXVIII (June 21, 1963), 357.
Wylder, Delbert E., "The Novels of William Eastlake,"
NMQ, XXXIV (Summer, 1964), 197-200.

ELKIN, STANLEY LAWRENCE, 1930-

BOSWELL: A MODERN COMEDY

Guttmann, Allen, "Stanley Elkin's Orphans," MR, VII (Summer, 1966), 598-600.

ELLIOTT, GEORGE PAUL, 1918-

GENERAL

Gelfant, Blanche H., "Beyond Nihilism: The Fiction of
George P. Elliott," HC, V (December, 1968), 1-12.

DAVID KNUDSEN

Greenberg, Alvin, "The Novel of Disintegration: Paradoxical Impossibility in Contemporary Fiction," WSCL, VII
(Winter-Spring, 1966), 108-9.
Slatoff, Walter, "George P. Elliott," Epoch, XII (Spring,
1962), 60-2.
Trachtenberg, Alan, Crit, V, i (Spring-Summer, 1962), 83-
9.

IN THE WORLD

Kramer, Hilton, "Liberal Verities," New Leader, XLVIII
(October 11, 1965), 22-3.
Slatoff, Walter, Epoch, XV (Winter, 1966), 190-1.

ELLISON, RALPH, 1914-

GENERAL

Bone, Robert, "Ralph Ellison and the Uses of Imagination,"
TriQ, No. 6 (1966), 39-54. Also in Hill, Herbert, ed.,
Anger and Beyond: The Negro Writer in the United States,
N. Y.: Harper, 1966, 86-111.
Britt, David D., "The Image of the White Man in the Fiction
of Langston Hughes, Richard Wright, James Baldwin and
Ralph Ellison," DA, XIX (1968), 1532A (Emory).
Chester, Alfred, and Vilma Howard, "The Art of Fiction
VIII: Ralph Ellison," ParisR, No. 8 (Spring, 1955). Al-
so in Writers at Work, 2nd ser., 317-34. Also in Elli-
son, Ralph, Shadow and Act, N. Y.: Random House,
1964, 167-83.
Ellison, Ralph, "That Same Pain, That Same Pleasure: An
Interview," Shadow and Act, N. Y.: Random House, 1964,
3-23. Also in December, III (Winter, 1961).
Geller, Allen, "An Interview with Ralph Ellison," TamR, No.
32 (Summer, 1964), 3-24. Also in Bigsby, C. W. E., ed.,
Black American Writer, Vol. I, 153-68.
Isaacs, Harold R., "Five Writers and Their African Ancestors," Phylon, XXI (1960), 317-22.
Klein, M., After Alienation, 71-107.

Kostelanetz, Richard, "The Negro Genius," TC, 1033 (1967), 49-50.
Lehan, Richard, "The Strange Silence of Ralph Ellison," CEJ, I (1965), 63-8. (Not seen.)
O'Daniel, Therman B., "The Image of Man as Portrayed by Ralph Ellison," CLAJ, X (June, 1967), 277-84.
Thompson, James, Lennox Raphael, and Steve Cannon, " 'A Very Stern Discipline': An Interview with Ralph Ellison," Harpers, CCXXXIV (March, 1967), 76-95.
Zietlow, Edward R., "Wright to Hansberry: The Evolution of Outlook in Four Negro Writers," DA, XXVIII (1967), 701A (Un. of Wash.).

INVISIBLE MAN

Allen, Michael, "Some Examples of Faulknerian Rhetoric in Ellison's INVISIBLE MAN," in Bigsby, C. W. E., ed., Black American Writer, Vol. I, 143-51.
Allen, W., Modern Novel, 317-20.
Baumbach, Jonathan, "Nightmare of a Native Son: Ralph Ellison's INVISIBLE MAN," Crit, VI, i (Spring, 1963), 48-65. Also in Baumbach, J., Landscape of Nightmare, 68-86.
Bennett, John Z., "The Race and the Runner: Ellison's IN-VISIBLE MAN, XUS, V (March, 1966), 12-26.
Bloch, Alice, "Sight Imagery in INVISIBLE MAN," EJ, LV (November, 1966), 1019-21, 1024.
Bluestein, Gene, "The Blues as a Literary Theme," MR, VIII (Autumn, 1967), 600-17.
Bone, R. A., Negro Novel in America, 197-212.
Bontemps, Arna, in Griffin, W., ed., Literature in the Modern World, 119-22.
Breit, Harvey, in Balakian, N., and C. Simmons, eds., Creative Present, 18-21.
Ellison, Ralph, "Light on INVISIBLE MAN," Crisis, LX (March, 1953), 157-8.
Ford, Nick A., "Four Popular Negro Novelists," Phylon, XV (1954), 34-7.
Fraiberg, Selma, "Two Modern Incest Heroes," PR, XXVIII, No. 5-6 (1961), 655-61.
Geller, Allen, "An Interview with Ralph Ellison," TamR, No. 32 (Summer, 1964), 3-24.
Gérard, Albert, "Humanism and Negritude: Notes on the Contemporary Afro-American Novel," Diogenes, No. 37 (Spring, 1962), 121-4.
Girson, Rochelle, "Sidelights on Invisibility," SatR, XXXVI (March 14, 1953), 20+.

Glicksberg, Charles I., "The Symbolism of Vision," SWR,
    XXXIX (1954), 259-65.
Hassan, I., Radical Innocence, 169-78.
Horowitz, Ellin, in Kostelanetz, R., ed., Contemporary
    Literature, 330-46.
Horowitz, Floyd R., "The Enigma of Ellison's Intellectual
    Man," CLAJ, VII (December, 1963), 126-32.
_____, "Ralph Ellison's Modern Version of Brer Bear and
    Brer Rabbit in INVISIBLE MAN," MASJ, IV, ii (Fall,
    1963), 21-7.
Howe, I., World More Attractive, 112-15.
Hux, Samuel H., "American Myth and Existential Vision:
    The Indigenous Existentialism of Mailer, Bellow, Styron,
    and Ellison," DA, XXVI (1966), 5437. (Conn.).
Jackson, Esther M., "The American Negro and the Image
    of the Absurd," Phylon, XXIII (Winter, 1962), 368-71.
Klein, M., After Alienation, 107-46. Also in Gross, S.L.,
    and J.E. Hardy, eds., Images of the Negro in American
    Literature, 249-64.
Knox, George, "The Negro Novelist's Sensibility and the Out-
    sider Theme," WHR, XI (Spring, 1957), 137-48.
Kostelanetz, Richard, "The Politics of Ellison's Booker:
    INVISIBLE MAN as Symbolic History," ChiR, XIX, ii
    (1967), 5-26.
Lee, L.L., "The Proper Self: Ralph Ellison's INVISIBLE
    MAN," Descant, X (Spring, 1966), 38-48.
Lehan, Richard, "Existentialism in Recent American Fiction:
    The Demonic Quest," TSLL, I (Summer, 1959), 195-6,
    199-200.
_____, "The Strange Silence of Ralph Ellison," CEJ, I,
    ii (1965), 63-8.
Lewis, R.W.B., "Days of Wrath and Laughter," Trials of
    the Word, 218-20.
Littlejohn, D., Black on White, 110-19.
Ludwig, J., Recent American Novelists, 19-24.
Marcus, Steven, "The American Negro in Search of Iden-
    tity," Ctary, XVI (November, 1953), 458-9.
Margolies, E., "History as Blues: Ralph Ellison's INVIS-
    IBLE MAN," Native Sons, 127-48.
Mengeling, Marvin E., "Whitman and Ellison: Older Sym-
    bols in a Modern Mainstream," WWR, XII (September,
    1966), 67-70.
Miller, Stuart, The Picaresque Novel, Cleveland: Case
    Western Reserve Un., 1967, 134-5.
Nash, R.W., "Stereotypes and Social Types in Ellison's
    INVISIBLE MAN," Sociological Qtly, VI (1965), 349-60.
O'Daniel, Therman B., "The Image of Man as Portrayed

by Ralph Ellison," CLAJ, X (June, 1967), 277-84.
Olderman, Raymond M., "Ralph Ellison's Blues and INVIS-
    IBLE MAN," WSCL, VII (Summer, 1966), 142-59.
Randall, John H., III, "Ralph Ellison: INVISIBLE MAN,"
    RLV, XXXI (1965), 24-45.
Rao, B. R., "The INVISIBLE MAN: A Study," in Maini,
    Darsan Singh, ed., Variations on American Literature,
    New Delhi: U.S. Educ. Foundation in India, 1968, 93-8.
Rovit, Earl H., "Ralph Ellison and the American Comic Tra-
    dition," WSCL, I, iii (Fall, 1960), 34-42.   Also in Wald-
    meir, J.J., ed., Recent American Fiction, 167-74.
Schafer, William J., "Ralph Ellison and the Birth of the
    Anti-Hero," Crit, X, II (1968), 81-93.
Scott, Nathan A., Jr., "Judgment Marked by a Cellar: The
    American Negro Writer and the Dialectic of Despair,"
    UDQ, II, ii (1967), 30-34.   Also in Mooney, H.J., and
    T.F. Staley, eds., Shapeless God, 164-8.
Singleton, M.K., "Leadership Mirages as Antagonists in IN-
    VISIBLE MAN," ArQ, XXII (Summer, 1966), 157-71.
Waghmare, J.M., "Invisibility of the American Negro:
    Ralph Ellison's INVISIBLE MAN," Quest, LIX (1968), 23-
    30.
West, A., Principles and Persuasions, 212-18.

BIBLIOGRAPHY

Gross, S.L., and J.E. Hardy, eds.   Images of the Negro
    in American Literature, 305.

FARRELL, JAMES (T)HOMAS, 1904-

GENERAL

Aldridge, John W., "The Education of James Farrell," In
    Search of Heresy, 186-91.
Alexis, Gerhard T., "Farrell Since Our Days of Anger,"
    CE, XXVII (December, 1965), 221-6.
Blake, N.M., "The World of Fifty-eighth Street," Novelist's
    America, 195-225.
Blankenship, R., American Literature, 755-8.
Branch, Edgar M., "American Writer in the Twenties:
    James T. Farrell and the University of Chicago," ABC,
    XI, x (Summer, 1961), 25-32.
_____, James T. Farrell.
Curley, Thomas F., "Catholic Novels and the American Cul-
    ture," Ctary, XXXVI (July, 1963), 34-8.

Douglas, Wallace, "The Case of James T. Farrell," TriQ,
No. 2 (Winter, 1965), 105-23.
Eisinger, C. E., Fiction of the Forties, 64-6.
Farrell, James T., "C'est Droll," ABC, XI, x (Summer,
1961), 33.
_____, "Farrell Revisits Studs Lonigan's Neighborhood,"
NYTBR, (June 20, 1954), 4-5+.
_____, "James Farrell," NYHTBR, XXIX (October 12,
1952), 14.
_____, Reflections at Fifty, N. Y.: Vanguard, 1954.
Frohock, W. H., "James Farrell: The Precise Content,"
SWR, XXXV (Winter, 1950), 39-48.   Also in Novel of
Violence in America, 69-85.
Gelfant, B. H., "James T. Farrell: The Ecological Novel,"
American City Novel, 175-227.
Grattan, C. Hartley, "James T. Farrell: Moralist,"
Harpers, CCIX (October 8, 1954), 93-4, 96-8.
Gregory, Horace, "James T. Farrell: Beyond the Provinces
of Art," in New World Writing, No. 5, N. Y.: New Am-
erican Library, 1954, 52-65.
Hobsbaum, Philip, "The Great American Novel: A Study of
James T. Farrell," Gemini, II (Summer, 1959), 39-42.
Morris, L., "Thunder on the Left," Postscript to Yester-
day, 162-6.
O'Malley, Frank, "James T. Farrell: Two Twilight Im-
ages" in Gardiner, H. C., ed., Fifty Years of the Ameri-
can Novel, 237-56.
Reiter, Irene M., "A Study of James T. Farrell's Short
Stories and Their Relation to His Longer Fiction," DA,
XXV (1965), 5285 (Penn.).
Shannon, W. V., American Irish, 249-58.
Snell, G., Shapers of American Fiction, 288-300.
Stock, Irvin, "Farrell and His Critics," ArQ, VI (Winter,
1950), 328-38.
Thorp, W., American Writing in the Twentieth Century,
123-6, 170-3.
Van Gelder, Robert, Writers on Writing, 278-82.
Walcutt, Charles C., "James T. Farrell and the Reversible
Topcoat," ArQ, VII (Winter, 1951), 293-310.
Willingham, Calder, "Note on James T. Farrell," QRL, II
(1945), 120-4.

BERNARD CARR Trilogy

Branch, E. M., James T. Farrell, 29-35.
Kligerman, Jack, "The Quest for Self; James T. Farrell's
Character Bernard Carr," UKCR, XXIX (October, 1962),
9-16.

BERNARD CLARE (See also BERNARD CARR Trilogy)

Snell, G., Shapers of American Fiction, 298-300.
Walcutt, Charles C., "James T. Farrell and the Reversible
Topcoat," ArQ, VII (Winter, 1951), 302-6.
_____, "Naturalism in 1946," Accent, VI (Summer, 1946),
266-8. Also in Walcutt, C. C., American Literary Natur-
alism, 250-6.

DANNY O'NEILL Pentalogy

Beach, J. W., American Fiction, 295-305. Also in Aldridge,
J. W., ed., Critiques and Essays on Modern Fiction, 407-
14.
Branch, E. M., James T. Farrell, 22-9.
Douglas, Wallace, "The Case of James T. Farrell," TriQ,
No. 2 (Winter, 1965), 117-19.
Dyer, Henry H., "James T. Farrell's STUDS LONIGAN and
DANNY O'NEILL Novels," DA, XXVI (1965), 3332 (Un. of
Penn.).
Hobsbaum, Philip, "The Great American Novel: A Study of
James T. Farrell," Gemini, II (Summer, 1959), 39-40.
Snell, G., Shapers of American Fiction, 294-6.
Walcutt, Charles C., American Literary Naturalism, 245-9.
_____, "James T. Farrell and the Reversible Topcoat,"
ArQ, VII (Winter, 1951), 297-301.

ELLEN ROGERS

Snell, G., Shapers of American Fiction, 297-8.

THE FACE OF TIME (See also DANNY O'NEILL Pentalogy)

Allen, W., Urgent West, 102-3.
Douglas, Wallace, "The Case of James T. Farrell," TriQ,
No. 2 (Winter, 1965), 119-20.

GAS-HOUSE MCGINTY

Beach, J. W., American Fiction, 287-94. Also in Aldridge,
J. W., ed., Critiques and Essays on Modern Fiction,
402-7.

JUDGMENT DAY (See also STUDS LONIGAN Trilogy)

Berry, Newton, "A Preface to the Death Fantasy Sequence
of JUDGMENT DAY," TriQ, No. 2 (1965), 124-6.

Farrell, James T. , in Madden, C. F. , ed. , Talks with Authors, 89-102.

MY DAYS OF ANGER (See also DANNY O'NEILL Pentalogy)

Lyons, J. O. , College Novel in America, 92-3.
Rosenfeld, Isaac, "The Anger of James T. Farrell," NRep,
CIX (November 8, 1943), 657-8. Also in Rosenfeld, I. ,
Age of Enormity, 81-5.

THE ROAD BETWEEN (See also BERNARD CARR Trilogy)

Stock, Irvin, "Farrell and His Critics," ArQ, VI (Winter,
1950), 335-8.

STUDS LONIGAN Trilogy

Allen, W. , Modern Novel, 148-53.
Beach, J. W. , American Fiction, 273-83. Also (excerpted)
in Rubin, L. D. , Jr. , and J. R. Moore, eds. , Idea of an
American Novel, 340-3.
Branch, Edgar M. , "Destiny, Culture, and Technique:
STUDS LONIGAN," UKCR, XXIX (December, 1962), 103-
13.
_____, James T. Farrell, 16-22.
_____, "James T. Farrell's STUDS LONIGAN," ABC, XI,
x (Summer, 1961), 9-19.
_____, in Krause, S. J. , ed. , Essays in Determinism,
79-93.
_____, "STUDS LONIGAN Symbolism and Theme," CE,
XXIII (December, 1961), 191-6.
Douglas, Wallace, "The Case of James T. Farrell," TriQ,
No. 2 (Winter, 1965), 10 8-15.
Dyer, Henry H. , "James T. Farrell's STUDS LONIGAN and
DANNY O'NEILL Novels," DA, XXVI (1965), 3332 (Un.
of Penn.).
Farrell, James T. , "The Author as Plaintiff: Testimony in
a Censorship Case," Reflections at Fifty and other essays,
N. Y. : Vanguard, 1954, 188-233. Also in Downs, Robert
B. , ed. , First Freedom: Liberty and Justice in the
the World of Books, Chicago: American Library Assn. ,
1960, 286-301.
_____, "How STUDS LONIGAN Was Written," in Targ,
William, ed. , A Reader for Writers, N. Y. : Hermitage
House, 1951, 148-54.
Gurko, L. , Angry Decade, 119-25.
Hobsbaum, Philip, "The Great American Novel: A Study of

James T. Farrell," Gemini, II (Summer, 1959), 40-2.

McElroy, Davis D., Existentialism and Modern Literature:
An Essay in Existential Criticism, N.Y.: Citadel, 1963,
25-6.

Mitchell, Richard, "James T. Farrell's Scientific Novel,"
DA, XXIV (1964), 5413 (Syracuse).

_____, "STUDS LONIGAN: Research in Morality," CRAS,
VI (Spring, 1962), 202-14.

Newcomer, James, "Longinus in a Modern Instance," CJ,
LIII (1957), 113-18.

Rosenthal, T.G., "STUDS LONIGAN and the Search for an
American Tragedy," BAASB, No. 7 (December, 1963),
46-54.

Snell, G., Shapers of American Fiction, 289-94.

Walcutt, Charles C., American Literary Naturalism, 240-5.

_____, "James T. Farrell and the Reversible Topcoat,"
ArQ, VII, (Winter, 1951), 293-7.

WHAT TIME COLLECTS

Douglas, Wallace, "The Case of James T. Farrell," TriQ,
No. 2 (Winter, 1965), 120-3.

A WORLD I NEVER MADE
(See also DANNY O'NEILL Pentalogy)

Cowley, M., "A Portrait of James T. Farrell as a Young
Man," Look Back on Us, 304-7. Also in NRep (November 18, 1936).

YOUNG LONIGAN (See also STUDS LONIGAN Trilogy)

Beach, J.W., American Fiction, 276-80.

Woodbridge, Hensley C., "Slang in Farrell's YOUNG LONI-
GAN," AS, XXXVI (October, 1961), 225-9.

Woolf, H.B., "Bede, the Sparrow, and Farrell," N&Q,
CXCVIII (1953), 263-4.

BIBLIOGRAPHY

Branch, E.M., in Krause, S.J., ed., Essays in Determinism, 93-4.

FAST, Howard Melvin, 1914-

GENERAL

Eisinger, C. E., Fiction of the Forties, 90-3.
Hicks, Granville, "Howard Fast's One-Man Reformation,"
 CE, VII (October, 1945), 1-6.
Lifka, Marion, "Howard Fast: Wool Puller?" CathW,
 CLXXVII (September, 1953), 446-51.
Meisler, Stanley, "The Lost Dreams of Howard Fast," Na-
 tion, CLXXXVIII (May 30, 1959), 498-500.   Also in Na-
 tion (Periodical), View of the Nation, 40-6.
Rideout, W., Radical Novel in the United States, 275-85.

THE AMERICAN

Rideout, W., Radical Novel in the United States, 278-9.

CONCEIVED IN LIBERTY

Hicks, Granville, "Howard Fast's One-Man Reformation,"
 CE, VII (October, 1945), 1-6 passim.

THE LAST FRONTIER

Hicks, Granville, "Howard Fast's One-Man Reformation,"
 CE, VII (October, 1945), 1-6 passim.
Rideout, W., Radical Novel in the United States, 279-80.

THE PROUD AND THE FREE

Fast, Howard, "Reply to the Critics," M&M, III (December,
 1950), 53-64.
Rideout, W., Radical Novel in the United States, 281-3.

SPARTACUS

Rideout, W., Radical Novel in the United States, 283-5.

THE UNVANQUISHED

Eisinger, C. E., Fiction of the Forties, 92-3.

FAULKNER, WILLIAM, 1897-1962

GENERAL

Adams, Percy G., "The Franco-American Faulkner," TSL,

V (1960), 1-13.

Adams, Richard P., "The Apprenticeship of William Faulkner," TSE, XII (1962), 113-56.

_____, Faulkner.

_____, "Faulkner and the Myth of the South," MissQ, XIV (Summer, 1961), 131-7.

_____, "Some Key Words in Faulkner," TSE, XVI (1968), 135-48.

Aiken, Conrad, "William Faulkner: The Novel as Form," Atlantic, CLXIV (November, 1939), 650-4. Also in Aiken, Conrad, ABC: Collected Criticism from 1916 to the Present, N.Y.: Meridian, 1958, 200-7. Also in Aiken, C., Reviewer's ABC, 200-7. Also in HarvardA, CXXXV (November, 1951), 13, 24-6. Also in Hoffman, F.J., and O.W. Vickery, eds., William Faulkner, 135-42. Also in Hoffman, F.J., and O.W. Vickery, eds., William Faulkner: Two Decades of Criticism, 139-47. Also in Rubin, L.D., Jr., and J.R. Moore, eds., Idea of an American Novel, 354-9. Also in Warren, R.P., ed., Faulkner, 46-52.

Akai, Yasumitsu, "A Study on the Negro English in W. Faulkner's Works," Anglica, IV (January, 1961), 72-90; IV (September, 1961), 44-56.

Allen, Charles A., "William Faulkner: Comedy and the Purpose of Humor," ArQ, XVI (Spring, 1960), 59-69.

_____, "William Faulkner's Vision of Good and Evil," PacSp, X (Summer, 1956), 236-41.

Alter, Jean V., "Faulkner, Sartre, and the 'nouveau roman'," Sym, XX (Summer, 1966), 101-12.

Anderson, Charles, "Faulkner's Moral Center," EA, VII (January, 1954), 48-58.

Antrim, Harry D., "Faulkner's Suspended Style," UR, XXXII (December, 1965), 122-8.

Archer, Lewis F., "Coleridge's Definition of the Poet and the Works of Herman Melville and William Faulkner," DA, XXVIII (1967), 1810A-1811A (Drew).

Arthos, John, "Ritual and Humor in the Writing of William Faulkner," Accent, IX (Autumn, 1948), 17-30. Also in Hoffman, F.J., and O.W. Vickery, eds., William Faulkner: Two Decades of Criticism, 101-18.

Backman, M., Faulkner.

_____, "Sickness and Primitivism: A Dominant Pattern in William Faulkner's Work," Accent, XIV (Winter, 1954), 61-73.

Baker, Carlos, "William Faulkner: The Doomed and the Damned," in Bode, C., ed., Young Rebel in American Literature, 145-69.

Baker, James R., "The Symbolic Extension of Yoknapataw-
pha County," ArQ, VIII (Autumn, 1952), 223-8.
Baldanza, Frank, "Faulkner's '1699-1945: The Compsons',"
Expl., XIX (May, 1961), Item 59.
Baldwin, James, "Faulkner and Desegregation," PR, XXIII
(Summer, 1956), 568-73.
Barth, J. Robert, "Faulkner and the Calvinist Tradition,"
Thought, XXXIX (Spring, 1964), 100-20.
Beach, J. W., American Fiction, 123-69.
Beck, Warren, "William Faulkner's Style," American Pref-
aces, VI (Spring, 1941), 195-211. Also in Hoffman, F. J.,
and O. W. Vickery, eds., William Faulkner, 142-56. Al-
so in Hoffman, F. J., and O. W. Vickery, eds., William
Faulkner: Two Decades of Criticism, 147-64. Also in
Warren, R. P., ed., Faulkner, 53-65.
Beja, Morris, "A Flash, a Glare: Faulkner and Time,"
Ren, XVI (Spring, 1964), 133-41, 145.
Beringause, A. F., "Faulkner's Yoknapatawpha Register,"
BuR, XI, iii (May, 1963), 71-82.
Berner, Robert L., "The Theme of Responsibility in the
Later Fiction of William Faulkner," DA, XXI (1960), 1561
(Wash.).
Blackwell, Louise, "Faulkner and the Womenfolk," KM (1967),
73-7.
Blake, N. M., "The Decay of Yoknapatawpha County," Novel-
ist's America, 75-109.
Blöcker, Günter, "William Faulkner," in Warren, R. P.,
ed., Faulkner, 122-6.
Boswell, George W., "Picturesque Faulknerisms," UMSE,
IX (1968), 47-56. (Not seen.)
_____, "Traditional Verse and Music Influence in Faulk-
ner," NMW, I (Spring, 1968), 23-31.
Bouvard, Loic, "Conversation with William Faulkner," MFS,
V (Winter, 1959-60), 361-4.
Bowling, Lawrence E., "William Faulkner: The Importance
of Love," DR, XLIII (Winter, 1963-64), 474-82.
Bradford, Melvin E., "Faulkner, James Baldwin and the
South," GaR, XX (Winter, 1966), 431-43.
_____, "On the Importance of Discovering God: Faulkner
and Hemingway's THE OLD MAN AND THE SEA," MissQ,
XX (Summer, 1967), 158-62.
_____, "Spring Paradigm: Faulkner's Living Legacy,"
ForumH, VI, ii (1968), 4-7.
Brady, Emily K., "The Literary Faulkner: His Indebtedness
to Conrad, Lawrence, Hemingway, and Other Modern Nov-
elists," DA, XXIII (1962), 2131-2 (Brown).
Breaden, Dale G., "William Faulkner and the Land," AQ,

X (Fall, 1958), 344-57.

Breit, Harvey, "William Faulkner," Atlantic CLXXXVIII
(October, 1951), 53-6.

Brennan, Joseph X., and S. L. Gross, "The Problem of Moral Values in Conrad and Faulkner," Person, XLI (January, 1960), 60-70.

Brien, Dolores E., "William Faulkner and the Myth of
Woman," RS, XXXV (June, 1967), 132-40.

Brooks, Cleanth, "Faulkner's Vision of Good and Evil," MR,
III (Summer, 1962), 692-712. Also in Brooks, C., Hidden God, 22-43.

Brooks, C., William Faulkner.

Brown, Calvin S., "Faulkner's Geography and Topography,"
PMLA, LXXVII (December, 1962), 652-9.

————, "Faulkner's Manhunts: Fact into Fiction," GaR,
XX (Winter, 1966), 388-95.

————, "Faulkner's Use of the Oral Tradition," GaR,
XXII (1968), 160-9.

Brown, William R., "William Faulkner's Use of the Material
of Abnormal Psychology in Characterization," DA, XXVI
(1965), 1036-37 (Arkansas).

Brumm, Ursula, "Wilderness and Civilization: A Note on
William Faulkner," PR, XXII (Summer, 1955), 340-50.
Also in Hoffman, F. J., and O. W. Vickery, eds., William
Faulkner, 125-34.

Brylowski, W., Faulkner's Olympian Laugh.

Buckley, G. T., "Is Oxford the Original of Jefferson in William Faulkner's Novels?" PMLA, LXXVI (September,
1961), 447-54.

Burrows, Robert N., "Institutional Christianity as Reflected
in the Works of William Faulkner," MissQ, XIV (Summer,
1961), 138-47.

Callen, Shirley P., "Bergsonian Dynamism in the Writings
of William Faulkner," DA, XXIII (1963), 2521 (Tulane).

Campbell, Harry M., "Structural Devices in the Works of
Faulkner," Per, III (Autumn, 1950), 209-26.

————, and R. E. Foster, William Faulkner.

Carey, Glenn O., "William Faulkner as a Critic of Society,"
ArQ, XXI (Summer, 1965), 101-8.

————, "William Faulkner: Critic of Society," DA,
XXIII (1963), 2522 (Illinois).

Carnes, Frank F., "On the Aesthetics of Faulkner's Fiction," DA, XXIX (1968), 894A-5A (Vanderbilt).

Carpenter, Robert A., "Faulkner 'Discovered'," Delta Rev,
II (July-August, 1965), 27-9.

Church, M., "William Faulkner: Myth and Duration,"
Time and Reality, 227-50.

Ciancio, Ralph A., "Faulkner's Existentialist Affinities," in
Woodruff, N., Jr., and Others, eds., Studies in Faulk-
ner, 69-91.
Coffee, Jessie A., "Empty Steeples: Theme, Symbol, and
Irony in Faulkner's Novels," ArQ, XXIII (Autumn, 1967),
197-206.
Collins, Carvel, in Griffin, William, ed., Literature in the
Modern World, 65-71.
_____, in Stegner, W., ed., American Novel, 219-28.
Colson, Theodore L., "The Characters of Hawthorne and
Faulkner: A Typology of Sinners," DA, XXVIII (1967),
2204A-5A (Michigan).
Cook, Albert, "Plot as Discovery," The Meaning of Fiction,
Detroit: Wayne State Un. Pr., 1960, 232-41.
Couch, John P., "Camus and Faulkner: The Search for the
Language of Modern Tragedy," YFS, No. 25 (1960), 120-
5.
Coughlan, Robert, The Private World of William Faulkner,
N.Y.: Harper, 1954. Also (excerpted) as "The Private
World of William Faulkner," Life, XXXV (September 28,
1953), 118-36; (October 5, 1953), 55-68. Also in Life
(Periodical), Great Reading from Life: a Treasury of the
Best Stories and Articles Chosen by the Editors, N.Y.:
Harper, 1960, 204-16. Also in Prize Articles, 1954; the
Benjamin Franklin Magazine Awards, administered by the
Un. of Illinois, ed. by Llewellyn Miller, N.Y.: Ballan-
tine, 1954, 121-56.
Cowley, Malcolm, The Faulkner-Cowley File: Letters and
Memories, 1944-1962, N.Y.: Viking, 1966.
_____, "A Fresh Look at Faulkner," SatR, XLIX (June
11, 1966), 22-6.
_____, "An Introduction to William Faulkner," in Ald-
ridge, J.W., ed., Critiques and Essays on Modern Fic-
tion, 427-46. Also (in part) as "Introduction," in The
Portable Faulkner, N.Y.: Viking, 1946, 1-24. Also in
Hoffman, F.J., and O.W. Vickery, eds., William Faulkner, 94-109. Also in Hoffman, F.J., and O.W. Vickery,
eds., William Faulkner: Two Decades of Criticism, 63-
82. Also (condensed) in Warren, R.P., ed., Faulkner,
34-45. Also (in part) as "William Faulkner's Legend of
the South," SR, LIII (Summer, 1945), 343-61. Also in
Tate, Allen, ed., A Southern Vanguard, N.Y.: Prentice-
Hall, 1947, 13-27. Also in West, Ray B., ed., Essays
in Modern Literary Criticism, N.Y.: Holt, 1952, 513-26.
Cullen, John B., and F.C. Watkins, Old Times in the Faulkner Country, Chapel Hill: Un. of No. Carolina Pr., 1961.
Dike, Donald, "The World of Faulkner's Imagination," DA,

XV (1955), 365 (Syracuse).

Dillingham, William B., "William Faulkner and the 'Tragic Condition'," Edda, LXVI (1966), 322-35.

Ditsky, John M., "Land-Nostalgia in the Novels of Faulkner, Cather, and Steinbeck," DA, XXVIII (1967), 1072A (N. Y. U.).

Donnelly, William and Doris, "William Faulkner: In Search of Peace," Person, XLIV (Autumn, 1963), 490-8.

Doran, Leonard, "Form and the Story Teller," HarvardA, CXXXV (November, 1951), 12+.

Dorsch, Robert L., "An Interpretation of the Central Themes in the Work of William Faulkner," ESRS, XI, i (September, 1962), 5-42.

Doster, William C., "The Several Faces of Gavin Stevens," MissQ, XI (Fall, 1958), 191-5.

_____, "William Faulkner and the Negro," DA, XX (1959), 1094 (Florida).

Douglas, Harold J., and Robert Daniel, "Faulkner and the Puritanism of the South," TSL, II (1957), 1-13.

Dowell, Bobby R., "Faulkner's Comic Spirit," DA, XXIII (1963), 4355 (Denver).

Doyle, Charles, "The Moral World of Faulkner," Ren, XIX (Fall, 1966), 3-12.

Eby, Cecil D., "Faulkner and the Southwestern Humorists," Shen, XI, i (Autumn, 1959), 13-21.

Edmonds, Irene C., "Faulkner and the Black Shadow," in Rubin, L., and R. D. Jacobs, eds., Southern Renascence, 192-206.

Eisinger, C. E., Fiction of the Forties, 178-86.

Elkin, Stanley L., "Religious Themes and Symbolism in the Novels of William Faulkner," DA, XXII (1962), 3659-60 (Illinois).

Emerson, O. B., "Prophet Next Door," in Walker, W. E., and Welker, R. E., eds., Reality and Myth, 237-74.

Emmanuel, Pierre, "Faulkner and the Sense of Sin," HarvardA, CXXXV (November, 1951), 20.

Everett, W. K., Faulkner's Art and Characters.

Fadiman, C., Party of One, 98-125.

Falkner, Murry C., The Falkners of Mississippi: A Memoir, Baton Rouge: La. St. Un. Pr., 1967.

Fant, Joseph L., III, and Robert Ashley, eds., Faulkner at West Point, N. Y.: Random House, 1964.

Farnham, James F., "They Who Endure and Prevail: Characters of William Faulkner," Unpub. Doct. Diss., Western Reserve Un., 1962.

Faulkner, John, My Brother Bill: An Affectionate Reminiscence, N. Y.: Trident, 1963.

Faulkner, William, "The Stockholm Address," (Nobel Prize) in Hoffman, F. J., and O. W. Vickery, eds., William Faulkner, 347-8.

Fazio, Rocco R., "The Fury and the Design: Realms of Being and Knowing in Four Novels of William Faulkner," DA, XXV (1964), 1910 (Rochester).

Fiedler, Leslie, "An American Dickens," Ctary, X (October, 1950), 384-7. Also in Fiedler, L., No! In Thunder, 111-18.

———, "The Death of the Old Men," A&S, (Winter, 1963-64), 1-5. Also in Fiedler, L. A., Waiting For the End, 9-19.

———, Love and Death in the American Novel, 309-15, passim.

Finkelstein, S., Existentialism and Alienation in American Literature, 184-97.

———, "William Faulkner," Mainstream, XV, viii (August, 1962), 3-6.

Flanagan, John T., "Faulkner's Favorite Word," GaR, XVII (Winter, 1963), 429-34.

Flint, R. W., "Faulkner as Elegist," HudR, VII (Summer, 1954), 246-57.

Ford, Margaret P., and Suzanne Kincaid, Who's Who in Faulkner, Baton Rouge: La. State Un. Pr., 1963.

Foster, Ruel, "Dream as Symbolic Act in Faulkner," Per, II (Summer, 1949), 179-94.

———, "Social Order and Disorder in Faulkner's Fiction," Approach, No. 55 (Spring, 1965), 20-8.

Freedman, Morris, "Sound and Sense in Faulkner's Prose," CEA, XIX, vi (1957), 1, 4-5. (Not seen.)

French, Warren, "The Background of Snopesism in Mississippi Politics," MASJ, V (Fall, 1964), 3-17.

———, "William Faulkner and the Art of the Detective Story," in French, W., ed., Thirties, 55-62.

Friend, George L., "Levels of Maturity: The Theme of Striving in the Novels of William Faulkner," DA, XXV (1965), 6622-23 (Illinois).

Frohock, W. M., "Faulkner and the Roman Nouveau: An Interim Report," BuR, X (March, 1962), 186-93.

———, "William Faulkner: The Private View versus the Public Vision," SWR, XXXIV (Summer, 1949), 281-94.

———, "William Faulkner: The Private Vision," Novel of Violence in America, 144-65.

Garrett, George, "The Influence of William Faulkner," GaR, XVIII (1964), 419-27.

Geismar, M., Writers in Crisis, 143-83.

Gerard, Albert, "Justice in Yoknapatawpha County: Some

Symbolic Motifs in Faulkner's Later Writing," Faulkner
Studies, II (Winter, 1953), 49-57.
Giorgini, J., "Faulkner and Camus," Delta Rev, II, iii
(1965), 31+.
Glicksberg, Charles I., "The Art of Faulkner's Fiction,"
Meanjin, XII (Autumn, 1953), 69-78.
_____, "William Faulkner and the Negro Problem," Phy-
lon, X (June, 1949), 153-60.
_____, "The World of William Faulkner," ArQ, V (Spring,
1949), 46-57.
Gold, Joseph, "The Humanism of William Faulkner," Human-
ist, XX (January-February, 1960), 113-17.
_____, William Faulkner.
Gossett, L. Y., Violence in Recent Southern Fiction, 29-47.
Green, A. Wigfall, "William Faulkner at Home," SR, XL
(Summer, 1932), 294-36. Also in Hoffman, F. J., and
O. W. Vickery, eds., William Faulkner: Two Decades of
Criticism, 33-47.
Green, M., "Faulkner: the triumph of rhetoric," Re-Ap-
praisals, 167-94.
Greer, Dorothy D., "Dilsey and Lucas: Faulkner's Use of
the Negro as a Gauge of Moral Character," ESRS, XI, i
(September, 1962), 43-61.
Grenier, Cynthia, "The Art of Fiction: An Interview with
William Faulkner- September, 1955," Accent, XVI (Sum-
mer, 1956), 167-77.
Gresham, Jewell H., "Narrative Techniques of William Faulk-
ner's Form," Nassau Rev (Nassau Community College), I,
iii (1966), 103-19.
Griffin, William C., "How to Misread Faulkner: A Power-
ful Plea for Ignorance," TSL, No. 1 (1956), 27-34.
Gurko, L., Angry Decade, 128-36.
Guttmann, Allen, "Collisions and Confrontations," ArQ, XVI
(Spring, 1960), 46-52.
Gwynn, F. L., and J. L. Blotner, eds., Faulkner in the Uni-
versity.
_____, "Faulkner in the University," CE, XIX (October,
1957), 1-6.
_____, "William Faulkner on Dialect," UVMag, II, i
(1958), 7-13; II, ii (1958), 32-7.
Hagopian, John V., "Style and Meaning in Hemingway and
Faulkner," JA, Band 4 (1959), 170-9.
Hall, J., Lunatic Giant in the Drawing Room, 56-77.
Hamilton, Edith, "Faulkner: Sorcerer or Slave?" SatR,
XXV (July 12, 1952), 8-10, 39. Also in Saturday Review
(Periodical), Saturday Review Gallery, N. Y.: Simon and
Schuster, 1959, 419-29. Also as "William Faulkner,"

The Ever-Present Past, N.Y.: Norton, 1964, 159-73.

Hammond, Donald, "Faulkner's Levels of Awareness,"
FloQ, I, ii (1967), 73-81.

Harder, Kelsie B., "Charactonyms in Faulkner's Novels,"
BuR, VIII, iii (May, 1959), 189-201.

Hardy, J. E., "William Faulkner: The Legend Behind the
Legend," Man in the Modern Novel, 137-58.

Harkness, Bruce, "Faulkner and Scott," MissQ, XX (Summer, 1967), 164.

Hawkins, E. O., Jr., "A Handbook of Yoknapatawpha," DA,
XXI (1961), 3457-8 (Arkansas).

Hayakawa, Hiroshi, "Negation in William Faulkner," in
Araki, Kazuo, and others, Studies in English Grammar
and Linguistics. A Miscellany in Honour of Takanobu
Otsuka, Tokyo: Kenkyusha, 1958, 103-16.

Hirano, Nobuyuki, "Reconsideration of Moral Order and Disorder in Faulkner's Works," HJAS, VIII, i (September,
1967), 7-32.

Hoadley, Frank M., "Folk Humor in the Novels of William
Faulkner," TFSB, XXIII (1957), 75-82.

_____, "The World View of William Faulkner," DA, XVI
(1956), 338 (Oklahoma).

Hoffman, Frederick J., in French, W. G., and W. E. Kidd,
American Winners of the Nobel Literary Prize, 138-57.

_____, William Faulkner.

_____, and O. W. Vickery, eds., William Faulkner.

_____, "William Faulkner: A Review of Recent Criticism,"
Ren, XIII (Autumn, 1960), 3-9+.

_____, and O. W. Vickery, eds., William Faulkner:
Three Decades of Criticism.

Hogan, Patrick G., Jr., "Critical Misconceptions of Southern Thought: Faulkner's Optimism," MissQ, X (January,
1957), 19-28.

Holman, C. H., "William Faulkner: The Anguished Dream
of Time," Three Modes of Modern Southern Fiction, 27-
47.

Holmes, Edward M., Faulkner's Twice-Told Tales: His Re-
Use of His Material, The Hague, The Netherlands:
Mouton, 1966.

Hopper, Vincent, "Faulkner's Paradise Lost," VQR, XXIII
(Summer, 1947), 405-20.

Hornback, Vernon T., Jr., "William Faulkner and the Terror of History: Myth, History, and Moral Freedom in
the Yoknapatawpha Cycle," DA, XXV (1964), 476 (St.
Louis).

Horsch, Janice, "Faulkner on Man's Struggle with Communi-
cation," KM, (1964), 77-83.

Hovde, Carl F., "Faulkner's Democratic Rhetoric," SAQ, LXIII (Autumn, 1964), 530-41.

Howe, Irving, "Faulkner and the Negroes," in Gross, S. L., and J. E. Hardy, eds., Images of the Negro in American Literature, 204-20.

_____, "William Faulkner and the Negroes," Ctary, XII (October, 1951), 359-67.

_____, "Faulkner and the Southern Tradition," in Rahv, P., ed., Literature in America, 409-14.   Also in Howe, I., William Faulkner, 22-9.

_____, "The Quest for a Moral Style," A World More Attractive, 73-6.

_____, "The Southern Myth and William Faulkner," AQ, III (Winter, 1951), 357-62.

_____, "A Talent of Wild Abundance," in Brown, F., ed., Opinions and Perspectives, 194-8.

_____, William Faulkner.

_____, "William Faulkner's Enduring Power," NYTBR (April 4, 1954), 1+.

Howell, Elmo, "Mark Twain, William Faulkner and the First Families of Virginia," MTJ, XIII, ii (1966), 1-3+.

_____, "A Name for Faulkner's City," Names, XVI (December, 1968), 415-21.

_____, "A Note on Faulkner's Negro Characters," MissQ, XI (Fall, 1958), 201-3.

_____, "William Faulkner and Tennessee," THQ, XXI (September, 1962), 251-62.

_____, "William Faulkner and the New Deal," MQ, V (July, 1964), 323-32.

_____, "William Faulkner and the Plain People of Yoknapatawpha County," Jnl of Miss Hist, XXIV (April, 1962), 73-87.

_____, "William Faulkner's New Orleans," LaH, VII (Summer, 1966), 229-39.

_____, "William Faulkner's Southern Baptists," ArQ, XXIII (Autumn, 1967), 220-6.

Hubank, Roger, "William Faulkner: A Perspective View," Delta, No. 10 (Autumn, 1956), 13-21.

Hudson, Tommy, "William Faulkner: Mystic and Traditionalist," Per, III (Autumn, 1950), 227-35.

Hughes, Richard, "Faulkner and Bennett," Encounter, XXI, No. 120 (September, 1963), 59-61.

Hunt, J. W., William Faulkner.

Hutchinson, James D., "TIME: The Fourth Dimension in Faulkner," SDR, VI (Autumn, 1968), 91-103.

Inge, M. Thomas, ed., with an introd. by "Donald Davidson on Faulkner: An Early Recognition," GaR, XX (Winter,

1966), 454-62.

_____, "William Faulkner and George Washington Harris:
In the Tradition of Southwestern Humor," TSL, VII (1962),
47-59.

Jackson, Naomi, "Faulkner's Woman: 'Demon-Nun and An-
gel-Witch'," BSUF, VIII, i (Winter, 1967), 12-20.

Jacobs, Robert D., "Faulkner's Tragedy of Isolation," Hopkins Rev, VI (Spring-Summer, 1953), 162-83.   Also in
Rubin, L. D., and R. D. Jacobs, eds., Southern Renascence, 170-91.

_____, "How Do You Read Faulkner?" Prov, I, iv (April,
1957), 3-5.

_____, "William Faulkner: The Passion and the Pretense,"
in Rubin, L. D., Jr., and R. D. Jacobs, eds., South, 141-
76.

Jordan, Robert M., "The Limits of Illusion: Faulkner,
Fielding, and Chaucer," Criticism, II (Summer, 1960),
278-89.

Kaluza, I., "William Faulkner's Subjective Style," KN, XI,
i (1964), 13-29.

Kartiganer, Donald M., "The Individual and the Community:
Values in the Novels of William Faulkner," DA, XXV
(1965), 4701-02 (Brown).

Kay, Wallace G., "Faulkner's Mississippi: The Myth and the
Microcosm," SoQ, VI (October, 1967), 13-24.

Kazin, Alfred, "Faulkner in His Fury," The Inmost Leaf,
N.Y.: Noonday Pr., 1959, 257-73. Also in Litz, A. W.,
ed., Modern American Fiction, 166-78.

_____, "Faulkner's Vision of Human Integrity," HarvardA,
CXXXV (November, 1951), 8-9+.

Kerr, Elizabeth M., "William Faulkner and the Southern
Concept of Woman," MissQ, XV (Winter, 1961-62), 1-16.

_____, "Yoknapatawpha and the Myth of the South,"
WisSL, No. 1 (1964), 85-93.

_____, Yoknapatawpha: Faulkner's 'Little Postage Stamp
of Native Soil', N.Y.: Fordham Un. Pr., 1969.

Kirk, Robert W., and Marvin Klotz, Faulkner's People: A
Complete Guide and Index to Characters in the Fiction of
William Faulkner, Berkeley: Un. of Calif. Pr., 1963.

Klotz, Marvin, "The Triumph Over Time: Narrative Form
in William Faulkner and William Styron," MissQ, XVII
(Winter, 1963-64), 9-20.

Kohler, Dayton, "William Faulkner and the Social Conscience," EJ, XXXVIII (December, 1949), 545-52. Also
in CE, XI (December, 1949), 119-27.

Kowalczyk, Richard L., "From Addie Bundren to Gavin
Stevens: The Direction from Reality," CEJ, II, i (1966),
45-52.

Larsen, Eric, "The Barrier of Language: The Irony of Language in Faulkner," MFS, XIII, i (Spring, 1967), 19-31.

Leaver, Florence, "Faulkner: The Word as Principle and Power," SAQ, LVII (Autumn, 1958), 464-76. Also in Hoffman, F. J., and O. W. Vickery, eds., William Faulkner, 199-209. Also in ICTE Yearbook, (Fall, 1958), 14-19.

Linneman, William R., "Faulkner's Ten-Dollar Words," AS, XXXVIII (May, 1963), 158-9.

Linscott, Robert N., "Faulkner Without Fanfare," Esquire, LX, i (July, 1963), 36, 38.

Litz, Walton, "William Faulkner's Moral Vision," SWR, XXXVII (Summer, 1952), 200-9.

Longley, J. L., Jr., Tragic Mask.

Loughrey, Thomas F., "Values and Love in the Fiction of William Faulkner," DA, XXIII (1963), 2915 (Notre Dame).

McClennen, Joshua, "William Faulkner and Christian Complacency," PMASAL, XLI (1956), 315-22.

McCorquodale, Marjorie K., "Alienation in Yoknapatawpha County," ForumH, I, ii (January, 1957), 4-8.

_____, "William Faulkner and Existentialism," Unpub. Doct. Diss., Un. of Texas, 1956.

McGrew, Julia, "Faulkner and the Icelanders," SS, XXXI (February, 1959), 1-14.

Maclachlan, John M., "William Faulkner and the Southern Folk," SFQ, IX (September, 1945), 153-67.

McLauglin, Carrol D., "Religion in Yoknapatawpha County," DA, XXIII (1963), 2915-16 (Denver).

MacLeish, Archibald, "Faulkner and the Responsibility of the Artist," HarvardA, CXXXV (November, 1951), 18+.

MacLure, Millar, "William Faulkner: Soothsayer of the South," QQ, LXIII (Autumn, 1956), 334-43.

Magny, Claude-Edmonde, "Faulkner or Theological Inversion," in Warren, R. P., ed., Faulkner, 66-78.

Malin, Irving, William Faulkner: An Interpretation, Stanford: Stanford Un. Pr., 1957.

Marcović, Vida, "Interview with Faulkner," TSLL, V (1964), 463-6.

Mascitelli, David W., "Faulkner's Characters of Sensibility," DA, XXIX (1968), 608A-9A (Duke).

Mayoux, Jean-Jacques, "The Creation of the Real in William Faulkner," in Hoffman, F. J., and O. W. Vickery, eds., William Faulkner, 156-73.

Mellard, James M., "Humor in Faulkner's Novels: Its Development, Forms, and Functions," DA, XXV (1964), 480-1 (Texas).

Meriwether, James B., "Faulkner and the New Criticism,"

BA, XXXVII (Summer, 1963), 265-8.

————, and Michael Millgate, eds., Lion in the Garden:
Interviews with William Faulkner, 1926-1962, N.Y.:
Random House, 1968.

————, "Sartoris and Snopes: An Early Notice," LCUT,
VII, ii (1962), 36-9.

————, "The Text of Faulkner's Books: An Introduction
and Some Notes," MFS, IX (Summer, 1963), 159-70.

————, "William Faulkner," Shen, X (Winter, 1959), 18-
24.

Mickelson, Joel C., "Faulkner's Military Figures of Speech,"
WisSL, No. 4 (1967), 46-55. (Not seen.)

Miller, David M., "Faulkner's Women," MFS, XIII, i
(Spring, 1967), 3-17.

Miller, Douglas T., "Faulkner and the Civil War: Myth and
Reality," AQ, XV (Summer, 1963), 200-9.

Miller, James, "William Faulkner: Descent into the Vor-
tex," Quests Surd and Absurd, 41-75.

Millgate, M., Achievement of William Faulkner.

————, William Faulkner.

————, "William Faulkner: The Problem of Point of
View," in La France, Marston, ed., Patterns of Commit-
ment in American Literature, Toronto: Un. of Toronto
Pr., 1967.

Miner, Ward L., "Faulkner and Christ's Crucifixion," NM,
LVII (1956), 260-9.

————, The World of William Faulkner, Durham, No.
Carolina: Duke Un. Pr., 1952.

Mizener, A., Twelve Great American Novels, 142-6.

Moloney, Michael, "The Enigma of Time: Proust, Virginia
Woolf, and Faulkner," Thought, XXXII (1957), 69-85.

Moreland, Agnes L., "A Study of Faulkner's Presentation of
Some Problems That Relate to Negroes," DA, XXI (1960),
1192-3 (Columbia).

Morris, L., "Sphinx in the South," Postscript to Yesterday,
160-2.

Morris, W., "The Function of Rage: William Faulkner,"
Territory Ahead, 171-84.

————, "The Violent Land: Some Observations on the
Faulkner Country," Magazine of Art, XLV (March, 1952),
99-103.

Nicholson, Norman, "William Faulkner," in Martin, E.W.,
ed., The New Spirit, London: Dennis Dobson, 1946, 32-
41.

Nilon, Charles H., "Faulkner and the Negro," UCSSLL,
No. 8 (September, 1962), 1-111. Also in Nilon, C.H.,
Faulkner and the Negro.

Noble, D. W. , Eternal Adam and the New World Garden,
    163-6.
Nonaka, Ryo, "Faulkner's 'Stream of Consciousness'," SEL,
    XXXVI (1959), 179-80. (Not seen.)
O'Brien, Frances B. , "Faulkner and Wright, Alias S. S.
    Van Dine," MissQ, XIV (Spring, 1961), 101-7.
O'Connor, William Van, "Faulkner's Legend of the Old
    South," WHR, VII (Autumn, 1953), 293-301.
_____, "Faulkner's One-Sided 'Dialogue' with Hemingway,"
    CE, XXIV (December, 1962), 208-15.
_____, "Hawthorne and Faulkner: Some Common Ground,"
    VQR, XXXIII (Winter, 1957), 105-23. Also in O'Connor,
    W. V. , Grotesque, 59-77.
_____, "Protestantism in Yoknapatawpha County," Hopkins
    Rev, V (Spring, 1952), 26-42. Also in Rubin, L. , and
    R. D. Jacobs, eds. , Southern Renascence, 153-91.
_____, "Rhetoric in Southern Writing: Faulkner," GaR,
    XII (Spring, 1958), 83-6.
_____, Tangled Fire of William Faulkner.
_____, William Faulkner. Also in O'Connor, W. V. , ed. ,
    Seven Modern American Novelists, 118-52.
_____, "William Faulkner's Apprenticeship," SWR,
    XXXVIII (Winter, 1953), 1-14.
O'Dea, Richard J. , "Faulkner's Vestigial Christianity," Ren,
    XXI (Autumn, 1968), 44-54.
O'Donnell, George M. , "Faulkner's Mythology," KR, I (Sum-
    mer, 1939), 285-99. Also in Hoffman, F. J. , and O. W.
    Vickery, eds. , William Faulkner, 82-93. Also in Hoff-
    man, F. J. , and O. W. Vickery, eds. , William Faulkner:
    Two Decades of Criticism, 49-62. Also in Warren, R. P. ,
    ed. , Faulkner, 23-33.
Odum, Howard W. , "On Southern Literature and Southern
    Culture," Hopkins Rev, VII (Winter, 1953), 60-76. Also
    in Odum, H. W. , Folk Religion and Society; Selected Pa-
    pers of Howard W. Odum; arr. and ed. by Katherine
    Jocher (and others), Chapel Hill: Un. of No. Carolina,
    1964, 202-18. Also in Rubin, L. D. , Jr. , and R. D.
    Jacobs, eds. , Southern Renascence, 84-100.
O'Faolain, S. , Vanishing Hero, 73-111.
Oldenburg, Egbert W. , "William Faulkner's Early Experi-
    ments With Narrative Techniques," DA, XXVII (1967),
    2158A (Michigan).
Otten, Terry, "Faulkner's Use of the Past: A Comment,"
    Ren, XX (Summer, 1968), 198-207, 214.
Parks, Edd W. , "Faulkner and Hemingway: Their Thought,"
    SAB, XXII, iv (1957), 1-2.
Patil, Vimala, "William Faulkner- America's Literary Giant,"

UA, XIV (September, 1962), 523-5.
Penick, Edwin A., Jr., "The Testimony of William Faulk-
ner," ChS, XXXVIII (June, 1955), 121-33.
Phillips, William L., "Sherwood Anderson's Two Prize Pu-
pils," Un. of Chicago Mag., XLVII (January, 1955), 9-12.
Also in White, Ray L., ed., The Achievement of Sherwood
Anderson, Chapel Hill: Un. of No. Carolina Pr., 1966,
202-10.
Player, Raleigh P., Jr., "The Negro Character in the Fic-
tion of William Faulkner," DA, XXVII (1966), 483A-4A
(Un. of Michigan).
Pollack, Agnes S., "The Current of Time in the Novels of
William Faulkner," DA, XXV (1965), 7276-7 (U.C.L.A.).
Pouillon, Jean, "Time and Destiny in Faulkner," in Warren,
R.P., ed., Faulkner, 79-87.
Powers, Lyall H., "Hawthorne and Faulkner and the Pearl
of Great Price," PMASAL, LII (1967), 391-401.
Prescott, O., In My Opinion, 85-91.
Price-Stephens, Gordon, "Faulkner and the Royal Air Force,"
MissQ, XVII (Summer, 1964), 123-8.
Pritchett, V.S., "Books in General," NS&Nation, XLI (June
2, 1951), 624-6. Also in Pritchett, V.S., Books in Gen-
eral, 242-7.
Rabi, "Faulkner and the Exiled Generation," in Hoffman, F.
J., and O.W. Vickery, eds., William Faulkner: Two
Decades of Criticism, 118-38.
Ranald, Ralph A., "William Faulkner's South: Three De-
grees of Myth," Landfall, XVIII (December, 1964), 329-
38.
Ransom, John Crowe, "William Faulkner: An Impression,"
HarvardA, CXXXV (November, 1951), 17.
Richards, Lewis A., "The Literary Styles of Jean-Paul
Sartre and William Faulkner: An Analysis, Comparison,
and Contrast," DA, XXIV (1964), 3755-6 (So. Calif.).
Richardson, H. Edward, "Anderson and Faulkner," AL,
XXXVI (November, 1964), 298-314.
_____, William Faulkner.
Richardson, K.E., Force and Faith in the Novels of William
Faulkner.
Riedel, F.C., "Faulkner as Stylist," SAQ, LVI (Autumn,
1957), 462-79.
Rinaldi, Nicholas M., "Game-Consciousness and Game-
Metaphor in the Work of William Faulkner," DA, XXIV
(1964), 4196-7. (Fordham).
_____, "Game Imagery and Game-Consciousness in
Faulkner's Fiction," TCL, X (October, 1964), 108-18.
Robb, Mary C., William Faulkner: An Estimate of His

Contribution to the Modern Novel (Critical Essays in English and American Literature, No. 1), Pittsburgh: Un. of Pittsburgh Pr., 1957.

Roberts, James A., "William Faulkner: A Thematic Study," DA, XVII (1958), 3023 (Iowa).

Roberts, James L., "Experimental Exercises- Faulkner's Early Writings," Discourse, VI (Summer, 1963), 183-97.

Roscoe, Lavon, "An Interview with William Faulkner," WR, XV (Summer, 1951), 300-4.

Roth, Russell, "William Faulkner: The Pattern of Pilgrimage," Per, II (1949), 246-54.

Rubel, Warren G., "The Structural Function of the Christ Figure in the Fiction of William Faulkner," DA, XXV (1965), 5941-2 (Ark.).

Rubin, L.D., Jr., "Chronicles of Yoknapatawpha: The Dynasties of William Faulkner," Faraway Country, 43-71.

Runyan, Harry, A Faulkner Glossary, N.Y.: Citadel, 1964.

Saito, Kazue, "Ethics in Faulkner's Works," Ushione, X (1957), 1-12. (Not seen.)

Sandeen, Ernest, "William Faulkner: Tragedian of Yoknapatawpha," in Gardiner, H.C., ed., Fifty Years of the American Novel, 165-82.

Scott, Arthur L., "The Faulknerian Sentence," PrS, XXVII (Spring, 1953), 91-8.

Shanaghan, Father Malachy M., O.S.B., "A Critical Analysis of the Fictional Techniques of William Faulkner," DA, XX (1960), 4663 (Notre Dame).

Shaw, Joe C., "Sociological Aspects of Faulkner's Writing," MissQ, XIV (Summer, 1961), 148-52.

Sherwood, J.C., "The Traditional Element in Faulkner," Faulkner Studies, III (1954), 17-23.

Sidney, George, "William Faulkner and Hollywood," ColQ, IX (Spring, 1961), 367-77.

Simon, John K., "Faulkner and Sartre: Metamorphosis and the Obscene," CL, XV (Summer, 1963), 216-25.

_____, "The Glance of the Idiot: A Thematic Study of Faulkner and Modern French Fiction," DA, XXV (1964), 1220 (Yale).

Slabey, Robert M., "William Faulkner: 'The Waste Land' Phase (1926-1936)," DA, XXII (1961), 1632 (Notre Dame).

Slatoff, Walter J., "The Edge of Order: The Pattern of Faulkner's Rhetoric," TCL, III (October, 1957), 107-27. Also in Hoffman, F.J., and O.W. Vickery, eds., William Faulkner, 173-98.

_____, Quest for Failure.

Snell, George, "The Fury of William Faulkner," WR, XI (Autumn, 1946), 29-40. Also in Snell, G., ed., Shapers of American Fiction, 87-104.

Spiller, R. E., Cycle of American Literature, 291-303.

Stanford, Raney, "Of Mules and Men: Faulkner and Silone,"
Discourse, VI (Winter, 1962-63), 73-8.

Stavrou, C. N., "Ambiguity in Faulkner's Affirmation," Person, XL (April, 1959), 169-77.

Steene, Birgitta, "William Faulkner and the Myth of the
American South," MS, LIV (1960), 271-9.

Stein, Jean, "William Faulkner," Paris Rev, IV (Spring,
1956), 28-52. Also in Cowley, Malcolm, ed., Writers
at Work, N. Y.: Viking, 1958, 119-41.

Steinberg, Aaron, "Faulkner and the Negro," DA, XXVII
(1966), 1385A (N. Y. U.).

Stewart, David H., "William Faulkner and Mikhail Sholokhov:
A Comparative Study of Two Representatives of the Re-
gional Conscience, Their Affinities and Meanings," DA,
XIX (1959), 3309-10. (Mich.).

Stewart, Randall, "Hawthorne and Faulkner," CE, XVII
(February, 1956), 258-62.

_____, "Poetically the Most Accurate Man Alive," ModA,
VI (Winter, 1961-62), 81-90.

Strandberg, Victor, "Faulkner's Poor Parson and the Technique of Inversion (or William Faulkner: An Epitaph),"
SR, LXXIII (Spring, 1965), 181-90.

Sullivan, William P., "William Faulkner and the Community,"
DA, XXII (1962), 4355 (Columbia).

Sutton, George W., "Primitivism in the Fiction of William
Faulkner," DA, XXVIII (1967), 695A-6A (Miss.).

Swiggart, P., Art of Faulkner's Novels.

_____, "The Snopes Trilogy," SR, LXVIII (Spring, 1960),
319-25.

_____, "Time in Faulkner's Novels," MFS, I (May, 1955),
25-9.

Tate, Allan, "William Faulkner 1897-1962," SR, LXXI
(Winter, 1963), 160-4.

Taylor, Nancy D., "The River of Faulkner and Mark Twain,"
MissQ, XVI (Fall, 1963), 191-9.

Taylor, Walter F., Jr., "The Roles of the Negro in William
Faulkner's Fiction," DA, XXV (1964), 2990 (Emory).

Thompson, L., William Faulkner.

Thorp, W., "Southern Renaissance," American Writing in the
Twentieth Century, 263-74.

Tischler, Nancy P., "William Faulkner and the Southern Negro," SUS, VII, iv (1965), 261-5.

Tolliver, Kenneth R., "Truth and the Poet," Delta Rev, II,
iii (1965), 48+.

Tomlinson, T. B., "Faulkner and American Sophistication,"

MCR, No. 7 (1964), 92-103.

Tritschler, Donald, "The Unity of Faulkner's Shaping Vision,"
MFS, V (Winter, 1959-60), 337-43.

Tuck, D., Crowell's Handbook of Faulkner.

Turner, Arlin, "William Faulkner and the Literary Flowering in the American South," DUJ, XXIX (March, 1968),
109-18.

_____, "William Faulkner, Southern Novelist," MissQ,
XIV (Summer, 1961), 117-30.

Van Nostrand, A.D., "The Poetic Dialogues of William
Faulkner," Everyman His Own Poet, 175-96.

Vickery, Olga W., "Faulkner and the Contours of Time,"
GaR, XII (Summer, 1958), 192-201.

_____, "Language as Theme and Technique," Novels of
William Faulkner, 266-81. Also in Litz, A.W., ed.,
Modern American Fiction, 179-93.

_____, Novels of William Faulkner.

_____, "William Faulkner and the Figure in the Carpet,"
SAQ, LXIII (Summer, 1964), 318-35.

Vorpahl, Ben M., "Such Stuff as Dreams Are Made On: History, Myth and the Comic Vision of Mark Twain and William Faulkner," DA, XXVIII (1967), 698A (Wisconsin).

Wagenknecht, E., Cavalcade of the American Novel, 417-25.

Waggoner, H.H., William Faulkner.

_____, "William Faulkner: The Definition of Man," BBr,
XVIII (March, 1958), 116-22.

_____, "William Faulkner's Passion Week of the Heart,"
in Scott, Nathan A., ed., The Tragic Vision and The
Christian Faith, N.Y.: Association Pr., 1957, 306-23.

Wall, Carey G., "Faulkner's Rhetoric," DA, XXV (1965),
5947 (Stanford).

Warren, Robert Penn, "Cowley's Faulkner," NRep, CXV
(August 12, 1946), 176-80; (August 26, 1946), 234-7. Al-
so in Hoffman, F.J., and O.W. Vickery, eds., William
Faulkner, 109-24. Also in Hoffman, F.J., and O.W.
Vickery, eds., William Faulkner: Two Decades of Criti-
cism, 82-101. Also in O'Connor, William Van, ed.,
Forms of Modern Fiction, 125-43. Also in Gibson, Wil-
liam M., and George Arms, eds., Twelve American
Writers, N.Y.: Macmillan, 1962, 786-95. Also in Rahv,
P., ed., Literature in America, 415-30. Also in Zabel,
M.D., ed., Literary Opinion in America, 464-77. Also
(rev. and expanded) in Beaver, Harold, ed., American
Critical Essays, London: Oxford Un. Pr., 1959, 211-33.
And in Litz, A.W., ed., Modern American Fiction, 150-
65. And (in part) in Rubin, L.D., Jr., and J.R. Moore,
eds., Idea of an American Novel, 359-63. And in War-

ren, R. P. , Selected Essays, 59-79.
_____, ed. , Faulkner.
_____, "Faulkner: The South, the Negro, and Time,"
SoR, n. s. , I (Summer, 1965), 501-29. Also in Warren,
R. P. , ed. , Faulkner, 251-71.
_____, "Introduction: Faulkner: Past and Future," in
Warren, R. P. , ed. , Faulkner, 1-22.
Watkins, Floyd, "Faulkner and His Critics," TSLL, X (Sum-
mer, 1968), 317-29.
_____, "The Gentle Reader and Mr. Faulkner's Morals,"
GaR, XIII (Spring, 1959), 68-75.
_____, "William Faulkner, the Individual, and the World,"
GaR, XIV (Fall, 1960), 238-47.
Way, Brian, "William Faulkner," CritQ, III (Spring, 1961),
42-53.
Webb, James W. , and A. Wigfall Green, eds. , William
Faulkner of Oxford, Baton Rouge: Louisiana St. Un. Pr. ,
1965.
Weisgerber, Jean, "Faulkner's Monomaniacs: Their Indebt-
edness to Raskolnikov," CLS, V (1968), 181-93.
West, Anthony, et al. , "William Faulkner: A Critical Con-
sensus," Study of Current English (Tokyo), X (September,
1955), 28-9. (Not seen.)
Wheeler, Otis B. , "Faulkner's Wilderness," AL, XXXI (May,
1959), 127-36.
_____, "Some Uses of Folk Humor by Faulkner," MissQ,
XVII (Spring, 1964), 107-22.
Wilson, C. , Strength to Dream, 36-40.
Wyld, Lionel D. , "Faulkner and Yoknapatawpha: Out of the
'Waste Land'," Amer Lit Rev (Japan), XXX (December,
1959), 4-12.
Wynn, Lelia C. , "A Bookman's Faulkner," Delta Rev, II
(July-August, 1965), 33-5+.
Wynne, Carolyn, "Aspects of Space: John Marin and William
Faulkner," AQ, XVI (Spring, 1964), 59-71.
Yorks, Samuel A. , "Faulkner's Woman: The Peril of Man-
kind," ArQ, XVII (Summer, 1961), 119-29.
Young, T. D. , and Floyd C. Watkins, "Faulkner's Snopeses,"
MissQ, XI (Fall, 1958), 196-200.
Zink, Karl E. , "Faulkner's Garden: Woman and the Im-
memorial Earth," MFS, II (Autumn, 1956), 139-49.
_____, "Flux and the Frozen Moment: The Imagery of
Stasis in Faulkner's Prose," PMLA, LXXI (June, 1956),
285-301.
_____, "William Faulkner: Form as Experience," SAQ,
LIII (July, 1954), 384-403.

ABSALOM, ABSALOM!

Adams, R. P. , Faulkner, 172-214.
Allen, W. , Modern Novel, 121-4.
_____ , Urgent West, 88-90.
Aswell, Duncan, "The Puzzling Design of ABSALOM, AB-
SALOM!" KR, XXX (Winter, 1968), 67-84.
Backman, M. , Faulkner, 88-112.
_____ , "Sutpen and the South: A Study of ABSALOM, AB-
SALOM!" PMLA, LXXX (December, 1965), 596-604.
Baldanza, Frank, "Faulkner and Stein: A Study in Stylistic
Intransigence," GaR, XIII (Fall, 1959), 274-86.
Bashiruddin, Zeba, "The Lost Individual in ABSALOM, AB-
SALOM!" Newsletter Number 11, American Studies Re-
search Centre, Hyderabad, 1967, 49-52.
Beach, J. W. , American Fiction, 138-42, 164-9.
Beja, Morris, "A Flash, a Glare: Faulkner and Time,"
Ren, XVI (Spring, 1964), 137-41.
Bjork, Lennart, "Ancient Myths and the Moral Framework of
Faulkner's ABSALOM, ABSALOM!" AL, XXXV (May,
1963), 196-204.
Brooks, Cleanth, "ABSALOM, ABSALOM!: The Definition
of Innocence," SR, LIX (Autumn, 1951), 543-8.
_____ , "The American 'Innocence'": in James, Fitzger-
ald, and Faulkner," Shen, XVI (Autumn, 1964), 21-37.
_____ , "History, Tragedy, and the Imagination in ABSA-
LOM, ABSALOM!" YR, LII (Spring, 1963), 340-51.
_____ , William Faulkner, 295-324, 424-43. Also (con-
densed) in Warren, R. P. , ed. , Faulkner, 186-203.
Brylowski, W. , Faulkner's Olympian Laugh, 17-42.
Burgum, E. B. , Novel and the World's Dilemma, 221-2.
Callen, Shirley, "Planter and Poor White in ABSALOM, AB-
SALOM!, "Wash", and The Mind of the South," SCB,
XXIII, iv (Winter, 1963), 24-36.
Campbell, Harry M. , "Faulkner's ABSALOM, ABSALOM!"
Explicator, VII (December, 1948), Item 24.
Church, M. , "William Faulkner: Myth and Duration,"
Time and Reality, 241-3.
Clark, William G. , "Is King David a Racist?" UR, XXXIV
(December, 1967), 121-6.
Coanda, Richard, "ABSALOM, ABSALOM!: The Edge of
Infinity," Ren, XI (Autumn, 1958), 3-9.
Connolly, Thomas E. , "A Skeletal Outline of ABSALOM, AB-
SALOM!" CE, XXV (November, 1963), 110-14.
_____ , in Krause, S. J. , ed. Essays in Determinism,
45-7.
Dillingham, William B. , "William Faulkner and 'Tragic Con-

dition'," Edda, LXVI (1966), 327-30.
Everett, W. K., Faulkner's Art and Characters, 1-6.
Fazio, Rocco R., "The Fury and the Design: Realms of
    Being and Knowing in Four Novels of William Faulkner,"
    DA, XXV (1964), 1910 (Rochester).
Fiedler, L., Love and Death in the American Novel, 394-8,
    443-6.
Geismar, M., Writers in Crisis, 170-6.
Glicksberg, Charles I., "William Faulkner and the Negro
    Problem," Phylon, X (1949), 153-6.
Gold, J., William Faulkner, 30-8.
Gossett, L. Y., Violence in Recent Southern Fiction, 35-8.
Guetti, James, Limits of Metaphor, N. Y.: Ithaca: Cornell
    Un. Pr., 1967, 69-108.
_____, "The Failure of the Imagination: A Study of Mel-
    ville, Conrad, and Faulkner," DA, XXV (1965), 4145-6
    (Cornell).
Gwynn, F. L., and J. L. Blotner, eds., Faulkner in the Uni-
    versity.
Hagan, John, "Déjà vu and the Effect of Timelessness in
    Faulkner's ABSALOM, ABSALOM!" BuR, XI, ii (March,
    1963), 31-52.
_____, "Fact and Fancy in ABSALOM, ABSALOM!" CE,
    XXIV (December, 1962), 215-18.
Hammond, Donald, "Faulkner's Levels of Awareness,"
    FloQ, I, ii (1967), 75-8.
Hartt, J. N., Lost Image of Man, 39-45.
Hawkins, E. O., "Faulkner's 'Duke John of Lorraine',"
    AN&Q, IV (September, 1965), 22.
Hoffman, A. C., "Faulkner's ABSALOM, ABSALOM!" Expl,
    X (November, 1951), Item 12.
_____, "Point of View in ABSALOM, ABSALOM!" UKCR,
    XIX (Summer, 1953), 233-9.
Hoffman, F. J., William Faulkner, 74-9.
_____, in French, W. G., and W. E. Kidd, eds., Ameri-
    can Winners of the Nobel Literary Prize, 150-2.
Holman, C. H., Three Modes of Modern Southern Fiction,
    37-44+.
Howe, I., William Faulkner, 71-8, 221-32.
Hunt, J. W., William Faulkner, 101-36.
Jacobs, Robert D., "Faulkner's Tragedy of Isolation," in
    Rubin, L. D., and R. D. Jacobs, eds., Southern Renas-
    cence, 184-91.
_____, "William Faulkner: The Passion and the Penance,"
    in Rubin, L. D., Jr., and R. D. Jacobs, eds., South,
    163-9.
Justus, James H., "The Epic Design of ABSALOM, ABSA-

LOM!" TSLL, IV (Summer, 1962), 157-76.
Kartiganer, Donald M., "Faulkner's ABSALOM, ABSALOM!:
The Discovery of Values," AL, XXXVII (November, 1965),
291-306.
_____, "The Role of Myth in ABSALOM, ABSALOM!"
MFS, IX (Winter, 1963-64), 357-69.
Lind, Ilse D., "The Design and Meaning of ABSALOM, AB-
SALOM!" PMLA, LXX (December, 1955), 887-912. Also
in Hoffman, F.J., and O.W. Vickery, eds., William
Faulkner, 278-304.
Longley, J.L., Jr., Tragic Mask, 206-18.
Lorch, Thomas M., "Thomas Sutpen and the Female Prin-
ciple," MissQ, XX (Winter, 1966-67), 38-42.
Loughry, Thomas F., "Aborted Sacrament in ABSALOM, AB-
SALOM!" FQ, XIV (November, 1964), 13-21.
McClennen, Joshua, "ABSALOM, ABSALOM! and the Meaning
of History," PMASAL, XLII (1956), 357-69.
MacLure, Millar, "Allegories of Innocence," DR, XL (Sum-
mer, 1960), 146-9.
Marshall, Sarah L., "Fathers and Sons in ABSALOM, AB-
SALOM!" UMSE, VIII (1967), 19-29.
Mascitelli, David W., "Faulkner's Characters of Sensibility,"
DA, XXIX (1968), 608A-9A (Duke).
Mathews, James W., "The Civil War of 1936: GONE WITH
THE WIND and ABSALOM, ABSALOM!" GaR, XXI (Winter,
1967), 462-9.
Millgate, M., Achievement of William Faulkner, 150-64.
_____, William Faulkner, 52-9.
Minter, David L., The Interpreted Design as a Structural
Principle in American Prose, New Haven, Conn.: Yale
Un. Pr., 1969, 191-219.
Muehl, Lois, "Faulkner's Humor in Three Novels and One
'Play'," LC, XXXIV (Spring, 1968), 78-93.
Nilon, Charles H., "Faulkner and the Negro," UCSSLL, No.
8 (September, 1962), 93-6. Also in Nilon, C.H., Faulk-
ner and the Negro, 93-6.
Nishiyama, Tamotsu, "The Structure of ABSALOM, ABSA-
LOM!" KAL, No. 1 (June, 1958), 9-13.
O'Connor, William Van, "Faulkner's Legend of the Old
South," WHR, VII (Autumn, 1953), 294-9.
_____, "Protestantism in Yoknapatawpha County," in Ru-
bin, L.D., and R.D. Jacobs, Southern Renascence, 156-
8.
_____, Tangled Fire of William Faulkner, 94-100.
_____, William Faulkner, 25-8. Also in O'Connor, W.V.,
ed., Seven Modern American Novelists, 138-40.
Paterson, John, "Hardy, Faulkner, and the Prosaics of

Tragedy," CRAS, V (Spring, 1961), 156-75.

Poirier, William R. , " 'Strange Gods' in Jefferson, Missis-
sippi: Analysis of ABSALOM, ABSALOM!" in Hoffman,
F. J. , and O. W. Vickery, eds. , William Faulkner: Two
Decades of Criticism, 217-43.

Richardson, K. E. , Force and Faith in the Novels of William
Faulkner, 29-35.

Rinaldi, Nicholas M. , "Game-Consciousness and Game-Metaphor in the Work of William Faulkner," DA, XXIV
(1964), 4196-7 (Fordham).

Rubin, L. D. , Jr. , Faraway Country, 50-4.

Scott, Arthur L. , "The Faulknerian Sentence," PrS, XXVII
(1953), 91-8.

_____, "The Myriad Perspectives of ABSALOM, ABSA-
LOM!" AQ, VII (Fall, 1954), 210-20.

Seiden, Melvin, "Faulkner's Ambiguous Negro," MR, IV
(Summer, 1963), 675-90

Sewall, Richard B. , The Vision of Tragedy, New Haven:
Yale Un. Pr. , 1959, 133-47.

Singleton, Marvin K. , "Personae at Law and Equity: The
Unity of Faulkner's ABSALOM, ABSALOM!" PLL, III
(Fall, 1967), 354-70.

Slabey, Robert M. , "Faulkner's 'Waste Land': Vision in
ABSALOM, ABSALOM!" MissQ, XIV (Summer, 1961),
153-61.

_____, "Quentin Compson's 'Lost Childhood,' " SSF, I
(Spring, 1964), 173-83.

Slatoff, W. J. , Quest for Failure, 13-14, 71-2, 118-19,
198-202, 256.

Sowder, William J. , "Colonel Thomas Sutpen as Existentialist Hero," AL, XXXIII (January, 1962), 485-99.

Steinberg, Aaron, "ABSALOM, ABSALOM!: The Irretriev-
able Bon," CLAJ, IX (September, 1965), 61-7.

_____, "Faulkner and the Negro," DA, XXVII (1966),
1385A (N. Y. U.).

Stewart, David H. , "ABSALOM Reconsidered," UTQ, XXX
(October, 1960), 31-44.

Sullivan, Walter, "The Tragic Design of ABSALOM, ABSA-
LOM!" SAQ, L (October, 1951), 552-66.

Sullivan, William P. , "William Faulkner and the Community," DA, XXII (1962), 4355 (Columbia).

Swiggart, P. , Art of Faulkner's Novels, 149-70.

Thomas, Douglas M. , "Memory-Narrative in ABSALOM, AB-
SALOM!" Faulkner Studies, II (Summer, 1953), 19-22.

Thompson, Lawrance, "A Defense of Difficulties in William
Faulkner's Art," Carrell, IV (December, 1963), 7-16.

_____, William Faulkner, 53-65, 191-3.

Tindall, W. Y., Literary Symbol, 264-7.
Tritschler, Donald H., "Whorls of Form in Faulkner's Fiction," DA, XVII (1957), 3025 (Northwestern).
Tuck, D., Crowell's Handbook of Faulkner, 56-66.
Van Nostrand, A. D., "The Poetic Dialogues of William Faulkner," Everyman His Own Poet, 184-9.
Vickery, O. W., Novels of William Faulkner, 84-102.
Volpe, E. L., Reader's Guide to William Faulkner, 184-212.
Waggoner, H. H., William Faulkner, 148-69. Also (condensed) in Warren, R. P., ed., Faulkner, 175-85.
Watkins, Floyd C., "What Happens in ABSALOM, ABSALOM!?" MFS, XIII, i (Spring, 1967), 79-87.
Weatherby, H. L., "Sutpen's Garden," GaR, XXI (Fall, 1967), 354-69.
Whan, Edgar, "ABSALOM, ABSALOM! as Gothic Myth," Per, III (Autumn, 1950), 192-201.
Wigley, Joseph A., "An Analysis of the Imagery of William Faulkner's ABSALOM, ABSALOM!" DA, XVI (1956), 2464-65 (Northwestern).
Williams, Philip E., "The Biblical View of History: Hawthorne, Mark Twain, Faulkner, and Eliot," DA, XXV (1965), 4159-60 (Un. of Pennsylvania).
_____, "Faulkner's Satan Sutpen and the Tragedy of ABSALOM, ABSALOM!" ESELL, Nos. 45-46 (December, 1964), 179-99.
Zoellner, Robert H., "Faulkner's Prose Style in ABSALOM, ABSALOM!" AL, XXX (January, 1959), 486-502.

AS I LAY DYING

Adams, R. P., Faulkner, 71-84.
Allen, Charles A., "William Faulkner: Comedy and the Purpose of Humor," ArQ, XVI (Spring, 1960), 61-4.
Backman, M., Faulkner, 50-66.
Baker, Carlos, "William Faulkner: The Doomed and the Damned," in Bode, C., ed., Young Rebel in American Literature, 150-4.
Beach, J. W., American Fiction, 132-5.
Bedient, Calvin, "Pride and Nakedness: AS I LAY DYING," MLQ, XXIX (March, 1968), 61-76.
Beidler, Peter G., "Faulkner's Techniques of Characterization: Jewel in AS I LAY DYING," EA, XXI (1968), 236-42.
Blotner, Joseph L., "AS I LAY DYING: Christian Lore and Irony," TCL, III (April, 1957), 14-19.
Bridgman, Richard, "As Hester Prynne Lay Dying," ELN, II (June, 1965), 294-6.

Brooks, C., William Faulkner, 141-66, 398-401.

Brylowski, W., Faulkner's Olympian Laugh, 86-96.

Burgum, E. B., Novel and the World's Dilemma, 215-17.

Chase, R., American Novel and It's Tradition, 207-10.

Church, M., "William Faulkner: Myth and Duration," Time and Reality, 235-7.

Collins, Carvel, "The Pairing of THE SOUND AND THE FURY and AS I LAY DYING," PULC, XVIII (Spring, 1957), 115-19.

Cross, Barbara M., "Apocalypse and Comedy in AS I LAY DYING," TSLL, III (Summer, 1961), 251-8.

Dickerson, Mary J., "AS I LAY DYING and THE WASTE LAND: Some Relationships," MissQ, XVII (Summer, 1964), 129-35.

_____, "Some Sources of Faulkner's Myth in AS I LAY DYING," MissQ, XIX (Summer, 1966), 132-42.

Everett, W. K., Faulkner's Art and Characters, 7-15.

Fazio, Rocco R., "The Fury and the Design: Realms of Being and Knowing in Four Novels of William Faulkner," DA, XXV (1964), 1910 (Rochester).

Franklin, Rosemary, "Animal Magnetism in AS I LAY DYING," AQ, XVIII (Spring, 1966), 24-34.

_____, "Narrative Management in AS I LAY DYING," MFS, XIII, i (Spring, 1967), 57-65.

Garrett, George P., "Some Revisions in AS I LAY DYING," MLN, LXXIII (June, 1958), 414-19.

Geismar, M., Writers in Crisis, 161-2.

Goellner, Jack G., "A Closer Look at AS I LAY DYING," Per, VII (Spring, 1954), 42-54.

Gossett, L. Y., Violence in Recent Southern Fiction, 32-4.

Gwynn, F. L., and J. L. Blotner, eds., Faulkner in the University.

Hammond, Donald, "Faulkner's Levels of Awareness," FloQ, I, ii (1967), 78-81.

Handy, William J., "AS I LAY DYING: Faulkner's Inner Reporter," KR, XXI (Summer, 1959), 437-51. Also in Westbrook, M., ed., Modern American Novel, 153-69.

Harwick, Robert D., "Humor in the Novels of William Faulkner," DA, XXVI (1965), 1646 (Nebraska).

Hirano, Nobuyuki, "Reconsideration of Moral Order and Disorder in Faulkner's Works," HJAS, VIII, i (September, 1967), 19-25.

Hoffman, F. J., William Faulkner, 60-5.

Howe, I., William Faulkner, 52-6, 175-91.

Howell, Elmo, "Faulkner's Jumblies: The Nonsense World of AS I LAY DYING," ArQ, XVI (Spring, 1960), 70-8.

Humphrey, R., Stream of Consciousness in the Modern Novel.

Jacobs, Robert D., "William Faulkner: The Passion and the Penance," in Rubin, L. D., Jr., and R. D. Jacobs, eds., South, 153-5.

Kerr, Elizabeth M., "AS I LAY DYING as Ironic Quest," WSCL, III, i (Winter, 1962), 5-19.

King, Roma, Jr., "The Janus Symbol in AS I LAY DYING," UKCR, XXI (Summer, 1955), 287-90.

Kirk, Robert W., "Faulkner's Anse Bundren," GaR, XIX (Winter, 1965), 446-52.

Lewis, R. W. B., Picaresque Saint, 218-19.

Mellard, James M., "Faulkner's Philosophical Novel: Ontological Themes in AS I LAY DYING," Person, XLVIII (Autumn, 1967), 509-23.

Millgate, M., Achievement of William Faulkner, 104-12.

_____, William Faulkner, 34-9.

O'Connor, W. V., Tangled Fire of William Faulkner, 45-53.

_____, William Faulkner, 14-17. Also in O'Connor, W. V., ed., Seven Modern American Novelists, 128-31.

Presley, Delma E., "Is Reverend Whitfield a Hypocrite?" RS, XXXVI (March, 1968), 57-61.

Randall, Julia, "Some Notes on AS I LAY DYING," Hopkins Rev, IV (Summer, 1951), 47-51.

Reaver, J. Russell, "This Vessel of Clay: A Thematic Comparison of Faulkner's AS I LAY DYING and Latorre's THE OLD WOMAN OF PERALILLO," Fla. St. Un. Studies, No. 14 (1954), 131-40.

Richardson, K. E., Force and Faith in the Novels of William Faulkner, 73-6.

Roberts, James L., "The Individual and the Family: Faulkner's AS I LAY DYING," ArQ, XVI (Spring, 1960), 26-38.

Rossky, William, "AS I LAY DYING: The Insane World," TSLL, IV (Spring, 1962), 87-95.

Rubin, L. D., Jr., Faraway Country, 62-3.

Sadler, David F., "The Second Mrs. Bundren: Another Look at the Ending of AS I LAY DYING," AL, XXXVII (March, 1965), 65-9.

Sawyer, K. B., "Hero in AS I LAY DYING," Faulkner Studies, III (Autumn, 1954), 30-3.

Simon, John K., "The Glance of the Idiot: A Thematic Study of Faulkner and Modern French Fiction," DA, XXV (1964), 1220 (Yale).

_____, "The Scene and the Imagery of Metamorphosis in AS I LAY DYING," Criticism, VII (Winter, 1965), 1-22.

_____, "What Are You Laughing At, Darl?" CE, XXV (November, 1963), 104-10.

Slabey, Robert M., "AS I LAY DYING as an Existential Novel," BuR, XI, iv (December, 1963), 12-23.

Slatoff, W. J., Quest for Failure, 9-11, 104-6, 158-73.
Stallman, Robert W., "A Cryptogram: AS I LAY DYING,"
    The Houses that James Built and Other Literary Studies,
    Lansing: Mich. St. Un. Pr., 1961, 200-11.
Stonesifer, Richard J., "In Defense of Dewey Dell," EL,
    XXII (July, 1958), 27-33.
Sutherland, Ronald, "AS I LAY DYING: A Faulkner Micro-
    cosm," QQ, LXXIII (Winter, 1966), 541-9.
Swiggart, P., Art of Faulkner's Novels, 57-9, 108-30.
Tuck, D., Crowell's Handbook of Faulkner, 34-9.
Vickery, Olga W., "AS I LAY DYING," Per, III (Autumn, 1950),
    179-91. Also in Vickery, O. W., Novels of William Faulkner,
    50-65. Also in Hoffman, F. J., and O. W. Vickery, eds.,
    William Faulkner, 232-47. Also in Hoffman, F. J., and O. W.
    Vickery, eds., William Faulkner: Two Decades of Criticism,
    189-205.
Volpe, E. L., Reader's Guide to William Faulkner, 126-40.
Waggoner, H. H., William Faulkner, 62-87.
Wasiolek, Edward, "AS I LAY DYING: Distortion in the Slow
    Eddy of Current Opinion," Crit, III, i (Spring-Fall, 1959),
    15-23.
Watkins, Floyd C., and W. B. Dillingham, "The Mind of Varda-
    man Bundren," PQ, XXXIX (April, 1960), 247-51.

A FABLE

Adams, R. P., Faulkner, 161-9.
Baker, Carlos, "William Faulkner: The Doomed and the
    Damned," in Bode, C., ed., Young Rebel in American
    Literature, 166-8.
Barth, J. Robert, "A Rereading of Faulkner's FABLE,"
    America, XCII (October 9, 1954), 44-6.
Brylowski, W., Faulkner's Olympian Laugh, 183-200.
Cabaniss, Allen, "A Source of Faulkner's FABLE," UMSE,
    VI (1965), 87-9.
Carter, Thomas H., "Dramatization of an Enigma," WR,
    XIX (Winter, 1955), 147-58.
Chametzky, Jules, "Some Remarks on A FABLE," Faulkner
    Studies, III (Summer-Autumn, 1954), 39-40.
Church, M., "William Faulkner: Myth and Duration,"
    Time and Reality, 248-50.
Connolly, Thomas E., "Faulkner's A FABLE in the Class-
    room," CE, XXI (December, 1959), 165-71.
_____, "The Three Plots of A FABLE," TCL, VI (July,
    1960), 70-5.
Cottrell, Beekman W., "Faulkner's Cosmic FABLE: The
    Extraordinary Family of Man," in Woodruff, N., Jr.,
    and Others, eds., Studies in Faulkner, 17-27.

Dillistone, F. W. , The Novelist and the Passion Story, N. Y. : Sheed and Ward, 1960, 92-118.

Dorsch, Robert L. , "An Interpretation of the Central Themes in the Work of William Faulkner," ESRS, XI, i (September, 1962), 27-35.

Everett, W. K. , Faulkner's Art and Characters, 15-21.

Flint, R. W. , "What Price Glory?" HudR, VII (Winter, 1955), 602-6.

Gardiner, H. C. , "William Faulkner's A FABLE," In All Conscience, 129-31.

Geismar, M. , SatR, XXXVII (July 31, 1954), 11. Also in Geismar, M. , American Moderns, 97-101.

Gold, Joseph, "Delusion and Redemption in Faulkner's A FABLE," MFS, VII (Summer, 1961), 145-56.

_____, William Faulkner, 111-47.

Gwynn, F. L. , and J. L. Blotner, eds. , Faulkner in the University.

Hafley, James, "Faulkner's FABLE: Dream and Transfiguration," Accent, XVI (Winter, 1956), 3-14.

Hartt, J. N. , Lost Image of Man, 110-11.

_____, "Some Reflections on Faulkner's FABLE," Religion in Life, XXIV (Fall, 1955), 601-7.

Hoffman, Frederick J. , in French, W. G. , and Kidd, W. E. , eds. , American Winners of the Nobel Literary Prize, 154-6.

_____, William Faulkner, 111-15.

Howe, I. , William Faulkner, 268-81.

Kenner, Hugh, "A FABLE," Shen, VI (Spring, 1955), 44-53.

King, Roma A. , Jr. , "Everyman's Warfare: A Study of Faulkner's FABLE," MFS, II (Autumn, 1956), 132-8.

Kohler, Dayton, "A FABLE: The Novel as Myth," CE, XVI (May, 1955), 471-8. Also in EJ, XLIV (May, 1955), 253-60.

Kunkel, Francis L. , "Christ Symbolism in Faulkner: Prevalence of the Human," Ren, XVII (Spring, 1965), 151-6.

Lewis, R. W. B. , Picaresque Saint, 210-17.

Lytle, Andrew N. , "The Son of Man: He Will Prevail," SR, LXIII (Winter, 1955), 114-37. Also in Lytle, A. , Hero with the Private Parts, 103-28.

Millgate, M. , Achievement of William Faulkner, 227-34.

_____, William Faulkner, 99-101.

Mills, Ralph J. , Jr. , "Faulkner's Essential Vision: Notes on A FABLE," ChS, XLIV (Fall, 1961), 187-98.

Milton, John R. , "American Fiction and Man," Cresset, XVIII, iii (1955), 16-20.

Miner, Ward L. , "Faulkner and Christ's Crucifixion," NM, LVII (1956), 260-9.

Podhoretz, Norman, "William Faulkner and the Problem of
    War," Ctary, XVIII (September, 1954), 227-32. Also in
    Podhoretz, N., Doings and Undoings, 13-24. Also in
    Warren, R. P., ed., Faulkner, 243-50.
Pritchett, V. S., "Time Frozen: A FABLE," PR, XXI, v
    (September-October, 1954), 557-61. Also in Warren, R.
    P., ed., Faulkner, 238-42.
Raymund, Bernard, "A FABLE," ArQ, X (Winter, 1954),
    361-3.
Rice, Philip B., "Faulkner's Crucifixion," KR, XVI (Autumn,
    1954), 661-70.
Richardson, K. E., Force and Faith in the Novels of William
    Faulkner, 156-62.
Sandeen, Ernest, "William Faulkner: His Legend and His
    Fable," RPol, XVIII (January, 1956), 47-68.
Schendler, Sylvan, "William Faulkner's A FABLE," DA,
    XVII (1957), 366-7 (Northwestern).
Schwartz, Delmore, "William Faulkner's A FABLE," Per-
    spectives U. S. A., No. 10 (Winter, 1955), 126-36.
Slatoff, W. J., Quest for Failure, 221-37.
Smith, Julian, "A Source for Faulkner's A FABLE," AL,
    XL (November, 1968), 394-7.
Sowder, William J., "Faulkner and Existentialism: A Note
    on the Generalissimo," WSCL, IV, ii (Spring-Summer,
    1963), 163-71.
Stavrou, C. N., "William Faulkner's Apologia: Some Notes
    on A FABLE," ColQ, III (Spring, 1955), 432-9.
Stein, Randolph E., "The World Outside Yoknapatawpha: A
    Study of Five Novels by William Faulkner," DA, XXVI
    (1965), 2225 (Ohio Un.).
Straumann, Heinrich, "An American Interpretation of Exist-
    ence: Faulkner's A FABLE," in Hoffman, F. J., and O.
    W. Vickery, eds., William Faulkner, 349-72.
Stuckey, W. J., Pulitzer Prize Novels, 170-5.
Swiggart, P., Art of Faulkner's Novels, 184-94.
Taylor, Walter F., "William Faulkner: The Faulkner Fable,"
    ASch, XXVI (Autumn, 1957), 471-7.
Tsagari, Myrto, "A FABLE: Faulkner's Message to the
    World," nota bene (Lake Erie College, Painesville, Ohio),
    I (1958), 30-4.
Tuck, D., Crowell's Handbook of Faulkner, 143-56.
Turaj, Frank, "The Dialectic in Faulkner's A FABLE,"
    TSLL, VIII (Spring, 1966), 93-102.
Vickery, O. W., Novels of William Faulkner, 209-27.
Volpe, E. L., Reader's Guide to William Faulkner, 282-304.
Waggoner, H. H., William Faulkner, 225-32.
Wagner, Geoffrey, "Faulkner's Contemporary Passion Play,"

TC, CLVI (December, 1954), 527-38.
Webb, James W., "Faulkner Writes A FABLE," UMSE, VII
(1966), 1-13.

THE HAMLET (See also SNOPES Trilogy)

Adams, R. P., Faulkner, 115-20.
Backman, M., Faulkner, 139-59.
Beach, J. W., American Fiction, 147-9.
Brooks, Cleanth, "Faulkner's Savage Arcadia: Frenchman's
Bend," VQR, XXXIX (Autumn, 1963), 598-611.
Brooks, C., William Faulkner, 167-91, 402-10.
Brylowski, W., Faulkner's Olympian Laugh, 139-49.
Burgum, E. B., Novel and the World's Dilemma, 220-1.
Campbell, H. M., and R. E. Foster, William Faulkner, 79-
81.
Cowley, M., "Faulkner by Daylight," NRep, CII (April 15,
1940), 510. Also in Cowley, M., Look Back on Us, 358-
60.
Cross, Richard K., "The Humor of THE HAMLET," TCL,
XII (January, 1967), 203-15.
Dirksen, Sherland N., "William Faulkner's Snopes Family:
THE HAMLET, THE TOWN, and THE MANSION," ESRS,
XI, ii (December, 1962), 12-22.
Eby, Cecil D., "Faulkner and the Southwestern Humorists,"
Shen, XI (Autumn, 1959), 13-21.
_____, "Ichabod Crane in Yoknapatawpha," GaR, XVI
(Winter, 1962), 465-9.
Everett, W. K., Faulkner's Art and Characters, 37-43.
French, Warren, "The Background of Snopesism in Missis-
sippi Politics," MASJ, V (Fall, 1964), 3-17.
_____, Social Novel, 18-49, passim.
Gates, Allen, "The Old Frenchman Place: Symbol of a Lost
Civilization," IEY, No. 13 (Fall, 1968), 44-50.
Gold, Joseph, "The 'Normality' of Snopesism: Universal
Themes in Faulkner's THE HAMLET," WSCL, III, i (Win-
ter, 1962), 25-34.
Gossett, L. Y., Violence in Recent Southern Fiction, 43-4.
Greet, T. Y., "The Theme and Structure of Faulkner's THE
HAMLET," PMLA, LXXII (September, 1957), 775-90. Al-
so in Hoffman, F. J., and O. W. Vickery, eds., William
Faulkner, 330-47.
Gwynn, F. L., and J. L. Blotner, eds., Faulkner in the Uni-
versity.
Hall, J., Lunatic Giant in the Drawing Room, 58-9, 62-74.
_____, "Play, the Training Camp, and American Angry
Comedy," HAB, XV (Spring, 1964), 7-9.

Harder, Kelsie B., "Proverbial Snopeslore," TFSB, XXIV
   (September, 1958), 89-95.
Harwick, Robert D., "Humor in the Novels of William Faulk-
   ner," DA, XXVI (1965), 1646 (Nebraska).
Hayes, Ann L., "The World of THE HAMLET," in Woodruff,
   N., Jr. and Others, eds., Studies in Faulkner, 3-16.
Hoffman, F. J., William Faulkner, 85-92.
Hopkins, Viola, "William Faulkner's THE HAMLET: A Study
   in Meaning and Form," Accent, XV (Spring, 1955), 125-44.
Howe, I., William Faulkner, 78-88, 243-52.
Jacobs, Robert D., "William Faulkner: The Passion and the
   Penance," in Rubin, L. D., Jr., and Jacobs, R. D., eds.,
   South, 169-71.
Lawson, Strang, "Faulkner's THE HAMLET," CEA Critic,
   X (December, 1948), 3.
Lawson, Lewis A., "The Grotesque-Comic in the SNOPES
   Trilogy," L&P, XV (1965), 107-19. Also in Manheim,
   L., and E., eds., Hidden Patterns, 243-58.
Leaver, Florence, "The Structure of THE HAMLET," TCL,
   I (July, 1955), 77-84.
Lisca, Peter, "THE HAMLET: Genesis and Revisions,"
   Faulkner Studies, III (Spring, 1954), 5-13.
McClennen, Joshua, "Why Read Faulkner," MAQR, LXII
   (Summer, 1956), 342-5.
McDonald, W. V., Jr., "The Time Scheme of THE HAM-
   LET," MidR, V (1963), 22-9.
Mercer, Caroline, and Susan J. Turner, "Restoring Life to
   Faulkner's THE HAMLET," CEA, XXI (December, 1959),
   1, 4-5.
Millgate, M., Achievement of William Faulkner, 180-200.
   _____, William Faulkner, 84-90.
O'Connor, W. V., Tangled Fire of William Faulkner, 111-24.
   _____, William Faulkner, 31-4. Also in O'Connor, W.
   V., ed., Seven Modern American Novelists, 144-6.
Richardson, K. E., Force and Faith in the Novels of William
   Faulkner, 118-24.
Rinaldi, Nicholas M., "Game-Consciousness and Game-Met-
   aphor in the Work of William Faulkner," DA, XXIV
   (1964), 4196-7 (Fordham).
Roberts, James L., "Snopeslore: THE HAMLET, THE
   TOWN, THE MANSION," UKCR, XXVIII (1961), 65-71.
Shanaghan, Father Malachy M., O. S. B., "A Critical Analy-
   sis of the Fictional Techniques of William Faulkner," DA,
   XX (1960) 4663 (Notre Dame).
Slatoff, W. J., Quest for Failure, 85-6.
Stone, Edward, A Certain Morbidness: A View of American
   Literature, Carbondale and Edwardsville: So. Ill. Un.

Pr., 1969, 100-20.
Stonesifer, Richard J., "Faulkner's THE HAMLET in the
Classroom," CE, XX (November, 1958), 71-7.
Swiggart, P., Art of Faulkner's Novels, 49-51.
Thompson, L., William Faulkner, 133-47, 199-200.
Thonan, Robert, "William Faulkner: From THE HAMLET
to THE TOWN," ESA, II (September, 1959), 190-202.
Tuck, D., Crowell's Handbook of Faulkner, 74-81.
Vickery, O.W., Novels of William Faulkner, 167-81.
Volpe, E.L., Reader's Guide to William Faulkner, 306-17.
Vorpahl, Ben M., "Such Stuff as Dreams Are Made On:
History, Myth and the Comic Vision of Mark Twain and
William Faulkner," DA, XXVIII (1967), 698A (Wisconsin).
Waggoner, H.H., William Faulkner, 183-93.
Wall, Carey, "Drama and Technique in Faulkner's THE HAM-
LET," TCL, XIV (April, 1968), 17-33.
Watkins, Floyd C., and T.D. Young, "Revisions of Style in
Faulkner's THE HAMLET," MFS, V (Winter, 1959-60),
327-36.

INTRUDER IN THE DUST

Adams, R.P., Faulkner, 155-6.
Baker, Carlos, "William Faulkner: The Doomed and the
Damned," in Bode, C., ed., Young Rebel in American
Literature, 154-6.
Brooks, C., William Faulkner, 279-94; 420-4.
Brylowski, W., Faulkner's Olympian Laugh, 168-73.
Bunker, Robert, "Faulkner: A Case for Regionalism,"
NMQ, XIX (Spring, 1949), 108-15.
Carter, Everett, "The Meaning of, and in, Realism," AR,
XII (Spring, 1952), 92-4.
Cohen, B. Bernard, "Study Aids for Faulkner's INTRUDER
IN THE DUST," Exercise Exchange, VII (October, 1959),
12-13.
Connolly, Thomas E., in Krause, S.J., ed., Essays in De-
terminism, 49-52.
Elias, Robert H., "Gavin Stevens: Intruder?" Faulkner
Studies, III (Spring, 1954), 1-4.
Everett, W.K., Faulkner's Art and Characters, 43-7.
Geismar, M., SatR, XXXI (September 25, 1948), 8. Also in
Geismar, M., American Moderns, 91-3.
Gerstenberger, Donna, "Meaning and Form in INTRUDER IN
THE DUST," CE, XXIII (December, 1961), 223-5.
Glicksberg, Charles, "INTRUDER IN THE DUST," ArQ, V
(Spring, 1949), 85-8.
Gloster, Hugh M., "Southern Justice," Phylon, X (1949), 93-5.

Gold, J., William Faulkner, 76-94.
Greer, Dorothy D., "Dilsey and Lucas: Faulkner's Use of
    the Negro as a Gauge of Moral Character," ESRS, XI, i
    (September, 1962), 54-60.
Gwynn, F.L., and J.L. Blotner, eds., Faulkner in the Uni-
    versity.
Hardwick, Elizabeth, "Faulkner and the South Today," PR,
    XV (October, 1948), 1130-5. Also in Hoffman, F.J.,
    and O.W. Vickery, eds., William Faulkner: Two Decades
    of Criticism, 244-50. Also in Warren, R.P., ed.,
    Faulkner, 226-30.
Hart, John A., "That Not Impossible He: Faulkner's Third-
    Person Narrator," in Woodruff, N., Jr., and Others,
    eds., Studies in Faulkner, 34-41.
Hoffman, F.J., William Faulkner, 99-101.
Howe, Irving, "The South and Current Literature," AmMerc,
    LXVII (October, 1948), 495-8.
_____, William Faulkner, 23-4, 98-102, 104-5.
Howell, Elmo, "William Faulkner's Caledonia: A Note on
    INTRUDER IN THE DUST," SSL, III (April, 1966), 248-
    52.
Hudson, Tommy, "William Faulkner: Mystic and Tradition-
    alist," Per III (Autumn, 1950), 227-35.
Little, Gail B., "Three Novels for Comparative Study in the
    Twelfth Grade," EJ, LII (1963), 501-5.
Lytle, Andrew, "Regeneration for the Man," SR, LVII, i
    (Winter, 1949), 120-7. Also in Warren, R.P., ed.,
    Faulkner, 231-7. Also in Lytle, A., Hero with the Pri-
    vate Parts, 129-36. Also in Hoffman, F.J., and O.W.
    Vickery, eds., William Faulkner: Two Decades of Criti-
    cism, 251-9.
Maxwell, D.E.S., American Fiction, 275-8.
Millgate, M., Achievement of William Faulkner, 215-20.
_____, William Faulkner, 94-5.
Mizener, A., Twelve Great American Novels, 146-7.
Muehl, Lois, "Faulkner's Humor in Three Novels and One
    'Play'," LC, XXXIV (Spring, 1968), 78-93.
Nilon, Charles H., "Faulkner and the Negro," UCSSLL, No.
    8 (September, 1962), 4-12, 25-30. Also in Nilon, C.H.,
    Faulkner and the Negro, 4-12, 25-30.
O'Connor, W.V., Tangled Fire of William Faulkner, 136-
    42.
O'Faolain, S., Vanishing Hero, 104-6.
Richardson, K.E., Force and Faith in the Novels of William
    Faulkner, 103-7.
Rollins, Ronald G., "Ike McCaslin and Chick Mallison:
    Faulkner's Emerging Southern Hero," WVUPP, XIV (Oc-

LIGHT IN AUGUST

Beach, J.W. American Fiction, 135-8, 162-4.

Beja, Morris, "A Flash, a Glare: Faulkner and Time,"
Ren, XVI (Spring, 1964), 134-7.

Benson, Carl, "Thematic Design in LIGHT IN AUGUST,"
SAQ, LIII (October, 1954), 540-55.

Berland, Alwyn, "LIGHT IN AUGUST: The Calvinism of
William Faulkner," MFS, VIII (Summer, 1962), 159-70.

Bernberg, Raymond E., "LIGHT IN AUGUST: A Psychological View," MissQ, XI (Fall, 1958), 173-6.

Bowden, E.T., "The Commonplace and the Grotesque,"
Dungeon of the Heart, 124-38.

Brooks, Cleanth, "The Community and the Pariah," VQR,
XXXIX (Spring, 1963), 236-53.

_____, Hidden God, 35-40.

_____, "Notes on Faulkner's LIGHT IN AUGUST," Har-
vardA, CXXXV (November, 1951), 10-11, 27.

Brown, William R., "Faulkner's Paradox in Pathology and
Salvation: SANCTUARY, LIGHT IN AUGUST, REQUIEM
FOR A NUN," TSLL, IX (1967), 429-49.

Brylowski, W., Faulkner's Olympian Laugh, 102-17.

Campbell, H.M., and R.E. Foster, William Faulkner, 67-
74.

Chase, R., American Novel and Its Tradition, 210-19.

_____, "The Stone and the Crucifixion: Faulkner's LIGHT
IN AUGUST," KR, X (Autumn, 1948), 539-51. Also in
Aldridge, J.W., ed., Critiques and Essays on Modern
Fiction, 190-9. Also in Hoffman, F.J., and O.W. Vick-
ery, eds., William Faulkner: Two Decades of Criticism,
205-17. Also in Kenyon Review. Kenyon Critics, 115-
26. Also in Oldsey, Bernard S., and Arthur O. Lewis,
Jr., eds., Visions and Revisions in Modern American
Literary Criticism, N.Y.: Dutton, 1962, 271-83.

Church, M., "William Faulkner: Myth and Duration," Time
and Reality, 238-41.

Clark, William G., "Faulkner's LIGHT IN AUGUST," Expl,
XXVI (March, 1968), Item 54.

Coffee, Jessie A., "Empty Steeples: Theme, Symbol and
Irony in Faulkner's Novels," ArQ, XXIII (Autumn, 1967),
198-201.

Collins, Robert G., "Four Critical Interpretations in the
Modern Novel," DA, XXII (1962), 3642 (Denver).

Connolly, Thomas E., in Krause, S.J., ed., Essays in Determinism, 41-5.

Cottrell, Beekman W., "Christian Symbols in LIGHT IN
AUGUST," MFS, II (Winter, 1956-57), 207-13.

Dorsch, Robert L., "An Interpretation of the Central
Themes in the Work of William Faulkner," ESRS, XI, i

(September, 1962), 8-20.

Dunn, Richard J., "Faulkner's LIGHT IN AUGUST, Chapter 5," Expl, XXV (October, 1966), Item 11.

Everett, W. K., Faulkner's Art and Characters, 47-52.

Fazio, Rocco R., "The Fury and the Design: Realms of Being and Knowing in Four Novels of William Faulkner," DA, XXV (1964), 1910 (Rochester).

Flint, R. W., "Faulkner as Elegist," HudR, VII (Summer, 1954), 249-50.

Frazier, David L., "Lucas Burch and the Polarity of LIGHT IN AUGUST," MLN, LXXIII (June, 1958), 417-19.

Gavin, Jerome, "LIGHT IN AUGUST: The Act of Involvement," HarvardA, CXXXV (November, 1951), 14-15, 34-7.

Geismar, M., Writers in Crisis, 163-9.

Glicksberg, Charles, "William Faulkner and the Negro Problem," Phylon, X (1949), 157-60.

Gold, Joseph, "The Two Worlds of LIGHT IN AUGUST," MissQ, XVI (Summer, 1963), 160-7.

_____, William Faulkner, 38-42.

Gossett, L. Y., Violence in Recent Southern Fiction, 30-1.

Greer, Scott, "Joe Christmas and the 'Social Self'," MissQ, XI (Fall, 1958), 160-6.

Gwynn, F. L., and J. L. Blotner, eds., Faulkner in the University.

Hammond, Donald, "Faulkner's Levels of Awareness," FloQ, I, ii (1967), 73-5.

Hartt, J. N., Lost Image of Man, 45-8.

Hirano, Nobuyuki, "Reconsideration of Moral Order and Disorder in Faulkner's Works," HJAS, VIII, i (September, 1967), 25-30.

Hirshleifer, Phyllis, "As Whirlwinds in the South: An Analysis of LIGHT IN AUGUST," Per, II (Summer, 1949), 225-38.

Hoffman, F. J., in French, W. G., and Kidd, W. E., eds., American Winners of the Nobel Literary Prize, 148-50.

_____, William Faulkner, 69-74.

Holman, C. Hugh, "The Unity of Faulkner's LIGHT IN AUGUST," PMLA, LXXIII (March, 1958), 155-66.

Howe, I., William Faulkner, 61-70, 125-6, 200-14.

Howell, Elmo, "A Note on Faulkner's Presbyterian Novel," PLL, II (Spring, 1966), 182-7.

_____, "Reverend Hightower and the Uses of Southern Adversity," CE, XXIV (December, 1962), 183-7.

Hunt, J. W., William Faulkner, 13-16.

Jackson, Esther M., "The American Negro and the Image of the Absurd," Phylon, XXIII (Winter, 1962), 360-4.

Jacobs, Robert D., "Faulkner's Tragedy of Isolation," in

Rubin, L. D. , and R. D. Jacobs, eds. , Southern Renas-
cence, 174-84.
_____, "William Faulkner: The Passion and the Penance,"
in Rubin, L. D. , Jr. , and R. D. Jacobs, eds. , South, 157-
63.
Kaplan, H. , "The Inert and the Violent: Faulkner's LIGHT
IN AUGUST," Passive Voice, 111-30.
Kazin, Alfred, "The Stillness in LIGHT IN AUGUST," PR,
XXIV (Fall, 1957), 519-38. Also in Kazin, A. , Con-
temporaries, 130-49. Also in Feidelson, C. , Jr. , and
P. Brodtkorb, Jr. , eds. , Interpretations of American Lit-
erature, 349-68. Also in Shapiro, C. , ed. , Twelve Orig-
inal Essays, 257-83. Also in Hoffman, F. J. , and O. W.
Vickery, eds. , William Faulkner, 247-65. Also in War-
ren, R. P. , ed. , Faulkner, 147-62.
Kimmey, John L. , "The Good Earth in LIGHT IN AUGUST,"
MissQ, XVII (Winter, 1963-64), 1-8.
Kirk, Robert W. , "Faulkner's Lena Grove," GaR, XXI
(Spring, 1967), 57-64.
Kunkel, Francis L. , "Christ Symbolism in Faulkner: Preva-
lence of the Human," Ren, XVII (Spring, 1965), 148-51.
Lamont, William H. F. , "The Chronology of LIGHT IN AU-
GUST," MFS, III (Winter, 1957-58), 360-1.
Langston, Beach, "The Meaning of Lena Grove and Gail
Hightower in LIGHT IN AUGUST," BUSE, V (Spring,
1961), 46-63.
Levith, Murray J. , "Unity in Faulkner's LIGHT IN AUGUST,"
Thoth, VII (Winter, 1966), 31-4.
Lind, Ilse D. , "The Calvinistic Burden of LIGHT IN AU-
GUST," NEQ, XXX (September, 1957), 307-29.
Longley, John L. , Jr. , "Faulkner's Byron Bunch," GaR, XV
(Summer, 1961), 197-208.
_____, "Joe Christmas: the Hero in the Modern World,"
VQR, XXXIII (Spring, 1957), 233-49. Also in Hoffman,
F. J. , and O. W. Vickery, eds. , William Faulkner, 265-
78. Also (revised) in Longley, J. L. , Jr. , Tragic Mask,
192-205. Also in Warren, R. P. , ed. , Faulkner, 163-74.
_____, Tragic Mask, 50-62.
McElderry, B. R. , Jr. , "The Narrative Structure of LIGHT
IN AUGUST," CE, XIX (February, 1958), 200-7. Also
in MissQ, XI (Fall, 1958), 177-87.
Millgate, M. , Achievement of William Faulkner, 124-37.
_____, William Faulkner, 44-52.
Miner, Ward L. , "Faulkner and Christ's Crucifixion," NM,
LVII (1956), 265.
Morrison, Sister Kristin, "Faulkner's Joe Christmas: Char-
acter Through Voice," TSLL, II (Winter, 1961), 419-43.

Moseley, E. M., Pseudonyms of Christ in the Modern Novel, 135-51.

Nemerov, H., "Calculation Raised to Mystery: The Dialectics of LIGHT IN AUGUST," Poetry and Fiction, 246-59.

Nilon, Charles H., "Faulkner and the Negro," UCSSLL, No. 8 (September, 1962), 73-93. Also in Nilon, C. H., Faulkner and the Negro, 73-93.

Noble, D. W., Eternal Adam and the New World Garden, 166-76.

O'Connor, William Van, "Protestantism in Yoknapatawpha County," Hopkins Rev, V, iii (Spring, 1952), 31-42. Also in Rubin, L. D., and R. D. Jacobs, Southern Renascence, 158-69.

_____, Tangled Fire of William Faulkner, 72-86.

_____, William Faulkner, 19-23. Also in O'Connor, W. V., ed., Seven Modern American Novelists, 133-5.

O'Faolain, S., Vanishing Hero, 101-4.

Pearce, Richard C., "Faulkner's One Ring Circus," WSCL, VII (Autumn, 1966), 270-83.

Pearson, Norman H., "Lena Grove," Shen, III (Spring, 1952), 3-7.

Pommer, Henry F., "LIGHT IN AUGUST: A Letter by Faulkner," ELN, IV (September, 1966), 47-8.

Powers, Lyall H., "Hawthorne and Faulkner and the Pearl of Great Price," PMASAL, LII (1967), 391-401.

Richardson, K. E., Force and Faith in the Novels of William Faulkner, 35-42, 80-7, 93-6.

Rinaldi, Nicholas M., "Game-Consciousness and Game-Metaphor in the Work of William Faulkner," DA, XXIV (1964), 4196-7 (Fordham).

Roberts, James L., "The Individual and the Community: Faulkner's LIGHT IN AUGUST," in McNeir, Waldo, and L. B. Levy, eds., Studies in American Literature (LSUSHS, No. 8), Baton Rouge: La. St. Un. Pr., 1960, 132-53.

Rovere, Richard, "Introduction," in LIGHT IN AUGUST, N. Y.: Modern Library, 1950.

Rubin, L. D., Jr., Curious Death of the Novel, 139-44. Also in Vandiver, Frank E., ed., The Idea of the South, Chicago: Un. of Chicago Pr., 1964, 32-6.

_____, Faraway Country, 60-2.

Sandstrom, Glenn, "Identity Diffusion: Joe Christmas and Quentin Compson," AQ, XIX (Summer, 1967), 207-23.

Shanaghan, Father Malachy M., O. S. B., "A Critical Analysis of the Fictional Technique of William Faulkner," DA, XX (1960), 4663 (Notre Dame).

Slabey, Robert M., "Faulkner's Geography and Hightower's House," AN&Q, III (February, 1965), 85-6.

_____, "Joe Christmas, Faulkner's Marginal Man," Phylon, XXI (Fall, 1960), 266-77.

_____, "Myth and Ritual in LIGHT IN AUGUST," TSLL, II (Autumn, 1960), 328-49.

Slatoff, W. J., Quest for Failure, 30-1, 36-7, 58-9, 65-6, 70-1, 84-5, 88-9, 109-10, 115-16, 139-41, 173-98, 259.

Smith, Hallet, "Summary of a Symposium on LIGHT IN AUGUST," MissQ, XI (Fall, 1958), 188-90.

Sowder, William J., "Christmas as Existentialist Hero," UR, XXX (June, 1964), 279-84.

Steinberg, Aaron, "Faulkner and the Negro," DA, XXVII (1966), 1385A (N. Y. U.).

Sullivan, William P., "William Faulkner and the Community," DA, XXII (1962), 4355 (Columbia).

Swiggart, P., Art of Faulkner's Novels, 41-7, 131-48.

Thompson, L., William Faulkner, 66-80, 193-5.

Tritschler, Donald H., "Whorls of Form in Faulkner's Fiction," DA, XVII (1957), 3025 (Northwestern).

Tuck, D., Crowell's Handbook of Faulkner, 46-55.

_____, "The Inwardness of Understanding," in Unterecker, John, ed., Approaches to the Twentieth Century Novel, N. Y.: Crowell, 1965, 79-107.

Vickery, Olga W., "Gavin Stevens: From Rhetoric to Dialectic," Faulkner Studies, II (Spring, 1953), 1-4.

_____, Novels of William Faulkner, 66-83.

Volpe, E. L., Reader's Guide to William Faulkner, 151-74.

Waggoner, H. H., William Faulkner, 100-20.

West, Ray B., Jr., "Faulkner's LIGHT IN AUGUST: A View of Tragedy," WSCL, I, i (Winter, 1960), 5-12. Also in West, R. B., Jr., Writer in the Room, 175-84.

Widmer, K., "Naturalism and the American Joe," Literary Rebel, 118-20.

Williams, John S., " 'The Final Copper Light of Afternoon': Hightower's Redemption," TCL, XIII (January, 1968), 205-15.

Yorks, Samuel A., "Faulkner's Woman: The Peril of Mankind," ArQ, XVII (Summer, 1961), 119-29.

Zink, Karl E., "William Faulkner: Form as Experience," SAQ, LIII (1954), 384-403, passim.

THE MANSION (See also SNOPES Trilogy)

Beck, Warren, "Faulkner in THE MANSION," VQR, XXXVI (Spring, 1960), 272-92.

Brooks, C., William Faulkner, 219-43, 412-14.

Brylowski, W., Faulkner's Olympian Laugh, 206-14.

Chugunov, Konstantin, "Faulkner's MANSION in the U. S.

S. R. ," Soviet Literature, (1962), 171-2.
Dirksen, Sherland N. , "William Faulkner's Snopes Family:
    THE HAMLET, THE TOWN, and THE MANSION," ESRS,
    XI, ii (December, 1962), 33-40.
Everett, W. K. , Faulkner's Art and Characters, 52-7.
Gold, J. , William Faulkner, 162-73.
Greene, Theodore M. , "The Philosophy of Life Implicit in
    Faulkner's THE MANSION," TSLL, II (Winter, 1961),
    401-18.
Gwynn, F. L. , and J. L. Blotner, eds. , Faulkner in the Uni-
    versity.
Howe, Irving, "Faulkner: End of a Road," NRep, CXLI
    (December 7, 1959), 17-21.
_____, William Faulkner, 110-14, 282-94.
Howell, Elmo, "Mink Snopes and Faulkner's Moral Conclu-
    sion," SAQ, LXVII (Winter, 1968), 13-22.
Hunt, J. W. , William Faulkner, 154-6.
Lawson, Lewis A. , "The Grotesque-Comic in the SNOPES
    Trilogy," in Manheim, L. , and E. , eds. , Hidden Pat-
    terns, 243-58. Also in L&P, XV (1965), 107-19.
Millgate, M. , Achievement of William Faulkner, 245-52.
_____, William Faulkner, 92-3.
Moses, W. R. , "The Limits of Yoknapatawpha County," GaR,
    XVI (Fall, 1962), 297-305.
O'Connor, William Van, "The Old Master, the Sole Pro-
    prietor," VQR, XXXVI (Winter, 1960), 147-51.
Richardson, K. E. , Force and Faith in the Novels of William
    Faulkner, 163-71.
Roberts, James L. , "Snopeslore: THE HAMLET, THE
    TOWN, THE MANSION," UKCR, XXVIII (1961), 65-71.
Rossky, William, "Faulkner: The Image of the Child in
    THE MANSION," MissQ, XV (1962), 17-20.
Tuck, D. , Crowell's Handbook of Faulkner, 86-94.
Vickery, O. W. , Novels of William Faulkner, 191-208.
Volpe, E. L. , Reader's Guide to William Faulkner, 331-43.
Whitbread, Thomas, "The Snopes Trilogy: The Setting of
    THE MANSION," in Sutherland, W. O. S. , ed. , Six Con-
    temporary Novels, 76-88.

MOSQUITOES

Adams, R. P. , Faulkner, 40-9.
Aiken, C. , "William Faulkner," New York Post (June 11,
    1927), Sec. III, 7. Also in Aiken, C. , Reviewer's ABC,
    197-200.
Brylowski, W. , Faulkner's Olympian Laugh, 48-51.
Carnes, Frank F. , "On the Aesthetics of Faulkner's Fic-

174   FAULKNER (cont.)

tion," DA, XXIX (1968), 894A-5A (Vanderbilt).
Davidson, Donald, Nashville Tennessean (July 3, 1927). Also
    in GaR, XX (Winter, 1966), 458-9.
Everett, W. K. , Faulkner's Art and Characters, 57-65.
Geismar, M. , Writers in Crisis, 148-50.
Gold, Joseph, "William Faulkner's 'One Compact Thing',"
    TCL, VIII, i (April, 1962), 3-4.
Gwynn, F. L. , and J. L. Blotner, eds. , Faulkner in the Uni-
    versity.
_____, "Faulkner's Prufrock- and Other Observations,"
    JEGP, LII (January, 1953), 63-70.
Harwick, Robert D. , "Humor in the Novels of William Faulk-
    ner," DA, XXVI (1965), 1646 (Nebraska).
Hoffman, F. J. , William Faulkner, 42-4.
Howe, I. , William Faulkner, 19-20.
Millgate, M. , Achievement of William Faulkner, 68-75.
_____, William Faulkner, 20-2.
O'Connor, W. V. , Tangled Fire of William Faulkner, 30-3.
_____, "William Faulkner's Apprenticeship," SWR,
    XXXVIII (Winter, 1953), 10-12.
Richardson, H. Edward, "Faulkner, Anderson, and Their
    Tall Tale," AL, XXXIV (May, 1962), 287-91.
_____, William Faulkner, 134-8.
Rideout, Walter B. , and James B. Meriwether, "On the Col-
    laboration of Faulkner and Anderson," AL, XXXV (March,
    1963), 85-7.
Roberts, James L. , "Experimental Exercises- Faulkner's
    Early Writings," Discourse, VI (Summer, 1963), 191-6.
Slabey, Robert M. , "Faulkner's MOSQUITOES and Joyce's
    ULYSSES," RLV, XXVIII, v (1962), 435-7.
Smart, G. K. , Religious Elements in Faulkner's Early
    Novels.
Stein, Randolph E. , "The World Outside Yoknapatawpha: A
    Study of Five Novels by William Faulkner," DA, XXVI
    (1965), 2225 (Ohio Un.).
Swiggart, P. , Art of Faulkner's Novels, 32-3.
Tuck, D. , Crowell's Handbook of Faulkner, 129-31.
Vickery, Olga W. , "Faulkner's MOSQUITOES," UKCR, XXIV
    (March, 1958), 219-24.
_____, Novels of William Faulkner, 8-14.
Volpe, E. L. , Reader's Guide to William Faulkner, 56-66.
Waggoner, H. H. , William Faulkner, 8-19.
Warren, Joyce W. , "Faulkner's 'Portrait of the Artist',"
    MissQ, XIX (Summer, 1966), 121-31.

THE OLD MAN (See also THE WILD PALMS)

Everett, W. K. , Faulkner's Art and Characters, 127-9.
Feaster, John, "Faulkner's OLD MAN: A Psychoanalytic
    Approach," MFS, XIII, i (Spring, 1967), 89-93.
Howell, Elmo, "William Faulkner and the Plain People of
    Yoknapatawpha County," Jnl of Miss Hist, XXIV (April,
    1962), 82-5.
Moses, W. R. , "Water, Water Everywhere: OLD MAN and
    A FAREWELL TO ARMS," MFS, V (Summer, 1959), 172-
    4.
Reed, John Q. , "Theme and Symbol in Faulkner's OLD
    MAN," EdL, XXI (January, 1958), 25-31.
Richardson, K. E. , Force and Faith in the Novels of William
    Faulkner, 96-9.
Stonesifer, Richard J. , "Faulkner's OLD MAN in the Class-
    room," CE, XVII (February, 1956), 254-7.
Swiggart, P. , Art of Faulkner's Novels, 51-7.
Taylor, Nancy D. , "The River of Faulkner and Mark Twain,"
    MissQ, XVI (Fall, 1963), 191-9, passim.
Tuck, D. , Crowell's Handbook of Faulkner, 136-42.
Watkins, Floyd C. , "William Faulkner, the Individual, and
    the World," GaR, XIV (Fall, 1960), 242-6.

PYLON

Adams, R. P. , Faulkner, 95-102.
Beach, J. W. , American Fiction, 149-50.
Brylowski, W. , Faulkner's Olympian Laugh, 117-20.
Cowley, M. , "Faulkner: Voodoo Dance," NRep, LXXXII
    (April 10, 1935), 254. Also in Cowley, M. , Think Back
    on Us, 268-71.
Everett, W. K. , Faulkner's Art and Characters, 65-9.
Geismar, M. , Writers in Crisis, 169-70.
Guereschi, Edward, "Ritual and Myth in William Faulkner's
    PYLON," Thoth, III (Spring, 1962), 101-10.
Hoffman, F. J. , William Faulkner, 80-2.
Howe, I. , William Faulkner, 215-20.
Longley, J. L. , Jr. , Tragic Mask, 133-7.
Marvin, John R. , "PYLON: The Definition of Sacrifice,"
    Faulkner Studies, I (Summer, 1952), 20-3.
Millgate, M. , Achievement of William Faulkner, 138-49.
————, "Faulkner and the Air: The Background of PY-
    LON," LitR, III (Winter, 1964), 271-7.
Monteiro, George, "Bankruptcy in Time: A Reading of Wil-
    liam Faulkner's PYLON," TCL, IV (Spring-Summer,
    1958), 9-20.

O'Connor, W. V. , Tangled Fire of William Faulkner, 89-93.
_____, William Faulkner, 23-5. Also in O'Connor, W.
    V. , ed. , Seven Modern American Novelists, 135-8.
Price, Reynolds, "PYLON: The Posture of Worship, Shen,
    XIX (Spring, 1968), 29-45.
Slatoff, W. J. , Quest for Failure, 95-6, 211-15.
Stein, Randolph E. , "The World Outside Yoknapatawpha: A
    Study of Five Novels by William Faulkner," DA, XXVI
    (1965), 2225 (Ohio Un.).
Swiggart, P. , Art of Faulkner's Novels, 27-9.
Torchiana, Donald T. , "Faulkner's PYLON and the Structure
    of Modernity," MFS, III (Winter, 1957-58), 291-308.
_____, "The Reporter in Faulkner's PYLON," HINL, IV
    (Spring, 1958), 33-9.
Tuck, D. , Crowell's Handbook of Faulkner, 132-5.
Vickery, O. W. , Novels of William Faulkner, 145-55.
Vickery, John B. , "William Faulkner and Sir Philip Sidney,"
    MLN, LXX (May, 1955), 349-50.
Volpe, E. L. , Reader's Guide to William Faulkner, 174-84.
Waggoner, H. H. , William Faulkner, 121-32, 145-7.

THE REIVERS

Adams, R. P. , Faulkner, 169-70.
Brooks, C. , William Faulkner, 349-68, 446.
Brylowski, W. , Faulkner's Olympian Laugh, 215-19.
Cronin, Mary A. , "Mississippi Revisited," Lit, No 5 (1964),
    11-14.
Everett, W. K. , Faulkner's Art and Characters, 69-73.
Gold, J. , William Faulkner, 174-87.
Harwick, Robert D. , "Humor in the Novels of William Faulk-
    ner," DA, XXVI (1965), 1646 (Nebraska).
Hoffman, F. J. , William Faulkner, 115-17.
Howell, Elmo, "In Ole Mississippi: Faulkner's Reminis-
    cence," KM (1965), 77-81.
Kerr, Elizabeth M. , "THE REIVERS: The Golden Book of
    Yoknapatawpha County," MFS, XIII, i (Spring, 1967),
    95-113.
Mellard, J. M. , "Faulkner's 'Golden Book': THE REIVERS
    as Romantic Comedy," BuR, XIII, iii (December, 1965),
    19-31.
Millgate, M. , Achievement of William Faulkner, 253-8.
Muehl, Lois, "Faulkner's Humor in Three Novels and One
    'Play'," LC, XXXIV (Spring, 1968), 78-93.
Mueller, William R. , "THE REIVERS: William Faulkner's
    Valediction," ChC, LXXX (September 4, 1963), 1079-81.
Rossky, William, "THE REIVERS and HUCKLEBERRY FINN:

Faulkner and Twain," HLQ, XXVIII (August, 1965), 373-87.
_____, "THE REIVERS: Faulkner's TEMPEST," MissQ,
XVIII (Spring, 1965), 82-93.
Swiggart, P., Art of Faulkner's Novels, 207-14.
Thompson, L., William Faulkner, 14-15.
Tuck, D., Crowell's Handbook of Faulkner, 121-4.
Vickery, O.W., Novels of William Faulkner, 228-39.
Volpe, E.L., Reader's Guide to William Faulkner, 343-9.

REQUIEM FOR A NUN

Adams, R.P., Faulkner, 157-8.
Babbage, Stuart B., The Mark of Cain: Studies in Litera-
ture and Theology, Grand Rapids: William B. Eerdmans,
1966, 75-7.
Baker, Carlos, "William Faulkner: The Doomed and the
Damned," in Bode, C., ed., Young Rebel in American
Literature, 163-6.
Baker, James R., "Ideas and Queries," Faulkner Studies,
I (Spring, 1952), 4-7.
Brooks, C., William Faulkner, 138-40, 394-5, 449-51.
Brown, William R., "Faulkner's Paradox in Pathology and
Salvation: SANCTUARY, LIGHT IN AUGUST, REQUIEM
FOR A NUN," TSLL, IX (1967), 429-49.
Brylowski, W., Faulkner's Olympian Laugh, 173-83.
English, H.M., "REQUIEM FOR A NUN," Furioso, VII
(Winter, 1952), 60-3.
Everett, W.K., Faulkner's Art and Characters, 73-7.
Gardiner, H.C., "Two Southern Tales," In All Conscience,
128-9. Also in America (October 6, 1951), 18.
Geismar, M., New York Post (September 23, 1951). Also
in American Moderns, 93-5.
Gold, J., William Faulkner, 94-110.
Graham, Philip, "Patterns in Faulkner's SANCTUARY and
REQUIEM FOR A NUN," TSL, VIII (1963), 39-46.
Guerard, Albert L., "REQUIEM FOR A NUN: An Examina-
tion," HarvardA, CXXXV (November, 1951), 19, 41-2.
Gwynn, F.L., and J.L. Blotner, eds., Faulkner in the Uni-
versity.
Hamblen, Abigail A., "Faulkner's Pillar of Endurance:
SANCTUARY and REQUIEM FOR A NUN," MQ, VI (Sum-
mer, 1965), 369-75.
Haugh, R.F., "Faulkner's Corrupt Temple," ESA, IV (March,
1961), 7-16.
Hawkins, E.O., Jr., "Jane Cook and Cecilia Farmer,"
MissQ, XVIII (Fall, 1965), 248-51.
Heilman, Robert B., "Schools for Girls," SR, LX (April-

June, 1952), 304-9.

Hoffman, F. J., William Faulkner, 109-11.

Howe, I., William Faulkner, 105-7, 114-15.

Jacobs, Robert D., "William Faulkner: The Passion and the Penance," in Rubin, L. D., Jr., and R.D. Jacobs, eds., South, 173-4.

McHaney, Thomas N., "Faulkner Borrows from the Mississippi Guide," MissQ, XIX (Summer, 1966), 116-20.

Millgate, M., Achievement of William Faulkner, 221-6.

_____, William Faulkner, 96-8.

O'Connor, W. V., Tangled Fire of William Faulkner, 157-9.

Richardson, K. E. Force and Faith in the Novels of William Faulkner, 150-4.

Simpson, Louis, "Isaac McCaslin and Temple Drake: The Fall of New World Man," in Sanford, D. E., ed., Nine Essays in Modern Literature, 101-6.

Slatoff, W. J., Quest for Failure, 208-10.

Swiggart, P., Art of Faulkner's Novels, 181-4.

Thompson, L., William Faulkner, 117-32, 198-9.

Tuck, D., Crowell's Handbook of Faulkner, 115-20.

Ulrey, Pamela A., "Faulkner's SANCTUARY and REQUIEM FOR A NUN: Songs of Innocence and Experience," DA, XXIV (1963), 2043-4 (Cornell).

Vickery, Olga W., "Gavin Stevens: From Rhetoric to Dialectic," Faulkner Studies, II (Spring, 1953), 1-4.

_____, Novels of William Faulkner, 114-23.

Volpe, E. L., Reader's Guide to William Faulkner, 265-81.

Waggoner, H. H., William Faulkner, 219-25.

West, Ray B., Jr., "William Faulkner: Artist and Moralist," WR, XVI (Winter, 1952), 162-7.

SANCTUARY

Adams, R. P., Faulkner, 59-71.

Backman, M., Faulkner, 41-9.

Beach, J. W., American Fiction, 131-2.

Beck, Warren, "Faulkner: A Preface and a Letter," YR, LII (Autumn, 1962), 157-60.

Bergel, Lienhard, "Faulkner's SANCTUARY," Expl, VI (December, 1947), Item 20.

Borgström, Greta I., "The Roaring Twenties and William Faulkner's SANCTUARY," MSpr, LXII (1968), 237-48.

Brooks, Cleanth, "Faulkner's SANCTUARY: The Discovery of Evil," SR, LXXI (Winter, 1963), 1-24. Also in William Faulkner, 116-40, 387-98.

_____, Hidden God, 25-6, 27-8.

Brown, James, "Shaping the World of SANCTUARY," UKCR,

XXV (Winter, 1958), 137-42.

Brown, William R. , "Faulkner's Paradox in Pathology and Salvation: SANCTUARY, LIGHT IN AUGUST, REQUIEM FOR A NUN," TSLL, IX (Autumn, 1967), 429-49.

Brylowski, W. , Faulkner's Olympian Laugh, 97-102.

Burgum, E. B. , Novel and the World's Dilemma, 217-20.

Campbell, Harry M. , and J. P. Pilkington," Faulkner's SANCTUARY," Expl, IV (June, 1946), Item 61.

_____, and R. E. Foster, William Faulkner, 61-2.

Cantwell, Robert, "Faulkner's 'Popeye'," Nation, CLXXXVI (February 15, 1958), 140-1, 148.

Chase, R. , "SANCTUARY vs. THE TURN OF THE SCREW," in American Novel and Its Tradition, 237-41.

Church, M. , "William Faulkner: Myth and Duration," Time and Reality, 237-8.

Cole, Douglas, "Faulkner's SANCTUARY: Retreat from Responsibility," WHR, XIV (Summer, 1960), 291-8.

Collins, Carvel, "Nathanael West's THE DAY OF THE LOCUST and SANCTUARY," Faulkner Studies, II (Summer, 1953), 23-4.

_____, "A Note on SANCTUARY," HarvardA, CXXXV (November, 1951), 16.

Cypher, James R. , "The Tangled Sexuality of Temple Drake," AI, XIX (Fall, 1962), 243-52.

Everett, W. K. , Faulkner's Art and Characters, 77-83.

Faulkner, William, "Introduction," in SANCTUARY, N. Y.: Modern Library, 1931. Also in Essays, Speeches and Public Letters by William Faulkner, ed. by James B. Meriwether, N. Y.: Random House, 1965, 176-8.

Fiedler, L. , Love and Death in the American Novel, 311-13.

Flynn, Robert, "The Dialectic of SANCTUARY," MFS, II (Autumn, 1956), 109-13.

Foster, Ruel, "Dream as Symbolic Act in Faulkner," Per, II (Summer, 1949), 191-4.

Frazier, David L. , "Gothicism in SANCTUARY: The Black Pall and the Crap Table," MFS, II (Autumn, 1956), 114-24.

Geismar, M. , Writers in Crisis, 159-61.

Gold, Joseph, "No Refuge: Faulkner's SANCTUARY," UR, XXXIII (December, 1966), 129-35.

Gossett, L. Y. , Violence in Recent Southern Fiction, 34-5.

Graham, Philip, "Patterns in Faulkner's SANCTUARY and REQUIEM FOR A NUN," TSL, VIII (1963), 39-46.

Gwynn, F. L. , and J. L. Blotner, eds. , Faulkner in the University.

Hamblen, Abigail A. , "Faulkner's Pillar of Endurance: SANCTUARY and REQUIEM FOR A NUN," MQ, VI (Sum-

mer, 1965), 369-75.

Hashiguchi, Yasuo, "Popeye Extenuated," KAL, No. 5 (1962), 1-9.

Haugh, R. F., "Faulkner's Corrupt Temple," ESA, IV (March, 1961), 7-16.

Hoffman, F. J., William Faulkner, 66-8.

Howe, I., William Faulkner, 57-61, 192-9.

Howell, Elmo, "The Quality of Evil in Faulkner's SANCTUARY," TSL, IV (1959), 99-107.

Jacobs, Robert D., "William Faulkner: The Passion and the Penance," in Rubin, L.D., Jr., and R.D. Jacobs, eds., South, 155-7.

Kubie, Lawrence S., "Literature of Horror; SANCTUARY," SRL, XI (October 20, 1934), 218+. Also in Warren, R. P., ed., Faulkner, 137-46.

Lisca, Peter, "Some New Light on Faulkner's SANCTUARY," Faulkner Studies, II (Spring, 1953), 5-9.

Malraux, André, "A Preface for Faulkner's SANCTUARY," YFS, No. 10 (Fall, 1952), 92-4.

Mason, Robert L., "A Defense of Faulkner's SANCTUARY," GaR, XXI (Winter, 1967), 430-8.

Massey, Linton, "Notes on the Unrevised Galleys of Faulkner's SANCTUARY," SB, VIII (1956), 195-208.

Meriwether, James B., "Some Notes on the Text of Faulkner's SANCTUARY, PBSA, LV (1961), 192-206.

Millgate, M., Achievement of William Faulkner, 113-23.

_____, " 'A Fair Job': A Study of Faulkner's SANCTUARY," REL, IV, iv (October, 1963), 47-62.

_____, William Faulkner, 41-4.

Monteiro, George, "Initiation and the Moral Sense in Faulkner's SANCTUARY, MLN, LXXIII (November, 1958), 500-4.

Nishiyama, Tamotsu, "What Really Happens in SANCTUARY?" SELit, XLII (1966), 235-43.

O'Connor, William Van, "A Short View of Faulkner's SANCTUARY," Faulkner Studies, I (Fall, 1952), 33-9.

_____, Tangled Fire of William Faulkner, 55-64.

_____, William Faulkner, 17-19. Also in O'Connor, W. V., ed., Seven Modern American Novelists, 131-3.

Richardson, K. E., Force and Faith in the Novels of William Faulkner, 77-80, 116-17.

Simpson, Louis, "Isaac McCaslin and Temple Drake: The Fall of New World Man," in Sanford, D. E., ed., Nine Essays in Modern Literature, 97-101.

Slabey, Robert M., "Faulkner's SANCTUARY," Expl, XXII (1963), Item 45.

Slatoff, W. J., Quest for Failure, 210-11.

Stein, William B., "The Wake in Faulkner's SANCTUARY,"
  MLN, LXXV (January, 1960), 28-9.
Swiggart, P., Art of Faulkner's Novels, 29-31, 208-11.
Tate, Allen, "Faulkner's SANCTUARY and the Southern
  Myth," VQR, XLIV (Summer, 1968), 418-27.
Thompson, L., William Faulkner, 99-116, 197-8.
Tuck, D., Crowell's Handbook of Faulkner, 40-5.
Ulrey, Pamela A., "Faulkner's SANCTUARY and REQUIEM
  FOR A NUN: Songs of Innocence and Experience," DA,
  XXIV (1963), 2043-4 (Cornell).
Vickery, O. W., Novels of William Faulkner, 103-14. Also
  in Warren, R. P., ed., Faulkner, 127-36.
Volpe, E. L., Reader's Guide to William Faulkner, 140-51.
Waggoner, H. H., William Faulkner, 88-100, 118-20.
Wasiolek, Edward, "Dostoevsky and SANCTUARY," MLN,
  LXXIV (February, 1959), 114-17.
Way, Brian, "William Faulkner," CritQ, III (Spring, 1961),
  44-7.
Williams, Aubrey, "William Faulkner's 'Temple' of Inno-
  cence," RIP, XLVII, iii (October, 1960), 51-67.
Wilson, C., Strength to Dream, 36-8.

SARTORIS

Adams, R. P., Faulkner, 49-56.
Backman, M., Faulkner, 3-12.
_____, "Faulkner's Sick Heroes: Bayard Sartoris and
  Quentin Compton," MFS, II (Autumn, 1956), 96-100.
Beach, J. W., American Fiction, 127-8.
Bell, Haney H., "A Reading of Faulkner's SARTORIS and
  THERE WAS A QUEEN," Forum (Texas), IV (Fall-Winter,
  1965), 23-6.
Brooks, C., William Faulkner, 100-15, 384-6, 450-1.
Bruccoli, Matthew, "A Source for SARTORIS?" MissQ, XX
  (1967), 163.
Brylowski, W., Faulkner's Olympian Laugh, 51-8.
Cantwell, Robert, "Introduction," in SARTORIS, N. Y.: Sig-
  net Bks., 1953, vii-xxv.
Carnes, Frank F., "On the Aesthetics of Faulkner's Fic-
  tion," DA, XXIX (1968), 894A-5A (Vanderbilt).
Carpenter, Richard C., "Faulkner's SARTORIS," Expl, XIV
  (April, 1956), Item 41.
Church, M., "William Faulkner: Myth and Duration," Time
  and Reality, 232-3.
Collins, Carvel, "Are These Mandalas?" L&P, III, v (1953),
  3-6.
Connolly, Thomas, in Krause, S. J., ed., Essays on De-

terminism, 37-9.

Davidson, Donald, Nashville Tennessean (April 14, 1929).
    Also in GaR, XX (Winter, 1966), 459-62.

Everett, W. K., Faulkner's Art and Characters, 83-94.

Geismar, M., Writers in Crisis, 146-7.

Gold, Joseph, "William Faulkner's 'One Compact Thing',"
    TCL, VIII, i (April, 1962), 7-9.

Gwynn, F. L., and J. L. Blotner, eds., Faulkner in the Uni-
    versity.

Hirano, Nobuyuki, "Reconsideration of Moral Order and Dis-
    order in Faulkner's Works," HJAS, VIII, i (September,
    1967), 7-11.

Hoffman, F. J., William Faulkner, 44-8.

Howe, I., William Faulkner, 12-13, 33-41.

Howell, Elmo, "Faulkner's SARTORIS," Expl, XVII (Febru-
    ary, 1959), Item 33.

_____, "Faulkner's SARTORIS and the Mississippi Country
    People," SFQ, XXV (June, 1961), 136-46.

Jacobs, Robert D., "William Faulkner: The Passion and the
    Penance," in Rubin, L. D., Jr., and R. D. Jacobs, eds.,
    South, 143-6.

Millgate, M., Achievement of William Faulkner, 76-85.

_____, William Faulkner, 22-6.

Muehl, Lois, "Faulkner's Humor in Three Novels and One
    'Play'," LC, XXXIV (Spring, 1968), 78-93.

Nilon, Charles H., "Faulkner and the Negro," UCSSLL, No.
    8 (September, 1962), 70-3. Also in Nilon, C. H., Faulk-
    ner and the Negro, 70-3.

Nishiyama, Tamotsu, "SARTORIS," KAL, No. 2 (May, 1959),
    28-32.

O'Connor, W. V., Tangled Fire of William Faulkner, 33-6.

_____, "William Faulkner's Apprenticeship," SWR,
    XXXVIII (Winter, 1953), 12-14.

Page, Ralph, "John Sartoris: Friend or Foe," ArQ, XXIII
    (Spring, 1967), 27-33.

Richardson, H. E., William Faulkner, 167-84.

Richardson, K. E., Force and Faith in the Novels of William
    Faulkner, 20-5.

Sartre, Jean-Paul, "William Faulkner's SARTORIS," YFS,
    No. 10 (Fall, 1952), 95-9. Also in Sartre, J.-P., Lit-
    erary and Philosophical Essays, 73-8.

Scholes, Robert, "Myth and Manners in SARTORIS," GaR,
    XVI (Summer, 1962), 195-201.

Smart, G. K., Religious Elements in Faulkner's Early Novels.

Swiggart, P., Art of Faulkner's Novels, 34-6.

Thompson, Lawrance, "Afterword," in SARTORIS, N. Y.:
    Signet Bks, 1964.

Tuck, D., <u>Crowell's Handbook of Faulkner,</u> 16-21.
Vickery, Olga W., "The Making of a Myth: SARTORIS,"
    <u>WR,</u> XXII (Spring, 1958), 209-19.
_____, <u>Novels of William Faulkner,</u> 15-27.
Volpe, E. L., <u>Reader's Guide to William Faulkner</u>, 66-76.
Waggoner, H. H., <u>William Faulkner,</u> 20-33.
Way, Brian, "William Faulkner," <u>CritQ,</u> III (Spring, 1961),
    43-4.

SNOPES Trilogy

Adams, Percy G., "Humor as Structure and Theme in Faulk-
    ner's Trilogy," <u>WSCL,</u> V, iii (Autumn, 1964), 205-12.
Adams, R. P., <u>Faulkner,</u> 158-61.
Barth, J. R., "Faulkner and the SNOPES Trilogy," <u>America,</u>
    CII (February 27, 1960), 638-40.
Beck, Warren, <u>Man in Motion: Faulkner's Trilogy,</u> Madi-
    son: Un. of Wisconsin Pr., 1961.
Bigelow, Gordon E., "Faulkner's SNOPES Saga," <u>EJ,</u> XLIX
    (December, 1960), 595-605.
Dirksen, Sherland N., "William Faulkner's Snopes Family:
    THE HAMLET, THE TOWN, and THE MANSION," <u>ESRS,</u>
    XI, ii (December, 1962), 5-45.
Farmer, Norman, Jr., "The Love Theme: A Principal
    Source of Thematic Unity in Faulkner's SNOPES Trilogy,"
    <u>TCL,</u> VIII (October, 1962-January, 1963), 111-23.
Farnham, James F., "Faulkner's Unsung Hero: Gavin
    Stevens," <u>ArQ,</u> XXI (Summer, 1965), 115-32.
Geismar, M., "The Meaning of Faulkner's Humor," <u>Ameri-</u>
    <u>can Moderns,</u> 101-6.
Hartt, J. N., <u>Lost Image of Man,</u> 89-92.
Howe, Irving, "Faulkner: End of a Road," <u>NRep,</u> CXLI
    (December 7, 1959), 17-21.
Howell, Elmo, "The Meaning of 'Snopesism'," <u>SSJ,</u> XXXI
    (Spring, 1966), 223-5.
Hyman, S. E., <u>Standards,</u> 259-63.
Kerr, Elizabeth M., "Snopes," <u>WSCL,</u> I, ii (Spring-Sum-
    mer, 1960), 66-84.
Lawson, Lewis A., "The Grotesque-Comic in the SNOPES
    Trilogy," <u>L&P,</u> XV (Spring, 1965), 107-19.
Leibowitz, Herbert A., "The Snopes Dilemma and the South,"
    <u>UKCR,</u> XXVIII (June, 1962), 273-84.
Létargez, Joseph, "William Faulkner's SNOPES Trilogy,"
    <u>RLV,</u> No. 5 (1961), 446-51.
Levine, Paul, "Love and Money in the SNOPES Trilogy,"
    <u>CE,</u> XXIII (December, 1961), 196-203.
Longley, J. L., Jr., <u>Tragic Mask,</u> 41-9, 63-78, 150-64.

Maclure, Millar, "Snopes- A Faulkner Myth," CanF, XXXIX
(February, 1960), 245-50.
Palmer, William J., "The Mechanistic World of SNOPES,"
MissQ, XX (1967), 185-94.
Podhoretz, N., "Faulkner in the Fifties: Snopesishness,"
Doings and Undoings, 24-9. Also in (slightly different
form) NY, XXXIII (June 1, 1957), 110.
Richardson, K. E., Force and Faith in the Novels of William
Faulkner, 118-29.
Roberts, James L., "Snopeslore: THE HAMLET, THE
TOWN, THE MANSION," UKCR, XXVIII (October, 1961),
65-71.
Ross, Maude C., "Moral Values of the American Woman as
Presented in Three Major American Authors," DA, XXV
(1965), 5262-3 (Texas).
Rubin, L. D., Jr., Faraway Country, 58-9.
Swiggart, P., Art of Faulkner's Novels, 195-202.
_____, "The SNOPES Trilogy," SR, LXVIII (Spring, 1960),
319-25. Also in Litz, A. W., ed., Modern American Fic-
tion, 194-200.
Tuck, D., Crowell's Handbook of Faulkner, 72-94.
Watson, James G., " 'The Snopes Dilemma': Morality and
Amorality in Faulkner's SNOPES Trilogy," DA, XXIX
(1968), 1237A-8A (Pittsburgh).

SOLDIERS' PAY

Adams, R. P., Faulkner, 34-40.
Beach, J. W., American Fiction, 125-6.
Bross, Addison C., "SOLDIERS' PAY and the Art of Aubrey
Beardsley," AQ, XIX (Spring, 1967), 3-23.
Brylowski, W., Faulkner's Olympian Laugh, 43-51.
Carnes, Frank F., "On the Aesthetics of Faulkner's Fic-
tion," DA, XXIX (1968), 894A-5A (Vanderbilt).
Church, M., "William Faulkner: Myth and Duration," Time
and Reality, 231-2.
Coffee, Jessie A., "Empty Steeples: Theme, Symbol, and
Irony in Faulkner's Novels," ArQ, XXIII (Autumn, 1967),
201-3.
Cooperman, S., World War I and the American Novel, 159-
61, passim.
Davidson, Donald, Nashville Tennessean (April 11, 1926).
Also in GaR, XX (Winter, 1966), 456-8.
Everett, W. K., Faulkner's Art and Characters, 94-101.
Frederick, John T., "Anticipation and Achievement in Faulk-
ner's SOLDIERS' PAY," ArQ, XXIII (Autumn, 1967), 243-
9.

Gold, Joseph, "William Faulkner's 'One Compact Thing',"
TCL, VIII, i (April, 1962), 6-7.
Gwynn, F. L., and J. L. Blotner, eds., Faulkner in the Uni-
versity.
Hirano, Nobuyuki, "Reconsideration of Moral Order and Dis-
order in Faulkner's Works," HJAS, VIII, i (September,
1967), 7-11.
Hoffman, F. J., William Faulkner, 40-2.
Howe, I., William Faulkner, 17-19.
Millgate, M., Achievement of William Faulkner, 61-7.
_____, William Faulkner, 18-20.
Nilon, Charles H., "Faulkner and the Negro," UCSSLL, No.
8 (September, 1962), 67-70.   Also in Nilon, C. H., Faulk-
ner and the Negro, 67-70.
O'Connor, W. V., Tangled Fire of William Faulkner, 27-30.
_____, "William Faulkner's Apprenticeship," SWR,
XXXVIII (Winter, 1953), 8-10.
Pritchett, V. S., "SOLDIERS' PAY," NS&Nation, XLI (June
2, 1951), 624-6.
Richardson, H. Edward, "The Decadence in Faulkner's
First Novel: The Faun, the Worm, and the Tower," EA,
XXI (July-September, 1968), 225-35.
_____, William Faulkner, 142-63.
Roberts, James L., "Experimental Exercises- Faulkner's
Early Writings," Discourse, VI (Summer, 1963), 186-91.
Slabey, Robert M., "SOLDIERS' PAY: Faulkner's First
Novel," RLV, XXX, iii (1964), 234-43.
Smart, G. K., Religious Elements in Faulkner's Early Nov-
els.
Stein, Randolph E., "The World Outside Yoknapatawpha: A
Study of Five Novels by William Faulkner," DA, XXVI
(1965), 2225 (Ohio Un.).
Swiggart, P., Art of Faulkner's Novels, 31-2.
Tuck, D., Crowell's Handbook of Faulkner, 125-8.
Vickery, Olga, "Faulkner's First Novel," WHR, XI (Sum-
mer, 1957), 251-6.
_____, Novels of William Faulkner, 1-8.
Volpe, E. L., Reader's Guide to William Faulkner, 49-56.
Waggoner, H. H., William Faulkner, 1-8, 15-19.

THE SOUND AND THE FURY

Absalom, H. P., "Order and Disorder in THE SOUND AND
THE FURY," DUJ, LVIII (December, 1965), 30-9.
Adams, Robert M., "Poetry in the Novel: or Faulkner
Esemplastic," VQR, XXIX (Summer, 1953), 420-34.
_____, Strains of Discord: Studies in Literary Openness,

Ithaca: Cornell Un. Pr., 1958, 190-4.

Adams, R.P., Faulkner, 215-48.

Allen, W., Modern Novel, 115-18.

Aswell, Duncan, "The Recollection and the Blood: Jason's Role in THE SOUND AND THE FURY," MissQ, XXI (Summer, 1968), 211-18.

Backman, M., Faulkner, 13-40.

＿＿＿＿, "Faulkner's Sick Heroes: Bayard Sartoris and Quentin Compton," MFS, II (Autumn, 1956), 100-08.

Backus, Joseph M., "Names of Characters in Faulkner's THE SOUND AND THE FURY," Names, VI (December, 1958), 226-33.

Bass, Eben, "Meaningful Images in THE SOUND AND THE FURY," MLN, LXXVI (December, 1961), 728-31.

Bassan, Maurice, "Benjy at the Monument," ELN, II (September, 1964), 46-50.

Baum, Catherine B., " 'The Beautiful One': Caddy Compson as Heroine of THE SOUND AND THE FURY," MFS, XIII, i (Spring, 1967), 33-44.

Beach, J.W., American Fiction, 128-31.

Beatty, Richard C., and others, eds., The Literature of the South, Chicago: Scott, Foresman, 1952, 626-7.

Bowling, Lawrence E., "Faulkner and the Theme of Innocence," KR, XX (Summer, 1958), 466-87.

＿＿＿＿, "Faulkner and the Theme of Isolation," GaR, XVIII (Spring, 1964), 50-66.

＿＿＿＿, "Faulkner: Technique of THE SOUND AND THE FURY," KR, X (Autumn, 1948), 552-66. Also in Hoffman, F.J., and O.W. Vickery, eds., William Faulkner: Two Decades of Criticism, 165-79.

＿＿＿＿, "Faulkner: The Theme of Pride in THE SOUND AND THE FURY," MFS, XI (Summer, 1965), 129-39.

Broderick, John C., "Faulkner's THE SOUND AND THE FURY," Expl, XIX (1960), Item 12.

Brooks, C., Hidden God, 40-3.

＿＿＿＿, "Primitivism in THE SOUND AND THE FURY," in English Institute Essays, 1952, 5-28.

＿＿＿＿, William Faulkner, 325-48, 443-6. Also, condensed, in Cowan, M.H., ed., Twentieth Century Interpretations of THE SOUND AND THE FURY, 63-70.

Brylowski, W., Faulkner's Olympian Laugh, 59-85.

Burgum, E.B., Novel and the World's Dilemma, 208-15.

Campbell, H.M., and R.E. Foster, William Faulkner, 50-60.

Carns, Frank F., "On the Aesthetics of Faulkner's Fiction," DA, XXIX (1968), 894A-5A (Vanderbilt).

Chase, R., American Novel and Its Tradition, 219-36.

Chisholm, William S., "Sentence Patterns in THE SOUND
    AND THE FURY," DA, XXV (1965), 7254-5 (Michigan).
Church, M., "William Faulkner: Myth and Duration," Time
    and Reality, 233-5.
Clerc, Charles, "Faulkner's THE SOUND AND THE FURY,"
    Expl, XXIV (November, 1965), Item 29.
Coffee, Jessie A., "Empty Steeples: Theme, Symbol, and
    Irony in Faulkner's Novels," ArQ, XXIII (Autumn, 1967),
    204-6.
_____, "Faulkner's THE SOUND AND THE FURY," Expl,
    XXIV (October, 1965), Item 21.
Collins, Carvel, "A Conscious Literary Use of Freud?"
    L&P, III, III (June, 1953), 2-4.
_____, "Faulkner's THE SOUND AND THE FURY," Expl,
    XVII (December, 1958), Item 19.
_____, "The Interior Monologues of THE SOUND AND
    THE FURY," in Malin, I., ed., Psychoanalysis and Am-
    erican Fiction, 223-43. Also in English Institute Essays,
    1952, 29-56. Also in Mass. Inst. of Tech. Publications
    in the Humanities, No. 6.
_____, in Griffin, William, ed., Literature in the Mod-
    ern World, 67-9.
_____, "Miss Quentin's Paternity Again," TSLL, II (Au-
    tumn, 1960), 253-60.
_____, "The Pairing of THE SOUND AND THE FURY and
    AS I LAY DYING," PULC, XVIII (Spring, 1957), 115-19.
    Also, condensed, in Cowan, M.H., ed., Twentieth Cen-
    tury Interpretations of THE SOUND AND THE FURY, 71-
    4.
_____, "William Faulkner, THE SOUND AND THE FURY,"
    in Stegner, W., ed., American Novel, 219-28.
Connolly, Thomas, in Krause, S.J., ed., Essays on Deter-
    minism, 39-41.
Cowan, Michael H., "Introduction," in Cowan, M.H., ed.,
    Twentieth Century Interpretations of THE SOUND AND THE
    FURY, 1-13.
Cross, Barbara M., "THE SOUND AND THE FURY: The
    Pattern of Sacrifice," ArQ, XVI (Spring, 1960), 5-16.
Dauner, Louise, "Quentin and the Walking Shadow: The Di-
    lemma of Nature and Culture," ArQ, XVIII (Summer,
    1965), 159-71. Also, condensed, in Cowan, M.H., ed.,
    Twentieth Century Interpretations of THE SOUND AND THE
    FURY, 75-80.
Dillingham, William B., "William Faulkner and the 'Tragic
    Condition'," Edda, LXVI (1966), 323-7.
Dorsch, Robert L., "An Interpretation of the Central Themes
    in the Work of William Faulkner," ESRS, XI, i (Septem-

ber, 1962), 21-6.
Dove, George N., "Shadow and Paradox: Imagery in THE
    SOUND AND THE FURY," in Burton, Thomas G., ed.,
    Essays in Memory of Christine Burleson in Language and
    Literature by Former Colleagues and Students, Johnson
    City: Res. Advisory Council, East Tennessee St. Un.,
    1969, 89-95.
Edel, Leon, "How to Read THE SOUND AND THE FURY,"
    The Modern Psychological Novel, rev. and enl., N.Y.:
    Grosset and Dunlop, 1964, 162-76.   Also in Burnshaw,
    Stanley, Varieties of Literary Experience, N.Y.: N.Y.U.
    Pr., 1962, 241-57.
_____, The Psychological Novel, 1900-1950, N.Y. and
    Philadelphia: Lippincott, 1955, 149-54.   Also in Edel,
    L., Modern Psychological Novel, N.Y.: Grosset, 1964,
    97-102.
England, Martha W., "Quentin's Story: Chronology and Ex-
    plication," CE, XXII (January, 1961), 228-35.
_____, "Teaching THE SOUND AND THE FURY," CE,
    XVIII (January, 1957), 221-4.
Everett, W.K., Faulkner's Art and Characters, 101-14.
Fasel, Ida, "A Conversation Between Faulkner and Eliot,"
    MissQ, XX (1967), 195-206.
_____, "Spatial Form and Spatial Time," WHR, XVI
    (Summer, 1962), 230-4.
Faulkner, William, "Faulkner Discusses THE SOUND AND
    THE FURY," in Cowan, M.H., ed., Twentieth Century
    Interpretations of THE SOUND AND THE FURY, 14-24.
_____, "1699-1945: The Compsons," Appendix to The
    Portable Faulkner, N.Y.: Modern Library, 1946. Rev.
    as Forward to Faulkner, W., THE SOUND AND THE
    FURY, N.Y.: Modern Library, 1946.   Also in Kirk, Ro-
    bert W., with Marvin Klotz, Faulkner's People, Berke-
    ley and Los Angeles: Un. of Calif. Pr., 1963, 38-49.
Fazio, Rocco R., "The Fury and the Design: Realms of
    Being and Knowing in Four Novels of William Faulkner,"
    DA, XXV (1964), 1910 (Rochester).
Foster, Ruel, "Dream as Symbolic Act in Faulkner," Per,
    II (Summer, 1949), 185-91.
Frederickson, Michael A., "A Note on 'The Idiot Boy' as a
    Probable Source for THE SOUND AND THE FURY,"
    MinnR, VI, iv (Winter, 1966), 368-70.
Freedman, William A., "The Technique of Isolation in THE
    SOUND AND THE FURY," MissQ, XV (Winter, 1961-62),
    21-6.
Friedman, M.J., Stream of Consciousness, 8-11.
Garmon, Gerald M., "Faulkner's THE SOUND AND THE

FURY, Expl, XXV (September, 1966), Item 2.

Gatlin, Jesse C., Jr., "Of Time and Character in THE SOUND AND THE FURY," HAB, XVII, ii (Autumn, 1966), 27-35.

Geismar, M., Writers in Crisis, 154-9.

Gibbons, Kathryn G., "Quentin's Shadow," L&P, XII (Winter, 1962), 16-24.

Gibson, William M., "Faulkner's THE SOUND AND THE FURY," Expl, XXII (January, 1963), Item 33.

Gold, Joseph, "Faulkner's THE SOUND AND THE FURY," Expl, XIX (February, 1961), Item 29.

Gossett, L. Y., Violence in Recent Southern Fiction, 38-41.

Graves, T. W., Jr., "A Portrait of Benjy," William & Mary Rev, II (Winter, 1964), 53-7.

Greer, Dorothy D., "Dilsey and Lucas: Faulkner's Use of the Negro as a Gauge of Moral Character," ESRS, XI, i (September, 1962), 44-54.

Gresset, Michel, "Psychological Aspects of Evil in THE SOUND AND THE FURY," MissQ, XIX (Summer, 1966), 143-53.

Griffin, Robert J., "Ethical Point of View in THE SOUND AND THE FURY," in Langford, R. E., ed., Essays in Modern American Literature, 55-64.

Gross, Beverly, "Form and Fulfillment in THE SOUND AND THE FURY," MLQ, XXIX (December, 1968), 439-49.

Guetti, James, Limits of Metaphor, Ithaca: Cornell Un. Pr., 1967, 148-53.

Gwynn, F. L., and J. L. Blotner, eds., Faulkner in the University.

_____, "Faulkner's Raskolnikov," MFS, IV (Summer, 1958), 169-72.

Hagopian, John V., "Nihilism in Faulkner's THE SOUND AND THE FURY," MFS, XIII, i (Spring, 1967), 45-55.

Hall, J. E., Lunatic Giant in the Drawing Room, 61-2.

Harris, Wendell V., "Faulkner's THE SOUND AND THE FURY," Expl, XXI (March, 1963), Item 54.

_____, "Of Time and the Novel," BuR, XVI (March, 1968), 114-29. (DAVID COPPERFIELD, NOSTROMO, THE SOUND AND THE FURY.)

Hathaway, Baxter, "The Meanings of Faulkner's Structures," EngR, XV (December, 1964), 22-7.

Hirano, Nobuyuki, "Reconsideration of Moral Order and Disorder in Faulkner's Works," HJAS, VIII, i (September, 1967), 11-19.

Hoffman, Frederick J., in French, W. G., and W. E. Kidd, eds., American Winners of the Nobel Literary Prize, 146-8.

_____, Twenties, 214-16.
_____, William Faulkner, 49-60.
Hornback, Vernon T., Jr., "The Uses of Time in Faulkner's
    THE SOUND AND THE FURY," PELL, I (Winter, 1965),
    50-8.
Howe, Irving, "The Passing of a World," in Cowan, M.H.,
    ed., Twentieth Century Interpretations of THE SOUND
    AND THE FURY, 33-9. Condensed from Howe, I., Wil-
    liam Faulkner, 46-8, 158-74.
_____, William Faulkner, 46-52, 123-4, 134-6, 157-74.
Howell, John M., "Hemingway and Fitzgerald in Sound and
    Fury," PLL, II (Summer, 1966), 234-42.
_____, "The Waste Land Tradition in the American Novel,"
    DA, XXIV (1964), 3337 (Tulane).
Humphrey, Robert, "Form and Function of Stream of Con-
    sciousness in William Faulkner's THE SOUND AND THE
    FURY," UKCR, XIX (Autumn, 1952), 34-40.
_____, Stream of Consciousness in the Modern Novel,
    17-20, 57-8, 65-70, 73-4, 106-11.
Hunt, J.W., William Faulkner, Chapter 2.   Also condensed,
    in Cowan, M.H., ed., Twentieth Century Interpretations
    of THE SOUND AND THE FURY, 83-92.
Izsak, Emily K., "The Manuscript of THE SOUND AND THE
    FURY: The Revisions in the First Section," SB, XX
    (1967), 189-202.
Jacobs, Robert D., "Faulkner's Tragedy of Isolation," in
    Rubin, L.D., and R.D. Jacobs, eds., Southern Renas-
    cence, 171-4, 179.
_____, "William Faulkner: The Passion and the Penance,"
    in Rubin, L.D., Jr., and R.D. Jacobs, eds., South, 146-
    53.
Kaluža, Irena, The Functioning of Sentence Structure in the
    Stream-of-Consciousness Technique of William Faulkner's
    THE SOUND AND THE FURY: A Study in Linguistic Sty-
    listics, Krakow: UJ, 1967.
Kermenli, Leylâ, William Faulkner's THE SOUND AND THE
    FURY," Litera, VIII (1965), 99-113.
Klotz, Marvin, "The Triumph Over Time: Narrative Form
    in William Faulkner and William Styron," MissQ, XVII
    (Winter, 1963-64), 10-12.
Labor, Earle, "Faulkner's THE SOUND AND THE FURY,"
    Expl, XVII (January, 1959), Item 29.
Lee, E.B., "A Note on the Ordonnance of THE SOUND AND
    THE FURY," Faulkner Studies, III (Summer-Autumn,
    1954), 37-9.
Lowrey, Perrin, "Concepts of Time in THE SOUND AND
    THE FURY," in English Institute Essays, 1952, 57-82. ·

Also, condensed, in Cowan, M. H., ed., Twentieth Century Interpretations of THE SOUND AND THE FURY, 53-62.

Meriwether, James B., "Notes on the Textual History of THE SOUND AND THE FURY," PBSA, LVI (1962), 285-316.

Millgate, Jane, "Quentin Compson as Poor Player: Verbal and Social Cliches in THE SOUND AND THE FURY," RLV, XXXIV (1968), 40-9.

Millgate, M., Achievement of William Faulkner, 86-103. Also in Warren, R. P., ed., Faulkner, 94-108.
_____, William Faulkner, 26-34.

Miner, Ward L., "Faulkner and Christ's Crucifixion," NM, LVII (1956), 260-2.

Mizener, A., Twelve Great American Novels, 147-59.

Morillo, Marvin, "Faulkner's THE SOUND AND THE FURY," Expl, XXIV (February, 1966), Item 50.

Mueller, W. R., "The Theme of Suffering: William Faulkner's THE SOUND AND THE FURY," Prophetic Voice, 110-35.

O'Connor, William Van, "THE SOUND AND THE FURY and the Impressionist Novel," Northern Rev (Montreal), VI (June-July, 1953), 17-22.
_____, Tangled Fire of William Faulkner, 37-45.
_____, William Faulkner, 11-14. Also in O'Connor, W. V., ed., Seven Modern American Novelists, 125-8.

O'Faolain, S., Vanishing Hero, 94-100.

O'Nan, Martha, The Role of Mind in Hugo, Faulkner, Beckett and Grass, N. Y.: Philosophical Library, 1969, 13-22.

Pate, Willard, "Benjy's Names in the Compson Household," FurmS, XV, iv (May, 1968), 37-8.

Peavy, Charles D., "Did You Ever Have a Sister? Holden, Quentin, and Sexual Innocence," FloQ, I, iii (Winter, 1968), 82-95.
_____, "The Eyes of Innocence: Faulkner's The Kingdom of God," PLL, II (Spring, 1966), 178-82.
_____, "Faulkner's Use of Folklore in THE SOUND AND THE FURY," JAF, LXXIX (July, 1966), 437-47.
_____, "A Note on the "Suicide Pact" in the SOUND AND THE FURY," ELN, V (March, 1968), 207-9.

Powell, Sumner C., "William Faulkner Celebrates Easter, 1928," Per, II (Summer, 1949), 195-218.

Powers, Lyall H., "Hawthorne and Faulkner and the Pearl of Great Price," PMASAL, LII (1967), 391-401.

Pratt, J. Norwood, "Faulkner's THE SOUND AND THE FURY," Expl, XXIII (January, 1965), Item 37.

Richardson, K. E. , Force and Faith in the Novels of William
    Faulkner, 24-9, 70-3, 100-3.
Rinaldi, Nicholas M. , "Game-Consciousness and Game-Meta-
    phor in the Work of William Faulkner," DA, XXIV (1964),
    4196-7 (Fordham).
Rodrigues, Eusebio L. , "Time and Technique in THE SOUND
    AND THE FURY," LCrit, VI, iv (1965), 61-7.
Rubin, L. D. , Jr. , Faraway Country, 54-8.
Ryan, Marjorie, "The Shakespearean Symbolism in THE
    SOUND AND THE FURY," Faulkner Studies, II (Autumn,
    1953), 40-3.
Sandstrom, Glenn, "Identity Diffusion: Joe Christmas and
    Quentin Compson," AQ, XIX (Summer, 1967), 207-23.
Sartre, J. -P. , "On THE SOUND AND THE FURY: Time in
    the Work of Faulkner," Literary and Philosophical Essays,
    79-87. Also as "Time in Faulkner: THE SOUND AND
    THE FURY," in Hoffman, F. J. , and O. W. Vickery, eds. ,
    William Faulkner: Three Decades of Criticism, 225-32.
    Also in Hoffman, F. J. , and O. W. Vickery, eds. , William
    Faulkner: Two Decades of Criticism, 180-8. Also in
    Warren, R. P. , ed. , Faulkner, 87-93.
Scott, Evelyn, in Cowan, M. H. , ed. , Twentieth Century In-
    terpretations of THE SOUND AND THE FURY, 25-9.
Simpson, Hassell A. , "Faulkner's THE SOUND AND THE
    FURY. Appendix," Expl, XXI (December, 1962), Item 27.
Slabey, Robert M. , "Quentin Compson's 'Lost Childhood',"
    SSF, I (Spring, 1964), 173-83.
_____, "The 'Romanticism' of THE SOUND AND THE
    FURY," MissQ, XVI (Summer, 1963), 146-59. Also, con-
    densed, in Cowan, M. H. , ed. , Twentieth Century Interpre-
    tations of THE SOUND AND THE FURY, 81-2.
Slatoff, Walter J. , "The Edge of Order: The Pattern of
    Faulkner's Rhetoric," TCL, III (October, 1957), 107-27.
    Also in Slatoff, W. J. , Quest for Failure, 137-9, 155-8.
    Also, condensed, in Cowan, M.H. , ed. , Twentieth Century
    Interpretations of THE SOUND AND THE FURY, 93-6.
_____, Quest for Failure, 12-13, 69-70, 138-9, 149-58,
    254-5.
Steinberg, Aaron, "Faulkner and the Negro," DA, XXVII
    (1966), 1385A (N. Y. U).
Stewart, George R. , and Joseph M. Backus, " 'Each in Its
    Ordered Place': Structure and Narrative in 'Benjy's Sec-
    tion' of THE SOUND AND THE FURY," AL, XXIX (Janu-
    ary, 1958), 440-56.
Strandberg, Victor, "Faulkner's Poor Parson and the Tech-
    nique of Inversion (or William Faulkner: An Epitaph),"
    SR, LXXIII (Spring, 1965), 184-90.

Swiggart, P., Art of Faulkner's Novels, 38-40, 61-70, 87-107.

_____, "Faulkner's THE SOUND AND THE FURY," Expl, XXII (December, 1963), Item 31.

_____, "Moral and Temporal Order in THE SOUND AND THE FURY," SR, LXI (Spring, 1953), 221-37.

Thompson, Lawrance, "Mirror Analogues in THE SOUND AND THE FURY," in English Institute Essays, 1952, 83-106. Also in Hoffman, F.J., and O.W. Vickery, eds., William Faulkner, 211-25. Also in Westbrook, M., ed., Modern American Novel, 134-53. Also in Warren, R.P., ed., Faulkner, 109-21.

_____, William Faulkner, 29-52, 187-91.

Tilley, Winthrop, "The Idiot Boy in Mississippi: Faulkner's THE SOUND AND THE FURY," American Jnl of Mental Deficiency, LIX (January, 1955), 374-7.

Tuck, D., Crowell's Handbook of Faulkner, 22-33.

Underwood, Henry J., Jr., "Sartre on THE SOUND AND THE FURY: Some Errors," MFS, XII (Winter, 1966-67), 477-9.

Vahanian, Gabriel, "William Faulkner: Rendez-vous with Existence," Wait Without Idols, N.Y.: Braziller, 1964, 93-116.

Van Nostrand, A.D., "The Poetic Dialogues of William Faulkner," Every Man His Own Poet, 181-4.

Vickery, Olga W., "THE SOUND AND THE FURY: A Study in Perspective," PMLA, LXIX (December, 1954), 1017-37. Also in Vickery, O.W., Novels of William Faulkner, 28-49. Also, condensed, in Cowan, M.H., ed., Twentieth Century Interpretations of THE SOUND AND THE FURY, 40-52.

Volpe, E.L., "Chronology and Scene Shifts in Benjy's and Quentin's Sections," in Cowan, M.H., ed., Twentieth Century Interpretations of THE SOUND AND THE FURY, 103-8. Adapted from Volpe, E.L., Reader's Guide to William Faulkner, 353, 363-5, 373-7.

_____, Reader's Guide to William Faulkner, 87-126.

Waggoner, H.H., William Faulkner, 34-61. Also, condensed, in Cowan, M.H., ed., Twentieth Century Interpretations of THE SOUND AND THE FURY, 97-101.

Walters, Paul S., "Theory and Practice in Faulkner: THE SOUND AND THE FURY," ESA, X (March, 1967), 22-39.

Way, Brian, "William Faulkner," CritQ, III (Spring, 1961), 47-9.

Weisgerber, Jean, "Faulkner and Dostoievski: THE SOUND AND THE FURY," RLC, XXXIX (1965), 406-21.

Whicher, Stephen E., "The Compsons' Nancies: A Note on

THE SOUND AND THE FURY and 'That Evening Sun',"
  AL, XXVI (May, 1954), 253-5.
Wilder, Amos N., Theology and Modern Literature, Cam-
  bridge: Harvard Un. Pr., 1958, 119-28.
Young, James D., "Quentin's Maundy Thursday," TSE, X
  (1960), 143-51.

THE TOWN (See also SNOPES Trilogy)

Brooks, C., William Faulkner, 192-218.
Brylowski, W., Faulkner's Olympian Laugh, 201-6.
Dirksen, Sherland N., "William Faulkner's Snopes Family:
  THE HAMLET, THE TOWN, and THE MANSION," ESRS,
  XI, ii (December, 1962), 23-32.
Everett, W. K., Faulkner's Art and Characters, 115-19.
Gold, Joseph, "Truth or Consequences: Faulkner's THE
  TOWN," MissQ, XIII (Summer, 1960), 112-16.
_____, William Faulkner, 148-61.
Gwynn, F. L., and J. L. Blotner, eds., Faulkner in the Uni-
  versity.
Harder, Kelsie B., "Proverbial Snopeslore," TFSB, XXIV
  (1958), 89-95.
Howe, I., William Faulkner, 107-10, 282-94.
Kazin, A., Contemporaries, 150-4.
Lawson, Lewis A., "The Grotesque-Comic in the SNOPES
  Trilogy," in Manheim, L. and E., eds., Hidden Patterns,
  243-58. Also in L&P, XV (1965), 107-19.
Longley, John L., "Galahad Gavin and a Garland of Snopeses,"
  VQR, XXXIII (Autumn, 1957), 623-8.
Lytle, Andrew, "THE TOWN: Helen's Last Stand," SR, LXV
  (Summer, 1957), 475-84. Also in Lytle, A., Hero with
  the Private Parts, 137-47.
Marcus, Steven, "Faulkner's Town: Mythology as History,"
  PR, XXIV (Summer, 1957), 432-41. Also in Hoffman, F.
  J., and O. W. Vickery, eds., William Faulkner, 382-91.
Meriwether, James B., "The Snopes Revisited," SatR (April
  27, 1957), 12-13.
Millgate, M., Achievement of William Faulkner, 235-44.
_____, William Faulkner, 90-2.
Mooney, Stephen L., "Faulkner's THE TOWN: A Question of
  Voices," MissQ, XIII (Summer, 1960), 117-22.
Richardson, K. E., Force and Faith in the Novels of William
  Faulkner, 124-6.
Roberts, James L., "Snopeslore: THE HAMLET, THE
  TOWN, THE MANSION," UKCR, XXVIII (1961), 65-71.
Rogers, Thomas H., "Farce and Anecdote," ChiR, VI (Au-
  tumn, 1957), 110-14.

Rubin, Louis D., Jr., "Snopeslore: or, Faulkner, Clears
the Deck," WR, XXII (Autumn, 1957), 73-6.
Shanaghan, Father Malachy M., O.S.B., "A Critical Analy-
sis of the Fictional Techniques of William Faulkner," DA,
XX (1960), 4663 (Notre Dame).
Slatoff, W.J., Quest for Failure, 204-5.
Sullivan, William P., "William Faulkner and the Community,"
DA, XXII (1962), 4355 (Columbia).
Swiggart, P., Art of Faulkner's Novels, 195-202.
Thompson, L., William Faulkner, 148-58, 200-2.
Thonan, Robert, "William Faulkner: From THE HAMLET to
THE TOWN," ESA, II (September, 1959), 190-202.
Tuck, D., Crowell's Handbook of Faulkner, 81-6.
Vickery, O.W., Novels of William Faulkner, 181-91.
Volpe, E.L., Reader's Guide to William Faulkner, 317-31.
Waggoner, H.H., William Faulkner, 232-7.

THE WILD PALMS

Adams, R.P., Faulkner, 111-14.
Backman, M., Faulkner, 127-38.
_____, "Faulkner's THE WILD PALMS: Civilization
Against Nature," UKCR, XXVIII (March, 1962), 199-204.
Baker, Carlos, "William Faulkner: The Doomed and the
Damned," in Bode, C., ed., Young Rebel in American Lit-
erature, 160-3.
Beach, J.W., American Fiction, 150-2, passim.
Brylowski, W., Faulkner's Olympian Laugh, 127-39.
Church, M., "William Faulkner: Myth and Duration," Time
and Reality, 243-4.
Everett, W.K., Faulkner's Art and Characters, 124-7.
Galharn, Carl, "Faulkner's Faith: Roots from THE WILD
PALMS," TCL, I (October, 1955), 139-60.
Gwynn, F.L., and J.L. Blotner, eds., Faulkner in the Uni-
versity.
Hoffman, Frederick J., in French, W.G., and W.E. Kidd,
eds., American Winners of the Nobel Literary Prize, 143-
5.
_____, William Faulkner, 83-5.
Howe, I., William Faulkner, 233-42.
Jewkes, W.T., "Counterpoint in Faulkner's THE WILD
PALMS," WSCL, II, i (Winter, 1961), 39-53.
Merton, Thomas, "Baptism in the Forest: Wisdom and Initi-
ation in William Faulkner," in Panichas, G.A., ed., Man-
sions of the Spirit, 34-42. Also (excerpted) in CathW,
CCVII (June, 1968), 128-30.
Millgate, M., Achievement of William Faulkner, 171-9.

_____, William Faulkner, 69-73.
Moldenhauer, Joseph J., "Unity of Theme and Structure in
    THE WILD PALMS," in Hoffman, F. J., and O. W. Vick-
    ery, eds., William Faulkner, 305-22.
Moses, W. R., "The Unity of THE WILD PALMS," MFS, II
    (Autumn, 1956), 125-31.
O'Connor, William Van, "Faulkner, Hemingway, and the
    1920's," in Langford, R. E., and Taylor, W. E., eds.,
    Twenties, 95-8.
_____, William Faulkner, 29-31. Also, revised, in O'-
    Connor, W. V., ed., Seven Modern American Novelists,
    142-4.
Reeves, Caroline H., "THE WILD PALMS: Faulkner's Cha-
    otic Cosmos," MissQ, XX (1967), 148-57.
Richards, Lewis A., "The Literary Styles of Jean-Paul
    Sartre and William Faulkner: An Analysis, Comparison
    and Contrast," DA, XXIV (1964), 3755-6 (So. Calif.).
Richardson, H. Edward, "The 'Hemingwaves' in Faulkner's
    WILD PALMS," MFS, IV (Winter, 1958-59), 357-60.
Richardson, K. E., Force and Faith in the Novels of William
    Faulkner, 67-70, 96-9, 117-18.
Slatoff, W. J., Quest for Failure, 205-8.
Stein, Randolph E., "The World Outside Yoknapatawpha: A
    Study of Five Novels by William Faulkner," DA, XXVI
    (1965), 2225 (Ohio Un.).
Swiggart, P., Art of Faulkner's Novels, 51-7.
Tuck, D., Crowell's Handbook of Faulkner, 136-42.
Vickery, O. W., Novels of William Faulkner, 156-66.
Volpe, E. L., Reader's Guide to William Faulkner, 212-30.
Waggoner, H. H., William Faulkner, 121-2, 132-47.
Way, Brian, "William Faulkner," CritQ, III (Spring, 1961),
    51-3.

                         BIBLIOGRAPHY

Beebe, Maurice, "Criticism of William Faulkner: A Se-
    lected Checklist," MFS, XIII, i (Spring, 1967), 115-61.
Massey, Linton R., comp., "Man Working," 1919-1962,
    William Faulkner, A Catalogue of the William Faulkner
    Collections at the University of Virginia, Charlottesville:
    Un. Pr. of Virginia, 1968.
Sleeth, Irene L., "William Faulkner: A Bibliography of
    Criticism," TCL, VIII (April, 1962), 18-43.
Vickery, Olga W., "A Selective Bibliography," in Hoffman,
    F. J., and O. W. Vickery, eds., William Faulkner, 393-
    428.

FIELDING, GABRIEL, PSEUD. (ALAN GABRIEL BARNS-LEY), 1916-

GENERAL

Grande, Brother Luke M., F.S.C., "Gabriel Fielding, New
    Master of the Catholic Classic?" CathW, CXCVII (June,
    1963), 172-9.
Stanford, Derek, "Gabriel Fielding and the Catholic Novel,"
    Month, CCXII (December, 1961), 352-6.
Towne, Frank, "The Tragicomic Moment in the Art of Gabri-
    el Fielding," in Grosshans, H., ed., To Find Something
    New, 104-16.

THE BIRTHDAY KING

Bowers, Frederick, "Gabriel Fielding's THE BIRTHDAY
    KING," QQ, LXXIV (Spring, 1967), 149-58.
Grande, Brother Luke M., F.S.C., "Gabriel Fielding, New
    Master of the Catholic Classic?" CathW, CXCVII (June,
    1963), 172-9.
Kunkel, Francis L., "Clowns and Saviors: Two Contempo-
    rary Novels," Ren, XVIII (Autumn, 1965), 40-4.
Towne, Frank, "The Tragicomic Moment in the Art of Gab-
    riel Fielding," in Grosshans, H., ed., To Find Something
    New, 111-13.

BROTHERLY LOVE

Towne, Frank, "The Tragicomic Moment in the Art of Gab-
    riel Fielding," in Grosshans, H., ed., To Find Something
    New, 105-7.

EIGHT DAYS

Towne, Frank, "The Tragicomic Moment in the Art of Gab-
    riel Fielding," in Grosshans, H., ed., To Find Something
    New, 110-11.

GENTLEMEN IN THEIR SEASON

"Novels of 1966. Gabriel Fielding, GENTLEMEN IN THEIR
    SEASON," in T.L.S. Essays and Reviews, 1966, 69-71.
    Also in TLS (June 23, 1966).
Towne, Frank, "The Tragicomic Moment in the Art of Gab-
    riel Fielding," in Grosshans, H., ed., To Find Something

New, 113-16.

IN THE TIME OF GREENBLOOM

Bowers, Frederick, "The Unity of Fielding's GREENBLOOM,"
Ren, XVIII (Spring, 1966), 147-55.
Price, Martin, in YaleR, XLVII (Autumn, 1957), 143-6.
Towne, Frank, "The Tragicomic Moment in the Art of Gab-
riel Fielding," in Grosshans, H., ed., To Find Something
New, 107-9.

THROUGH STREETS BROAD AND NARROW

Stanford, Derek, "Gabriel Fielding and the Catholic Novel,"
Month, CCXII (December, 1961), 352-6.
Towne, Frank, "The Tragicomic Moment in the Art of Gab-
riel Fielding," in Grosshans, H., ed., To Find Something
New, 109-10.

FISHER, VARDIS, 1895-

GENERAL

Bishop, J. P., "The Strange Case of Vardis Fisher," SoR,
(Autumn, 1937), 348-59.   Also in Bishop, J. P., Collected
Essays, 56-65.
Day, George F., "The Uses of History in the Novels of Var-
dis Fisher," DA, XXIX (1968), 1225A (Colorado).
Fisher, Vardis, "The Novelist and His Characters," ABC,
XIV (September, 1963), 25-30.
_____, "The Novelist and His Work," Thomas Wolfe as I
Knew Him and Other Essays, Denver: Alan Swallow, 1963,
103-15.
Flora, Joseph M., "The Early Power of Vardis Fisher,"
ABC, XIV (September, 1963), 15-19.
_____, Vardis Fisher.
Snell, G., Shapers of American Fiction, 276-88.
Swallow, Alan, "The Mavericks," Crit, II, iii (Winter, 1959),
79-84.
Taber, Ronald W., "Vardis Fisher: New Directions for the
Historical Novel," WAL, I (Winter, 1967), 285-96.

ADAM AND THE SERPENT
(See also THE TESTAMENT OF MAN Series)

Flora, J. M., Vardis Fisher, 84-5.

APRIL: A FABLE OF LOVE

Flora, J.M., Vardis Fisher, 109-13.

CHILDREN OF GOD: AN AMERICAN EPIC

Davis, David B., "CHILDREN OF GOD: An Historian's Eval-
uation," WHR, VIII (Winter, 1953-54), 49-56.
Flora, J.M., Vardis Fisher, 131-8.
Snell, G., Shapers of American Fiction, 285-6.

CITY OF ILLUSION

Flora, J.M., Vardis Fisher, 129-31.

DARK BRIDWELL

Flora, J.M., Vardis Fisher, 106-9.

DARKNESS AND THE DEEP
(See also THE TESTAMENT OF MAN Series)

Flora, J.M., Vardis Fisher, 74-8.

THE DIVINE PASSION
(See also THE TESTAMENT OF MAN Series)

Flora, J.M., Vardis Fisher, 85-7.

A GOAT FOR AZAZEL
(See also THE TESTAMENT OF MAN Series)

Flora, J.M., Vardis Fisher, 92-3.

THE GOLDEN ROOMS
(See also THE TESTAMENT OF MAN Series)

Duncan Kirby L., "William Golding and Vardis Fisher: A
Study in Parallels and Extensions," CE, XXVII (December,
1965), 232-5.
Flora, J.M., Vardis Fisher, 78-82.

IN TRAGIC LIFE
(See also THE VRIDAR HUNTER Tetralogy)

Bishop, J.B., "The Strange Case of Vardis Fisher," Collected Essays, 56-65. Also in SoR (Autumn, 1937).

Flora, J. M. , <u>Vardis Fisher</u>, 35-6, 67-8.
Snell, G. , <u>Shapers of American Fiction</u>, 281-5.

INTIMATIONS OF EVE
(See also THE TESTAMENT OF MAN Series)

Flora, J. M. , <u>Vardis Fisher</u>, 82-4.

THE ISLAND OF THE INNOCENT
(See also THE TESTAMENT OF MAN Series)

Flora, J. M. , <u>Vardis Fisher</u>, 89-91.

JESUS CAME AGAIN
(See also THE TESTAMENT OF MAN Series)

Flora, J. M. , <u>Vardis Fisher</u>, 91-2.

THE MOTHERS: AN AMERICAN SAGA OF COURAGE

Flora, J. M. , <u>Vardis Fisher</u>, 119-22.
Robinson, Francis C. , "The Donner Party in Fiction," in
    Emery, J. K. , ed. , <u>University of Colorado Studies</u> (Series
    in Language and Literature, 10), Boulder: Un. of Colora-
    do Pr. , 1966, 87-93.

MOUNTAIN MAN

Angleman, Sydney W. , <u>UHQ</u>, XXXIV (Fall, 1966), 349-50.

MY HOLY SATAN
(See also THE TESTAMENT OF MAN Series)

Flora, J. M. , <u>Vardis Fisher</u>, 95-7.

NO VILLAIN NEED BE
(See also THE VRIDAR HUNTER Tetralogy)

Flora, J. M. , <u>Vardis Fisher</u>, 45-8, 53-4, 69-70.

ORPHANS IN GETHSEMANE
(See also THE TESTAMENT OF MAN Series)

Flora, J. M. , <u>Vardis Fisher</u>, 49-72.

PASSIONS SPIN THE PLOT
(See also THE VRIDAR HUNTER Tetralogy)

Flora, J.M., Vardis Fisher, 36-7, 68-9.
Lyons, J.O., College Novel in America, 85-7.

PEACE LIKE A RIVER
(See also THE TESTAMENT OF MAN Series)

Flora, J.M., Vardis Fisher, 93-5.

PEMMICAN

Flora, J.M., Vardis Fisher, 124-8.

TALE OF VALOR

Flora, J.M., Vardis Fisher, 122-4.

THE TESTAMENT OF MAN Series

Fisher, Vardis, "Vardis Fisher Comments on His TESTA-
    MENT OF MAN Series," ABC, XIV (September, 1963),
    31-6. Also in Fisher, V., Thomas Wolfe as I Knew Him
    and Other Essays, Denver: Alan Swallow, 1963, 64-78.
Flora, J.M., Vardis Fisher, 73-98.
Margarick, P., "Vardis Fisher and His TESTAMENT OF
    MAN," ABC, XIV (September, 1963), 20-4.
Thomas, Alfred K., "The Epic of Evolution, Its Etiology and
    Art: A Study of Vardis Fisher's TESTAMENT OF MAN,"
    DA, XIX (1968), 277A-8A (Penn State).

TOILERS OF THE HILLS

Flora, Joseph M., "The Early Power of Vardis Fisher,"
    ABC, XIV (September, 1963), 15-19.
_____, Vardis Fisher, 99-106.
Folsom, J.K., American Western Novel, 185-6.

THE VALLEY OF VISION
(See also THE TESTAMENT OF MAN Series)

Flora, J.M., Vardis Fisher, 87-9.

THE VRIDAR HUNTER Tetralogy

Flora, J.M., Vardis Fisher, 26-48, 52-9.

WE ARE BETRAYED
(See also THE VRIDAR HUNTER Tetralogy)

Flora, J.M., <u>Vardis Fisher,</u> 37-9.

BIBLIOGRAPHY

Flora, J.M., <u>Vardis Fisher,</u> 149-52.

FOOTE, SHELBY, 1916-

GENERAL

Breit, Harvey, "Talk With Shelby Foote," <u>NYTBR</u> (April 27, 1952), 16.

FOLLOW ME DOWN

Sullivan, Walter, in Rubin, L.D., Jr., and R.D. Jacobs, eds., <u>South,</u> 377-9.

FOWLES, JOHN, 1926-

THE COLLECTOR

Churchill, Thomas, "Waterhouse, Storey, and Fowles: <u>Which Way Out of the Room</u>?" <u>Crit,</u> X, iii (1968), 72-87.

THE FRENCH LIEUTENANT'S WOMAN

Fowles, John, "Notes on an Unfinished Novel," in McCormack, T., ed., <u>Afterwards,</u> 160-75.

THE MAGUS

Churchill, Thomas, "Waterhouse, Storey, and Fowles: <u>Which Way Out of the Room</u>?" <u>Crit,</u> X, iii (1968), 72-87.

FRAME, JANET, 1924-

GENERAL

Frame, Janet, "Beginnings," <u>Landfall,</u> XIX (March, 1965), 40-7.

OWLS DO CRY

Stevens, J., <u>New Zealand Novel,</u> 98-100, 121-3.

SCENTED GARDENS FOR THE BLIND

Hyman, S. E., "Reason in Madness," Standards, 239-43.

FRIEDMAN, BRUCE JAY, 1930-

A MOTHER'S KISSES

Schulz, M. F., "Wallant and Friedman: The Glory and Agony
    of Love," Crit, X, iii (1968), 31-47. Also in Schulz, M.
    F., Radical Sophistication, 186-97.
Sherman, B., Invention of the Jew, 224-8.

STERN

Hyman, S. E., "An Exceptional First Novel," Standards, 98-
    102.
Kaplan, Charles, "Escape into Hell: Friedman's STERN,"
    CEJ, I (1965), 25-30.
Schulz, M. F., "Wallant and Friedman: The Glory and Agony
    of Love," Crit, X, iii (1968), 31-47. Also in Schulz, M.
    F., Radical Sophistication, 186-97.
Trachtenberg, Stanley, "The Humiliated Hero: Bruce Jay
    Friedman's STERN," Crit, VII (Spring-Summer, 1965), 91-
    3.

GASS, WILLIAM HOWARD, 1924-

OMENSETTER'S LUCK

Gass, William, "A Letter to the Editor," in McCormack,
    T., ed., Afterwords, 89-105.
Gilman, R., Confusion of Realms, 69-79.

GODDEN, RUMER, 1907-

GENERAL

Hartley, Lois, "The Indian Novels of Rumer Godden," Mah-
    fil, III, ii-iii (1966), 65-75.
Prescott, O., In My Opinion, 203-8.
Tindall, William Y., "Rumer Godden, Public Symbolist,"

CE, XIII (March, 1952), 297-303.

BLACK NARCISSUS

Hartley, Lois, "The Indian Novels of Rumer Godden," Mahfil,
III, ii-iii (1966), 68-70.
Tindall, William Y., "Rumer Godden, Public Symbolist,"
CE, XIII (March, 1952), 300-1.

BREAKFAST WITH THE NIKOLIDES

Hartley, Lois, "The Indian Novels of Rumer Godden," Mahfil, III, ii-iii (1966), 70-2.

KINGFISHERS CATCH FIRE

Hartley, Lois, "The Indian Novels of Rumer Godden," Mahfil,
III, ii-iii (1966), 73-5.

THE RIVER

Hartley, Lois, "The Indian Novels of Rumer Godden," Mahfil,
III, ii-iii (1966), 72-3.
Tindall, William Y., "Rumer Godden, Public Symbolist,"
CE, XIII (March, 1952), 297-9.

TAKE THREE TENSES: A FUGUE IN TIME

Frey, John R., "Past or Present Tense? A Note on the
Technique of Narration," JEGP, XLVI (April, 1947), 205-
8.
Tindall, William Y., "Rumer Godden, Public Symbolist," CE,
XIII (March, 1952), 301-2.

GOLD, HERBERT, 1924-

GENERAL

Hicks, Granville, in Balakian, N., and C. Simmons, eds.,
Creative Present, 224-32.
Moore, Harry T., "The Fiction of Herbert Gold," in Moore,
H. T., ed., Contemporary American Novelists, 170-81.

THE MAN WHO WAS NOT WITH IT

Seiden, Melvin, "Characters and Ideas: The Modern Novel,"

<u>Nation,</u> CLXXXVIII (April 25, 1959), 387-92.
Widmer, K., "Contemporary American Outcasts," <u>Literary Rebel,</u> 126-7.

THE OPTIMIST

Hassan, I., <u>Radical Innocence,</u> 180-7.
Moore, Harry T., in Moore, H.T., ed., <u>Contemporary American Novelists,</u> 179-81.
Nemerov, Howard, in <u>PR,</u> XXVII (Winter, 1960), 180-4. Also in Nemerov, H., <u>Poetry and Fiction,</u> 283-6.
Seiden, Melvin, "Characters and Ideas: The Modern Novel," <u>Nation,</u> CLXXXVIII (April 25, 1959), 387-92.

SALT

Moore, Harry T., in Moore, H.T., ed., <u>Contemporary American Novelists,</u> 177-9.

THEREFORE BE BOLD

Sherman, B., <u>Invention of the Jew,</u> 211-14.

GOLDING, WILLIAM GERALD, 1911-

GENERAL

Allen, W., <u>Modern Novel,</u> 288-92.
Baker, J.R., <u>William Golding.</u>
Bowen, John, "Bending over Backwards," <u>TLS</u> (October 23, 1959), 608. Also in Nelson, W., <u>William Golding's LORD OF THE FLIES,</u> 55-60.
Bufkin, Ernest C., Jr., "The Novels of William Golding: A Descriptive and Analytic Study," <u>DA,</u> XXV (1964), 469-70 (Vanderbilt).
Dick, Bernard F., "The Novelist as Displaced Person: An Interview with William Golding," <u>CE,</u> XXVI (March, 1965), 480-2.
_____, <u>William Golding.</u>
Elmen, P., <u>William Golding.</u>
Freedman, Ralph, "The New Realism: The Fancy of William Golding," <u>Per,</u> X (Summer-Autumn, 1958), 118-28.
Gallagher, Michael P., "The Human Image in William Golding," <u>Studies,</u> LIV (Summer-Autumn, 1965), 197-216.
Gindin, James, " 'Gimmick' and Metaphor in the Novels of William Golding," <u>MFS,</u> VI (Summer, 1960), 145-52. Also

in Gindin, J., Underline: Postwar British Fiction, 196-206. Also in
Nelson, W., William Golding's LORD OF THE FLIES,
132-40.

Green, Martin, "Distaste for the Contemporary," Nation,
CXC (May 21, 1960), 451-4. Also in Nelson, W., William
Golding's LORD OF THE FLIES, 75-82.

Green, Peter, "The World of William Golding," EDH, XXXII
(1963), 37-57.

_____, "The World of William Golding," REL, I, ii (April,
1960), 62-72. Also, revised, in Nelson, W., William
Golding's LORD OF THE FLIES, 170-89. Also, revised,
in TPRSL, XXXII (1963), 37-57.

Hainsworth, J.D., "William Golding," HJ, LXIV (Summer,
1966), 122-3.

Hodson, L., Golding.

Hynes, Sam, "Novels of a Religious Man," Cweal, LXXI
(March 18, 1960), 673-5. Also in Nelson, W., William
Golding's LORD OF THE FLIES, 70-5.

_____, William Golding.

Irwin, Joseph J., "The Serpent Coiled Within," Motive (Nashville), XXIII (May, 1963), 1-5.

Karl, F.R., "The Metaphysical Novels of William Golding,"
Contemporary English Novel, 254-60.

Kermode, F., "The Later Golding," Continuities, 186-94.

_____, and William Golding, "The Meaning of it All,"
Books and Bookmen, V (October, 1959), 9-10.

_____, "The Novels of William Golding," ILA, III (1961),
11-29. Also in Kermode, F., Puzzles and Epiphanies,
198-213. Also in Kostelanetz, R., ed., On Contemporary
Literature, 366-81.

Kinkead-Weekes, M., and I. Gregor, William Golding.

MacLure, Millar, "William Golding's Survivor Stories,"
TamR, V (Summer, 1957), 60-7.

MacShane, Frank, "The Novels of William Golding," DR,
XLII (Summer, 1962), 171-83.

Malin, Irving, in Shapiro, C., ed., Contemporary British
Novelists, 36-47.

Marcus, Steven, "The Novel Again," PR, XXIX (Spring, 1962),
180-4.

Marsden, Arthur, "The Novels of William Golding," Delta,
No. 10 (Autumn, 1956), 26-9.

Mitchell, Juliet, "Concepts and Technique in William Golding," New Left Review, No. 15 (May-June, 1962), 63-71.

Nelson, W., William Golding's LORD OF THE FLIES.

Nossen, Evon, "The Beast-Man Theme in the Work of William Golding," BSUF, IX, ii (1968), 60-9.

Oldsey, B.S., and S. Weintraub, Art of William Golding.

Pemberton, C., <u>William Golding</u>.
Pendry, E. D., "William Golding and 'Mankind's Essential Ill-
    ness'," <u>MSpr</u>, LV (1961), 1-7.
Peter, John, "The Fables of William Golding," <u>KR</u>, XIX
    (Autumn, 1957), 577-92.
Pritchett, V. S., "God's Folly," <u>NStat</u>, LXVII (April 10, 1964),
    562-3.
_____, "Pain and Mr. Golding," <u>Living Novel</u>, 309-15.
Rexroth, Kenneth, "William Golding," <u>Atlantic Mthly</u>, CCXV
    (May, 1965), 96-8.
Sullivan, Walter, "William Golding: The Fables and the Art,"
    <u>SR</u>, LXXI (Autumn, 1963), 660-4.
Thomson, George H., "The Real World of William Golding,"
    <u>Alphabet</u>, No. 9 (November, 1964), 26-33.
Walters, Margaret, "Two Fabulists: Golding and Camus,"
    <u>MCR</u>, No. 4 (1961), 18-29. Also in Nelson, W., <u>William
    Golding</u>'s LORD OF THE FLIES, 95-107.
Williams, H. M., "The Art of William Golding," <u>BDEC</u>, III,
    Nos. 3 & 4 (1962), 20-31. (Not seen.)
Young, Wayland, "Letter from London," <u>KR</u>, XIX (Summer,
    1957), 478-82. Also in Nelson, W., <u>William Golding's
    LORD OF THE FLIES</u>, 18-21.

FREE FALL

Axthelm, P. M., <u>Modern Confessional Novel</u>, 113-27.
Babb, Howard S., "Four Passages from William Golding's
    Fiction," <u>MinnR</u>, V (1965), 57-8.
Baker, J. R., <u>William Golding</u>, 55-70.
Boyle, Ted E., "The Denial of the Spirit: An Explication of
    William Golding's FREE FALL," <u>WascanaR</u>, I (1966), 3-
    10.
Broes, Arthur T., "The Two Worlds of William Golding," in
    Carnegie Institute of Technology, <u>Lectures on Modern Nov-
    elists</u>, 13-14.
Cox, C. B., <u>Free Spirit</u>, 181-4.
Dick, B. F., <u>William Golding</u>, 67-76, 99-100.
Elmen, P., <u>William Golding</u>, 31-5.
Gallagher, Michael P., "The Human Image in William Gold-
    ing," <u>Studies</u>, LIV (Summer-Autumn, 1965), 205-8.
Gindin, J., " 'Gimmick' and Metaphor in the Novels of Wil-
    liam Golding," <u>MFS</u>, VI (1960), 149-52. Also in Gindin,
    J., <u>Postwar British Fiction</u>, 202-6.
Goldberg, Gerald J., "The Search for the Artist in Some Re-
    cent British Fiction," <u>SAQ</u>, LXII (Summer, 1963), 392-4.
Green, Peter, "The World of William Golding," <u>REL</u>, I, ii
    (April, 1960), 71-2. Also, revised, in Nelson, W., <u>Wil-</u>

liam Golding's LORD OF THE FLIES, 185-9. Also, re-
vised, in TPRSL, XXXII (1963), 52-6. Also in EDH,
XXXII (1963), 52-7.
Gregor, Ian, and M. Kinkead-Weekes, "The Strange Case of
Mr. Golding and His Critics," TC, CLXVII (February,
1960), 115-25. Also in Nelson, W., William Golding's
LORD OF THE FLIES, 60-70.
Harris, Wendell V., "Golding's FREE FALL," Expl, XXIII
(May, 1965), Item 76.
Hartt, J.N., Lost Image of Man, 101-2.
Hodson, L., Golding, 72-87.
Hynes, S., William Golding, 33-40.
Karl, F.R., "The Metaphysical Novels of William Golding,"
Contemporary English Novel, 254-7.
Kermode, Frank, "The Novels of William Golding," ILA, III
(1961), 25-9. Also in Kermode, F., Puzzles and Epipha-
nies, 210-12. Also in Nelson, W., William Golding's
LORD OF THE FLIES, 118-20. Also in Kostelanetz, R.,
ed., On Contemporary Literature, 379-81.
Kinkead-Weekes, M., and I. Gregor, William Golding, 165-
99.
MacShane, Frank, "The Novels of William Golding," DR,
XLII (Summer, 1962), 178-83.
Malin, Irving, in Shapiro, C., ed., Contemporary British
Novelists, 44-5.
Oldsey, B.S., and S. Weintraub, Art of William Golding,
103-22.
Pemberton, C., William Golding, 18-20.
Rippier, J.S., Some Postwar English Novelists, 62-7.
Wain, John, "Lord of the Agencies," Aspect, No. 3 (April,
1963), 56-67.

THE INHERITORS

Babb, Howard S., "Four Passages from William Golding's
Fiction," MinnR, V (1965), 52-4.
Baker, J.R., William Golding, 18-31.
Broes, Arthur T., "The Two Worlds of William Golding,"
in Carnegie Institute of Technology, Lectures on Modern
Novelists, 7-10.
Bufkin, E.C., "The Ironic Art of William Golding's THE IN-
HERITORS," TSLL, IX (1968), 567-8.
Dick, B.F., William Golding, 37-48.
Duncan, Kirby L., "William Golding and Vardis Fisher: A
Study in Parallels and Extensions," CE, XXVII (1965),
232-5.
Elmen, P., William Golding, 21-5.

Freedman, Ralph, "The New Realism: The Fancy of William
  Golding," Per, X (Spring-Autumn, 1958), 118-28.
Gallagher, Michael P., "The Human Image in William Gold-
  ing," Studies, LIV (Summer-Autumn, 1965), 201-2.
Gindin, J., "'Gimmick' and Metaphor in the Novels of Wil-
  liam Golding," MFS, VI (1960), 147-8, 151-2. Also in
  Gindin, J., Postwar British Fiction, 198-200, 204-6.
Green, Peter, "The World of William Golding," EDH, XXXII
  (1963) 45-8. Also in REL, I, ii (April, 1960), 67-8. Al-
  so, revised, in Nelson, W., William Golding's LORD OF
  THE FLIES, 177-81. Also, revised, in TPRSL, XXXII
  (1963), 45-8.
Hodson, L., Golding, 39-54.
Hurt, James R., "Grendel's Point of View: BEOWULF and
  William Golding," MFS, XIII (Summer, 1967), 264-5.
Hynes, S., William Golding, 16-23.
Kermode, Frank, and William Golding, "The Meaning of it
  All," Books and Bookmen, V (October, 1959), 10.
_____, "The Novels of William Golding," ILA, III (1961),
  19-22. Also in Kermode, F., Puzzles and Epiphanies,
  205-7. Also in Kostelanetz, ed., On Contemporary Litera-
  ture, 373-5. Also in Nelson, W., William Golding's
  LORD OF THE FLIES, 113-15.
Kinkead-Weekes, M., and I. Gregor, William Golding, 67-
  118.
MacShane, Frank, "The Novels of William Golding," DR,
  XLII (Summer, 1962), 174-5.
Malin, Irving, in Shapiro, C., ed., Contemporary British
  Novelists, 40-1.
Oldsey, B.S., and S. Weintraub, Art of William Golding, 43-
  72.
Pemberton, C., William Golding, 11-14.
Peter, John, "The Fables of William Golding," KR, XIX
  (Autumn, 1957), 585-7.
Rippier, J.S., Some Postwar English Novelists, 53-7.
Sternlicht, Sanford, "Songs of Innocence and Songs of Experi-
  ence in LORD OF THE FLIES and THE INHERITORS,"
  MQ, IX (July, 1968), 383-90.

LORD OF THE FLIES

Allen, W., Modern Novel, 288-90.
Babb, Howard S., "Four Passages from William Golding's
  Fiction," MinnR, V (1965), 50-2.
Babbage, Stuart B., "The End of Innocence," The Mark of
  Cain: Studies in Literature and Theology, Grand Rapids:
  Eerdmans, 1966, 24-8.

Baker, James R. , "Why It's No Go: A Study of William
    Golding's LORD OF THE FLIES," ArQ, XIX (Winter,
    1963), 293-305. Also, later version, in Baker, J. R. ,
    William Golding, 3-17. Also in Baker, J. R. , and A. P.
    Ziegler, Jr. , eds. , Casebook Edition of LORD OF THE
    FLIES, " xiii-xxiv.
Biles, Jack I. , "Piggy: Apologia Pro Vita Sua," SLitI, I, ii
    (October, 1968), 83-108.
Broes, Arthur T. , "The Two Worlds of William Golding," in
    Carnegie Institute of Technology, Lectures on Modern Nov-
    elists, 1-7.
Bufkin, E. C. , "LORD OF THE FLIES: An Analysis," GaR,
    XIX (Spring, 1965), 40-57.
Clark, George, "An Illiberal Education: William Golding's
    Pedagogy," in Whitbread, T. B. , ed. , Seven Contemporary
    Authors, 75-84.
Cohn, Alan M. , "The Berengaria Allusion in LORD OF THE
    FLIES," N&Q, XIII (November, 1966), 419-20.
Coskren, Thomas M. , O. P. , "Is Golding Calvinistic?"
    America, CIX (July 6, 1963), 18-20. Also in Baker, J.
    R. , and A. P. Ziegler, Jr. , eds. , Casebook Edition of
    William Golding's LORD OF THE FLIES," 253-60.
Cox, C. B. , Free Spirit, 173-9.
_____, "LORD OF THE FLIES," CritQ, II (Summer, 1960),
    112-17. Also in Nelson, W. , William Golding's LORD OF
    THE FLIES, 82-8.
Davis, W. Eugene, "Mr. Golding's Optical Delusion," ELN,
    III (December, 1965), 125-6.
Dick, Bernard F. , "LORD OF THE FLIES and the BACCHAE,"
    CW (January, 1964), 145-6.
_____, William Golding, 18-36, 96-8.
Drew, Philip, "Second Reading," Cambridge Rev, (October
    27, 1956), 79-84.
Egan, John M. , O. P. , "Golding's View of Man," America,
    CVIII (January 26, 1963), 140-1. Also in Nelson, W. ,
    William Golding's LORD OF THE FLIES, 145-7.
Elmen, P. , William Golding, 11-20.
Ely, Sister M. Amanda, O. P. , "The Adult Image in Three
    Novels of Adolescent Life," EJ, LVI (November, 1967),
    1127-8.
Epstein, E. L. , "Notes on LORD OF THE FLIES," in LORD
    OF THE FLIES, N. Y.: Putnam's, 1959, 249-55. Also in
    Baker, J. R. , and A. P. Ziegler, Jr. , eds. , Casebook Edi-
    tion of William Golding's LORD OF THE FLIES, 277-81.
Forster, E. M. , "Introduction," in LORD OF THE FLIES,
    N. Y.: Coward-McCann, 1962, ix-xii. Also in Baker, J.
    R. , and A. P. Ziegler, Jr. , eds. , Casebook Edition of

William Golding's LORD OF THE FLIES, 207-10.

Freedman, Ralph, "The New Realism: The Fancy of William Golding," Per, X (Summer-Autumn, 1958), 118-28.

Fuller, Edmund, "Behind the Vogue, a Rigorous Understanding," NYHTBR, XXXIX (November 4, 1962), 3. Also in Nelson, W., William Golding's LORD OF THE FLIES, 143-5.

Gaskin, J. C. A., "Beelzebub," HJ, LXVI (1968), 58-61.

Gindin, J., " 'Gimmick' and Metaphor in the Novels of William Golding," MFS, VI (1960), 145-7, 151-2. Also in Gindin, J., Postwar British Fiction, 196-8, 204-6.

Golding, J. T. C., "A World of Violence and Small Boys," in Baker, J. R. and A. P. Ziegler, Jr., eds., Casebook Edition of William Golding's LORD OF THE FLIES, 225-7.

Golding, William, "The Fable," The Hot Gates and Other Occasional Pieces, N. Y.: Harcourt, Brace & World, 1966, 85-101.

Gordon, Robert C., "Classical Themes in LORD OF THE FLIES," MFS, XI (Winter, 1965-66), 424-7.

Grande, Luke M., "The Appeal of Golding," Cweal, LXXVII (January 25, 1963), 457-9. Also in Nelson, W., William Golding's LORD OF THE FLIES, 156-9.

Green, Peter, "The World of William Golding," EDH, XXXII (1963), 41-5. Also in REL, I, ii (April, 1960), 63-7. Also, revised, in Nelson, W., William Golding's LORD OF THE FLIES, 173-7. Also, revised, in TPRSL, XXXII (1963), 41-5.

Gregor, Ian, and M. Kinkead-Weekes, "Introduction," in LORD OF THE FLIES, London: Faber and Faber School Editions, 1962, i-xii. Also in Baker, J. R., and A. P. Ziegler, Jr., eds., Casebook Edition of William Golding's LORD OF THE FLIES," 235-43.

Gulbin, Suzanne, "Parallels and Contrasts in LORD OF THE FLIES and ANIMAL FARM," EJ, LV (January, 1966), 86-90, 92.

Hampton, T., "An Error in LORD OF THE FLIES," N&Q, XII (July, 1965), 275.

Herndl, George C., "Golding and Salinger: A Clear Choice," WiseR, No. 502 (Winter, 1964), 309-22.

Hodson, L., Golding, 19-38.

Hynes, S., William Golding, 6-16.

Karl, F. R., "The Metaphysical Novels of William Golding," Contemporary English Novel, 257-8.

Kearns, Francis E., and L. M. Grande, "An Exchange of Views," Cweal, LXXVII (February 22, 1963), 569-71. Also in Nelson, W., William Golding's LORD OF THE FLIES, 160-4.

_____, "Golding Revisited," in Nelson, W., William Gold-
ing's LORD OF THE FLIES, 165-9.
_____, "Salinger and Golding: Conflict on the Campus,"
America, CVIII (January 26, 1963), 136-9. Also in Nel-
son, W., William Golding's LORD OF THE FLIES, 148-55.
Keating, James, and William Golding, "The Purdue Inter-
view," (in part) in Baker, J.R., and A.P. Ziegler, Jr.,
eds., Casebook Edition of William Golding's LORD OF THE
FLIES, 189-95.
Kermode, Frank, "Coral Islands," Spectator, CCI (August 22,
1958), 257. Also in Nelson, W., William Golding's LORD
OF THE FLIES, 39-42.
_____, and William Golding, "The Meaning of It All,"
Books and Bookmen, V (October, 1959), 9-10. Also in
Baker, J.R., and A.P. Ziegler, Jr., eds., Casebook Edi-
tion of William Golding's LORD OF THE FLIES, 197-201.
_____, "The Novels of William Golding," International
Literary Annual, No. 3 (1961), 16-19. Also in F. Ker-
mode, Puzzles and Epiphanies, 202-5. Also (selection) in
Baker, J.R., and A.P. Ziegler, Jr., eds., Casebook Edi-
tion of William Golding's LORD OF THE FLIES, 203-6.
Also in Nelson, W., William Golding's LORD OF THE
FLIES, 111-13. Also in Kostalanetz, R., ed., On Con-
temporary Literature, 368-73.
Kinkead-Weekes, M., and I. Gregor, William Golding, 15-
64.
Lederer, Richard H., "Student Reactions to LORD OF THE
FLIES," EJ, LIII (1964), 575-9.
Leed, Jacob, "Golding's LORD OF THE FLIES, Chapter 7,"
Expl, XXIV (September, 1965), Item 8.
"Lord of the Campus," Time, LXXIX (June 22, 1962), 64.
Also in Baker, J.R., and A.P. Ziegler, Jr., eds., Case-
book Edition of William Golding's LORD OF THE FLIES,"
283-5. Also in Nelson, W., William Golding's LORD OF
THE FLIES, 141-2.
MacLure, Millar, "Allegories of Innocence," DR, XL (Sum-
mer, 1960), 149-51.
MacShane, Frank, "The Novels of William Golding," DR,
XLII (Summer, 1962), 172-3.
Malin, Irving, in Shapiro, C., ed., Contemporary British
Novelists, 37-40.
Marcus, Steven, "The Novel Again," PR, XXIX (Spring,
1962), 181-2.
Merren, John, "LORD OF THE FLIES as an Anatomy,"
CCTE, XXXI (September, 1966), 28-9. (Abstract).
Michel-Michot, Paulette, "The Myth of Innocence," RLV,
XXVIII, vi (1962), 510-20.

Mitchell, Charles, "THE LORD OF THE FLIES and the Es-
cape from Freedom," ArQ, XXII (Spring, 1966), 27-40.
Moody, Philippa, A Critical Commentary on William Gold-
ing's LORD OF THE FLIES, London: Macmillan, 1966.
Mueller, William R. , "An Old Story Well Told," ChC, LXXX
(October 2, 1963), 1203-6.   Also, condensed, in Baker, J.
R. , and A. P. Ziegler, Jr. , eds. , Casebook Edition of
William Golding's LORD OF THE FLIES, 245-51.
Nelson, W. , William Golding's LORD OF THE FLIES.
Niemeyer, Carl, "The Coral Island Revisited," CE, XXII
(1961), 241-5.   Also, condensed, in Baker, J. R. , and A.
P. Ziegler, Jr. , eds. , Casebook Edition of William Gold-
ing's LORD OF THE FLIES, 217-23.   Also in Nelson, W. ,
William Golding's LORD OF THE FLIES, 88-94.
O'Hara, John D. , "Mute Choirboys and Angelic Pigs: The
Fable in LORD OF THE FLIES," TSLL, VII (Winter,
1966), 411-20.
Oldsey, Bern, and Stanley Weintraub, "LORD OF THE FLIES:
Beelzebub Revisited," CE, XXV (November, 1963), 90-9.
Also (expanded) in Oldsey, B. S. , and S. Weintraub, Art of
William Golding, 15-40.
Padovano, A. , Estranged God, 149-54.
Page, Norman, "LORD OF THE FLIES," Use of English, XVI
(Autumn, 1964), 44-5, 57.
Pemberton, C. , William Golding, 7-11.
Peter, John, "The Fables of William Golding," KR, XIX
(Autumn, 1957), 581-5.   Also, condensed, in Baker, J. R. ,
and A. P. Ziegler, Jr. , eds. , Casebook Edition of William
Golding's LORD OF THE FLIES, 229-34.   Also in Nelson,
W. , William Golding's LORD OF THE FLIES, 25-8.
Pritchett, V. S. , "Pain and Mr. Golding," Working Novelist,
56-61.
_____, "Secret Parables," NStat (August 2, 1958), 146-7.
Also in Nelson, W. , William Golding's LORD OF THE
FLIES, 35-9.
Rippier, J. S. , Some Postwar English Novelists, 46-53.
Rosenberg, Bruce A. , "Lord of the Fire-Flies," CRAS, XI
(Winter, 1967), 128-39.
Rosenfield, Claire, " 'Men of a Smaller Growth': A Psycho-
logical Analysis of William Golding's LORD OF THE
FLIES," L&P, XI (Autumn, 1961), 93-101.   Also, re-
vised, in Baker, J. R. , and A. P. Ziegler, Jr. , eds. ,
Casebook Edition of William Golding's LORD OF THE
FLIES, 261-76.   Also in Manheim, E. , and L. , eds. ,
Hidden Patterns, 259-74.   Also in Nelson, W. , William
Golding's LORD OF THE FLIES, 121-32.
_____, "Reply by Miss Rosenfield," L&P, XII (Winter,

1962), 11-12.

Spangler, Donald R., "Simon," in Baker, J.R., and A.P.
   Ziegler, Jr., eds., Casebook Edition of William Golding's
   LORD OF THE FLIES, 211-15.

Spector, Robert D., "Islands of Good and Evil: TOM SAW-
   YER and LORD OF THE FLIES," in Twain, Mark, THE
   ADVENTURES OF TOM SAWYER, N.Y.: Bantam, 1966.

Sternlicht, Sanford, "Songs of Innocence and Songs of Experience in LORD OF THE FLIES and THE INHERITORS,"
   MQ, IX (July, 1968), 383-90.

_____, "A Source for Golding's LORD OF THE FLIES:
   Peter Pan?" EngR, XIV (December, 1963), 41-2.

Talon, Henri, "Irony in LORD OF THE FLIES," EIC, XVIII
   (July, 1968), 296-309.

Taylor, Harry H., "The Case Against William Golding's
   Simon-Piggy," ConR (September, 1966), 155-60.

Townsend, R.C., "LORD OF THE FLIES: Fool's Gold?"
   JGE, XVI (July, 1964), 153-60.

Trilling, Lionel, "LORD OF THE FLIES," Mid-Century, Issue 45 (October, 1962), 10-12.

Veidemanis, Gladys, "LORD OF THE FLIES in the Class-
   room--No Passing Fad," EJ, LIII (1964), 569-74.

Walters, Margaret, "Two Fabulists: Golding and Camus,"
   MCR, IV (1961), 20-3. Also in Nelson, W., William
   Golding's LORD OF THE FLIES, 97-101.

Warner, Oliver, "Mr. Golding and Marryat's LITTLE SAV-
   AGE," REL, V, i (1964), 51-5.

Wasserstrom, William, "Reason and Reverence in Art and
   Science," L&P, XII (Winter, 1962), 2-3.

Watson, Kenneth, "A Reading of LORD OF THE FLIES,"
   English, XV (Spring, 1964), 2-7.

White, Robert J., "Butterfly and Beast in LORD OF THE
   FLIES," MFS, X (Summer, 1964), 163-70.

PINCHER MARTIN
(THE TWO DEATHS OF CHRISTOPHER MARTIN)

Babb, Howard, "Four Passages from William Golding's Fiction," MinnR., V (1965), 54-7.

_____, "On the Ending of PINCHER MARTIN," EIC, XIV
   (January, 1964), 106-8.

Baker, J.R., William Golding, 32-47.

Blake, Ian, "PINCHER MARTIN: William Golding and 'Taf-
   frail'," N&Q, IX (August, 1962), 309-10.

Braybrooke, Neville, "The Return of Pincher Martin," Cweal,
   LXXXIX (October 25, 1968), 115-18.

Broes, Arthur T., "The Two Worlds of William Golding,"

in Carnegie Institute of Technology, Lectures on Modern
    Novelists, 10-12.
Clark, George, "An Illiberal Education: William Golding's
    Pedagogy," Whitbread, T. B., ed., Seven Contemporary
    Authors, 84-95.
Cox, C. B., Free Spirit, 180-1.
_____, "William Golding's PINCHER MARTIN," Listener,
    LXXI (March 12, 1964), 430-1.
Dick, B. F., William Golding, 49-62, 98-9.
Elmen, P., William Golding, 25-30.
Freedman, Ralph, "The New Realism: The Fancy of William
    Golding," Per, X (Spring-Autumn, 1958), 118-28.
Gallagher, Michael P., "The Human Image in William Gold-
    ing," Studies, LIV (Summer-Autumn, 1965), 202-4.
Gindin, J., " 'Gimmick' and Metaphor in the Novels of Wil-
    liam Golding," MFS, VI (1960), 148-9, 151-2. Also in
    Gindin, J., Postwar British Fiction, 200-2, 204-6.
Green, Peter, "The World of William Golding," EDH, XXXII
    (1963), 49-52. Also in REL, I, ii (April, 1960), 69-71.
    Also, revised, in Nelson, W., William Golding's LORD OF
    THE FLIES, 181-5. Also, revised, in TPRSL, XXXII
    (1963), 49-52.
Hodson, L., Golding, 55-71.
Hynes, S., William Golding, 23-32.
Kermode, Frank, and William Golding, "The Meaning of it
    All," Books and Bookmen, V (October, 1959), 10.
_____, "The Novels of William Golding," ILA, III (1961),
    22-5. Also in Kermode, F., Puzzles and Epiphanies,
    207-10. Also in Kostelanetz, R., ed., On Contemporary
    Literature, 375-9. Also in Nelson, W., William Golding's
    LORD OF THE FLIES, 115-18.
Kinkead-Weekes, M., and I. Gregor, William Golding, 121-
    61.
MacLure, Millar, "William Golding's Survival Stories,"
    TamR, V (Summer, 1957), 60-7.
MacNeice, Louis, Varieties of Experience, London: Cam-
    bridge Un. Pr., 1965, 147-51.
MacShane, Frank, "The Novels of William Golding," DR,
    XLII (Summer, 1962), 175-8.
Malin, Irving, in Shapiro, C., ed., Contemporary British
    Novelists, 41-4.
Marcus, Steven, "The Novel Again," PR, XXIX (Spring,
    1962), 182-3.
Maxwell, J. C., "PINCHER MARTIN," TLS (August 21, 1959),
    483. Comments: Green, Peter, and Edward Morgan (Au-
    gust 28, 1959), 495; Daisch, W. G. (September 4, 1959),
    507; Webster, Owen (September 11, 1959), 519.

Morgan, Edwin, "PINCHER MARTIN and THE CORAL IS-
    LAND," N&Q, VII (April, 1960), 150.
Oldsey, B. S. , and S. Weintraub, Art of William Golding, 75-
    100.
Pearson, Anthony, "H. G. Wells and PINCHER MARTIN,"
    N&Q, XII (July, 1965), 275-6.
Pemberton, C. , William Golding, 14-17.
Peter, John, "The Fables of William Golding," KR, XIX (Au-
    tumn, 1957), 587-91.
Quinn, Michael, "An Unheroic Hero: William Golding's
    PINCHER MARTIN," CritQ, IV (Autumn, 1962), 247-56.
Rippier, J. S. , Some Postwar English Novelists, 58-61.
Sasso, Laurence J. , Jr. , "A Note on the Dwarf in PINCHER
    MARTIN," MSE, I (Spring, 1968), 66-8.
Sternlicht, Sanford, "PINCHER MARTIN: A Freudian Crusoe,"
    EngR, XV (April, 1965), 2-4.

THE PYRAMID

Henry, Avril, "William Golding: THE PYRAMID," SoRA, III
    (1968), 5-31.
Hodson, L. , Golding, 102-6.
Pemberton, C. , William Golding, 24-7.
Trickett, Rachel, "Recent Novels: Craftmanship in Violence
    and Sex," YR, LVII (Spring, 1968), 444-6.
Whitehead, John, "A Conducted Tour to the Pyramid," Lon-
    don Mag, n. s. , VII (June, 1967), 100-4.

THE SPIRE

Baker, J. R. , William Golding, 70-88.
Carmichael, D. , "A God in Ruins," Quadrant, No. 33 (Janu-
    ary, 1965), 72-5.
Crompton, D. W. , "THE SPIRE," CritQ, IX (Spring, 1967),
    63-79.
Dick, Bernard F. , and Raymond J. Porter, "Jocelin and
    Oedipus," Cithara, VI, i (November, 1966), 43-8.
_____, William Golding, 77-87, 100-1.
Elman, P. , William Golding, 35-40.
Freehof, Solomon B. , "Nostalgia for the Middle Ages: Wil-
    liam Golding's THE SPIRE," Carnegie Mag, XXXIX (Janu-
    ary, 1965), 13-16.
Gallagher, Michael P. , "The Human Image in William Gold-
    ing," Studies, LIV (Summer-Autumn, 1965), 208-16.
Hodson, L. , Golding, 88-99.
Hyman, S. E. , "The Spire of Babel," Standards, 219-23.
Hynes, S. , William Golding, 40-6.

Kermode, Frank, "The Case for William Golding," NYRB, II
    (April 30, 1964), 3-4.   Also in Kermode, F., Continui-
    ties, 186-94.   Also in Kostelanetz, R., ed., On Contempo-
    rary Literature, 381-7.
Kinkead-Weekes, M., and I. Gregor, William Golding, 203-
    35.
Kort, Wesley, "The Groundless Glory of Golding's Spire,"
    Ren, XX (1968), 75-8.
Livingston, James C., William Golding's THE SPIRE (Re-
    ligious Dimensions in Literature), N.Y.: Seabury, 1967.
Malin, Irving, in Shapiro, C., ed., Contemporary British
    Novelists, 45-7.
"Novels of 1964.   William Golding: THE SPIRE," in T.L.S.
    Essays and Reviews from The Times Literary Supplement,
    1964, 35-41.   Also in TLS (April 16, 1964).
Oldsey, B.S., and S. Weintraub, Art of William Golding,
    125-46.
Pemberton, C., William Golding, 22-4.
Roper, Derek, "Allegory and Novel in Golding's THE SPIRE,"
    WSCL, VIII (Winter, 1967), 19-30.
Spender, Stephen, "Traditional vs. Underground Novels," in
    Encyclopaedia Britannica, Great Ideas Today, 1965, 188-90.
Sternlicht, Sanford, "The Sin of Pride in Golding's THE
    SPIRE," MinnR, V (January-April, 1965), 59-60.
Sullivan, Walter, "The Long Chronicle of Guilt: William
    Golding's THE SPIRE," HC, I, iii (June, 1964), 1-12.
Temple, E.R.A., "William Golding's THE SPIRE: A Cri-
    tique," Ren, XX (Summer, 1968), 171-3.

THE TWO DEATHS OF CHRISTOPHER MARTIN,
See PINCHER MARTIN

BIBLIOGRAPHY

Baker, J.R., and A.P. Ziegler, Jr., eds., Casebook Edi-
    tion of William Golding's LORD OF THE FLIES, 287-91.
    _____, William Golding, 97-102.
Hodson, L., Golding, 110-16.

GORDIMER, NADINE, 1923-

GENERAL

Abrahams, Lionel, "Nadine Gordimer: The Transparent
    Ego," ESA, III (September, 1960), 146-51.
McGuinness, Frank, "The Novels of Nadine Gordimer,"

LonM, n. s. , V (June, 1965), 97-102.
Woodward, Anthony, "Nadine Gordimer," Theoria, XVI
   (1961), 1-12.

THE LATE BOURGEOIS WORLD

"Prose out of Africa. Nadine Gordimer. THE LATE BOUR-
   GEOIS WORLD," in T. L. S. Essays and Reviews, 1966,
   45-6. Also in TLS (July 7, 1966).

A WORLD OF STRANGERS

Tucker, M. , Africa in Modern Literature, 222-3.

BIBLIOGRAPHY

Nell, Racilia J. , Nadine Gordimer, Novelist and Short Story
   Writer: A Bibliography of Her Works and Selected Literary Criticism, Johannesburg; Un. of Witwatersrand, 1964.

GORDON, CAROLINE, 1895-

GENERAL

Brown, Ashley, "The Achievement of Caroline Gordon," SHR,
   II (Summer, 1968), 279-90.
Brown, Samuel A. , Jr. , "Caroline Gordon and the Impres-
   sionist Novel," DA, XVIII (1958), 1795 (Vanderbilt).
Cheney, Brainard, "Caroline Gordon's Ontological Quest,"
   Ren, XVI (Fall, 1963), 3-12.
Cowan, Louise, "Nature and Grace in Caroline Gordon,"
   Crit, I (Winter, 1956), 11-27.
Fletcher, Marie, "The Fate of Women in a Changing South:
   A Persistant Theme in the Fiction of Caroline Gordon,"
   MissQ, XXI (Winter, 1967-68), 17-28.
Hoffman, F. J. , Art of Southern Fiction. 36-9. Also, basi-
   cally the same, as "Caroline Gordon: The Special Yield,"
   Crit, I (Winter, 1956), 29-35.
King, Lawrence T. , "The Novels of Caroline Gordon,"
   CathW, CLXXXI (July, 1955), 274-9.
Koch, Vivienne, "The Conservatism of Caroline Gordon," in
   Rubin, L. D. , Jr. , and R. D. Jacobs, eds. , Southern Ren-
   ascence, 325-37.
Lytle, Andrew, "Caroline Gordon and the Historic Image,"
   SR, LVII (Autumn, 1949), 560-86. Also in Lytle, A. ,
   Hero with the Private Parts, 148-70.

McDowell, F. P. W. , <u>Caroline Gordon.</u>
O'Connor, William Van, "Art and Miss Gordon," in Rubin,
    L. D. , Jr. , and R. D. Jacobs, eds. , <u>South,</u> 314-22.   Also
    in O'Connor, W. V. , <u>Grotesque,</u> 168-76.
Rocks, James E. , "The Mind and Art of Caroline Gordon,"
    <u>DA,</u> XXVII (1966), 1835A (Duke).   Also, in part, in
    <u>MissQ,</u> XXI (Winter, 1967-68), 1-16.
Thorp, W. , "Southern Renaissance," <u>American Writing in the</u>
    <u>Twentieth Century,</u> 249-53.
_____, "The Way Back and the Way Up: The Novels of
    Caroline Gordon," <u>BuR,</u> VI, iii (December, 1956), 1-15.

ALECK MAURY, SPORTSMAN

Brown, Ashley, "The Achievement of Caroline Gordon," <u>SHR,</u>
    II (1968), 283-4.
Hoffman, Frederick J. , "Caroline Gordon: The Special Yield,"
    <u>Crit,</u> I (1956), 29-31, 33-4.   Also in Hoffman, F. J. , <u>Art</u>
    <u>of Southern Fiction,</u> 36-7.
McDowell, F. P. W. , <u>Caroline Gordon,</u> 17-19.

THE GARDEN OF ADONIS

Brown, Ashley, "The Achievement of Caroline Gordon," <u>SHR,</u>
    II (1968), 285-6.
Fletcher, Marie, "The Fate of Women in a Changing South:
    A Persistant Theme in the Fiction of Caroline Gordon,"
    <u>MissQ,</u> XXI (Winter, 1967-68), 22-4.
McDowell, F. P. W. , <u>Caroline Gordon,</u> 19-21.

GREEN CENTURIES

Brown, Ashley, "The Achievement of Caroline Gordon," <u>SHR,</u>
    II (1968), 286-7.
Lytle, Andrew, "Caroline Gordon and the Historic Image,"
    <u>SR,</u> LVII (Autumn, 1949), 569-75.   Also in Lytle, A. ,
    <u>Hero with the Private Parts,</u> 156-61.
McDowell, F. P. W. , <u>Caroline Gordon,</u> 26-30.
Thorp, Willard, "The Way Back and the Way Up: The Novels
    of Caroline Gordon," <u>BuR,</u> VI (December, 1956), 9-11.

THE MALEFACTORS

Brown, Ashley, "The Novel as Christian Comedy: Gordon's
    THE MALEFACTORS," in Walker, W. E. , and Welker, R.
    L. , eds. , <u>Reality and Myth,</u> 161-78.
Koch, Vivienne, "Companions in the Blood," <u>SR,</u> LXIV (Au-

tumn, 1956), 645-51.
McDowell, F. P. W. , Caroline Gordon, 38-44.
Thorp, Willard, "The Way Back and the Way Up: The Novels
of Caroline Gordon," BuR, VI (December, 1956), 13-15.

NONE SHALL LOOK BACK

Allen, W. , Modern Novel, 113-14.
Brown, Ashley, "The Achievement of Caroline Gordon," SHR,
II (1968), 284-5.
Lytle, Andrew, "Caroline Gordon and the Historic Image,"
SR, LVII (Autumn, 1949), 578-80.   Also in Lytle, A. ,
Hero with the Private Parts, 164-6.
McDowell, F. P. W. , Caroline Gordon, 21-6.

PENHALLY

Brown, Ashley, "The Achievement of Caroline Gordon," SHR,
II (1968), 281-3.
Eisinger, C. E. , "Class and American Fiction: The Aristoc-
racy in Some Novels of the Thirties," in Lanzinger, K. ,
ed. , Americana-Austriaca, 144-6.
Fletcher, Marie, "The Fate of Women in a Changing South:
A Persistant Theme in the Fiction of Caroline Gordon,"
MissQ, XXI (Winter, 1967-68), 21-2.
Lytle, Andrew, "Caroline Gordon and the Historic Image,"
SR, LVII (Autumn, 1949), 575-80.   Also in Lytle, A. ,
Hero with the Private Parts, 161-3.
McDowell, F. P. W. , Caroline Gordon, 14-17.
Thorp, Willard, "The Way Back and the Way Up: The Novels
of Caroline Gordon," BuR, VI (December, 1956), 3-5.

THE STRANGE CHILDREN

Fletcher, Marie, "The Fate of Women in a Changing South:
A Persistant Theme in the Fiction of Caroline Gordon,"
MissQ, XXI (Winter, 1967-68), 26-7.
Gardiner, H. C. , "Two Southern Tales," In All Conscience,
128-9.   Also in America, LXXXVI (October 6, 1951), 18 .
Hartman, Carl, "Charades at Benfolly," WR, XVI (Summer,
1952), 322-4.
Heilman, Robert B. , "Schools for Girls," SR, LX (April-
June, 1952), 299-304.
King, Lawrence T. , "The Novels of Caroline Gordon,"
CathW, CLXXXI (July, 1955), 277-9.
Koch, Vivienne, in Rubin, L. D. , and R. D. Jacobs, eds. ,
Southern Renascence, 333-7.

McDowell, F. P. W. , Caroline Gordon, 33-8.
Rocks, James E. , "The Christian Myth as Salvation: Caro-
line Gordon's THE STRANGE CHILDREN," TSE, XVI
(1968), 149-60.
Smith, Patrick J. , "Typology and Peripety in Four Catholic
Novels," DA, XXVIII (1967), 2265A (Calif. , Davis).
Thorp, Willard, "The Way Back and the Way Up: The Novels
of Caroline Gordon," BuR, VI (December, 1956), 12-13.

THE WOMEN ON THE PORCH

Cowan, Louise, "Nature and Grace in Caroline Gordon,"
Crit, I (1956), 22-7.
Fletcher, Marie, "The Fate of Women in a Changing South:
A Persistant Theme in the Fiction of Caroline Gordon,"
MissQ, XXI (Winter, 1967-68), 24-6.
Lytle, Andrew, "Caroline Gordon and the Historic Image,"
SR, LVII (Autumn, 1949), 581-5. Also in Lytle, A. ,
Hero with the Private Parts, 166-70.
McDowell, F. P. W. , Caroline Gordon, 30-3.
Thorp, Willard, "The Way Back and the Way Up: The Novels
of Caroline Gordon," BuR, VI (December, 1956), 11-12.

BIBLIOGRAPHY

Griscom, Joan, "Bibliography of Caroline Gordon," Crit, I
(Winter, 1956), 74-8.
McDowell, F. P. W. , Caroline Gordon, 46-8.

GOVER, ROBERT, 1929-

GENERAL

Southern, Terry, "Rechy and Gover," in Moore, H. T. , ed. ,
Contemporary American Novelists, 222-7.

GOYEN, WILLIAM, 1918-

GENERAL

Gossett, L. Y. , "The Voices of Distance: William Goyen,"
Violence in Recent Southern Fiction, 131-44.

THE HOUSE OF BREATH

Hoffman, F. J. , Art of Southern Fiction, 124-7.

IN A FARTHER COUNTRY

Hoffman, F. J. , Art of Southern Fiction, 127-9.

GRAU, SHIRLEY ANN, 1929-

GENERAL

Berland, Alwyn, "The Fiction of Shirley Ann Grau," Crit, VI,
    i (Spring, 1963), 78-84.
Gossett, L. Y. , "Primitives and Violence: Shirley Ann Grau,"
    Violence in Recent Southern Fiction, 177-95.
Hoffman, F. J. , Art of Southern Fiction, 106-9.
Keith, Don L. , "New Orleans Notes," Delta Rev, II, iii
    (1965), 11-12+.   (Not seen.)

THE HARD BLUE SKY

Berland, Alwyn, "The Fiction of Shirley Ann Grau," Crit, VI,
    i (Spring, 1963), 80-2.
Gossett, L. Y. , Violence in Recent Southern Fiction, 180-6.

THE HOUSE ON COLISEUM STREET

Berland, Alwyn, "The Fiction of Shirley Ann Grau," Crit, VI,
    i (Spring, 1963), 82-4.

THE KEEPERS OF THE HOUSE

Going, William T. , "Alabama Geography in Shirley Ann
    Grau's THE KEEPERS OF THE HOUSE," AlaR, XX (Janu-
    ary, 1967), 62-8.
Gossett, L. Y. , Violence in Recent Southern Fiction, 189-94.
Hoffman, F. J. , Art of Southern Fiction, 108-10.

GREEN, HENRY, PSEUD. (HENRY VINCENT YORKE), 1905-

GENERAL

Allen, Walter, "Greening," NS&Nation, LVII (May 2, 1959),
    615-16.

_____, "Henry Green," in Baker, D.V., ed., Modern British Writing, 258-71. Also in Penguin New Writing, XXV (1945), 144-55.

_____, Modern Novel, 214-19.

Bain, Bruce, "Henry Green: The Man and His Work," World Rev (May, 1949), 55-8, 80.

Cottrell, Beekman W., "Conversation Piece: Four Twentieth Century English Dialogue Novelists," DA, XVI (1956), 2159 (Columbia).

Dennis, Nigel, "The Double Life of Henry Green," Life (August 4, 1952), 83-94.

Fraser, G.S., Writer and His World, 167-9.

Hall, James, "The Fiction of Henry Greene (sic): Paradoxes of Pleasure-and-Pain," KR, XIX (Winter, 1957), 76-88. Also in Hall, J., Tragic Comedians, 66-81.

Johnson, Bruce, "Henry Green's Comic Symbolism," BSUF, VI (Autumn, 1965), 29-35.

_____, "Loving: A Study of Henry Green," DA, XX (1959), 2292 (Northwestern).

Karl, F.R., "Normality Defined: The Novels of Henry Green," Contemporary English Novel, 183-200.

Melchiori, Giorgio, "The Abstract Art of Henry Green," The Tightrope Walkers; Studies of Mannerism in Modern English Literature, London: Routledge and Kegan Paul, 1956, 188-212.

Odom, Keith C., "Symbolism and Diversion: Birds in the Novels of Henry Green," Descant, VI (Winter, 1962), 30-41.

Phelps, Robert, "The Vision of Henry Green," HudR, V (Winter, 1953), 614-20.

Prescott, O., In My Opinion, 92-8.

Russell, J., Henry Green.

_____, "There It Is," KR, XXVI (Summer, 1964), 433-65.

Ryf, R.S., Henry Green.

Schorer, Mark, "Introduction to Henry Green's World," NYTBR (October 9, 1949), 1, 22.

Southern, Terry, ed., "The Art of Fiction, XXII. Henry Green," ParisR, No. 19 (1958), 60-77. (Interview.)

Stokes, Edward, "Henry Green, Dispossessed Poet," AusQ, XXVIII (December, 1956), 84-91.

_____, The Novels of Henry Green, N.Y.: Macmillan, 1959.

Toynbee, Philip, "The Novels of Henry Green," PR, XVI (May, 1949), 487-97.

Turner, Myron, "The Imagery of Wallace Stevens and Henry Green," WSCL, VIII (Winter, 1967), 60-77.

Weatherhead, A.K., Reading of Henry Green.

_____, "Structure and Texture in Henry Green's Latest
   Novels," Accent, XIX (Spring, 1959), 111-22.
Weaver, Robert L., "Novels of Henry Green," CanF, XXX
   (January, 1951), 227-8.
Welty, Eudora, "Henry Green, a Novelist of the Imagina-
   tion," TQ, IV, iii (Autumn, 1961), 246-56.

BACK

Prescott, O., In My Opinion, 97-8.
Russell, J., Henry Green, 160-78.
Ryf, R. S., Henry Green, 29-33.
Shapiro, Stephen A., "Henry Green's BACK: The Presence
   of the Past," Crit, VII (Spring, 1964), 87-96.
Weatherhead, A. K., Reading of Henry Green, 93-105.

BLINDNESS

Russell, J., Henry Green, 50-73.
Ryf, R. S., Henry Green, 4-10.
Weatherhead, A. K., Reading of Henry Green, 7-20.

CAUGHT

Allen, Walter, "Henry Green," in Baker, D. V., ed., Mod-
   ern British Writing, 267-9.
_____, Modern Novel, 216-17.
Russell, J., Henry Green, 141-60, 172-8.
Ryf, R. S., Henry Green, 22-6.
Schorer, Mark, "The Unreal Worlds of Henry Green,"
   NYTBR (December 31, 1950), 5+.
Weatherhead, A. K., Reading of Henry Green, 55-72.

CONCLUDING

Hall, James, "The Fiction of Henry Greene (sic): Paradoxes
   of Pleasure-and-Pain," KR, XIX (1957), 86-8.   Also in
   Hall, J., Tragic Comedians, 75-81.
Karl, F. R., "Normality Defined: The Novels of Henry
   Green," Contemporary English Novel, 194-6.
Russell, J., Henry Green, 179-201.
Ryf, R. S., Henry Green, 33-6.
Schorer, Mark, "The Unreal Worlds of Henry Green,"
   NYTBR (December 31, 1950), 5+.
Weatherhead, A. K., Reading of Henry Green, 106-22.
_____, "Structure and Texture in Henry Green's Latest
   Novels," Accent, XIX (Spring, 1959), 111-15.

DOTING

Russell, J., <u>Henry Green,</u> 202-25.
Ryf, R. S., <u>Henry Green,</u> 39-42.
Taylor, Donald S., "Catalytic Rhetoric: Henry Green's The-
    ory of the Modern Novel," <u>Criticism,</u> VII (Winter, 1965),
    81-99.
Weatherhead, A. K., <u>Reading of Henry Green,</u> 135-43.
_____, "Structure and Texture in Henry Green's Latest
    Novels," <u>Accent,</u> XIX (Spring, 1959), 120-1.

LIVING

Allen, Walter, "Henry Green," in Baker, D. V., ed., <u>Mod-
    ern British Writing,</u> 262-4.
_____, <u>Modern Novel,</u> 214-16.
Russell, J., <u>Henry Green,</u> 74-97.
Ryf, R. S., <u>Henry Green,</u> 10-15.
Weatherhead, A. K., <u>Reading of Henry Green,</u> 21-39.

LOVING

Churchill, Thomas, "LOVING: A Comic Novel," <u>Crit,</u> IV, ii
    (1961), 29-38.
Davidson, Barbara, "The World of LOVING," <u>WSCL,</u> II, i
    (Winter, 1961), 65-78.
Hall, James, "The Fiction of Henry Greene (sic): Paradoxes
    of Pleasure-and-Pain," <u>KR,</u> XIX (1957), 78-85. Also in
    Hall, J., <u>Tragic Comedians,</u> 69-74.
Labor, Earle, "Henry Green's Web of Loving," <u>Crit,</u> IV, i
    (1961), 29-40.
Mehoke, James S., "Sartre's Theory of Emotion and Three
    English Novelists: Waugh, Green, and Amis," <u>WisSL,</u>
    No. 3 (1966), 108-10.
Quinton, Anthony, "A French View of LOVING," <u>LonM,</u> VI
    (April, 1959), 25-35.
Russell, J., <u>Henry Green,</u> 114-40.
Ryf, R. S., <u>Henry Green,</u> 26-9.
Shorer, Mark, "Introduction to Henry Green's World,"
    <u>NYTBR</u> (October 9, 1949), 1+.
Tindall, W. Y., <u>Literary Symbol,</u> 95-7.
Weatherhead, A. K., <u>Reading of Henry Green,</u> 73-92.

NOTHING

Russell, J., <u>Henry Green,</u> 202-25.
Ryf, R. S., <u>Henry Green,</u> 37-9.

Weatherhead, A. K. , Reading of Henry Green, 123-35.
_____, "Structure and Texture in Henry Green's Latest
    Novels," Accent, XIX (Spring, 1959), 115-20.

PARTY GOING

Allen, Walter, "Henry Green," in Baker, D. V. , ed. , Mod-
    ern British Writing, 264-6.
Johnson, Bruce, "Henry Green's Comic Symbolism," BSUF,
    VI (Autumn, 1965), 31-6.
Kettle, A. , Introduction to the English Novel, 190-7.
Russell, J. , Henry Green, 97-113.
Ryf, R. S. , Henry Green, 15-20.
Tindall, W. Y. , Literary Symbol, 92-5.
Weatherhead, A. K. , Reading of Henry Green, 40-54.

BIBLIOGRAPHY

Ryf, R. S. , Henry Green, 47-8.
Weatherhead, A. K. , Reading of Henry Green, 169-70.

GREENE, GRAHAM, 1904-

GENERAL

Allen, W. Gore, "Evelyn Waugh and Graham Greene," IrM,
    LXXVII (January, 1949), 16-22.
_____, "The World of Graham Greene," IrEccRec, LXXI
    (January, 1949), 42-9.
Allen, Walter, "Graham Greene," in Baker, D. V. , ed. ,
    Writers of Today, 15-28. Also, as "The Novels of Gra-
    ham Greene," in Penguin New Writing, 18, 1943, 148-60.
_____, Modern Novel, 202-7.
Allott, Kenneth, and Miriam Farris, Art of Graham Greene.
Anon. , "Shocker," Time, LVIII (October 29, 1951), 98-104.
Atkins, J. , Graham Greene.
Barnes, Robert J. , "Two Modes of Fiction: Hemingway and
    Greene," Ren, XIV (Summer, 1962), 193-8.
Battock, Marjorie, "The Novels of Graham Greene," Norse-
    man, XIII (January-February, 1955), 45-52.
Bedard, Bernard J. , "The Thriller Pattern in the Major
    Novels of Graham Greene," DA, XX (1959), 1779-80
    (Michigan).
Boardman, Gwenn R. , "Graham Greene: The Aesthetics of
    Exploration," DA, XXIV (1963), 2474 (Claremont Gradu-
    ate School).

Boyle, Alexander, "Graham Greene," IrM, LXXVII (November, 1949), 519-25.

_____, "Symbolism of Graham Greene," IrM, LXXX (March, 1952), 98-102.

Braybrooke, Neville, "Graham Greene," Envoy, III (September, 1950), 10-23.

_____, "Graham Greene: A Pioneer Novelist," CE, XII (October, 1950), 1-9. Also in EJ, XXXIX (October, 1950), 415-23.

Bryden, Ronald, "Graham Greene, Alas," Spectator (September 28, 1962), 441-2.

Burgess, A., "The Greene and the Red: Politics in the Novels of Graham Greene," Urgent Copy, 13-20.

_____, "The Politics of Graham Greene," NYTBR (September 10, 1967), 2, 32, 34.

Cargas, H. J., ed., Graham Greene.

Chapman, Raymond, "The Vision of Graham Greene," in Scott, Nathan A., ed., Forms of Extremity in the Modern Novel, Richmond: John Knox Pr., 1965, 75-94.

Clancy, L. J., "Graham Greene's Battlefield," CritR, X (1967), 99-108.

Connolly, Francis X, "Inside Modern Man: The Spiritual Adventures of Graham Greene," Ren, I (Spring, 1949), 16-24.

Consolo, Dominick P., "Graham Greene: Style and Stylistics in Five Novels," in Evans, R. O., ed., Graham Greene, 61-95.

_____, "The Technique of Graham Greene: A Stylistic Analysis of Five Novels," DA, XX (1959), 297 (State Un. of Iowa).

Cosman, Max, "Disquieted Graham Greene," ColQ, VI (Winter, 1958), 319-25.

_____, "An Early Chapter in Graham Greene," ArQ, XI (Summer, 1955), 143-7.

Costello, Donald P., "Graham Greene and the Catholic Press," Ren, XII (Autumn, 1959), 3-28.

Currie, John S., "Supernaturalism in Graham Greene: A Comparison of Orthodox Catholicism with Religious Vision in the Major Novels," DA, XXVIII (1968), 3176A-77A (Alabama).

De Hegedus, Adam, "Graham Greene and the Modern Novel," Tomorrow, VIII (October, 1948), 54-6.

_____, "Graham Greene: The Man and His Work," WoR (August, 1948), 57-61.

De Vitis, A. A., "The Catholic as Novelist: Graham Greene and François Mauriac," in Evans, R. O., ed., Graham Greene, 112-26.

_____, "The Entertaining Mr. Greene," Ren, XIV (Autumn, 1961), 8-24.

_____, Graham Greene.

_____, "Religious Aspects in the Novels of Graham Greene," in Mooney, H. J., Jr., and T. F. Staley, eds., Shapeless God, 41-65.

Dinkins, Paul, "Graham Greene: The Incomplete Version," CathW, CLXXVI (November, 1952), 96-102.

Duffy, Joseph M., Jr., "The Lost World of Graham Greene," Thought, XXXIII (Summer, 1958), 229-47.

Ellis, William D., Jr., "The Grand Theme of Graham Greene," SWR, (Summer, 1956), 239-50.

Fielding, Gabriel, "Graham Greene: The Religious Englishman," Listener, LXXII (September 24, 1964), 465-6. Also in Critic, XXIII (October-November, 1964), 24-8.

Fowler, Alastair, "Novelist of Damnation," Theology, LVI (July, 1953), 259-64.

Fraser, G. S., Modern Writer and His World, 133-7.

Fytton, Francis, "Graham Greene: Catholicism and Controversy," CathW, CLXXX (December, 1954), 172-5.

Gardiner, Harold C., "Graham Greene, Catholic Shocker," Ren, I (Spring, 1949), 12-15.

Glicksberg, Charles I., "Graham Greene: Catholicism in Fiction," Criticism, I (Autumn, 1959), 339-53.

Graef, H., Modern Gloom and Christian Hope, 84-97.

Gregor, Ian, "The Green Baize Door," Blackfriars, XXXVI (September, 1955), 327-33.

Gusdorf, Barbara N., "Concepts of Sainthood in the Novels of Albert Camus and Graham Greene," DA, XXIX (1968), 1895A-6A (Mich. St. Un.).

Hall, J., Lunatic Giant in the Drawing Room, 111-23.

Herling, Gustav, "Two Sanctities: Greene and Camus," Adam, No. 201 (December, 1949), 10-18.

Hesla, David H., "Theological Ambiguity in the 'Catholic Novels'," in Evans, R. O., ed., Graham Greene, 96-111.

Hortmann, Wilhelm, "Graham Greene: The Burnt-Out Catholic," TCL, X (July, 1964), 64-76.

Hughes, Catharine, "Innocence Revisited," Ren, XII (Autumn, 1959), 29-34.

Jacobsen, Josephine, "A Catholic Quartet," ChS, XLVII (Summer, 1964), 143-6.

Jerrold, Douglas, "Graham Greene, Pleasure-Hater," Harper's, CCV (August, 1952), 50-2.

Johnston, J. L., "Graham Greene--The Unhappy Man," The Central Literary Magazine (Birmingham), XXXVIII (July, 1954), 43-9. (Not seen.)

Jones, James L., "Graham Greene and the Structure of Moral Imagination," PhoenixC, No. 2 (1966), 34-56. (Not seen.)

Joselyn, Sister M., O.S.B., "Graham Greene's Novels: The Conscience in the World," in Slote, Bernice, ed., Literature and Society: Nineteen Essays by Germaine Brée and Others, Lincoln: Un. of Neb. Pr., 1964, 153-72.

Karl, F.R., "Graham Greene's Demoniacal Heroes," Contemporary English Novel, 85-106.

Kelleher, James P., "The Orthodoxy and Values of Graham Greene," DA, XXVII (1966), 1825A (Boston Un.).

Kenny, Herbert A., "Graham Greene," CathW, CLXXXV (August, 1957), 326-9.

Kermode, Frank, "The House of Fiction: Interviews with Seven English Novelists," PR, XXX (Spring, 1963), 65-8.

_____, Puzzles and Epiphanies, 182-7.

Kohn, L., Graham Greene.

Kunkel, F.L., Labyrinthine Ways of Graham Greene.

_____, "The Theme of Sin and Grace in Graham Greene," in Evans, R.O., ed., Graham Greene, 49-60. Also, as "Greene's Catholic Themes," in Kunkel, F.L., Labyrinthine Ways of Graham Greene.

Lanina, T., "Paradoxes of Graham Greene," Inostrannaja Literatura, No. 3 (March, 1959), 188-96.

Lees, F.N., "Graham Greene: A Comment," Scrutiny, XIX (October, 1952), 31-42.

Lerner, Laurence, "Graham Greene," CritQ, V (Autumn, 1963), 217-31.

Lewis, R.W.B., "The Fiction of Graham Greene: Between the Horror and the Glory," KR, XIX (Winter, 1957), 56-75.

_____, "The 'Trilogy' of Graham Greene," MFS, III (Autumn, 1957), 195-215. Also in Cargas, H.J., ed., Graham Greene, 45-74.

Lodge, D., Graham Greene.

Lohf, Kenneth A., "Graham Greene and the Problem of Evil," CathW, CLXXIII (June, 1951), 196-9.

Marković, Vida E., "Graham Greene in Search of God," TSLL, V (Summer, 1963), 271-82.

Marshall, Bruce, "Graham Greene and Evelyn Waugh," Cweal, LI (March 3, 1950), 551-3.

Maurois, A., Points of View from Kipling to Graham Greene, 384-409.

Mesnet, Marie-Beatrice, Graham Greene and The Heart of the Matter.

Miller, J.D.B., "Graham Greene," Meanjin, V (Spring, 1946), 193-7.

Monroe, N. Elizabeth, "The New Man in Fiction," Ren, VI

(August, 1953), 9-12.

Mosley, Nicholas, "A New Puritanism," The European, No. 3 (May, 1953), 28-35, 38-40. (Reply to article by Neame, A. J.).

Neame, A. J., "Black and Blue: A Study of the Catholic Novel," The European, No. 2 (April, 1953), 26-30, 36.

O'Donnell, Donat, "Graham Greene," Chimera, V (Summer, 1947), 18-30.

O'Faolain, S., Vanishing Hero, 45-72.

Osterman, Robert, "Interview with Graham Greene," CathW, CLXX (February, 1950), 356-61.

Peters, W., "The Concern of Graham Greene," Month, X (November, 1953), 281-90.

Poole, Roger C., "Graham Greene's Indirection," Blackfriars, XLV (June, 1964), 257-68. Also in Cargas, H. J., ed., Graham Greene, 29-44.

Prescott, O., In My Opinion, 106-9.

Pryce-Jones, D., Graham Greene.

Puentevella, Renato, "Ambiguity in Greene," Ren, XII (1959), 35-7.

Rolo, Charles J., "Graham Greene: The Man and the Message," Atlantic, CCVII (May, 1961), 60-5.

Scott, Carolyn D., "The Urban Romance: A Study of Graham Greene's Thrillers," in Cargas, H. J., ed., Graham Greene, 1-28.

Scott, N. A., Jr., "Graham Greene: Christian Tragedian," Volusia Review, I, i (1954), 29-42. Also (expanded and revised) in Scott, N. A., Jr., Craters of the Spirit, 201-32. Also in Evans, R. O., ed., Graham Greene, 25-48.

Sewall, Elizabeth, "Graham Greene," DubR, No. 463 (First Quarter, 1954), 12-21.

_____, "The Imagination of Graham Greene," Thought, XXIX (March, 1954), 51-60.

Seward, Barbara, "Graham Greene: A Hint of an Explanation," WR, XXII (Winter, 1958), 83-95.

Shuttleworth, Martin, and Simon Raven, "The Art of Fiction III: Graham Greene," ParisR, I (Autumn, 1953), 24-41.

Slate, Audrey N., "Technique and Form in the Novels of Graham Greene," DA, XXI (1960), 629-30 (Wisconsin).

Smith, A. J. M., "Graham Greene's Theological Thrillers," QQ, LXVIII (Spring, 1961), 15-33.

Sternlicht, Sanford, "The Sad Comedies: Graham Greene's Later Novels," FloQ, I, iv (1968), 65-77.

Stratford, P., Faith and Fiction.

_____, "Graham Greene: Master of Melodrama," TamR, No. 19 (Spring, 1961), 67-86.

Tracy, Honor, "The Life and Soul of the Party," NRep,

CXL (April 20, 1959), 15-16.

Traversi, Derek, "Graham Greene," TC, CXLIX (1951), 231-40, 319-28.

Turnell, M., Graham Greene.

_____, "Graham Greene: The Man Within," Ramparts, IV (June, 1965), 54-64.

_____, "The Religious Novel," Cweal, LV (October 26, 1951), 55-7.

Voorhees, Richard J., "Recent Greene," SAQ, LXII (Spring, 1963), 244-55.

_____, "The World of Graham Greene," SAQ, L (July, 1951), 389-98.

Wassmer, Thomas A., "Graham Greene: A Look at His Sinners," Critic, XVIII (December, 1959-January, 1960), 16-17, 72-4.

_____, "The Problem and the Mystery of Sin in the Works of Graham Greene," ChS, XLIII (Winter, 1960), 309-15.

_____, "The Sinners of Graham Greene," DR, XXXIX (Autumn, 1959), 326-32.

Webster, Harvey C., in Evans, R.O., ed., Graham Greene, 1-24.

West, Paul, "Knowing the Worst: Graham Greene," The Wine of Absurdity, University Park and London: Penn. St. Un. Pr., 1966, 174-85.

Wilshere, A.D., "Conflict and Conciliation in Graham Greene," E&S, XIX (1966), 122-37.

Wilson, C., Strength to Dream, 46-55.

Woodcock, G., Writer and Politics, 125-53.

Wyndham, F., Graham Greene.

Zabel, Morton D., "Graham Greene," Nation, CLVII (July 3, 1943), 18-20. Also in Aldridge, J.W., ed., Critiques and Essays in Modern Fiction, 518-25. Also in O'Connor, W.V., ed., Forms of Modern Fiction, 287-93. Also (revised and expanded) in Zabel, M.D., Craft and Character, 276-96.

BRIGHTON ROCK

Allen, W., Modern Novel, 204-5.

Allott, K., and M. Farris, Art of Graham Greene, 147-60.

Atkins, J., Graham Greene, 88-101.

Braybrooke, Neville, "Graham Greene: A Pioneer Novelist," CE, XII (October, 1950), 4-6.

Clancy, L.J., "Graham Greene's Battlefield," CritR, X (1967), 99-101.

Consolo, Dominick P., "Graham Greene: Style and Stylistics in Five Novels," in Evans, R.O., ed., Graham

Greene, 68-74.

_____, "Music as Motif: The Unity of BRIGHTON ROCK,"
Ren, XV (Fall, 1962), 12-20. Also in Cargas, H. J., ed.,
Graham Greene, 75-87.

Currie, John S., "Supernaturalism in Graham Greene: A
Comparison of Orthodox Catholicism and Religious Vision
in the Major Novels," DA, XXVIII (1968), 3176A-77A
(Alabama).

De Vitis, A. A., "Allegory in BRIGHTON ROCK," MFS, III
(Autumn, 1957), 216-24.

_____, Graham Greene, 56-9, 80-7.

_____, "Religious Aspects in the Novels of Graham
Greene," in Mooney, H. J., Jr., and T. F. Staley, eds.,
Shapeless God, 42-4.

Ellis, William D., Jr., "The Grand Theme of Graham
Greene," SWR, XLI (Summer, 1956), 245-50.

Evans, Robert O., "The Satanist Fallacy of BRIGHTON
ROCK," in Evans, R. O., ed., Graham Greene, 78-85.

Glicksberg, Charles I., "Graham Greene: Catholicism in
Fiction," Criticism, I (Fall, 1959), 342-3.

Haber, Herbert R., "The Two Worlds of Graham Greene,"
MFS, III (Autumn, 1957), 257-64.

Hall, J., Lunatic Giant in the Drawing Room, 115-16.

Karl, F. R., "Graham Greene's Demoniacal Heroes," Contemporary English Novel, 93-5.

Kohn, L., Graham Greene, 2-10.

Kunkel, F. L., Labyrinthine Ways of Graham Greene, 106-
12.

Lewis, R. W. B., "The 'Trilogy' of Graham Greene," MFS,
III (Autumn, 1957), 198-203. Also in Lewis, R. W. B.,
Picaresque Saint, 242-8. Also in Cargas, H. J., ed.,
Graham Greene, 49-56.

Lodge, D., Graham Greene, 20-3.

McCall, Dan, "BRIGHTON ROCK: The Price of Order,"
ELN, III (June, 1966), 290-4.

McGowan, F. A., "Symbolism in BRIGHTON ROCK," Ren,
VIII (1955), 25-35.

Marian, Sister I. H. M., "Graham Greene's People: Becoming and Becoming," Ren, XVIII (Autumn, 1965), 17-18.

Maurois, A., Points of View from Kipling to Graham Greene,
386-7.

Mesnet, M. -B., Graham Greene, 13-19, 48-55, 84-6, passim.

O'Donnell, Donat, "Graham Greene," Chimera, V (Summer,
1947), 23-5.

Pryce-Jones, D., Graham Greene, 29-38.

Ruotolo, Lucio P., "BRIGHTON ROCK's Absurd Heroine,"

MLQ, XXV (December, 1964), 425-33.
Scott, Nathan A. , Jr. , "Graham Greene: Christian Trage-
dian," The Volusia Review, I, i (1954). Also, revised,
in Evans, R.O. , ed. , Graham Greene, 32-5. Also in
Scott, N.A. , Jr. , Craters of the Spirit, 208-11.
Smith, A. J. M. , "Graham Greene's Theological Thrillers,"
QQ, LXVIII (Spring, 1961), 18-22.
Stephens, Martha, "Flannery O'Connor and the Sanctified-
Sinner Tradition," ArQ, XXIII (Winter, 1967), 229-31.
Stewart, Douglas, Ark of God, 72-81.
Stratford, Philip, "Graham Greene: Master of Melodrama,"
TamR, No. 19 (1961), 71-6.
Traversi, Derek, "Graham Greene," TC, CXLIX (1951), 237-
40.
Turnell, M. , Graham Greene, 15-22.
Wilshere, A.D. , "Conflict and Conciliation in Graham
Greene," in English Association, Essays and Studies,
1966, 124-8.
Wilson, C. , Strength to Dream, 53-4.
Wyndham, F. , Graham Greene, 13-14.

A BURNT-OUT CASE

Atkins, J. , Graham Greene, 245-9.
De Vitis, A. A. , Graham Greene, 120-5.
Dooley, D. J. , "A BURNT-OUT CASE Reconsidered," WiseR,
CCXXXVII (Summer, 1963), 168-78.
_____, "The Suspension of Disbelief: Greene's BURNT-
OUT CASE," DR, XLIII (Autumn, 1963), 343-52.
Hardwick, E. , A View of My Own, 96-102. Also in PR,
XXVIII, Nos. 5-6 (1961), 702-7.
Hess, M. W. , "Graham Greene's Travesty on THE RING AND
THE BOOK," CathW, CXCIV (October, 1961), 37-42.
Hughes, R. E. , WSCL, II, i (Winter, 1961), 117-18.
Jarrett-Kerr, Martin, "The 491 Pitfalls of the Christian
Artist," in Scott, Nathan A. , Jr. , ed. , The Climate of
Faith in Modern Literature, N. Y.: Seabury Pr. , 1964,
195-7.
Kermode, Frank, "Mr. Greene's Eggs and Crosses," En-
counter, XVI (April, 1961), 69-75.
_____, Puzzles and Epiphanies, 176-82.
Lodge, D. , Graham Greene, 39-42.
Marian, Sister I. H. M. , "Graham Greene's People: Becom-
ing and Becoming," Ren, XVIII (Autumn, 1959), 20-2.
Noxon, James, "Kierkegaard's Stages and A BURNT-OUT
CASE," REL, III (January, 1962), 90-101.
O'Brien, C. C. , "Our Men in Africa," Maria Cross, 252-6.

Pryce-Jones, D. , Graham Greene, 93-7.
Sackville-West, Edward, "Time-Bomb," Month, XXV (1961),
    175-8.
Scott, N. A. , Jr. , "Graham Greene: Christian Tragedian,"
    Craters of the Spirit, 229-31.
Simon, John K. , "Off the Voie royale: The Failure of
    Greene's A BURNT-OUT CASE," Sym, XVIII (Summer,
    1964), 163-9.
Smith, Francis J. , "The Anatomy of A BURNT-OUT CASE,"
    America (September 9, 1961), 711-12.
Sternlicht, Sanford, "The Sad Comedies: Graham Greene's
    Later Novels," FloQ, I, iv (1968), 70-2.
Stratford, Philip, "Chalk and Cheese: A Comparative Study
    of A KISS FOR THE LEPER and A BURNT-OUT CASE,"
    UTQ, XXXIII (1964), 200-18. Also, revised, in Stratford,
    P. , Faith and Fiction, 1-30, 328-9.
Turnell, M. , Graham Greene, 32-4.
Van Kaam, Adrian, and Kathleen Healy, "Querry in Greene's
    A BURNT-OUT CASE," The Demon and the Dove: Per-
    sonality Growth Through Literature, Pittsburgh: Duquesne
    Un. Pr. , 1967, 259-85.
Voorhees, Richard J. , "Recent Greene," SAQ, LXII (Spring,
    1963), 252-5.

                        THE COMEDIANS

Allen, Walter, LonM, n. s. V (March, 1966), 73-80.
Bedford, Sybille, "Tragic Comedians," NYRB, VI (March 3,
    1966), 25-7.
De Vitis, A. A. , "Greene's THE COMEDIANS: Hollower
    Men," Ren, XVIII (1966), 129-36, 146. Also in Mooney,
    H. J. , Jr. , and T. F. Staley, eds. , Shapeless God, 57-65.
Lodge, D. , Graham Greene, 42-5.
_____, "Graham Greene's Comedians," Cweal, LXXXIII
    (February 25, 1966), 604-6.
Mayhew, Alice, "THE COMEDIANS," Nat. Catholic Reporter,
    (March 30, 1966). Also in Cargas, H. J. , ed. , Graham
    Greene, 134-41.
Pritchett, V. S. , "Brown's Hotel, Haiti," NStat (January 28,
    1966), 129.
Sternlicht, Sanford, "The Sad Comedies: Graham Greene's
    Later Novels," FloQ, I, iv (1968), 72-7.
Turnell, M. , Graham Greene, 34-7.

                    THE CONFIDENTIAL AGENT

Allott, K. , and M. Farris, Art of Graham Greene, 139-47.

Atkins, J. , Graham Greene, 102-9.
De Vitis, A. A. , Graham Greene, 59-61.
Karl, F. R. , "Graham Greene's Demoniacal Heroes," Con-
temporary English Novel, 88-9.
Kunkel, F. L. , Labyrinthine Ways of Graham Greene, 66-8.
Pryce-Jones, D. , Graham Greene, 64-6.

THE END OF THE AFFAIR

Allen, W. , Modern Novel, 206-7.
Anon. , "Shocker," Time, LVIII (October 29, 1951), 98-9.
Arnold, G. L. , "Adam's Tree," TC, CLIV (October, 1951),
337-42.
Atkins, J. , Graham Greene, 193-203.
Bogan, Louise, "Good Beyond Evil," NRep, CXXV (Decem-
ber 10, 1951), 29-30.
Boyle, Alexander, "Symbolism of Graham Greene," IrM,
LXXX (1952), 98-102.
Braybrooke, Neville, "Graham Greene and the Double Man:
An Approach to THE END OF THE AFFAIR," DubR, No.
455 (1st Quarter, 1952), 61-73. Also in Cargas, H. J. ,
ed. , Graham Greene, 114-29.
Clancy, L. J. , "Graham Greene's Battlefield," CritR, X
(1967), 105-8.
Consolo, Dominick P. , "Graham Greene: Style and Stylis-
tics in Five Novels," in Evans, R. O. , ed. , Graham
Greene, 87-91.
Currie, John S. , "Supernaturalism in Graham Greene: A
Comparison of Orthodox Catholicism with Religious Vision
in the Major Novels," DA, XXVII (1968), 3176A-77A (Ala-
bama).
De Vitis, A. A. , Graham Greene, 104-16.
_____ , "Religious Aspects in the Novels of Graham
Greene," in Mooney, H. J. , Jr. , and T. F. Staley, eds. ,
Shapeless God, 51-5.
Gardiner, H. C. , "Mr. Greene Does It Again," In All Con-
science, 96-8. Also in America, LXXXVI (October 27,
1951), 100-1.
_____ , "Second Thoughts on Greene's Latest," In All
Conscience, 98-102. Also in America, LXXXVI (Decem-
ber 15, 1951), 312-13.
Glicksberg, Charles I. , "Graham Greene: Catholicism in
Fiction," Criticism, I (Fall, 1959), 349-50.
Graef, H. , Modern Gloom and Christian Hope, 93-6.
Gregor, Ian, and Brian Nicholas, "Grace and Morality:
'THÉRÈSE DESQUEYROUX' (1927); THE END OF THE AF-
FAIR (1951)," The Moral and the Story, London: Faber

and Faber, 1962, 185-216.
Haber, Herbert R., "The End of the Catholic Cycle: The
   Writer Versus the Saint," in Evans, R.O., ed., Graham
   Greene, 127-50.
Hartt, J.M., Lost Image of Man, 117-18.
Kohn, L., Graham Greene, 22-31.
Kunkel, F.L., Labyrinthine Ways of Graham Greene, 128-32.
Lees, F.N., "Graham Greene: A Comment," Scrutiny, XIX
   (October, 1952), 40-2.
Lewis, R.W.B., Picaresque Saint, 268-70.
Lodge, D., Graham Greene, 31-5.
_____, "The Use of Key-Words in the Novels of Graham
   Greene- Love, Hate, and THE END OF THE AFFAIR,"
   Blackfriars, XLII (November, 1961), 468-74.
Poole, Roger C., "Graham Greene's Indirection," Blackfri-
   ars, XLV (June, 1964), 260-4. Also in Cargas, H.J.,
   ed., Graham Greene, 33-8.
Pryce-Jones, D., Graham Greene, 82-8.
Scott, Nathan A., Jr., "Graham Greene: Christian Tragedi-
   an," The Volusia Review, I, i (1954). Also, revised, in
   Evans, R.O., ed., Graham Greene, 41-7. Also in Scott,
   N.A., Jr., Craters of the Spirit, 217-23.
Smith, A.J.M., "Graham Greene's Theological Thrillers,"
   QQ, LXVIII (Spring, 1961), 28-30.
Spier, Ursula, "Melodrama in Graham Greene's THE END OF
   THE AFFAIR," MFS, III (Autumn, 1957), 235-40.
Sternlicht, Sanford, "The Sad Comedies: Graham Greene's
   Later Novels," FloQ, I, iv (1968), 65-6.
Stewart, Douglas, Ark of God, 87-90.
Wansbrough, John, "Graham Greene: The Detective in the
   Wasteland," HarvardA, CXXXVI (December, 1962), 11-13,
   29-31.
Waugh, Evelyn, Month, VI (September, 1951), 174-6.
West, A., Principles and Persuasions, 195-200.

ENGLAND MADE ME (THE SHIPWRECKED)

Allott, K., and M. Farris, Art of Graham Greene, 100-17.
Atkins, J., Graham Greene, 50-7.
De Vitis, A.A., Graham Greene, 75-9.
Fraser, G.S., Modern Writer and His World, 135-6.
Kunkel, F.L., Labyrinthine Ways of Graham Greene, 43-56.
Lewis, R.W.B., "The Fiction of Graham Greene: Between
   the Horror and the Glory," KR, XIX (Winter, 1957), 62-5.
_____, Picaresque Saint, 228-34.
Lodge, D., Graham Greene, 18-19.
Pryce-Jones, D., Graham Greene, 22-8.

Scott, N. A., Jr., "Graham Greene: Christian Tragedian,"
  Craters of the Spirit, 205-7.
Stratford, P., Faith and Fiction, 132-7.
Traversi, Derek, "Graham Greene," TC, CXLIX (1951),
  233-7.

A GUN FOR SALE

Allott, K., and M. Farris, Art of Graham Greene, 130-9.
Atkins, J., Graham Greene, 72-7.
De Vitis, A. A., Graham Greene, 55-9.
Lodge, D., Graham Greene, 14-16.
Pryce-Jones, D., Graham Greene, 62-4.
Stratford, P., Faith and Fiction, 188-92, 214-16.
Wyndham, F., Graham Greene, 11-13.

THE HEART OF THE MATTER

Allen, W. Gore, "Evelyn Waugh and Graham Greene," IrM,
  LXXXVII (January, 1949), 18-19.
Allott, K., and M. Farris, Art of Graham Greene, 214-44.
Atkins, J., Graham Greene, 159-67.
Barratt, Harold, "Adultery as Betrayal in Graham Greene,"
  DR, XLV (Autumn, 1965), 324-32.
Braybrooke, Neville, "Graham Greene, a Pioneer Novelist,"
  CE, XII (October, 1950), 7-8.
Clancy, L. J., "Graham Greene's Battlefield," CritR, X
  (1967), 103-5.
Consolo, Dominick P., "Graham Greene: Style and Stylistics
  in Five Novels," in Evans, R. O., ed., Graham Greene,
  78-85.
Currie, John S., "Supernaturalism in Graham Greene: A
  Comparison of Orthodox Catholicism with Religious Vision
  in the Major Novels," DA, XXVIII (1968), 3176A-77A
  (Alabama).
De Vitis, A. A., "The Church and Major Scobie," Ren, X
  (Spring, 1958), 115-20.
_____, Graham Greene, 97-104.
_____, "Religious Aspects in the Novels of Graham Greene,"
  in Mooney, H. J., Jr., and T. F. Staley, eds., Shapeless
  God, 48-51.
Glicksberg, Charles I., "Graham Greene: Catholicism in
  Fiction," Criticism, I (Fall, 1959), 347-9.
Gordon, Caroline, "Some Readings and Misreadings," SR,
  LXI (July-September, 1953), 393-6.
Graef, H., Modern Gloom and Christian Hope, 84-5, 89-93.
Haber, Herbert R., "The Two Worlds of Graham Greene,"

MFS, III (Autumn, 1957), 256-68.

Hall, J., Lunatic Giant in the Drawing Room, 119-21.

Hardwick, E., A View of My Own, 93-6. Also in PR, XV
(August, 1948), 937-9.

Herling, Gustav, "Two Sanctities: Greene and Camus,"
Adam, No. 201 (December, 1949), 12-16.

Howes, Jane, "Out of the Pit," CathW, CLXXI (April, 1950),
36-40.

Jefferson, Mary E., "THE HEART OF THE MATTER: The
Responsible Man," CarQ, IX (Summer, 1957), 23-31. Also in Cargas, H. J., ed., Graham Greene, 88-100.

Kettle, A., Introduction to the English Novel, 170-7.

King, Bruce, "Graham Greene's Inferno," EA, XXI (January-
March, 1968), 35-51.

Kohn, L., Graham Greene, 10-22.

Kunkel, F. L., Labyrinthine Ways of Graham Greene, 122-8.

Laitinen, Kai, "The Heart of the Novel: The Turning Point
in THE HEART OF THE MATTER," in Evans, R. O., ed.,
Graham Greene, 169-80.

Lees, F. N., "Graham Greene: A Comment," Scrutiny, XIX
(October, 1952), 36-40.

Levi, A. W., Literature, Philosophy, and the Imagination,
266-8.

Lewis, R. W. B., "The 'Trilogy' of Graham Greene," MFS,
III (Autumn, 1957), 211-15. Also in Lewis, R. W. B.,
Picaresque Saint, 258-64. Also in Cargas, H. J., ed.,
Graham Greene, 66-72.

Maurois, A., Points of View from Kipling to Graham Greene,
393-8.

Mesnet, M.-B., Graham Greene, 28-34, 61-8, 86-9, and
passim.

Moré, Marcel, "The Two Holocausts of Scobie," CC, I
(Winter, 1951), 44-63.

Mueller, W. R., "The Theme of Love: Graham Greene's
THE HEART OF THE MATTER," Prophetic Voice, 136-
57.

O'Donnell, Donat, "Graham Greene: The Anatomy of Pity,"
Maria Cross, 63-91. Also in O'Brien, C. C., Maria
Cross, 57-84.

O'Faoláin, Seán, "The Novels of Graham Greene; THE HEART
OF THE MATTER," Britain Today, No. 148 (August,
1948), 32-6.

Poole, Roger C., "Graham Greene's Indirection," Blackfriars, XLV (June, 1964), 265-6. Also in Cargas, H. J.,
ed., Graham Greene, 38-41.

Pryce-Jones, D., Graham Greene, 78-82.

Scott, Nathan A., Jr., "Graham Greene: Christian Trage-

dian," The Volusia Review, I, i (1954). Also, revised,
in Evans, R.O., ed., Graham Greene, 38-41. Also in
Scott, N.A., Jr., Craters of the Spirit, 214-17.
Smith, A.J.M., "Graham Greene's Theological Thrillers,"
QQ, LXVIII (Spring, 1961), 23-6.
Stewart, Douglas, Ark of God, 93-5.
Stratford, P., Faith and Fiction, 234-7.
_____, "Graham Greene: Master of Melodrama," TamR,
No. 19 (1961), 76-83.
Traversi, Derek, "Graham Greene," TC, CXLIX (1951),
323-8.
Turnell, M., Graham Greene, 27-31.
_____, "Graham Greene: The Man Within," Ramparts,
IV (June, 1965), 62-3.
Wansbrough, John, "Graham Greene: The Detective in the
Wasteland," HarvardA, CXXXVI (December, 1952), 11-13,
29-31.
Waugh, Evelyn, "Felix Culpa?" Cweal, XLVIII (July 16, 1948),
322-5.
Wilshere, A.D., "Conflict and Conciliation in Graham
Greene," in English Association, Essays and Studies,
1966, 132-7.
Wyndham, F., Graham Greene, 18-21.

IT'S A BATTLEFIELD

Allott, K., and M. Farris, Art of Graham Greene, 85-100.
Atkins, J., Graham Greene, 38-46.
Braybrooke, Neville, "Graham Greene, a Pioneer Novelist,"
CE, XII (October, 1950), 3-4.
De Vitis, A.A., Graham Greene, 72-5.
Kunkel, F.L., Labyrinthine Ways of Graham Greene, 34-43.
O'Donnell, Donat, "Graham Greene," Chimera, V (Summer,
1947), 22-3.
Pryce-Jones, D., Graham Greene, 20-2.
Stratford, P., Faith and Fiction, 120-2.

THE LABYRINTHINE WAYS
see THE POWER AND THE GLORY

LOSER TAKES ALL

De Vitis, A.A., Graham Greene, 67-8.
Kunkel, F.L., Labyrinthine Ways of Graham Greene, 92-7.
Voorhees, Richard J., "Recent Greene," SAQ, LXII (Spring,
1963), 245-6.

THE MAN WITHIN

Allott, K., and M. Farris, Art of Graham Greene, 51-60.
Atkins, J., Graham Greene, 17-21.
Kunkel, F. L., Labyrinthine Ways of Graham Greene, 24-33.
Lewis, R. W. B., "The Fiction of Graham Greene: Between
   the Horror and the Glory," KR, XIX (Winter, 1957), 62-5.
_____, Picaresque Saint, 228-32.
Lodge, D., Graham Greene, 11-12.
Maxwell, J. C., " 'The Dry Salvages': A Possible Echo of
   Graham Greene," N&Q, XI (October, 1964), 387.
Pryce-Jones, D., Graham Greene, 15-16.
Stratford, P., Faith and Fiction, 91-8.
Turnell, M., Graham Greene, 11-13.

THE MINISTRY OF FEAR

Allott, K., and M. Farris, Art of Graham Greene, 193-214.
Atkins, J., Graham Greene, 128-39, 144-8.
Auden, W. H., "The Heresy of Our Time," Ren, I (Spring,
   1949), 23-4.
De Vitis, A. A., Graham Greene, 61-5.
Duffey, Joseph M., Jr., "The Lost World of Graham Greene,"
   Thought, XXXIII (Summer, 1958), 237-45.
Grubbs, Henry A., "Albert Camus and Graham Greene,"
   MLQ, X (1949), 33-42.
Kunkel, F. L., Labyrinthine Ways of Graham Greene, 68-72,
   76-9.
Lodge, D., Graham Greene, 27-31.
Pryce-Jones, D., Graham Greene, 66-8.
Stratford, P., Faith and Fiction, 106-9.

THE NAME OF ACTION (Withdrawn at Author's Request)

Allott, K., and M. Farris, Art of Graham Greene, 60-71.
Atkins, J., Graham Greene, 24-7.
Lewis, R. W. B., Picaresque Saint, 228-30.
Stratford, P., Faith and Fiction, 98-102.

ORIENT EXPRESS see STAMBOUL TRAIN

OUR MAN IN HAVANA

Atkins, J., Graham Greene, 241-5.
De Vitis, A. A., Graham Greene, 68-71.
Kazin, A., "Graham Greene and the Age of Absurdity," Con-
   temporaries, 158-61.

Kunkel, F. L., Labyrinthine Ways of Graham Greene, 97-100.
Sternlicht, Sanford, "The Sad Comedies: Graham Greene's
   Later Novels," FloQ, I, iv (1968), 69-70.
Stratford, P., Faith and Fiction, 318-25.
Voorhees, Richard J., "Recent Greene," SAQ, LXII (Spring,
   1963), 249-52.

THE POWER AND THE GLORY (THE LABYRINTHINE WAYS)

Allen, W., Modern Novel, 207.
_____, Reading a Novel, 34-8. Also in Rev. ed., Lon-
   don: Phoenix Books, 1956, 37-42.
_____, in Baker, D. V., ed., Writers of Today, 25-7.
Allott, K., and M. Farris, Art of Graham Greene, 173-93.
Atkins, John, "Altogether Amen: A Reconsideration of THE
   POWER AND THE GLORY," in Evans, R. O., ed., Gra-
   ham Greene, 181-7.
_____, Graham Greene, 119-27.
Beary, Thomas J., "Religion and the Modern Novel," CathW,
   CLXVI (December, 1947), 204-5.
Braybrooke, Neville, "Graham Greene, a Pioneer Novelist,"
   CE, XII (October, 1950), 6-7.
Clancy, L. J., "Graham Greene's Battlefield," CritR, X
   (1967), 101-3.
Consolo, Dominick P., "Graham Greene: Style and Stylis-
   tics in Five Novels," in Evans, R. O., ed., Graham
   Greene, 74-8.
Currie, John S., "Supernaturalism in Graham Greene: A
   Comparison of Orthodox Catholicism with Religious Vision
   in the Major Novels," DA, XXVIII (1968), 3176A-77A
   (Alabama).
Davies, H., A Mirror of the Ministry in Modern Novels,
   103-10.
De Vitis, A. A., Graham Greene, 87-96.
_____, "Notes on THE POWER AND THE GLORY," An-
   notator (Purdue Un. Dept. of English), No. 5 (May, 1955),
   7-10.
_____, "Religious Aspects in the Novels of Graham
   Greene," in Mooney, H. J., Jr., and T. F. Staley, eds.,
   Shapeless God, 45-8.
Gardiner, Harold C., "Taste and Worth," America, LXXV
   (1946), 53.
Glicksberg, Charles I., "Graham Greene: Catholicism in
   Fiction," Criticism, I (Fall, 1959), 343-5.
Graef, H., Modern Gloom and Christian Hope, 86-9.
Haber, Herbert R., "The Two Worlds of Graham Greene,"
   MFS, III (Autumn, 1957), 256-68.

Hall, J., Lunatic Giant in the Drawing Room, 116-19.
Harmer, Ruth M., "Greene World of Mexico: The Birth of
    a Novelist," Ren, XV (Summer, 1963), 171-82, 194.
Hartt, J. N., Lost Image of Man, 116-17.
Herling, Gustav, "Two Sanctities: Greene and Camus,"
    Adam, No. 201 (December, 1949), 10-12.
Hoggart, Richard, "The Force of Caricature: Aspects of the
    Art of Graham Greene with Particular Reference to THE
    POWER AND THE GLORY," EIC, III (October, 1953),
    447-62.
Karl, F. R., "Graham Greene's Demoniacal Heroes," Con-
    temporary English Novel, 98-106.
Kohn, L., Graham Greene, 31-50.
Kunkel, F. L., Labyrinthine Ways of Graham Greene, 112-22.
Lees, F. N., "Graham Greene: A Comment," Scrutiny, XIX
    (October, 1952), 32-6.
Lewis, R. W. B., "The 'Trilogy' of Graham Greene," MFS,
    III (Autumn, 1957), 203-10. Also in Lewis, R. W. B.,
    Picaresque Saint, 248-58. Also in Cargas, H. J., ed.,
    Graham Greene, 56-66.
Lodge, D., Graham Greene, 24-7.
Marian, Sister I. H. M., "Graham Greene's People: Becom-
    ing and Becoming," Ren, XVIII (Autumn, 1965), 18-20.
Mauriac, François, "Graham Greene," in Great Men, Lon-
    don: Rockliff, 1952, 117-21. Also in Mauriac, F., Men
    I Hold Great, N. Y.: Philosophical Library, 1951, 124-8.
Maurois, A., Points of View from Kipling to Graham Greene,
    399-404.
Mesnet, M.-B., Graham Greene, 19-28, 55-60, 89-92, and
    passim.
Michener, Richard L., "Apocalyptic Mexico: THE PLUMED
    SERPENT and THE POWER AND THE GLORY," UR,
    XXXIV (June, 1968), 313-16.
O'Donnell, Donat, "Graham Greene," Chimera, V (Summer,
    1947), 28-30.
Patten, Karl, "The Structure of THE POWER AND THE
    GLORY," MFS, III (Autumn, 1957), 225-34. Also in Car-
    gas, H. J., ed., Graham Greene, 101-13.
Poole, Roger C., "Graham Greene's Indirection," Blackfri-
    ars, XLV (June, 1964), 259-60. Also in Cargas, H. J.,
    ed., Graham Greene, 32-3.
Pryce-Jones, D., Graham Greene, 47-58.
Sandra, Sister Mary, S. S. A., "The Priest-Hero in Modern
    Fiction," Person, XLVI (October, 1965), 538-42.
Smith, A. J. M., "Graham Greene's Theological Thrillers,"
    QQ, LXVIII (Spring, 1961), 30-2.
Stewart, Douglas, Ark of God, 81-7.

Traversi, Derek, "Graham Greene," TC, CXLIX (1951), 319-23.

Turnell, M., Graham Greene, 22-7.

————, "Graham Greene: The Man Within," Ramparts, IV (June, 1965), 58-62.

Wansbrough, John, "Graham Greene: The Detective in the Wasteland," HarvardA, CXXXVI (December, 1952), 11-13, 29-31.

Wells, Arvin R., in Hagopian, J.V., and M. Dolch, eds., Insight II, 153-64.

Wichert, Robert A., "The Quality of Graham Greene's Mercy," CE, XXV (November, 1963), 99-103.

Wilshere, A.D., "Conflict and Conciliation in Graham Greene," in English Association, Essays and Studies, 1966, 128-32.

Woodcock, George, "Mexico and the English Novelist," WR, XXI (Autumn, 1956), 29-32.

Wyndham, F., Graham Greene, 14-17.

THE QUIET AMERICAN

Allen, Walter, "Awareness of Evil: Graham Greene," Nation, CLXXXII (April 21, 1956), 344-6.

Allott, Miriam, "The Moral Situation in THE QUIET AMER-ICAN," in Evans, R.O., ed., Graham Greene, 188-206.

Atkins, J., Graham Greene, 227-36.

Consolo, Dominick P., "Graham Greene: Style and Stylis-tics in Five Novels," in Evans, R.O., ed., Graham Greene, 91-4.

De Vitis, A.A., Graham Greene, 116-20.

————, "Religious Aspects in the Novels of Graham Greene," in Mooney, H.J., Jr., and T.F. Staley, eds., Shapeless God, 55-6.

Elistratova, Anna, "Graham Greene and His New Novel," SovLit, VIII (1956), 149-55.

Evans, Robert O., "Existentialism in Greene's THE QUIET AMERICAN," MFS, III (Autumn, 1957), 241-8.

Freedman, Ralph, "Novel of Contention: THE QUIET AMER-ICAN," WR, XXI (Autumn, 1956), 76-81.

Hall, J., Lunatic Giant in the Drawing Room, 121-3.

Hinchliffe, Arnold P., "The Good American," TC, CLXVIII (December, 1960), 534-7.

Hughes, R.E., "THE QUIET AMERICAN: The Case Re-opened," Ren, XII (Autumn, 1959), 41-2+. Also in Car-gas, H.J., ed., Graham Greene, 130-3.

Kunkel, F.L., Labyrinthine Ways of Graham Greene, 148-53.

Lewis, R.W.B., "The Fiction of Graham Greene: Between

the Horror and the Glory," KR, XIX (Winter, 1957), 56-60.

Lodge, D., Graham Greene, 35-7.

McCormick, John O., "The Rough and Lurid Vision: Henry James, Graham Greene and the International Novel," JA, II (1957), 158-67.

McMahon, J., "Graham Greene and THE QUIET AMERICAN," Jammu and Kashmir Un. Rev., I (November, 1958), 64-73.

O'Brien, C.C., "Mr. Greene's Battlefield," Maria Cross, 249-51. Also in NStat&Nation, X (December, 1955).

Pryce-Jones, D., Graham Greene, 90-3.

Rahv, Philip, "Wicked American Innocence," Ctary, XXI (May, 1956), 488-90.

Rudman, Harry W., "Clough and Graham Greene's THE QUIET AMERICAN," VN, No. 19 (1961), 14-15.

Scott, Nathan A., Jr., "Christian Novelists Dilemma," ChC, LXXIII (August 1, 1956), 901-2. Also, as "Graham Greene: Christian Tragedian," Craters of the Spirit, 223-7.

Sternlicht, Sanford, "The Sad Comedies: Graham Greene's Later Novels," FloQ, I, iv (1968), 66-9.

Stratford, P., Faith and Fiction, 308-16.

Trilling, Diana, and Philip Rahv, "America and THE QUIET AMERICAN," Ctary, XII (July, 1956), 166-71.

Voorhees, Richard J., "Recent Greene," SAQ, LXII (Spring, 1963), 246-9.

RUMOUR AT NIGHTFALL (Withdrawn at Author's Request)

Allott, K., and M. Farris, Art of Graham Greene, 60-71.
Atkins, J., Graham Greene, 27-9.
Stratford, P., Faith and Fiction, 103-6, 171-3.

THE SHIPWRECKED see ENGLAND MADE ME

STAMBOUL TRAIN (ORIENT EXPRESS)

Allott, K., and M. Farris, Art of Graham Greene, 79-85.
Atkins, J., Graham Greene, 30-7.
De Vitis, A.A., Graham Greene, 54-5.
Kunkel, F.L., Labyrinthine Ways of Graham Greene, 83-9.
Lodge, D., Graham Greene, 12-14.
Pryce-Jones, D., Graham Greene, 17-20.
Stratford, P., Faith and Fiction, 111-16.

THE THIRD MAN

Alloway, Lawrence, "Symbolism in THE THIRD MAN," WoR, (March, 1950), 57-60.

BIBLIOGRAPHY

Beebe, Maurice, "Criticism of Graham Greene: A Selected Checklist with an index to Studies of Separate Works," MFS, III (Autumn, 1957), 281-8.
Birmingham, William, "Graham Greene Criticism: A Bibliographical Study," Thought, XXVII (Spring, 1952), 72-100.
Brennan, Neil, "Bibliography," in Evans, R. O., ed., Graham Greene, 245-76.
De Vitis, A. A., "Selected Bibliography," Graham Greene, 161-71.

GUTHRIE, A(LFRED) B(ERTRAM), JR., 1901-

GENERAL

Ford, T. W. A. B. Guthrie, Jr.
Kohler, Dayton, "A. B. Guthrie, Jr., and the West," CE, XII (February, 1951), 249-56.

THE BIG SKY

Folsom, J. K., American Western Novel, 64-70.
Ford, T. W., A. B. Guthrie, Jr., 10-18.
Kohler, Dayton, "A. B. Guthrie, Jr., and the West," EJ, XL (February, 1951), 67-70. Also in CE, XII (February, 1951), 251-4.
Prescott, O., In My Opinion, 141-3.
Stegner, Wallace, "Foreward" to Sentry Edition, THE BIG SKY, Boston: Houghton, 1965.

THESE THOUSAND HILLS

Folsom, J. K., American Western Novel, 74-5.
Ford, Thomas W., A. B. Guthrie, Jr., 27-33.

THE WAY WEST

Folsom, J. K., American Western Novel, 70-3.
Ford, T. W., A. B. Guthrie, Jr., 18-26.

Kohler, Dayton, "A. B. Guthrie, Jr. , and the West," EJ,
    XL (February, 1951), 70-2.   Also in CE, XII (February,
    1951), 254-6.
Prescott, O. , In My Opinion, 143-5.
Stuckey, W. J. , Pulitzer Prize Novels, 152-4.

HANLEY, JAMES, 1901-

GENERAL

Allen, W. , Modern Novel, 227-8.
Anon. , "The Kingdom of the Sea," TLS (February 27, 1953),
    136.
Moore, Reginald, "The Sea Around Him," John o' London's
    Weekly, LXI (September 19, 1952), 861-2.
Stokes, E. , Novels of James Hanley.

BOY

Stokes, E. , Novels of James Hanley, 28-34.

CAPTAIN BOTTELL

Stokes, E. , Novels of James Hanley, 96-103.

THE CLOSED HARBOUR

Stokes, E. , Novels of James Hanley, 158-65.

DRIFT

Stokes, E. , Novels of James Hanley, 19-28.

EBB AND FLOOD

Stokes, E. , Novels of James Hanley, 35-9.

EMILY

Stokes, E. , Novels of James Hanley, 150-2.

AN END AND A BEGINNING

Stokes, E. , Novels of James Hanley, 76-85.

THE FURYS

Stokes, E., Novels of James Hanley, 46-54.

HOLLOW SEA

Stokes, E., Novels of James Hanley, 110-19.

THE HOUSE IN THE VALLEY

Stokes, E., Novels of James Hanley, 182-6.

LEVINE

Stokes, E., Novels of James Hanley, 165-74.

NO DIRECTIONS

Stokes, E., Novels of James Hanley, 142-9.

THE OCEAN

Stokes, E., Novels of James Hanley, 119-27.

OUR TIME IS GONE

Stokes, E., Novels of James Hanley, 61-8.

RESURREXIT DOMINUS

Stokes, E., Novels of James Hanley, 175-81.

SAILOR'S SONG

Stokes, E., Novels of James Hanley, 127-38.

SAY NOTHING

Stokes, E., Novels of James Hanley, 193-200.

THE SECRET JOURNEY

Stokes, E., Novels of James Hanley, 54-61.

STOKER BUSH

Stokes, E., Novels of James Hanley, 103-10.

THE WELSH SONATA

Stokes, E., Novels of James Hanley, 186-93.

WHAT FARRAR SAW

Stokes, E., Novels of James Hanley, 152-5.

WINTER SONG

Stokes, E., Novels of James Hanley, 68-76.

HARRIS, MARK, 1922-

GENERAL

Enck, John, "Mark Harris: An Interview," WSCL, VI
(1965), 15-26.

SOMETHING ABOUT A SOLDIER

Sherman, B., Invention of the Jew, 220-1.

TRUMPET TO THE WORLD

Harris, Mark, "How to Write," in McCormack, T., ed.,
Afterwords, 65-79.

WAKE UP, STUPID

Oliphant, Robert, "Public Voices and Wise Guys," VQR,
XXXVII (Autumn, 1961), 528-37, passim.

HARTLEY, L(ESLIE) P(OLES), 1895-

GENERAL

Athos, John, "L. P. Hartley and the Gothic Infatuation," TCL,
VII (January, 1962), 172-9.
Bien, P., L. P. Hartley.
Bloomfield, P., L. P. Hartley and Anthony Powell.
Hall, J., Tragic Comedians, 111-28.
Melchiori, Giorgio, "The English Novelist and the American
Tradition," SR, LXVIII (Summer, 1960), 502-15. Also in
SA, I (1955).

Reynolds, Donald L., Jr., "The Novels of L. P. Hartley,"
DA, XXVIII (1968), 4186A (Un. of Washington).
Webster, Harvey C., "The Novels of L. P. Hartley," Crit,
IV, ii (1961), 39-51.

THE BOAT

Bien, P., L. P. Hartley, 106-66.
Bloomfield, P., L. P. Hartley and Anthony Powell, 17-18.
Fraser, G. S., Modern Writer and His World, 160.
Hall, J., Tragic Comedians, 114-21.

EUSTACE AND HILDA
(See also EUSTACE AND HILDA Trilogy)

Bloomfield, P., L. P. Hartley and Anthony Powell, 14-15.
Karl, F. R., Contemporary English Novel, 277-8.

EUSTACE AND HILDA Trilogy

Allen, W., Modern Novel, 253-7.
Bien, P., L. P. Hartley, 46-98.
Cecil, Lord David, "Introduction" to EUSTACE AND HILDA:
A TRILOGY, London: British Book Centre; N. Y.: Put-
nam, 1958.
Fraser, G. S., Modern Writer and His World, 160-1.

FACIAL JUSTICE

Bien, P., L. P. Hartley, 215-28.
Bloomfield, P., L. P. Hartley and Anthony Powell, 20-2.
Webster, Harvey C., "The Novels of L. P. Hartley," Crit,
IV, ii (1961), 41-4.

THE GO-BETWEEN

Athos, John, "L. P. Hartley and the Gothic Infatuation,"
TCL, VII (January, 1962), 174-5.
Bien, P., L. P. Hartley, 33-6, 167-83.
Bloomfield, P., L. P. Hartley and Anthony Powell, 16-17.
Davison, Richard A., "Graham Greene and L. P. Hartley:
'The Basement Room' and THE GO-BETWEEN," N&Q,
XIII (1966), 101-2.
Kitchin, Laurence, "Imperial Weekend," Listener, LXXIV
(October 28, 1965), 662-3, 667.

THE HIRELING

Athos, John, "L. P. Hartley and the Gothic Infatuation,"
    TCL, VII (January, 1962), 177-8.
Bien, P. , L. P. Hartley, 204-15.

MY FELLOW DEVILS

Athos, John, "L. P. Hartley and the Gothic Infatuation,"
    TCL, VII (January, 1962), 175-7.
Bien, P. , L. P. Hartley, 24-5, 184-91.
Hall, J. , Tragic Comedians, 122-7.

A PERFECT WOMAN

Bien, P. , L. P. Hartley, 191-204.
Kreutz, Irving, "L. P. Hartley, Who Are U? or: Luncheon
    in the Lounge," KR, XXV (Winter, 1963), 150-4.

THE SHRIMP AND THE ANEMONE
(See also EUSTACE AND HILDA Trilogy)

Bloomfield, P. , L. P. Hartley and Anthony Powell, 9-11.

SIMONETTA PERKINS

Bloomfield, P. , L. P. Hartley and Anthony Powell, 5-8.

THE SIXTH HEAVEN
(See also EUSTACE AND HILDA Trilogy)

Bloomfield, P. , L. P. Hartley and Anthony Powell, 11-14.

HAWKES, JOHN, 1925-

GENERAL

Enck, John, "John Hawkes: An Interview," WSCL, VI
    (1965), 141-55.
Fiedler, Leslie A. , "A Lonely American Eccentric: The
    Pleasures of John Hawkes," New Leader, XLIII (Decem-
    ber 12, 1960), 12-14.
Frohock, W. M. , "John Hawkes's Vision of Violence," SWR,
    L (Winter, 1965), 69-79.
Guerard, Albert J. , "The Prose Style of John Hawkes,"
    Crit, VI, ii (Fall, 1963), 19-29.

Littlejohn, David, "The Anti-realists," Daedalus, XIII
    (Spring, 1963), 256-8.
Malin, Irving, "The Gothic Family," in Psychoanalysis and
    American Fiction, 271-5.
Matthews, Charles, "The Destructive Vision of John Hawkes,"
    Crit, VI, ii (Fall, 1963), 38-52.
Oberbeck, S.K., "John Hawkes: The Smile Slashed by a
    Razor," in Moore, H.T., ed., Contemporary American
    Novelists, 193-204.
Ratner, Marc, "The Constructed Vision: The Fiction of
    John Hawkes," SA, XI (1965), 345-57.
Rovit, Earl, "The Fiction of John Hawkes: An Introductory
    View," MFS, X (Summer, 1964), 150-62.
Scholes, R., Fabulators, 66-74.
Schott, Webster, "John Hawkes, American Original," NYTBR
    (May 29, 1966), 4, 24-5.
Scott, Henry E., Jr., " 'The Terrifying Similarity': The
    Themes and Techniques of John Hawkes," DA, XXIX
    (1968), 878A-9A (Wisconsin).
Trachtenberg, Alan, "Barth and Hawkes: Two Fabulists,"
    Crit, VI, ii (Fall, 1963), 4-18.

THE BEETLE LEG

Matthews, Charles, "The Destructive Vision of John Hawkes,"
    Crit, VI, ii (Fall, 1963), 44-6.

THE CANNIBAL

Fiedler, L., Love and Death in the American Novel, 467-8.
Graham, John, "John Hawkes on His Novels; an Interview,"
    MR, VII (Summer, 1966), 449-53.
Malin, Irving, "The Gothic Family," in Psychoanalysis and
    American Fiction, 272-4.
_____, "Self-love," in New American Gothic, 38-41, 71-
    4.
Matthews, Charles, "The Destructive Vision of John Hawkes,"
    Crit, VI, ii (Fall, 1963), 40-4.
Ratner, Marc, "The Constructed Vision: The Fiction of
    John Hawkes," SA, XI (1965), 350-7.
Reutlinger, D.P., "THE CANNIBAL: 'The Reality of Vic-
    tim'," Crit, VI, ii (Fall, 1963), 30-7.
Scholes, R., Fabulator, 74-9.

THE GOOSE ON THE GRAVE

Malin, I., New American Gothic, 74-5.

THE LIME TWIG

Edenbaum, Robert I., "John Hawkes: THE LIME TWIG and
    Other Tenuous Horrors," MR, VII (Summer, 1966), 462-
    75.
Graham, John, "John Hawkes on His Novels; an Interview,"
    MR, VII (Summer, 1966), 453-7.
Malin, I., "Self-love," New American Gothic, 42-4.
Matthews, Charles, "The Destructive Vision of John Hawkes,"
    Crit, VI, ii (Fall, 1963), 48-52.
Scholes, R., Fabulators, 79-94.

THE OWL

Malin, I., "Self-love," in New American Gothic, 41-2.

SECOND SKIN

Galloway, David D., "Clown and Saint: The Hero in Cur-
    rent American Fiction," Crit, VII (Spring-Summer, 1965),
    53-4.
Graham, John, "John Hawkes on His Novels; an Interview,"
    MR, VII (Summer, 1966), 457-61.
Ricks, Christopher, "Chamber of Horrors," NStat (March 11,
    1966), 339-40.

BIBLIOGRAPHY

Bryer, Jackson R., "John Hawkes," Crit, VI, ii (Fall,
    1963), 89-94.

HAYES, ALFRED, 1911-

GENERAL

Aldridge, J.W., After the Lost Generation, 110-11, 114-16.

ALL THY CONQUESTS

Waldmeir, J.J., American Novels of the Second World War,
    83-8.

THE GIRL ON THE VIA FLAMINIA

Healey, Robert C., in Gardiner, H.C., ed., Fifty Years of
    the American Novel, 266-7.

HELLER, JOSEPH, 1923-

GENERAL

Ritter, Jesse P., "Fearful Comedy: The Fiction of Joseph
Heller, Gunter Grass, and the Social Surrealist Genre,"
DA, XXVIII (1967), 1447A (Arkansas).

CATCH-22

Anon., "A Review: CATCH-22," in Smith, Roger, ed., The
American Reading Public (The Daedalus Symposium),
N.Y.: Bowker, 1963, 234-7. Also in Daedalus (Winter,
1962), 155-64.
Cheuse, Alan, "Laughing on the Outside," StL, III (Fall,
1963), 81-7.
Cockburn, Alex, "CATCH-22," New Left Rev, No. 18 (Janu-
ary-February, 1963), 87-92.
Day, Douglas, "CATCH-22: A Manifesto for Anarchists,"
Carolina Qtly, XV (Summer, 1963), 86-92.
Denniston, Constance, "The American Romance-Parody: A
Study of Purdy's MALCOLM and Heller's CATCH-22,"
ESRS, XIV, ii (1965), 42-59, 63-4.
Doskow, Minna, "The Night Journey in CATCH-22," TCL,
XII (January, 1967), 186-93.
Galloway, David D., "Clown and Saint: The Hero in Current
American Fiction," Crit, VII (Spring-Summer, 1965), 50-
2.
Gordon, Caroline, and Jeanne Richardson, "Flies in Their
Eyes? A Note on Joseph Heller's CATCH-22," SoR, III
(January, 1967), 96-105.
Greenberg, Alvin, "The Novel of Disintegration: Paradoxi-
cal Impossibility in Contemporary Fiction," WSCL, VII
(Winter-Spring, 1966), 115-17.
Hoffman, F.J., Mortal No, 261-3.
Hunt, John W., "Comic Escape and Anti-Vision: The Novels
of Joseph Heller and Thomas Pynchon," in Scott, N.A.,
Jr., Adversity and Grace, 90-8, passim.
Karl, Frederick R., "Joseph Heller's CATCH-22: Only
Fools Walk in Darkness," in Moore, H.T., ed., Contempo-
rary American Novelists, 134-42.
Kostelanetz, Richard, "The New American Fiction," in Kos-
telanetz, R., ed., New American Arts, 212-14.
Lehan, Richard, and Jerry Patch, "CATCH-22: The Making
of a Novel," MinnR, VII, iii (1967), 238-44.
Lewis, R.W.B., "Days of Wrath and Laughter," Trials of

the World, 226-7.

Littlejohn, David, "The Anti-realists," Daedalus, XCII
(Spring, 1963), 258-9.

McDonald, James M., "I See Everything Twice: The Structure of Joseph Heller's CATCH-22," UR, XXXIV (March,
1968), 175-80.

McK. Henry, G. B. "Significant Corn: CATCH-22," CritR,
IX (1966), 133-44.

McNamara, Eugene, "The Absurd Style in Contemporary
American Literature," HAB, XIX, i (Winter, 1968), 44-9.

Mellard, James M., "CATCH-22: Deja-vu and the Labyrinth
of Memory," BuR, XVI, ii (May, 1968), 29-44.

Muste, John M., "Better to Die Laughing: The War Novels
of Joseph Heller and John Ashmead," Crit, V, ii (Fall,
1962), 16-27.

Pinsker, Sanford, "Heller's CATCH-22. The Protest of a
Puer Eternis," Crit, VII, ii (Winter, 1964-65), 150-62.

Podhoretz, N., "The Best Catch There Is," Doings and Undoings, 228-35.

Ramsey, Vance, "From Here to Absurdity: Heller's CATCH-
22," in Whitbread, T. B., ed., Seven Contemporary Authors, 100-18.

Ritter, Jesse P., Jr., "Fearful Comedy: The Fiction of
Joseph Heller, Günter Grass, and the Social Surrealist
Genre," DA, XXVIII (1967), 1447A (Arkansas).

Solomon, Jan, "The Structure of Joseph Heller's CATCH-
22," Crit, IX, ii (1967), 46-57.

Stern, J. P., "War and the Comic Muse," CL, XX (Summer,
1968), 193-216.

Wain, John, "A New Novel About Old Troubles," CritQ, V
(Summer, 1963), 168-73.

Waldmeir, J. J., American Novels of the Second World War,
160-5.

_____, "Two Novelists of the Absurd: Heller and Kesey,"
WSCL, V, iii (Autumn, 1964), 192-6.

Way, Brian, "Formal Experiment and Social Discontent:
Joseph Heller's CATCH-22," JAmS, II (1968), 253-70.

Wincelberg, Shimon, "A Deadly Serious Lunacy," in Kostelanetz, R., Contemporary Literature, 388-91. Also in
New Leader (May 14, 1962).

HEMINGWAY, ERNEST, 1898-1961

GENERAL

Aberg, Gilbert, "White Hope--Somewhat Sunburned; The Maturity of Hemingway," ChiR, VII (Spring, 1953), 18-24.

Akmakjian, Hiag, "Hemingway and Haiku," CUF, IX, ii
(Spring, 1966), 45-8.

Aldridge, John W., "Hemingway and Europe," Shen, XII, iii
(Spring, 1961), 11-24.

_____, "Hemingway: Nightmare and the Correlative of
Loss," After the Lost Generation, 23-43.

_____, "Hemingway: The Etiquette of the Beserk," Man-
drake, II (Autumn-Winter, 1954-55), 331-41. Also in Aldridge, J.W., In Search of Heresy, 149-65.

Algren, Nelson, "Hemingway: The Dye That Did Not Run,"
Nation, CXCIII (November 18, 1961), 387-90.

_____, Notes From a Sea Diary: Hemingway All the Way,
N.Y.: Putnam, 1965.

Allen, Charles A., "Ernest Hemingway's Clean Well-Lighted
Heroes," PacSp, IX (Autumn, 1955), 383-9.

Amiran, Minda R., "Hemingway as Lyric Novelist," Scripta
Hierosolymitana, XVII (1966), 292-300.

Anderson, David D., "Ernest Hemingway, the Voice of an
Era," Person, XLVII (April, 1966), 234-47.

Asselineau, Roger, ed., The Literary Reputation of Hemingway in Europe, N.Y.: New York Un. Pr., 1965.

Atkins, J., Art of Ernest Hemingway.

Backman, Melvin, "Hemingway: The Matador and the Crucified," MFS, I (August, 1955), 2-11. Also in Baker, C.,
ed., Hemingway and His Critics, 245-58. Also in Litz,
A.W., ed., Modern American Fiction, 201-14.

Bagchi, K., "The Hemingway Hero," Banasthali Patrika
(Rajasthan), No. 11 (1968), 91-4. (Not seen.)

Baker, C., Hemingway.

_____, "Hemingway," SatR, XLIV (July 29, 1961), 10-13.

_____, ed., Hemingway and His Critics.

_____, "Hemingway's Wastelanders," VQR, XXVIII (Sum-
mer, 1952), 373-92.

Baker, S., Ernest Hemingway.

Bardacke, Theodore, "Hemingway's Women," in McCaffery,
J.K.M., ed., Ernest Hemingway, 340-51.

Barnes, Lois L., "The Helpless Hero of Ernest Hemingway,"
S&S, XVII (Winter, 1953), 1-25.

Barnes, Robert J., "Two Modes of Fiction: Hemingway and
Greene," Ren, XIV (Summer, 1962), 193-8.

Beach, J.W., American Fiction, 69-119.

_____, "How Do You Like It Now, Gentlemen?" SR, LIX
(1951), 311-28. Also in Baker, C., ed., Hemingway and
His Critics, 227-44.

Beaver, Joseph, " 'Technique' in Hemingway," CE, XIV
(March, 1953), 325-8.

Benson, J. J. , Hemingway.
Bhai, Indira, "Hemingway's Hero," EMD, No. 2 (1963), 57-
   62. (Not seen.)
Bishop, John P. , "Homage to Hemingway," in Cowley, M. ,
   ed. , After the Genteel Tradition, 147-58. Also in Bish-
   op, J. P. , Collected Essays, 37-46. Also in NRep,
   LXXXIX (November 11, 1936), 39-42.
Blankenship, R. , American Literature, 731-42.
Bovie, Vernett, "The Evolution of a Myth: A Study of the
   Major Symbols in the Works of Ernest Hemingway," DA,
   XVII (1957), 1080 (Pennsylvania).
Brashers, H. C. , Introduction to American Literature, 135-8.
Bridgman, Richard, The Colloquial Style in America, N. Y. :
   Oxford Un. Pr. , 1966, 195-230.
Brooks, C. , "Ernest Hemingway: Man on His Moral Up-
   pers," Hidden God, 6-21.
Bryan, James E. , "Hemingway as Vivisector," UR, XXX
   (October, 1963), 3-12.
Burgum, E. B. , "Ernest Hemingway and the Psychology of
   the Lost Generation," Novel and the World's Dilemma,
   184-204.
Burnam, Tom, "Primitivism and Masculinity in the Work of
   Ernest Hemingway," MFS, I (August, 1955), 20-4.
Carpenter, Frederic I. , "Hemingway Achieves the Fifth Di-
   mension," PMLA, LXIX (September, 1954), 711-18. Al-
   so in Carpenter, F. I. , American Literature and The
   Dream, 185-93. Also in Baker, C. , ed. , Hemingway
   and His Critics, 192-201.
Clemens, Cyril, ed. , "Ernest Hemingway Memorial Number,"
   MTJ, XI, iv (Summer, 1962), 1-19.
Clendenning, John, "Hemingway's Gods, Dead and Alive,"
   TSLL, III (1962), 489-502.
Connolly, C. , Previous Convictions, 293-8.
Cooke, Alistair, "Hemingway: Master of the Mid-West Ver-
   nacular," MGW, (November 11, 1954), 7. (Not seen.)
Cowley, Malcolm, "Ernest Hemingway," in Baker, D. V. , ed. ,
   Writers of Today: 2, 3-17.
_____, "Nightmare and Ritual in Hemingway," Introduc-
   tion to The Portable Hemingway, N. Y. : Viking, 1945.
   Also in Weeks, R. P. , ed. , Hemingway, 40-51.
_____, "Papa and the Parricides," Esquire, LXVII, vi
   (June, 1967), 100-1+.
Curran, Ronald T. , "The Individual and the Military Institu-
   tion in Hemingway's Novels and Collier's Dispatches,"
   RLV, XXXIV (1968), 26-39.
D'Agostino, Nemi, "The Later Hemingway (1956)," SR,
   LXVIII (Summer, 1960), 482-93. Also in Weeks, R. P. ,

ed., Hemingway, 152-60.

Daniel, Robert A., "Hemingway and His Heroes," QQ, LIV (Winter, 1947-48), 471-85.

Dillingham, William B., "Hemingway and Death," EUQ, XIX (Summer, 1963), 95-101.

Dring, John R., "The Religious Element in Ernest Hemingway's Novels," DESB, VII (1962), 63-72, 104-12.

Drinnon, Richard, "In the American Heartland: Hemingway and Death," PsyR, LII (Summer, 1965), 5-31.

Edel, Leon, "The Art of Evasion," Folio, XX (Spring, 1955), 18-20. Also in Weeks, R.P., ed., Hemingway, 169-71.

Evans, Robert, "Hemingway and the Pale Cast of Thought," AL, XXXVIII (May, 1966), 161-76.

Farquhar, Robin H., "Dramatic Structure in the Novels of Ernest Hemingway," MFS, XIV (Autumn, 1968), 271-82.

Fenton, Charles A., The Apprenticeship of Ernest Hemingway: The Early Years, N.Y.: Farrar, 1954.

Fiedler, Leslie, "An Almost Imaginary Interview: Hemingway in Ketchum," PR, XXIX (Summer, 1962), 395-405.

_____, "The Death of the Old Men," A&S, (Winter, 1963-64), 1-5. Also in Fiedler, L.A., Waiting for the End, 9-19.

_____, "Men Without Women," in Weeks, R.P., ed., Hemingway, 86-92. Also in Fiedler, L., Love and Death in the American Novel, 304-9.

Floor, Richard, "Fate and Life: Determinism in Ernest Hemingway," Ren, XV (Fall, 1962), 23-7.

Friedrich, Otto, "Ernest Hemingway: Joy Through Strength," ASch, XXVI (Autumn, 1957), 470, 518-30.

Frohock, W.M., "Ernest Hemingway: Violence and Discipline," SWR, XXXII (1947), 89-97, 184-93. Also in Frohock, W.M., Novel of Violence in America, 166-98. Also in McCaffery, J.K.M., Ernest Hemingway, 262-91.

Fuchs, Daniel, "Ernest Hemingway, Literary Critic," AL, XXXVI (January, 1965), 431-51.

Fussell, Edwin, "Hemingway and Mark Twain," Accent, XIV (Summer, 1954), 199-206.

Gado, Frank, "The Curious History of the Hemingway Hero," Symposium (Union College), IV, i (1965), 18-22.

Galligan, Edward L., "Hemingway's Staying Power," MR, VIII (Summer, 1967), 431-9.

Garlington, Jack, "The Intelligence Quotient of Lady Brett Ashley," San Francisco Rev, I (September, 1959), 23-8.

Geismar, M., American Moderns, 54-8. Also in NYTBR (July 31, 1949), 1, 21.

_____, American Moderns, 61-4. Also in SatR (November 13, 1954), 24, 34.

_____, "Was 'Papa' Truly a Great Writer?" in Brown,
    F., ed., Opinions and Perspectives, 162-8.
_____, Writers in Crisis, Boston: Houghton, 1942, 39-85.
    Also in McCaffery, J.K.M., ed., Ernest Hemingway,
    143-89. Also, condensed, in VQR, XVII (1941), 517-34.
Gifford, William, "Ernest Hemingway: The Monsters and the
    Critics," MFS, XIV (Autumn, 1968), 255-70.
Gillespie, Gerald, "Hemingway and the Happy Few," OL,
    XXIII (1968), 287-99.
Goldhurst, William, F. Scott Fitzgerald and His Contempo-
    raries, Cleveland and N.Y.: World, 1963, 155-216.
Goodheart, Eugene, "The Legacy of Ernest Hemingway,"
    PrS, XXX (Fall, 1956), 212-18.
Gordon, Caroline, "Notes on Hemingway and Kafka," SR,
    LVII (Spring, 1949), 215-26.
Gordon, David, "The Son and the Father: Patterns of Re-
    sponse to Conflict in Hemingway's Fiction," L&P, XVI
    (1966), 122-38.
Graham, John, "Ernest Hemingway: The Meaning of Style,"
    MFS, VI (Winter, 1960-61), 298-313. Also in Baker, C.,
    ed., Ernest Hemingway, 183-92.
Gray, James, "Tenderly Tolls the Bell," On Second Thought,
    74-82. Also in McCaffery, J.K.M., ed., Ernest Heming-
    way, 226-35.
Grebstein, Sheldon, "Controversy," ASch, XXVII (Spring,
    1958), 229-31.
_____, "Sex, Hemingway, and the Critics," Humanist, XXI
    (July-August, 1961), 212-18.
_____, "The Tough Hemingway and His Hard-Boiled Chil-
    dren," in Madden, D., ed., Tough Guy Writers of the
    Thirties, 18-41.
Griffin, Gerald R., "Hemingway's Fictive Use of the Negro:
    'the curious quality of incompleteness'," Husson Rev, I
    (1968), 104-11.
Gurko, Leo, "The Achievement of Ernest Hemingway," EJ,
    XLI (June, 1952), 291-8. Also in CE, XIII (April, 1952),
    368-75.
_____, Ernest Hemingway and the Pursuit of Heroism.
_____, "Hemingway in Spain," in The Angry Decade,
    N.Y.: Dodd, 1947, 187-90. Also in McCaffery, J.K.M.,
    ed., Ernest Hemingway, 258-61.
Hagopian, John V., "Style and Meaning in Hemingway and
    Faulkner," JA, Band 4 (1959), 170-9.
Hale, Nancy, "Hemingway and the Courage to Be," VQR,
    XXXVIII (Autumn, 1962), 620-39.
Halliday, E.M., "Hemingway's Ambiguity: Symbolism and
    Irony," AL, XXVIII (March, 1956), 1-22. Also in Feidel-

son, C., Jr., and P. Brodtkorb, Jr., Interpretations of American Literature, 297-318. Also in Weeks, R. P., ed., Hemingway, 52-71.

_____, "Hemingway's Narrative Perspective," SR, LX (Spring, 1952), 202-18. Also in Baker, C., ed., Ernest Hemingway, 174-82. Also in Litz, A. W., ed., Modern American Fiction, 215-27.

Hand, Harry E., "Transducers and Hemingway's Heroes," EJ, LV (October, 1966), 870-1.

Hart, Robert C., "Hemingway on Writing," CE, XVIII (March, 1957), 314-20.

Hemingway, Leicester, "Ernest Hemingway's Boyhood Reading," MTJ, XII, ii (Spring, 1964), 4-5.

_____, My Brother, Ernest Hemingway, Cleveland: World, 1962. Also, excerpted, in Playboy, VIII (December, 1961), 48ff.

Hertzel, Leo J., "Hemingway and the Problem of Belief," CathW, CLXXXIV (October, 1956), 29-33.

_____, "The Look of Religion: Hemingway and Catholicism," Ren, XVII (Winter, 1964), 77-81.

Hoffman, Frederick J., "No Beginning and No End: Hemingway and Death," EIC, III (January, 1953), 73-84. Also in Feidelson, C., Jr., and P. Brodtkorb, Jr., Interpretations of American Literature, 320-31. Also, in part, as "The Unreasonable Wound," Twenties, 66-76.

Holder, Alan, "The Other Hemingway, TCL, IX (October, 1963), 153-7.

Holman, C. Hugh, "Ernest Hemingway," Shen, X (Winter, 1959), 4-11.

_____, "Ernest Hemingway: A Tribute," BA, XXXVI (Winter, 1962), 5-8.

_____, "Hemingway and Emerson," MFS, I (August, 1955), 12-16.

Hovey, R. B., Hemingway.

Howe, Irving, "Hemingway: The Conquest of Panic," NRep, CXLV (July 24, 1961), 19-20.

_____, "The Quest for a Moral Style," World More Attractive, 65-70.

Isabelle, J., Hemingway's Religious Experience.

Ishi, Ichiro, "Understanding of E. Hemingway," Hotogogisu, V (February, 1956), 12-13. (Not seen.)

Johnson, Edgar, "Farewell the Separate Peace," SR, XLVIII (July-September, 1940), 289-300. Also in McCaffery, J. K. M., ed., Ernest Hemingway, 130-42.

Jones, John A., "Hemingway: The Critics and the Public Legend," WHR, XIII (Autumn, 1959), 387-400.

Joost, Nicholas, Ernest Hemingway and the Little Magazines:

The Paris Years, Barre, Mass.: Barre Publishers, 1968.
Kaplan, H., "Hemingway and the Passive Hero," Passive
    Voice, 93-110.
Kashkeen, Ivan, "Alive in the Midst of Death," Soviet Litera-
    ture, No. 7 (1956), 160-72. Also in Baker, C., ed.,
    Hemingway and His Critics, 162-79.
_____, "What is Hemingway's Style?" Soviet Literature,
    No. 6 (1964), 172-80.
Kazin, Alfred, "Ernest Hemingway as His Own Fable," Corn-
    hill, No. 1040 (Summer, 1964), 139-47.
_____, On Native Grounds, Garden City, N.Y.: Double-
    day, 1956, 253-66. Also, revised, in McCaffery, J.K.
    M., ed., Ernest Hemingway, 190-204.
Kelly, John C., "Ernest Hemingway (1899-1961)," Studies,
    L (Autumn, 1961), 312-26.
Kerr, Johnny F., "Hemingway's Use of a Physical Setting
    and Stage Props in His Novels: A Study in Craftsmanship,"
    DA, XXVI (1965), 2217 (Texas).
Killinger, John, "Hemingway and Our 'Essential Worldliness',"
    in Scott, Nathan A., Jr., ed., Forms of Extremity in the
    Modern Novel, Richmond: John Knox Pr., 1965, 35-54.
_____, Hemingway and the Dead Gods: A Study in Exis-
    tentialism, Lexington: Un. of Kentucky Pr., 1960.
Kinnamon, Kenneth, "Hemingway, the Corrida, and Spain,"
    TSLL, I (Spring, 1959), 44-61.
Kirshner, Sumner, "From the Gulf Stream into the Main
    Stream: Siegfried Lenz and Hemingway," RS, XXXV
    (June, 1967), 141-7.
Knapp, Daniel, "Hemingway: The Naming of the Hero," StL,
    II, ii (1961), 30-41.
Kobler, Jasper, "Journalist and Artist: The Dual Role of
    Ernest Hemingway," DA, XXIX (1968), 606A-7A (Texas).
Lair, Robert L., "Hemingway and Cézanne: An Indebted-
    ness," MFS, VI (Summer, 1960), 165-8.
Lehan, Richard, "Camus and Hemingway," WSCL, I, ii
    (Spring-Summer, 1960), 37-48.
Levin, Harry, "Observations on the Style of Hemingway,"
    KR, XIII (Autumn, 1951), 581-609. Also in Baker, C.,
    ed., Hemingway and His Critics, 93-115. Also in Beaver,
    Harold, ed., American Critical Essays, London: Oxford
    Un. Pr., 1959, 286-313. Also in Levin, H., Contexts of
    Criticism, 140-67. Also, abridged, in Weeks, R.P., ed.,
    Hemingway, 72-85.
Levine, M.H., "Hemingway and the 'Lost Generation,'"
    KAL, No. 9 (1966), 19-26. (Not seen.)
Lewis, R.W., Jr., Hemingway on Love.
Linderoth, Leon W., "The Female Characters of Ernest

Hemingway," DA, XXVII (1966), 1060A (Florida State).

Lupan, Radu, "The Old Man and the World: Some Final Thoughts on Ernest Hemingway," LitR, X (Winter, 1966-67), 159-65.

McCaffery, J. K. M., ed., Ernest Hemingway.

McCormick, John, "Hemingway and History," WR, XVII (Winter, 1953), 87-98.

Macdonald, Dwight, "Ernest Hemingway," Encounter, XVIII (January, 1962), 115-21.

Madariaga, Salvador de, et al., "The World Weighs a Writer's Influence," SatR, XLIV (July 29, 1961), 18-22.

Marin, Dave, "Seven Hours with Papa," SWR, LIII (Spring, 1968), 167-77.

Matsuda, Sumio, "Symbolism and the Rhetoric of Fiction in Hemingway's Novels," DA, XXVIII (1968), 2689A (So. Calif.).

Maurois, Andre, "Ernest Hemingway," in Baker, C., ed., Hemingway and His Critics, 38-54.

Mizener, Arthur, "The Two Hemingways," in Bode, Carl, ed., The Great Experiment in American Literature, N. Y.: Praeger, 1961, 135-51.

Moloney, Michael F., "Ernest Hemingway: The Missing Third Dimension," in Gardiner, H. C., ed., Fifty Years of the American Novel, 183-96.

Moritz, Ken, in French, W. G., and W.E. Kidd, American Winners of the Nobel Literary Prize, 158-92.

Morris, L., "Salvage," Postscript to Yesterday, 154-6.

Morris, W., "The Function of Style: Ernest Hemingway," Territory Ahead, 133-46. Also in New World Writing, No. 13 (June, 1958), N. Y.: New American Library, 34-51.

————, "One Law for the Lion," PR, XXVIII (1961), 541-51.

Motola, Gabriel, "Hemingway's Code: Literature and Life," MFS, X (Winter, 1964-65), 319-29.

Noble, D. W., Eternal Adam and the New World Garden, 144-52.

Nozaki, Takashi, "An Embodiment of Sensibility: The Work of Ernest Hemingway," SEL, XXXVI (October, 1959), 93-108. (Not seen.)

O'Connor, William Van, "Faulkner's One-Sided 'Dialogue' with Hemingway," CE, XXIV (December, 1962), 208-15.

O'Faolain, S., Vanishing Hero, 112-45.

O'Hara, John L., et al., "Who the Hell is Hemingway?" True, XXXVI (February, 1956), 14-19, 25-31, 68. (Not seen.)

Oldsey, Bernard S., "Hemingway's Old Men," MFS, I

(August, 1955), 31-5.

_____, "The Snows of Ernest Hemingway," WSCL, IV, ii
(Spring-Summer), 172-98.

Parks, Edd W., "Hemingway and Faulkner: The Pattern of
Their Thought," Dagens Nyheter (Copenhagen) (February
12, 1956), 4-5. Also in SAB, XII, iv (1957), 1-2.

Pendleton, Harold E., "Ernest Hemingway: A Theory of
Learning," DA, XX (1960), 3302-3 (Illinois).

Peterson, Richard K., "Hemingway: Direct and Oblique,"
DA, XXII (1962), 4353-4 (Un. of Washington). Also The
Hague, The Netherlands: Mouton, 1969.

Phillips, William L., "Sherwood Anderson's Two Prize Pu-
pils," Un. of Chicago Mag, XLVII (January, 1955), 9-12.
Also in White, R. L., ed., The Achievement of Sherwood
Anderson, Chapel Hill: Un. of No. Carolina Pr., 1966,
202-10.

Plimpton, George, "The Art of Fiction, XXI: Hemingway,"
ParisR, No. 18 (1958), 61-89. (Interview). Also in
Writers at Work, 2nd ser., 215-39. Also in Baker, C.,
ed., Hemingway and His Critics, 19-37.

Portuondo, José A., "The Old Man and Society," Americas,
IV (December, 1952), 6-7+.

Prescott, O., In My Opinion, 64-8.

Reardon, John, "Hemingway's Esthetic and Ethical Sports-
men," UR, XXXIV (October, 1967), 13-23.

Rosenfeld, Isaac, "A Farewell to Hemingway," KR, XIII
(Winter, 1951), 147-55. Also in Rosenfeld, I., Age of
Enormity, 258-67.

Ross, Lillian, "Profiles," NY (May 13, 1950), 36-62.

Rovit, E., Ernest Hemingway.

Rubinstein, Annette T., "Brave and Baffled Hunter," Mainstream, XIII, i (January, 1960), 1-23.

Sanders, David, "Ernest Hemingway's Spanish Civil War Experience," AQ, XII (Summer, 1960), 133-43.

Sanderson, S. F., Ernest Hemingway.

Savage, D. S., Withered Branch, 23-43.

Schwartz, Delmore, "Ernest Hemingway's Literary Situation,"
SoR, III (Spring, 1938), 769-82. Also in McCaffery, J.
K. M., ed., Ernest Hemingway, 114-29.

_____, "The Fiction of Ernest Hemingway," PUSA, No.
13 (Autumn, 1955), 70-88.

Scott, N. A., Jr., Ernest Hemingway.

Shockley, Martin S., "Hemingway's Moment of Truth,"
ColQ, V (Spring, 1957), 380-8.

Slochower, H., No Voice is Wholly Lost, 36-40.

Snell, G., "Ernest Hemingway and the 'Fifth Dimension',"
Shapers of American Fiction, 156-72.

Soucie, Gary, "Reflections on Hemingway," Carolina Qtly, XII (Spring, 1960), 57-63.

Spiller, R. E. , Cycle of American Literature, 269-74.

_____, The Third Dimension: Studies in Literary History, N. Y.: Macmillan, 1965, 168-71.

Spivey, Ted R. , "Hemingway's Pursuit of Happiness on the Open Road," EUQ, XI (December, 1955), 240-52.

Stavrou, C. N. , "Nada, Religion and Hemingway," Topic, VI (Fall, 1966), 5-20.

Stephens, Robert O. , "The Escape Motif in the Works of Ernest Hemingway," DA, XIX (1958), 1079-80 (Texas).

Sykes, Robert H. , "Ernest Hemingway's Style: A Descriptive Analysis," DA, XXIV (1963), 2043 (Pittsburgh).

Tanner, T. , "Ernest Hemingway's Unhurried Sensations," Reign of Wonder, 228-57.

Thorp, W. , "The Persistance of Naturalism in the Novel," American Writing in the Twentieth Century, 185-95.

Trilling, Lionel, "Hemingway and His Critics," PR, VI (Winter, 1939), 52-60.

Vandiver, Samuel E. , "The Architecture of Hemingway's Prose," DA, XXVIII (1967), 2268A (Texas).

Van Gelder, Robert, Writers on Writing, 95-8.

Wagenknecht, E. , "Ernest Hemingway: Legend and Reality," Cavalcade of the American Novel, 368-81.

Waggoner, Hyatt H. , "Ernest Hemingway," ChS, XXXVIII (June, 1955), 114-20.

Walcutt, C. C. , American Literary Naturalism, 270-80.

Warren, Robert Penn, "Hemingway," KR, IX (Winter, 1947), 1-28. Also in Warren, R. P. , Selected Essays, 80-118. Also in Aldridge, J. W. , ed. , Critiques and Essays on Modern Fiction, 447-73. Also in Zabel, M. D. , ed. , Literary Opinion in America, 444-63. Also, Introduction to A FAREWELL TO ARMS, N. Y.: Scribner, 1949. Also in Horizon, XV (1947), 156-80.

Webster, Harvey C. , "Ernest Hemingway: The Pursuit of Death," TQ, VII (Summer, 1964), 149-59.

Weeks, R. P. , ed. , Hemingway.

_____, "Hemingway and the Spectorial Attitude," WHR, XI (Summer, 1957), 277-81.

_____, "Hemingway and the Uses of Isolation," UKCR, XXIV (December, 1957), 119-25.

Wegelin, Christof, "Hemingway and the Decline of International Fiction," SR, LXXIII (Spring, 1965), 285-98.

West, Ray B. , Jr. , "Ernest Hemingway: The Failure of Sensibility," in O'Connor, W. V. , ed. , Forms of Modern Fiction, 87-101. Also in SR, LIII (Winter, 1945), 120-35.

White, William, "Ernest Hemingway: Violence, Blood, Death," Orient/West (Tokyo), VI (November, 1961), 11-23.

_____, "Father and Son: Some Comments on Hemingway's Psychology," DR, XXXI (Winter, 1952), 276-84.

_____, "Novelist as Reporter: Ernest Hemingway," OW, IX, v (1964), 77-92.

Whitfield, E., "Hemingway: The Man," Why, I (April, 1953), 10-19. (Not seen.)

Wilson, Edmund, "Hemingway: Gauge of Morale," The Wound and the Bow: Seven Studies in Literature, N.Y.: Oxford Un. Pr., 1947, 214-42. Also in Atlantic, CLXIV (July, 1939). Also in Caldwell, Guy, ed., Readings from the Americas: An Introduction to Democratic Thought, N.Y.: Ronald Pr., 1947, 246-48. Also in McCaffery, J. K. M., ed., Ernest Hemingway, 236-57. Also in Rahv, P., ed., Literature in America, 373-90. Also in Wilson, E., Eight Essays, Garden City, N.Y.: Doubleday, 1954, 92-114.

Wyatt, Bryant N., "Huckleberry Finn and the Art of Ernest Hemingway," MTJ, XIII, iv (Summer, 1967), 1-8.

Wylder, D.E., Hemingway's Heroes.

Wylder, Robert C., "An Investigation of Hemingway's Fictional Method, Its Sources, and Its Influence on American Literature," DA, XV (1955), 2535 (Wisconsin).

Wyrick, Green D., "Hemingway and Bergson: The Elan Vital," MFS, I (August, 1955), 17-19.

_____, "The World of Ernest Hemingway: A Critical Study," ESRS, II (September, 1953), 3-32.

Yokelson, Joseph B., "Symbolism in the Fiction of Ernest Hemingway," DA, XXIII (1962), 1714 (Brown).

Young, Philip, "Crane and Hemingway," in Bassan, Maurice, ed., Stephen Crane: A Collection of Critical Essays, Englewood Cliffs, N.J.: Prentice-Hall, 1967, 52-6. Also in Young, P., Ernest Hemingway, 191-6.

_____, Ernest Hemingway.

_____, Ernest Hemingway (UMPAW, 1). Also in O'Connor, W.V., ed., Seven Modern American Novelists, 153-88.

_____, "Hemingway: A Defense," Folio, XX (Spring, 1955), 20-2. Also in Weeks, R.P., ed., Hemingway, 172-4.

Yu, Beongcheon, "The Still Center of Hemingway's World," PhoenixK, XII (1968), 15-44. (Not seen.)

Yunck, John A., "The Natural History of a Dead Quarrel: Hemingway and the Humanists," SAQ, LXII (Winter, 1963), 29-42.

ACROSS THE RIVER AND INTO THE TREES

Baker, C., Hemingway, 264-88.
Baker, S., Ernest Hemingway, 121-6.
Beach, Joseph W., "How Do You Like It Now, Gentlemen?"
SR, LIX (1951), 311-17. Also in Baker, C., ed., Hem-
ingway and His Critics, 227-33.
Benson, J.J., Hemingway, 48-54.
Connolly, C., Previous Convictions, 290-2.
Dring, John R., "The Religious Element in Ernest Heming-
way's Novels," DESB, VII (1962), 107-9.
Gardiner, H.C., "He-Man Whimpering," In All Conscience,
124-5. Also in America, LXXXIII (September 16, 1950),
628, 630.
Geismar, M., SatR, XXXIII (September 9, 1950), 18. Also
in Geismar, M., American Moderns, 59-61.
Gurko, L., Ernest Hemingway and the Pursuit of Heroism,
152-8.
Hovey, R.B., Hemingway, 173-4, 177-90.
Lewis, R.W., Jr., Hemingway on Love, 181-96.
Lisca, Peter, "The Structure of Hemingway's ACROSS THE
RIVER AND INTO THE TREES," MFS, XII (Summer,
1966), 232-50.
Oppel, Horst, "Hemingway's ACROSS THE RIVER AND IN-
TO THE TREES," in Baker, C., ed., Hemingway and
His Critics, 213-26.
Prescott, O., In My Opinion, 68-70.
Rahv, Philip, in Ctary, X (October, 1950), 400-2. Also in
Rahv, P., Image and Idea, 188-92. Also in Rahv, P.,
Literature and the Sixth Sense, 351-5. Also in Rahv, P.,
Myth and the Powerhouse, 193-8.
Rosenfeld, Isaac, "A Farewell to Hemingway," KR, XIII
(Winter, 1951), 147-55. Also in Rosenfeld, I., Age of
Enormity, 258-67.
Sanderson, S.F., Ernest Hemingway, 103-12.
Seyppel, Joachim H., "Two Variations on a Theme: Dying
in Venice (Thomas Mann and Ernest Hemingway)," L&P,
VII (February, 1957), 8-12.
Stephens, Robert O., "Hemingway's ACROSS THE RIVER
AND INTO THE TREES: A Reprise," TxSE, XXXVII
(1958), 92-101.
Waugh, Evelyn, "The Case of Mr. Hemingway," Cweal
(November 3, 1950), 97-8.
Wylder, D.E., Hemingway's Heroes, 165-98.
Young, P., Ernest Hemingway, 114-21.
_____, Ernest Hemingway (UMPAW, 1), 17-19. Also in
O'Connor, W.V., ed., Seven Modern American Novel-

ists, 166-8.
Zabel, M. D., "A Good Day for Mr. Tolstoy," Nation,
    CLXXI (September 9, 1950), 9. Also in Zabel, M. D.,
    Craft and Character, 317-21.

A FAREWELL TO ARMS

Aldridge, J. W., After the Lost Generation, 6-10, 38-9,
    passim.
Allen, W., Modern Novel, 97-8.
Anderson, Charles R., "Hemingway's Other Style," MLN,
    LXXVI (May, 1961), 434-42. Also in Baker, C., ed.,
    Ernest Hemingway, 41-6.
Baker, Carlos, in Stegner, W., ed., American Novel, 192-
    205.
_____, "The Mountain and the Plain," VQR, XXVII
    (Summer, 1951), 410-18. Also in Baker, C., Hemingway,
    94-6, 98-109. Also in Baker, C., ed., Ernest Heming-
    way, 47-60.
_____, "On Ernest Hemingway," in Madden, C. F., ed.,
    Talks With Authors, 74-88.
Baker, S., Ernest Hemingway, 62-73.
Beach, J. W., American Fiction, 84-9, passim.
Benson, J. J., Hemingway, 81-112.
Brashers, H. C., An Introduction to American Literature,
    137-8.
Burgum, E. B., Novel and the World's Dilemma, 184-6.
Cecil, L. Moffit, "The Color of A FAREWELL TO ARMS,"
    RS, XXXVI (June, 1968), 168-73.
Cooperman, Stanley, "Death and Cojones: Hemingway's A
    FAREWELL TO ARMS," SAQ, LXIII (Winter, 1964), 85-
    92.
_____, World War I and the American Novel, 181-90,
    passim.
Davidson, Donald, The Spyglass: Views and Reviews, 1924-
    1930, Nashville: Vanderbilt Un. Pr., 1963, 88-92.
Dring, John R., "The Religious Element in Ernest Heming-
    way's Novels," DESB, VII (1962), 67-71.
Farquhar, Robin H., "Dramatic Structure in the Novels of
    Ernest Hemingway," MFS, XIV (Autumn, 1968), 275-7.
Friedman, Norman, "Criticism and the Novel," AR, XVIII
    (Fall, 1958), 352-6. Also in Westbrook, M., ed., Mod-
    ern American Novel, 113-18.
_____, "Hardy, Hemingway, Crane, Woolf and Conrad,"
    AR, XVIII (Fall, 1958), 343-8, 352-6.
Friedrich, Otto, "Ernest Hemingway: Joy Through Strength,"
    ASch, XXVI (1957), 519-24, passim.

Frohock, W. M. , Ernest Hemingway: Violence and Disci-
pline: I," SWR, XXXII (1947), 95-7. Also in Frohock,
W. M. , Novel of Violence in America, 176-9+. Also in
McCaffery, J. K. M. , ed. , Ernest Hemingway, 272-5.

Geismar, M. , Writers in Crisis, 46-7.

Gelfant, Blanche, "Language as a Moral Code in A FARE-
WELL TO ARMS," MFS, IX (1963), 173-6.

Gerstenberger, Donna, "THE WASTELAND in A FAREWELL
TO ARMS," MLN, LXXVI (1961), 24-5.

Gibson, Walker, "Tough Talk: The Rhetoric of Frederick
Henry," in Tough, Sweet, and Stuffy, Bloomington: Indiana Un. Pr. , 1966, 28-42.

Glasser, William A. , "A FAREWELL TO ARMS, SR, LXXIV
(Spring, 1966), 453-69.

_____, "Hemingway's A FAREWELL TO ARMS, Expl, XX
(October, 1961), Item 18.

Gurko, L. , Ernest Hemingway and the Pursuit of Heroism,
81-109.

Hackett, Francis, "Hemingway: A FAREWELL TO ARMS,"
SRL, XXXII (August 6, 1949), 32-3.

Halliday, E. M. , "Hemingway's Ambiguity: Symbolism and
Irony," AL, XXVIII (March, 1956), 7-18. Also in Baker,
C. , ed. , Ernest Hemingway, 61-74. Also in Feidelson,
C. , Jr. , and P. Brodtkorb, Jr. , Interpreations of Amer-
ican Literature, 303-13. Also in Weeks, R. P. , ed. ,
Hemingway, 52-71.

Hallman, Ralph J. , Psychology of Literature: A Study of
Alienation and Tragedy, N. Y. : Philosophical Library,
1961, 119-21.

Hardy, J. E. , Man in the Modern Novel, 123-36.

Hashiguchi, Yasuo, "A FAREWELL TO ARMS and 'A Farewell to Arms'," KAL, No. 3 (May, 1960), 1-8.

Hemingway, Ernest, "The Original Conclusion to A FARE-
WELL TO ARMS," in Baker, C. , ed. , Ernest Hemingway,
75.

Hoffman, Frederick J. , "No Beginning and No End: Hemingway and Death," EIC, III (1953), 78-80. Also in Feidelson, C. , Jr. , and P. Brodtkorb, eds. , Interpretations of
American Literature, 325-6.

Hovey, Richard B. , "A FAREWELL TO ARMS: Hemingway's
Liebestod," UR, XXXIII (December, 1966), 93-100.

_____, "A FAREWELL TO ARMS: Hemingway's Liebe-
stod II," UR, XXXIII (March, 1967), 163-8.

_____, Hemingway, 73-91.

Keeler, Clinton, "A FAREWELL TO ARMS: Hemingway and
Peele," MLN, LXXVI (November, 1961), 622-5.

Knapp, Daniel, "Hemingway: The Naming of the Hero," StL,

II, ii (1961), 31-4.

Labor, Earle, "Crane and Hemingway: Anatomy of Trauma,"
Ren, XI (1959), 189-96.

Lewis, R.W., Jr., Hemingway on Love, 39-54.

Liedloff, Helmut, "Two War Novels: A Critical Comparison," RLC, XLII (1968), 390-406.

Light, James F., "The Religion of Death in A FAREWELL
TO ARMS," MFS, VII (Summer, 1961), 169-73. Also in
Baker, C., ed., Ernest Hemingway, 37-40.

McAleer, John J., "A FAREWELL TO ARMS: Frederic
Henry's Rejected Passion," Ren, XIV (Winter, 1961), 72-
9, 89.

Marcus, Fred H., "A FAREWELL TO ARMS: The Impact
of Irony and the Irrational," EJ, LII (November, 1962),
527-35.

Marcus, Mordecai, "A FAREWELL TO ARMS: Novel into
Film," JCMVASA, II (1961), 69-71.

Mazzaro, Jerome L., "George Peele and A FAREWELL TO
ARMS: A Thematic Tie?" MLN, LXXV (February, 1960),
118-19.

Meriwether, James B., "The Dashes in Hemingway's A
FAREWELL TO ARMS," PBSA, LVIII, iv (1964), 449-57.

Morioka, Sakae, "HUCK FINN and A FAREWELL TO ARMS,"
KAL, No. 5 (1962), 27-35.

Moses, W.R., "Victory in Defeat: 'Ad Astra' and A FARE-
WELL TO ARMS," MissQ, XIX (Spring, 1966), 85-9.

_____, "Water, Water Everywhere: OLD MAN and A FARE-
WELL TO ARMS," MFS, V (Summer, 1959), 172-4.

Richardson, H. Edward, "The 'Hemingwaves' in Faulkner's
WILD PALMS," MFS, IV (Winter, 1958-59), 357-60.

Robinson, Forrest D., "The Tragic Awareness of Hemingway's First-Person Narrators: A Study of THE SUN AL-
SO RISES and A FAREWELL TO ARMS," DA, XXVII
(1967), 2543A (Ohio).

Ross, Frank, "The Assailant-Victim in Three War Protest
Novels," Paunch, XXXII (1968), 46-57.

Rossky, William, "Sudden Love: An Approach to A FARE-
WELL TO ARMS," EngR, XII (Spring, 1961), 4-6.

Rovit, E., Ernest Hemingway, 98-106.

Russell, H.K., "The Catharsis in A FAREWELL TO ARMS,"
MFS, I, iii (August, 1955), 25-30.

Sanderson, S.F., Ernest Hemingway, 51-61.

Savage, D.S., "Ernest Hemingway," HudR, I (Autumn, 1949),
389-401.

Schneider, Daniel J., "Hemingway's A FAREWELL TO
ARMS: The Novel as Pure Poetry," MFS, XIV (Autumn,
1968), 283-96.

Scott, N.A., Jr., Ernest Hemingway, 33-5.
Simpson, Herbert, "The Problem of Structure in A FARE-
    WELL TO ARMS," ForumH, IV, iv (Spring-Summer,
    1964), 20-4.
Slattery, Sister Margaret P., "Hemingway's A FAREWELL
    TO ARMS," Expl, XXVII (October, 1968), Item 8.
Stone, Edward, A Certain Morbidness: A View of American
    Literature, Carbondale: So. Ill. Un. Pr., 1969, 161-3.
    (Dream Sequence--Chap. 28).
Strandberg, Victor H., "A Palm for Pamela: Three Studies
    in the Game of Love," WHR, XX (Winter, 1966), 37-47.
Toole, William B., "Religion, Love and Nature in A FARE-
    WELL TO ARMS: The Dark Shape of Irony," CEA, XXIX,
    (May 1967), 10-11.
Warren, Robert Penn, "Ernest Hemingway," KR, IX (1947),
    1-28. Also in Warren, R.P., Introduction to A FARE-
    WELL TO ARMS, N.Y.: Scribner, 1949. Also in War-
    ren, R.P., Selected Essays, 80-118. Also in Horizon,
    XV (1947), 156-80. Also in Aldridge, J.W., ed., Crit-
    iques and Essays on Modern Fiction, 447-73. Also in
    Zabel, M.D., ed., Literary Opinion in America, 443-63.
Way, Brian, "The Early Novels of Ernest Hemingway,"
    Delta, No. 16 (Autumn, 1958), 15-24.
West, Ray B., Jr., in West, R.B., Jr., and R.W. Stall-
    man, eds., Art of Modern Fiction, N.Y.: Holt, 1949,
    622-33. Also in Baker, C., ed., Ernest Hemingway,
    28-36. Also in Weeks, R.P., ed., Hemingway, 139-51.
    Also in West, R.B., Writer in the Room, 158-74.
Wylder, D.E., Hemingway's Heroes, 66-95.
Yokelson, Joseph B., "Symbolism in the Fiction of Ernest
    Hemingway," DA, XXIII (1962), 1714 (Brown).
Young, P., Ernest Hemingway, 88-95.
_____, Ernest Hemingway (UMPAW, 1), 11-13. Also in
    O'Connor, W.V., ed., Seven Modern American Novelists,
    161-3.
_____, "Hemingway's A FAREWELL TO ARMS," Expl,
    VII (1948), Item 7.
_____, Carlos Baker, and George D. Crothers, "A FARE-
    WELL TO ARMS," in Crothers, G.D., ed., Invitation to
    Learning, N.Y.: Basic Bks., 1966, 329-36.

FOR WHOM THE BELL TOLLS

Adler, Jack, "Theme and Character in Hemingway: FOR
    WHOM THE BELL TOLLS," UR, XXX (June, 1964), 293-
    9.
Aldridge, J.W., After the Lost Generation, 34-8.

Allen, John J., "The English of Hemingway's Spaniards,"
SAB, XXVII (November, 1961), 6-7.
Atkins, J., Art of Ernest Hemingway, 27-45.
Backman, Melvin, "Hemingway: The Matador and the Cruci-
fied," MFS, I (August, 1955), 6-9. Also in Baker, C.,
ed., Hemingway and His Critics, 250-4.
Baker, C., Hemingway, 237-63. Also in Baker, C., ed.,
Ernest Hemingway, 108-30.
Baker, S., Ernest Hemingway, 109-18.
Barea, Arturo, "Not Spain But Hemingway," Horizon, III
(May, 1941), Also in Baker, C., ed., Hemingway and
His Critics, 202-12.
Beach, J. W., American Fiction, 89-93, 112-19. Also in
Baker, C., ed., Ernest Hemingway, 82-6.
_____, "How Do You Like It Now, Gentlemen?" SR, LIX
(1951), 322-8. Also in Baker, C., ed., Hemingway and
His Critics, 238-44.
Benson, J. J., Hemingway, 153-68.
Bessie, Alvah C., New Masses, XXXVII (November 5, 1940),
25-9. Also in Baker, C., ed., Ernest Hemingway, 90-4.
Brooks, C., Hidden God, 16-20.
Burgum, Edwin B., "Ernest Hemingway and the Psychology
of the Lost Generation," Novel and the World's Dilemma,
197-204. Also in McCaffery, J. K. M., ed., Ernest Hem-
ingway, 321-8.
Bury, John P., "Hemingway in Spain," ConR, No. 1118
(February, 1959), 103-5.
Carpenter, Frederic I., "Hemingway Achieves the Fifth Di-
mension," PMLA, LXIX (September, 1954), 714-17. Also
in Carpenter, F. I., American Literature and The Dream,
185-93. Also in Baker, C., ed., Hemingway and His
Critics, 196-9.
Cooperman, Stanley, "Hemingway's Blue-eyed Boy: Robert
Jordan and 'Purging Ecstasy'," Criticism, VIII (Winter,
1966), 87-96.
Cowley, M., "Hemingway's 'Nevertheless'," Look Back on
Us, 361-4. Also as "Death of a Hero," NRep (January
20, 1941), 89-90.
Dring, John R., "The Religious Element in Ernest Heming-
way's Novels," DESB, VII (1962), 105-7.
Eby, Cecil D., "The Real Robert Jordan," AL, XXXVIII
(November, 1966), 380-6.
Eisinger, C. E., Fiction of the Forties, 115-16.
Evans, Robert, "Hemingway and the Pale Cast of Thought,"
AL, XXXVIII (May, 1966), 168-72.
Farquhar, Robin H., "Dramatic Structure in the Novels of
Ernest Hemingway," MFS, XIV (Autumn, 1968), 277-9.

Fenimore, Edward, "English and Spanish in FOR WHOM THE
BELL TOLLS," ELH, X (June, 1943), 73-86. Also in
McCaffery, J. K. M., ed., Ernest Hemingway, 205-20.
French, W., Social Novel at the End of an Era, 87-124,
passim.
Frohock, W. M., "Ernest Hemingway: Violence and Disci-
pline: II," SWR, XXXII (1947), 189-93. Also in Frohock,
W. M., Novel of Violence in America, 188-94+. Also in
McCaffery, J. K. M., ed., Ernest Hemingway, 285-91.
Geismar, Maxwell, Writers in Crisis, 79-84. Also in Mc-
Caffery, J. K. M., ed., Ernest Hemingway, 183-9. Also,
condensed, in VQR, XVII (1941), 533-4.
Gleaves, Edwin S., "The Spanish Influence on Ernest Hem-
ingway's Concepts of Death, Nada, and Immortality," DA,
XXV (1964), 2511-12, (Emory).
Gray, J., On Second Thought, 79-81.
Gurko, L., Angry Decade, 188-90.
_____, Ernest Hemingway and the Pursuit of Heroism,
110-36.
Guttmann, Allen, " 'Mechanized Doom': Ernest Hemingway
and the Spanish Civil War," MR, I (May, 1960), 541-61.
Also in Guttmann, A., The Wound in the Heart: America
and the Spanish Civil War, N. Y.: Free Pr. of Glencoe,
1962, 167-75. Also, revised, in Baker, C., ed., Ernest
Hemingway, 95-107.
Halliday, F. M., "Hemingway's Ambiguity: Symbolism and
Irony," AL, XXVIII (1956), 18-21. Also in Feidelson,
C., Jr., and P. Brodtkorb, Jr., Interpretations of Amer-
ican Literature, 313-16.
Hovey, R. B., Hemingway, 151-72.
Kazin, Alfred, On Native Grounds, Garden City, N. Y.:
Doubleday, 1956, 262-5. Also, revised, in McCaffery,
J. K. M., ed., Ernest Hemingway, 202-4.
Koskimies, Rafael, "Notes on Ernest Hemingway's FOR
WHOM THE BELL TOLLS," OL, XXIII (1968), 276-86.
Krzyzanowski, Jerzy R., "FOR WHOM THE BELL TOLLS:
The Origin of General Golz," PolR, VII, iv (Autumn,
1962), 69-74.
Lewis, R. W., Jr., Hemingway on Love, 143-78.
Motola, Gabriel, "Hemingway's Code: Literature and Life,"
MFS, X (Winter, 1964-65), 325-9.
Moynihan, William T., "The Martyrdom of Robert Jordan,"
CE, XXI (December, 1959), 127-32.
Muste, John M., Say That We Saw Spain Die: Literary Con-
sequences of the Spanish Civil War, Seattle: Un. of
Washington Pr., 1966, 94-119.
Parsons, Thornton H., "Hemingway's Tyrannous Plot,"

UKCR, XXVII (June, 1961), 261-6.

Ramsey, Paul, "Hemingway as Moral Thinker: A Look at Two Novels," in Langford, R. E., and W. E. Taylor, eds., Twenties, 92-4.

Rovit, E., Ernest Hemingway, 74-6, 136-46.

Sanders, David, "Ernest Hemingway's Spanish Civil War Experience," AQ, XII (Summer, 1960), 133-43, passim.

Sanderson, S. F., Ernest Hemingway, 92-102.

Savage, D. S., "Ernest Hemingway," HudR, I (Autumn, 1948), 389-401.

_____, Withered Branch, 36-43.

Schorer, Mark, "The Background of a Style," KR, III (Winter, 1941), 101-5. Also in Baker, C., ed., Ernest Hemingway, 87-9.

Slochower, H., No Voice is Wholly Lost, 37-40.

Snell, G., "Ernest Hemingway and the 'Fifth Dimension'," Shapers of American Fiction, 166-71.

Trilling, Lionel, "An American in Spain," in Philips, William, and Philip Rahv, eds., The Partisan Reader, N. Y.: Dial, 1946, 639-44. Also in Baker, C., ed., Ernest Hemingway, 78-81.

Walcutt, C. C., American Literary Naturalism, 276-9.

Weeks, Robert P., "The Power of the Tacit in Crane and Hemingway," MFS, VIII (Winter, 1962-63), 415-18.

Weintraub, S., Last Great Cause, 215-20.

West, Ray B., Jr., "Ernest Hemingway: The Failure of Sensibility," SR, LIII (Winter, 1945), 120-35. Also in West, R. B., Jr., Writer in the Room, 142-57. Also in Litz, A. W., ed., Modern American Fiction, 244-55. Also in O'Connor, W. V., ed., Forms of Modern Fiction, 89-96.

Williams, Stanley T., "Some Spanish Influences on American Fiction: Mark Twain to Willa Cather," Hispania, XXXVI (1953), 133-6.

Wylder, D. E., Hemingway's Heroes, 127-64.

Young, P., Ernest Hemingway, 103-14.

_____, Ernest Hemingway (UMPAW, 1), 16-17. Also in O'Connor, W. V., ed., Seven Modern American Novelists, 165-6.

THE OLD MAN AND THE SEA

Aldridge, J. W., "A Last Look at the Old Man," Time to Murder and Create, 185-91.

Atkins, J., Art of Ernest Hemingway, 244-7.

Backman, Melvin, "Hemingway: The Matador and the Crucified," MFS, I (August, 1955), 9-11. Also, corrected version, in Baker, C., ed., Hemingway and His Critics, 255-8. Also in Baker, C., ed., Ernest Hemingway, 135-43.

Baker, Carlos, "The Boy and the Lions," in Jobes, K. T., ed., Twentieth Century Interpretations of THE OLD MAN AND THE SEA, 27-33. Also in Baker, C., Hemingway: The Writer as Artist, 304-11.

_____, Hemingway, 292-328. Also, revised, in Baker, C., ed., Ernest Hemingway, 156-72.

_____, "The Marvel Who Must Die," SatR, XXXV (September 6, 1952), 10-11. Also in Wagenknecht, Edward C., ed., A Preface to Literature, N.Y.: Holt, 1954, 341-4.

Baker, S., Ernest Hemingway, 126-33.

Barnes, Lois L., "The Helpless Hero of Ernest Hemingway," S&S, XVII (Winter, 1953), 1-11.

Benson, J. J., Hemingway, 123-7, 169-85.

Bluefarb, Samuel, "The Sea--Mirror and Maker of Character in Fiction and Drama," EJ, XLVIII (December, 1959), 505-7.

Bovie, Vernett, "The Evolution of a Myth: A Study of the Major Symbols in the Works of Ernest Hemingway," DA, XVII (1957), 1080 (Pennsylvania).

Bradford, Melvin E., "On the Importance of Discovering God: Faulkner and Hemingway's THE OLD MAN AND THE SEA," MissQ, XX (Summer, 1967), 158-62.

Broadus, Robert N., "The New Record Set by Hemingway's Old Man," N&Q, X (April, 1963), 152-3.

Burhans, Clinton S., Jr., "THE OLD MAN AND THE SEA: Hemingway's Tragic Vision," AL, XXXI (January, 1960), 446-55. Also in Baker, C., ed., Ernest Hemingway, 150-5. Also in Baker, C., ed., Hemingway and His Critics, 259-68. Also in Jobes, K. T., ed., Twentieth Century Interpretations of THE OLD MAN AND THE SEA, 72-80. Also in Westbrook, M., ed., Modern American Novel, 118-30.

Cooperman, Stanley, "Hemingway and Old Age: Santiago as a Priest of Time," CE, XXVII (December, 1965), 215-20.

Corin, Fernand, "Steinbeck and Hemingway: A Study in Literary Economy," RLV, XXIV (January-February, 1958), 60-75; (March-April, 1958), 153-63.

Cotten, L., "Hemingway's OLD MAN AND THE SEA," Expl, XI (March, 1953), Item 38.

Cotter, Janet M., "THE OLD MAN AND THE SEA: An 'Open' Literary Experience," EJ, LI (1962), 459-63.

Dring, John R., "The Religious Element in Ernest Hemingway's Novels," DESB, VII (1962), 109-11.

274   HEMINGWAY (cont.)

Dupee, F. W. , "Hemingway Revealed," KR, XV (Winter,
    1953), 150-5.
Fagan, Edward R. , "Teaching Enigmas of THE OLD MAN
    AND THE SEA," EngR, VIII (Autumn, 1957), 13-20.
Farquhar, Robin H. , "Dramatic Structure in the Novels of
    Ernest Hemingway," MFS, XIV (Autumn, 1968), 279-82.
Frohock, W. M. , "Mr. Hemingway's Truly Tragic Bones,"
    SWR, XXXVIII (Winter, 1953), 74-7.
        , Novel of Violence in America, 196-7.
Gahlot, Jai S. , "THE OLD MAN AND THE SEA: A Read-
    ing," in Maini, Darshan Singh, ed. , Variations on Ameri-
    can Literature, New Delhi: U. S. Educ. Foundation in
    India, 1968, 89-92.
Gardiner, H. C. , "Pathetic Fallacy," In All Conscience, 125-
    6. Also in America, LXXXVII (September 13, 1952), 569.
Gurko, L. , Ernest Hemingway and the Pursuit of Heroism,
    159-74.
        , "The Heroic Impulse in THE OLD MAN AND THE
    SEA," CE, XVII (October, 1955), 11-15. Also in EJ,
    XLIV (October, 1955), 377-82. Also in Jobes, K. T. , ed. ,
    Twentieth Century Interpretations of THE OLD MAN AND
    THE SEA, 64-71.
Halverson, John, "Christian Resonance in THE OLD MAN
    AND THE SEA," ELN, II (September, 1964), 50-4.
Handy, William J. , "A New Dimension for a Hero: Santiago
    of THE OLD MAN AND THE SEA," in Sutherland, W. O.
    S. , Jr. , ed. , Six Contemporary Novels, 58-75.
Harada, Keiichi, "The Marlin and the Shark," Journal of the
    College of Literature (Aryama Gakuin Un. , Tokyo), (1960),
    49-54. Also in Baker, C. , ed. , Hemingway and His
    Critics, 269-76.
Harlow, Benjamin C. , "Some Archetypal Motifs in THE OLD
    MAN AND THE SEA," McNR, XVII (1966), 74-9.
Hofling, Charles K. , "Hemingway, THE OLD MAN AND THE
    SEA and the Male Reader," AI, XX (Summer, 1963), 161-
    73.
Hovey, R. B. , Hemingway, 191-203.
        , "THE OLD MAN AND THE SEA: A New Heming-
    way Hero," Discourse, IX, (Summer, 1966), 283-94.
Jobes, Katharine T. , "Introduction," in Jobes, K. T. , ed. ,
    Twentieth Century Interpretations of THE OLD MAN AND
    THE SEA, 1-17.
Krim, Seymour, "Ernest Hemingway: Valor and Defeat,"
    Views of a Nearsighted Cannoneer, New Enlarged Ed. ,
    N. Y. : Dutton, 1968, 159-62. Also in Cweal, LVI (Sep-
    tember 19, 1952), 584-6.
Lewis, R. W. , Jr. , Hemingway on Love, 199-213.

Mertens, Gerard M., "Hemingway's OLD MAN AND THE
   SEA and Mann's THE BLACK SWAN," L&P, VI (1956),
   96-9.
Milton, John R., "American Fiction and Man," Cresset,
   XVIII, iii (1955), 16-20.
Morris, W., "The Function of Style: Ernest Hemingway,"
   Territory Ahead, 133-41.
Moseley, E. H., Pseudonyms of Christ in the Modern Novel,
   205-12.
Phillips, William, "Male-ism and Moralism," AmMerc,
   LXXV (October, 1952), 93-8.
Politicus, "How We Swallowed THE OLD MAN AND THE
   SEA," AmMerc, LXXXIX (August, 1959), 73-6.
Rahv, Philip, Ctary, XIV (October, 1952), 390-1.   Also in
   Rahv, P., Image and Idea, 192-5.   Also in Rahv, P.,
   Literature and the Sixth Sense, 355-7.   Also in Rahv, P.,
   Myth and the Powerhouse, 198-201.
Rosenfield, Claire, "New World, Old Myths," in Jobes, K.
   T., ed., Twentieth Century Interpretations of THE OLD
   MAN AND THE SEA, 41-55.
Rovit, E., Ernest Hemingway, 85-94.
Sanderson, S. F., Ernest Hemingway, 113-18.
Schorer, Mark, "With Grace Under Pressure," NRep,
   CXXVII (October 6, 1952), 19-20.   Also in Baker, C.,
   ed., Ernest Hemingway, 132-4.
Schwartz, Delmore, "The Fiction of Ernest Hemingway:
   Moral Historian of the American Dream," PUSA, No. 13
   (Autumn, 1955), 82-8.   Also in Jobes, K. T., ed., Twen-
   tieth Century Interpretations of THE OLD MAN AND THE
   SEA, 97-102.
Scoville, Samuel, "The Weltanschauung of Steinbeck and Hem-
   ingway: An Analysis of Themes," EJ, LVI (January,
   1967), 60-3, 66.
Spector, Robert D., "Hemingway's THE OLD MAN AND THE
   SEA," Expl, XI (March, 1953), Item 38.
Stephens, Robert O., "Hemingway's Old Man and the Ice-
   berg," MFS, VII (Winter, 1961-62), 295-304.
Stuckey, W. J., Pulitzer Prize Novels, 167-70.
Sylvester, Bickford, "Hemingway's Extended Vision: THE
   OLD MAN AND THE SEA," DA, XXVII (1966), 1841A
   (Un. of Washington).
_____, "Hemingway's Extended Vision: THE OLD MAN
   AND THE SEA," PMLA, LXXXI (March, 1966), 130-8.
   Also in Jobes, K. T., ed., Twentieth Century Interpreta-
   tions of THE OLD MAN AND THE SEA, 81-96.
_____, " 'They Went Through this Fiction Every Day':
   Informed Illusion in THE OLD MAN AND THE SEA,"

MFS, XII (Winter, 1966-67), 473-7.

Ueno, Naozo, "An Oriental View of THE OLD MAN AND THE SEA," EWR, II (Spring, 1965), 67-76.

Walcutt, C. C., American Literary Naturalism, 279-80.

Waldmeir, Joseph, "Confiteor Hominem: Ernest Hemingway's Religion of Man," PMASAL, XLII (1957), 349-56. Also in Baker, C., ed., Ernest Hemingway, 144-9. Also in Weeks, R. P., ed., Hemingway, 161-8.

Weeks, Robert P., "Fakery in THE OLD MAN AND THE SEA," CE, XXIV (December, 1962), 188-92. Also in Jobes, K. T., ed., Twentieth Century Interpretations of THE OLD MAN AND THE SEA, 34-40.

Wells, Arvin R., in Hagopian, John V., and Martin Dolch, eds., Insight I: Analyses of American Literature, Frankfurt am Main: Hirschgraben-Verlag, 1964, 111-22.
_____, "A Ritual of Transfiguration: THE OLD MAN AND THE SEA," UR, XXX (December, 1963), 95-101. Also in Jobes, K. T., ed., Twentieth Century Interpretations of THE OLD MAN AND THE SEA, 56-63.

Wilner, Herbert, "Aspects of American Fiction: A Whale, a Bear, and a Marlin," in Lanzinger, Klaus, ed., Americana-Austriaca, 229-46.

Wood, Cecil, "On the Tendency of Nature to Intimate Art," MinnR, VI (1966), 140-8.

Wylder, D. E., Hemingway's Heroes, 199-222.

Young, P., Ernest Hemingway (UMPAW, 1), 19-21. Also in O'Connor, W. V., ed., Seven Modern American Novelists, 168-70.
_____, "THE OLD MAN AND THE SEA: Vision/Revision," in Jobes, K. T., ed., Twentieth Century Interpretations of THE OLD MAN AND THE SEA, 18-26. Also in Young, P., Ernest Hemingway: A Reconsideration, 123-33, 274-5.

Zabel, M. D., Craft and Character, 321-6. Also in TLS, No. 2746 (September 17, 1954).

THE SUN ALSO RISES

Adams, Richard P., "Sunrise out of the Waste Land," TSE, IX (1959), 119-31.

Aldridge, J. W., After the Lost Generation, 30-2.

Allen, W., Modern Novel, 94-7.

Amiran, Minda R., "Hemingway as Lyric Novelist," Scripta Hierosolymitana (Hebrew Un., Jerusalem), XVII (1966), 294-300.

Backman, Melvin, "Hemingway: The Matador and the Crucified," MFS, I (August, 1955), 3-4. Also in Baker, C., ed. , Hemingway and His Critics, 246-9.

Baker, C. , Hemingway, 77-93. Also in Baker, C. , ed. ,
Ernest Hemingway, 11-17. Also in White, W. , comp. ,
Merrill Studies in THE SUN ALSO RISES, 26-36.

_____, "Hemingway's Wastelanders," VQR, XXVIII (Sum-
mer, 1952), 373-92.

Baker, S. , Ernest Hemingway, 46-55. Also in White, W. ,
comp. , Merrill Studies in THE SUN ALSO RISES, 37-52.

Beach, J. W. , American Fiction, 79-84, passim.

Benson, J. J. , Hemingway, 30-43.

Brooks, C. , Hidden God, 20-1.

Burgum, E. B. , Novel and the World's Dilemma, 187-94.

Bury, John P. , "Hemingway in Spain," ConR, No. 1118
(February, 1959), 103-5.

Cochran, Robert W. , "Circularity in THE SUN ALSO RISES,"
MFS, XIV (Autumn, 1968), 297-305.

Cohen, Joseph, "Wouk's Morningstar and Hemingway's Sun,"
SAQ, LVIII (Spring, 1959), 213-14.

Cowley, Malcolm, "Introduction," THE SUN ALSO RISES,
Scribner, 1962. Also in White, W. , comp. , Merrill
Studies in THE SUN ALSO RISES, 91-106.

Dring, John R. , "The Religious Element in Ernest Hemingway's Novels," DESB, VII (1962), 71-2, 104.

Evans, Oliver, "The Arrow Wounds of Count Mippipopoulos,"
PMLA, LXXVII (March, 1962), 175.

Farquhar, Robin H. , "Dramatic Structure in the Novels of
Ernest Hemingway," MFS, XIV (Autumn, 1968), 273-5.

Farrell, James T. , NYTBR (August 1, 1943), 6+. Also in
Farrell, J. T. , The League of Frightened Philistines,
N. Y. : Vanguard, 1945, 20-4. Also in Baker, C. , ed. ,
Ernest Hemingway, 4-6. Also in McCaffery, J. K. M. ,
ed. , Ernest Hemingway, 221-5. Also in White, W. ,
comp. , Merrill Studies in THE SUN ALSO RISES, 53-7.

Frohock, W. M. , "Ernest Hemingway: Violence and Disci-
pline: I," SWR, XXXII (1947), 90-5. Also in Frohock,
W. M. , Novel of Violence in America, 167-75+. Also in
McCaffery, J. K. M. , ed. , Ernest Hemingway, 261-71.

Ganzel, Dewey, "Cabestro and Vaquilla: The Symbolic Structure of THE SUN ALSO RISES," SR, LXXVI (Winter,
1968), 26-48.

Geismar, M. , Writers in Crisis, 51-3.

Gurko, L. , Ernest Hemingway and the Pursuit of Heroism.
55-80.

Hoffman, Frederick J. , "No Beginning and No End: Hemingway and Death," EIC, III (1953), 81-2. Also in Feidelson, C. , Jr. , and P. Brodtkorb, Jr. , eds. , Interpretations of American Literature, 327-9.

_____, "The Text: Hemingway's THE SUN ALSO RISES,"
    Twenties, 80-5.
Holman, C. Hugh, "Hemingway and Vanity Fair," CarQ,
    VIII (Summer, 1956), 31-7.
Hovey, R. B. , Hemingway, 60-73.
_____, "THE SUN ALSO RISES: Hemingway's Inner De-
    bate," ForumH, IV (Summer, 1966), 4-10.
Howell, John M. , "The Waste Land Tradition in the Ameri-
    can Novel," DA, XXIV (1964), 3337 (Tulane).
Hyman, S. E. , "The Best of Hemingway," Standards, 28-30.
Isabelle, J. , Hemingway's Religious Experience, 38-41.
Knapp, Daniel, "Hemingway: The Naming of the Hero,"
    StL, II, ii (1961), 35-7.
Kobler, Jasper F. , "Confused Chronology in THE SUN ALSO
    RISES," MFS, XIII (Winter, 1967-68), 517-20.
Lauter, Paul, "Plato's Stepchildren, Gatsby and Cohn,"
    MFS, IX (Winter, 1963-64), 338-46.
Levy, Alfred J. , "Hemingway's THE SUN ALSO RISES,"
    Expl, XVII (February, 1959), Item 37.
Lewis, R. W. , Jr. , Hemingway on Love, 19-35. Also in
    Westbrook, M. , ed. , The Modern American Novel, 93-
    113.
McCormick, J. , Catastrophe and Imagination, 209-13.
_____, "Hemingway and History," WR, XVII (Winter,
    1953), 90-8.
Mizener, A. , Twelve Great American Novels, 120-41.
Moore, Geoffrey, "THE SUN ALSO RISES: Notes Toward an
    Extreme Fiction," REL, IV, iv (October, 1963), 31-46.
Moss, Sidney P. , "Character, Vision, and Theme in THE
    SUN ALSO RISES," IEY, No. 9 (1964), 64-7.
Munson, Gorham, "A Comedy of Exiles," LitR, XII (1968),
    41-75.
Newman, Paul B. , "Hemingway's Grail Quest," UKCR,
    XXVIII (June, 1962), 295-303.
Nishiyama, Tamotsu, "Hemingway's Post-War Generation
    Reconsidered," NDQ, XXVIII (1960), 129-33.
Ramsey, Paul, "Hemingway as Moral Thinker: A Look at
    Two Novels," in Langford, R. E. , and W. E. Taylor, eds. ,
    Twenties, 92-4.
Robinson, Forrest D. , "The Tragic Awareness of Heming-
    way's First-Person Narrators: A Study of THE SUN AL-
    SO RISES and A FAREWELL TO ARMS," DA, XXVII
    (1967), 2543A (Ohio).
Rouch, John S. , "Jake Barnes as Narrator," MFS, XI
    (Winter, 1965-66), 361-70.
Rovit, E. , Ernest Hemingway, 147-62. Also in White, W. ,
    comp. , Merrill Studies in THE SUN ALSO RISES, 58-72.

_____, "Ernest Hemingway: THE SUN ALSO RISES," in
Cohen, Hennig, ed., Landmarks of American Writing,
N. Y.: Basic Bks., 1969, 303-14.
Sanderson, S. F., Ernest Hemingway, 40-50.
Schneider, Daniel J., "The Symbolism of THE SUN ALSO
RISES," Discourse, X (Summer, 1967), 334-42.
Schroeter, James, "Hemingway's THE SUN ALSO RISES,"
Expl, XX (November, 1961), Item 28.
Scott, Arthur L., "In Defense of Robert Cohn," CE, XVIII
(March, 1957), 309-14.
Scott, N. A., Jr., Ernest Hemingway, 29-33.
Skipp, Francis E., "What Was the Matter with Jacob Barnes?"
Carrell, VII (1965), 17-22.
Spilka, Mark, "The Death of Love in THE SUN ALSO RISES,"
in Shapiro, C., ed., Twelve Original Essays on Great
American Novels, 238-56.   Also in Baker, C., ed.,
Hemingway and His Critics, 80-92.   Also in Baker, C.,
ed., Ernest Hemingway, 18-25.   Also in Weeks, R. P.,
ed., Hemingway, 127-38.   Also in White, W., comp.,
Merrill Studies in THE SUN ALSO RISES, 73-85.
Stallman, Robert W., "THE SUN ALSO RISES--But No Bells
Ring," The Houses that James Built and Other Literary
Studies, Lansing: Michigan State Un. Pr., 1961, 173-93.
Stephens, Robert O., "Ernest Hemingway and the Rhetoric
of Escape," in Langford, R. E., and W. E. Taylor, eds.,
Twenties, 82-6.
_____, and James Ellis, "Hemingway, Fitzgerald, and
the Riddle of 'Henry's Bicycle'," ELN, V (1967), 46-9.
_____, "Hemingway's Don Quixote in Pamplona," CE,
XXIII (December, 1961), 216-18.
Tamke, Alexander, "Jacob Barnes' 'Bibliocal Name': Cen-
tral Irony in THE SUN ALSO RISES," EngR, XVIII (De-
cember, 1967), 2-7.
Torchiana, Donald T., "THE SUN ALSO RISES: A Recon-
sideration," in Bruccoli, Matthew J., ed., Fitzgerald/
Hemingway Annual, 1969, Washington, D. C.: Microcard
Editions, 1969, 77-103.
Vance, William L., "Implications of Form in THE SUN AL-
SO RISES," in Langford, R. E., and W. E. Taylor, eds.,
Twenties, 87-91.
Walcutt, C. C., Man's Changing Mask, 309-14.
Way, Brian, "The Early Novels of Ernest Hemingway,"
Delta, No. 16 (Autumn, 1958), 15-24.
Wertheim, Stanley, "The Conclusion of Hemingway's THE
SUN ALSO RISES," L&P, XVII, i (1967), 55-6.
Wilson, Edmund, "The Sportsman's Tragedy," NRep, XLVI
(May 1926), 404-5.   Also in Wilson, E., Shores of

Light, 342-4.
Wood, Dean C., "The Significance of Bulls and Bullfighters
    in THE SUN ALSO RISES," Wingover, I (Fall-Winter,
    1958-59), 28-30.
Wylder, D. E., Hemingway's Heroes, 31-65.
Yevish, Irving A., "The Sun Also Exposes: Hemingway and
    Jake Barnes," MQ, X (1968), 89-97.
Yokelson, Joseph B., "Symbolism in the Fiction of Ernest
    Hemingway," DA, XXIII (1962), 1714 (Brown).
Young, P., Ernest Hemingway, 82-8. Also in Baker, C.,
    ed., Ernest Hemingway, 7-10. Also in White, W., comp.,
    Merrill Studies in THE SUN ALSO RISES, 86-90.
_____, Ernest Hemingway (UMPAW, 1), 9-11. Also in
    O'Connor, W. V., ed., Seven Modern American Novelists,
    160-1.

TO HAVE AND HAVE NOT

Aldridge, J. W., After the Lost Generation, 32-4.
Baker, C., Hemingway, 205-22.
Baker, S., Ernest Hemingway, 102-6.
Cowley, M., "Hemingway: Work in Progress," Look Back
    on Us, 310-14. Also in NRep (October 20, 1937), 305-6.
Dring, John R., "The Religious Element in Ernest Heming-
    way's Novels," DESB, VII (1962), 104-5.
French, W., Social Novel at the End of an Era, 99-102.
Geismar, M., Writers in Crisis, 66-7, 72-6. Also in Mc-
    Caffery, J. K. M., ed., Ernest Hemingway, 176-83. Also,
    condensed, in VQR, XVII (1941), 529-30.
Grebstein, Sheldon N., in Madden, D., ed., Tough Guy
    Writers of the Thirties, 36-41.
Gurko, L., Ernest Hemingway and the Pursuit of Heroism,
    143-52.
Hovey, R. B., Hemingway, 131-44.
Knapp, Daniel, "Hemingway: The Naming of the Hero,"
    StL, II, ii (1961), 37-8.
Lewis, R. W., Jr., Hemingway on Love, 113-40.
Ryan, William J., "Uses of Irony in TO HAVE AND HAVE
    NOT," MFS, XIV (Autumn, 1968), 329-36.
Sanderson, S. F., Ernest Hemingway, 78-88.
Schwartz, Delmore, "Ernest Hemingway's Literary Situation,"
    SoR, III (Spring, 1938), 777-82. Also in McCaffery, J.
    K. M., ed., Ernest Hemingway, 123-9.
Wylder, D. E., Hemingway's Heroes, 96-126.
Young, P., Ernest Hemingway, 98-102, 198-200.
_____, Ernest Hemingway (UMPAW, 1), 14-15. Also in
    O'Connor, W. V., ed., Seven Modern American Novelists,

164-5.

_____, "Focus on TO HAVE AND HAVE NOT: To Have
Not: Tough Luck," in Madden, D., ed., Tough Guy
Writers of the Thirties, 42-50.

THE TORRENTS OF SPRING

Baker, C., Hemingway, 37-42.
Flanagan, John T., "Hemingway's Debt to Sherwood Ander-
son," JEGP, LIV (1955), 507-20. Also in Illinois Un.
English Dept., Studies by Members of the English Depart-
ment in Honor of John Jay Parry, Urbana: Un. of Illi-
nois Pr., 1955, 47-60.
Geismar, M., Writers in Crisis, 68-71. Also in McCaffery,
J. K. M., ed., Ernest Hemingway, 172-6.
Gurko, L., Ernest Hemingway and the Pursuit of Heroism,
137-43.
Hovey, R. B., Hemingway, 55-60.
_____, "THE TORRENTS OF SPRING: Prefigurations in
the Early Hemingway," CE, XXVI (March, 1965), 460-4.
White, Ray L., "Hemingway's Private Explanation of THE
TORRENTS OF SPRING," MFS, XIII (Summer, 1967), 261-
3.
Wylder, D. E., Hemingway's Heroes, 11-30.
_____, "Hemingway's THE TORRENTS OF SPRING," SDR,
V (Winter, 1967-68), 23-47.
Young, P., Ernest Hemingway, 80-2.

BIBLIOGRAPHY

Baker, C., ed., Hemingway and His Critics, 279-98.
Beebe, Maurice, and John Feaster," Criticism of Ernest
Hemingway: A Selected Checklist," MFS, XIV (Autumn,
1968), 337-69.
Hanneman, Audre, Ernest Hemingway; A Comprehensive Bib-
liography, Princeton, N. J.: Princeton Un. Pr., 1967.

HERSEY, JOHN, 1914-

GENERAL

Geismar, M., "John Hersey: The Revival of Conscience,"
American Moderns, 182-6.
Guilfoil, Kelsey, "John Hersey: Fact and Fiction," EJ,
XXXIX (September, 1950), 355-60.
McDonnell, Thomas P., "Hersey's Allegorical Novels,"

CathW, CXCV (July, 1962), 240-5.
Rugoff, Milton, "John Hersey--From Documentary Journal-
    ism to the Novelist's Art," NYHTBR, XXVII (August 20,
    1950), 3+.
Sanders, D., John Hersey.
    _____, "John Hersey: War Correspondent Into Novelist,"
    in Browne, Ray B., and Others, eds., New Voices in
    American Studies, Lafayette, Ind.: Purdue Un. Studies,
    1966, 49-58.
Werner, Alfred, "With a Pen of Iron," AmHebrew, CLX
    (August 11, 1950), 4-5.

A BELL FOR ADANO

Prescott, O., In My Opinion, 151-2.
Sanders, D., John Hersey, 31-7.

THE CHILD BUYER

Burton, Arthur, "Existential Conceptions in John Hersey's
    Novel, THE CHILD BUYER," Jnl of Existential Psychol-
    ogy, II (Fall, 1961), 243-58.
Sanders, D., John Hersey, 108-21.

THE MARMOT DRIVE

Sanders, D., John Hersey, 75-82.
Tindall, W. Y., Literary Symbol, 100-1.

A SINGLE PEBBLE

Sanders, D., John Hersey, 83-94.

THE WALL

Daiches, David, "Record and Statement," Ctary (April, 1950),
    385-8.
Eisinger, C. E., Fiction of the Forties, 52.
Geismar, M., American Moderns, 180-2. Also in SatR,
    XXXIII (March 4, 1950), 14.
Green, L. C., "THE WALL," AmHebrew, CLIX (1951), 7-8+.
Guilfoil, Kelsey, "John Hersey: Fact and Fiction," EJ,
    XXXIX (September, 1950), 358-60.
Healey, Robert C., in Gardiner, H. C., ed., Fifty Years of
    the American Novel, 269-71.
Prescott, O., In My Opinion, 238-40.
Rovere, Richard, in Harper's, CC (March, 1950), 102-7.

Rugoff, Milton, "John Hersey--From Documentary Journalism to the Novelist's Art," NYHTBR, XXVII (August 20, 1950), 3+.
Samuel, Maurice, "The Story That Must Build Itself," in Ribalow, H., ed., Mid-Century, 228-49.
Sanders, D., John Hersey, 56-73.
Werner, Alfred, "With a Pen of Iron," AmHebrew, CLX (August 11, 1950), 4-5.

THE WAR LOVER

Sanders, D., John Hersey, 95-107.
Waldmeir, J.J., American Novels of the Second World War, 30-2.

WHITE LOTUS

Sanders, D., John Hersey, 122-36.

BIBLIOGRAPHY

Sanders, D., John Hersey, 150-6.

HINDE, THOMAS, PSEUD. (THOMAS CHITTY), 1926-

THE DAY THE CALL CAME

"Novels of 1964. Thomas Hinde: THE DAY THE CALL CAME," in T.L.S. Essays and Reviews from The Times Literary Supplement, 1964, 107-9. Also in TLS (June 11, 1964).

HAPPY AS LARRY

Allsop, K., Angry Decade, 70-3.
Podhoretz, N., "The New Nihilism and the Novel," Doings and Undoings, 171-3.

HIGH

"Fiction of 1968. Thomas Hinde: HIGH," in T.L.S. Essays and Reviews from The Times Literary Supplement, 1968, 190-2. Also in TLS (November 7, 1968).

MR. NICHOLAS

Allsop, K., Angry Decade, 69-70.
Gindin, J., Postwar British Fiction, 94-5.

HOLMES, (JOHN) CLELLON, 1926-

GO

Hassan, I., Radical Innocence, 91-3.

HOPKINS, BILL, 1928-

THE DIVINE AND THE DECAY

Allsop, K., Angry Decade, 183-7.
Gindin, J., Postwar British Fiction, 223-4.

HUGHES, RICHARD, 1900-

THE FOX IN THE ATTIC

Allen, W., Modern Novel, 61-2.
Bosano, J., "Richard Hughes," EA, XVI (July, 1963), 262-9.
Wiley, Paul, WSCL, IV, ii (Spring-Summer, 1963), 229-30.

A HIGH WIND IN JAMAICA

Allen, W., Modern Novel, 58-9.
Brown, Daniel R., "A HIGH WIND IN JAMAICA: Comedy of
   the Absurd," BSUF, IX, i (Winter, 1968), 6-12.
Henighan, T. J., "Nature and Convention in A HIGH WIND IN
   JAMAICA," Crit, IX, i (1967), 5-18.
Woodward, Daniel H., "The Delphic Voice: Richard Hughes's
   A HIGH WIND IN JAMAICA," PLL, III (Winter, 1967), 57-
   74.

IN HAZARD

Allen, W., Modern Novel, 59-61.

HUMPHREY, WILLIAM, 1924-

GENERAL

Lee, J. W., William Humphrey.

HOME FROM THE HILL

Lee, J. W., William Humphrey, 21-33.
Meeker, Richard, in Simonini, R. C., Jr., ed., Southern
Writers, 170-1.

THE ORDWAYS

Hoffman, F. J., Art of Southern Fiction, 103-6.
Lee, J. W., William Humphrey, 34-43.
Rubin, L. D., Jr., The Curious Death of the Novel, 263-5.
_____, "Southerners and Jews," SoR, II (1966), 698-700.

HUXLEY, ALDOUS, 1894-1963

GENERAL

Allen, W., Modern Novel, 41-4.
Aninger, Thomas, "The Essay Element in the Fiction of Al-
dous Huxley," DA, XXIX (1968), 892A-3A (UCLA).
Atkins, John, Aldous Huxley: A Literary Study, New and
Rev. Ed., N. Y.: Orion, 1967.
Bald, R. C., "Aldous Huxley as a Borrower," CE, XI (Janu-
ary, 1950), 183-7.
Bartlett, Norman, "Aldous Huxley and D. H. Lawrence,"
AusQ, XXXVI, i (March, 1964), 76-84.
Beerman, Hans, "An Interview with Aldous Huxley," MQ, V
(April, 1964), 223-30.
Bentley, Joseph G., "Aldous Huxley and the Anatomical Vi-
sion," DA, XXII (1962), 3655-6 (Ohio State).
_____, "Huxley's Ambivalent Responses to the Ideas of
D. H. Lawrence," TCL, XIII (October, 1967), 139-53.
Birnbaum, Milton, "Aldous Huxley: A Study of His Quest
for Values," DA, XVII (1957), 360 (N. Y. U.).
_____, "Aldous Huxley: An Aristocrat's Comments on
Popular Culture," JPC, II (Summer, 1968), 106-12.
_____, "Aldous Huxley's Animadversions Upon Sexual
Love," TSLL, VIII (Summer, 1966), 285-96.
_____, "Aldous Huxley's Conception of the Nature of Real-
ity," Person, XLVII (July, 1966), 297-314.
_____, "Aldous Huxley's Quest for Values: A Study in
Religious Syncretism," CLS, III (1966), 169-82.

_____, "Aldous Huxley's Treatment of Nature," HJ, LXIV
(Midsummer, 1966), 150-2.
_____, "Aldous Huxley's Views on Education," XUS, VI
(May, 1967), 81-91.
Bowering, P., Aldous Huxley.
Brooke, J., Aldous Huxley.
Bullough, Geoffrey, "Aspects of Aldous Huxley," ES, XXX
(October, 1949), 233-43.
Burgum, E. B., Novel and the World's Dilemma, 140-56.
Also in AR, II (Spring, 1942), 62-75.
Church, Margaret, "Aldous Huxley's Attitude toward Dura-
tion," CE, XVII (April, 1956), 358-91.
_____, "Aldous Huxley: Perennial Time," Time and Real-
ity, 102-19.
Coates, J. B., "Aldous Huxley," in Baker, D. V., ed.,
Writers of Today, 1-13.
Cottrell, Beekman W., "Conversation Piece: Four Twentieth
Century English Dialogue Novelists," DA, XVI (1956),
2159 (Columbia).
Dooley, David, "The Impact of Satire on Fiction: Studies in
Norman Douglas, Sinclair Lewis, Aldous Huxley, Evelyn
Waugh and George Orwell," DA, XV (1955), 2203-4 (Iowa).
Dykstra, Emmanuel D., "Aldous Huxley: The Development
of a Mystic," DA, XVII (1957), 3013 (Iowa).
Dyson, A. E., "Aldous Huxley and the Two Nothings," CritQ,
III (Winter, 1961), 293-309. Also in Dyson, A. E., Crazy
Fabric, 166-86.
Enroth, Clyde A., "The Movement Toward Mysticism in the
Novels of Aldous Huxley," DA, XVI (1956), 1905 (Minne-
sota).
Firchow, Peter E., "Aldous Huxley and the Art of Satire:
A Study of His Prose Fiction to BRAVE NEW WORLD,"
DA, XXVI (1966), 5433 (Wisc.).
Ghose, S., Aldous Huxley.
Glicksberg, Charles I., "Aldous Huxley: Art and Mysticism,"
PrS, XXVII (Winter, 1953), 344-53.
_____, "Huxley: The Experimental Novelist," SAQ, LII
(January, 1953), 98-110.
Godfrey, D. R., "The Essence of Aldous Huxley," ES, XXXII
(June, 1951), 97-106.
Gray, J., On Second Thought, 167-74.
Greenblatt, S. J., Three Modern Satirists, 77-101, 105-17.
Gurtoff, Stanley A., "The Impact of D. H. Lawrence on His
Contemporaries," DA, XXVI (1966), 5412-13 (Minnesota).
Hamill, Elizabeth, These Modern Writers; An Introduction
for Modern Readers, Melbourne: Georgian House, 1946,
100-12.

Hamilton, Robert, "The Challenge of Aldous Huxley: 'The Perennial Philosophy'," Horizon, XVII (June, 1948), 441-56.

Hart, Hubert N., "Aldous Huxley," CathW, CLXXV (June, 1952), 204-8.

Heard, Gerald, "The Poignant Prophet," KR, XXVII (Winter, 1965), 49-70.

Hines, B., Social World of Aldous Huxley.

Hoffmann, Charles G., "The Change in Huxley's Approach to the Novel of Ideas," Person, XLII (January, 1961), 85-90.

Holmes, Charles M., "Aldous Huxley's Struggle with Art," WHR, XV (Spring, 1961), 149-56.

_____, "The Novels of Aldous Huxley," DA, XX (1960), 3743 (Columbia).

Huxley, Aldous, and John Morgan, "Aldous Huxley on Contemporary Society," Listener, LXVI (August 17, 1961), 237-9.

Huxley, Julian, ed., Aldous Huxley, 1894-1963: A Memorial Volume, London: Chatto and Windus, 1965; N.Y.: Harper, 1965.

_____, "My Brother, Aldous," Humanist, XXV (January-February, 1965), 25.

Jog, D.V., Aldous Huxley.

Jones, W.S. Handley, "The Modern Hamlet," London Quarterly and Holborn Rev (July, 1950), 240-7.

Ketser, G., "Aldous Huxley: A Retrospect," RLV, XXX, ii (1964), 179-84.

King, Carlyle, "Aldous Huxley and Music," QQ, LXX (Autumn, 1963), 336-51.

_____, "Aldous Huxley's Way to God," QQ, LXI (Spring, 1954), 80-100.

Kumler, Alan D., "Aldous Huxley's Novel of Ideas," DA, XVIII (1958), 1432 (Michigan).

Lockridge, Ernest H., "Aldous Huxley and the Novel of Diversity," DA, XXV (1965), 4703 (Yale).

Maini, Darshan Singh, "Aldous Huxley--A Study in Disintegration," Indian Rev, LIV (July, 1953), 294-6. (Not seen.)

Matson, Floyd W., "Aldous and Heaven Too: Religion Among the Intellectuals," AR, XIV (September, 1954), 293-309.

Maurois, André, Points of View from Kipling to Graham Greene, 287-312. Also in Maurois, André, Prophets and Poets, N.Y.: Harper, 1935.

Meckier, Jerome, Aldous Huxley.

_____, "Aldous Huxley: Satire and Structure," WSCL, VII (Autumn, 1966), 284-94.

Misra, G.S.P., and Nora Satin, "The Meaning of Life in Aldous Huxley," MQ, IX (July, 1968), 351-63.

Murray, Donald C., "A Study of the Novels of Aldous Hux-
    ley," DA, XXVII (1967), 4261A (Syracuse).
Nazareth, Peter, "Aldous Huxley and His Critics," ESA, VII
    (March, 1964), 65-81.
O'Faolain, S., Vanishing Hero, 3-23.
Pandey, Nand Kumar, "The Influence of Hindu and Buddhist
    Thought on Aldous Huxley," DA, XXV (1964), 1921 (Stan-
    ford).
Quina, James H., Jr., "The Philosophical Phase of Aldous
    Huxley," CE, XXIII (May, 1962), 636-41.
Rolo, Charles J., "Aldous Huxley," Atlantic, CLXXX (Au-
    gust, 1947), 109-15. Also in Rolo, C., ed., Introduction
    to The World of Aldous Huxley, N.Y.: Harper, 1947.
Savage, D.S., "Aldous Huxley and the Dissociation of Per-
    sonality," in Rajan, B., ed., Novelist as Thinker, 9-34.
_____, Withered Branch, 129-55. Also in Aldridge, J.
    W., ed., Critiques and Essays on Modern Fiction, 340-
    61. Also in SR, LV (Autumn, 1947), 537-68.
Scales, Derek P., Aldous Huxley and French Literature,
    Sydney, Australia: Sydney Un. Pr., 1969.
Schmerl, Rudolf B., "Aldous Huxley's Social Criticism,"
    ChiR, XIII (Winter-Spring, 1959), 37-58.
Sponberg, Florence L., "Huxley's Perennial Preoccupation,"
    MSCS, III (December, 1968), 1-18. (Not seen.)
Stewart, Douglas, Ark of God, 44-70.
_____, "Significant Modern Writers: Aldous Huxley," ET,
    LXXI (1960), 100-3. (Not seen.)
Vincour, Jacob, "Aldous Huxley: Themes and Variations,"
    DA, XVI (1956), 1392-93 (Wisconsin).
Voorhees, Richard J., "The Perennial Huxley," PrS, XXIII
    (1949), 189-92.
Wajc-Tenenbaum, R., "Aldous Huxley and D.H. Lawrence,"
    RLV, XXXII (1966), 598-610.
Watts, H.H., Aldous Huxley.
Webster, H.T., "Aldous Huxley: Notes on a Moral Evolu-
    tion," SAQ, XLV (July, 1946), 372-83.
Wickes, George, and R. Frazer, "The Art of Fiction XXIV,"
    ParisR, VI (Spring, 1960), 57-80. Also in Writers at
    Work, 2nd ser., 193-214.
Wilson, Colin, "Existential Criticism and the Work of Aldous
    Huxley," LonM, V (September, 1958), 46-59. Also in
    Wilson, C., Strength to Dream, 213-38.
Zolla, Elemire, "Aldous Huxley and the Doom of Reason,"
    Letterature Moderne, V (September-December, 1954),
    523-30.

AFTER MANY A SUMMER DIES THE SWAN

Bowering, P., Aldous Huxley, 141-59.
Dyson, A. E., Crazy Fabric, 183-4.
Gordon, Caroline, How to Read a Novel, N. Y.: Viking,
     1957, 222-4.
Hines, B., Social World of Aldous Huxley, 40-2.
Jog, D. V., Aldous Huxley, 85-90.
Meckier, J., Aldous Huxley, 37-9, 159-62.
Nagarjan, S., "Religion in Three Recent Novels of Aldous
     Huxley," MFS, V (Summer, 1959), 153-65.
Salter, K. W., and A. E. Dyson, "Aldous Huxley," CritQ,
     IV (Summer, 1962), 177-9.
Savage, D. S., "Aldous Huxley and the Dissociation of Per-
     sonality," in Rajan, B., ed., Novelist as Thinker, 29-32.
     _____, Withered Branch, 150-3. Also in SR, LV (Au-
     tumn, 1947), 563-7.
Wagner, Linda W., "Satiric Masks: Huxley and Waugh,"
     SNL, III (Spring, 1966), 160-2.
Wain, John, "Tracts Against Materialism," LonM, II (Au-
     gust, 1955), 59-60.
Watts, H. H., Aldous Huxley, 97-106.
Wilson, C., "Existential Criticism and the Work of Aldous
     Huxley," Strength to Dream, 230-1.

ANTIC HAY

Bowering, P., Aldous Huxley, 46-60, 215-18.
Brooke, J., Aldous Huxley, 15-17.
Dyson, A. E., "Aldous Huxley and the Two Nothings," CritQ,
     III (Winter, 1961), 294-7. Also in Dyson, A. E., Crazy
     Fabric, 167-71.
Enroth, Clyde, "Mysticism in Two of Aldous Huxley's Early
     Novels," TCL, VI (1960), 123-32.
Greenblatt, S. J., Three Modern Satirists, 89-95, passim.
Hall, J., Tragic Comedians, 31-44, passim.
Hines, B., Social World of Aldous Huxley, 18-22.
Karl, Frederick R., "The Play Within the Novel in ANTIC
     HAY," Ren, XIII (Winter, 1961), 59-68.
     _____, and M. Magalaner, Reader's Guide to Great Twen-
     tieth Century Novels, 262-7.
Meckier, J., Aldous Huxley, 66-70.
Montgomery, Marion, "Aldous Huxley's Incomparable Man in
     ANTIC HAY," Discourse, III (October, 1960), 227-32.
Savage, D. S., "Aldous Huxley and the Dissociation of Per-
     sonality," in Rajan, B., ed., Novelist as Thinker, 13-14.
     _____, Withered Branch, 133-4. Also in Aldridge, J. W.,

ed. , Critiques and Essays on Modern Fiction, 343-4.
Also in SR, LV (Autumn, 1947), 542-4.
Watts, H. H. , Aldous Huxley, 49-56.
Waugh, Evelyn, "Youth at the Helm and Pleasure at the
Prow," LonM, II (August, 1955), 51-3.
Wilson, C. , "Existential Criticism and the Work of Aldous
Huxley," Strength to Dream, 217-19.

APE AND ESSENCE

Gump, Margaret, "From Ape to Man from Man to Ape,"
KFLQ, IV (1957), 177-85.
Hines, B. , Social World of Aldous Huxley, 46-7.
Jog, D. V. , Aldous Huxley, 98-102.
Meckier, J. , Aldous Huxley, 175-6, 189-97.
Schmerl, Rudolf B. , "The Two Future Worlds of Aldous Hux-
ley," PMLA, LXXVII (June, 1962), 328-34.
Watts, H. H. , Aldous Huxley, 113-18.

BRAVE NEW WORLD

Bowering, P. , Aldous Huxley, 98-113.
Brooke, J. , Aldous Huxley, 22-3.
Browning, Gordon, "Zamiatin's WE: An Anti-Utopian Clas-
sic," Cithara, VII (May, 1968), 13-20.
Clareson, Thomas D. , "The Classic: Aldous Huxley's
BRAVE NEW WORLD," Extrapolation, II (May, 1961), 33-
40.
Coleman, D. C. , "Bernard Shaw and BRAVE NEW WORLD,"
ShawR, X (January, 1967), 6-8.
Curle, Adam, "Huxley's BRAVE NEW WORLD," NS&N,
XLIX (April 9, 1955), 508-9.
Dyson, A. E. , "Aldous Huxley and the Two Nothings," CritQ,
III (Winter, 1961), 300-3. Also in Dyson, A. E. , Crazy
Fabric, 175-8.
Ehrenpreis, Irvin, "Orwell, Huxley, Pope," RLV, XXIII
(1957), 215-30, passim.
Enroth, Clyde, "Mysticism in Two of Aldous Huxley's Early
Novels," TCL, VI (1960), 123-32.
Firchow, Peter E. , "The Satire of Huxley's BRAVE NEW
WORLD," MFS, XII (Winter, 1966-67), 451-60.
Gable, Sister Mariella, "Prose Satire and the Modern Chris-
tian Temper," ABR, XI (March-June, 1960), 23-6.
Ghose, S. , Aldous Huxley, 50-3.
Greenblatt, S. J. , Three Modern Satirists, 95-101, passim.
Grushow, Ira, "BRAVE NEW WORLD and THE TEMPEST,"
CE, XXIV (October, 1962), 42-5.

Hacker, Andrew, "Dostoyevsky's Disciples: Man and Sheep in Political Theory," Jnl of Politics, XVII (November, 1955), 600-2.

Hall, J., Tragic Comedians, 42-4.

Hines, B., Social World of Aldous Huxley, 34-6.

Jog, D. V., Aldous Huxley, 66-73.

Jones, Joseph, "Utopia as Dirge," AQ, II (Fall, 1950), 214-26.

Jones, William M., "The Iago of BRAVE NEW WORLD," WHR, XV (Summer, 1961), 275-8.

Karl, F., and M. Magalaner, Reader's Guide to Great Twentieth Century Novels, 275-9.

Kessler, Martin, "Power and the Perfect State: A Study in Disillusionment as Reflected in Orwell's NINETEEN EIGHTY-FOUR and Huxley's BRAVE NEW WORLD," PSQ, LXXII (December, 1957), 565-77.

King, Almeda, "Christianity Without Tears: Man Without Humanity," EJ, LVII (September, 1968), 820-4.

Leeper, Geoffrey, "The Happy Utopias of Aldous Huxley and H. G. Wells," Meanjin, XXIV (March, 1965), 120-4.

Le Roy, Gaylord C., "A. F. 632 to 1984," CE, XII (December, 1950), 135-8.

Leyburn, E. D., Satiric Allegory, 114-25.

Meckier, J., Aldous Huxley, 17-19, 22-3, 112-13, 175-83, 186-7, 199-202, 204-5.

Miles, O. Thomas, "Three Authors in Search of a Character," Person, XLVI (January, 1965), 65-72.

Pendexter, Hugh, III, "Huxley's BRAVE NEW WORLD," Expl, XX (March, 1962), Item 58.

Richards, D., "Four Utopias," SEER, XL (1962), 224-8.

Rosenfeld, Isaac, "Second Thoughts on Huxley's BRAVE NEW WORLD," Nation, CLXIII (October 19, 1945), 445-7. Also in Rosenfeld, I., An Age of Enormity, 144-8.

Schmerl, Rudolf B., "The Two Future Worlds of Aldous Huxley," PMLA, LXXVII (June, 1962), 328-34.

Thomas, W. K., "BRAVE NEW WORLD and the Houyhnhnms," RUO, XXXVII (1967), 688-96.

Wain, John, "Tracts Against Materialsim," LonM, II (August, 1955), 60-1.

Watts, H. H., Aldous Huxley, 72-84.

Wells, Arvin R., in Hagopian, J. V., and M. Dolch, eds., Insight II, 176-85.

Wilson, Robert H., "BRAVE NEW WORLD as Shakspere Criticism," SAB, XXI (1946), 99-107.

_____, "Versions of BRAVE NEW WORLD," LCUT, VIII iv (Spring, 1968), 28-41.

Woodcock, George, "Utopias in Negative," SR, LXIV (Winter,

1956), 81-97.

CROME YELLOW

Bowering, P., Aldous Huxley, 6-9, 33-45.
Brooke, J., Aldous Huxley, 12-13.
Burgum, E. B., Novel and the World's Dilemma, 143-6. Al-
so in AR, II (March, 1942), 64-7.
Greenblatt, S. J., Three Modern Satirists, 79-89, passim.
Hines, B., Social World of Aldous Huxley, 14-18.
Karl, F., and M. Magalaner, Reader's Guide to Great Twen-
tieth Century Novels, 259-62.
Meckier, J., Aldous Huxley, 64-7.
Savage, D. S., "Aldous Huxley and the Dissociation of Per-
sonality," in Rajan, B., ed., Novelist as Thinker, 12-13.
_____, Withered Branch, 132-3. Also in Aldridge, J. W.,
ed., Critiques and Essays on Modern Fiction, 342-3. Al-
so in SR, LV (Autumn, 1947), 540-2.
Watts, H. H., Aldous Huxley, 45-9.
Wilson, Angus, "The House Party Novels," LonM, II (Au-
gust, 1955), 53-6.
Wilson, C., "Existential Criticism and the Work of Aldous
Huxley," Strength to Dream, 216-17.

EYELESS IN GAZA

Bowering, P., Aldous Huxley, 19-20, 114-40, 229-30.
Brooke, J., Aldous Huxley, 23-5.
Dyson, A. E., "Aldous Huxley and the Two Nothings," CritQ,
III (Winter, 1961), 303-6. Also in Dyson, A. E., Crazy
Fabric, 178-83.
Gray, J., On Second Thought, 169-70.
Hines, B., Social World of Aldous Huxley, 36-9.
Jog, D. V., Aldous Huxley, 75-85.
Karl, F., and M. Magalaner, Reader's Guide to Great Twen-
tieth Century Novels, 279-84.
Meckier, J., Aldous Huxley, 150-2, 154-8.
Savage, D. S., "Aldous Huxley and the Dissociation of Per-
sonality," in Rajan, B., ed., Novelist as Thinker, 21-7.
_____, Withered Branch, 142-6. Also in Aldridge, J. W.,
ed., Critiques and Essays on Modern Fiction, 350-5. Al-
so in SR, LV (Autumn, 1947), 553-60.
Watts, H. H., Aldous Huxley, 86-96.

THE GENIUS AND THE GODDESS

Jog, D. V., Aldous Huxley, 102-8.

Meckier, J., <u>Aldous Huxley</u>, 162-4.
Nagarjan, S., "Religion in Three Novels of Aldous Huxley,"
   <u>MFS</u>, V (Summer, 1959), 153-65.
Watts, H. H., <u>Aldous Huxley</u>, 118-25.

ISLAND

Bowering, P., <u>Aldous Huxley,</u> 181-212, 230-3.
Gorer, Geoffrey, "There is a Happy Land..." <u>Encounter,</u>
   XIX (July, 1962), 83-6.
Jog, D. V., <u>Aldous Huxley</u>, 108-15.
Kennedy, Richard S., "Aldous Huxley: The Final Wisdom,"
   <u>SWR,</u> L (Winter, 1965), 37-47.
Leeper, Geoffrey, "The Happy Utopias of Aldous Huxley and
   H. G. Wells," <u>Meanjin,</u> XXIV (March, 1965), 120-4.
McMichael, Charles T., "Aldous Huxley's ISLAND: The Fi-
   nal Vision," <u>SLitI</u>, I, ii (October, 1968), 73-82.
Meckier, J., <u>Aldous Huxley</u>, 196-205.
Stewart, D. H., "Aldous Huxley's ISLAND," <u>QQ,</u> LXX (Au-
   tumn, 1963), 326-35.
Watt, Donald J., "Vision and Symbol in Aldous Huxley's IS-
   LAND," <u>TCL</u>, XIV (October, 1968), 149-60.
Watts, H. H., <u>Aldous Huxley,</u> 139-45.

POINT COUNTER POINT

Baldanza, Frank, "POINT COUNTER POINT: Aldous Hux-
   ley on 'The Human Fugue'," <u>SAQ,</u> LVIII (Spring, 1959),
   248-57.
Bentley, Joseph, "Huxley's Ambivalent Responses to the Ideas
   of D. H. Lawrence," <u>TCL</u>, XIII (October, 1967), 144-53.
Bowering, P., <u>Aldous Huxley</u>, 9-10, 77-97, 221-3, 226-7,
   228-9.
Brooke, J., <u>Aldous Huxley,</u> 18-22.
Burgum, E. B., <u>Novel and the World's Dilemma,</u> 150-4. Al-
   so in <u>AR,</u> II (Spring, 1942), 68-73.
Dyson, A. E., "Aldous Huxley and the Two Nothings," <u>CritQ,</u>
   III (Winter, 1961), 297-300. Also in Dyson, A. E., <u>Crazy</u>
   <u>Fabric,</u> 171-5.
Ehrenpreis, Irwin, "Orwell, Huxley, Pope," <u>RLV</u>, XXIII
   (1957), 215-30, <u>passim.</u>
Glicksberg, Charles I., "Huxley; The Experimental Novelist,"
   <u>SAQ,</u> LII (1953), 101-6.
Hamilton, Robert, "The Challenge of Aldous Huxley: 'The
   Perennial Philosophy'," <u>Horizon,</u> XVII (June, 1948), 446-
   8.
Hines, B., <u>Social World of Aldous Huxley</u>, 27-34.

Hoffman, Frederick J., "Aldous Huxley and the Novel of
    Ideas," CE, VIII (December, 1946), 129-37. Also in O'-
    Connor, W. V., ed., Forms of Modern Fiction, 189-200.
Jog, D. V., Aldous Huxley, 58-66.
Karl, F., and M. Magalaner, Reader's Guide to Great Twen-
    tieth Century Novels, 267-75.
Kettle, A., Introduction to the English Novel, 167-70.
King, Carlyle, "Aldous Huxley's Way to God," QQ, LXI
    (Spring, 1954), 86-9.
Levi, A. W., Literature, Philosophy, and the Imagination,
    262-4.
Meckier, J., Aldous Huxley, 26-7, 32-5, 41-52, 60-1, 78-
    82, 86-90, 102-10.
Patty, James S., "Baudelaire and Huxley," SAB, XXIII
    (November, 1968), 5-8.
Savage, D. S., "Aldous Huxley and the Dissociation of Per-
    sonality," in Rajan, B., ed., Novelist as Thinker, 19-21.
Slochower, H., No Voice is Wholly Lost, 33-5.
Smyser, H. M., "Huxley's POINT COUNTER POINT, Chapter
    XI," Expl, VI (December, 1947), Item 22.
Thompson, Leslie L., "A Lawrence-Huxley Parallel: WOM-
    EN IN LOVE and POINT COUNTER POINT," N&Q, XV
    (February, 1968), 58-9.
Watts, H. H., Aldous Huxley, 62-71.
_____, Introduction, POINT COUNTER POINT, N. Y.:
    Harper, 1947.
Wilson, C., "Existential Criticism and the Work of Aldous
    Huxley," Strength to Dream, 220-2.

THOSE BARREN LEAVES

Aiken, C., Reviewer's ABC, 225-30. Also in Criterion,
    III (April, 1925), 449-53.
Bowering, P., Aldous Huxley, 61-76, 218-19.
Brooke, J., Aldous Huxley, 17-18.
Church, Margaret, "Concepts of Time in the Novels of Virginia
    Woolf and Aldous Huxley," MFS, I (May, 1955), 19-24.
Ghose, S., Aldous Huxley, 78-80.
Hines, B., Social World of Aldous Huxley, 22-6.
Meckier, J., Aldous Huxley, 24-7, 70-7.
O'Faolain, S., Vanishing Hero, 10-19.
Savage, D. S., "Aldous Huxley and the Dissociation of Per-
    sonality," in Rajan, B., ed., Novelist as Thinker, 14-19.
Watts, H. H., Aldous Huxley, 56-62.
Wilson, Angus, "The House Party Novels," LonM, II (August,
    1955), 53-6.

TIME MUST HAVE A STOP

Beary, Thomas J., "Religion and the Modern Novel," CathW,
    CLXVI (December, 1947), 206-9.
Bowering, P., Aldous Huxley, 160-80.
Church, Margaret, "Concepts of Time in the Novels of Vir-
    ginia Woolf and Aldous Huxley," MFS, I (May, 1955), 19-
    24.
Hamilton, Robert, "The Challenge of Aldous Huxley: 'The
    Perennial Philosophy'," Horizon, XVII (June, 1948), 450-
    3.
Hara, Ichiro, "On A. Huxley's TIME MUST HAVE A STOP,"
    Rising Generation (Japan), XCIII (1947), No. 11.
Hines, B., Social World of Aldous Huxley, 43-6.
Jog, D. V., Aldous Huxley, 90-8.
Lebowitz, Martin, "The Everlasting Mr. Huxley," in Kenyon
    Review. Kenyon Critics, 289-93. Also in KR, VII
    (Winter, 1945), 135-8.
Meckier, J., Aldous Huxley, 164-72.
Nagarajan, S., "Religion in Three Recent Novels of Aldous
    Huxley," MFS, V (Summer, 1959), 153-65.
Savage, D. S., "Aldous Huxley and the Dissociation of Per-
    sonality," in Rajan, B., ed., Novelist as Thinker, 32-4.
    _____, Withered Branch, 154-5. Also in Aldridge, J. W.,
    ed., Critiques and Essays on Modern Fiction, 360-1. Al-
    so in SR, LV (Autumn, 1947), 567-8.
Watts, H. H., Aldous Huxley, 106-13.
Wilson, Edmund, "Aldous Huxley in the World Beyond Time,"
    NY (September 2, 1944), 64-6. Also in Wilson, E.,
    Classics and Commercials, 209-14.

BIBLIOGRAPHY

Clareson, Thomas D., and Carolyn S. Andrews, "Aldous
    Huxley: A Bibliography 1960-1964," Extrapolation, VI
    (December, 1964), 2-21.
Eschelbach, Claire John, and J. L. Shober, Aldous Huxley:
    A Bibliography, 1916-1959, Berkeley: Un. of Calif.,
    1961.
Watts, H. H., Aldous Huxley, 169-76.

ISHERWOOD, CHRISTOPHER, 1904-

GENERAL

Bantock, G. H., "The Novels of Christopher Isherwood," in

Rajan, B., ed., Novelist as Thinker, 46-57.
Isherwood, Christopher, "A Conversation on Tape," LonM,
    n.s. I (June, 1961), 41-58.
Karl, F.R., Contemporary English Novel, 290-2.
Maes-Jelinek, Hena, "The Knowledge of Man in the Works of
    Christopher Isherwood," RLV, No. 5 (1960), 341-60.
Mayne, Richard, "The Novel and Mr. Norris," Cambridge
    Jnl, VI (June, 1953), 561-70.
Pryce-Jones, David, "Isherwood Reassessed," T&T, XLI
    (October 1, 1960), 1162-3.
Solway, Clifford, "An Interview with Christopher Isherwood,"
    TamR, No. 39 (Spring, 1966), 22-35.
Whitehead, John, "Christophananda: Isherwood at Sixty,"
    LonM, n.s. V (July, 1965), 90-100.
Wickes, Gerald, "An Interview with Christopher Isherwood,"
    Shen, XVI (Spring, 1965), 23-52.

ALL THE CONSPIRATORS

Allen, W., Modern Novel, 234-5.

DOWN THERE ON A VISIT

Dienstfrey, Harris, Ctary, XXXIV (October, 1962), 360-3.
Jebb, Julian, LonM, n.s. II (April, 1962), 87-9.
Wiley, Paul, WSCL, IV, ii (Spring-Summer, 1963), 225-8.

GOODBYE TO BERLIN

Allen, W., Modern Novel, 237-8.

THE MEMORIAL

Allen, W., Modern Novel, 235-7.
Kermode, F., Puzzles and Epiphanies, 125-6.

PRATER VIOLET

Bantock, G.H., "The Novels of Christopher Isherwood," in
    Rajan, B., ed., Novelist as Thinker, 55-7.
Farrell, James T., "When Graustark Is in Celluloid," Lit-
    erature and Morality, N.Y.: Vanguard, 1947, 125-32.
Rosenfeld, Isaac, "Isherwood's Master Theme," KR, VIII
    (Summer, 1946), 488-92. Also in Rosenfeld, I., Age of
    Enormity, 149-54.

A SINGLE MAN

Kuehn, Robert E., "Fiction Chronicle," WSCL, VI (1965), 134-5.

Raban, J., "Narrative: Some Problems and Conventions," Technique of Modern Fiction, 29-32.

Solway, Clifford, "An Interview with Christopher Isherwood," TamR, No. 39 (Spring, 1966), 22-35.

Spender, Stephen, "Must There Always be a Red Brick England?" in Encyclopaedia Britannica, Great Ideas Today, 1965, 184-6.

THE WORLD IN THE EVENING

Gunn, Thom, LonM, I (October, 1954), 81-5.

Kermode, F., Puzzles and Epiphanies, 121-5.

Maes-Jelinek, Hena, "The Knowledge of Man in the Works of Christopher Isherwood," RLV, No. 5 (1960), 351-9.

BIBLIOGRAPHY

Westby, Selmer, and Clayton M. Brown, Christopher Isherwood: A Bibliography 1923-1967, Los Angeles: California State College, 1968.

JACKSON, SHIRLEY, 1920-1965

HANGSAMAN

Lyons, J.O., College Novel in America, 62-9.

WE HAVE ALWAYS LIVED IN THE CASTLE

Woodruff, Stuart C., "The Real Horror Elsewhere: Shirley Jackson's Last Novel," SWR, LII (Spring, 1967), 152-62.

BIBLIOGRAPHY

Phillips, Robert S., "Shirley Jackson: A Checklist," PBSA, LX (1966), 203-13.

JACOBSON, DAN, 1929-

GENERAL

Girling, H. K., "Compassion and Detachment in the Novels of
   Dan Jacobson," The Purple Renoster, II (Spring, 1957),
   16-23. (Not seen.)
Winegarten, Renée, "The Novels of Dan Jacobson," Midstream, XII (May, 1966), 69-73.

THE BEGINNERS

"Prose Out of Africa. Dan Jacobson: THE BEGINNERS," in
   T. L. S. Essays and Reviews, 1966, 42-3. Also in TLS
   (June 2, 1966), 812.
Ricks, Christopher, "One Little Liberal," NStat (June 3,
   1966), 812.
Winegarten, Renée, "The Novels of Dan Jacobson," Mid-
   stream, XII (1966), 72-3.

A DANCE IN THE SUN

Durrant, G. H., "Promising Young Men," Standpunte, XI
   (December, 1956-January, 1957), 64-6.

EVIDENCE OF LOVE

Alvarez, A., "The Difficulty of Being South African," NS&-
   Nation, LIX (June 4, 1960), 827-8.
Dienstfrey, Harris, "Tales of Hate and Love," Ctary, XXX
   (September, 1960), 261-4.
Miller, Karl, "Annals of Lyndhurst," Spectator (June 3,
   1960), 806-7.

THE PRICE OF DIAMONDS

Decter, Midge, "Novelist of South Africa," Ctary, XXV
   (June, 1958), 539-44.

THE TRAP

Durrant, G. H., "Promising Young Men," Standpunte, XI
   (December, 1956-January, 1957), 63-4.

BIBLIOGRAPHY

Yudelman, Myra, comp., Dan Jacobson: A Bibliography,
   Johannesburg: Un. of Witwatersrand, Dep't of Bibliography, Librarianship and Typography, 1967.

JOHNSON, PAMELA HANSFORD, 1912-

GENERAL

Karl, F. R., Contemporary English Novel, 275-6.
Quigly, I., Pamela Hansford Johnson.

AN AVENUE OF STONE (See also TRILOGY)

Raymond, J., "A Corvo of Our Day," Doge of Dover, 157-8.

CATHERINE CARTER

Quigly, I., Pamela Hansford Johnson, 28-31.

CORK STREET, NEXT TO THE HATTERS

Quigly, I., Pamela Hansford Johnson, 37-8.

AN ERROR OF JUDGEMENT

Quigly, I., Pamela Hansford Johnson, 41-3.

THE HUMBLER CREATION

Quigly, I., Pamela Hansford Johnson, 38-40.

AN IMPOSSIBLE MARRIAGE

Quigly, I., Pamela Hansford Johnson, 31-3.

THE LAST RESORT

Allen, W., Modern Novel, 258-60.
Quigly, I., Pamela Hansford Johnson, 33-5.

NIGHT AND SILENCE WHO IS HERE?

Webster, Harvey C., "Farce and Faith," KR, XXV (Autumn, 1963), 747-51.

THE PHILISTINES

Quigly, I., Pamela Hansford Johnson, 26-8.

THIS BED THY CENTRE

Quigly, I., Pamela Hansford Johnson, 9-13.

TRILOGY

Quigly, I., <u>Pamela Hansford Johnson</u>, 17-23.

THE TROJAN BROTHERS

Quigly, I., <u>Pamela Hansford Johnson</u>, 24-6.

THE UNSPEAKABLE SKIPTON

Allen, W., <u>Modern Novel</u>, 260.
Quigly, I., <u>Pamela Hansford Johnson</u>, 35-6.
Raymond, John, "A Corvo of Our Day," <u>Doge of Dover</u>,
    158-63.

WINTER QUARTERS

Quigly, I., <u>Pamela Hansford Johnson</u>, 23-4.

<u>JONES, JAMES, 1921-</u>

GENERAL

Aldrich, Nelson W., Jr., "The Art of Fiction XXIII: James
    Jones," <u>ParisR</u>, XX (Autumn-Winter, 1958-59), 34-55.
    Also in <u>Writers at Work</u>, 3rd ser., 231-50.
Jones, James, and William Styron, "Two Writers Talk It
    Over," <u>Esquire</u>, LX, i (July, 1963), 57-9.
Sheed, Wilfrid, "The Jones Boy Forever," <u>Atlantic Monthly</u>,
    CCXIX (June, 1967), 68-72.
Stevenson, David L., in Balakian, N., and C. Simmons, eds.,
    <u>Creative Present</u>, 195-206+.
Volpe, Edmond L., in Moore, H. T., ed., <u>Contemporary
    American Novelists</u>, 106-12.

FROM HERE TO ETERNITY

Adams, Richard P., "A Second Look at FROM HERE TO
    ETERNITY," <u>CE</u>, XVII (1956), 205-10.
Bryant, Jerry H., "The Last of the Social Protest Writers,"
    <u>ArQ</u>, XIX (Winter, 1963), 320-3.
Burress, Lee A., Jr., "James Jones on Folklore and Bal-
    lad," <u>CE</u>, XXI (1959), 161-5.
De Voto, Bernard, "Dull Novels Make Dull Reading,"
    <u>Harper's</u>, CCII (June, 1951), 67-70.
Dinkins, Paul, "FROM HERE TO ETERNITY and the New

Sentimentality," CathW, CLXXIII (September, 1951), 422-
8.
Eisinger, C. E., Fiction of the Forties, 41-3.
Fiedler, Leslie, "Dead-End Werther: The Bum as American
Culture Hero," An End to Innocence, Boston: Beacon Pr.,
1955, 183-90.
_____, "James Jones' Dead-End Young Werther," Ctary,
XII (1951), 252-5.
Gardiner, H. C., " 'Damned' is the Missing Word," In All
Conscience, 17-21. Also in America (March 10, 1951),
672-4.
Geismar, M., American Moderns, 225-34.
Glicksberg, Charles I., "Racial Attitudes in FROM HERE TO
ETERNITY," Phylon, XIV (1953), 384-9.
Griffith, Ben W., Jr., "Rear Rank Robin Hood: James
Jones's Folk Hero," GaR, X (1956), 41-6.
Hassan, I., Radical Innocence, 83-6.
Healey, Robert C., in Gardiner, H. C., ed., Fifty Years
of the American Novel, 263-4.
Macauley, Robie, "Private Jones's Revenge," KR, XIII
(Summer, 1951), 526-9.
Prescott, O., In My Opinion, 159-62.
Stevenson, David L., in Balakian, N., and C. Simmons,
eds., Creative Present, 200-3+.
Volpe, Edmond L., in Moore, H. T., ed., Contemporary
American Novelists, 108-9.

GO TO THE WIDOW-MAKER

Sheed, Wilfrid, "The Jones Boy Forever," Atlantic Monthly,
CCXIX (June, 1967), 68-72.

SOME CAME RUNNING

Geismar, M., American Moderns, 234-8.
Hicks, Granville, "James Jones's SOME CAME RUNNING:
A Study in Arrogant Primitivism," New Leader (January
27, 1958), 120-2.
Stevenson, David L., in Balakian, N., and C. Simmons,
eds., Creative Present, 203-5.

THE THIN RED LINE

Allen, Donald A., "The Way it Was," Reporter, XXVII
(October 25, 1962), 61-5.
Michel-Michot, Paulette, "Jones's THE THIN RED LINE:
The End of Innocence," RLV, XXX, i (1964), 15-26.

Pritchett, V. S., "American Soldiers," NStat (February 8, 1963), 207.
Volpe, Edmond L., in Moore, H. T., ed., Contemporary American Novelists, 110-12.

KEROUAC, JACK, 1922-1969

GENERAL

Allen, Eliot D., "That Was No Lady... That Was Jack Kerouac's Girl," in Langford, R. E., ed. Essays in Modern American Literature, 97-102.
Ashida, Margaret E., "Frogs and Frozen Zen," PrS, XXXIV (1960), 199-206.
Berrigan, Ted, "The Art of Fiction XLI: Jack Kerouac (an interview), ParisR, XI (Summer, 1968), 60-105.
Duffey, Bernard, "The Three Worlds of Jack Kerouac," in Waldmeir, W. W., ed., Recent American Fiction, 175-84.
Frohock, W. M., Strangers to this Ground, 132-47.
Jones, Granville H., "Jack Kerouac and the American Conscience," in Carnegie Institute of Technology, Lectures on Modern Novelists, 25-39.
Kerouac, Jack, "Beatific: On the Origins of a Generation," Encounter, XIII (August, 1959), 57-61.
Krim, Seymour, "King of the Beats," Cweal, LXIX (January 2, 1959), 359-60.
Stevenson, David L., in Balakian, N., and C. Simmons, eds., Creative Present, 195-200, 206-12.
Tallman, Warren, "Kerouac's Sound," TamR, No. 11 (Spring, 1959), 58-74. Also in EvR, IV, No. 11, 153-69. Also in Parkinson, T., ed., Casebook on the Beat, 215-29.
Vaidyanathan, T. G., "Jack Kerouac and Existentialist Anxiety," OJES, No. 2 (1962), 61-6.
Webb, Howard W., Jr., "The Singular Worlds of Jack Kerouac," in Moore, H. T., ed., Contemporary American Novelists, 120-33.

DESOLATION ANGELS

Mazzocco, Robert, "Our Gang," NYRB (May 20, 1965), 8-9.
Spender, Stephen, "Traditional vs. Underground Novels," in Encyclopaedia Britannica, Great Ideas Today, 1965, 194-6.
Wakefield, Dan, "Jack Kerouac Comes Home," Atlantic Mthly, CCXVI (July, 1965), 69-72.

THE DHARMA BUMS

Bellman, Samuel, "On the Mountain," ChiR, XIII (Winter-Spring, 1959), 68-72.

Champney, Freeman, "Beat-up or Beatific?" AR, XIX (Spring, 1959), 117-20.

Feied, F., No Pie in the Sky, 73-80, passim.

Feldman, Irving, "Stuffed Dharma," Ctary, XXVI (December, 1958), 543-4.

Jackson, Robert P., "The Dharma Bums," American Buddhist, II (October, 1958), 1+.

Leer, Norman, "Three American Novels and Contemporary Society; A Search for Commitment," WSCL, III, iii (Fall, 1962), 81-4.

Rubin, Louis D., Jr., "Two Gentlemen of San Francisco: Notes on Kerouac and Responsibility," WR, XXIII (Spring, 1959), 278-83.

ON THE ROAD

Askew, Melvin W., "Quests, Cars, and Kerouac," UKCR, XXVIII (March, 1962), 231-40.

Champney, Freeman, "Beat-up or Beatific?" AR, XIX (Spring, 1959), 115-17.

Feied, F., No Pie in the Sky, 57-73, passim.

Fuller, Edmund, Man in Modern Fiction; Some Minority Opinions on Contemporary American Writing, N.Y.: Random House, 1958, 148-54.

Gleason, Ralph, "Kerouac's 'Beat Generation'," SatR, XLI (January 11, 1958), 75.

Gold, Herbert, "Hip, Cool, Beat--and Frantic," Nation, CLXXXV (November 16, 1957), 349-55.

Goodman, Paul, "Wingless Wandervogel, 1957," Midstream, IV (Winter, 1958), 98-101.

Hassan, I., Radical Innocence, 93-4.

Podhoretz, Norman, "The Know-Nothing Bohemians," Doings and Undoings, 143-58. Also in PR, XXV (Spring, 1958), 305-18. Also in Parkinson, T., ed., Casebook on the Beat, 201-12. Also in Krim, Seymour, ed., The Beats, N.Y.: Fawcett, 1960, 111-24.

Sigal, Clancy, "Nihilism's Organization Man," Universities and Left Rev, No. 4 (Summer, 1958), 59-65.

Vaidyanathan, T.G., "Jack Kerouac and Existentialist Anxiety," OJES, No. 2 (1962), 61-6.

THE SUBTERRANEANS

Kerouac, Jack, "Written Address to the Italian Judge," EvR,
VII (October-November, 1963), 108-10.

Miller, Henry, Preface to THE SUBTERRANEANS, N.Y.:
Avon, 1959, 5-7. Also in Parkinson, T., ed., Casebook
on the Beat, 230-1.

Podhoretz, Norman, "The Know-Nothing Bohemians," Doings
and Undoings, 143-58. Also in PR, XXV (Spring, 1958),
305-18. Also in Parkinson, T., ed., Casebook on the
Beat, 201-12. Also in Krim, Seymour, ed., The Beats,
N.Y.: Fawcett, 1960, 111-24.

Russell, William, "Kerouac's THE SUBTERRANEANS,"
Mainstream, XV, vi (June, 1962), 61-4.

Straumann, H., American Literature in the Twentieth Century, 81-2.

KESEY, KEN, 1935-

ONE FLEW OVER THE CUCKOO'S NEST

Boyers, Robert, "Attitudes Toward Sex in American 'High
Culture'," AAAPSS, CCCLXXVI (March, 1968), 44-7.

Malin, Irving, "Ken Kesey: ONE FLEW OVER THE CUCK-
OO'S NEST," Crit, V, ii (Fall, 1962), 81-4.

Waldmeir, Joseph J., "Two Novelists of the Absurd: Heller
and Kesey," WSCL, V, iii (Autumn, 1964), 196-204.

Widmer, L., "Contemporary American Outcasts," Literary
Rebel, 133-6.

KNOWLES, JOHN, 1926-

GENERAL

Halio, Jay L., "John Knowles's Short Novels," SSF, I
(Winter, 1964), 107-12.

McDonald, James L., "The Novels of John Knowles," ArQ,
XXIII (Winter, 1967), 335-42.

INDIAN SUMMER

Ellis, James, "John Knowles: INDIAN SUMMER," Crit, IX,
ii (1967), 92-5.

McDonald, James L., "The Novels of John Knowles," ArQ,
XXIII (Winter, 1967), 338-42.

MORNING IN ANTIBES

Halio, Jay L. , "John Knowles's Short Novels," SSF, I
(Winter, 1964), 109-12.
McDonald, James L. , "The Novels of John Knowles," ArQ,
XXIII (Winter, 1967), 337-8.

A SEPARATE PEACE

Crabbe, John K. , "On the Playing Fields of Devon," EJ, LII
(1963), 109-11.
Ellis, James, "A SEPARATE PEACE: The Fall from Inno-
cence," EJ, LIII (1964), 313-18.
Ely, Sister M. Amanda, O. P. , "The Adult Image in Three
Novels of Adolescent Life," EJ, LVI (November, 1967),
1128-30.
Foster, Milton P. , "Levels of Meaning in A SEPARATE
PEACE," EngR, XVIII, iv (1968), 34-40.
Greiling, Franzika L. , "The Theme of Freedom in A SEPA-
RATE PEACE," EJ, LVI (December, 1967), 1269-72.
Halio, Jay L. , "John Knowles's Short Novels," SSF, I (Win-
ter, 1964), 107-9.
McDonald, James L. , "The Novels of John Knowles," ArQ,
XXIII (Winter, 1967), 335-7.
Mellard, James M. , "Counterpoint and 'Double Vision' in A
SEPARATE PEACE," SSF, IV (Winter, 1967), 127-34.
Nora, Sister M. , S. S. N. D. , "A Comparison of Actual and
Symbolic Landscape in A SEPARATE PEACE," Discourse,
XI (Summer, 1968), 356-62.
Weber, Ronald, "Narrative Method in A SEPARATE PEACE,"
SSF, III (Fall, 1965), 63-72.
Witherington, Paul, "A SEPARATE PEACE: A Study in
Structural Ambiguity," EJ, LIV (December, 1965), 795-
800.

KOESTLER, ARTHUR, 1905-

GENERAL

Atkins, J. , Arthur Koestler.
Bantock, G. H. , "Arthur Koestler," P&L, I (Summer, 1948),
41-7.
Burgess, A. , Urgent Copy, 147-9.
Calder, J. , Chronicles of Conscience.
Hicks, Granville, "Arthur Koestler and the Future of the
Left," AR, V (June, 1945), 212-23.

Kahn, Lothar, "Arthur Koestler and the Jews," CJF, XVIII
  (Summer, 1960), 341-6.
Klingopulos, G.D., "Arthur Koestler," Scrutiny, XVI (June,
  1949), 82-92.
Mortimer, Raymond, "Arthur Koestler," Cornhill, CLXII
  (Winter, 1946), 213-22.
Prescott, O., In My Opinion, 31-9.
Pritchett, V.S., "The Art of Koestler," Books in General,
  155-72. Also in Horizon, XV (May, 1947), 233-47.
_____, "Koestler: A Guilty Figure," Harper's Mag,
  CXCVI (January, 1948), 84-92.
Rahv, P., Image and Idea, 173-81.
_____, "Koestler and Homelss Radicalism," Literature
  and the Sixth Sense, 126-33.
Redman, Ben Ray, "Arthur Koestler: Radical's Progress,"
  CE, XIII (December, 1951), 131-6.
Rivett, Kenneth, "In Defence of Arthur Koestler," AusQ,
  XIX (September, 1947), 90-4.
Stanford, Derek, "Arthur Koestler," in Baker, D.V., ed.,
  Modern British Writing, 271-80. Also in Baker, D.V.,
  ed., Writers of Today, 85-95.
Winegarten, Renée, "Arthur Koestler as Witness," Mid-
  stream, XII (February, 1966), 71-7.
Woodcock, G., Writer and Politics, 175-96.

THE AGE OF LONGING

Calder, J., Chronicles of Conscience, 220-2.
Prescott, O., In My Opinion, 38-9.

ARRIVAL AND DEPARTURE

Atkins, J., Arthur Koestler, 81-90.
Bantock, G.H., "Arthur Koestler," P&L, I (Summer, 1948),
  46-7.
Calder, J., Chronicles of Conscience, 141-4, 155-60.
Fuerst, Rudolph A., PsyR, XXXIII (1946), 102-7.
Gray, J., On Second Thought, 237-40.
Prescott, O., In My Opinion, 35-6.
Pritchett, V.S., "The Art of Koestler," Books in General,
  166-7.
Rahv, P., "Koestler and Homeless Radicalism," Literature
  and the Sixth Sense, 128-30.
Roland, Albert, "Christian Implications in Anti-Stalinist
  Novels," Religion in Life, XXII (1953), 407-8.
Stanford, Derek, "Arthur Koestler," in Baker, D.V., ed.,
  Modern British Writing, 279-80. Also in Baker, D.V.,

ed. , Writers of Today, 91-3.
Woodcock, G. , Writer and Politics, 187-9.

DARKNESS AT NOON

Atkins, J. , Arthur Koestler, 177-84, 189-91.
Axthelm, P. M. , Modern Confessional Novel, 97-113.
Bantock, G. H. , "Arthur Koestler," P&L, I (Summer, 1948), 44-6.
Beum, Robert, "Epigraphs for Rubashov: Koestler's DARK-NESS AT NOON," DR, XLII (1962), 86-91.
Calder, J. , Chronicles of Conscience, 127-35, 149-53.
Downing, Francis, "Koestler Revisited," Cweal (February 9, 1951), 444-6.
Garaudy, Roger, "The Lie in its Pure State: Arthur Koestler," in Garaudy, R. , Literature of the Graveyard, N. Y.: International Pubs. , 1948, 50-5.
Geering, R. G. , "DARKNESS AT NOON and NINETTEN EIGHTY-FOUR--A Comparative Study," AusQ, XXX, iii (1958), 90-6.
Glicksberg, Charles I. , "Arthur Koestler and Communism," QQ, LIII (Winter, 1946-47), 420-3.
Hartt, J. N. , Lost Image of Man, 76-9.
Hoffman, Frederick J. , ['DARKNESS AT NOON: The Consequences of Secular Grace," GaR, XIII (1959), 331-45. Also in Hoffman, F. J. , Mortal No, 126-35.
Howe, I. , Politics and the Novel, 227-32.
Klingopulos, G. D. , "Arthur Koestler," Scrutiny, XVI (June, 1949), 83-7.
Moseley, E. M. , Pseudonyms of Christ in the Modern Novel, 189-94.
Prabhakar, M. S. , "Two Inconsistencies in DARKNESS AT NOON," N&Q, XI (October, 1964), 387-8.
Prescott, O. , In My Opinion, 33-5.
Pritchett, V. S. , "The Art of Koestler," Books in General, 164-6. Also in Horizon, XV (May, 1947), 240-3.
_____, "Koestler: A Guilty Figure," Harper's Mag, CXCVI (January, 1948), 88-90.
Roland, Albert, "Christian Implications in Anti-Stalinist Novels," Religion in Life, XXII (1953), 406-7.
Stanford, Derek, "Arthur Koestler," in Baker, D. V. , ed. , Modern British Writing, 276-7. Also in Baker, D. V. , ed. , Writers of Today, 89-91.
Strachey, J. , Strangled Cry, 11-23. Also in Encounter, XV (November, 1960), 3-9.
Weintraub, S. , Last Great Cause, 138-42.
Woodcock, G. , Writer and Politics, 183-7.

THE GLADIATORS

Atkins, J., Arthur Koestler, 99-100, 111-13, 117-21, 156-7.
Bantock, G. H., "Arthur Koestler," P&L, I (Summer, 1948),
    43-4.
Calder, J., Chronicles of Conscience, 121-4, 146-8.
Pritchett, V. S., "The Art of Koestler," Books in General,
    160-3. Also in Horizon, XV (May, 1947), 237-40.
_____, "Koestler: A Guilty Figure," Harper's Mag,
    CXCVI (January, 1948), 86-8.
Stanford, Derek, "Arthur Koestler," in Baker, D. V., ed.,
    Modern British Writing, 274-6. Also in Baker, D. V.,
    ed., Writers of Today, 87-9.
Winegarten, Renée, "Arthur Koestler as Witness," Mid-
    stream, XII (February, 1966), 73-4.

THIEVES IN THE NIGHT

Calder, J., Chronicles of Conscience, 200-2, 212-20.
Glicksberg, Charles, "Anti-Semitism and the Jewish Novel-
    ist," in Ribalow, H., ed., Mid-Century, 344-6.
Klingopulos, G. D., "Arthur Koestler," Scrutiny, XVI (June,
    1949), 90-2.
Lerner, Max, Actions and Passions: Notes on the Multiple
    Revolution of Our Time, N. Y.: Simon & Schuster, 1949,
    51-3.
Mortimer, Raymond, "Arthur Koestler," Cornhill, CLXII
    (Winter, 1946), 216-22.
Prescott, O., In My Opinion, 37.
Pritchett, V. S., "The Art of Koestler," Books in General,
    167-72. Also in Horizon, XV (May, 1947), 244-6.
_____, "Koestler: A Guilty Figure," Harper's Mag,
    CXCVI (January, 1948), 90-2.
Ribalow, Harold, "Zion in Contemporary Fiction," in Riba-
    low, H., ed., Mid-Century, 581-3.
Winegarten, Renée, "Arthur Koestler as Witness," Mid-
    stream, XII (February, 1966), 75-6.
Woodcock, G., Writer and Politics, 191-6.

LARKIN, PHILIP, 1922-

GENERAL

Wain, John, "Engagement or Withdrawal? Some Notes on
    the Work of Philip Larkin," CritQ, VI (Summer, 1964),
    175-8.

A GIRL IN WINTER

Gindin, J., "Education and the Contemporary Class Structure," Postwar British Fiction, 104-5.
O'Connor, W. V., New University Wits, 20-3.

JILL

Gindin, J., "Education and the Contemporary Class Structure,
Postwar British Fiction, 85-108.
O'Connor, W. V., New University Wits, 18-20.

LEHMANN, ROSAMOND, 1903-

GENERAL

Le Stourgeon, D. E., Rosamond Lehmann.
Pendry, E. D., New Feminism of English Fiction, 153-72.
Raven, Simon, "The Game That Nobody Wins: The Novels
of Rosamond Lehmann," LonM, n. s. III (April, 1963), 59-
64.
Shuman, R. Baird, "Personal Isolation in the Novels of Rosamond Lehmann," RLV, XXVI, i (1960), 76-80.

THE BALLAD AND THE SOURCE

Le Stourgeon, D. E., Rosamond Lehmann, 89-107.

DUSTY ANSWER

Le Stourgeon, D. E., Rosamond Lehmann, 29-42.

THE ECHOING GROVE

Allen, W., Modern Novel, 195-7.
Balakian, Nona, "Three English Novelists," KR, XV (Sum-
mer, 1953), 494-6.
Bowen, Elizabeth, "The Modern Novel and the Theme of
Love," NRep, CXXVIII (May 11, 1953), 18-19. Also in
Bowen, E., Seven Winters and Afterthoughts, 218-23.
Le Stourgeon, D. E., Rosamond Lehmann, 108-21.
McCormick, J., Catastrophe and Imagination, 85-6; 89-92.

INVITATION TO THE WALTZ

Le Stourgeon, D. E., Rosamond Lehmann, 57-75.

A NOTE IN MUSIC

Le Stourgeon, D. E. , Rosamond Lehmann, 43-56.

THE WEATHER IN THE STREETS

Le Stourgeon, D. E. , Rosamond Lehmann, 76-88.

LESSING, DORIS, 1919-

GENERAL

Allen, Walter, in Kostelanetz, R. , ed. , Contemporary Lit-
erature, 400-1.
Brewster, D. , Doris Lessing.
Burkom, Selma R. , " 'Only Connect': Form and Content in
the Works of Doris Lessing," Crit, XI, i (1968), 51-68.
Carey, Father Alfred Augustine, "Doris Lessing: The Search
for Reality. A Study of the Major Themes in Her Novels,"
DA, XXVI (1965), 3297 (Wisconsin).
Gindin, J. , "Doris Lessing's Intense Commitment," Postwar
British Fiction, 65-86.
McDowell, Frederick P. W. , "The Fiction of Doris Lessing:
An Interim View," ArQ, XXI (Winter, 1965), 315-45.
Schlueter, Peter, "Doris Lessing: Free Woman's Commit-
ment" in Shapiro, C. , ed. , Contemporary British Novel-
ists, 48-61.
Tucker, M. , Africa in Modern Literature, 175-83.

THE ANTHEAP

Brewster, D. , Doris Lessing, 53-8.

CHILDREN OF VIOLENCE Series

Allen W. , Modern Novel, 276-7.
Brewster, D. , Doris Lessing, 33; 103.
Howe, Florence, "Doris Lessing's Free Women," Nation,
CC (January 11, 1965), 34-7.
Karl, F. R. , Contemporary English Novel, 282-3.
McDowell, Frederick P. W. , "The Fiction of Doris Lessing:
An Interim View," ArQ, XXI (Winter, 1965), 330-45.
Owen, Roger, "Good Man is Hard to Find," Ctary, XXXIX
(April, 1965), 79-82.
Schlueter, Peter, "Doris Lessing: Free Woman's Commit-
ment" in Shapiro, C. , ed. , Contemporary British Novel-

ists, 51-5.

ELDORADO

Brewster, D., Doris Lessing, 51-3.

THE GOLDEN NOTEBOOK

Anon., "The Fog of War," TLS (April 27, 1962), 280.
Bergonzi, Bernard, "In Pursuit of Doris Lessing," NYRB,
    IV (February 11, 1965), 13-14.
Brewster, D., Doris Lessing, 138-57.
Burkom, Selma R., " 'Only Connect': Form and Content in
    the Works of Doris Lessing," Crit, XI, i (1968), 54-6.
Howe, Florence, "A Talk with Doris Lessing," Nation, CCIV
    (March 7, 1967), 311-13.
McDowell, Frederick P.W., " 'The Devious Involutions of
    Human Character and Emotions': Reflections on Some Re-
    cent British Novels," WSCL, IV, iii (Autumn, 1963), 746-
    50.
_____, "The Fiction of Doris Lessing: An Interim View,"
    ArQ, XXI (Winter, 1965), 328-30.
Schlueter, Peter, "Doris Lessing: Free Woman's Commit-
    ment" in Shapiro, C., ed., Contemporary British Novel-
    ists, 55-8.
Taubman, Howard, "Free Women," NStat, LXIII (April 20,
    1962), 569. Also in Kostelanetz, R., ed., On Contempo-
    rary Literature, 402-3.

THE GRASS IS SINGING

Brewster, D., Doris Lessing, 34-41.
Karl, F.R., Contemporary English Novel, 281-2.
McDowell, Frederick P.W., "The Fiction of Doris Lessing:
    An Interim View," ArQ, XXI (Winter, 1965), 317-18.
Schlueter, Peter, "Doris Lessing: Free Woman's Commit-
    ment" in Shapiro, C., ed., Contemporary British Novel-
    ists, 50-1.
Tucker, M., Africa in Modern Literature, 177-9.

A HOME FOR THE HIGHLAND CATTLE

Brewster, D., Doris Lessing, 42-7.

HUNGER

Brewster, D., Doris Lessing, 42-7.

LANDLOCKED (See also CHILDREN OF VIOLENCE Series)

Brewster, D., <u>Doris Lessing</u>, 129-35.

MARTHA QUEST (See also CHILDREN OF VIOLENCE Series)

Bergonzi, Bernard, "In Pursuit of Doris Lessing," <u>NYRB,</u>
   IV (February 11, 1965), 12-13.
Brewster, D., <u>Doris Lessing</u>, 103-8.
Tucker, M., <u>Africa in Modern Literature</u>, 180-2.

THE OTHER WOMAN

Brewster, D., <u>Doris Lessing</u>, 74-8.

A PROPER MARRIAGE
(See also CHILDREN OF VIOLENCE Series)

Bergonzi, Bernard, "In Pursuit of Doris Lessing," <u>NYRB,</u>
   IV (February 11, 1965), 12-13.
Brewster, D., <u>Doris Lessing</u>, 108-18.

RETREAT TO INNOCENCE

Brewster, D., <u>Doris Lessing</u>, 98-103.

A RIPPLE IN THE STORM
(See also CHILDREN OF VIOLENCE Series)

Brewster, D., <u>Doris Lessing</u>, 118-28.

BIBLIOGRAPHY

Brewster, D., <u>Doris Lessing</u>, 165-70.
Burkom, Selma R., "A Doris Lessing Checklist," <u>Crit,</u> XI,
   i (1968), 69-81.
Ipp, Catharina, <u>Doris Lessing; a Bibliography,</u> Johannesburg:
   University of the Witwatersrand, 1967.

<u>LEWIS, SINCLAIR, 1885-1951</u>

GENERAL

Ames, Russell, "Sinclair Lewis Again," <u>CE</u>, X (November,
   1948), 77-80.
Austin, Allen, "An Interview with Sinclair Lewis," <u>UKCR,</u>

XXIV (Spring, 1958), 199-210.

Babcock, C. Merton, "Americanisms in the Novels of Sinclair Lewis," AS, XXV (May, 1960), 110-16.

Beck, Warren, "How Good is Sinclair Lewis?" CE, IX (January, 1948), 173-80.

Becker, George J., "Sinclair Lewis: Apostle to the Philistines," ASch, XXI (Autumn, 1952), 423-32.

Blankenship, R., American Literature, 657-64; 722-4.

Brooks, Van Wyk, Confident Years, 497-506.

Brown, Daniel, "Lewis's Satire---A Negative Emphasis," Ren, XVIII (Winter, 1966), 63-72.

Brown, Deming, "Sinclair Lewis: The Russian View," AL, XXV (March, 1953), 1-12.

Bucco, Martin, "The Serialized Novels of Sinclair Lewis: A Comparative Analysis of Periodical and Book," DA, XXIV (1964), 4692-3 (Missouri).

Cantwell, Robert, "Sinclair Lewis," NRep, LXXXVIII (October 21, 1936), 298-301. Also in Cowley, M., ed., After the Genteel Tradition, 92-102. Also in Schorer, M., ed., Sinclair Lewis, 111-18. Also in Zabel, M.D., ed., Literary Opinion in America, 494-501.

Carpenter, Frederick I., "Sinclair Lewis and the Fortress of Reality," CE, XVI (1955), 416-22. Also in Carpenter, F.I., American Literature and the Dream, 116-25.

Coard, Robert L., "Names in the Fiction of Sinclair Lewis," GaR, XVI (Fall, 1962), 318-29.

Coleman, Arthur B., "The Genesis of Social Ideas in Sinclair Lewis," DA, XV (1955), 1069 (N.Y.U.).

Conroy, Stephen S., "The American Culture and the Individual in the Novels of Sinclair Lewis," DA, XXVII (1966), 473A-74A (Iowa).

Couch, William, Jr., The Emergence, Rise and Decline of Sinclair Lewis, Dissertation, Un. of Chicago, 1954.

_____, "Sinclair Lewis: Crisis in the American Dream," CLAJ, VII (March, 1964), 224-34.

Dooley, D.J., Art of Sinclair Lewis.

_____, "The Impact of Satire on Fiction: Studies in Norman Douglass, Sinclair Lewis, Aldous Huxley, Evelyn Waugh and George Orwell," DA, XV (1955), 2203-4 (Iowa).

Feinberg, Leonard, Sinclair Lewis as a Satirist, Dissertation, Un. of Illinois, 1946.

Fife, Jim L., "Two Views of the American West," WAL, I (Spring, 1966), 34-43.

Flanagan, John T., "A Long Way to Gopher Prairie: Sinclair Lewis's Apprenticeship," SWR, XXXII (Autumn, 1947), 403-14.

_____, "The Minnesota Backgrounds of Sinclair Lewis'

Fiction," Minn. Hist., XXXVII (March, 1960), 1-13.

Forster, E. M., "Our Photography: Sinclair Lewis," NYHTBR (April 28, 1929). Also in Forster, E. M., Abinger Harvest, N. Y.: Harcourt, 1936. Also in Schorer, M., ed., Sinclair Lewis, 95-9.

Geismar, Maxwell, "Sinclair Lewis: Forgotten Hero," SatR, XLIII (June 25, 1960), 29-30.

_____, "Sinclair Lewis: The Cosmic Bourjoyce," Last of the Provincials, 69-150. Also (condensed) in SatR, XXX (November 1, 1947), 9-10; 42-5. Also (condensed and revised) in Geismar, M., American Moderns, 107-14. Also (selections) in Schorer, M., ed., Sinclair Lewis, 10-16; 129-38.

Grattan C. Hartley, "Sinclair Lewis: The Work of a Lifetime," NRep, CXXV (April 2, 1951), 19.

Griffin, Robert J., in French, W. G., and W. E. Kidd, eds., American Winners of the Nobel Literary Prize, 16-53.

Grebstein, S. N., Sinclair Lewis.

_____, "Sinclair Lewis's Unwritten Novel," PQ, XXVII (October, 1958), 400-9.

_____, "Sinclair Lewis and the Nobel Prize," WHR, XIII (Spring, 1959), 163-71.

Guthrie, Ramon, "The 'Labor Novel' That Sinclair Lewis Never Wrote," NYHTBR, XXVIII (February 10, 1952), 1+.

Hilfer, A. C., Revolt from the Village, 224-30.

Hollis, C. Carroll, "Sinclair Lewis: Reviver of Character" in Gardiner, H. C., ed., Fifty Years of the American Novel, 89-106.

Hughes, Serge, "From Main Street to the World So Wide," Cweal, LIII (April 6, 1951), 648-50.

Johnson, Gerald W., "Romance and Mr. Babbitt," NRep, CXXIV (January 29, 1951), 14-15. Also in NRep, CXXXI (November 22, 1954), 29-30.

Kazin, Alfred, "The folksiest and most comradely of American novelists," On Native Grounds, N. Y.: Harcourt, Brace, 1942, 219-21. Also in Rubin, L. D., Jr., and J. R. Moore, eds., Idea of an American Novel, 301-3.

_____, "The New Realism: Sherwood Anderson and Sinclair Lewis," On Native Grounds, N. Y.: Harcourt, Brace, 1942. Also in Schorer, M., ed., Sinclair Lewis, 119-28.

Kramer, Maurice, "Sinclair Lewis and the Hollow Center" in Langford, R. E., and W. E. Taylor, eds., Twenties, 67-9.

Krutch, Joseph W., "Sinclair Lewis," Nation, CLXXII (February 24, 1951), 179-80. Also in Schorer, M., ed., Sinclair Lewis, 147-50.

Lewis, Grace Hegger, With Love From Gracie: Sinclair
Lewis, 1912-1925, N.Y.: Harcourt, 1956.
Lewis, S., Man From Main Street.
Light, Martin, "H. G. Wells and Sinclair Lewis: Friendship,
Literary Influence, and Letters," EFT, V, iv (1962), 1-
20.

_____, "Lewis' Finicky Girls and Faithful Workers," UR,
XXX (December, 1963), 151-9.

_____, "A Study of Characterization in Sinclair Lewis's
Fiction," DA, XXI (1960), 1957 (Illinois).
Lippman, Walter, Men of Destiny, N.Y.: Macmillan, 1927.
Also in Schorer, M., ed., Sinclair Lewis, 84-94.
Lockerbie, D. Bruce, "Sinclair Lewis and William Ridgway,"
AL, XXXVI (March, 1964), 68-72.
Lovett, Robert M., "An Interpreter of American Life," Dial,
LXXVIII (June, 1925), 515-18. Also in Schorer, M., ed.,
Sinclair Lewis, 32-5.
Miller, Perry, "The Incorruptible Sinclair Lewis," Atlantic,
CLXXXVII (April, 1951), 30-4.
Millgate, M., American Social Fiction, 93-106.

_____, "Sinclair Lewis and the Obscure Hero," SA, VIII
(1962), 111-27.
Moore, Geoffrey, "Sinclair Lewis: A Lost Romantic" in
Bode, C., ed., Young Rebel in American Literature, 51-
76. Also in Schorer, M., ed., Sinclair Lewis, 151-65.
Morris, L., "The National Gadfly," Postscript to Yesterday,
134-42.
Mumford, Lewis, "The America of Sinclair Lewis," Current
History, (January, 1931). Also in Schorer, M., ed.,
Sinclair Lewis, 102-7.
Park, Sue S., "Satire of Characterization in the Fiction of
Sinclair Lewis," DA, XXVII (1967) 2158A (Texas Tech).
Parrington, Vernon L., "Sinclair Lewis: Our Own Diogenes,"
Main Currents in American Thought, N.Y.: Harcourt,
1927. Also in University of Washington Chapbooks, No.
5, 1927. Also in Schorer, M., ed., Sinclair Lewis, 62-
70.
Petrullo, Helen B., "Satire and Freedom: Sinclair Lewis,
Nathaniel West, and James Thurber," DA, XXVIII (1967)
1445A (Syracuse).
Prescott, O., In My Opinion, 52-8.
Rourke, C., American Humor, N.Y.: Harcourt, 1931. Al-
so in Schorer, M., ed., Sinclair Lewis, 29-31.
Schorer, M., Sinclair Lewis. Also in O'Connor, W.V., ed.,
Seven Modern American Novelists, 46-80.

_____, ed., Sinclair Lewis.

_____, Sinclair Lewis: An American Life.

_____, "Sinclair Lewis and His Critics," World We Im-
agine, 183-94.   Also in Schorer, M. , ed. , Sinclair
Lewis, 1-9.
_____, "Sinclair Lewis and the Method of Half-Truths" in
Schorer, M. , ed. , Society and Self in the Novel: English
Institute Essays, 1955, N. Y.: Columbia Un. Pr. , 1956,
117-44.   Also in Litz, A. W. , ed. , Modern American Fiction, 95-111.   Also in Schorer, M. , ed. , Sinclair Lewis,
46-61.
_____, "Two Houses, Two Ways: The Florentine Villas
of Lewis and Lawrence Respectively" in New World Writ-
ing, Fourth Mentor Selection, 1953, 136-54.
Smith, Harrison, ed. , From Main Street to Stockholm: Let-
ters of Sinclair Lewis, 1919-1930, N. Y.: Harcourt,
Brace, 1962.
Straumann, H. , American Literature in the Twentieth Cen-
tury, 17-22.
Thompson, Dorothy, "Sinclair Lewis: A Postscript," At-
lantic, CLXXXVII (June, 1951), 73-4.
Thorp, W. , "Class and Caste in the Novel, 1920-1950," Am-
erican Writing in the Twentieth Century, 119-23.
Van Gelder, W. , Writers on Writing, 77-81.
Wagenknecht, E. , Cavalcade of the American Novel, 354-67.
Waterman, Margaret, "Sinclair Lewis as a Teacher," CE,
XIII (1951), 87-90.
West, T. R. , Flesh of Steel, 116-31.
Whipple, T. K. , in NRep (April 15, 1925).   Also (revised) in
Whipple, T. E. , Spokesmen, N. Y.: Appleton, 1928.   Al-
so in Schorer, M. , ed. , Sinclair Lewis, 71-83.
Yoshida, Hiroshige, "Satirical Techniques in Sinclair Lewis's
Works; Contrastive and Contradictory Expressions," SELit,
XLII (1966), 209-22.
_____, "Some Devices and Techniques of Expression in
the Works of Sinclair Lewis," Hiroshima University Stud-
ies, XXIV, No. 3.

ANN VICKERS

Dooley, D. J. , Art of Sinclair Lewis, 181-6.
Geismar, M. , Last of the Provincials, 115-17.
Grebstein, S. N. , Sinclair Lewis, 125-9.
Schorer, M. , Sinclair Lewis, 31-2.   Also in O'Connor, V.
W. , ed. , Seven Modern American Novelists, 69-70.
_____, Sinclair Lewis: An American Life, 580-3.

ARROWSMITH

Anon., "Martin Arrowsmith," TLS, XXIV (March 5, 1925),
153. Also in Griffin, R. J., ed., Twentieth Century Interpretations of ARROWSMITH, 99-100.
Blake, N. M., Novelist's America, 35-6.
Canby, Henry S., "Fighting Success," SRL, I (March 7,
1925), 575. Also in Griffin, R. J., ed., Twentieth Century Interpretations of ARROWSMITH, 110-12.
Carpenter, F. I., "Sinclair Lewis and the Fortress of Reality," American Literature and the Dream, 121-2.
Davidson, Donald, The Spyglass: Views and Reviews, 1924-
1930, Nashville: Vanderbilt Un. Pr., 1963, 63-7.
Dooley, D. J., Art of Sinclair Lewis, 99-103; 105-17. Also
in Griffin, R. J., ed., Twentieth Century Interpretations
of ARROWSMITH, 61-7.
Emerson, Haven, M. D., "A Doctor Looks at ARROWSMITH,"
Survey, LIV (May 1, 1925), 180. Also in Griffin, R. J.,
ed., Twentieth Century Interpretations of ARROWSMITH,
107-8.
Fyvel, T. R., "Martin Arrowsmith and His Habitat," NRep,
CXXXIII (July 18, 1955), 16-18. Also in Griffin, R. J.,
ed., Twentieth Century Interpretations of ARROWSMITH,
93-7.
Geismar, M., Last of the Provincials, 97-101.
Grebstein, S. N., Sinclair Lewis, 85-96. Also in Griffin,
R. J., ed., Twentieth Century Interpretations of ARROW-
SMITH, 68-76.
Griffin, R. J., in French, W. J., and W. E. Kidd, eds., Am-
erican Winners of the Nobel Literary Prize, 39-41.
_____, ed., Twentieth Century Interpretations of ARROW-
SMITH.
Hashiguchi, Yasuo, "ARROWSMITH and Escapism," KAL,
No. 8 (1965), 14-18.
Hazard, Lucy L., "The Frontier in ARROWSMITH," The
Frontier in American Literature, N. Y.: Crowell, 1928,
283-5; N. Y.: Ungar, 1960, 282-5. Also in Griffin, R.
J., ed., Twentieth Century Interpretations of ARROW-
SMITH, 113-14.
Karfeldt, Erik, A., "Why Sinclair Lewis Got the Nobel
Prize" in Griffin, R. J., ed., Twentieth Century Interpre-
tations of ARROWSMITH, 77-82.
Krutch, Joseph W., "A Genius on Main Street," Nation,
CXX (April 1, 1925), 359-60. Also in Griffin, R. J., ed.,
Twentieth Century Interpretations of ARROWSMITH, 105-7.
Lovett, Robert M., "An Interpreter of American Life,"
Dial, LXXVIII (June, 1925), 515-18. Also in Schorer,

M., ed., Sinclair Lewis, 32-5. Also in Griffin, R. J.,
    ed., Twentieth Century Interpretations of ARROWSMITH,
    103-5.
Mencken, H. L., "ARROWSMITH," AmMerc, IV (April,
    1925), 507-9. Also (condensed) in Griffin, R. J., ed.,
    Twentieth Century Interpretations of ARROWSMITH, 100-2.
Muir, Edwin, "Melodrama in America," Nation & The Athen-
    aeum, XXXVI (March 14, 1925), 818. Also in Griffin,
    R./J., ed., Twentieth Century Interpretations of ARROW-
    SMITH, 109-10.
Ober, William, M. D., "ARROWSMITH and THE LAST
    ADAM," Carleton Miscellany, IV (Fall, 1963), 101-6. Al-
    so in Griffin, R. J., ed., Twentieth Century Interpreta-
    tions of ARROWSMITH, 57-60.
Richardson, Lyon, N., "ARROWSMITH: Genesis, Develop-
    ment, Versions," AL, XXVII (May, 1955), 225-44. Also
    (condensed) in Griffin, R. J., ed., Twentieth Century In-
    terpretations of ARROWSMITH, 24-33.
Rosenberg, Charles E., "Martin Arrowsmith: The Scientist
    as Hero," AQ, XV (Fall, 1963), 447-58. Also in Griffin,
    R. J., ed.; Twentieth Century Interpretations of ARROW-
    SMITH, 47-56.
Schorer, Mark, "On ARROWSMITH," Afterword to Signet
    Classic edition of ARROWSMITH, N. Y.: New American
    Library, 1961, 431-8. Also in Griffin, R. J., ed.,
    Twentieth Century Interpretations of ARROWSMITH, 40-6.
    _____, Sinclair Lewis, 17-19. Also in O'Connor, W. V.,
    ed., Seven Modern American Novelists, 57-9.
    _____, Sinclair Lewis: An American Life, 414-20.
Sherman, Stuart P., "A Way Out: Sinclair Lewis Discovers
    a Hero," NYHTB (March 8, 1925), 1-2. Also (condensed)
    in Griffin, R. J., ed., Twentieth Century Interpretations
    of ARROWSMITH, 19-23.
Spitz, Leon "Sinclair Lewis' Prof. Gottlieb," American He-
    brew, CLVIII (December 3, 1948).
Stuckey, W. J., Pulitzer Prize Novels, 60-7.
Van Doren, Carl, "Sinclair Lewis and the Revolt from the
    Village" The American Novel, 1789-1939, N. Y.: Mac-
    millan, 1940, 303-14. Also (condensed) in Griffin, R. J.,
    ed., Twentieth Century Interpretations of ARROWSMITH,
    83-92.
West, T. R., Flesh of Steel, 122-5.
Whipple, T. K., "Sinclair Lewis: ARROWSMITH," NRep,
    XLII (April 15, 1925), Part II, 3-5. Also in Griffin, R.
    J., ed., Twentieth Century Interpretations of ARROW-
    SMITH, 34-9.
W. P. K., "Martin Arrowsmith," Nature, CXV (May 22, 1925),

797. Also in Griffin, R. J., ed., Twentieth Century Interpretations of ARROWSMITH, 109.

BABBITT

Allen, W., Modern Novel, 69-70.
_____, Urgent West, 199-200.
Bruccoli, Matthew, "Textual Variants in Sinclair Lewis's BABBITT," SB, XI (1958), 263-8.
Cole, E. R., "George Babbitt: Mock-Hero of a Mock-Epic," Descant, X (Winter, 1966), 21-5.
Dooley, D. J., Art of Sinclair Lewis, 81-95.
Falke, Wayne C., "The Novel of Disentanglement: A Thematic Study of Lewis's BABBITT, Bromfield's MR. SMITH and Updike's RABBIT, RUN," DA, XXVIII (1967), 194A (Michigan).
Friedman, Philip A., "BABBITT: Satiric Realism in Form and Content," SNL, IV (Fall, 1966), 20-9.
Geismar, M., Last of the Provincials, 88-96. Also in Westbrook, M., ed., Modern American Novel, 48-56.
Grebstein, S. N., Sinclair Lewis, 73-85.
Griffin, Robert J., in French, W. G., and W. E. Kidd, eds., American Winners of the Nobel Literary Prize, 47-50.
Hilfer, A. C., "Sinclair Lewis: Cariacturist of the Village Mind," Revolt from the Village, 167-76.
Hoffman, F. J., "The Text: Sinclair Lewis's BABBITT," Twenties, 364-70.
Kishler, Thomas C., " 'The Sacred Rites of Pride': An Echo of THE RAPE OF THE LOCK in BABBITT," SNL, III (1965), 28-9.
Krutch, Joseph W., "Sinclair Lewis," Nation (February 24, 1951). Also in Schorer, M., ed., Sinclair Lewis, 147-50.
Lewis, S., "Unpublished Introduction to BABBITT," Man from Main Street, 21-9.
Manfred, N. M., Novelist's America, 23-33; 36-8.
Mencken, H. L., "Portrait of an American Citizen," Smart Set, (October, 1922). Also in Schorer, M., ed., Sinclair Lewis, 20-2.
Nichols, James W., "Nathaniel West, Sinclair Lewis, Alexander Pope and Satiric Contrasts," SNL, V (Spring, 1968), 119-22.
Oldham, Janet, "Dr. ZHIVAGO and BABBITT," EJ, XLVIII (May 1959), 24-26.
Rothwell, Kenneth S., "From Society to Babbittry: Lewis' Debt to Edith Wharton," JCMVASA, I, i (Spring, 1960), 32-7.
Schorer, M., Sinclair Lewis, 11-17. Also in O'Connor,

W. V., ed., Seven Modern American Novelists, 52-7.
_____, Sinclair Lewis: An American Life, 343-57.
_____, "Sinclair Lewis: BABBITT" in Cohen, Hennig,
  ed., Landmarks of American Writing, N.Y.: Basic
  Books, 1969, 315-27.
Walcutt, C.C., Man's Changing Mask, 241-7.
West, Rebecca, "BABBITT," Newstatesman (October 21,
  1922). Also in Schorer, M., ed., Sinclair Lewis, 23-6.

BETHEL MERRIDAY

Geismar, M., Last of the Provincials, 135-7. Also in
  Schorer, M., ed., Sinclair Lewis, 129-30.
Gray, J., On Second Thought, 15-17.
Grebstein, S.N., Sinclair Lewis, 134-6.

CASS TIMBERLANE

Dooley, D.J., Art of Sinclair Lewis, 217-24.
Gardiner, Harold C., "Neither Hot Nor Cold" America (Oc-
  tober 6, 1945). Also in Gardiner, H.C., In All Con-
  science, 138-9.
Geismar, M., Last of the Provincials, 140-3. Also in
  Schorer, M., ed., Sinclair Lewis, 132-4.
Gray, J., On Second Thought, 18-20.
Grebstein, S.N., Sinclair Lewis, 148-52.
Prescott, O., In My Opinion, 55-6.
Schorer, M., Sinclair Lewis: An American Life, 738-41.
Wilson, Edmund, "Salute to an Old Landmark: Sinclair Lew-
  is," NY (October 13, 1945). Also in Schorer, M., ed.,
  Sinclair Lewis, 139-42.

DODSWORTH

Ausmus, Martin R., "Sinclair Lewis, DODSWORTH, and the
  Fallacy of Reputation," BA, XXXIV (Autumn, 1960), 349-
  55.
Blake, N.M., Novelist's America, 33-5.
Dooley, D.J., Art of Sinclair Lewis, 150-60.
Fadiman, Clifton, Introduction to DODSWORTH, N.Y.: Mod-
  ern Library, 1947. Also in Fadiman, C., Party of One,
  132-5.
Ford, Ford Madox, "DODSWORTH," Bookman (April, 1929).
  Also in Schorer, M., ed., Sinclair Lewis, 100-1.
Geismar, M., Last of the Provincials, 112-15.
Grebstein, S.N., Sinclair Lewis, 109-17.
Griffin, Robert J., in French, W.G., and W.E. Kidd, eds.,

American Winners of the Nobel Literary Prize, 44-6.
Schorer, M., Sinclair Lewis, 25-7.   Also in O'Connor, W.
    V., ed., Seven Modern American Novelists, 63-5.
_____, Sinclair Lewis: An American Life, 515-18.
West, T. R., Flesh of Steel, 127-9.

ELMER GANTRY

Blake, Nelson M., "How to Learn History from Sinclair Lew-
    is and Other Uncommon Sources," Stetson Univ. Bulletin,
    LXIV, ii (1964).   Also in Hague, John A., ed., American
    Character and Culture: Some Twentieth Century Perspec-
    tives, DeLand, Fla.: Everett Edwards Pr., 1964, 41-7.
    Also in Blake, N. M., Novelist's America, 39-44.
Davies, H., Mirror of the Ministry in Modern Novels, 28-
    34.
Dooley, D. J., Art of Sinclair Lewis, 121-2; 125-35.
Genthe, Charles V., "THE DAMNATION OF THERON WARE
    and ELMER GANTRY," RS, XXXII (December, 1964),
    334-43.
Geismar, M., Last of the Provincials, 101-5.
Grebstein, S. N., Art of Sinclair Lewis, 99-107.
Griffin, Robert J., in French, W. G., and W. E. Kidd, eds.,
    American Winners of the Nobel Literary Prize, 41-4.
Hilfer, A. C., "Elmer Gantry and That Old Time Religion,"
    Revolt from the Village, 177-92.
Krutch, Joseph W., "Mr. Babbitt's Spiritual Guide: A Re-
    view of Sinclair Lewis's ELMER GANTRY," Nation (March
    16, 1927).   Also in Schorer, M., ed., Sinclair Lewis, 36-
    8.
Moore, James B., "The Sources of ELMER GANTRY,"
    NRep, CXLIII (August 8, 1960), 6.
Schorer, Mark, "The Monstrous Self-Deception of Elmer
    Gantry," NRep, CXXXIII (October 31, 1955), 13-5.   Ex-
    panded as "Sinclair Lewis and the Method of Half-Truths"
    in Schorer, M., ed., Society and Self in the Novel: Eng-
    lish Institute Essays, 1955, N. Y.: Columbia Un. Pr.,
    1956, 129-44.   Also in Schorer, M., ed., Sinclair Lewis,
    50-61.   Also in Litz, A. W., ed., Modern American Fic-
    tion, 102-11.   Also in Schorer, M., World We Imagine,
    162-82.
_____, Sinclair Lewis, 20-4.   Also in O'Connor, W. V.,
    ed., Seven Modern American Novelists, 59-63.
_____, Sinclair Lewis: An American Life, 475-83.
West, Rebecca, "Sinclair Lewis Introduces ELMER GANTRY,"
    NYHTB (March 13, 1927).   Also in West, R., The Strange
    Necessity, N. Y.: Viking, 1927, 1955.   Also in Schorer,

M., ed., Sinclair Lewis, 39-45.

FREE AIR

Dooley, D. J., Art of Sinclair Lewis, 50-2.
Flanagan, John T., "A Long Way to Gopher Prairie: Sinclair Lewis's Apprenticeship," SWR, XXXII (Autumn, 1947), 408-9, & passim.
Geismar, M., Last of the Provincials, 81-3.
Griffin, Robert J., in French, W. G., and W. E. Kidd, eds., American Winners of the Nobel Literary Prize, 28-31.

GIDEON PLANISH

Dooley, D. J., Art of Sinclair Lewis, 208-11.
Geismar, M., Last of the Provincials, 137-9; 144-5. Also (part) in Schorer, M., ed., Sinclair Lewis, 130-1.
Grebstein, S. N., Sinclair Lewis, 157-9.
Schorer, M., Sinclair Lewis: An American Life, 697-9.

THE GODSEEKER

Davies, H., Mirror of the Ministry in Modern Novels, 35-40.
Dooley, D. J., Art of Sinclair Lewis, 227-30.

THE INNOCENTS

Dickson, James K., "Note on Sinclair Lewis's THE INNOCENTS, 1917," PBSA, XXXIX (1945), 167-8.
Grebstein, S. N., Sinclair Lewis, 50-3.

IT CAN'T HAPPEN HERE

Blackmur, Richard P., "Utopia, or Uncle Tom's Cabin," Nation (October 30, 1935). Also in Schorer, M., ed., Sinclair Lewis, 108-10.
Blotner, J., Modern American Political Novel, 153-6.
Dooley, D. J., Art of Sinclair Lewis, 191-5.
Geismar, M., Last of the Provincials, 117-22.
Grebstein, S. N., Sinclair Lewis, 139-47.
Milne, G., American Political Novel, 128-32.
Schorer, M., Sinclair Lewis, 33-4. Also in O'Connor, W. V., ed., Seven Modern American Novelists, 71-2.
_____, Sinclair Lewis: An American Life, 608-12.

THE JOB

Dooley, D. J., <u>Art of Sinclair Lewis</u>, 41-7.
Flanagan, John T., "A Long Way to Gopher Prairie: Sinclair Lewis's Apprenticeship," <u>SWR</u>, XXXII (Autumn, 1947), 407-8, & <u>passim</u>.
Geismar, M., <u>Last of the Provincials</u>, 76-9.
Grebstein, S. N., <u>Sinclair Lewis</u>, 55-8.
Schorer, M., <u>Sinclair Lewis: An American Life</u>, 242-6.

KINGSBLOOD ROYAL

Beck, Warren, "How Good is Sinclair Lewis?" <u>CE</u>, IX (January, 1948), 173-80.
Dooley, D. J., <u>Art of Sinclair Lewis</u>, 224-7.
Grebstein, S. N., <u>Sinclair Lewis</u>, 152-6.
Hand, Harry E., "The Rise of a Modern American Hero," LauR, VI, i (Spring, 1966), 14-20.
Lewis, S., "A Note about KINGSBLOOD ROYAL," <u>Man from Main Street</u>, 36-42.
Prescott, O., <u>In My Opinion</u>, 56-8.
Redman, Ben R., "Sinclair Lewis on Intolerance," <u>AmMerc</u>, LXV (July, 1947), 111-17.
Schorer, M., <u>Sinclair Lewis: An American Life</u>, 758-60.
Thomas, J. D., "Three American Tragedies: Notes on the Responsibilities of Fiction," <u>SCB</u>, XX, iv (Winter, 1960), 11-5.

MAIN STREET

Aaron, Daniel, in Stegner, W., ed., <u>American Novel</u>, 166-79.
Allen, W., <u>Modern Novel</u>, 66-9.
Blake, N. M., <u>Novelist's America</u>, 12-23.
Dooley, D. J., <u>Art of Sinclair Lewis</u>, 57-82.
Duffus, R. L., "MAIN STREET Thirty-five Years Later," NYTMag (August 7, 1955), 24; 62-3.
Gannett, Lewis, "Sinclair Lewis: MAIN STREET," <u>SRL</u>, XXXII (August 7, 1949), 31-2.
Geismar, M., <u>Last of the Provincials</u>, 84-8.
Grebstein, S. N., <u>Sinclair Lewis</u>, 61-73.
Griffin, Robert J., in French, W. G., and W. E. Kidd, eds., <u>American Winners of the Nobel Literary Prize</u>, 32-4.
Hackett, Francis, "God's Country," <u>NRep</u>, XXV (December 1, 1920). Also in Rubin, L. D., Jr., and J. R. Moore, eds., <u>Idea of an American Novel</u>, 297-300.
Hilfer, A. C., "Sinclair Lewis: Caricaturist of the Village

Mind," Revolt from the Village, 158-67.

Krutch, Joseph W., "Sinclair Lewis," Nation (February 24,
1951).   Also in Schorer, M., ed., Sinclair Lewis, 147-
50.

Lewis, S., "Introduction to MAIN STREET," Man from
Main Street, 213-17.

Mencken, H.L., "Consolation," Smart Set (January 1921).
Also in Schorer, M., ed., Sinclair Lewis, 17-19.

Schier, Donald, "MAIN STREET, by Sinclair Lewis," Carleton Miscellany, IV (Fall, 1963), 95-101.

Schorer, Mark, "Afterword" in Lewis, S., Main Street,
N.Y.: New American Library, 1961.

_____, "MAIN STREET," AH, XII (October, 1961), 28-31;
74-7.

_____, Sinclair Lewis, 9-11. Also in O'Connor, W.V.,
ed., Seven Modern American Novelists, 50-1.

_____, Sinclair Lewis: An American Life, 267-97.

Tanselle, G. Thomas, "Sinclair Lewis and Floyd Dell: Two
Views of the Midwest," TCL, IX (January, 1964), 175-84.

MANTRAP

Dooley, D.J., Art of Sinclair Lewis, 118-20.

Greene, D.J., "With Sinclair Lewis in Darkest Saskatchewan:
The Genesis of MANTRAP," Saskatchewan Hist., VI
(1953), 47-52.

Griffin, Robert J., in French, W.G., and W.E. Kidd, eds.,
American Winners of the Nobel Literary Prize, 36-9.

Schorer, M., Sinclair Lewis: An American Life, 438-9.

THE MAN WHO KNEW COOLIDGE

Dooley, D.J., Art of Sinclair Lewis, 141-8.

Geismar, M., Last of the Provincials, 105-8.

Grebstein, S.N., Sinclair Lewis, 108-9.

Richardson, Lyon N., "Revision in Sinclair Lewis's THE
MAN WHO KNEW COOLIDGE," AL, XXV (1953), 326-33.

OUR MR. WRENN

Dooley, D.J., Art of Sinclair Lewis, 16-28.

Flanagan, John T., "A Long Way to Gopher Prairie: Sinclair Lewis's Apprenticeship," SWR, XXXII (Autumn,
1947), 405-6.

Geismar, M., Last of the Provincials, 75-6.

Grebstein, S.N., Sinclair Lewis, 37-44.

Griffin, Robert J., in French, W.G., and W.E. Kidd, eds.,

American Winners of the Nobel Literary Prize, 22-3.
Knight, Grant C., New Freedom in American Literature, Lexington: Mrs. Grant C. Knight, 1961, 69-70.
West, T. R., Flesh of Steel, 118-20.

THE PRODIGAL PARENTS

Dooley, D. J., Art of Sinclair Lewis, 198-202.
Geismar, M., Last of the Provincials, 124-8.
Grebstein, S. N., Sinclair Lewis, 132-4.
Schorer, M., Sinclair Lewis: An American Life, 635-6.

THE TRAIL OF THE HAWK

Dooley, D. J., Art of Sinclair Lewis, 28-35.
Flanagan, John T., "A Long Way to Gopher Prairie: Sinclair Lewis's Apprenticeship," SWR, XXXII (Autumn, 1947), 406-7 & passim.
Geismar, M., Last of the Provincials, 73-5; 79-80.
Grebstein, S. N., Sinclair Lewis, 44-7; 54-5.
Griffin, Robert J., in French, W. G., and W. E. Kidd, eds., American Winners of the Nobel Literary Prize, 24-6.
Schorer, M., Sinclair Lewis: An American Life, 221-7.

WORK OF ART

Geismar, M., Last of the Provincials, 122-4.
Grebstein, S. N., Sinclair Lewis, 129-31.
Schorer, M., Sinclair Lewis, 32-3. Also in O'Connor, W. V., ed., Seven Modern American Novelists, 70-1.

WORLD SO WIDE

Cowley, Malcolm, "The Last Flight from Main Street," NYTBR (March 25, 1951). Also in Schorer, M., ed., Sinclair Lewis, 143-6. Also in Brown, Francis, ed., Highlights of Modern Literature, N. Y.: New American Library, 1954.
Dooley, D. J., Art of Sinclair Lewis, 231-4.
Gardiner, Harold C., "Sauk Center Was Home Still," America (April 7, 1951). Also in Gardiner, H. C., In All Conscience, 140-41.
Grebstein, S. N., Sinclair Lewis, 160-1.

BIBLIOGRAPHY

Dooley, D. J., Art of Sinclair Lewis, 269-77.

Grebstein, S. N. , Sinclair Lewis, 180-8.

LOWRY, MALCOLM, 1909-1957

GENERAL

Aiken, Conrad, "Malcolm Lowry," TLS (February 16, 1967),
   127.
_____, "Malcolm Lowry--A Note," CanL,. No. 8 (Spring,
   1961), 29-30.
Birney, Earle, "Glimpses Into the Life of Malcolm Lowry,"
   TamR, No. 19 (Spring, 1961), 31-8.
Breit, Harvey, and Marjorie B. Lowry, eds. , Selected Let-
   ters of Malcolm Lowry, Philadelphia: Lippincott, 1965.
Chittick, V. L. O. , "USHANT's Malcolm Lowry," QQ, LXXI
   (Spring, 1964), 67-75.
Donohue, Denis, "Ultra-Writer," NYRB, VI (March 3, 1966),
   16-18.
Edmonds, Dale H. , II, "Malcolm Lowry: A Study of His
   Life and Work," DA, XXVI (1966), 7315 (Texas).
Epstein, P. S. , Private Labyrinth of Malcolm Lowry.
Magee, A. Peter, "The Quest for Love," Emeritus, I
   (Spring, 1965), 24-9. (Not seen.)
Malcolm Lowry Issue. PrS, XXXVII (1963), 284-362.
Woodcock, George, "Under Seymour Mountain," CanL, No.
   8 (Spring, 1961), 3-6.

ULTRAMARINE

Woodcock, George, "Malcolm Lowry as Novelist," QQ, XXIV
   (April, 1961), 26-8.

UNDER THE VOLCANO

Allen, Walter, in NStat, XXXIV (December 1947), 455-6.
_____, "The Masterpiece of the Forties" in Kostelanetz,
   R. , ed. , On Contemporary Literature, 419-22.
_____, Modern Novel, 263-5.
Anon. , "A Prose Waste Land," TLS (May 11, 1962), 332.
Barnes, Jim, "The Myth of Sisyphus in UNDER THE VOL-
   CANO," PrS, XLII (1968), 341-8.
Casari, Laura E. , "Malcolm Lowry's Drunken Divine Com-
   edy: UNDER THE VOLCANO and Shorter Fiction," DA,
   XXVIII (1967), 2238A (Nebraska).
Christella Marie, Sister, "UNDER THE VOLCANO: A Con-
   sideration of the Novel by Malcolm Lowry," XUS, IV

(March, 1965), 13-27.
Costa, Richard H. , "The Lowry/Aiken Symbiosis," Nation, CCIV (June 26, 1967), 823-6.
_____, "ULYSSES, Lowry's VOLCANO and the VOYAGE Between: A Study of An unacknowledged Literary Kinship," UTQ, XXXVI (July, 1967), 335-52.
Day, Douglas, "Of Tragic Joy," PrS, XXXVII (Winter, 1963), 354-62.
Donohue, Denis, "Ultra-Writer," NYRB, VI (March 3, 1966), 15-17.
Edelstein, J. M. , "On Re-Reading UNDER THE VOLCANO," PrS, XXXVII (Winter, 1963), 336-9.
Edmonds, Dale H. , "Malcolm Lowry: A Study of His Life and Work," DA, XXVI (1966), 7315 (Texas).
_____, "UNDER THE VOLCANO: A Reading of the 'Immediate Level'," TSE, XVI (1968), 63-105.
Enright, D. J. , "Malcolm Lowry," NStat (January 27, 1967), 117-8.
Epstein, P. S. , Private Labyrinth of Malcolm Lowry.
Flint, R. W. , in KR, IX (Summer, 1947), 474-7.
Heilman, Robert B. , in SR, LV (Summer, 1947), 483-92.
_____, "The Possessed Artist and the Ailing Soul," CanL, No. 8 (Spring, 1961), 7-16.
Hirschman, Jack, "Kabbala/Lowry, etc. ," PrS, XXXVII (Winter, 1963), 347-53.
Kilgallin, Anthony R. , "Faust and UNDER THE VOLCANO," CanL, No. 26 (Autumn, 1965), 34-54.
Leech, Clifford, "The Shaping of Time: NOSTROMO and UNDER THE VOLCANO" in Mack, M. , and I. Gregor, eds. , Imagined Worlds, 323-41.
Lytle, A. , Hero with the Private Parts, 54-8.
McCormick, J. , Catastrophe and Imagination, 85-9.
Markson, David, "Myth in UNDER THE VOLCANO," PrS, XXXVII (Winter, 1963), 336-9.
Tindall, W. Y. , Literary Symbol, 98-9.
Widmer, Eleanor, "The Drunken Wheel: Malcolm Lowry and UNDER THE VOLCANO," in French, W. , ed. , Forties, 217-26.
Wild, Bernadette, "Malcolm Lowry: A Study of the Sea Metaphor in UNDER THE VOLCANO," UWR, IV, i (1968), 46-60.
Woodcock, George, "Malcolm Lowry as Novelist," BCLQ, XXIII-XXIV (April, 1961), 25-30.
_____, "Malcolm Lowry's UNDER THE VOLCANO," MFS, IV (Summer, 1958), 151-6.
_____, "On the Day of the Dead (Some Reflections on Malcolm Lowry's UNDER THE VOLCANO)," NoR, VI (Decem-

ber-January, 1953-54), 15-21.
Young, Vernon, in ArQ, III (Autumn, 1947), 281-3.

LYTLE, ANDREW NELSON, 1902-

GENERAL

Bradbury, J.M., Fugitives, 265-93.
Carter, Thomas H., in Rubin, L.D., Jr., and R.D. Jacobs,
   eds., South, 287-300.

AT THE MOON'S END

Carter, Thomas H., in Rubin, L.D., Jr., and R.D. Jacobs,
   eds., South, 291-4.
Eisinger, C.E., Fiction of the Forties, 194-5.

THE LONG NIGHT

Carter, Thomas H., in Rubin, L.D., Jr., and R.D. Jacobs,
   eds., South, 289-91.
Hoffman, F.J., Art of Southern Fiction, 99-101.

A NAME FOR EVIL

Bradbury, J.M., Fugitives, 270-1.
Carter, Thomas H., in Rubin, L.D., Jr., and R.D. Jacobs,
   eds., South, 294-5.
De Bellis, Jack, "Andrew Lytle's A NAME FOR EVIL: A
   Transformation of THE TURN OF THE SCREW," Crit,
   VIII, iii (Spring-Summer, 1966), 26-40.
Eisinger, C.E., Fiction of the Forties, 195-6.

THE VELVET HORN

Carter, Thomas H., in Rubin, L.D., Jr., and R.D. Jacobs,
   eds., South, 295-9.
Ghiselin, Brewster, "Trial of Light," SR, LXV (1957), 657-
   65.
Hoffman, F.J., Art of Southern Fiction, 101-2.
Lytle, Andrew, "The Working Novelist and the Mythmaking
   Process," Daedulus, LXXXVIII (Spring, 1959), 326-38.
   Also in Murray, Henry A., ed., Myth and Mythmaking,
   N.Y.: Braziller, 1960, 141-56. Also in Lytle, A., Hero
   with the Private Parts, 178-92. Also in Vickery, John
   B., ed., Myth and Literature; Contemporary Theory and

Practice, Lincoln: Un. of Nebraska Pr., 1966, 99-108.
Trowbridge, Clinton W., "The World Made Flesh: Andrew
Lytle's THE VELVET HORN," Crit, X, ii (1968), 53-68.

McCARTHY, MARY, 1912-

GENERAL

Aldridge, J.W., "Mary McCarthy: Princess Among the
Trolls," Time to Murder and Create, 95-132.
Auchincloss, L., Pioneers and Caretakers, 170-86.
Baumbach, J., Landscape of Nightmare, 8-9.
Brower, Brook, "Mary McCarthyism," Esquire, LVIII (July,
1962), 62-7; 113.
Chamberlain, John, "The Conservative Miss McCarthy,"
NatR, XV (October 22, 1963), 353-5.
_____, "The Novels of Mary McCarthy" in Balakian, N.,
and C. Simmons, eds., Creative Present, 241-55.
Cook, Bruce, "Mary McCarthy: One of Ours?" CathW,
CXCIX (April, 1964), 34-42.
Eisinger, C.E., Fiction of the Forties, 128-35.
Enright, D.J., "Contrary Wise: the Writings of Mary Mc-
Carthy," NStat (July 27, 1962), 115-16. Also in Enright,
D.J., Conspirators and Poets, 127-33.
Fitch, Robert E., "The Cold Eye of Mary McCarthy," NRep,
CXXXVIII (May 5, 1958), 17-19.
Grumbach, D., Company She Kept.
Hardwick, E., View of My Own, 33-9.
McKenzie, B., Mary McCarthy.
Niebuhr, Elisabeth, "The Art of Fiction XXVII: Mary Mc-
Carthy," ParisR, No. 27 (Winter-Spring, 1962), 58-94.
Also in Writers at Work, 2nd ser., 283-315.
Ohmann, Carol B., and Richard Ohmann, "Class Notes from
Vassar," Cweal, LXXIX (September 27, 1963), 12-15.
Ross, T.J., "Passion---Moral and Otherwise," NRep,
CXXXIX (August 18, 1958), 23-6.
Schlueter, Paul, "The Dissections of Mary McCarthy" in
Moore, H.T., ed., Contemporary American Novelists,
53-64.
Stock, I., Mary McCarthy.
Symons, J., "That Elegant Miss McCarthy," Critical Occa-
sions, 90-5.

A CHARMED LIFE

Auchincloss, L., Pioneers and Caretakers, 178-80.

Grumbach, D. , Company She Kept, 174-80.
McKenzie, B. , Mary McCarthy, 122-34.
Podhoretz, Norman, "Gibbsville and New Leeds: The Amer-
    ica of John O'Hara and Mary McCarthy," Ctary, XXI
    (March, 1956), 271-2. Also in Podhoretz, N. , Doings and
    Undoings, 81-7.
Schlueter, Paul, "The Dissections of Mary McCarthy" in
    Moore, H. T. , ed. , Contemporary American Novelists, 59-
    61.
Stock, I. , Mary McCarthy, 29-35.

THE COMPANY SHE KEEPS

Grumbach, D. , Company She Kept, 91-111.
Rees, David, "The Exorcism," Spectator (September 17, 1965)
    353-4.
Stock, I. , Mary McCarthy, 14-20.

THE GROVES OF ACADEME

Auchincloss, L. , Pioneers and Caretakers, 176-8.
Chamberlain, John, "The Conservative Miss McCarthy," NatR
    XV (October 22, 1963), 353-5.
Eisinger, C. E. , Fiction of the Forties, 133-5.
Grumbach, D. , Company She Kept, 159-72.
Latham, Earl, "The Managerialization of the Campus," Pub-
    lic Administration Rev. , XIX (Winter, 1959), 48-57 pas-
    sim.
Lyons, J. O. , College Novel in America, 169-74.
McKenzie, B. , Mary McCarthy, 112-21.
Millgate, M. , American Social Fiction, 166-8.
Schlueter, Paul, "The Dissections of Mary McCarthy" in
    Moore, H. T. , ed. , Contemporary American Novelists, 57-
    9.
Schutter, Howard N. , "Academic Freedom and the American
    College Novel of the Nineteen Fifties," DA, XXVIII (1968),
    5070A (Michigan).
Stock, I. , Mary McCarthy, 24-9.
Walcutt, C. C. , Man's Changing Mask, 292-4.

THE GROUP

Aldridge, J. W. , "Mary McCarthy: Princess Among the
    Trolls," Time to Murder and Create, 95-100; 124-32.
Auchincloss, L. , Pioneers and Caretakers, 181-4.
Cook, Bruce, "Mary McCarthy: One of Ours?" CathW,
    CXCIX (April, 1964), 34-42.

DeMott, Benjamin, in Harpers, CCXXVII (October, 1963), 98; 102.

Grumbach, D., Company She Kept, 189-210.

Hicks, Granville, "The Group in Second Meeting," SatR, (February 22, 1964), 51-2.

McCarthy, Mary, "Letters to a Translator: About THE GROUP," Encounter, XXIII, v (November, 1964), 69-71+.

McKenzie, B., Mary McCarthy, 134-54.

Mailer, Norman, "The Mary McCarthy Case," NYRB, I (October 17, 1963), 1-3. Also in Mailer, N., Cannibals and Christians, N.Y.: Dial, 1966, 133-40.

Mathewson, Ruth, "The Vassar Joke," CUF, VI, iv (Fall, 1963), 10-16.

Ohmann, Carol B., and Richard Ohmann, "Class Notes from Vassar," Cweal, LXXIX (September 27, 1963), 12-15.

Podhoretz, N., "Miss McCarthy and the Leopard's Spots," Doings and Undoings, 87-93.

Raban, J., "Character and Manners," Techniques of Modern Fiction, 97-100.

Rogers, Thomas, in Ctary, XXXVI (December, 1963), 488-9.

Schlueter, Paul, "The Dissections of Mary McCarthy" in Moore, H.T., ed., Contemporary American Novelists, 61-2.

Soule, George, "Must a Novelist Be an Artist?" Carleton Miscellany, V (Spring, 1964), 92-8.

Stock, I., Mary McCarthy, 35-43.

Whitehorn, Katharine, "Three Women," Encounter, XXI (December, 1963), 78-9.

THE OASIS

Eisinger, C.E., Fiction of the Forties, 132-3.

Gottfried, Alex, and Sue Davidson, "Utopia's Children: An Interpretation of Three Political Novels," Western Pol. Quart., XV (March, 1962), 24-32.

Grumbach, D., Company She Kept, 128-47.

McKenzie, B., Mary McCarthy, 104-12.

Schlueter, Paul, "The Dissections of Mary McCarthy" in Moore, H.T., ed., Contemporary American Novelists, 56-7.

Stock, I., Mary McCarthy, 20-4.

McCULLERS, CARSON, 1917-1967

GENERAL

Auchincloss, L., Pioneers and Caretakers, 161-9.

Baldanza, Frank, "Plato in Dixie," GaR, XII (Summer, 1958), 151-67.

Dodd, Wayne D., "The Development of the Theme Through Symbol in the Novels of Carson McCullers," GaR, XVII (Summer, 1963), 206-13.

Drake, Robert, "The Lonely Heart of Carson McCullers," ChC, LXXXV (January 10, 1968), 50-1.

Edmonds, D., Carson McCullers.

Eisinger, C. E., Fiction of the Forties, 243-58.

Evans, Oliver, "The Achievement of Carson McCullers," EJ, LI (May, 1962), 301-8.

————, "The Case of Carson McCullers," GaR, XVIII (Spring, 1964), 40-5.

————, "The Theme of Spiritual Isolation in Carson Mc-Cullers" in New World Writing, First Mentor Selection, N. Y.: New American Library, 1952, 297-310. Also in Rubin, L. D., Jr., and R. D. Jacobs, eds., South, 333-48.

Felheim, Maxwell, in Moore, H. T., ed., Contemporary American Novelists, 48-53.

Folk, Barbara N., "The Sad Sweet Music of Carson McCullers," GaR, XVI (Spring, 1962), 202-9.

Gossett, L. Y., "Dispossessed Love: Carson McCullers," Violence in Recent Southern Fiction, 159-77.

Graver, L., Carson McCullers.

Hart, Jane, "Carson McCullers, Pilgrim of Loneliness," GaR, XI (Spring, 1957), 53-8.

Hassan, Ihab H., "Carson McCullers: The Alchemy of Love and Aesthetics of Pain," MFS, V (Winter, 1959-60), 311-26. Also in Hassan, I., Radical Innocence, 205-11. Also in Waldmeir, J., ed., Recent American Fiction, 215-30.

Hendrick, George, " 'Almost Everyone Wants to be the Lover': The Fiction of Carson McCullers," BA, XLII (Summer, 1968), 389-91.

Hoffman, F. J., Art of Southern Fiction, 65-73.

Joost, Nicholas, in Gardiner, H. C., ed., Fifty Years of the American Novel, 284-6.

Kohler, Dayton, "Carson McCullers: Variations on a Theme," EJ, XL (October, 1951), 415-22. Also in CE, XIII (1951), 1-8.

Lubbers, Klaus, "The Necessary Order: A Study of the Theme and Structure in Carson McCullers' Fiction," JA, VIII (1963), 187-204.

McCullers, Carson, "The Flowering Dream: Notes on Writing," Esquire, LII (December, 1959), 162-4.

McPherson, Hugh, "Carson McCullers: Lonely Huntress," TamR, No. 11 (Spring, 1959), 28-40.

Malin, I., "Self-Love," New American Gothic, 19-26.
Meeker, Richard K., in Simonini, R. C., Jr., ed., Southern
    Writers, 184-6.
Rechnitz, Robert M., "Perception, Identity, and the Gro-
    tesque; A Study of Three Southern Writers," DA, XXVIII
    (1967), 2261A (Colorado).
Robinson, W. R., "The Life of Carson McCullers' Imagina-
    tion," SHR, II (Summer, 1968), 291-302.
Schorer, Mark, "McCullers and Capote: Basic Patterns" in
    Balakian, N., and C. Simmons, eds., Creative Present,
    83-94. Also in Schorer, M., World We Imagine, 274-85.
Smith, Simeon M., Jr., "Carson McCullers: A Critical In-
    troduction," DA, XXV (1964), 3583-84 (Penn.).
Sullivan, Walter S., "Carson McCullers, 1917-1947: The
    Conversion of Experience," DA, XXVIII (1968), 4648A
    (Duke).
Symons, J., "The Lonely Hear," Critical Occasions, 106-11.
Vickery, John B., "Carson McCullers: A Map of Love,"
    WSCL, I, i (Winter, 1960), 13-24.

THE BALLAD OF THE SAD CAFÉ

Auchincloss, L., Pioneers and Caretakers, 166-7.
Edmonds, D., Carson McCullers, 19-24.
Eisinger, C. E., Fiction of the Forties, 256-8.
Evans, O., Ballad of Carson McCullers, 126-38.
_____, "The Theme of Spiritual Isolation in Carson Mc-
    Cullers" in New World Writing, First Mentor Selection,
    N. Y.: New American Library, 1952, 304-10. Also in
    Rubin, L. D., Jr., and R. D. Jacobs, eds., South, 340-8.
Graver, L., Carson McCullers, 24-33.
Griffith, Albert J., "Carson McCullers' Myth of the Sad
    Café," GaR, XXI (Spring, 1967), 46-56.
Hassan Ihab H., "Carson McCullers: The Alchemy of Love
    and Aesthetics of Pain," MFS, V (Winter, 1959-60), 313-
    15. Also in Hassan, I. H., Radical Innocence, 223-6. Al-
    so in Waldmeir, J., ed., Recent American Fiction, 217-
    18; 227-30.
Hoffman, F. J., Art of Southern Fiction, 68-71.
Lubbers, Klaus, "The Necessary Order: A Study of Theme
    and Structure in Carson McCullers' Fiction," JA, VIII
    (1963), 198-201.
Phillips, Robert S., "Dinesen's MONKEY and McCullers'
    BALLAD: A Study in Literary Affinity," SSF, I (Spring,
    1964), 184-90.

_____, "Painful Love, Carson McCullers' Parable," SWR, LI (Winter, 1966), 80-6.

Rechnitz, Robert M., "The Failure of Love: The Grotesque in Two Novels by Carson McCullers," GaR, XXII (Winter, 1968), 458-63.

Schorer, Mark, "McCullers and Capote: Basic Patterns" in Balakian, N., and C. Simmons, eds., Creative Present, 92-3. Also in Schorer, M., World We Imagine, 282-3.

Vickery, John B., "Carson McCullers: A Map of Love," WSCL, I, i (Winter, 1960), 14-16.

CLOCK WITHOUT HANDS

Allen, W., Modern Novel, 136-7.

Auchincloss, L., Pioneers and Caretakers, 167-9.

Edmonds, D., Carson McCullers, 30-2.

Emerson, Donald, "The Ambiguities of CLOCK WITHOUT HANDS," WSCL, III, iii (Fall, 1962), 15-28.

Evans, Oliver, "The Achievement of Carson McCullers," EJ, LI (May, 1962), 306-8.

_____, Ballad of Carson McCullers, 170-82.

Ford, Nick A., "Search for Identity: A Critical Survey of Significant Belles-Lettres by and about Negroes Published in 1961," Phylon, XXIII (1962), 130-3.

Graver, L., Carson McCullers, 42-5.

Hartt, J.N., "The Return of Moral Passion, YR, LI, ii (Winter, 1962), 300-1.

Hicks, Granville, "The Subtler Corruptions," SatR, XLIV (September 23, 1961), 14-15; 49.

Hughes, Catherine, "A World of Outcasts," Cweal, LXXV (October 13, 1961), 73-5.

Lubbers, Klaus, "The Necessary Order: A Study of Theme and Structure in Carson McCullers' Fiction," JA, VIII (1963), 201-2.

Parker, Dorothy, "CLOCK WITHOUT HANDS Belongs in Yesterday's Ivory Tower," Esquire, LVI (December, 1961), 72-3.

Rolo, Charles, "A Southern Drama," Atlantic, CCVIII (October, 1961), 126-7.

Schorer, Mark, "McCullers and Capote: Basic Patterns" in Balakian, N., and C. Simmons, eds., Creative Present, 92-3. Also in Schorer, M., World We Imagine, 283-5.

Sullivan, Walter, in GaR, XV (Winter, 1961), 467-9.

Vidal, Gore, "The World Outside," Reporter, XXV (September 28, 1961), 50-2. Also in Vidal, G., Rocking the Boat, 178-83.

THE HEART IS A LONELY HUNTER

Allen, W., Modern Novel, 132-4.
Auchincloss, L., Pioneers and Caretakers, 161-3.
Carpenter, Frederick I., "The Adolescent in American Fic-
    tion," EJ, XLVI (1957), 316-17.
Durham, Frank, "God and No God in THE HEART IS A
    LONELY HUNTER," SAQ, LVI (Autumn, 1957), 494-9.
Edmonds, D., Carson McCullers, 9-14.
Eisinger, C. E., Fiction of the Forties, 245-51.
Evans, O., Ballad of Carson McCullers, 98-117.
_____, "The Case of the Silent Singer: A Revaluation of
    THE HEART IS A LONELY HUNTER," GaR, XIX (Summer,
    1965), 188-203.
_____, "The Theme of Spiritual Isolation in Carson Mc-
    Cullers" in New World Writing, First Mentor Selection,
    N. Y.: New American Library, 1952, 298-300. Also in
    Rubin, L. D., Jr., and R. D. Jacobs, eds., South, 334-6.
Graver, L., Carson McCullers, 10-20.
Hassan, Ihab H., "Carson McCullers: The Alchemy of Love
    and Aesthetics of Pain," MFS, V (Winter, 1959-60), 315-
    18. Also in Hassan, I., Radical Innocence, 211-15. Also
    in Waldmeir, J., ed., Recent American Fiction, 219-22.
Knowles, A. S., Jr., "Six Bronze Petals and Two Red: Car-
    son McCullers in the Forties" in French, W., ed., For-
    ties, 86-94.
Lubbers, Klaus, "The Necessary Order: A Study of Theme
    and Structure in Carson McCullers' Fiction," JA, VIII
    (1963), 188-94.
McPherson, Hugo, "Carson McCullers: Lonely Huntress,"
    TamR, No. 11 (Spring, 1959), 31-4.
Madden, David, "The Paradox of the Need for Privacy and
    the Need for Understanding in Carson McCullers' THE
    HEART IS A LONELY HUNTER," L&P, XVII (1967), 128-
    40.
Malin, I., New American Gothic, 54-7. Also in Malin, I.,
    ed., Psychoanalysis in American Fiction, 258-60.
Mizuta, J., "Carson McCullers' THE HEART IS A LONELY
    HUNTER," Rikkyo Review, XXII (1961), 79-95. (Not
    seen.)
Moore, Jack B., "Carson McCullers: The Heart is a Time-
    less Hunter," TCL, XI (July, 1965), 76-81.
Schorer, Mark, "McCullers and Capote: Basic Patterns" in
    Balakian, N., and C. Simmons, eds., Creative Present,
    87-8. Also in Schorer, M., World We Imagine, 277-9.
Sherrill, Roland A., "McCullers' THE HEART IS A LONELY
    HUNTER," KyR, II (1968), 5-17.

Symons, J., "The Lonely Heart," Critical Occasions, 106-
11.
Taylor, Horace, "THE HEART IS A LONELY HUNTER: A
Southern Wasteland" in McNeir, Waldo, and Leo B. Levy,
eds., Studies in American Literature (LSUSHS, No. 8),
Baton Rouge: Louisiana State Un. Pr., 1960, 154-60.
Vickery, John B., "Carson McCullers: A Map of Love,"
WSCL, I, i (Winter, 1960), 16-18.

THE MEMBER OF THE WEDDING

Allen, W., Modern Novel, 134-5.
Auchincloss, L., Pioneers and Caretakers, 165-6.
Edmonds, D., Carson McCullers, 24-9.
Eisinger, C. E., Fiction of the Forties, 254-6.
Evans, O., Ballad of Carson McCullers, 98-117.
_____, "The Theme of Spiritual Isolation in Carson Mc-
Cullers" in New World Writing, First Mentor Selection,
N. Y.: New American Library, 1952, 301-4. Also in
Rubin, L. D., Jr., and R. D. Jacobs, eds., South, 337-
40.
Graver, L., Carson McCullers, 33-42.
Hassan, Ihab B., "Carson McCullers: The Alchemy of Love
and Aesthetics of Pain," MFS, V (Winter, 1959-60), 320-
3. Also in Hassan, I., Radical Innocence, 219-23. Also
in Waldmeir, J., ed., Recent American Fiction, 224-7.
Knowles, A. S., Jr., "Six Bronze Petals and Two Red: Car-
son McCullers in the Forties" in French, W., ed., Forties, 94-7.
Lubbers, Klaus, "The Necessary Order: A Study of Theme
and Structure in Carson McCullers' Fiction," JA, VIII
(1963), 196-8.
Malin, I., New American Gothic, 57-9. Also in Malin, I.,
ed., Psychoanalysis and American Fiction, 261-2.
Phillips, Robert S., "The Gothic Architecture of THE MEM-
BER OF THE WEDDING," Ren, XVI (Winter, 1964), 59-
72.
Schorer, Mark, "McCullers and Capote: Basic Patterns" in
Balakian, N., and C. Simmons, eds., Creative Present,
90-3. Also in Schorer, M., World We Imagine, 281-2.
Tinkham, Charles B., "The Member of the Sideshow," Phy-
lon, XVIII (Fourth Quarter, 1958), 383-90.
Vickery, John B., "Carson McCullers: A Map of Love,"
WSCL, I, i (Winter, 1960), 21-3.
Young, Marguerite, "Metaphysical Fiction," KR, IX (Winter,
1947), 151-5.

REFLECTIONS IN A GOLDEN EYE

Auchincloss, L., Pioneers and Caretakers, 163-5.
Edmonds, D., Carson McCullers, 14-19.
Eisinger, C. E., Fiction of the Forties, 251-4.
Evans, O., Ballad of Carson McCullers, 60-71.
_____, "The Theme of Spiritual Isolation in Carson Mc-
Cullers" in New World Writing, First Mentor Selection,
N. Y.: New American Library, 1952, 300-1. Also in
Rubin, L. D., Jr., and R. D. Jacobs, eds., South, 336-7.
Graver, L., Carson McCullers, 20-4.
Hassan, Ihab H., "Carson McCullers: The Alchemy of Love
and Aesthetics of Pain," MFS, V (Winter, 1959-60), 318-
20. Also in Hassan, I., Radical Innocence, 216-18. Al-
so in Waldmeir, J., ed., Recent American Fiction, 222-
4.
Hoffman, F. J., Art of Southern Fiction, 67-8.
Lubbers, Klaus, "The Necessary Order: A Study of Theme
and Structure in Carson McCullers' Fiction," JA, VIII
(1963), 194-6.
McPherson, Hugo, "Carson McCullers: Lonely Huntress,"
TamR, No. 11 (Spring, 1959), 34-8.
Rechnitz, Robert M., "The Failure of Love: The Grotesque
in Two Novels by Carson McCullers," GaR, XXII (Winter,
1968), 454-8.
Schorer, Mark, "McCullers and Capote: Basic Patterns" in
Balakian, N., and C. Simmons, eds., Creative Present,
88-90. Also in Schorer, M., World We Imagine, 279-80.
Vickery, John B., "Carson McCullers: A Map of Love,"
WSCL, I, i (Winter, 1960), 18-21.
Williams, Tennessee, Introduction to REFLECTIONS IN A
GOLDEN EYE, Norfolk: New Directions, 1950, i-xxi.

BIBLIOGRAPHY

Phillips, Robert S., "Carson McCullers: 1956-1964: A Selected Checklist, BB, XXIV (September-December, 1964),
113-16.
Stewart, Stanley, "Carson McCullers, 1940-1956: A Selected
Checklist," BB, XXII (April, 1959), 182-5.

MacLENNAN, HUGH, 1907-

GENERAL

Chambers, Robert D., "The Novels of Hugh MacLennan,"

Journal of Canadian Studies. Rev D' Etudes Canadiennes,
  II (August, 1967), 3-11.
Goetsch, Paul, "Too Long to the Courtly Muses: Hugh Mac-
  Lennan as Contemporary Writer," CanL, No. 10 (Autumn,
  1961), 19-31.
McPherson, Hugo, "The Novels of Hugh MacLennan," QQ,
  LX (Summer, 1953), 186-98.
Pacey, Desmond, Creative Writing in Canada, 217-21.
Watters, R. E. , "Hugh MacLennan and the Canadian Charac-
  ter" in Morrison, Edmund, and William Robbins, eds. ,
  As a Man Thinks, Toronto: W. J. Gage and Co. , 1953,
  228-43.
Wilson, E. , O Canada, 57-80.
Woodcock, George, "A Nation's Odyssey: The Novels of
  Hugh MacLennan," REL, II, iv (October, 1951), 77-90.
  Also in CanL, No. 10 (Autumn, 1961), 7-18. Also in
  Smith, A. J. M. , ed. , Masks of Fiction, 128-40. Also in
  Canadian Literature. Choice of Critics, 79-100.

BAROMETER RISING

Goetsch, Paul, "Too Long to the Courtly Muses: Hugh Mac-
  Lennan as Contemporary Writer," CanL, No. 10 (Autumn,
  1961), 20-1.
McPherson, Hugo, "The Novels of Hugh MacLennan," QQ,
  LX (Summer, 1953), 187-90.
New, William H. , "The Storm and After: Imagery and Sym-
  bolism in Hugh MacLennan's BAROMETER RISING," QQ,
  LXXIV (Summer, 1967), 302-13.
O'Donnell, Kathleen, "The Wanderer in BAROMETER RISING,"
  UWR, III, ii (1968), 12-18.
Woodcock, George, "Hugh MacLennan," NoR, III (April-May,
  1950), 2-7.
_____, "A Nation's Odyssey: The Novels of Hugh Mac-
  Lennan," REL, II, iv (October, 1961), 77-82. Also in
  CanL, No. 10 (Autumn, 1961), 7-11. Also in Smith, A.
  J. M. , ed. , Masks of Fiction, 130-2. Also in Canadian
  Literature. Choice of Critics, 79-84.

EACH MAN'S SON

Goetsch, Paul, "Too Long to the Courtly Muses: Hugh Mac-
  Lennan as Contemporary Writer," CanL, No. 10 (Autumn,
  1961), 23-5.
McPherson, Hugo, "The Novels of Hugh MacLennan," QQ,
  LX (Summer, 1953), 195-8.
Phelps, A. L. , Canadian Writers, 82-4.

Tallman, Warren, in Canadian Literature. Choice of Critics,
    64-7+.
_____, "Wolf in the Snow," CanL, No. 5 (Summer, 1960),
    18-20; No. 6 (Autumn, 1960), 41-4.
Woodcock, George, "A Nation's Odyssey: The Novels of
    Hugh MacLennan," REL, II, iv (October, 1961), 85-7. Al-
    so in CanL, No. 10 (Autumn, 1961), 14-15. Also in
    Smith, A. J. M. , ed. , Masks of Fiction, 136-7. Also in
    Canadian Literature. Choice of Critics, 87-9.

THE PRECIPICE

Goetsch, Paul, "Too Long to the Courtly Muses: Hugh Mac-
    Lennan as Contemporary Writer," CanL, No. 10 (Autumn,
    1961), 22-3.
McPherson, Hugo, "The Novels of Hugh MacLennan," QQ,
    LX (Summer, 1953), 192-5.
Phelps, A. L. , Canadian Writers, 81.
Wilson, E. , O Canada, 64-6.
Woodcock, George, "Hugh MacLennan," NoR, III (April-May,
    1950), 9-10.
_____, "A Nation's Odyssey: The Novels of Hugh Mac-
    Lennan," REL, II, iv (October, 1961), 84-5. Also in
    CanL, No. 10 (Autumn, 1961), 13-14. Also in Smith, A.
    J. M. , ed. , Masks of Fiction, 135-6. Also in Canadian
    Literature. Choice of Critics, 86-7.

RETURN OF THE SPHINX

New, William H. , "Winter and the Night People," CanL, No.
    36 (Spring, 1968), 26-33.
Spettigue, Douglas, "Beauty and the Beast," QQ, LXXIV
    (Winter, 1967), 762-5.

TWO SOLITUDES

Chambers, Robert D. , "The Novels of Hugh MacLennan,"
    Journal of Canadian Studies. Rev. d'Etudes Canadiennes,
    II (August, 1967), 5-6.
Goetsch, Paul, "Too Long to the Courtly Muses: Hugh Mac-
    Lennan as Contemporary Writer," CanL, No. 10 (Autumn,
    1961), 21-2.
McPherson, Hugo, "The Novels of Hugh MacLennan," QQ,
    LX (Summer, 1953), 190-2.
Phelps, A. L. , Canadian Writers, 78-81.
Woodcock, George, "Hugh MacLennan," NoR, III (April-May,
    1950), 7-9.

_____, "A Nation's Odyssey: The Novels of Hugh Mac-
Lennan," REL, II, iv (October, 1961), 82-4. Also in
CanL, No. 10 (Autumn, 1961), 11-13. Also in Smith, A.
J.M., ed., Masks of Fiction, 133-5. Also in Canadian
Literature. Choice of Critics, 84-6.

THE WATCH THAT ENDS THE NIGHT

Chambers, Robert D., "The Novels of Hugh MacLennan,"
Journal of Canadian Studies. Rev. d'Etudes Canadiennes,
II (August, 1967), 7-10.
Davies, Robertson, "MacLennan's Rising Sun," Saturday
Night, LXXIV (March 28, 1959), 29-31.
Goetsch, Paul, "Too Long to the Courtly Muses: Hugh Mac-
Lennan as Contemporary Writer," CanL, No. 10 (Autumn,
1961), 25-8.
Hirano, Keiichi, "Jerome Martell and Norman Bethune: A
Note on Hugh MacLennan's THE WATCH THAT ENDS THE
NIGHT," SELit, English Number (1968), 37-59.
MacLennan, Hugh, "The Story of a Novel" in Smith, A.J.M.,
ed., Masks of Fiction, 137-40. Also in CanL, No. 10
(Autumn, 1961), 15-18.
New, William, "The Apprenticeship of Discovery," CanL,
No. 29 (1966), 18-33.
Watt, F.W., in UTQ, XXIX (July, 1960), 461-3.
Woodcock, George, "A Nation's Odyssey: The Novels of
Hugh MacLennan," REL, II, iv (October, 1961), 87-9.
Also in CanL, No. 10 (Autumn, 1961), 15-18. Also in
Smith, A.J.M., ed., Masks of Fiction, 137-40. Also in
Canadian Literature. Choice of Critics, 89-92.

MAILER, NORMAN, 1923-

GENERAL

Aldridge, J.W., "Norman Mailer: The Energy of New Suc-
cess," Time to Murder and Create, 149-63.
Baumbach, J., Landscape of Nightmare, 9-11.
Breslow, Paul, "The Hipster and the Radical," StL, I (1960),
102-5.
Cook, Bruce A., "Norman Mailer: The Temptation of Pow-
er," Ren, XIV (Summer, 1962), 206-15; 222.
Dupee, F.W., "The American Norman Mailer," Ctary, XXIX
(February, 1960), 128-32.
Finkelstein, S., Existentialism and Alienation in American
Literature, 269-75.

Foster, Richard, "Mailer and the Fitzgerald Tradition,"
Novel, I (Spring, 1968), 219-30.
_____, Norman Mailer.
Gilman, R., Confusion of Realms, 81-153.
Glicksberg, Charles I., "Norman Mailer: The Angry Young
Novelist in America," WSCL, I, i (Winter, 1960), 25-34.
Goldstone, Herbert, "The Novels of Norman Mailer," EJ,
XLV (March, 1956), 113-21.
Harper, H. M., "Norman Mailer: A Revolution in the Con-
sciousness of Time," Desperate Faith, 96-136.
Hesla, David, "The Two Roles of Norman Mailer" in Scott,
N. A., Jr., ed., Adversity and Grace, 211-23.
Hoffman, Frederick J., "Norman Mailer and the Revolt of
the Ego: Some Observations on Recent American Litera-
ture," WSCL, I, iii (Fall, 1960), 5-12.
Howe, I., "A Quest for Peril: Norman Mailer," World
More Attractive, 123-9.
Hux, Samuel H., "American Myth and Existential Vision:
The Indigenous Existentialism of Mailer, Bellow, Styron
and Ellison," DA, XXVI (1966), 5437 (Conn.).
Kaufmann, D. L., Norman Mailer.
Lakin, R. D., "D. W.'s: The Displaced Writer in America,"
MQ, IV (July, 1963), 295-303.
Langbaum, Robert, "Mailer's New Style," Novel, II (Fall,
1968), 69-78.
Leeds, B. H., Structured Vision of Norman Mailer.
Marcus, Steven, "The Art of Fiction XXIII: Norman Mailer,"
ParisR, VIII, No. 31 (Winter-Spring, 1964), 28-58. Also
in Writers at Work, 3rd ser., 251-78.
Mudrick, Marvin, "Mailer and Styron: Guests of the Estab-
lishment," HudR, XVII (Autumn, 1964), 346-66.
Newman, Paul B., "Mailer: The Jew as Existentialist,"
North American Review, II, iii (July, 1965), 48-55.
Noble, D. W., Eternal Adam and the New World Garden,
197-209.
"Playboy Interview: Norman Mailer," Playboy, XV (January,
1968), 69-84.
Podhoretz, Norman, "Norman Mailer: The Embattled Vision,"
PR, XXVI (Summer, 1959), 371-91. Also in Podhoretz,
N., Doings and Undoings, 179-204. Also in Waldmeir, J.
J., ed., Recent American Fiction, 185-202. Also Intro-
duction to Barbary Shore, N. Y.: Grosset & Dunlop, 1963.
Richler, Mordecai, "Norman Mailer," Encounter, XXV (July,
1965), 61-4.
Schrader, George A., "Norman Mailer and the Despair of
Defiance," YR, LI (December, 1961), 267-80.
Schulz, Max F., "Mailer's Divine Comedy," WSCL, IX (1968),

36-57. Also (expanded) in Schulz, M. F. , Radical Sophistication, 69-109.

Scott, James B. , "The Individual and Society: Norman
Mailer vs. William Styron," DA, XXV (1965), 5942 (Syracuse).

Shaw, Peter, "The Tough Guy Intellectual," CritQ, VIII
(Spring, 1966), 13-28.

Solotaroff, Robert, "Down Mailer's Way," ChiR, XIX, iii
(June, 1967), 11-25.

Steiner, George, "Naked But Not Dead," Encounter, XVII
(December, 1961), 67-70.

Stern, Richard, "Hip, Hell and the Navigator: An Interview
with Norman Mailer," WR, XXIII (Winter, 1959), 101-9.
Also in Mailer, Norman, Advertisements for Myself, N. Y. :
Putnam, 1959, 383-5.

Toback, James, "Norman Mailer Today," Ctary, XLIV (October, 1967), 68-76.

Trilling, Diana, "Norman Mailer," Encounter, XIX (November, 1962), 45-56. Also in Balakian, N. , and C. Simmons, eds. , Creative Present, 145-71. Also in Trilling,
D. , Claremont Essays, 175-202.

Volpe, Edmond L. , in Moore, H. T. , ed. , Contemporary
American Novelists, 112-19.

Wilson, Robert A. , "Negative Thinking: The New Art of the
Brave," Realist, No. 22 (December, 1960), 5; 11-13.
(Not seen.)

Winegarten, Renée, "Norman Mailer, Genuine or Counter-
feit?" Midstream, XI (September, 1965), 91-5.

AN AMERICAN DREAM

Aldridge, James W. , "The Big Comeback of Norman Mailer,"
Life, LVIII (March 19, 1965), 12. Also as "Norman Mailer: The Energy of New Success" in Aldridge, J. W. , Time
to Murder and Create, 160-3.

Alvarez, A. , "Norman X," Spectator, No. 7141 (May 7,
1965), 603.

Bersani, Leo, "The Interpretation of Dreams," PR, XXXII
(Fall, 1965), 603-8.

Boyers, Robert, "Attitudes Toward Sex in American 'High
Culture'," AAAPSS, Vol. 376 (March, 1968), 38-41, 43-4.

Corrington, John W. , "An American Dreamer," ChiR, XVIII,
i (Spring, 1965), 58-66.

Didion, Joan, "A Social Eye," NatR, XVII (April 20, 1965),
329-30.

Fiedler, Leslie A. , "Master of Dreams," PR, XXXIV (Sum-

mer, 1967), 352-6.
Finkelstein, S., Existentialism and Alienation in American
Literature, 274-5.
Foster, R., Norman Mailer, 18-19.
Hardwick, Elizabeth, "Bad Boy," PR, XXXII (Spring, 1965),
291-4.
Harper, H.M., Jr., Desperate Faith, 120-4.
Hesla, David, "The Two Roles of Norman Mailer" in Scott,
N.A., Jr., ed., Adversity and Grace, 223-8.
Hux, Samuel, "Mailer's Dream of Violence," MinnR, VIII
(1968), 152-7.
Hyman, Stanley E., "Norman Mailer's Yummy Rump," New
Leader, (March 15, 1965), 16-17. Also in Hyman, S.E.,
Standards, 274-8.
Kaufmann, D.L., Norman Mailer, 35-50; 67-9; 76-9; 80-3;
91-7; 123-8; 132-42; 144-7; 166-8.
Langbaum, Robert, "Mailer's New Style," Novel, II (Fall,
1968), 70-5.
Leeds, B.H., Structured Vision of Norman Mailer, 125-77;
231-6.
Noble, D.W., Eternal Adam and the New World Garden, 207-
9.
Poirier, Richard, "Morbid Mindedness," Ctary, XXXIX
(June, 1965), 91-4.
_____, "T.S. Eliot and the Literature of Waste," NRep,
CLVI (May 20, 1967), 21-2.
Rahv, Philip, "Crime Without Punishment," NYRB (March 25,
1965), 1-4. Also in Rahv, P., Myth and the Powerhouse,
234-43. Also in Rahv, P., Literature and the Sixth
Sense, 409-17.
Richler, Mordecai, "Norman Mailer," Encounter, XXV (July,
1965), 61-4.
Schulz, Max F., "Mailer's Divine Comedy," WSCL, IX
(1968), 51-7. Also in Schulz, M.F., Radical Sophistica-
tion, 91-9.
Solotaroff, Robert, "Down Mailer's Way," ChiR, XIX, iii
(June, 1967), 20-5.
Spender, Stephen, "Mailer's American Melodrama" in En-
cyclopedia Britannica. Great Ideas Today, 1965, 173-6.
Toback, James, "Norman Mailer Today," Ctary, XLIV (Oc-
tober, 1967), 20-5.
Wagenheim, Allan J., "Square's Progress. AN AMERICAN
DREAM," Crit, X, i (Winter, 1968), 45-68.
Weber, Brom, "A Fear of Dying: Norman Mailer's AN
AMERICAN DREAM," HC, II, iii (June, 1965), 1-6; 8-11.
Wood, Margery, "Norman Mailer and Nathalie Sarraute: A
Comparison of Existential Novels," MinnR, VI (Spring,

1966), 67-72.

BARBARY SHORE

Cook, Bruce A., "Norman Mailer: The Temptation to Power," Ren, XIV (Summer, 1962), 210-11.
Dienstfrey, Harris, in Kostelanetz, R., ed., On Contemporary Literature, 425-31.
Eisinger, C. E., Fiction of the Forties, 93-4.
Foster, R., Norman Mailer, 12-14.
Geismar, Maxwell, in SatR, XXXIV (May 26, 1951), 15. Also in Geismar, M., American Moderns, 173-4.
Goldstone, Herbert, "The Novels of Norman Mailer," EJ, XLV (March, 1956), 116-18.
Harper, H. M., Jr., Desperate Faith, 103-9.
Kaufmann, D. L., Norman Mailer, 12-33; 53-7; 115-17.
Leeds, B. H., Structured Vision of Norman Mailer, 53-103.
Ludwig, J., Recent American Novelists, 26-7.
Noble, D. W., Eternal Adam and the New World Garden, 201-2.
Podhoretz, Norman, "Norman Mailer: The Embattled Vision," PR, XXVI (Summer, 1959), 377-83. Also in Podhoretz, N., Doings and Undoings, 187-94. Also in Waldmeir, J. J., ed., Recent American Fiction, 190-5. Also, "Introduction," BARBARY SHORE, N. Y.: Grosset & Dunlop, 1963.
Schulz, Max F., "Norman Mailer's Divine Comedy," WSCL, IX (1968), 39-45. Also in Schulz, M. F., Radical Sophistication, 73-81.
Trilling, Diana, "Norman Mailer," Encounter, XIX (November, 1962), 49-50. Also in Balakian, N., and C. Simmons, eds., Creative Present, 154-8. Also in Trilling, D., Claremont Essays, 185-9.

THE DEER PARK

Cook, Bruce A., "Norman Mailer: The Temptation to Power," Ren, XIV (Summer, 1962), 212-14.
Dienstfrey, Harris, in Kostelanetz, R., ed., On Contemporary Literature, 431-4.
Dupee, F. W., "The American Norman Mailer," Ctary, XXIX (February, 1960), 131-2.
Foster, R., Norman Mailer, 14-18.
Geismar, M., American Moderns, 174-9.
Goldstone, Herbert, "The Novels of Norman Mailer," EJ, XLV (March, 1956), 118-20.
Harper, H. M., Jr., Desperate Faith, 109-15.

Kaufmann, D. L. , Norman Mailer, 24-34; 58-9; 117-20; 161-3.

Kramer, Maurice, "The Secular Mode of Jewishness," Works, I (Autumn, 1967), 107.

Leeds, B. H. , Structured Vision of Norman Mailer, 105-23; 164-7.

Ludwig, J. , Recent American Novelists, 26-7.

Mailer, Norman, "The Last Draft of THE DEER PARK" in McCormack, T. , ed. , Afterwords, 193-231.

Millgate, M. , American Social Fiction, 159-62.

Noble, D. W. , Eternal Adam and the New World Garden, 202-4.

Podhoretz, Norman, "Norman Mailer: The Embattled Vision," PR, XXVI (Summer, 1959), 383-90. Also in Podhoretz, N. , Doings and Undoings, 194-200. Also in Waldmeir, J. J. , ed. , Recent American Fiction, 195-201.

Schulz, Max F. , "Mailer's Divine Comedy," WSCL, IX (1968), 45-51. Also in Schulz, M. F. , Radical Sophistication, 81-90.

Solotaroff, Robert, "Down Mailer's Way," ChiR, XIX, iii (June, 1967), 16-20.

Trilling, Diana, "Norman Mailer," Encounter, XIX (November, 1962), 51-3. Also in Balakian, N. , and C. Simmons, eds. , Creative Present, 159-63. Also in Trilling, D. , Claremont Essays, 190-3.

THE NAKED AND THE DEAD

Aldridge, J. W. , After the Lost Generation, 133-41.

Allen, W. , Modern Novel, 296-8.

Baumbach, J. , Landscape of Nightmare, 9-10.

Bryant, Jerry H. , "The Last of the Social Protest Writers," ArQ, XIX (Winter, 1963), 317-20.

Cook, Bruce A. , "Norman Mailer: The Temptation to Power," Ren, XIV (Summer, 1962), 207-9.

Dienstfrey, Harris, in Kostelanetz, R. , ed. , On Contemporary Literature, 422-5.

Eisinger, C. E. , Fiction of the Forties, 33-8.

_____, "Introduction," THE NAKED AND THE DEAD, N. Y.: Holt, Rinehart and Winston, 1968.

Enkvist, Nils E. , "Re-readings. Norman Mailer. THE NAKED AND THE DEAD," MSpr, LVI (1962), 60-4.

Finkelstein, S. , Existentialism and Alienation in American Literature, 270-2.

_____, "Norman Mailer and Edward Albee," American Dialog, II (February-March, 1965), 23-5.

Foster, R. , Norman Mailer, 8-12.

French, Warren, in French, W. , ed. , Forties, 21-5.
Geismar, Maxwell, SatR, XXXI (May 8, 1948), 10+. Also
in Geismar, M. , American Moderns, 171-3.
Goldstone, Herbert, "The Novels of Norman Mailer," EJ,
XLV (March, 1956), 114-16.
Harper, H. M. , Jr. , Desperate Faith, 96-102.
Hassan, I. , Radical Innocence, 140-51.
Healy, Robert C. , in Gardiner, H. C. , ed. , Fifty Years of
the American Novel, 260-3.
Kaufmann, D. L. , Norman Mailer, 1-12; 51-3; 70-2; 100-3;
112-15; 142-3.
Leeds, B. H. , Structured Vision of Norman Mailer, 9-51.
Ludwig, J. , Recent American Novelists, 24-6.
Millgate, M. , American Social Fiction, 146-50.
Newman, Paul B. , "Mailer: The Jew as Existentialist,"
North American Review, II, iii (July, 1965), 48-55.
Noble, D. W. , Eternal Adam and the New World Garden,
198-201.
Podhoretz, Norman, "Norman Mailer: The Embattled Vi-
sion," PR, XXVI (Summer, 1959), 371-7. Also in Pod-
horetz, N. , Doings and Undoings, 180-7. Also in Wald-
meir, W. W. , ed. , Recent American Fiction, 185-90.
Prescott, O. , In My Opinion, 155-9.
Rideout, W. B. , Radical Novel in the U. S. , 270-3.
Ross, Frank, "The Assailant-Victim in Three War Protest
Novels," Paunch, XXXII (August, 1968), 46-57.
Solotaroff, Robert, "Down Mailer's Way," ChiR, XIX, iii
(June, 1967), 12-14.
Thorp, W. , "The Persistence of Naturalism in the Novel,"
American Writing in the Twentieth Century, 145-7.
Trilling, Diana, "Norman Mailer," Encounter, XIX (Novem-
ber, 1962), 47-9+. Also in Balakian, N. , and C. Sim-
mons, eds. , Creative Present, 151-4+. Also in Trilling,
D. , Claremont Essays, 182-5+.
Volpe, Edmund L. , in Moore, H. T. , ed. , Contemporary
American Novelists, 114-16.
Waldmeir, J. J. , American Novels of the Second World War,
110-18.

WHY ARE WE IN VIETNAM?

Aldridge, John W. , "From Vietnam to Obscenity," Harpers,
CCXXXVI (February, 1968), 91-7.
Foster, R. , Norman Mailer, 19-21.
Langbaum, Robert, "Mailer's New Style," Novel, II (Fall,
1968), 75-8.

Leeds, B. H. , Structured Vision of Norman Mailer, 179-206.
Schulz, M. F. , Radical Sophistication, 109.

BIBLIOGRAPHY

Foster, R. , Norman Mailer, 44-6.
Kaufmann, D. L. , Norman Mailer, 177-84.

MALAMUD, BERNARD, 1914-

GENERAL

Alter, Robert, "Malamud as Jewish Writer," Ctary, XLII
    (September, 1966), 71-6. Also (revised) in Alter, R. ,
    After the Tradition, 116-30.
Baumbach, Jonathan, "The Economy of Love: The Novels of
    Bernard Malamud," KR, XXV (Summer, 1963), 438-57.
_____, "Malamud's Heroes," Cweal, LXXXV (October 28,
    1966), 97-9.
Bellman, Samuel I. , "Women, Children, and Idiot's First:
    The Transformation Psychology of Bernard Malamud,"
    Crit, VII, ii (Winter, 1965), 123-38.
Charles, Gerda, "Bernard Malamud, the 'Natural' Writer,"
    JewishQ, IX (Spring, 1962), 5-6.
Dupee, F. W. , "The Power of Positive Sex," PR, XXXI (Sum-
    mer, 1964), 425-9. Also as "Malamud: The Uses and
    Abuses of Commitment" in Dupee, F. W. , King of the
    Cats, 156-63.
Featherstone, Joseph, "Bernard Malamud," Atlantic, CCXIX
    (March, 1967), 95-8.
Frankel, Haskel, "Interview with Bernard Malamud," SatR,
    XLIX (September 10, 1966), 39-40.
Goldman, Mark, "Bernard|Malamud's Comic Vision and the
    Theme of Identity," Crit, VII, i (Winter, 1965), 92-109.
Gunn, Giles B. , "Bernard Malamud and the High Cost of
    Living" in Scott, N. A. , Jr. , Adversity and Grace, 59-82.
Hicks, Granville, "Generations of the Fifties: Malamud,
    Gold and Updike" in Balakian, N. , and C. Simmons, eds. ,
    Creative Present, 217-24.
_____, "His Hopes on the Human Heart," SatR, XLVI
    (October 12, 1963), 31-2.
Hoyt, Charles A. , "Bernard Malamud and the New Romanti-
    cism" in Moore, H. T. , ed. , Contemporary American Nov-
    elists, 65-79.
Kazin, Alfred, "Bernard Malamud: The Magic and the
    Dread" in Kostelanetz, R. , ed. , On Contemporary Litera-

ture, 437-41.   Also in Kazin, A., Contemporaries, 202-7.

Kermode, Frank, in NStat, LXIII (March 30, 1962), 452-3. Also in Kermode, F., Continuities, 216-22.

Klein, M., "Bernard Malamud: The Sadness of Goodness," After Alienation, 247-93.

Lewin, Lois, "The Theme of Suffering in the Work of Bernard Malamud and Saul Bellow," DA, XXVIII (1968), 5021A (Pittsburgh).

Malin, I., Jews and Americans.

Marcus, Steven, "The Novel Again," PR, XXIX (Spring, 1962), 184-6.

Meeter, G., Philip Roth and Bernard Malamud.

Mellard, James M., "Malamud's Novels: Four Versions of the Pastoral," Crit, IX, ii (1967), 5-19.

Mudrick, Marvin, "Who Killed Herzog? or, Three American Novelists," UDQ, I, i (Spring, 1966), 61-97.

Pinsker, Sanford S., "The Schlemiel as Metaphor: Studies in the Yiddish and American Jewish Novel," DA, XXVIII (1968), 3679A-80A (Un. of Washington).

Rahv, Philip, "Introduction," A Malamud Reader, N.Y.: Farrar, Straus and Giroux, 1967.   Also in Rahv, P., Literature and the Sixth Sense, 280-8.

Ratner, Marc L., "Style and Humanity in Malamud's Fiction," MR, V (Summer, 1964), 663-83.

Richman, S., Bernard Malamud.

Schulz, M. F., "Bernard Malamud's Mythic Proletarians," Radical Sophistication, 56-67.

Siegel, Ben, "Victims in Motion: Bernard Malamud's Sad and Bitter Clowns," NWR, V (Spring, 1962), 69-80. Also in Waldmeir, J.J., ed., Recent American Fiction, 203-14.

Solotaroff, Theodore, "Bernard Malamud's Fiction: The Old Life and the New," Ctary, XXXIII (March, 1962), 197-204.

Tajuddin, Mohammed, "The Tragicomic Novel: Camus, Malamud, Hawkes, Bellow," DA, XXVIII (1968), 2698A-99A (Indiana).

Tanner, Tony, "Bernard Malamud and the New Life," CritQ, X (Spring-Summer, 1968), 151-68.

Weiss, Samuel A., "Notes on Bernard Malamud," CJF, XXI (Winter, 1962-63), 155-8.

_____, "Passion and Purgation in Bernard Malamud," UWR, II, i (Fall, 1966), 93-9.

THE ASSISTANT

Allen, W. , Modern Novel, 330-2.
Alley, Alvin D. , and Hugh Agee, "Existential Heroes: Frank
  Alpine and Rabbit Angstrom," BSUF, IX, i (Winter, 1968),
  3-5.
Bailey, Anthony, "Insidious Patience," Cweal, LXVI (June
  21, 1957), 307-8.
Baumbach, J. , "All Men are Jews: THE ASSISTANT,"
  Landscape of Nightmare, 111-22.
_____, "The Economy of Love: The Novels of Bernard
  Malamud," KR, XXV (Summer, 1963), 448-57.
Bloomfield, Caroline, "Religion and Alienation in James
  Baldwin, Bernard Malamud, and James F. Powers," Re-
  ligious Education, LVII (March-April, 1962), 98-9.
Eigner, Edwin, "Malamud's Use of the Quest Romance,"
  Genre, I (January, 1968), 55-75.
Fiedler, Leslie, "The Commonplace as Absurd," Reconstruc-
  tionist, XXIV (February 21, 1958), 22-4. Also in Fied-
  ler, L. , No! In Thunder, 106-10.
Francis, H. E. , "Bernard Malamud's Everyman," Midstream,
  VII (Winter, 1961), 93-7.
Gunn, Giles B. , "Bernard Malamud and the High Cost of
  Living" in Scott, N. A. , Jr. , ed. , Adversity and Grace,
  70-6.
Hassan, I. , Radical Innocence, 161-8.
Hicks, Granville, in Balakian, N. , and C. Simmons, eds. ,
  Creative Present, 220-2.
Hoyt, Charles A. , "Bernard Malamud and the New Romanti-
  cism" in Moore, H. T. , ed. , Contemporary American
  Novelists, 65-71.
Kazin, Alfred, "Fantasist of the Ordinary," Ctary, XXIV
  (July, 1957), 89-92.
Klein, M. , "Bernard Malamud: The Sadness of Goodness,"
  After Alienation, 267-77.
Kramer, Maurice, "The Secular Mode of Jewishness,"
  Works, I (Autumn, 1967), 102-5, and passim.
Leer, Norman, "Three American Novels and Contemporary
  Society: A Search for Commitment," WSCL, III, iii
  (Fall, 1962), 72-6.
Mandel, Ruth B. , "Bernard Malamud's THE ASSISTANT and
  A NEW LIFE: Ironic Affirmation," Crit, VII, ii (Winter,
  1965), 110-21.
Meeter, G. , Philip Roth and Bernard Malamud, 34-9.
Mellard, James M. , "Malamud's THE ASSISTANT: The
  City Novel as Pastoral," SSF, V (Fall, 1967), 1-11.
Ratner, Marc L. , "Style and Humanity in Malamud's Fic-

tion," MR, V (Summer, 1964), 664-7.
Richman, S., Bernard Malamud, 25-6; 50-79.
Shear, Walter, "Culture Conflict in THE ASSISTANT," MQ,
   VII (Summer, 1966), 367-80.
Siegel, Ben, "Victims in Motion: Bernard Malamud's Sad
   and Bitter Clowns," NWR, V (Spring, 1962), 71-2. Also
   in Waldmeir, J.J., ed., Recent American Fiction, 205-6.
Swados, Harvey, "The Emergence of an Artist," WR, XXII
   (Winter, 1958), 149-51.
Tanner, Tony, "Bernard Malamud and the New Life," CritQ,
   X (Spring-Summer, 1968), 155-7.
Widmer, K., "Contemporary American Outcasts," Literary
   Rebel, 124-6.

THE FIXER

Alter, Robert, "Malamud as Jewish Writer," Ctary, XLII
   (September, 1966), 73-6. Also (revised) in Alter, R.,
   After the Tradition, 122-30.
Baumbach, Jonathan, "Malamud's Heroes," Cweal, LXXXV
   (October 28, 1966), 97-9.
Burgess, A., Urgent Copy, 136-40.
Davis, Robert G., "Invaded Selves," HudR, XIX (Winter,
   1966-67), 663-5.
Dregnan, James P., "The Ordeal of Yakov Bok," Critic,
   XXV (October, 1966), 102-4.
Eigner, Edwin M., "Malamud's Use of the Quest Romance,"
   Genre, I (January, 1968), 55-75.
Elkins, Stanley, in MR, VIII (Spring, 1967), 388-92.
Featherstone, Joseph, "Bernard Malamud," Atlantic, CCXIX
   (March, 1967), 97-8.
Friedberg, Maurice, "History and Imagination: Two Views
   of the Beiless Case," Midstream, XII (November, 1966),
   71-3.
Friedman, Alan W., "The Hero as Schnook," SoR, IV (Oc-
   tober, 1968), 927-44.
Gunn, Giles B., "Bernard Malamud and the High Cost of
   Living" in Scott, N.A., Jr., ed., Adversity and Grace,
   79-82.
Handy, William J., "Malamud's THE FIXER, Another Look,"
   NWR, VIII (Spring, 1967), 74-82.
Hicks, Granville, "One Man to Stand for Six Million," SatR,
   XLIX (September 10, 1966), 37-9.
Jacobson, Dan, "The Old Country," PR, XXXIV (Spring,
   1967), 307-9.
McColm, Pearlmarie, "The Revised New Syllabus and the
   Unrevised Old," UDQ, I (Autumn, 1966), 138-41.

Marcus, Mordecai, "The Unsuccessful Malamud," PrS, XLI
    (Spring, 1967), 88-9.
Meeter, G., Philip Roth and Bernard Malamud, 40-3.
Pritchett, C. S., "A Pariah," NYRB (September 22, 1966),
    8-9.
Ratner, Marc L., "The Humanism of Malamud's THE FIX-
    ER," Crit, IX, ii (1967), 81-4.
Richler, Mordecai, "Write, Boychick, Write," NStat, LXXII
    (April 7, 1967), 473-4.
Samuels, Charles T., "The Career of Bernard Malamud,"
    NRep, CLV (September 10, 1966), 19-21.
Scholes, Robert, "Malamud's Latest Novel," NWR, VIII
    (Winter, 1966), 106-8.
Tanner, Tony, "Bernard Malamud and the New Life," CritQ,
    X (1968), 161-8.

THE NATURAL

Baumbach, Jonathan, "The Economy of Love: The Novels
    of Bernard Malamud," KR, XXV (Summer, 1963), 443-8.
    _____, Landscape of Nightmare, 106-11.
Eigner, Edwin M., "Malamud's Use of the Quest Romance,"
    Genre, I (January, 1968), 55-75.
Fiedler, Leslie, "In the Interest of Surprise and Delight,"
    Folio, XX (Summer, 1955), 17-20. Also in Fiedler, L.,
    No! In Thunder, 101-5.
Greiff, Louis K., "Quest and Defeat in THE NATURAL,"
    Thoth, VIII (Winter, 1967), 23-34.
Gunn, Giles B., "Bernard Malamud and the High Cost of
    Living" in Scott, N.A., Jr., ed., Adversity and Grace,
    65-70.
Hoyt, Charles A., "Bernard Malamud and the New Romanti-
    cism" in Moore, H.T., ed., Contemporary American
    Novelists, 77-9.
Klein, M., "Bernard Malamud: The Sadness of Goodness,"
    After Alienation, 255-63.
Meeter, G., Philip Roth and Bernard Malamud, 24-6.
Podhoretz, Norman, "Achilles in Left Field," Ctary, XV
    (March, 1953), 321-6.
Ratner, Marc L., "Style and Humanity in Malamud's Fic-
    tion," MR, V (Summer, 1964), 668-70.
Richman, S., Bernard Malamud, 27-49.
Shulman, Robert, "Myth, Mr. Eliot, and the Comic Novel,"
    MFS, XII (Winter, 1966-67), 399-403.
Siegel, Ben, "Victims in Motion: Bernard Malamud's Sad

and Bitter Clowns," NWR, V (Spring, 1962), 69-70. Al-
so in Waldmeir, J. J., ed., Recent American Fiction,
203-4.
Solotaroff, Theodore, "Bernard Malamud's Fiction: The Old
Life and the New," Ctary, XXXIII (March, 1962), 198-200.
Tanner, Tony, "Bernard Malamud and the New Life," CritQ,
X (Spring-Summer, 1968), 152-5.
Turner, Frederick W., III., "Myth Inside and Out: Mala-
mud's THE NATURAL," Novel, I (Winter, 1968), 133-9.
Wasserman, Earl R., "THE NATURAL: Malamud's World
Ceres," CRAS, IX (Fall, 1965), 438-60.

A NEW LIFE

Baumbach, Jonathan, "The Economy of Love: The Novels of
Bernard Malamud," KR, XXV (Summer, 1963), 439-43.
_____, Landscape of Nightmare, 102-6.
Daniels, Sally, "Flights and Evasions," MinnR, II (Summer,
1962), 551-4.
Eigner, Edwin M., "Malamud's Use of the Quest Romance,"
Genre, I (January, 1968), 55-75.
Elman, Richard M., "Malamud on Campus," Cweal, LXXV
(October 27, 1961), 114-15.
Goodhart, Eugene, "Fantasy and Reality," Midstream, VII
(Autumn, 1961), 102-5.
Gunn, Giles B., "Bernard Malamud and the High Cost of
Living" in Scott, N.A., Jr., ed., Adversity and Grace,
76-9.
Halley, Anne, "The Good Life in Recent Fiction, MR, III
(Autumn, 1961), 190-6.
Hartt, J.N., "The Return of Moral Passion," YR, LI, ii
(Winter, 1962), 304-5.
Hicks, Granville, in Balakian, N., and C. Simmons, eds.,
Creative Present, 222-4.
Hollander, John, "To Find the Westward Path," PR, XXIX
(Winter, 1962), 137-9.
Hoyt, Charles A., "Bernard Malamud and the New Romanti-
cism" in Moore, H.T., ed., Contemporary American
Novelists, 75-6.
Hyman, Stanley E., "A New Life for a Good Man," New
Leader, XLIV (October 2, 1961), 24-5. Also in Koste-
lanetz, R., ed., On Contemporary Literature, 442-6.
Also in Hyman, S. E., Standards, 33-7.
Kermode, Frank, in NStat, LXIII (March 30, 1962), 453.
Also in Kermode, F., Continuities, 221-2.
Klein, M., "Bernard Malamud: The Sadness of Goodness,"
After Alienation, 280-93.

Ludwig, J., Recent American Novelists, 39-41.
Lyons, J. O., College Novel in America, 161-2.
Maloff, Saul, "Between the Real and the Absurd," Nation,
    CXCIII (November 18, 1961), 407-8.
Mandel, Ruth B., "Bernard Malamud's THE ASSISTANT and
    A NEW LIFE: Ironic Affirmations," Crit, VII, ii (Win-
    ter, 1965), 110-21.
Meeter, G., Philip Roth and Bernard Malamud, 27-30.
Ratner, Marc L., "Style and Humanity in Malamud's Fic-
    tion," MR, V (Summer, 1964), 670-7.
Richman, S., Bernard Malamud, 78-97.
Siegel, Ben, "Victims in Motion: Bernard Malamud's Sad
    and Bitter Clowns," NWR, V (Spring, 1962), 77-80. Al-
    so in Waldmeir, J.J., ed., Recent American Fiction,
    211-14.
Solotaroff, Theodore, "Bernard Malamud's Fiction: The Old
    Life and the New," Ctary, XXXIII (March, 1962), 201-4.
Tanner, Tony, "Bernard Malamud and the New Life," CritQ,
    X (Spring-Summer, 1968), 157-60.
White, Robert L., "The English Instructor as Hero... Two
    Novels by Roth and Malamud," ForumH, IV (Winter, 1963),
    16-22.

BIBLIOGRAPHY

Kosofsky, Rita N., Bernard Malamud; An Annotated Check-
    list, Kent, Ohio: Kent State Un. Pr., 1969.
Richman, S., Bernard Malamud, 150-3.

MANFRED, FREDERICK, PSEUD. (FEIKE FEIKEMA), 1912-

GENERAL

Anon., "West of the Mississippi: An Interview with Fred-
    erick Manfred," Crit, II, iii (Winter, 1959), 35-56.
DeBoer, Peter P., "Frederick Feikema Manfred: Spiritual
    Naturalist," The Reformed Journal, XIII (April, 1963), 19-
    23. (Not seen.)
Milton, John R., "Frederick Feikema Manfred," WR, XXII
    (Spring, 1958), 181-99.
_____, "Voice from Siouxland: Frederick Feikema Man-
    fred," CE, XIX (December, 1957), 104-11.
Swallow, Alan, "The Mavericks," Crit, II, iii (1959), 88-90.
    Also in Swallow, A., An Editor's Essays of Two Decades,
    Seattle and Denver: Experiment Pr., 353-55.
Ter Maat, Cornelius J., "Three Novelists and a Community:

A Study of American Novelists with Dutch Calvinist Origins," DA, XXIV (1963), 751 (Michigan).

BOY ALMIGHTY

Milton, John R., "Frederick Feikema Manfred," WR, XXII (Spring, 1958), 184-5.

THE BROTHER (See WORLD'S WANDERER)

THE CHOKECHERRY TREE

Milton, John R., "Voice from Siouxland: Frederick Feikema Manfred," CE, XIX (December, 1957), 106-7.

THE GIANT (See WORLD'S WANDERER)

THE GOLDEN BOWL

Milton, John R., "Frederick Feikema Manfred," WR, XXII (Spring, 1958), 181-2.
_____, "Voice from Siouxland: Frederick Feikema Manfred," CE, XIX (December, 1957), 105-6.

LORD GRIZZLY

Austin, James C., "Legend, Myth and Symbol in Frederick Manfred's LORD GRIZZLY," Crit, VI, iii (Winter, 1963-64), 122-30.
Milton, John R., "American Fiction and Man," Cresset, XVIII, iii (1955), 16-20.
_____, "Frederick Feikema Manfred," WR, XXII (Spring, 1958), 192-6.
_____, "LORD GRIZZLY: Rhythm, Form and Meaning in the Western Novel," WAL, I (Spring, 1966), 6-14.
_____, "Voice from Siouxland: Frederick Feikema Manfred," CE, XIX (December, 1957), 109-10.

MORNING RED

Milton, John R., "Frederick Feikema Manfred," WR, XXII (Spring, 1958), 190-2.
_____, in Cresset, XX (September, 1957), 27-8.
_____, "Voice from Siouxland: Frederick Feikema Manfred," CE, XIX (December 1957), 110-11.

THE PRIMITIVE (See also WORLD'S WANDERER)

Lyons, J. O. , College Novel in America, 88-9.

RIDERS OF JUDGMENT

Milton, John R. , "Recreation of the Old West: A Postscript
on RIDERS OF JUDGMENT," WR, XXII (Spring, 1958),
196-9.

THIS IS THE YEAR

Meyer, Roy W. , "The Farm Novelist as Social Critic," The
Middle Western Farm Novel in the Twentieth Century,
Lincoln: Un. of Nebraska Pr. , 1965, 122-6.
Milton, John R. , "Frederick Feikema Manfred," WR, XXII
(Spring, 1958), 182-3.
_____, "Voice from Siouxland: Frederick Feikema Man-
fred," CE, XIX (December, 1957), 106.

WORLD'S WANDERER

Milton, John R. , "The American Novel: The Search for
Home, Tradition, and Identity," WHR, XVI (Spring, 1962),
175-6.
_____, "Frederick Feikema Manfred," WR, XXII (Spring,
1958), 185-90.
_____, "Voice from Siouxland: Frederick Feikema Man-
fred," CE, XIX (December, 1957), 107-9.

BIBLIOGRAPHY

Kellogg, George, "Frederick Manfred: A Bibliography,"
TCL, XI (April, 1965), 30-5.   Reprinted in pamphlet form
by Swallow Pr. , 1968.

MANNING, OLIVIA

GENERAL

Pendry, E. D. , New Feminism of English Fiction, 172-84.

FRIENDS AND HEROES

Anon. , "The Irony of Survival," TLS (November 4, 1965),
973.   Also in T. L. S.: Essays and Reviews from the
Times Literary Supplement 1965, 36-9.

THE GREAT FORTUNE

Allen, W. , Modern Novel, 261-2.

THE SPOILT CITY

Allen, W. , Modern Novel, 261-2.

MARCH, WILLIAM, PSEUD. (W. E. M. CAMPBELL), 1894-
1954.

GENERAL

Cooke, Alastair, "Introduction," A William March Omnibus,
    N. Y. : Rinehart, 1956.
Crowder, Richard, "The Novels of William March," UKCR,
    XV (Winter, 1948), 111-29.
Going, William T. , "William March's Alabama," AlaR, XVI
    (1963), 243-58.
Silva, Frederick E. , "The Cracked Looking-Glass: A Criti-
    cal Study of the Novels of William March (1894-1954),"
    DA, XXVIII (1967), 2264A (Indiana).

THE BAD SEED

Going, William T. , "A Footnote to 'THE BAD SEED: A
    Modern Elsie Venner'," WHR, XVIII (Spring, 1964), 175.
Hamblen, Abigail A. , "THE BAD SEED: A Modern ELSIE
    VENNER," WHR, XVII (Autumn, 1963), 361-3.

COME IN AT THE DOOR

Crowder, Richard, "The Novels of William March," UKCR,
    XV (Winter, 1948), 117-21.

COMPANY K

Crowder, Richard, "The Novels of William March," UKCR,
    XV (Winter, 1948), 111-17.
Waldmeir, J. J. , American Novels of the Second World War,
    41-2.

THE LOOKING GLASS

Crowder, Richard, "The Novels of William March," UKCR,
    XV (Winter, 1948), 124-9.

THE TALLONS

Crowder, Richard, "The Novels of William March," UKCR, XV (Winter, 1948), 121-4.

MARQUAND, JOHN PHILLIPS, 1893-1960

GENERAL

Allen, W., Modern Novel, 183-5.

Auchincloss, Louis, "Marquand and O'Hara: The Novel of Manners," Nation, CLXCI (November 19, 1960), 383-4. Also in Auchincloss, L., Reflections of a Jacobite, Boston: Houghton-Mifflin, 1961, 142-8.

Beach, J. W., American Fiction, 253-70.

Benedict, Stewart H., "The Pattern of Determinism in J. P. Marquand's Novels," BSTCF, II, ii (Winter, 1961-62), 60-4.

Blankenship, R., American Literature, 751-5.

Brady, Charles A., "John Phillips Marquand: Martini-Age Victorian" in Gardiner, H. C., ed., Fifty Years of the American Novel, 107-34.

Brown, John M., and Maxwell Geismar, "John P. Marquand: The Man and the Writer," SatR, XLIII (August 13, 1960), 14-15; 39.

Cochran, Robert W., "In Search of Perspective: A Study of the Serious Novels of John P. Marquand," DA, XVIII (1958), 1427-28 (Mich.).

Geismar, M., American Moderns, 161-4.

Glick, Nathan, "Marquand's Vanishing American Aristocracy: Good Manners and the Good Life," Ctary, IX (May, 1950), 435-41.

Greene, George, "A Tunnel from Persepolis: The Legacy of John Marquand," QQ, LXXIII (Autumn, 1966), 345-56.

Gross, J. J., John P. Marquand.

Gurko, L., Angry Decade, 208-12.

_____, "The High-Level Formula of J. P. Marquand," ASch, XXI (Autumn, 1952), 443-53.

Harris, Bennett, "The Literary Achievement of John P. Marquand," DA, XXIII (1962), 1701-2 (Cincinnati).

Hicks, Granville, "Marquand of Newburyport," Harpers, CC (April, 1950), 101-8.

Holman, C. Hugh, John P. Marquand (UMPAW, 46), Minneapolis: Un. of Minn., 1965.

Johnson, Robert O., "Mr. Marquand and Lord Tennyson," RS, XXXII (March, 1964), 28-38.

Kazin, Alfred, "John P. Marquand and the American Failure," Atlantic, CCII (November, 1958), 152-6.
Kuhlman, Thomas A., "The Humane Social Criticism of John P. Marquand," DA, XXVIII (1968), 3188A-89A (Brown).
Millgate, M., American Social Fiction, 182-5.
Oppenheimer, Franz M., "Lament for Unbought Grace: The Novels of John P. Marquand," AR, XVIII (Spring, 1958), 41-61.
Prescott, O., In My Opinion, 174-9.
Roberts, Kenneth, "The Memories of John P. Marquand," SatR, XXXIX (September 15, 1956), 14-15.
Smith, William J., "J. P. Marquand, Esq.," Cweal, LXIX (November 7, 1958), 148-50.
Steiner, George, "Marquand Country," T&T (October 10, 1959), 1096+.
Van Gelder, Robert, "An Interview with a Best-Selling Author: John Marquand," Cosmopolitan, CXXII (March, 1947), 18; 150-2.
_____, Writers on Writing, 38-41.
Wagenknecht, E., Cavalcade of the American Novel, 438-43.
Weeks, Edward, "John P. Marquand," Atlantic, CCVI (October, 1960), 74-6.

B. F. 'S DAUGHTER

Gross, J. J., John P. Marquand, 101-10.
Oppenheimer, Franz, "Lament for Unbought Grace: The Novels of John P. Marquand," AR, XVIII (Spring, 1958), 51-2.

H. M. PULHAM, ESQUIRE
(DON'T ASK QUESTIONS, English title)

Greene, George, "A Tunnel from Persepolis: The Legacy of John P. Marquand," QQ, LXXIII (Autumn, 1966), 350-1.
Gross, J. J., John P. Marquand, 64-83.
Johnson, Robert O., "Mr. Marquand and Lord Tennyson," RS, XXXII (1964), 29-32.
Marquand, John P., "Apley, Wickford Point, and Pulham: My Early Struggles," Atlantic, CXCVIII (September, 1956), 73-4.
Oppenheimer, Franz, "Lament for Unbought Grace: The Novels of John P. Marquand," AR, XVIII (Spring, 1958), 46-8.

THE LATE GEORGE APLEY

Beach, J.W., American Fiction, 259-70.
Eisinger, Charles E., "Class and American Fiction: The
    Aristocracy in Some Novels of the Thirties" in Lanzinger,
    K., ed., Americana-Austriaca, 138-40.
Goodwin, George, Jr., "The Last Hurrahs: George Apley
    and Frank Skeffington," MR, I (May, 1960), 461-71.
Gordon, Edward J., "What's Happened to Humor?" EJ,
    XLVII (1958), 127-33.
Greene, George, "A Tunnel from Persepolis: The Legacy
    of John Marquand," QQ, LXXIII (Autumn, 1966), 343-9.
Gross, J.J., John P. Marquand, 31-50.
Johnson, Robert O., "John P. Marquand and the Novel of
    Manners," DA, XXV (1965), 7271-72 (Un. of Washington).
_____, "Mary Monahan: Marquand's Sentimental Slip?"
    RS, XXXIII (December, 1965), 208-13.
Macauley, Robie, "Let Me Tell You About the Rich...,"
    KR, XXVII (Autumn, 1965), 664-6.
Marquand, John P., "Apley, Wickford Point, and Pulham:
    My Early Struggles," Atlantic, CXCVIII (September, 1956),
    71-2.
Oppenheimer, Franz, "Lament for Unbought Grace: The Novels
    of John P. Marquand," AR, XVIII (Spring, 1958), 41-5.
Stuckey, W.J., Pulitzer Prize Novels, 112-16.
Warren, Austin, "The Last Puritans," The New England Con-
    science, Ann Arbor: Un. of Michigan Pr., 1966, 195-
    201.

LIFE AT HAPPY KNOLL

Cosman, N., "Speakable Gentleman," Nation, CLXXXV (Au-
    gust 3, 1957), 56-7.

MELVILLE GOODWIN, U.S.A.

Geismar, Maxwell, in SatR, XXXIV (September 19, 1951),
    11. Also in Geismar, M., American Moderns, 159-61.
Gross, J.J., John P. Marquand, 127-40.
Johnson, Robert O., "Mr. Marquand and Lord Tennyson,"
    RS, XXXII (1964), 35-8.
Oppenheimer, Franz, "Lament for Unbought Grace: The
    Novels of John P. Marquand," AR, XVIII (Spring, 1958),
    58-60.

POINT OF NO RETURN

Geismar, Maxwell, in NYTBR (March 6, 1949), 4.   Also in
Geismar, G. , American Moderns, 156-9.
Greene, George, "A Tunnel from Persepolis: The Legacy of
John Marquand," QQ, LXXIII (Autumn, 1966), 351-2.
Gross, J. J. , John P. Marquand, 111-26.
Haugh, Robert F. , "The Dilemma of John P. Marquand,"
MAQR, LIX (December 6, 1952), 19-24.
Hicks, Granville, "John Marquand of Newburyport," Harpers,
CC (April, 1950), 101-8.
Johnson, Robert O. , "John P. Marquand and the Novel of
Manners," DA, XXV (1965), 7271-72 (Un. of Wash.).
_____, "Mr. Marquand and Lord Tennyson," RS, XXXII
(1964), 32-5.
Oppenheimer, Franz, "Lament for Unbought Grace: The
Novels of John P. Marquand," AR, XVIII (Spring, 1958),
52-7.
Scott, W. B. , in Furioso, IV (Summer, 1949), 76-8.
Van Nostrand, Albert D. , "After Marquand, the Deluge,"
EJ, XLVIII (February, 1959), 55-65 passim.
_____, "Fiction's Flagging Man of Commerce," EJ,
XLVIII (January, 1959), 6-11.

REPENT IN HASTE

Gross, J. J. , John P. Marquand, 96-101.

SINCERELY, WILLIS WADE

Gross, J. J. , John P. Marquand, 141-52.
Oppenheimer, Franz, "Lament for Unbought Grace: The
Novels of John P. Marquand," AR, XVIII (Spring, 1958),
57-8.

SO LITTLE TIME

Gray, J. , On Second Thought, 91-3.
Gross, J. J. , John P. Marquand, 84-96.
Oppenheimer, Franz, "Lament for Unbought Grace: The
Novels of John P. Marquand," AR, XVIII (Spring, 1958),
50-1.

WICKFORD POINT

Beach, J. W. , American Fiction, 254-9.
Eisinger, Charles E. , "Class and American Fiction: The

Aristocracy in Some Novels of the Thirties" in Lanzinger, K., ed., Americana-Austriaca, 140-1.

Gray, J., On Second Thought, 88-90.

Greene, George, "A Tunnel from Persepolis: The Legacy of John Marquand," QQ, LXXIII (Autumn, 1966), 349-50.

Gross, J. J., John P. Marquand, 51-63.

Marquand, John P., "Apley, Wickford Point, and Pulham: My Early Struggles," Atlantic, CXCVIII (September, 1956), 72-3.

Oppenheimer, Franz, "Lament for Unbought Grace: The Novels of John P. Marquand," AR, XVIII (Spring, 1958), 48-50.

WOMEN AND THOMAS HARROW

Gardiner, H. C., "Hero as Yo-Yo," America, C, ii (October 11, 1958), 51; 53. Also in Gardiner, H. C., In All Conscience, 126-7.

Greene, George, "A Tunnel from Persepolis: The Legacy of John Marquand," QQ, LXXIII (Autumn, 1966), 352-6.

Gross, J. J., John P. Marquand, 158-75.

Johnson, Robert Owen, "John P. Marquand and the Novel of Manners," DA, XXV (1965), 7271-72 (Un. of Wash.).

Kazin, A., Contemporaries, 122-30.

_____, "John P. Marquand and the American Failure," Atlantic, CCII (November, 1958), 152-6.

Smith, William J., "J. P. Marquand, Esq.," Cweal, LXIX (November 7, 1958), 148-50.

BIBLIOGRAPHY

Gross, J. J., John P. Marquand, 181-5.

White, William, "John P. Marquand Since 1950," BB, XXI (May-August, 1956), 230-4.

_____, "Marquandiana," BB, XX (January-April, 1950), 8-12.

MILLER, HENRY, 1891-

GENERAL

Anon., "The Tropic Myth," TLS (November 1, 1963), 892.

Baxter, Annette K., Henry Miller, Expatriate (Critical Essays in English and American Literature, No. 5), Pittsburgh: Un. of Pittsburgh Pr., 1961.

Bedford, Richard C., "The Apocatastasis of Henry Miller,"

DA, XXI (1960), 1560-1 (Iowa).

Bode, Elroy, "The World on Its Own Terms: A Brief for
Steinbeck, Miller and Simenon," SWR, LIII (1968), 406-16.

Brophy, Brigid, "The Last Time I F___d Paris," LonM,
n. s. III (June, 1963), 74-9.

Brown, Lionel, "King of the Four Letter Words," Modern
Man, VI (August, 1956), 14-18; 50-1. (Not seen.)

Capouya, Emile, "Henry Miller," Salmagundi, I (Fall, 1965),
81-7.

Cockcroft, George P., "The Two Henry Millers," DA,
XXCIII (1967), 669A (Columbia).

Dick, Kenneth C., Henry Miller: Colossus of One, Sittard,
The Netherlands: Alberts, 1967.

Donohue, Denis, "Dry Dreams," NYRB, V (October 14,
1965), 5-8.

Durrell, Lawrence, ed., "Introduction," The Henry Miller
Reader, Norfolk: New Directions, 1959.

_____, "Studies in Genius: VIII--Henry Miller," Horizon,
XX (July, 1949), 45-61. Also in Seaver, Richard, Terry
Southern, and Alexander Trocchi, eds., Writers in Revolt: An Anthology, N. Y.: Frederick Fell, 1963, 130-
45. Also in Wickes, G., ed., Henry Miller and the Critics, 86-107.

_____, and Alfred Perlès, Art and Outrage: A Corre-
spondence About Henry Miller, N. Y.: Dutton, 1961.

Fiedler, Leslie A., "The Beginning of the Thirties: Depression, Return and Rebirth," Waiting for the End, 37-
45.

Finkelstein, S., Existentialism and Alienation in American
Literature, 203-10.

Fruchter, Norman, "In Defense of Henry Miller," T&T,
XLII (April 6, 1961), 572-3.

Glicksberg, Charles I., "Henry Miller: Individualist in Ex-
tremis," SWR, XXXIII (Summer, 1948), 289-95.

Gordon, William A., "Henry Miller and the Romantic Tradition," DA, XXIV (1964), 3335-6 (Tulane).

_____, Mind and Art of Henry Miller.

_____, Writer and Critic: A Correspondence with Henry
Miller, Baton Rouge: Louisiana State Un. Pr., 1968.

Hassan, I., Literature of Silence.

_____, "The Literature of Silence: From Henry Miller to
Beckett to Burroughs," Encounter, XXVIII (January, 1967),
74-82.

Haverstick, John, and William Barrett, "Henry Miller: Man
in Quest of Life," SatR, XL (August 3, 1957), 8-10.

Hoffman, Frederick J., Freudianism and the Literary Mind,
2nd ed., Baton Rouge: La. State Un. Pr., 1957, 290-6.

_____, "Henry Miller, Defender of the Marginal Life" in French, W. , ed. , Thirties, 73-80.

Jackson, Paul R. , "Henry Miller: The Autobiographical Romances," DA, XXVIII (1967), 678A (Columbia).

Kermode, Frank, "Henry Miller and John Betjeman," Encounter, XVI (March, 1961), 69-75.

_____, Puzzles and Epiphanies, 140-50.

Kleine, Don, "Innocence Forbidden: Henry Miller in the Tropics," PrS, XXXIII (Summer, 1959), 125-30.

Lee, Alwyn, "Henry Miller - The Pathology of Isolation" in New World Writing, Second Mentor Selection, N.Y.: New American Library, 1952, 340-7.

Lord, Russell, "Henry Miller," Harvard Wake, I (June, 1945), 13-16.

Lund, Mary G. , "Henry Miller: A Fierce Oracle," North Amer. Rev. , IV, i (January, 1967), 18-21.

Manning, Hugo, "Apropos Henry Miller," Wind and the Rain, II (Winter, 1945), 166-8. (Not seen.)

Mauriac, C. , New Literature, 51-9.

May, James B. , "Henry Miller: An Individualist as Social Thinker," Trace, No. 40 (January-March, 1961), 24-31.

Miller, Henry, The Books in My Life, N. Y.: New Directions, 1952.

_____, and others, Of-By-and About Henry Miller, a Collection of Pieces, Yonkers, N. Y.: Alicat Bookshop Pr. , 1947.

Mitchell, Edward B. , "Artists and Artists: The 'Aesthetics' of Henry Miller," TSLL, VIII (Spring, 1966), 103-15.

_____, "Henry Miller: The Artist as Seer," DA, XXVI (1965), 1047 (Conn.).

Moore, Thomas H. , ed. , Henry Miller on Writing, N. Y.: New Directions, 1964.

Moravia, Alberto, "Two American Writers (1949)," SR, LXVIII (Summer, 1960), 473-7.

Muller, Herbert J. , "The World of Henry Miller," KR, II, iii (Summer, 1940), 312-18. Also in Wickes, G. , ed. , Henry Miller and the Critics, 44-51.

Nelson, Jane A. , "Form and Image in the Fiction of Henry Miller," DA, XXVIII (1967), 2256A (Michigan).

Nicholson, Homer K. , Jr. , "O Altitudo: A Comparison of the Writings of Walt Whitman, D. H. Lawrence, and Henry Miller," DA, XVII (1957), 2614 (Vanderbilt).

Omarr, Sydney, Henry Miller: His World of Urania, London: Villiers Pubs. , 1960.

Perlès, Alfred, My Friend Henry Miller, London: Neville Spearman, 1955; N. Y.: John Day, 1956.

Porter, Bern, ed. , The Happy Rock, Berkeley: B. Porter,

1945.
Rahv, Philip, "Sketches in Criticism: Henry Miller," Image
and Idea, 159-66. Also in Wickes, G. , ed. , Henry Mil-
ler and the Critics, 77-85. Also in Rahv, P. , Litera-
ture and the Sixth Sense, 88-94.
Read, Herbert, "Henry Miller" in Wickes, G. , ed. , Henry
Miller and the Critics, 111-18.
_____, The Tenth Muse; Essays in Criticism, N. Y. :
Horizon Pr. , 1958, 250-55.
Rexroth, Kenneth, "The Neglected Henry Miller," Nation,
CLXXXI (November 5, 1955), 385-7. Also in Nation
(Periodical). A View of the Nation, 31-7.
_____, "The Reality of Henry Miller," Bird in the Bush;
Obvious Essays, N. Y. : New Directions, 1959, 154-67.
Also in Wickes, G. , ed. , Henry Miller and the Critics,
119-31.
Rode, Alex, "Henry Miller: The Novelist as Liberator,"
Américas, XVIII (January, 1966), 41-3.
Rose, Edward J. , "The Aesthetics of Civil Disobedience:
Henry Miller, Twentieth Century Transcendentalist,"
Edge (Edmonton, Canada), I, i (Autumn, 1963), 5-16.
Shapiro, Karl, "The Greatest Living Author," Two Cities
(December, 1959). Also in Shapiro, K. , In Defense of
Ignorance, N. Y. : Random House, 1960, 313-38.
Smithline, Arnold, "Henry Miller and the Transcendental
Spirit," ESQ, No. 43 (1966), 50-6. Also in IHML, No.
7 (March 1966), 3-10.
Southern, Terry, "Miller: Only the Beginning," Nation,
CXCIII (November 18, 1961), 399-401.
Stuhlmann, Gunter, ed. , Henry Miller Letters to Anaïs Nin,
N. Y. : Putnam's, 1965.
Traschen, Isador, "Henry Miller: The Ego and I," SAQ,
LXV (Summer, 1966), 345-54.
White, Emil, ed. , Henry Miller - Between Heaven and Hell:
A Symposium, Big Sur, Calif. : Emil White, 1961.
Widmer, K. , Henry Miller.
_____, "The Rebel-Buffoon: Henry Miller's Legacy" in
Wickes, G. , ed. , Henry Miller and the Critics, 132-46.
Wickes, George, "The Art of Fiction XXVIII: Henry Miller,"
ParisR, No. 28 (Summer-Fall, 1962), 129-59. Also in
Writers at Work, 2nd ser. , 165-91.
_____, Henry Miller.
_____, ed. , Henry Miller and the Critics.
_____, "Henry Miller at Seventy," ClareQ, IX, ii (Winter,
1962), 5-20.
_____, ed. , Lawrence Durrell and Henry Miller: A Pri-
vate Correspondence, N. Y. : Dutton, 1964.

Williams, John, "Henry Miller: The Success of Failure,"
   VQR, XLIV (Spring, 1968), 225-45.
Wood, Richard C., ed., Collector's Quest: The Correspondence of Henry Miller and J. Rives Childs, 1947-
   1965, Charlottesville: Un. Pr. of Virginia, 1968.

BLACK SPRING

Hassan, I., Literature of Silence, 67-72.
Wickes, G., Henry Miller, 24-7.
Widmer, K., Henry Miller, 41-51.

NEXUS (See also THE ROSY CRUCIFIXION)

Hassan, I., Literature of Silence, 100-4.

PLEXUS (See also THE ROSY CRUCIFIXION)

Anon., "The Tropic Myth," TLS (November 1, 1963), 892.
   Also in T.L.S.: Essays and Reviews from the Times
   Literary Supplement, 1963, 215-21.
Hassan, I., Literature of Silence, 93-100.
Symons, J., "Goodbye, Henry Miller," Critical Occasions,
   126-32.

THE ROSY CRUCIFIXION

Gordon, W. A., Mind and Art of Henry Miller, 138-74.
Hassan, I., Literature of Silence, 85-109.
Soroyan, Chesley, "THE ROSEY CRUCIFIXION: A Review,"
   Points, No. 4 (October-November, 1949), 79-83.
Wickes, G., Henry Miller, 38-40.
Widmer, K., Henry Miller, 81-95.

SEXUS (See also THE ROSY CRUCIFIXION)

Hassan, I., Literature of Silence, 87-92.

THE SMILE AT THE FOOT OF THE LADDER

Greer, Scott, et. al., "To Be or Not: 4 Opinions on Henry
   Miller's THE SMILE AT THE FOOT OF THE LADDER,"
   Tiger's Eye, I, No. 5 (October 20, 1948), 68-72.

TROPIC OF CANCER

Allen, W., Modern Novel, 180-1.

Anon., "Out of Bond. Henry Miller: TROPIC OF CANCER,"
TLS (April 12, 1963), 243.   Also in T. L. S.: Essays
and Reviews from The Times Literary Supplement, 1963,
212-15.

Brophy, Brigid, in LonM, III (June, 1963), 74-9. Also in
Brophy, B., Don't Never Forget, 231-8.

Ciardi, John, "A Critic's Verdict," SatR, XLV (June 30,
1962), 13.   Also in Girvetz, Harry K., ed., Contemporary Moral Issues, Belmont, Calif.: Wadsworth, 1963,
240-2.

Foster, Steven, "A Critical Appraisal of Henry Miller's
TROPIC OF CANCER," TCL, IX (January, 1964), 196-
208.

Friedman, Alan, "The Pitching of Love's Mansion in the
TROPICS of Henry Miller" in Whitbread, T. B., ed.,
Seven Contemporary Authors, 25-48.

Fuller, E., Books With the Men Behind Them, 21-5+.

Gordon, W. A., Mind and Art of Henry Miller, 85-109.

Hassan, I., Literature of Silence, 59-67.

Highet, Gilbert, "Henry Miller's Stream of Consciousness,"
Horizon, IV (November, 1961), 104-5.

Hyman, S. E., "The Innocence of Henry Miller," Standards,
12-16.

Kauffmann, Stanley, "An Old Shocker Comes Home," NRep,
CXLV (July 10, 1961), 17-19. Also in Wickes, G., ed.,
Henry Miller and the Critics, 154-60.

Levin, Harry, "Commonwealth of Massachusetts vs. TROPIC
OF CANCER," in Wickes, G., ed., Henry Miller and the
Critics, 168-74.

Littlejohn, David, "The Tropics of Miller," NRep, CXLVI
(March 5, 1962), 31-5.

Lowenfels, Walter, "A Note on TROPIC OF CANCER - Paris,
1931," in Wickes, G., ed., Henry Miller and the Critics,
16-19.

_____, "Unpublished Preface to TROPIC OF CANCER,"
MR, V (Spring, 1964), 481-91.

Moore, Harry T., "From Under the Counter to Front Shelf,"
in Wickes, G., ed., Henry Miller and the Critics, 149-
53.

Orwell, George, "Inside the Whale," Such, Such Were the
Joys, 154-66. Also in Collected Essays, Journalism and
Letters of George Orwell, Vol. I., ed. by Sonia Orwell,
and Ian August, N. Y.: Harcourt, 1968, 493-527. Also in
Wickes, G., ed., Henry Miller and the Critics, 149-53.

Robischon, Thomas, "A Day in Court with the Literary
Critics," MR, VI (Autumn-Winter, 1964-65), 101-10.

Schorer, Mark, "Commonwealth of Massachusetts vs. TROP-

IC OF CANCER," in Wickes, G., ed., Henry Miller and the Critics, 161-7.
Shapiro, Karl, "Introduction," Tropic of Cancer, N.Y.: Grove, 1961.
Way, Brian, "Sex and Language: Obscene Words in D.H. Lawrence and Henry Miller," New Left Rev., No. 27 (September-October, 1964), 66-80.
Wickes, G., Henry Miller, 21-4.
Widmer, K., Henry Miller, 17-40.
Wilson, Edmund, "Twilight of the Expatriates," NRep, LXXXIV (March 9, 1938), 140. Also in Wilson, E., Shores of Light, 705-10. Also in Wickes, G., ed., Henry Miller and the Critics, 25-30.
Yerbury, Grace D., "Of a City Beside a River," WWR, X (September, 1964), 70-3.

TROPIC OF CAPRICORN

Friedman, Alan, "The Pitching of Love's Mansion in the TROPICS of Henry Miller," in Whitbread, T.B., ed., Seven Contemporary Authors, 25-48.
Gordon, W.A., Mind and Art of Henry Miller, 110-37.
Hassan, I., Literature of Silence, 72-81.
Littlejohn, David, "The Tropics of Miller," NRep, CXLVI (March 5, 1962), 31-5.
Rosenfeld, Paul, "The Traditions of Henry Miller," Nation, CXLIX (November 4, 1939), 502-3. Also in Miller, H., and others, Of-By-And About Henry Miller, Yonkers, N.Y.: Alicat Bookshop Pr., 1947.
Way, Brian, "Sex and Language: Obscene Words in D.H. Lawrence and Henry Miller," New Left Rev., No. 27 (September-October, 1964), 66-80.
Wickes, G., Henry Miller, 27-9.
Widmer, K., Henry Miller, 71-3; 81-5; 99-110.

BIBLIOGRAPHY

Renken, Maxine, "Bibliography of Henry Miller: 1945-1961," TCL, VII (January, 1962), 90-180. Also in pamphlet form, Swallow Pr., 1962.
Riley, Esta Lou, Henry Miller: An Informal Bibliography, 1924-1960, (Fort Hays Studies. New Series: Bibliog Ser., No. 1) Hays, Kansas: Fort Kansas State College, 1962.

MILLER, MERLE, 1918-

THE SURE THING

Aldridge, J.W., After the Lost Generation, 163-9.

THAT WINTER

Aldridge, J.W., After the Lost Generation, 157-65.

MITFORD, NANCY, 1904-

GENERAL

Karl, F. R., Contemporary English Novel, 276-7.
Pendry, E. D., New Feminism of English Fiction, 54-6.

DON'T TELL ALFRED

Walcutt, C.C., Man's Changing Mask, 229-36.
Waugh, Evelyn, in LonM, VII (December, 1960), 65-8.

MOORE, BRIAN, 1921-

GENERAL

Dahlie, Hallvard, "Brian Moore: An Interview," TamR, No.
    46 (Winter, 1968), 7-29.
_____, "The Novels of Brian Moore," DA, XXIX (1968),
    255A (Un. of Wash.).
Foster, John W., "Crisis and Ritual in Brian Moore's Bel-
    fast Novels," Eire-Ireland, III (Autumn, 1968), 66-74.
French, Philip, "The Novels of Brian Moore," LonM, n. s.
    V (February, 1966), 86-91.
Fulford, Robert, "Robert Fulford Interviews Brian Moore,"
    TamR, No. 23 (Spring, 1962), 5-18.
Kersnowski, Frank L., "Exit the Anti-Hero," Crit, X, iii
    (1968), 60-71.
Ludwig, Jack, "Brian Moore: Ireland's Loss, Canada's
    Novelist," Crit, V, i (Spring-Summer, 1962), 5-13.
_____, "Exile from the Emerald Isle," Nation, CC (March
    15, 1965), 287-8.
Pacey, D., Creative Writing in Canada, 262-4.
Ricks, Christopher, "The Simple Excellence of Brian Moore,"
    NStat (February 18, 1966), 227-8.

AN ANSWER FROM LIMBO

Allen, Walter, "All for Art," NStat (March 26, 1963), 465-6.
Gilman, Richard, in Ctary, XXXVI (August, 1963), 176-7.
Hicks, Granville, "Asphalt in Bitter Soil," SatR, XLV (October 13, 1962), 20+.
Hornyansky, Michael, "Countries of the Mind," TamR, XXVI (Winter, 1963), 63-7.
Watt, F.W., in UTQ (July, 1963), 395-6.
Woodcock, George, "A Close Shave," CanL (Spring, 1962), 70-2.

THE EMPEROR OF ICE-CREAM

Anon., "Bombing Around Belfast," TLS (February 3, 1966), 77.
Buckeye, Robert, in DR, XLVI (Spring, 1966), 135-9.
Dahlie, Hallvard, "Brian Moore's Broader Vision: THE EMPEROR OF ICE-CREAM," Crit, IX, i (1967), 43-50.
French, Philip, "The Novels of Brian Moore," LonM, n.s., V (February, 1966), 88-90.
Galloway, David D., "Belfast Blues," Spectator (February 4, 1966), 142.
Hicks, Granville, "An Invitation to Live," SatR, XLVIII (September 18, 1965), 97-8.
Raban, J., "Narrative: Time," Techniques of Modern Fiction, 64-6.
Smith, Marion B., "Existential Morality," CanL, No. 28 (Spring, 1966), 68-70.
Taranth, Rajeev, "Deepening Experience: A Note on THE EMPEROR OF ICE-CREAM," LCrit, VI (Summer, 1966), 68-72.

THE FEAST OF LUPERCAL

Horchler, Richard, "A Wrench of Pity," Cweal, LXVI (July 12, 1957), 380-1.
LaFarge, Oliver, "Defeat in a Church School," SatR, XL (April 27, 1957), 15; 27.

THE LUCK OF GINGER COFFEY

Conacher, D.J., in QQ, LXVIII (Summer, 1961), 351-3.
Ludwig, Jack, "Fiction for the Majors," TamR, No. 17 (Autumn, 1960), 65-71.
_____, "A Mirror of Moore," TamR, No. 17 (Winter, 1961), 19-23.

Magid, Norma, "On Loneliness," Cweal   (September 30, 1960), 20-1.

Tallman, Warren, "Irishman's Luck," CanL   (Autumn, 1960), 69-70.

Watt, F.W., in UTQ, XXX (July, 1961), 404-6.

THE LONELY PASSION OF JUDITH HEARN

MacDougall, Robert, in CanF (August, 1956), 111-12.

BIBLIOGRAPHY

Dahlie, Hallvard, in Crit, IX, i (1967), 51-5.

MORGAN, CHARLES, 1894-1958

GENERAL

Duffin, H. C. , Novels and Plays of Charles Morgan.
Priestley, J. B. , "Morgan in a Mirror," NStat (July 2, 1960), 92-3.

A BREEZE IN MORNING

Duffin, H. C. , Novels and Plays of Charles Morgan, 204-9.

THE FOUNTAIN (See SPARKENBROKE TRILOGY)

THE GUNROOM

Brock, James, "Morgan in a Mirror," NStat (July 23, 1960), 125.

THE JUDGE'S STORY

Duffin, H. C. , Novels and Plays of Charles Morgan, 198-203.

PORTRAIT IN A MIRROR (See SPARKENBROKE TRILOGY)

SPARKENBROKE (See SPARKENBROKE TRILOGY)

SPARKENBROKE TRILOGY

Duffin, H. C. , Novels and Plays of Charles Morgan, 171-88.

THE VOYAGE

Duffin, H. C., Novels and Plays of Charles Morgan, 189-97.

MORRIS, WRIGHT, 1910-

GENERAL

Allen, W., Modern Novel, 315-17.
Bleufarb, Sam, "Point of View: An Interview with Wright
  Morris, July, 1958," Accent, XIX (Winter, 1959), 34-46.
Breit, Harvey, "Talk with Wright Morris," NYTBR (June 10,
  1951), 19.
Booth, Wayne C., "The Shaping of Prophecy: Craft and
  Idea in the Novels of Wright Morris," ASch, XXXI (Au-
  tumn, 1962), 608-26.
_____, "The Two Worlds in the Fiction of Wright Mor-
  ris," SR, LXV (Summer, 1957), 375-99.
Carpenter, Frederick, "Wright Morris and the Territory
  Ahead," CE, XXI (December, 1959), 147-56.
Eisinger, C. E., Fiction of the Forties, 328-41.
Fiedler, L., Love and Death in the American Novel, 471-2.
Flanagan, John T., "The Fiction of Wright Morris," SGG,
  III (1961), 209-31.
Guettinger, Roger J., "The Problem with Jigsaw Puzzles:
  Form in the Fiction of Wright Morris," TQ, XI (Spring,
  1968), 209-20.
Howard, L., Wright Morris.
Hunt, John W., Jr., "The Journey Back: The Early Novels
  of Wright Morris," Crit, V, i (Spring-Summer, 1962),
  41-60.
Klein, M., After Alienation, 196-246.
Madden, David, "The Great Plains in the Novels of Wright
  Morris," Crit, IV, iii (Winter, 1961-62), 5-23.
_____, "The Hero and the Witness in Wright Morris'
  Field of Vision," PrS, XXXIV (Fall, 1960), 263-78.
_____, Wright Morris.
Miller, James E., Jr., "The Nebraska Encounter: Willa
  Cather and Wright Morris," PrS, XLI (Summer, 1967),
  165-7.
Morris, Wright, "Letter to a Young Critic," MR, VI (Au-
  tumn-Winter, 1964-65), 93-100.
_____, "National Book Award Address," Crit, IV, iii
  (Winter, 1961-62), 72-5.
_____, "The Origin of a Species, 1942-1956," MR, VII
  (Winter, 1966), 121-35.

Shetty, M. Nalini, "The Fiction of Wright Morris," DA,
    XXVII (1967), 3471A (Pittsburgh).
Trachtenberg, Alan, "The Craft of Vision," Crit, IV, iii
    (Winter, 1961-62), 41-55.
Tucker, Martin, "The Landscape of Wright Morris," LHR,
    No. 7 (1965), 43-51.
Waterman, Arthur E., "The Novels of Wright Morris: An
    Escape from Nostalgia," Crit, IV, iii (Winter, 1961-62),
    24-40.

CAUSE FOR WONDER

Howard, L., Wright Morris, 31-4.
Klein, M., After Alienation, 242-6.

CEREMONY IN LONE TREE

Baumbach, Jonathan, "Wake Before Bomb: CEREMONY IN
    LONE TREE," Crit, IV, iii (Winter, 1961-62), 56-71.
    Also in Baumbach, J., Landscape of Nightmare, 152-69.
Gardiner, Harold C., in America, CIII (July 23, 1960), 481-
    2.
Howard, L., Wright Morris, 26-8.
Klein, M., After Alienation, 238-42.
Madden, D., Wright Morris, 131-55.
Tornquist, Elizabeth, "The New Parochialism," Ctary, XXXI
    (May, 1961), 449-52.
Waterman, Arthur E., "The Novels of Wright Morris: An
    Escape from Nostalgia," Crit, IV, iii (Winter, 1961-62),
    37-9.

THE DEEP SLEEP

Aldridge, John, "Heart of a Secret Tragedy," NYTBR
    (September 13, 1953), 4-5.
Howard, L., Wright Morris, 17-19.
Klein, M., After Alienation, 220-6.
Madden, D., Wright Morris, 92-100.

THE FIELD OF VISION

Hartman, Carl, "Mr. Morris and Some Others," WR, XXI
    (Summer, 1957), 307-13.
Hicks, Granville, in New Leader, XXXIX (October 1, 1956),
    24-5.
Howard, L., Wright Morris, 21-3.
Klein, M., After Alienation, 238-42.

Leer, Norman, "Three American Novels and Contemporary
    Society: A Search for Commitment," WSCL, III, iii
    (Fall, 1962), 76-81.
Madden, D., Wright Morris, 132-5; 140; 148; 153; 154.
Trachtenberg, Alan, "The Craft of Vision," Crit, IV, iii
    (Winter, 1961-62), 47-55.
Waterman, Arthur E., "The Novels of Wright Morris: An
    Escape from Nostalgia," Crit, IV, iii (Winter, 1961-62),
    35-7.

THE HOME PLACE

Eisinger, C. E., Fiction of the Forties, 34-6.
Howard, L., Wright Morris, 9-10.
Hunt, John W., Jr., "The Journey Back: The Early Novels
    of Wright Morris," Crit, V, i (Spring-Summer, 1962),
    46-50.
Madden, D., Wright Morris, 41-7.

THE HUGE SEASON

Allen, W., Modern Novel, 316-17.
Howard, L., Wright Morris, 19-21.
Klein, M., After Alienation, 226-9.
Madden, D., Wright Morris, 101-11.
Waterman, Arthur E., "The Novels of Wright Morris: An
    Escape from Nostalgia," Crit, IV, iii (Winter, 1961-62),
    33-5.

THE INHABITANTS

Howard, L., Wright Morris, 10-11.
Madden, D., Wright Morris, 48-51.

IN ORBIT

Garrett, George, "Morris the Magician: A Look at IN OR-
    BIT," HC, IV, iii (June, 1967), 1-12.
Howard, L., Wright Morris, 39-41.
Madden, David, "Wright Morris' IN ORBIT: An Unspoken
    Series of Poetic Gestures," Crit, X, ii (1968), 102-19.

LOVE AMONG THE CANNIBALS

Hartman, Carl, "An Expense of Flesh," WR, XXII (Winter,
    1958), 152-4.
Howard, L., Wright Morris, 24-5.

Klein, M., <u>After Alienation,</u> 230-4.
Madden, D., <u>Wright Morris,</u> 112-30.
Oliphant, Robert, "Public Voices and Wise Guys," <u>VQR,</u>
    XXXVII (Autumn, 1961), 528-37.
Price, Martin, in <u>YR,</u> XLVII (Autumn, 1957), 151-3.

MAN AND BOY

Eisinger, C. E., <u>Fiction of the Forties,</u> 337-8.
Fiedler, L., <u>Love and Death in the American Novel,</u> 323-4.
Howard, L., <u>Wright Morris,</u> 14-15.
Klein, M., <u>After Alienation,</u> 211-14.
Madden, D., <u>Wright Morris,</u> 83-91.

THE MAN WHO WAS THERE

Eisinger, C. E., <u>Fiction of the Forties,</u> 333-4.
Howard, L., <u>Wright Morris,</u> 9-10.
Hunt, John W., Jr., "The Journey Back: The Early Novels
    of Wright Morris," <u>Crit,</u> V, I (Spring-Summer, 1962), 46-
    50.
Madden, D., <u>Wright Morris,</u> 41-7.

MY UNCLE DUDLEY

Eisinger, C. E., <u>Fiction of the Forties,</u> 331-3.
Howard, L., <u>Wright Morris,</u> 7-9.
Hunt, John W., Jr., "The Journey Back: The Early Novels
    of Wright Morris," <u>Crit,</u> V, I (Spring-Summer, 1962), 41-
    6.
Klein, M., <u>After Alienation,</u> 198-200.
Madden, D., <u>Wright Morris,</u> 32-41.

ONE DAY

Howard, L., <u>Wright Morris,</u> 34-9.
Morris, Wright, in McCormack, T., ed., <u>Afterwords,</u> 11-27.
Waterman, Arthur E., "Wright Morris's ONE DAY: The
    Novel of Revelation," <u>FurmS,</u> XV, iv (May, 1968), 29-36.

WHAT A WAY TO GO

Booth, Wayne C., "The Shaping of Prophecy: Craft and Idea
    in the Novels of Wright Morris," <u>ASch,</u> XXXI (Autumn,
    1962), 620-6.
Howard, L., <u>Wright Morris,</u> 28-31.
Klein, M., <u>After Alienation,</u> 34-8.

Madden, D., Wright Morris, 112-30.

THE WORKS OF LOVE

Eisinger, C. E., Fiction of the Forties, 338-40.
Howard, L., Wright Morris, 15-17.
Klein, M., After Alienation, 214-20.
Madden, D., Wright Morris, 64-75.

THE WORLD IN THE ATTIC

Eisinger, C. E., Fiction of the Forties, 336-7.
Howard, L., Wright Morris, 12-14.
Hunt, John W., Jr., "The Journey Back: The Early Novels of Wright Morris," Crit, V, i (Spring-Summer, 1962), 53-8.
Klein, M., After Alienation, 209-11.
Madden, D., Wright Morris, 57-63.

BIBLIOGRAPHY

Linden, Stanton J., and David Madden, "A Wright Morris Bibliography," Crit, IV, iii (Winter, 1961-62), 77-87.
Howard, L., Wright Morris, 44-8.
Madden, D., Wright, Morris, 177-84.

MORTIMER, PENELOPE, 1918-

THE PUMPKIN EATER

Raban, J., "Character and Location," Techniques of Modern Fiction, 119-21.

MOTLEY, WILLARD, 1912-1965

GENERAL

Weissgärber, Alfred, "Willard Motley and the Sociological Novel," SA, VII (1961), 299-309.

KNOCK ON ANY DOOR

Bone, R. A., Negro Novel in America, 178-80.
Breit, Harvey, in Balakian, N., and C. Simmons, eds., Creative Present, 21-3.

Ford, Nick A., "Four Popular Negro Novelists," Phylon, XV (1954), 32-4.

Gelfand, B. H., American City Novel, 248-52.

Hughes, Carl M., The Negro Novelist, N. Y.: Citadel, 1953, 178-93; 273-4.

Rideout, W. B., Radical Novel in the U. S., 261-3.

Weissgärber, Alfred, "Willard Motley and the Sociological Novel," SA, VII (1961), 300-4.

LET NO MAN WRITE MY EPITAPH

Light, James F., in PrS, XXXIII (1959), 190-2.

WE FISHED ALL NIGHT

Rideout, W. B., Radical Novel in the U. S., 263-4.

MURDOCH, IRIS, 1918-

GENERAL

Allen, W., Modern Novel, 282-4.

Allott, Miriam, "The Novels of Iris Murdoch," Talks to Teachers of English, No. 2 (1962), 57-71. (Not seen.)

Allsop, K., Angry Decade, 88-95.

Anon., "In the Heart or in the Head," TLS (November 7, 1958), 640.

Baldanza, Frank, "Iris Murdoch and the Theory of Personality," Criticism, VII (Spring, 1965), 176-89.

Berthoff, Warner, "Fortunes of the Novel: Muriel Spark and Iris Murdoch," MR, VIII (Spring, 1967), 314-32.

Byatt, A. S., Degrees of Freedom.

Dick, Bernard F., "The Novels of Iris Murdoch: A Formula for Enchantment," BuR, XIV (May, 1966), 66-81.

Felheim, Marvin, "Symbolic Characterization in the Novels of Iris Murdoch," TSLL, II (Summer, 1960), 189-97.

Fraser, G. S., "Iris Murdoch and the Solidity of the Normal," ILA, No. 2 (1959), 37-54.

_____, Modern Writer and His World, 184-7.

Gindin, James, "Images of Illusion in the Works of Iris Murdoch," TSLL, II (Summer, 1960), 180-8. Also in Gindin, J., Postwar British Fiction, 178-89.

Hall, James, "Blurring the Will: The Growth of Iris Murdoch," ELH, XXXII (June, 1965), 256-73. Also (expanded) in Hall, J., Lunatic Giant in the Drawing Room, 181-212.

Hall, William, "The Third Way: The Novels of Iris Murdoch," DR, XLVI (Autumn, 1966), 306-18.

Heyd, Ruth, "An Interview with Iris Murdoch," UWR, I (Spring, 1965), 138-43.

Hope, Francis, "The Novels of Iris Murdoch," LonM, n.s., I (August, 1961), 84-7. Also in Kostelanetz, R., ed., On Contemporary Literature, 468-72.

Hoffman, Frederick J., "Iris Murdoch: The Reality of Persons," Crit, VII (Spring, 1964), 48-57.

_____, "The Miracle of Contingency: The Novels of Iris Murdoch," Shen, XVII, i (Autumn, 1965), 49-56.

Karl, F. R., Contemporary English Novel, 260-5.

Kaufmann, R. J., "The Progress of Iris Murdoch," Nation, CLXXXVIII (March 21, 1959), 255-6.

Kermode, Frank, "The House of Fiction: Interviews with Seven English Novelists," PR, XXX (Spring, 1963), 62-5.

Kriegel, Leonard, in Shapiro, C., ed., Contemporary British Novelists, 62-80.

McCabe, Bernard, "The Guises of Love," Cweal, LXXXIII (December 3, 1965), 270-3.

Maes-Jelinek, Hena, "A House for Free Characters: The Novels of Iris Murdoch," RLV, XXIX (1963), 45-69.

Martin, Graham, "Iris Murdoch and the Symbolist Novel," BJA, V (July, 1965), 296-300.

Meidner, Olga M., "The Progress of Iris Murdoch," ESA, IV (March, 1961), 17-38.

Morrell, Roy, "Iris Murdoch: The Early Novels," CritQ, IX (Autumn, 1967), 272-82.

O'Connor, William V., "Iris Murdoch: The Formal and the Contingent," Crit, III, ii (Winter-Spring, 1960), 34-46. Also in O'Connor, W. V., New University Wits, 53-74.

O'Sullivan, Kevin, "Iris Murdoch and the Image of Liberal Man," YLM, CXXXI (December, 1962), 27-32.

Pearson, Gabriel, "Iris Murdoch and the Romantic Novel," New Left Rev., Nos. 13-14 (January-April, 1962), 137-45.

Rabinovitz, R., Iris Murdoch.

Ricks, Christopher, "A Sort of Mystery Novel," NStat (October 22, 1965), 604-5.

Rose, W. K., "An Interview with Iris Murdoch," Shen, XIX, ii (Winter, 1968), 3-22.

Souvage, Jacques, "The Novels of Iris Murdoch," SGG, IV (1962), 225-52.

Stimpson, Catherine R., "The Early Novels of Iris Murdoch," DA, XXVIII (1968), 5073A-74A (Columbia).

Tucker, Martin, "The Odd Fish in Iris Murdoch's Kettle," NRep, CLIV (February 5, 1966), 26-8.

Whiteside, George, "The Novels of Iris Murdoch," Crit, VII

(Spring, 1964), 27-47.
Wolfe, P. , <u>Disciplined Heart.</u>
_____, "Philosophical Themes in the Novels of Iris Mur-
doch," <u>DA</u>, XXVI (1965), 3357-58 (Wisc.).

THE BELL

Allen, W. , <u>Modern Novel,</u> 283-4.
_____, <u>Reading a Novel,</u> 61-4.
Byatt, A. S. , <u>Degrees of Freedom,</u> 73-104.
Clayre, Alasdair, "Common Cause: A Garden in the Clear-
ing, <u>TLS,</u> LIX, No. 2997 (August 7, 1959), xxx-xxxi.
Dick, Bernard F. , "The Novels of Iris Murdoch: A Formu-
la for Enchantment," <u>BuR</u>, XIV (May, 1966), 72-5.
Felheim, Marvin, "Symbolic Characterization in the Novels
of Iris Murdoch, <u>TSLL,</u> II (1960), 194-6.
Fraser, G. S. , "Iris Murdoch: The Solidity of the Normal,"
<u>ILA,</u> No. 2 (1959), 42-54.
Graham, A. R. , "All Our Failures are Failures of Love,"
<u>NYTBR</u> (October 26, 1958), 4-5.
Hall, James, "Blurring of the Will: The Growth of Iris
Murdoch," <u>ELH,</u> XXXII (June, 1965), 266-73. Also in
Hall, J. , <u>Lunatic Giant in the Drawing Room,</u> 190-9.
Howe, Irving, "Realities and Fictions," <u>PR</u>, XXVI (Winter,
1959), 132-3.
Jones, Dorothy, "Love and Morality in Iris Murdoch's THE
BELL," <u>Meanjin,</u> XXVI (March, 1967), 85-90.
Kaehele, Sharon, and Howard German, "The Discovery of
Reality in Iris Murdoch's THE BELL," <u>PMLA,</u> LXXXII
(December, 1967), 554-63.
Karl, F. R. , <u>Contemporary English Novel,</u> 261-4.
Kimber, John, "THE BELL: Iris Murdoch," <u>Delta,</u> No. 18
(Summer, 1959), 31-4.
Kriegel, Leonard, in Shapiro, C. , ed. , <u>Contemporary Brit-
ish Novelists,</u> 69-72.
Maes-Jelinek, Hena, "A House for Free Characters: The
Novels of Iris Murdoch," <u>RLV,</u> XXIX (1963), 56-9.
Meidner, Olga M. , "The Progress of Iris Murdoch," <u>ESA,</u>
IV (March, 1961), 25-31.
Morrell, Roy, "Iris Murdoch: The Early Novels," <u>CritQ,</u>
IX (Autumn, 1967), 277-81.
O'Connor, William V. , "Iris Murdoch: The Formal and the
Contingent," <u>Crit,</u> III, ii (Winter-Spring, 1960), 42-3.
Also in O'Connor, W. V. , <u>New University Wits,</u> 65-6.
Rabinovitz, R. , <u>Iris Murdoch,</u> 24-8.
Raymond, John, "The Unclassifiable Image," <u>NStat,</u> LVI
(November 15, 1958), 697-8. Also in Raymond, J. , <u>Doge</u>

of Dover, 179-84.
Rippier, J.S., Some Postwar English Novelists, 78; 82-8.
Sisk, John P., "Melodramatic Story and Novel of Ideas,"
    Cweal, LXIX (November 7, 1958), 154-5.
Souvage, Jacques, "The Novels of Iris Murdoch," SGG, IV
    (1962), 244-6.
_____, "Symbol as Narrative Device: An Interpretation of
    Iris Murdoch's THE BELL," ES, XLIII (April, 1962), 81-
    96.
Wall, Stephen, "The Bell in THE BELL," EIC, XIII (July,
    1963), 265-73.
Whiteside, George, "The Novels of Iris Murdoch," Crit, VII
    (Spring, 1964), 37-9.
Wolfe, P., Disciplined Heart, 113-38.

THE FLIGHT FROM THE ENCHANTER

Allsop, K., Angry Decade, 90-1.
Byatt, A.S., Degrees of Freedom, 40-60.
Dick, Bernard F., "The Novels of Iris Murdoch: A Formu-
    la for Enchantment," BuR, XIV (May, 1966), 70-1.
Felheim, Marvin, "Symbolic Characterization in the Novels
    of Iris Murdoch," TSLL, II (1960), 191-3.
Fraser, G.S., "Iris Murdoch: The Solidity of the Normal,"
    ILA, No. 2 (1959), 40-1.
Kriegel, Leonard, in Shapiro, C., ed., Contemporary Brit-
    ish Novelists, 65-7.
Maes-Jelinek, Hena, "A House for Free Characters: The
    Novels of Iris Murdoch," RLV, XXIX (1963), 50-3.
Meidner, Olga M., "Reviewer's Bane: A Study of Iris Mur-
    doch's THE FLIGHT FROM THE ENCHANTER," EIC, XI
    (October, 1961), 435-47.
O'Connor, William V., "Iris Murdoch: The Formal and the
    Contingent," Crit, III, ii (Winter-Spring, 1960), 38-40.
    Also in O'Connor, W.V., New University Wits, 59-62.
O'Sullivan, Kevin, "Iris Murdoch and the Image of Liberal
    Man," YLM, CXXXI (December, 1962), 28-30.
Rabinovitz, R., Iris Murdoch, 13-18.
Rippier, J.S., Some Postwar English Novelists, 74-9.
Souvage, Jacques, "The Novels of Iris Murdoch," SGG, IV
    (1962), 238-41.
_____, "Theme and Structure in Iris Murdoch's THE
    FLIGHT FROM THE ENCHANTER," Spieghel Historiael
    van de Bond van Gentste Germanisten, III (June, 1961),
    73-88.
Van Ghent, Dorothy, in YR, XLVI (Autumn, 1956), 153-5.
Whiteside, George, "The Novels of Iris Murdoch," Crit,

VII (Spring, 1964), 32-5.
Wolfe, P., Disciplined Heart, 68-88.

THE ITALIAN GIRL

Barrett, William, in Atlantic, CCXIV (November, 1964), 201-2.
Dick, Bernard F., "The Novels of Iris Murdoch: A Formula for Enchantment," BuR, XIV (May, 1966), 79-80.
Furbank, P.N., "Gowned Mortality," Encounter, XXIII (November, 1964), 88-90.
Hoffman, Frederick J., "The Miracle of Contingency: The Novels of Iris Murdoch," Shen, XVII, i (Autumn, 1965), 5205.
Kriegel, Leonard, in Shapiro, C., ed., Contemporary British Novelists, 76-8.
Kuehn, Robert E., "Fiction Chronicle," WSCL, VI (1965), 135-7.
Pagones, Dorrie, "Wanton Waifs and a Roman Woman," SatR, XLVII (September 19, 1964), 48-9.
Rabinovitz, R., Iris Murdoch, 36-8.
Tracy, Honor, "Misgivings About Miss Murdoch," NRep, CLI (October 10, 1964), 21-2.
Tucker, Martin, "More Iris Murdoch," Cweal, LXXXI (October 30, 1964), 173-4.
Wolfe, P., Disciplined Heart, 203-8.

THE NICE AND THE GOOD

Anon., "Characters in Love," TLS (January 25, 1968), 77. Also in T.L.S.: Essays and Reviews from the Times Literary Supplement, 1968, 56-61.
Freemantle, Anne, in Reporter, XXXVIII (January 25, 1968), 47-9.
Hicks, Granville, "Love Runs Rampant," SatR, LI (January 6, 1968), 27-8.
Palmer, Tony, "Artistic Privilege," LonM, VIII (May, 1968), 47-52.
Rabinovitz, R., Iris Murdoch, 42-3.

THE RED AND THE GREEN

Anon., "Republic and Private," TLS (October 14, 1965), 912. Also in T.L.S.: Essays and Reviews from the Times Literary Supplement, 1965, 40-1.
Berthoff, Warner, "Fortunes of the Novel: Muriel Spark and Iris Murdoch," MR, VIII (Spring, 1967), 314-27.

Bowen, John, "One Must Say Something," NYTBR (November 7, 1965), 4-5.
Hicks, Granville, "Easter Monday Insights," SatR, XLVIII (October 30, 1965), 41-2.
Ricks, Christopher, "A Sort of Mystery Novel," NStat (October 22, 1965), 604-5.
Rabinovitz, R. , Iris Murdoch, 38-9.
Tucker, Martin, "The Odd Fish in Iris Murdoch's Kettle," NRep, CLIV (February 5, 1966), 26-8.

THE SANDCASTLE

Byatt, A. S. , Degrees of Freedom, 61-72.
Dick, Bernard F. , "The Novels of Iris Murdoch: A Formula for Enchantment," BuR, XIV (May, 1966), 71-2.
Felheim, Marvin, "Symbolic Characterization in the Novels of Iris Murdoch," TSLL, II (1960), 193-4.
Fraser, G. S. , "Iris Murdoch: The Solidity of the Normal, ILA, No. 2 (1959), 41-2.
Hall, James, "Blurring the Will: The Growth of Iris Murdoch," ELH, XXXII (June, 1965), 262-6. Also in Hall, J. , Lunatic Giant in the Drawing Room, 186-90.
Kriegel, Leonard, in Shapiro, C. , ed. , Contemporary British Novelists, 68-9.
Maes-Jelinek, Hena, "A House for Free Characters: The Novels of Iris Murdoch," RLV, XXIX (1963), 53-6.
Morrell, Roy, "Iris Murdoch: The Early Novels," CritQ, IX (Autumn, 1967), 271-4.
O'Connor, William V. , "Iris Murdoch: The Formal and the Contingent," Crit, III, ii (Winter-Spring, 1960), 40-2. Also in O'Connor, W. V. , New University Wits, 62-4.
O'Sullivan, Kevin, "Iris Murdoch and the Image of Liberal Man," YLM, CXXXI (December, 1962), 30-2.
Pearson, Gabriel, "Iris Murdoch and the Romantic Novel," New Left Rev. , Nos. 12-14 (January-April, 1962), 137-45.
Price, Martin, in YR, XLVII (Autumn, 1957), 146-8.
Raban, J. , "Character and Symbolism," Techniques of Modern Fiction, 108-11.
Rabinovitz, R. , Iris Murdoch, 18-22.
Rippier, J. S. , Some Postwar English Novelists, 78-82.
Sisk, John P. , "A Sea Change," Cweal, LXVI (May 31, 1957), 236-7.
Taylor, Griffin, " 'What Doth it Profit a Man...?' " SR, LXVI (January-March, 1958), 137-41.
Whiteside, George, "The Novels of Iris Murdoch," Crit, VII (Spring, 1964), 35-7.

Wolfe, P. , Disciplined Heart, 89-112.

A SEVERED HEAD

Baldanza, Frank, "Iris Murdoch and the Theory of Person-
ality," Criticism, VII (Spring, 1965), 181-9.
Byatt, A. S. , Degrees of Freedom, 105-21.
Cosman, Max, "Priapean Japes," Cweal, LXXIV (June 9,
1961), 286-7.
Dick, Bernard F. , "The Novels of Iris Murdoch: A Formu-
la for Enchantment," BuR, XIV (May, 1966), 75-6.
Gindin, J. , "Images of Illusion in the Works of Iris Mur-
doch," Postwar British Fiction, 189-95.
Gregor, Ian, "Towards a Christian Literary Criticism,"
Month, XXXIII (1965), 239-49.
Hall, J. , Lunatic Giant in the Drawing Room, 199-200.
Jacobson, Dan, "Farce, Totem and Taboo," NStat, LXI
(June 16, 1961), 956-7.
Maes-Jelinek, Hena, "A House for Free Characters: The
Novels of Iris Murdoch," RLV, XXIX (1963), 59-62.
Malcolm, Donald, in NY, XXXVII (May 6, 1961), 172-6.
Miner, Earl, "Iris Murdoch: The Uses of Love," Nation,
CXCIV (June 2, 1962), 498-9.
O'Connor, William V. , "Iris Murdoch: A SEVERED HEAD,"
Crit, V, i (Spring-Summer, 1962), 74-7. Also in O'Con-
nor, W. V. , New University Wits, 70-4.
O'Sullivan, Kevin, "Iris Murdoch and the Image of Liberal
Man," YLM, CXXXI (December, 1962), 33-4.
Rabinovitz, R. , Iris Murdoch, 28-31.
Rippier, J. S. , Some Postwar English Novelists, 88-92.
Rolo, Charles, in Atlantic, CCVII (May, 1961), 98-100.
Souvage, Jacques, "The Novels of Iris Murdoch," SGG, IV
(1962), 247-52.
Warnke, F. J. , in YR, L (June, 1961), 632-3.
Whiteside, George, "The Novels of Iris Murdoch," Crit, VII
(Spring, 1964), 39-41.
Wolfe, P. , Disciplined Heart, 139-60.

THE TIME OF THE ANGELS

Anon. , "Picking Up the Pieces," TLS (September 8, 1966),
798. Also in T. L. S.: Essays and Reviews, 1966, 33-6.
Berthoff, Warner, "The Enemy of Freedom is Fantasy," MR,
VIII (Summer, 1967), 580-4.
Eimerl, Sarel, "Choreography of Despair," Reporter, XXXV
(November 3, 1966), 45-6.
Hicks, Granville, "Rector for a Dead God," SatR, XLIX (Oc-

tober 29, 1966), 25-6.
Rabinovitz, R., Iris Murdoch, 39-42.
Taubman, Robert, "Uncle's War," NStat, LXXII (September 16, 1966), 401-2.
Weeks, Edward, in Atlantic, CCXVIII (October, 1966), 138-9.

UNDER THE NET

Allsop, K., Angry Decade, 88-90; 93-4.
Batchelor, Billie, "Revision in Iris Murdoch's UNDER THE NET," BI, VIII (1968), 30-6.
Bradbury, Malcolm, "Iris Murdoch's UNDER THE NET," CritQ, IV (Spring, 1962), 47-54.
Byatt, A.S., Degrees of Freedom, 14-39.
DeMott, Benjamin, "Dirty Words?" HudR, XVIII (Spring, 1965), 37-40.
Dick, Bernard F., "The Novels of Iris Murdoch: A Formula for Enchantment," BuR, XIV (May, 1966), 68-70.
Felheim, Marvin, "Symbolic Characterization in the Novels of Iris Murdoch," TSLL, II (1960), 190-1.
Fitzsimmons, Thomas, in SR, LXIII (Spring, 1955), 328-30.
Fraser, G.S., "Iris Murdoch: The Solidity of the Normal," ILA, No. 2 (1959), 38-40.
Goldberg, Gerald, "The Search for the Artist in Some Recent British Fiction," SAQ, LXII (Summer, 1963), 394-6.
Hall, James, "Blurring the Will: The Growth of Iris Murdoch," ELH, XXXII (June, 1965), 259-62. Also in Hall, J., Lunatic Giant in the Drawing Room, 183-6.
Kriegel, Leonard, in Shapiro, C., ed., Contemporary British Novelists, 64-5.
Maes-Jelinek, Hena, "A House for Free Characters: The Novels of Iris Murdoch," RLV, XXIX (1963), 45-50.
Morrell, Roy, "Iris Murdoch: The Early Novels," CritQ, XI (Autumn, 1967), 274-7.
O'Connor, William V., "Iris Murdoch: The Formal and the Contingent," Crit, III, ii (Winter-Spring, 1960), 40-2. Also in O'Connor, W.V., New University Wits, 54-9.
O'Sullivan, Kevin, "Iris Murdoch and the Image of Liberal Man," YLM, CXXXI (December, 1962), 27-8.
Rabinovitz, R., Iris Murdoch, 8-13.
Rippier, J.S., Some Postwar British Novelists, 71-4.
Shestakov, Dmitri, "An Iris Murdoch Novel in Russian," Soviet Lit, No. 7 (1966), 169-75.
Souvage, Jacques, "The Novels of Iris Murdoch," SGG, IV (1962), 234-8.
_____, "The Unresolved Tension: An Interpretation of

Iris Murdoch's UNDER THE NET," RLV, XXVI (1960),
420-30.
Whiteside, George, "The Novels of Iris Murdoch," Crit,
VII (Spring, 1964), 29-32.
Widmann, R. L., "Murdoch's UNDER THE NET: Theory and
Practice of Fiction," Crit, X, i (1968), 5-16.
Wolfe, P., Disciplined Heart, 46-67.

THE UNICORN

Anon., "Fable Mates," TLS (September 6, 1963), 669. Also
in T. L. S.: Essays and Reviews from the Times Literary
Supplement, 1963, 176-8.
Barrett, William, "English Opposites," Atlantic, CCXI (June,
1963), 131-2.
Byatt, A. S., Degrees of Freedom, 146-80.
Cook, Eleanor, "Mythical Beasts," CanF, XLIII (August,
1963), 113-14.
Detweiler, Robert, Iris Murdoch's THE UNICORN (Religious
Dimensions in Literature), N. Y.: Seabury, 1969.
Dick, Bernard F., "The Novels of Iris Murdoch: A Formu-
la for Enchantment," BuR, XIV (May, 1966), 78-9.
Grigson, Geoffrey, "Entre les Tombes," NStat, LXVI (Sep-
tember 13, 1963), 321-2.
Hall, J., Lunatic Giant in the Drawing Room, 206-11.
Hebblethwaite, Peter, "Out Hunting Unicorns," Month, n. s.,
XXX (October, 1963), 224-8.
Hicks, Granville, "Entrance to Enchantment," SatR, XLVI
(May 11, 1963), 27-8.
Kriegel, Leonard, in Shapiro, C., ed., Contemporary Brit-
ish Novelists, 74-6.
McDowell, Frederick P. W., " 'The Devious Involutions of
Human Character and Emotions': Reflections on Some Re-
cent British Novels," WSCL, IV, iii (Autumn, 1963), 355-
9.
Pondrom, Cyrena N., "Iris Murdoch: THE UNICORN," Crit,
VI, (Winter, 1963-64), 177-80.
Rabinovitz, R., Iris Murdoch, 34-6.
Rippier, J. S., Some Postwar English Novelists, 96-103.
Scholes, R., Fabulators, 106-32.
Tucker, Martin, "Love and Freedom: Golden and Hard
Words," Cweal, LXXVII (June 21, 1963), 357-8.
Whitehorn, Katharine, "Three Women," Encounter, XXI (De-
cember, 1963), 78-82.
Whiteside, George, "The Novels of Iris Murdoch," Crit, VII
(Spring, 1964), 43-6.
Wolfe, P., Disciplined Heart, 183-202.

AN UNOFFICIAL ROSE

Barrett, William, "Rose with Thorns," Atlantic, CCIX (June, 1962), 201-2.

Byatt, A. S., Degrees of Freedom, 122-45.

Dick, Bernard F., "The Novels of Iris Murdoch: A Formula for Enchantment," BuR, XIV (May, 1966), 77.

Hall, J., Lunatic Giant in the Drawing Room, 200-6.

Kriegel, Leonard in Shapiro, C., ed., Contemporary British Novelists, 73-4.

McDowell, Frederick P. W., " 'The Devious Involutions of Human Character and Emotions': Reflections on Some Recent British Novels," WSCL, IV, iii (Autumn, 1963), 352-5.

Maes-Jelinek, Hena, "A House for Free Characters: The Novels of Iris Murdoch," RLV, XXIX (1963), 62-6.

Miner, Earl, "Iris Murdoch: The Uses of Love," Nation, CXCIV (June 2, 1962), 498-9.

O'Sullivan, Kevin, "Iris Murdoch and the Image of Liberal Man," YLM, CXXXI (December, 1962), 34-5.

Pondrom, Cyrena N., "Iris Murdoch: An Existentialist," CLS, V (1968), 403-19.

Rabinovitz, R., Iris Murdoch, 31-4.

Rippier, J. S., Some Postwar English Novelists, 92-6.

Ryan, Marjorie, in Crit, V, iii (Winter, 1962-63), 117-21.

Whiteside, George, "The Novels of Iris Murdoch," Crit, VII (Spring, 1964), 41-3.

Wolfe, P., Disciplined Heart, 161-82.

BIBLIOGRAPHY

Widmann, R. L., "An Iris Murdoch Checklist," Crit, X, i (1968), 17-29.

Wolfe, P., Disciplined Heart, 216-20.

NABOKOV, VLADIMIR, 1899-

GENERAL

Anon., "Lolita's Creator - Author Nabokov, a 'Cosmic Joker'," Newsweek, LIX (June 25, 1962), 51-4.

_____, "Playboy Interview: Vladimir Nabokov," Playboy, XI (January, 1964), 35-41; 44-5. Also in The Twelfth Anniversary Playboy Reader, Chicago: Playboy Pr., 1965.

Appel, Alfred, Jr., "An Interview with Vladimir Nabokov," WSCL, VIII, ii (Spring, 1967), 127-52. Also in Dembo,

L. S. , ed. , Nabokov, 19-44.

Brenner, Conrad, "Nabokov: The Art of the Perverse,"
NRep, CXXXVIII (June 23, 1958), 18-21.

Brown, Clarence, "Nabokov's Pushkin and Nabokov's Nabokov," WSCL, VIII, ii (Spring, 1967), 280-93. Also in
Dembo, L. S. , ed. , Nabokov, 195-208.

Crofts, Robert F. , "Vladimir Nabokov - A Russian Wolf in
American Clothing," MSpr, LIX (1965), 11-29.

Dembo, L. S. , "Vladimir Nabokov: An Introduction," WSCL,
VIII, ii (Spring, 1967), 111-26. Also in Dembo, L. S. ,
ed. , Nabokov, 3-18.

Dillard, R. H. W. , "Not Text, but Texture: The Novels of
Vladimir Nabokov," HC, III, iii (June, 1966), 1-12.

Dupee, F. W. , "Nabokov: The Prose and Poetry of It All,"
NYRB, (December 12, 1963), 10-12. Also in Dupee, F.
W. , King of the Cats, 131-41.

Enright, D. J. , "Nabokov's Way," NYRB (November 3, 1966),
3-4.

Field, A. , Nabokov.

Gardner, Thomas, "Vladimir Nabokov," SG, XXI (1968), 94-
110.

Gold, Herbert, "The Art of Fiction XL: Vladimir Nabokov,
An Interview," ParisR, No. 41 (Summer-Fall, 1967), 92-
111.

Grosshans, Henry, "Vladimir Nabokov and the Dream of Old
Russia," TSLL, VII (Winter, 1966), 401-9.

Hayman, John G. , "A Conversation with Vladimir Nabokov -
with Digressions," TC, CLXVI (December, 1959), 444-50.

Ivask, George, "The World of Vladimir Nabokov," RusR, XX
(April, 1961), 134-42.

Lee, L. L. , "Vladimir Nabokov's Great Spiral of Being,"
WHR, XVIII (Summer, 1964), 225-36.

Merivale, Patricia, "The Flaunting of Artifice in Vladimir
Nabokov and Jorge Luis Borges," WSCL, VIII, ii (Spring,
1967), 294-309. Also in Dembo, L. S. , ed. , Nabokov,
209-24.

Nabokov, Vladimir, and Peter D. Smith, "Vladimir Nabokov
on His Life and Work," Listener, LXVIII (November 22,
1962), 856-8. Also in Vogue, CXLI (March 1, 1963),
152-5.

Pryce-Jones, David, "The Art of Nabokov," Harpers,
CCXXVI (April, 1963), 97-101. Also (revised and expanded) as "The Fabulist's Worlds: Vladimir Nabokov"
in Balakian, N. , and C. Simmons, eds., Creative Present, 65-78.

Purdy, Struther B. , "Solus Rex: Nabokov and the Chess
Novel," MFS, XIV (Winter, 1968-69), 379-95.

Stegner, P., Escape Into Aesthetics.
Struve, Gleb, "Notes on Nabokov as a Russian Writer,"
    WSCL, VIII, ii (Spring, 1967), 127-52. Also in Dembo,
    L. S., ed., Nabokov, 45-56.
Wain, John, "Nabokov's Beheading," NRep, CXLI (December
    21, 1959), 17-19.
Williams, Carol T., "Nabokov's Dialectical Structure,"
    WSCL, VIII, ii (Spring, 1967), 250-67. Also in Dembo,
    L. S., ed., Nabokov, 165-82.
_____, "The Necessary Ripple: The Art of Vladimir
Nabokov," DA, XXVIII (1968), 3203A-04A (Wisconsin).

BEND SINISTER

Field, A., Nabokov, 198-203.
Kermode, Frank, "Aesthetic Bliss," Encounter, XIV (June,
    1960), 81-6. Also in Kermode, F., Puzzles and Epi-
    phanies, 228-33.
Lee, L. L., "BEND SINISTER: Nabokov's Political Dream,"
    WSCL, VIII, ii (Spring, 1967), 193-203. Also in Dembo,
    L. S., ed., Nabokov, 95-105.
Stegner, P., Escape Into Aesthetics, 76-89.

CAMERA OBSCURA (LAUGHTER IN THE DARK)

Field, A., Nabokov, 158-65.
Simon, John, "Before LOLITA, What?" Mid-Century, XIX
    (November, 1960), 8-13.
Williams, Carol T., "Nabokov's Dialectical Structure,"
    WSCL, VIII, ii (Spring, 1967), 258-61. Also in Dembo,
    L. S., ed., Nabokov, 173-6.

THE DEFENSE

Adams, Robert M., "Nabokov's Game," NYRB (January 14,
    1965), 18-19.
Anon., "Strange Mating," TLS (November 19, 1964), 1033.
    Also in T. L. S.: Essays and Reviews from the Times
    Literary Supplement, 1964, 207-9.
Bradbury, Malcolm, "Grand Master," Spectator, No. 7116
    (November 13, 1964), 643-4.
Field, A., Nabokov, 175-9.
_____, "The View From Above," New Leader, XLVII
    (October 26, 1964), 22-3.
Furbank, P. N., "Chess and Jogsaw," Encounter, XXIV (Jan-
    uary, 1965), 83-6.
Hampshire, Stuart, "Among the Barbarians," NStat, LXVIII

(November 6, 1964), 702-3.

Purdy, Struther B., "Solus Rex: Nabokov and the Chess Novel," MFS, XIV (Winter, 1968-69), 382-4.

Thorpe, Day, "A Master Chess Player Loses in the Game of Life," Sunday Star (Washington, D. C.), September 27, 1964, C-5.

Updike, John, "Grandmaster Nabokov," NRep, CLI (September 26, 1964), 15-18.

DESPAIR

Anderson, Quentin, "Nabokov in Time," NRep, CLIV (June 4, 1966), 23-8.

Anon., "Looking-Glass Death," TLS (July 28, 1966), 655. Also in T. L. S.: Essays and Reviews from the Times Literary Supplement, 1966, 27-9.

Brophy, Brigid, "LOLITA and Other Games," Book Week (May 15, 1966), 2; 10.

Field, Andrew, "Hermann and Felix," NYTBR (May 15, 1966), 5; 36-7.

_____, Nabokov, 225-37.

Hyman, Stanley E., "Nabokov's Distorting Mirrors," New Leader, XLIX (May 9, 1966), 11-12.

King, Adele, "La Meprise," Geste (Univ. of Leeds), IV (March 12, 1959), 18-20.

Rosenfield, Claire, "DESPAIR and the Lust for Immortality," WSCL, VIII, ii (Spring, 1967), 174-92. Also in Dembo, L. S., ed., Nabokov, 66-84.

THE EXPLOIT

Field, A., Nabokov, 116-23.

THE EYE

Field, A., Nabokov, 165-72. Also in Dembo, L. S., ed., Nabokov, 57-63.

Koch, Stephen, "Nabokov as Novice," Nation, CCII (January 17, 1966), 81-2.

THE GIFT

Dupee, F. W., "Nabokov: The Prose and Poetry of It All," NYRB, (December, 1963), 10-12. Also in Dupee, F. W., King of the Cats, 134-8.

Field, A., Nabokov, 15-26; 29-32; 241-9.

Hyman, Stanley E., "Nabokov's Gift," New Leader, XLVI

(October 14, 1963), 21.   Also in Hyman, S. E. , Standards, 184-8.

Karlinsky, Simon, "Vladimir Nabokov's Novel DAR as a
  Work of Literary Criticism: A Structural Analysis," SEEJ,
  VII (Fall, 1963), 284-90.

Malcolm, Donald, "A Retrospect," NY, XL (April 25, 1964),
  198-205.

Spender, Stephen, "A Poet's Invented and Demolished Truth,"
  NYTBR (May 26, 1963), 4-5.

INVITATION TO A BEHEADING

Field, A. , Nabokov, 185-98.

Moynahan, Julian, "A Russian Preface for Nabokov's BE-
  HEADING," Novel, I (Fall, 1967), 12-18.

Williams, Carol T. , "Nabokov's Dialectical Structure,"
  WSCL, VIII, ii (Spring, 1967), 255-7.   Also in Dembo, L.
  S. , ed. , Nabokov, 170-2.

KING, QUEEN, KNAVE

Field, A. , Nabokov, 152-9.

Gass, William H. , "Mirror, Mirror," NYRB, X (June 6,
  1968), 3-5.

LAUGHTER IN THE DARK (See CAMERA OBSCURA)

LOLITA

Aldridge, A. Owen, "LOLITA and LES LIAISONS DANGER-
  EUSES," WSCL, II, iii (Fall, 1961), 20-6.

Amis, Kingsley, "She Was a Child and I Was a Child,"
  Spectator, No. 6854 (November 6, 1959), 635-6.

Appel, Alfred, Jr. , "The Art of Nabokov's Artifice," UDQ,
  III (Summer, 1968), 25-37.

_____ , "LOLITA: The Springboard of Parody," WSCL,
  VIII, ii (Spring, 1967), 204-41.   Also in Dembo, L. S. ,
  ed. , Nabokov, 106-43.

Baker, George, "LOLITA: Literature or Pornography?"
  SatR, XL (June 22, 1957), 18.

Beaver, Harold, "A Figure in the Carpet: Irony and the
  American Novel," E&S, XV (1962), 113-14.

Brick, Allen, "The Madman in His Cell: Joyce, Beckett,
  Nabokov, and the Stereotypes," MR, I (Fall, 1959), 52-5.

Butler, Diana, "Lolita Lepidoptera," New World Writing,
  No. 16 (1960), 58-84.

Campbell, Felicia C. , "A Princedom by the Sea," LHR, X

(1968), 39-46.

Dalwood, Hubert, "LOLITA - A Postscript," Geste (Univ. of Leeds), IV (March 12, 1959), 13-14.

Davies, R., "By Lo Possessed," Voice from the Attic, 242-6.

DuBois, Arthur E., "Poe and LOLITA," CEA, XXVI, vi (March, 1964), 1; 7.

Dupee, F.W., "LOLITA in America," Encounter, XII (February, 1959), 30-5. Also in CUF, II (Winter, 1959), 35-9.

_____, "A Preface to LOLITA," Anchor Rev., No. 2 (1957), 1-13. Also in Dupee, F.W., King of the Cats, 117-31.

Fiedler, L., Love and Death in the American Novel, 326-8.

_____, "The Profanation of the Child," New Leader, XLI (June 23, 1958), 26-9.

Field, A., Nabokov, 323-50.

Gardiner, Harold C., "Clichés Are Dangerous," America, XCIX (August 30, 1958), 26-9.

Gold, Joseph, "The Morality of LOLITA," Brit. Assn. for Amer. Studies Bull., n. s. I (September, 1960), 50-4.

Green, Martin, "The Morality of LOLITA," KR, XXVIII (June, 1966), 352-77. Also in Green, M., Yeats's Blessing on von Hügel, 128-50.

_____, "American Rococo: Salinger and Nabokov," Re-Appraisals, 211-29.

Hale, Nancy, "Hemingway and the Courage to Be," VQR, XXXVIII (Autumn, 1962), 621-3.

Harris, Harold J., "LOLITA and the Sly Forward," MRR, I, ii (1965), 29-38.

Hiatt, L.R., "Nabokov's LOLITA: A 'Freudian' Cryptic Crossword," AI, XXIV (Winter, 1967), 360-70.

Hicks, Granville, "LOLITA and Her Problems," SatR, XLI (August 16, 1958), 12, 38.

Hinchliffe, Arnold P., "Belinda in America," SA, VI (1960), 339-47.

Hollander, John, "The Perilous Magic of Nymphets," PR, XXIII (Fall, 1956), 557-60. Also in Kostelanetz, R., ed., On Contemporary Literature, 477-80.

Hughes, Daniel J., "Character in Contemporary Fiction," MR, III (Summer, 1962), 792-3.

_____, "Reality and the Hero: LOLITA and HENDERSON THE RAIN KING," MFS, VI (Winter, 1960-61), 345-64. Also in Malin, I., ed., Saul Bellow and the Critics, 69-91.

Josipovici, G.D., "LOLITA: Parody and the Pursuit of Beauty," CritQ, VI (Spring, 1964), 35-48.

King, Bruce, "LOLITA - Sense and Sensibility at Mid-century," Geste (Univ. of Leeds), IV (March 12, 1959), 3-9.

Lund, Mary G., "Don Quixote Rides Again or Some Coordinates Are Outside," Whetstone, III (Fall, 1959), 172-8.

Meyer, Frank S., "The Strange Fate of LOLITA - A Lance Into Cotton Wool," NatR, VI (November 22, 1958), 340-1.

Mitchell, Charles, "Mythic Seriousness in LOLITA," TSLL, V (Autumn, 1963), 329-43.

Nabokov, Vladimir, "On a Book Entitled LOLITA," Anchor Rev., No. 2 (1957), 1-13. Also in Encounter, XII (April, 1959), 4-21.

Nemerov, Howard, "The Morality of Art," KR, XXVIII (Spring, 1957), 313-21. Also in Nemerov, H., Poetry and Fiction, 260-6.

Oliphant, Robert, "Public Voices and Wise Guys," VQR, XXXVII (Autumn, 1961), 530-5.

Phillips, Elizabeth, "The Hocus-Pocus of LOLITA," L&P, X (Summer, 1960), 97-101.

Pritchett, V.S., in NStat, LVII (January 10, 1959), 38.

Probyn, Hugh, "LOLITA - Nabokov by Poe Out of Rabelais," Geste (Univ. of Leeds), IV (March 12, 1959), 10-12.

Proffer, Carl R., Keys to Lolita, Bloomington: Indiana Un. Pr., 1968.

Rougemont, Denis de, Love Declared: Essays on the Myths of Love, N.Y.: Pantheon, 1963, 48-54.

Rubinstein, E., "Approaching LOLITA," MinnR, VI (Winter, 1966), 361-7.

Schickel, Richard, "Nabokov's Artistry," The Progressive, XXII (November, 1958), 46-9. Also in Reporter, XVII (November 28, 1957), 45-7.

Scott, W.G., "The LOLITA Case," Landfall, XV (June, 1961), 134-8.

Seldon, E.S., "LOLITA and JUSTINE," EvR, II, vi (Autumn, 1958), 156-9.

Slonim, Marc, "DOCTOR ZHIVAGO and LOLITA," ILA, II (1959), 213-25.

Speakman, P.T., "LOLITA - What Are Humbert's Motives?" Geste (Univ. of Leeds), IV (March 12, 1959), 12-13.

Stegner, P., Escape Into Aesthetics, 102-15.

Strainchamps, Ethel, "Nabokov's Handling of English Syntax," AS, XXXVI (October, 1961), 234-5.

Teirlinch, Herman, "Notes on Nabokov's LOLITA," LitR, VII (Spring, 1964), 439-42.

Trilllng, Lionel, "The Last Lover: Vladimir Nabokov's LOLITA," Griffin, VII (August, 1958), 4-21. Also in Encounter, XI (October, 1958), 9-19.

Uphaus, Robert W., "Nabokov's KUNSTLERROMAN: Por-

trait of the Artist as Dying Man," TCL, XIII (July, 1967),
104-10.
West, Rebecca, "LOLITA: A Tragic Book With a Sly Gri-
mace," (London) Sunday Times (November 8, 1959), 16.
Williams, Carol T., "Nabokov's Dialectical Structure,"
WSCL, VIII, ii (Spring, 1967), 261-7. Also in Dembo,
L. S., ed., Nabokov, 176-82.
Zall, Paul M., "Lolita and Gulliver," SNL, III (Fall, 1965),
33-7.

PALE FIRE

Adams, Robert M., in HudR, XV (Autumn, 1962), 420-3.
Chester, Alfred, "Nabokov's Anti-Novel," Ctary, XXXIV
(November, 1962), 449-51.
Field, A., Nabokov, 291-322.
_____, "PALE FIRE: The Labyrinth of a Great Novel,"
TriQ, VIII (Winter, 1967), 13-36.
Handley, Jack, "To Die in English," NWR, VI (Spring, 1963),
23-40.
Highet, Gilbert, "To the Sound of Hollow Laughter," Horizon,
IV (July, 1962), 89-91.
Keir, Walter, "Nabokov's Score," New Saltire, No. 6 (De-
cember, 1962), 77-81.
Kermode, Frank, "Zemblances," NStat, LXIV (November 9,
1962), 671-2. Also in Kermode, F., Continuities, 176-
80.
Kostelanetz, Richard, "Nabokov's Obtuse Fool," Ramparts,
III (January-February, 1965), 60-1. Also in Kostelanetz,
R., ed., On Contemporary Literature, 481-5. Also
(abridged) in Kostelanetz, R., ed., New American Arts,
222-4.
Krueger, John R., "Nabokov's Zemblan: A Constructed Lan-
guage of Fiction," Linguistics, XXXI (May, 1967), 44-9.
Lee, L. L., "Vladimir Nabokov's Great Spiral of Being,"
WHR, XVIII (Summer, 1964), 225-36.
Lyons, John O., "PALE FIRE and the Fine Art of Annota-
tion," WSCL, VIII, ii (Spring, 1967), 242-9. Also in
Dembo, L. S., ed., Nabokov, 66-84.
McCarthy, Mary, "A Bolt from the Blue," NRep, CXVI
(June 4, 1962), 21-7. Also as "Vladimir Nabokov's PALE
FIRE" in Encounter, XIX (October, 1962), 71-84.
Macdonald, Dwight, "Virtuosity Rewarded, or Dr. Kinbote's
Revenge," PR, XXIX (Summer, 1962), 437-42.
Malin, Irving, in WSCL, IV (Spring-Summer, 1963), 252-5.
Maloff, Saul, "The World of Rococo," Nation, CXCIV (June
16, 1962), 541-2.

Murray, Michele, "Aesthetic Delight - The Author-Created
    Confusion is Deliberate," Catholic Reporter (Kansas City,
    Mo.), July 6, 1962, 11.
Purdy, Struther B., "Solus Rex: Nabokov and the Chess
    Novel," MFS, XIV (Winter, 1968-69), 391-5.
Raban, J., "Registers in the Language of Fiction," Tech-
    niques of Modern Fiction, 154-7.
Riemer, Andrew, "Dim Glow, Faint Blaze - The Meaning of
    PALE FIRE," Balcony, VI (1967), 41-8.
Stegner, P., Escape Into Aesthetics, 116-32.
Steiner, George, "Lament for Language Lost," Reporter,
    XXVI (June 7, 1962), 40-5.
Williams, Carol T., " 'Web of Sense': PALE FIRE in the
    Nabokov Canon," Crit, VI, iii (Winter, 1963-64), 29-45.

PNIN

Anon., "Pnin and Pan," Time, LXIX (March 18, 1957), 108-
    10.
Elliott, George P., in HudR, X (Summer, 1957), 289-91.
Field, A., Nabokov, 129-40.
Gordon, Ambrose, Jr., "The Double Pnin" in Dembo, L.S.,
    ed., Nabokov, 144-56.
High, Roger, "PNIN - A Preposterous Little Explosion,"
    Geste (Univ. of Leeds), IV (March 12, 1959), 16-18.
Lyons, J.O., College Novel in America, 117-19.
Mizener, Arthur, "The Seriousness of Vladimir Nabokov,"
    SR, LXXVI (Autumn, 1968), 655-64.
Stegner, P., Escape Into Aesthetics, 90-101.
Stern, Richard G., "PNIN and the Dust-Jacket," PrS, XXXI
    (Summer, 1957), 161-4.

THE REAL LIFE OF SEBASTIAN KNIGHT

Field, A., Nabokov, 26-32.
Fromberg, Susan, "The Unwritten Chapters in THE REAL
    LIFE OF SEBASTIAN KNIGHT," MFS, XIII (Winter, 1967-
    68), 427-42.
Johnson, W.R., "THE REAL LIFE OF SEBASTIAN KNIGHT,"
    Carleton Miscellany, IV (Fall, 1963), 111-14.
Nicol, Charles, "The Mirrors of Sebastian Knight" in Dembo,
    L.S., ed., Nabokov, 85-94.
Purdy, Struther B., "Solus Rex: Nabokov and the Chess
    Novel," MFS, XIV (Winter, 1968-69), 384-7.
Stegner, S. Page, "The Immortality of Art: Vladimir Nabo-
    kov's THE REAL LIFE OF SEBASTIAN KNIGHT," SoR,
    n.s. (April, 1966), 286-96. Also in Stegner, P., Escape

Into Aesthetics, 63-75.
Stuart, Dabney, "THE REAL LIFE OF SEBASTIAN KNIGHT:
    Angles of Perception," MLQ, XXIX (September, 1968),
    312-28.
Tanzy, C.E., in EJ, XLIX (February, 1960), 141-2.

SOLUS REX (Unfinished Novel)

Field, A., Nabokov, 292-310.

ULTIMA THULE (Unfinished Novel)

Field, A., Nabokov, 292; 296-7; 305-8.

BIBLIOGRAPHY

Bryer, Jackson R., and Thomas J. Bergin, Jr., "Vladimir
    Nabokov's Critical Reputation in English: A Note and a
    Checklist," WSCL, VIII, ii 'Spring, 1967), 312-64. Also
    in Dembo, L.S., ed., Nabokov, 225-78.

NATHAN, ROBERT, 1894-

GENERAL

Blankenship, R., American Literature, 696-8.
Laurence, Dan H., "Robert Nathan: Master of Fantasy,"
    YULG, XXXVII (July, 1962), 1-7.
Roberts, Francis, "Robert Nathan: Master of Fantasy and
    Fable: An Interview," PrS, XL (Winter, 1966-67), 348-
    61.
Sandelin, C.K., Robert Nathan.
Spitz, Leon, "Robert Nathan's Jewish Types," AmHebrew,
    CLVIII (November 2, 1948), 10; 14-15.
Trachtenberg, Stanley, "Robert Nathan's Fiction," DA, XXIV
    (1964), 3345 (N.Y.U.).

AUTUMN

Sandelin, C.K., Robert Nathan, 32-7.

THE BISHOP'S WIFE

Sandelin, C.K., Robert Nathan, 54-5.

THE COLOR OF EVENING

Sandelin, C. K. , Robert Nathan, 122-5.

THE DEVIL WITH LOVE

Sandelin, C. K. , Robert Nathan, 125-8.

THE FIDDLER IN BARLY

Sandelin, C. K. , Robert Nathan, 44-8.

JONAH

Sandelin, C. K. , Robert Nathan, 40-4.

LONG AFTER SUMMER

Sandelin, C. K. , Robert Nathan, 75-6.

THE MALLOT DIARIES

Sandelin, C. K. , Robert Nathan, 77-8.

MR. WHITTLE AND THE MORNING STAR

Sandelin, C. K. , Robert Nathan, 93-5.

ONE MORE SPRING

Gurko, L. , Angry Decade, 82-3.
Sandelin, C. K. , Robert Nathan, 59-60.

THE ORCHID

Sandelin, C. K. , Robert Nathan, 56-7.

PETER KINDRED

Sandelin, C. K. , Robert Nathan, 20-7.

PORTRAIT OF JENNIE

Sandelin, C. K. , Robert Nathan, 64-74.

THE PUPPET MASTER

Sandelin, C. K. , Robert Nathan, 37-9.

ROAD OF AGES

Sandelin, C. K. , Robert Nathan, 60-3.

SIR HENRY

Sandelin, C. K. , Robert Nathan, 109-10.

SO LOVE RETURNS

Sandelin, C. K. , Robert Nathan, 92-3.

A STAR IN THE WIND

Sandelin, C. K. , Robert Nathan, 115-21.

STONECLIFFE

Sandelin, C. K. , Robert Nathan, 151-3.

THERE IS ANOTHER HEAVEN

Sandelin, C. K. , Robert Nathan, 55-6.

THE WILDERNESS STONE

Sandelin, C. K. , Robert Nathan, 76-7.

WINTER IN APRIL

Sandelin, C. K. , Robert Nathan, 57-8.

THE WOODCUTTER'S HOUSE

Sandelin, C. K. , Robert Nathan, 47-8.

NEMEROV, HOWARD

GENERAL

Meinke, P. , Howard Nemerov.
_____, "The Writings of Howard Nemerov," DA, XXVII

(1966), 1830A-31A (Minn.).

FEDERIGO, OR, THE POWER OF LOVE

Meinke, P., Howard Nemerov, 35-8.

THE HOMECOMING GAME

Lytle, A., "The Displaced Family," Hero With the Private Parts, 82-9.
Meinke, P., Howard Nemerov, 38-40.
White, Robert L., "The Trying-Out of THE HOMECOMING GAME," ColQ, X (Summer, 1961), 84-96.

THE MELODRAMATISTS

Meinke, P., Howard Nemerov, 32-5.

NEWBY, P(ERCY) H(OWARD), 1918-

GENERAL

Anon., "Novelist on His Own," TLS (April 6, 1962), 232.
Bufkin, E. C., "Quest in the Novels of P. H. Newby," Crit, VIII, i (Fall, 1965), 51-62.
Karl, F. R., Contemporary English Novel, 269-73.
McCormick, J., Catastrophe and Imagination, 166-7.
Mathews, Francis X., "The Fiction of P. H. Newby," DA, XXV (1964), 2515-16 (Wisconsin).
Watts, Harold H., "P. H. Newby: Experience as Farce," Per, X (Summer-Autumn, 1958), 106-17.

THE BARBARY LIGHT

Anon., "A Novelist on His Own," TLS (April 6, 1962), 232. Also in T. L. S.: Essays and Reviews from The Times Literary Supplement, 1962, London: Oxford, 1963, 101-6.
Bufkin, E. C., "Quest in the Novels of P. H. Newby," Crit, VIII, i (Fall, 1965), 58-62.

A GUEST AND HIS GOING

Mathews, F. X., "Newby on the Nile," TCL, XIV (April, 1968), 12-15.

A JOURNEY TO THE INTERIOR

Bufkin, E.C., "Quest in the Novels of P.H. Newby," Crit,
   VIII, i (Fall, 1965), 51-6.
Karl, F.R., Contemporary English Novel, 269-71.

THE PICNIC AT SAKKARA

Halpern, Ben, "The Wisdom of Blindness," Midstream, III
   (Winter, 1957), 104-7.
Mathews, F.X., "Newby on the Nile," TCL, XIV (April,
   1968), 5-9.

THE RETREAT

Allen, W., Modern Novel, 267.
Balakian, Nona, "Three English Novels," KR, XV (Summer,
   1953), 490-4.
Bufkin, E.C., "Quest in the Novels of P.H. Newby," Crit,
   VIII, i (Fall, 1965), 56-8.

REVOLUTION AND ROSES

Mathews, F.X., "Newby on the Nile," TCL, XIV (April,
   1968), 10-12.

THE SNOW PASTURE

Dickerson, Lucia, "Portrait of the Artist as a Jung Man,"
   KR, XXI (Winter, 1959), 58-83.

A STEP TO SILENCE

Allen, W., Modern Novel, 266-7.

THE YOUNG MAN MOON

Dickerson, Lucia, "Portrait of the Artist as a Jung Man,"
   KR, XXI (Winter, 1959), 58-83.

O'CONNOR, EDWIN, 1918-1968

ALL IN THE FAMILY

Jones, Howard M., "Politics, Mr. O'Connor, and the Family Novel," Atlantic, CCXVIII (October, 1966), 117-20.

THE EDGE OF SADNESS

Galbraith, John K., "Sadness in Boston," NY, XXXVII (June 24, 1961), 87-94.
O'Donovan, Patrick, "In the Shadow of His Excellency," NRep, CXLV (July 24, 1961), 24-6.
Rank, Hugh, "O'Connor's Image of the Priest," NEQ, XLI (March, 1968), 3-29.
Sandra, Sister Mary, S. S. A., "The Priest-Hero in Modern Fiction," Person, XLVI (October, 1965), 528-31.
Stuckey, W. J., Pulitzer Prize Novels, 197-204.

THE LAST HURRAH

Blotner, J., Modern American Political Novel, 82-5.
Goodwin, George, Jr., "The Last Hurrahs: George Apley and Frank Skeffington," MR, I (May, 1960), 461-71.
Milne, G., American Political Novel, 165-71.
West, A., "It's Just Politics," Principles and Persuasions, 219-24.

O'CONNOR, FLANNERY, 1925-1964

GENERAL

Alice, Sister Rose, S. S. J., "Flannery O'Connor: Poet to the Outcast," Ren, XVI (Spring, 1964), 126-32.
Bassan, Maurice, "Flannery O'Connor's Way: Shock, with Moral Intent, Ren, XV (Summer, 1963), 195-9+.
Blackwell, Annie L., "The Artistry of Flannery O'Connor," DA, XXVII (1967), 3862A-3A (Fla. State).
Brittain, Joan, "The Fictional Family of Flannery O'Connor," Ren, XIX (Fall, 1966), 48-52.
Cheney, Brainard, "Flannery O'Connor's Campaign for Her Country," SR, LXXII (Autumn, 1964), 555-8. Also in Reiter, R. E., ed., Flannery O'Connor, 1-4.
_____, "Miss O'Connor Creates Unusual Humor Out of Ordinary Sin," SR, LXXI (Autumn, 1963), 644-52. Also in Reiter, R. E., ed., Flannery O'Connor, 39-49.
Coffey, Warren, "Flannery O'Connor," Ctary, XL (November, 1965), 93-9.
Connolly, Janet M., "The Fiction of Flannery O'Connor," DA, XXVIII (1967), 670A (Columbia).
Davis, Barnabas, "Flannery O'Connor: Christian Belief in Recent Fiction," Listening, O (Autumn, 1965), 5-21.
Detweiler, Robert, "The Curse of Christ in Flannery O'Con-

nor's Fiction," CLS, III (1966), 235-45. Also in Panichas,
G. A. , ed. , Mansions of the Spirit, 358-69.
Dinneen, Patricia M. , "Flannery O'Connor: Realist of Dis-
tances," DA, XXVIII (1968), 3635A (Penn State).
Dowell, Bob, "The Moment of Grace in the Fiction of Flan-
nery O'Connor," CE, XXVII (December, 1965), 235-9.
Drake, R. , Flannery O'Connor.
_____, "The Harrowing Evangel of Flannery O'Connor,"
ChC, LXXXI (September 30, 1964), 1200-2.
Duhamel, P. Albert, "The Novelist as Prophet" in Fried-
man, M. J. , and L. A. Lawson, eds. , Added Dimension,
88-107.
Dunn, Sister Francis M. , "Functions and Implications of
Setting in the Fiction of Flannery O'Connor," DA, XXVII
(1967), 3043A (Catholic Univ.).
Esprit (Univ. of Scranton), VIII (Winter, 1964).   Flannery
O'Connor Memorial edition.
Farnham, James F. , "The Grotesque in Flannery O'Connor,"
America, CV (May 13, 1961), 277, 280-1.
Feeley, Sister Kathleen M. , "Thematic Imagery in the Fic-
tion of Flannery O'Connor," SHR, III (Winter, 1968), 14-
31.
Friedman, M. J. , and L. A. Lawson, eds. , Added Dimension.
Friedman, Melvin J. , "Flannery O'Connor: Another Legend
in Southern Fiction," EJ, LI (April, 1962), 233-43.   Also
(rev. and enl.) in Friedman, M. J. , and Lawson, L. A. ,
eds. , Added Dimension, 1-31. Also in Waldmeir, J. J. ,
ed. , Recent American Fiction, 231-45. Also in Reiter,
R. E. , ed. , Flannery O'Connor, 5-24.
_____, "Flannery O'Connor's Sacred Objects" in Fried-
man, M. J. , and L. A. Lawson, eds. , Added Dimension,
196-205.
Gable, Sister Mariella, "Ecumenic Core in Flannery O'Con-
nor's Fiction," ABR, XV (June, 1964), 127-43.
Gardiner, Harold C. , "Flannery O'Connor's Clarity of Vi-
sion" in Friedman, M. J. , and L. A. Lawson, eds. , Added
Dimension, 184-95.
Gordon, Caroline, "An American Girl" in Friedman, M. J. ,
and L. A. Lawson, eds. , Added Dimension, 123-37.
_____, "Heresy in Dixie," SR, LXXVI (1968), 263-97.
Gosset, L. Y. , "The Test By Fire: Flannery O'Connor,"
Violence in Recent Southern Fiction, 75-97.
Gregory, Donald L. , "An Internal Analysis of the Fiction of
Flannery O'Connor," DA, XXVIII (1968), 5055A (Ohio
State).
Griffith, Albert, "Flannery O'Connor," America, CXIII (No-
vember 27, 1965), 674-5.

Hawkes, John, "Flannery O'Connor's Devil," SR, LXX
    (Summer, 1962), 395-407. Also in Reiter, R.E., ed.,
    Flannery O'Connor, 25-37.
Hoffman, F.J., Art of Southern Fiction, 81-6.
_____, "The Search for Redemption: Flannery O'Connor's
    Fiction," in Friedman, M.J., and L.A. Lawson, eds.,
    Added Dimension, 32-48.
Holman, C. Hugh, "Her Rue with a Difference: Flannery
    O'Connor and the Southern Literary Tradition," in Fried-
    man, M.J., and L.A. Lawson, eds., Added Dimension,
    73-87.
Hyman, S.E., Flannery O'Connor.
Jacobsen, Josephine, "A Catholic Quartet," ChS, XLVII
    (Summer, 1964), 149-52.
Kirkland, William M., "Flannery O'Connor, The Person and
    the Writer," East-West Review, III (Summer, 1967), 159-
    63.
Lensing, George, "De Chardin's Ideas in Flannery O'Connor,"
    Ren, XVIII (Summer, 1966), 171-5.
Malin, Irving, "Flannery O'Connor and the Grotesque," in
    Friedman, M.J., and L.A. Lawson, eds., Added Dimen-
    sion, 108-22.
Martin, C.W., "The Convergence of Actualities: Themes in
    the Fiction of Flannery O'Connor," DA, XXVIII (1968),
    4180A-1A (Vanderbilt).
_____, True Country.
Meaders, Margaret I., "Flannery O'Connor: 'literary witch',"
    ColQ, X (Spring, 1962), 377-86.
Merton, Thomas, "Flannery O'Connor," Jubilee, XII (Novem-
    ber, 1964), 49-53.
Montgomery, Marion, "Flannery O'Connor and the Natural
    Man," MissQ, XXI (1968), 235-42.
_____, "Miss O'Connor and the Christ-Haunted," SoR, IV
    (Summer, 1968), 665-72.
Muller, Gilbert H., "Flannery O'Connor and the Catholic
    Grotesque," DA, XXVIII (1968), 3193A (Stanford).
Mullins, C. Ross, Jr., "Flannery O'Connor: An Interview,"
    Jubilee, XI (June, 1963), 32-5.
Murray, James G., "Southland ala Russe," Critic, XXI
    (June-July, 1963), 26-8.
O'Connor, Flannery, "The Novelist and Free Will," Fresco,
    I, ii (Winter, 1961), 100-1.
_____, "The Role of the Catholic Novelist," Greyfriar
    (Siena Studies in Literature), VII (1964), 5-13.
Quinn, Sister M. Bernetta, O.S.F., "Flannery O'Connor, a
    Realist of Distances," in Friedman, M.J., and L.A. Law-
    son, eds., Added Dimension, 157-83.

Rechnitz, Robert M., "Perception, Identity, and the Gro-
    tesque: A Study of Three Southern Writers," DA, XXVIII
    (1967), 2261A (Colo.).
Rubin, Louis D., Jr., "Flannery O'Connor and the Bible
    Belt," in Friedman, M.J., and L.A. Lawson, eds.,
    Added Dimension, 49-72. Also in Rubin, L.D., Jr.,
    Curious Death of the Novel, 239-61.
Rupp, Richard H., "Flannery O'Connor," Cweal, LXXIX
    (December 6, 1963), 304-7.
Scott, Nathan A., Jr., "Flannery O'Connor's Testimony:
    The Pressure of Glory," in Friedman, M.J., and L.A.
    Lawson, eds., Added Dimension, 138-56. Also in Scott,
    N.A., Jr., Craters of the Spirit, 267-85.
Shear, Walter, "Flannery O'Connor: Character and Charac-
    terization," Ren, XX (Spring, 1968), 140-6.
Sherry, Gerard E., "An Interview with Flannery O'Connor,"
    Critic, XXI (June-July, 1963), 26-8.
Shinn, Thelma J., "Flannery O'Connor and the Violence of
    Grace," WSCL, IX (Winter, 1968), 58-73.
Stelzmann, Rainulf, "Shock and Orthodoxy: An Interpretation
    of Flannery O'Connor's Novels and Short Stories," XUS,
    II (March, 1963), 4-21.
Stephens, Martha, "Flannery O'Connor and the Sanctified-
    Sinner Tradition," ArQ, XXIII, iv (Winter, 1967), 223-39.
Sullivan, Walter, "The Achievement of Flannery O'Connor,"
    SHR, II (Summer, 1968), 303-9.
VandeKieft, Ruth M., "Judgement in the Fiction of Flannery
    O'Connor," SR, LXXVI (1968), 337-56.
Walter, Sarah, "Strange Prophets of Flannery O'Connor,"
    Censer (Spring, 1960), 5-12. (Not seen.)

THE VIOLENT BEAR IT AWAY

Allen, W., Modern Novel, 308-9.
Baiiif, Algene, "A Southern Allegory: THE VIOLENT BEAR
    IT AWAY, by Flannery O'Connor," Ctary, XXX (October,
    1960), 358-62.
Bowen, Robert O., "Hope vs. Despair in the New Gothic
    Novel," Ren, XIII (1961), 147-52.
Browning, Preston M., Jr., "Flannery O'Connor and the
    Grotesque Recovery of the Holy," in Scott, N.A., Jr.,
    ed., Adversity and Grace, 147-61.
Burns, Stuart L., "Flannery O'Connor's THE VIOLENT
    BEAR IT AWAY: Apotheosis in Failure," SR, LXXVI
    (1968), 319-36.
_____, "'Torn By the Lord's Eye': Flannery O'Connor's
    Use of Sun Imagery," TCL, XIII (October, 1967), 163-6.

Davis, Barnabas, "Flannery O'Connor: Christian Belief in Recent Literature," Listening, 0 (Autumn, 1965), 15-18.

Donner, Robert, in Sign, XL (March, 1961), 46-8.

Drake, Robert, "The Bleeding Stinking Mad Shadow of Jesus in the Fiction of Flannery O'Connor," CLS, III (1966), 194-5.

_____, Flannery O'Connor.

_____, "Miss O'Connor and the Scandal of Redemption," ModA, IV (Fall, 1960), 428-30.

Duhamel, P. Albert, "Flannery O'Connor's Violent View of Reality," CathW, CXC (February, 1960), 280-5. Also in Reiter, R. E., ed., Flannery O'Connor, 93-101.

_____, "The Novelist as Prophet," in Friedman, M. J., and L. A. Lawson, eds., Added Dimension, 88-106.

Dunn, Sister Francis M., P. B. V. M., "Functions and Implications of Setting in the Fiction of Flannery O'Connor," DA, XXVII (1967), 3043A (Catholic Univ.).

Emerson, Donald C., in ArQ, XVI (Autumn, 1960), 284-6.

Fahey, William A., "Out of the Eater: Flannery O'Connor's Appetite for Truth," Ren, XX (Autumn, 1967), 22-9.

Ferris, Sumner J., "The Outside and the Inside: Flannery O'Connor's THE VIOLENT BEAR IT AWAY," Crit, III, ii (Winter-Spring, 1960), 11-19.

Friedman, Melvin J., "Flannery O'Connor: Another Legend in Southern Fiction," EJ, LI (April, 1962), 242-3. Also in Waldmeir, J. J., ed., Recent American Fiction, 243-5.

_____, "Flannery O'Connor's Sacred Objects," in Friedman, M. J., and L. A. Lawson, eds., Added Dimension, 201-2.

Gable, Sister Mariella, O. S. B., "Ecumenic Core in Flannery O'Connor's Fiction," ABR, XV (June, 1964), 132-6.

Gossett, L. Y., Violence in Recent Southern Fiction, 90-3.

Hawkes, John, "Flannery O'Conner's Devil, SR, LXX (Summer, 1962), 395-407, passim.

Hoffman, F. J., Art of Southern Fiction, 90-5.

_____, "The Search for Redemption: Flannery O'Connor's Fiction," in Friedman, F. J., and L. A. Lawson, eds., Added Dimension, 58-71.

Hood, Edward M., "A Prose Altogether Alive," KR, XXIII (Winter, 1961), 170-2.

Hyman, S. E., Flannery O'Connor, 19-25.

Jeremy, Sister, C. S. J., "THE VIOLENT BEAR IT AWAY: A Linguistic Education," Ren, XVII (Fall, 1964), 11-16. Also in Reiter, R. E., ed., Flannery O'Connor, 103-10.

Lorch, Thomas M., "Flannery O'Connor: Christian Allegorist," Crit, X, ii (1968), 69-80.

McCarthy, John F., "Human Intelligence Versus Divine

Truth: The Intellectual in Flannery O'Connor's Works,"
EJ, LV (December, 1966), 1143-5.

McCown, Robert M., "The Education of a Prophet: A Study
of Flannery O'Connor's THE VIOLENT BEAR IT AWAY,"
KM (1962), 73-8.

Malin, Irving, "Flannery O'Connor and the Grotesque," in
Friedman, M. J., and L. A. Lawson, eds., Added Dimension, 118-22.

_____, "The Gothic Family," Psychoanalysis and Ameri-
can Fiction, 269-71. Also in Malin, I., New American
Gothic, 68-71.

Martin, C. W., True Country, 55-61; 77-82; 100-3; 125-9;
141-2; 182-5; 205-6; 236-7.

Merton, Thomas, "The Other Side of Despair," Critic,
XXIII (October-November, 1965), 14-15.

Nolde, Sister M. Simon, O. S. B., "THE VIOLENT BEAR IT
AWAY: A Study in Imagery," XUS, I (1962), 180-94.

Quinn, John, in Esprit, (Univ. of Scranton), VII (Winter,
1963), 28-31.

Quinn, Sister M. Bernetta, O. S. F., "Flannery O'Connor, a
Realist of Distances," in Friedman, M. J., and L. A.
Lawson, eds., Added Dimension, 178-81.

Rubin, L. D., Jr., "Flannery O'Connor and the Bible Belt,"
in Friedman, M. J., and L. A. Lawson, eds., Added Dimension, 58-71. Also in Rubin, L. D., Jr., Curious
Death of the Novel, 248-61.

Scott, Nathan A., Jr., "Flannery O'Connor's Testimony:
The Pressure of Glory," in Friedman, M. J., and L. A.
Lawson, eds., Added Dimension, 144-8. Also in Scott,
N. A., Jr., Craters of the Spirit, 274-8.

Smith, J. Oates, "Ritual and Violence in Flannery O'Connor,"
Thought, XLI (Winter, 1966), 545-60.

Smith, Patrick J., "Typology and Peripety in Four Catholic
Novels," DA, XXVIII (1967), 2265A (Calif., Davis).

Snow, Ollye T., "The Functional Gothic of Flannery O'Connor," SWR, L (1965), 286-99.

Stelzmann, Rainulf, "Shock and Orthodoxy: An Interpretation
of Flannery O'Connor's Novels and Short Stories," XUS,
II (March, 1963), 11-13; 19-20.

Sullivan, Sister Bede, in Catholic Library World, XXXI
(May-June, 1960), 518-21.

Taylor, Henry, "The Halt Shall Be Gathered Together: Physical Deformity in the Fiction of Flannery O'Connor," WHR,
XXII (Autumn, 1968), 335-8.

Trowbridge, Clinton W., "The Symbolic Vision of Flannery
O'Connor: Patterns of Imagery in THE VIOLENT BEAR
IT AWAY," SR, LXXVI (1968), 298-318.

WISE BLOOD

Alvis, John, "WISE BLOOD: Hope in the City of the Profane," Kerygma, IV (Winter-Spring, 1965), 19-29.

Baumbach, Jonathan, "The Acid of God's Grace: The Fiction of Flannery O'Connor," GaR, XVII (Fall, 1963), 334-46. Also in Baumbach, J., Landscape of Nightmare, 87-100.

Davis, Joe L., "Outraged, or Embarassed," KR, XV (Spring, 1963), 320-3; 324-5.

Drake, Robert, "The Bleeding Stinking Mad Shadow of Jesus in the Fiction of Flannery O'Connor," CLS, III (1966), 186-8.

_____, Flannery O'Connor, 18-23.

Dunn, Sister Francis M., P.B.V.M., "Functions and Implications of Setting in the Fiction of Flannery O'Connor," DA, XXVII (1967), 3043A (Catholic Univ.).

Friedman, Melvin J., "Flannery O'Connor: Another Legend in Southern Fiction," EJ, LI (April, 1962), 240-2. Also in Waldmeir, J.J., ed., Recent American Fiction, 241-3.

Gable, Sister Mariella, "Ecumenic Core in Flannery O'Connor's Fiction," ABR, XV (June, 1964), 136-8.

Gordon, Caroline, "Flannery O'Connor's WISE BLOOD," Crit, II, ii (Fall, 1958), 3-10.

Gossett, L.Y., Violence in Recent Southern Fiction, 89-91.

Goyen, William, in NYTBR (May 18, 1952), 4.

Hart, Jane, "Strange Earth, the Stories of Flannery O'Connor," GaR, XII (Summer, 1958), 217-19.

Hartman, Carl, "Jesus Without Christ," WR, XVII (Autumn, 1952), 76-81.

Hassan, I., Radical Innocence, 79-80.

Hoffman, F.J., Art of Southern Fiction, 86-90.

_____, "The Search for Redemption: Flannery O'Connor's Fiction," in Friedman, M.J., and L.A. Lawson, eds., Added Dimension, 37-41; 47-8.

Hyman, S.E., Flannery O'Connor, 9-15.

Lawson, Lewis A., "Flannery O'Connor and the Grotesque: WISE BLOOD," Ren, XVIII (Spring, 1965), 137-47+. Also in Reiter, R.E., ed., Flannery O'Connor, 51-67.

Lorch, Thomas, "Flannery O'Connor: Christian Allegorist," Crit, X, ii (1968), 69-80.

Malin, Irving, "Flannery O'Connor and the Grotesque," in Friedman, M.J., and L.A. Lawson, eds., Added Dimension, 109-13.

_____, New American Gothic, 34-5.

Martin, C.W., True Country, 47-55; 66-71; 117-25; 194-5; 233-5.

Rechnitz, Robert M., "Passionate Pilgrim: Flannery O'Con-
nor's WISE BLOOD," GaR, XIX (Fall, 1965), 310-16.
Rubin, Louis D., Jr., "Flannery O'Connor and the Bible
Belt," in Friedman, M. J., and L. A. Lawson, eds.,
Added Dimension, 55-8.   Also in Rubin, L. D., Jr., Curi-
ous Death of the Novel, 245-8.
Scott, Nathan A., Jr., "Flannery O'Connor's Testimony:
The Pressures of Glory," in Friedman, M. J., and L. A.
Lawson, eds., Added Dimension, 150-4.   Also in Scott,
N. A., Jr., Craters of the Spirit, 280-5.
Simons, J. W., "A Case of Possession," Cweal, LVI (June
27, 1952), 297-8.
Smith, J. Oates, "Ritual and Violence in Flannery O'Connor,"
Thought, XLI (Winter, 1966), 545-60.
Snow, Ollye T., "The Functional Gothic of Flannery O'Con-
nor," SWR, L (1965), 298-9.
Stelzmann, Rainulf, "Shock and Orthodoxy: An Interpreta-
tion of Flannery O'Connor's Novels and Short Stories,"
XUS, II (March, 1963), 8-9; 14-16; 18-19.
Stephens, Martha, "Flannery O'Connor and the Sanctified-
Sinner Tradition," ArQ, XXIII, iv (Winter, 1967), 229-36.
Taylor, Henry, "The Halt Shall Be Gathered Together: Phys-
ical Deformity in the Fiction of Flannery O'Connor," WHR,
XXII (Autumn, 1968), 335-8.

BIBLIOGRAPHY

Brittain, Joan T., "Flannery O'Connor: A Bibliography,"
BB, XXV (September-December, 1967), 98-100
_____, "Flannery O'Connor, Part 2," BB, XXV (January-
April, 1968), 123-4.
Drake, R., Flannery O'Connor, 44-8.
Hyman, S. E., Flannery O'Connor, 47-8.
Lawson, Lewis A., "Bibliography," in Friedman, M. J., and
L. A. Lawson, eds., Added Dimension, 290-302.
Martin, C. W., True Country, 243-7.
Wedge, George F., "Two Bibliographies: Flannery O'Con-
nor, J. F. Powers," Crit, II (Fall, 1958), 59-63.

O'HARA, JOHN, 1905-

GENERAL

Aldridge, J. W., "The Pious Pornography of John O'Hara,"
Time to Murder and Create, 24-9.
Anon., "John O'Hara at 58: A Rage to Write," Newsweek,

LXI (June 3, 1963), 53-7.
Auchincloss, Louis, "Marquand and O'Hara: The Novel of
    Manners Today," Nation, CXCI (November 19, 1960),
    386-8. Also in Auchincloss, L., Reflections of a Jacob-
    ite, Boston: Houghton-Mifflin, 1961, 148-55.
Barrick, Mac E., "Proverbs and Sayings from Gibbsville,
    Pa.: John O'Hara's Use of Proverbial Materials," KFQ,
    XII (1967), 55-80.
Bassett, Charles W., "The Fictional World of John O'Hara,"
    DA, XXVI (1965), 363-4 (Kansas).
Bazelton, David, "O'Hara and America," New Leader, XLI
    (December 29, 1958), 18-19.
Bishop, J. P., "John O'Hara," VQR, (Winter, 1937). Also
    in Bishop, J. P., Collected Essays, 249-50.
Carson, E. R., Fiction of John O'Hara.
Grebstein, S. N., John O'Hara.
Portz, John, "John O'Hara Up to Now," CE, XVI (May,
    1955), 493-9; 516.
Sedlack, Robert P., "Manners, Morals, and the Fiction of
    John O'Hara," DA, XXVI (1965), 2224 (Notre Dame).
Shannon, William, "The Irish in Literature," American Irish,
    244-9.
Van Gelder, R., Writers on Writing, 59-61.
Walcutt, C. C., John O'Hara.
Weaver, Robert, "Twilight Area of Fiction: The Novels of
    John O'Hara," QQ, LXVI (Summer, 1959), 320-5.
Wilson, Edmund, "The Boys in the Back Room: John O'Hara,"
    NRep, (November 11, 1940), 665-6. Also in Wilson, E.,
    The Boys in the Back Room, San Francisco: Colt Pr.,
    1941. Also in Wilson, E., Classics and Commercials,
    22-6.

APPOINTMENT IN SAMARRA

Allen, W., Modern Novel, 182-3.
Bier, Jesse, "O'Hara's APPOINTMENT IN SAMARRA: His
    First and Only Real Novel," CE, XXV (November 1963),
    135-41.
Bruccoli, Matthew J., "Focus on APPOINTMENT IN SA-
    MARRA: The Importance of Knowing What You Are Talk-
    ing About," in Madden, D., ed., Tough Guy Writers of
    the Thirties, 129-36.
Carson, E. R., Fiction of John O'Hara, 9-14.
Donaldson, Scott, "Appointment With the Dentist: O'Hara's
    Naturalistic Novel," MFS, XIV (Winter, 1968-69), 435-42.
Fadiman, Clifton, in NY (September 1, 1934). Also in Fadi-
    man, C., Party of One, 447-9.

Grebstein, S. N. , John O'Hara, 34-45.
Gurko, L. , Angry Decade, 113-15.
Hierth, Harrison E. , "The Class Novel," CEA, XXVII (December, 1964), 1-4.
Levi, A. W. , Literature, Philosophy and the Imagination, 264-6.
Podhoretz, Norman, "Gibbsville and New Leeds: The America of John O'Hara and Mary McCarthy," Ctary, XXI (March, 1956), 269-70. Also in Podhoretz, N. , Doings and Undoings, 77-9.
Sedlack, Robert P. , "Manners, Morals, and the Fiction of John O'Hara," DA, XXVI (1965), 2224 (Notre Dame).
Walcutt, C. C. , John O'Hara, 13-17.
Weaver, Robert, "Twilight Area of Fiction: The Novels of John O'Hara," QQ, LXVI (1959), 322-3.

THE BIG LAUGH

Grebstein, S. N. , John O'Hara, 112-16.
Walcutt, C. C. , John O'Hara, 29-32.

BUTTERFIELD 8

Fadiman, C. , Party of One, 449-52.
Grebstein, S. N. , John O'Hara, 92-7.

ELIZABETH APPLETON

Boroff, David, "A Rage to Relive," SatR, XLVI (June 8, 1963), 29-30.
Grebstein, S. N. , John O'Hara, 75-82.
Walcutt, C. C. , John O'Hara, 32-6.

A FAMILY PARTY

Grebstein, S. N. , John O'Hara, 85-7.

THE FARMER'S HOTEL

Grebstein, S. N. , John O'Hara, 83-5.

FROM THE TERRACE

Bazelton, David, "O'Hara and America," New Leader, XLI (December 29, 1958), 18-19.
Carson, E. R. , Fiction of John O'Hara, 29-40.
Gardiner, Harold C. , "A Terrace Bounded By Curbstones,"

America, C (December 13, 1958), 347-8. Also in Gardiner, H.C., In All Conscience, 141-2.

Grebstein, S. N., John O'Hara, 63-9.

Hicks, Granville, "The Problem of O'Hara," SatR, XLI (November 29, 1958), 14-15.

Kazin, A., Contemporaries, 161-8.

Maloff, Saul, in NRep, CXL (January 5, 1959), 20-1.

Mizener, Arthur, "Something Went Seriously Wrong," NYTBR (November 23, 1958), 1, 14.

Sedlack, Robert P., "Manners, Morals, and the Fiction of John O'Hara," DA, XXVI (1965), 2224 (Notre Dame).

Wain, John, "Snowed Under," NY, XXXIV (January 10, 1959), 112-14.

Walcutt, C. C., Man's Changing Mask, 314-16.

Weaver, Robert, "Twilight Area of Fiction: The Novels of John O'Hara," QQ, LXVI (1959), 320-5 passim.

West, P., Modern Novel, v. 2, 231-2.

HOPE OF HEAVEN

Fadiman, C., Party of One, 452-4.

See, Carolyn, in Madden, D., ed., Tough Guy Writers of the Thirties, 211-13.

THE LOCKWOOD CONCERN

Walcutt, C. C., John O'Hara, 37-45.

OURSELVES TO KNOW

Adams, Phoebe, "Lolita in Pa.," Atlantic, CCV (March, 1969), 120-1.

Carson, E. R., Fiction of John O'Hara, 40-5.

Grebstein, S. N., John O'Hara, 69-75.

Mizener, Arthur, "Some Kinds of Modern Novel," SR, LXIX (Winter, 1961), 156-8.

A RAGE TO LIVE

Carson, E. R., Fiction of John O'Hara, 14-21.

Grebstein, S. N., John O'Hara, 45-54.

Prescott, O., In My Opinion, 72-4.

Sedlack, Robert P., "Manners, Morals, and the Fiction of John O'Hara," DA, XXVI (1965), 2224 (Notre Dame).

TEN NORTH FREDERICK

Alexander, Sidney, "Another Visit to O'Haraville," Reporter, XIV (January 26, 1956), 44-7.

Carson, E. R., Fiction of John O'Hara, 21-9.

Fiedler, Leslie, "Old Pro at Work," NRep, CXXXIV (January 9, 1956), 16-17.

Gardiner, Harold C., "Drained of Drama," America, XCIV (December 10, 1955), 307-8.

Grebstein, S. N., John O'Hara, 54-63.

McKelway, St. Clair, "And Nothing But the Truth," NY, XXXI (December 17, 1955), 162, 165-6.

Podhoretz, Norman, "Gibbsville and New Leeds: The America of John O'Hara and Mary McCarthy," Ctary, XXI (March, 1956), 269-71. Also in Podhoretz, N., Doings and Undoings, 76-80.

Sedlack, Robert P., "Manners, Morals and the Fiction of John O'Hara," DA, XXVI (1965), 2224 (Notre Dame).

BIBLIOGRAPHY

Grebstein, S. N., John O'Hara, 161-71.

ORWELL, GEORGE, 1903-1950

GENERAL

Alldritt, K., Making of George Orwell.

Ashe, Geoffrey, "A Note on George Orwell," Cweal, LIV (June 1, 1951), 191-3.

Atkins, J., George Orwell.

Barr, Donald, "The Answer to George Orwell," SatR, XL (March 30, 1957), 21; 30-2.

Beker, Miroslav, "The Ambivalence of George Orwell: A Note," SRA, No. 13-14 (July-December, 1962), 117-21.

————, "The Duality of George Orwell," Geste (Leeds Univ.), VI (October 27, 1960), 15-17. (Not seen.)

Birrell, T. A., "Is Integrity Enough?" DubR, CCXXIV (3rd quarter, (1950), 49-65.

Brander, Laurence, George Orwell.

————, "George Orwell: Politics and Good Prose," LonM, I (April, 1954), 64-71.

Braybrooke, Neville, "George Orwell," CathW, CLXXVIII (December, 1953), 178-84.

————, "George Orwell," Fortnightly, CLXXV (June, 1951), 403-9.

_____, "George Orwell: An English Radical in the Chris-
tian Tradition," Christus Rex, VII (July, 1953), 617-24.
Buckley, David P., "The Novels of George Orwell," DA,
XXVI (1966), 7310-11 (Columbia).
Burns, Wayne, "George Orwell: our 'responsible Quixote',"
WCR, II (September, 1967), 13-21.
Calder, J., Chronicles of Conscience.
Colquitt, Betsy F., "Orwell: Traditionalist in Wonderland,"
Discourse, VIII (Autumn, 1965), 370-83.
Cook, Richard, "Rudyard Kipling and George Orwell," MFS,
VII (Summer, 1961), 125-35.
Cosman, Max, "George Orwell and the Autonomous Individu-
al," PacSp, IX (Winter, 1955), 74-84.
_____, "Orwell's Terrain," Person, XXXV (January,
1954), 41-9.
Crowcroft, Peter, "Politics and Writing. The Orwell Analy-
sis," NRep, CXXXII (January 3, 1953), 17-18.
Dooley, David, "The Impact of Satire on Fiction: Studies in
Norman Douglas, Sinclair Lewis, Aldous Huxley. Evelyn
Waugh, and George Orwell," DA, XV (1955), 2203-4
(Iowa).
_____, "The Limitations of George Orwell," UTQ, XXVIII
(April, 1959), 291-300.
Duffey, Paula, "Form and Meaning in the Novels of George
Orwell," DA, XXVIII (1967), 1816A (Pa.).
Duncan, Iris J.A., "The Theme of the Artist's Isolation in
Works by Three Modern British Novelists," DA, XXVI
(1965), 3332 (Okla.).
Dutscher, Alan, "Orwell and the Crisis of Responsibility,"
Contemporary Issues (London), VII (August-September,
1956), 308-16.
Edrich, Emanuel, "George Orwell and the Satire in Horror,"
TSLL, IV (Spring, 1962), 96-108.
_____, "Literary Technique and Social Temper in the Fic-
tion of George Orwell," DA, XXI (1960), 620-1 (Wiscon-
sin).
Elliott, George P., "A Failed Prophet," HudR, X (Spring,
1957), 149-54.
Fiderer, Gerald L., "A Psychoanalytic Study of the Novels
of George Orwell," DA, XXVIII (1967), 1074A-75A (Okla.).
Fitzgerald, John J., "George Orwell's Social Compassion,"
Discourse, IX (Spring, 1966), 219-26.
Fixler, Michael, "George Orwell and the Instrument of Lan-
guage," IEY, No. 9 (1964), 46-54. (Not seen.)
Fyvel, T.R., "George Orwell and Eric Blair: Glimpses of
a Dual Life," Encounter, XIII (July, 1959), 60-5.
Glicksberg, Charles I., "The Literary Contribution of

George Orwell," ArQ, X (Autumn, 1954), 234-45.

Greenblatt, S. J., Three Modern Satirists, 37-73; 105-17.

Greenfield, Robert M., "Discursive Orwell," DA, XXVIII (1967), 1818A-19A (Columbia).

Griffin, C. W., "Orwell and the English Language," Audience, VII (Winter, 1960), 63-76.

Hollis, C., Study of George Orwell.

Hopkinson, Tom, George Orwell.

_____, "George Orwell - Dark Side Out," Cornhill, CLXVI (Summer, 1953), 450-70.

Jackson, Alan S., "George Orwell's Utopian Vision," DA, XXVI (1965), 2215 (So. Calif.).

Karl, F. R., "George Orwell: The White Man's Burden," Contemporary English Novel, 148-66.

Kendall, Walter, "David and Goliath... A Study of the Political Ideas of George Orwell," Geste (Leeds Univ.), VI (October 27, 1960), 3-14. (Not seen.)

King, Carlyle, "The Politics of George Orwell," UTQ, XXVI (1956), 79-91.

Kirk, Russell, "George Orwell's Despair," Intercollegiate Rev. (Bryn Mawr), V, i (1968), 21-5.

Kubal, David L., "Outside the Whale: George Orwell's Search for Meaning and Form," DA, XXIX (1968), 265A (Notre Dame).

Leckie, Robert, "The Man Who Invented Big Brother," Saga, XXV (October, 1962), 36-8; 88-9. (Not seen.)

Lee, Robert A., Orwell's Fiction.

_____, "The Spanish Experience: George Orwell and the Politics of Language," DA, XXVII (1967), 3053A (Oregon).

Lief, R. A., Homage to Oceania.

Mander, John, "Orwell in the Sixties," The Writer and Commitment, London: Secker and Warburg, 1961, 71-102.

Mellichamp, Leslie, "George Orwell and the Ethics of Revolutionary Politics," ModA, IX (1965), 272-8.

North, Roy, "George Orwell," Visva-Bharati Q, XIX (Summer, 1953), 39-56.

O'Donnell, Donat, "Orwell Looks at the World," NStat, LXI (May 26, 1961), 837-8. Also in O'Brien, C. C., Writers and Politics, N. Y.: Pantheon, 1964, 31-5.

Orwell, George, "Some Letters of George Orwell," Encounter, XVIII (January, 1962), 55-65.

_____, "Why I Write," Such, Such Were the Joys, 3-11.

Oxley, B. T., George Orwell.

Petts, Paul, "Don Quixote on a Bicycle: In Memorium, George Orwell, 1903-1950," LonM, IV (March, 1957), 39-47.

Quintana, Ricardo, "George Orwell: The Satiric Resolution,"

<u>WSCL</u>, II, i (Winter, 1961), 31-8.

Rees, R., <u>George Orwell.</u>

Rieff, Philip, "George Orwell and the Post-Liberal Imagination," <u>KR</u>, XVI (Winter, 1954), 49-70.   Also in Howe, I.,
ed., <u>Orwell's NINETEEN EIGHTY-FOUR</u>, 227-37.

Rovere, Richard H., "George Orwell," <u>NRep</u>, CXXXV (September 10, 1956), 11-15.   Also (expanded) as "Introduction," <u>The Orwell Reader</u>, N.Y.: Harcourt, Brace, 1956, ix-xxi.   Also in Rovere, R.H., <u>The American Establishment, and Other Reports, Opinions and Speculations,</u> N.Y.: Harcourt, Brace & World, 1962, 167-81.

Scott, Nathan A., "The Example of George Orwell," <u>Chr&Cr</u>, XIX (July 20, 1959), 107-10.

Shibata, Toshihiko, "The Road to Nightmare: An Essay on George Orwell," <u>SELL</u>, No. 12 (1962), 41-53.

Smith, W.D., "George Orwell," <u>ConR</u>, CLXXXIX, No. 1085 (May, 1956), 283-6.

Smyer, Richard M., "Structure and Meaning in the Works of George Orwell," <u>DA</u>, XXIX (1968), 615A (Stanford).

Snyder, Philip J., "Doing the Necessary Task: The Bourgeois Humanism of George Orwell," <u>DA</u>, XXV (1965), 6636-7 (Western Reserve).

Stevens, A. Wilbur, "George Orwell and Southeast Asia," <u>YCGL</u>, XI (1962), 133-41.

Thirlby, Peter, "Orwell as a Liberal," <u>Marxist Q</u>, III, iv (October, 1956), 239-47.

Thomas, E.M., <u>Orwell.</u>

Thompson, Frank H., Jr., "Orwell's Image of the Man of Good Will," <u>CE</u>, XXII (January, 1961), 235-40.

Trilling, Lionel, "George Orwell and the Politics of Truth," <u>Ctary</u>, XIII (March, 1952), 218-27.   Also as "Introduction" to Orwell, G., <u>Homage to Catalonia</u>, N.Y.: Harcourt, Brace, 1952.   Also in Trilling, L., <u>The Opposing Self</u>, N.Y.: Viking, 1955.   Also in Howe, I., ed., <u>Orwell's NINETEEN EIGHTY-FOUR</u>, 217-26.

Voorhees, Richard J., "George Orwell: Rebellion and Responsibility," <u>SAQ</u>, LIII (October, 1954), 556-65.

_____, "Orwell's Secular Crusade," <u>Cweal</u>, LXI (January 28, 1955), 448-51.

_____, <u>Paradox of George Orwell.</u>

Wain, John, "Here Lies Lower Binfield," <u>Encounter</u>, XVII (October, 1961), 70-83.

_____, "Orwell in Perspective," in <u>New World Writing</u>, 12th Mentor Selection, N.Y.: New American Library, 84-96.   Also in Wain, J., <u>Essays on Literature and Ideas</u>, N.Y.: St. Martin's Pr., London: Macmillan, 180-93.

_____, "Orwell and the Intelligentsia," <u>Encounter</u>, XXXI

vi (1968), 72-80.
Warncke, Wayne, "The Permanence of Orwell," UR, XXXIII
(March, 1967), 189-96.
West, A., Principles and Persuasions, 164-76.
Williams, Raymond, Culture and Society, 1780-1950, N. Y.:
Columbia Un. Pr., 1958, N. Y.: Harper Torchbooks,
1966, 285-94.
Willison, Ian, "Orwell's Bad Good Books," TC, CLVII (April, 1955), 354-66.
Woodcock, George, Crystal Spirit.
_____, "The Deepening Solitude," Malahat Rev., No. 5
(January, 1968), 57-62.
_____, Writer and Politics, 111-24.
_____, "George Orwell, 19th Century Liberal," Politics,
III (December, 1946), 384-8.
World Review, n. s. XVI (June, 1950). Orwell issue.
Wulfsberg, Frederick, "George Orwell," Norseman (March-
April, 1950), 90-4.

ANIMAL FARM

Aickman, Robert F., in Nineteenth Century, CXXXVIII (December, 1945), 255-61.
Aldritt, K., Making of George Orwell, 147-50.
Atkins, J., George Orwell, 221-32.
Brander, L., George Orwell, 170-82.
Brown, Spencer, "Strange Doings at Animal Farm," Ctary,
XIX (February, 1955), 155-61.
Calder, J., Chronicles of Conscience, 223-8.
Colquitt, Betsy F., "Orwell: Traditionalist in Wonderland,"
Discourse, VIII (Autumn, 1965), 376-7.
Cooper, Nancy M., "ANIMAL FARM: An Explication for
Teachers of Orwell's Novel," CEJ, IV (Fall, 1968), 59-69.
Davis, Robert M., "Politics in the Pig-Pen," JPC, II (Fall,
1968), 314-20.
De Hegedus, Adam, in Cweal, XLIV (September 13, 1946),
528-30.
Dempsey, David, in AR, VII (March, 1947), 142-50.
Fraser, G. S., Modern Writer and His World, 157-8.
Greenblatt, S. J., Three Modern Satirists, 60-66, and passim.
Gulbin, Suzanne, "Parallels and Contrasts in LORD OF THE
FLIES and ANIMAL FARM," EJ, LV (January, 1966), 86-
90+.
Hollis, C., Study of George Orwell, 139-53.
Hopkinson, Tom, "ANIMAL FARM," World Rev., n. s., XVI
(June, 1950), 54-7.
_____, George Orwell, 28-31.

King, Carlyle, "The Politics of George Orwell," <u>UTQ,</u> XXVI (1956), 79-91.
Lee, R.A., <u>Orwell's Fiction,</u> 105-27.
Leyburn, E.D., <u>Satiric Allegory,</u> 68-70.
Maddison, Michael, "At the Crossroads of Ideology: George Orwell's ANIMAL FARM," <u>Geste</u> (Leeds Univ.), VI (October 27, 1960), 18-21.
Oxley, B.T., <u>George Orwell,</u> 75-82.
Rees, R., <u>George Orwell,</u> 82-6.
Schmerl, Rudolf B., "Orwell as Fantasist," <u>Cresset,</u> XXV (June, 1962), 11-13.
Siepmann, F.O., "Farewell to Orwell," <u>Nineteenth Century and After,</u> CXLVII (March, 1950), 141-7 <u>passim.</u>
Smythe, P.E., <u>A Guide to the Study of Orwell's ANIMAL FARM,</u> Sidney: College Pr., 1965.
Strachey, John, "Strangled Cry," <u>Encounter,</u> XV (November, 1960), 9. Also in Strachey, J., <u>Strangled Cry,</u> 23-5.
Thomas, E.M., <u>Orwell,</u> 71-7.
Walsh, James, "An Appreciation of an Individualist Writer," <u>Marxist Q,</u> III, i (January, 1956), 30-2.
Webb, Tim, "Orwell: ANIMAL FARM," in Harward, T.B., ed., <u>European Patterns: Contemporary Patterns in European Writing,</u> Chester Springs, Pa.: Dufour, 1966, 44-8.
Woodcock, G., <u>Crystal Spirit,</u> 192-8.
Woodhouse, C.M., "ANIMAL FARM," <u>TLS</u> (August 6, 1954), xxx-xxxi.

BURMESE DAYS

Aldritt, K., <u>Making of George Orwell,</u> 20-6.
Brander, L., <u>George Orwell,</u> 75-89.
Braybrooke, Neville, "George Orwell," <u>CathW,</u> CLXXVIII (December, 1953), 179-81.
Calder, J., <u>Chronicles of Conscience,</u> 82-7.
Greenblatt, S.J., <u>Three Modern Satirists,</u> 49-54, and <u>passim.</u>
Hollis, C., <u>Study of George Orwell,</u> 29-39.
Karl, F.R., "George Orwell: The White Man's Burden," <u>Contemporary English Novel,</u> 155-7.
Lee, R.A., <u>Orwell's Fiction,</u> 1-22.
Meyers, Jeffrey, "The Ethics of Responsibility: Orwell's BURMESE DAYS," <u>UR,</u> XXXV (December, 1968), 83-7.
Muggeridge, Malcolm, "BURMESE DAYS," <u>World Rev.,</u> n.s., XVI (June, 1950), 45-8.
Oxley, B.T., <u>George Orwell,</u> 84-92.
Rosenfeld, Isaac, "Decency and Death," <u>PR,</u> XVII (May-June, 1950), 515. Also in Rosenfeld, I., <u>Age of Enor-</u>

mity, 252-3.
Spence, J. E., "George Orwell," Theoria, XIII (1959), 16-19.
Stevens, Arthur Wilbur, "George Orwell and Contemporary
    British Fiction of Burma," DA, XVIII (1958), 1799-80
    (Univ. of Washington).
————, "George Orwell and Southeast Asia," YCGL, XI
    (1962), 133-41.
Thomas, E. M., Orwell, 8-12.
Voorhees, Richard J., "Orwell and Power-Hunger," CanF,
    XXXVI (July, 1961), 79.
————, Paradox of George Orwell, 75-8.
Wadsworth, Frank W., "Orwell as Novelist: The Early
    Work," UKCR, XXII (Winter, 1955), 93-7.
Woodcock, G., Crystal Spirit, 84-104; 346-8.

A CLERGYMAN'S DAUGHTER

Alldritt, K., Making of George Orwell, 27-31.
Brander, L., George Orwell, 93-100.
Calder, J., Chronicles of Conscience, 87-90.
Hollis, C., Study of George Orwell, 57-68.
Lee, R. A., Orwell's Fiction, 23-47.
Lief, R. A., Homage to Oceania, 79-83.
Oxley, B. T., George Orwell, 92-8.
Thomas, E. M., Orwell, 24-6.
Voorhees, R. J., Paradox of George Orwell, 44-9.
Wadsworth, Frank W., "Orwell as Novelist: The Early
    Work," UKCR, XXII (Winter, 1955), 97-9.
Woodcock, G., Crystal Spirit, 125-40.

COMING UP FOR AIR

Alldritt, K., Making of George Orwell, 37-41.
Brander, L., George Orwell, 150-69.
Calder, J., Chronicles of Conscience, 163-5.
Hollis, C., Study of George Orwell, 108-18.
Hopkinson, T., George Orwell, 25-6.
King, Carlyle, "The Politics of George Orwell," UTQ, XXVI
    (1956), 90-1.
Lee, R. A., Orwell's Fiction, 83-104.
Oxley, B. T., George Orwell, 105-12.
Rees, R., George Orwell, 73-9.
Rosenfeld, Isaac, "Decency and Death," PR, XVII (May-June,
    1950), 515-16. Also in Rosenfeld, I., Age of Enormity,
    253-4.
Thomas, E. M., Orwell, 52-9.
Voorhees, R. J., Paradox of George Orwell, 109-14.

Wadsworth, Frank, "Orwell as Novelist: The Middle Period,"
UKCR, XXII (March, 1956), 192-4.
Wain, John, "Here Lies Lower Binfield," Encounter, XVII
(October, 1961), 74-83. Also in Wain, J., Essays on
Literature and Ideas, London: Macmillan, N.Y.: St.
Martin's, 1963, 194-213.
Woodcock, G., Crystal Spirit, 176-87.

KEEP THE ASPIDISTRA FLYING

Alldritt, K., Making of George Orwell, 31-6.
Brander, L., George Orwell, 100-10.
Calder, J., Chronicles of Conscience, 90-8.
Greenblatt, S.J., Three Modern Satirists, 53-7; and passim.
Hollis, C., Study of George Orwell, 69-76.
Hopkinson, T., George Orwell, 18-19.
Karl, F.R., "George Orwell: The White Man's Burden,"
Contemporary English Novel, 161-2.
Lee, R.A., Orwell's Fiction, 48-65.
Lief, R.A., Homage to Oceania, 44-7; 64-5; 115-17.
Meredith, William, "Pilgrim and the Money-God," Nation,
CLXXXII (January 21, 1956), 55.
Oxley, B.T., George Orwell, 98-105.
Rees, R., George Orwell, 31-6.
Rosenfeld, Isaac, "Gentleman George," Ctary, XXI (June,
1956), 581-91. Also in Rosenfeld, I., Age of Enormity,
246-51.
Thomas, E.M., Orwell, 26-8.
Wadsworth, Frank, "Orwell as Novelist: The Middle Period,"
UKCR, XXII (March, 1956), 189-92.
West, Anthony, "Hidden Damage," NY, XXXI (January 28,
1956), 98-104. Also in West, A., Principles and Per-
suasions, 164-9.
Woodcock, G., Crystal Spirit, 140-50.

NINETEEN EIGHTY FOUR

Alldritt, K., Making of George Orwell, 150-78.
Anon., "Orwell's Strange World of 1984," Life, XXVII (July
4, 1948), 78-85.
Ashe, Geoffrey, "Second Thoughts on NINETEEN EIGHTY-
FOUR," Month, n.s., IV (November, 1950), 285-300.
Atkins, J., George Orwell, 237-54.
Bakker, J., "George Orwell's Newspeak in Light of A
PHILOSOPHY IN A NEW KEY," Levende Talen, CCXLII
(December, 1967), 674-83.
Barr, Alan, "The Paradise Behind 1984," EM, XIX (1968),

199-203.

Brander, L., George Orwell, 183-204.

Browning, Gordon, "Zamiatin's WE: An Anti-Utopian Classic," Cithara, VII (May, 1968), 13-20.

Calder, J., Chronicles of Conscience, 229-53.

Coe, Richard N., "NINETEEN EIGHTY-FOUR and the Anti-Utopian Tradition," Geste (Leeds Univ.), VI (October 27, 1960), 22-6.

Colquitt, Betsy F., "Orwell: Traditionalist in Wonderland," Discourse, VIII (Autumn, 1965), 377-83.

Deutscher, Isaac, "1984 - The Mysticism of Cruelty," Russia in Transition, N.Y.: Coward-McCann, 1957. Also in Rev. ed., N.Y.: Grove, 1960, 250-65. Also in Howe, I., ed., Orwell's NINETEEN EIGHTY-FOUR, 196-203.

Dutscher, Alan, "Orwell and the Crisis of Responsibility," Contemporary Issues (London), VII (August-September, 1956), 311-16.

Dyson, A.E., "George Orwell: Irony as Prophecy," Crazy Fabric, 197-219.

Edrich, Emanuel, "George Orwell and the Satire in Horror," TSLL, IV (1962), 96-108, passim.

Ehrenpreis, Irvin, "Orwell, Huxley and Pope," RLV, XXIII, iii (1957), 215-30, passim.

Elsbree, Langdon, "The Structured Nightmare of 1984," TCL, V (October, 1959), 135-41.

Fraser, G.S., Modern Writer and His World, 158-9.

Fromm, Erich, "Afterward" to 1984, N.Y.: New American Library, 1954, 257-67. Also in Howe, I., ed., Orwell's NINETEEN EIGHTY-FOUR, 204-10.

Gable, Sister Mariella, "Prose Satire and the Modern Christian Temper," ABR, XI (March-June, 1960), 23-6.

Geering, D.G., "DARKNESS AT NOON and NINETEEN EIGHTY-FOUR - A Comparative Study," AusQ, XXX (March, 1958), 90-6.

Gleckner, Robert F., "1984 or 1948?" CE, XVIII (November, 1956), 95-9.

Greenblatt, S.J., Three Modern Satirists, 66-72, and passim.

Hamilton, Kenneth M., "G.K. Chesterton and George Orwell: A Contrast in Prophecy," DR, XXXI (Autumn, 1951), 203-5.

Harris, Harold J., "Orwell's Essays and 1984," TCL, IV (January, 1959), 154-61.

Highet, G., Anatomy of Satire, 171-3.

Hollis, Christopher, in Horizon, XX (September, 1949), 200-8.

_____, Study of George Orwell, 188-201.

Hopkinson, T., George Orwell, 31-4.

Howe, Irving, "The Fiction of Anti-Utopia," NRep, CXLVI (April 23, 1962), 13-16. Also in Howe, I., ed., Orwell's NINETEEN EIGHTY-FOUR, 176-80.

_____, "History as Nightmare," ASch, XXV (Spring, 1956), 193-206. Also in Howe, I., Politics and the Novel, 235-51. Also (as "1984: History as Nightmare") in Howe, I., ed., Orwell's NINETEEN EIGHTY-FOUR, 188-96.

_____, Orwell's NINETEEN EIGHTY-FOUR.

_____, "1984 - Utopia Reversed," New International, XVI (November-December, 1950), 360-8.

Huxley, Aldous, "A Footnote About '1984'," World Rev (June, 1950), 60.

Jones, Joseph, "Utopias as Dirge," AQ, II (Fall, 1950), 214-26.

Karl, F. R., "George Orwell: The White Man's Burden," Contemporary English Novel, 159-61; 163-5.

Kegel, Charles H., "NINETEEN EIGHTY-FOUR: A Century of Ingsoc," N&Q, X (April, 1963), 151-2.

Kessler, Martin, "Power and the Perfect State: A Study in Disillusionment as Reflected in Orwell's NINETEEN EIGHTY-FOUR and Huxley's BRAVE NEW WORLD," PSQ, LXXII (December, 1957), 565-77.

King, Carlyle, "The Politics of George Orwell," UTQ, XXVI (1956), 79-91.

Knox, George, "The 'Divine Comedy' in '1984'," WHR, IX (Autumn, 1955), 371-2.

Lee, R. A., Orwell's Fiction, 128-55.

LeRoy, Gaylord C., "A. F. 632 to 1984," CE, XII (December, 1950), 135-8.

Leyburn, E. D., Satiric Allegory, 125-35.

Lief, R. A., Homage to Oceania, 41-3; 56-8; 69-70; 76-7; 84-8; 93-101; 107-14; 118-21.

Lockyer, Robert, "George Orwell's 1984," T&T, XXXVI (January 15, 1955), 78.

Lyons, John O., "George Orwell's Opaque Glass in 1984," WSCL, II, iii (Fall, 1961), 39-46.

McDowell, Jennifer, "1984 and Soviet Reality," Univ. of Cal. Graduate Jnl., No. 1 (Fall, 1962), 12-19.

Maddison, Michael, "1984: A Burnhamite Fantasy?" PolQ, XXXII (January-March, 1961), 71-9.

Nott, Kathleen, "Orwell's NINETEEN EIGHTY-FOUR," Listener, LXX (October 31, 1963), 687-8.

Oxley, B. T., George Orwell, 112-25.

Padovano, A., Estranged God, 154-7.

Prescott, O., In My Opinion, 27-31.

Raban, J., "Irony in the Language of Fiction," Technique of Modern Fiction, 187-91.

Rahv, Philip, "The Unfuture of Utopia," PR, XVI (July, 1949), 743-9. Also in Howe, I., ed., Orwell's NINE-TEEN EIGHTY-FOUR, 181-5. Also in Rahv, P., Literature and the Sixth Sense, 331-9.

Ranald, Ralph A., "George Orwell and the Mad World: The Anti-Universe of 1984," SAQ, LXVI (1967), 544-53.

Read, Herbert, "1984," World Rev (June, 1950), 60.

Reader, Mark, "The Political Criticism of George Orwell," DA, XXVIII (1967), 273A (Michigan).

Rees, David, "The View from Airstrip One," Spectator (December 3, 1965), 742-3.

Rees, R., George Orwell, 88-108; 116-17.

Richards, D., "Four Utopias," SEER, XL (1962), 224-8.

Roland, Albert, "Christian Implications in Anti-Stalinist Novels," Religion in Life, XXII (1953), 404-6.

Rosenfeld, Isaac, "Decency and Death," PR, XVII (May-June, 1950), 516-18. Also in Rosenfeld, I., Age of Enormity, 254-7. Also in Howe, I., ed., Orwell's NINETEEN EIGHTY-FOUR, 185-8.

Russell, Bertrand, "Symptoms of Orwell's 1984," Portraits from Memory and Other Essays, N.Y.: Simon & Schuster, 1956, 221-8.

Schmerl, Rudolf B., "Orwell as Fantasist," Cresset, XXV (June, 1962), 8-10.

Shibata, Toshihiko, "The Road to Nightmare: An Essay on George Orwell," SELL, No. 12 (1962), 41-53 passim.

Siepmann, E.O., "Farewell to Orwell," Nineteenth Century and After, CXLVII (March, 1950), 141-7 passim.

Sillen, Samuel, "Maggot-of-the-Month," M&M, II (August, 1949). Also in Howe, I., ed., Orwell's NINETEEN EIGHTY-FOUR, 210-12.

Slater, Joseph, "The Fictional Values of 1984," in Kirk, Rudolf, and C.F. Main, eds., Essays in Literary History, presented to J. Milton French, New Brunswick, N.J.: Rutgers Un. Pr., 1960, 249-64.

Smith, Marcus, "The Wall of Blackness: A Psychological Approach to 1984," MFS, XIV (Winter, 1968-69), 423-33.

Soskin, William, "What Can Be," SatR, XXXII (June 11, 1949), 12-13.

Spender, S., "Anti-Vision and Despair," Creative Element, 125-39.

Strachey, John, "The Strangled Cry," Encounter, XV (November, 1960), 10-13. Also in Strachey, J., Strangled Cry, 25-32.

Symons, J., "George Orwell's Utopia," Critical Occasions,

55-60.

Thale, Jerome, "Orwell's Modest Proposal," CritQ, IV (Winter, 1962), 365-8.

Thomas, E. M., Orwell, 82-99.

Thompson, Frank H., Jr., "Orwell's Image of the Man of Good Will," CE, XXII (January, 1961), 235-8.

Voorhees, Richard J., "NINETEEN EIGHTY-FOUR: No Failure of Nerve," CE, XVIII (November, 1956), 101-2.

_____, "Orwell and Power-Hunger," CanF, XXXVI (July, 1956), 79-80.

_____, Paradox of George Orwell, 60-2; 78-88.

Wadsworth, Frank, "Orwell's Later Work," UKCR, XXII (1956), 285-91.

Walsh, James, "An Appreciation of an Individualist Writer: George Orwell," Marxist Qtly, III, i (January, 1956), 32-9. Also in Howe, I., ed., Orwell's NINETEEN EIGHTY-FOUR, 212-16.

Warncke, Wayne, "A Note on 1984," Hartwick Rev, III (Fall, 1967), 60-1.

_____, "The Permanence of Orwell," UR, XXXIII (March, 1967), 190-1.

Way, Brian, "George Orwell: The Political Thinker We Might Have Had," Gemini/Dialogue, III (Spring, 1960), 8-18.

Wicker, Brian, "An Analysis of Newspeak," Blackfriars, XLIII (June, 1962), 272-85.

Woodcock, George, Crystal Spirit, 58-61; 67-70; 203-21; 262-4; 330-2; 348-9.

_____, "Utopias in Negative," SR, LXIV (Winter, 1956), 81-97.

Yorks, Samuel A., "George Orwell: Seer Over His Shoulder," BuR, IX (March, 1960), 32-45.

BIBLIOGRAPHY

Lee, R. A., Orwell's Fiction, 179-83.

McDowell, M. Jennifer, "George Orwell: Bibliographical Addenda," BB, XXIV (May-August, 1963), 19-24; XXIV (September-December, 1963), 36-40.

Zeke, Zoltan G., and W. White, "Orwelliana," BB, XXIII (September-December, 1961), 140-4.

PATON, ALAN, 1903-

GENERAL

Callan, E., Alan Paton.
Rooney, F. Charles, "The 'Message' of Alan Paton," CathW,
    CXCIV (November, 1961), 92-8. Also in Baker, S., ed.,
    Paton's CRY, THE BELOVED COUNTRY, 151-3.

CRY, THE BELOVED COUNTRY

Baker, Sheridan, "Paton's Beloved Country and the Morality
    of Geography," CE, XIX (November, 1957), 56-61. Also
    in Baker, S., ed., Paton's CRY, THE BELOVED COUN-
    TRY, 144-8.
_____, ed., Paton's CRY, THE BELOVED COUNTRY.
Bruell, Edwin, "Keen Scalpel on Racial Ills," EJ, LIII (1964),
    658-61.
Callan, E., Alan Paton, 49-66.
Collins, Harold R., "CRY, THE BELOVED COUNTRY and
    the Broken Tribe," CE, XIV (April, 1953), 379-85. Also
    in Baker, S., ed., Paton's CRY, THE BELOVED COUN-
    TRY, 138-43.
Davies, Horton, "Alan Paton: Literary Artist and Anglican,"
    HJ, L (April, 1952), 262-8.
_____, Mirror of the Ministry in Modern Novels, 128-36.
Fuller, E., "Alan Paton: Tragedy and Beyond," Books With
    the Men Behind Them, 94-9.
Gailey, Harry A., "Sheridan Baker's 'Paton's Beloved Coun-
    try'," CE, XX (December, 1958), 143-4. Also in Baker,
    S., ed., Paton's CRY, THE BELOVED COUNTRY, 149-
    50.
Gardiner, Harold C., "On Saying 'Boo' to Geese," America,
    LXXVIII (March 13, 1948), 661-3. Also in Gardiner, H.
    C., In All Conscience, 108-9.
Hartt, K.N., Lost Image of Man, 85-9.
Hester, Sister Mary, "Greek Tragedy and the Novels of Alan
    Paton," WisSL, No. 1 (1964), 54-61.
Marcus, Fred H., "CRY, THE BELOVED COUNTRY and
    STRANGE FRUIT: Exploring Man's Inhumanity to Man,"
    EJ, LI (December, 1962), 658-61.
Prescott, O., In My Opinion, 240-3.
Rolo, Charles J., "Reader's Choice," Atlantic, CLXXXI
    (April, 1948), 112-13. Also in Baker, S., ed., Paton's
    CRY, THE BELOVED COUNTRY, 137.
Rooney, F. Charles, "The 'Message' of Alan Paton," CathW,
    CXCIV (November, 1961), 94-5. Also in Baker, S., ed.,
    Paton's CRY, THE BELOVED COUNTRY, 152-3.

Tucker, M., Africa in Modern Literature, 223-5.

TOO LATE THE PHALAROPE

Baker, Sheridan, "Paton's Late Phalarope," ESA, III (September, 1960), 152-9.
Callan, E., Alan Paton, 67-84.
Fuller, E., "Alan Paton: Tragedy and Beyond," Books With the Men Behind Them, 83-95.
Gardiner, Harold C., "Alan Paton's Second Masterpiece," America, LXXXIX (August 29, 1953), 519-20. Also in Gardiner, H. C., In All Conscience, 112-16.
Gordimer, Nadine, "The Novel and the Nation in South Africa," TLS (August 11, 1961), 521-2.
Hester, Sister Mary, "Greek Tragedy and the Novels of Alan Paton," WisSL, No. 1 (1964), 54-61.
Rooney, F. Charles, "The 'Message' of Alan Paton," CathW, CXCIV (November, 1961), 95-7.
Tucker, M., Africa in Modern Literature, 225-7.

BIBLIOGRAPHY

Callan, E., Alan Paton, 145-54.

PERCY, WALKER, 1916-

GENERAL

Brown, Ashley, "An Interview with Walker Percy," Shen, XVIII, iii (Spring, 1967), 3-10.
Cremeens, Carlton, "Walker Percy. The Man and the Novelist: An Interview," SoR, IV (Spring, 1968), 271-90.
Maxwell, Robert, "Walker Percy's Fancy," MinnR, VII, iii (1967), 231-7.

THE LAST GENTLEMAN

Blouin, Michael T., "The Novels of Walker Percy: An Attempt at Synthesis," XUS, VI (February, 1967), 29-42.
Crews, Frederick C., "The Hero as 'Case'," Ctary, XLII (September, 1966), 100-2.
Douglas, Ellen, Walker Percy's THE LAST GENTLEMAN (Religious Dimensions in Literature), N.Y.: Seabury, 1969.
Hoffman, F. J., Art of Southern Fiction, 133-7.
Lehan, Richard, "The Way Back: Redemption in the Novels of Walker Percy," SoR, IV (Spring, 1968), 306-19.

THE MOVIEGOER

Atkins, Anselm, "Walker Percy and the Post-Christian
  Search," CentR, XII (Winter, 1968), 73-95.
Blouin, Michael T., "The Novels of Walker Percy: An At-
  tempt at Synthesis," XUS, VI (February, 1967), 29-42.
Cheney, Brainard, "To Restore a Fragmented Image," SR,
  LXIX (1961), 691-700.
Henisey, Sarah, "Intersubjectivity in Symbolization," Ren,
  XX (Summer, 1968), 208-14.
Hoffman, F. J., Art of Southern Fiction, 129-33.
Hoggard, James, "Death of the Vicarious," SWR, XLIX
  (Autumn, 1964), 366-74.
Hyman, S. E., "Moviegoing and Other Intimacies," Standards,
  63-7.
Kostelanetz, Richard, "The New American Fiction," in Kos-
  telanetz, R., ed., New American Arts, 224-5.
Lehan, Richard, "The Way Back: Redemption in the Novels
  of Walker Percy," SoR, IV (Spring, 1968), 306-19.
Tanner, T., Reign of Wonder, 349-56.
Thale, Jerome, "Alienation on the American Plan," ForumH,
  VI (Summer, 1968), 36-40.
Thale, Mary, "The Moviegoer of the 1950's," TCL, XIV
  (July, 1968), 84-9.

PORTER, KATHERINE ANNE, 1894-

GENERAL

Core, George, "The Best Residuum of Truth," GaR, XX
  (1966), 278-91.
Curley, Daniel, "Katherine Anne Porter: The Larger Plan,"
  KR, XXV (Autumn, 1963), 671-95.
Hartley, L., and G. Fore, eds., Katherine Anne Porter.
Hendrick, G., Katherine Anne Porter.
Krishnamurthi, Matighatta G., "Katherine Anne Porter: A
  Study in Themes," DA, XXVIII (1967), 682A-3A (Wiscon-
  sin).
Marsden, Malcolm M., "Love as Threat in Katherine Anne
  Porter's Fiction," TCL, XIII (April, 1967), 29-38.
Mooney, H. J., Jr., Fiction and Criticism of Katherine Anne
  Porter.
Nance, W. L., Katherine Anne Porter and the Art of Re-
  ligion.
Plante, Patricia R., "Katherine Anne Porter: Misanthrope
  Acquitted," XUS, II (December, 1963), 87-91.

Ruoff, James, "Katherine Anne Porter Comes to Kansas,"
    MQ, IV (July, 1963), 305-14.
Thompson, Barbara, "The Art of Fiction XXIX: Katherine
    Anne Porter," ParisR, VIII, No. 29 (Winter-Spring, 1963),
    87-114. Also in Writers at Work, 2nd ser., 137-63.

SHIP OF FOOLS

Abraham, William, "Progression Through Repetition," MR,
    IX (Summer, 1963), 805-9.
Adams, Robert Hickman, "The Significance of Point of View
    in Katherine Anne Porter's SHIP OF FOOLS," DA, XXVI
    (1965), 2001 (So. Calif.).
Alexander, Jean, "Katherine Anne Porter's Ship in the
    Jungle," TCL, XI (January, 1966), 179-88.
Auchincloss, L., Pioneers and Caretakers, 145-51.
Baker, Howard, "The Upward Path: Notes on the Works of
    Katherine Anne Porter," SoR, n. s., IV (Winter, 1968),
    15-19.
Bedford, Sybille, "Voyage to Everywhere," Spectator, No.
    7012 (November 16, 1962), 763-4.
Bode, Carl, "Miss Porter's SHIP OF FOOLS," WSCL, III
    (Fall, 1962), 90-2. Also in Bode, C., The Half-World of
    American Culture, Carbondale: So. Illinois Un. Pr.,
    1965, 220-5.
Curley, Daniel, "Katherine Anne Porter: The Larger Plan,"
    KR, XXV (Autumn, 1963), 671-95.
Daniels, Sally, in MinnR, III (Fall, 1962), 124-7.
Finkelstein, Sidney, "SHIP OF FOOLS," Mainstream, XV
    (September, 1962), 42-8.
Hartley, Lodwick, "Dark Voyagers: A Study of Katherine
    Anne Porter's SHIP OF FOOLS," UR, XXX (December,
    1963), 83-94. Also in Hartley, L., and G. Core, eds.,
    Katherine Anne Porter, 211-26.
Heilman, Robert B., "SHIP OF FOOLS: Notes on Style,"
    FQ, XII, i (November, 1962), 46-55. Also in Hartley, L.,
    and G. Core, eds., Katherine Anne Porter, 197-210.
Hendrick, George, "Hart Crane Aboard the Ship of Fools:
    Some Speculations," TCL, IX (April, 1963), 3-9.
_____, Katherine Anne Porter, 118-40.
Hertz, Robert N., "Rising Waters: A Study of Katherine
    Anne Porter," DA, XXV (December, 1964), 3571-72 (Cor-
    nell).
_____, "Sebastian Brant and Porter's SHIP OF FOOLS,"
    MQ, VI (Summer, 1964), 389-401.
Hoffman, F. J., Art of Southern Fiction, 47-50.
Holmes, Theodore, "The Literary Mode," Carleton Miscel-

lany, IV (Winter, 1963), 124-8.
Hyman, Stanley E., "Archetypal Woman," New Leader, XLV
    (April 2, 1962), 23-4.
Joselyn, Sister M., "Animal Imagery in Katherine Anne
    Porter's Fiction," in Slote, Bernice, ed., Myth and Sym-
    bol: Critical Approaches and Applications, Lincoln: Un.
    of Nebraska Pr., 1963, 101-15.
_____, "On the Making of THE SHIP OF FOOLS," SDR,
    I, ii (May, 1964), 46-52.
Kasten, Maurice, in Shen, XIII (Summer, 1962), 54-61.
Kauffmann, Stanley, "Katherine Anne Porter's Crowning
    Work," NRep, CXLVI (April 2, 1962), 23-4.
Kiely, Robert, "The Craft of Despondency--The Traditional
    Novelists," Daedulus, XCII (Spring, 1963), 226-30; 234-5.
Kirkpatrick, Smith, "SHIP OF FOOLS," SR, LXXI (Winter,
    1963), 94-8.
Krishnamurthi, Matighatta G., "Katherine Anne Porter: A
    Study in Themes," DA, XXVIII (1967), 682A-3A (Wiscon-
    sin).
Liberman, M. M., "The Responsibility of the Novelist: The
    Critical Reception of SHIP OF FOOLS," Criticism, VIII
    (Fall, 1966), 377-88. Also in Hartley, L., and G. Core,
    eds., Katherine Anne Porter, 185-96.
_____, "The Short Story as Chapter in SHIP OF FOOLS,"
    Criticism, X (Winter, 1968), 65-71.
McIntyre, John P., "SHIP OF FOOLS and Its Publicity,"
    Thought, XXXVIII (Summer, 1963), 211-20.
Marsden, Malcolm M., "Love as Threat in Katherine Anne
    Porter's Fiction," TCL, XIII (April, 1967), 35-8.
Miller, Paul W., "Katherine Porter's SHIP OF FOOLS, A
    Masterpiece Manqué," UR, XXXII (December, 1965), 151-
    7.
Mooney, H. J., Jr., Fiction and Criticism of Katherine Anne
    Porter, 56-63.
Moss, Howard, "No Safe Harbor," NY, XXXVIII (April 28,
    1962), 165-73. Also in Moss, H., Writing Against Time,
    45-54.
Nance, W. L., Katherine Anne Porter and the Art of Rejec-
    tion, 156-207.
Plante, Patricia R., "Katherine Anne Porter: Misanthrope
    Acquitted," XUS, II (December, 1963), 87-91.
Rubin, Louis D., Jr., " 'We Get Along Together Just
    Fine...'," FQ, XII (March, 1963), 30-1.
Ruoff, James, "Katherine Anne Porter Comes to Kansas,"
    MQ, IV (July, 1963), 310-13.
_____, and Del Smith, "Katherine Anne Porter on SHIP
    OF FOOLS," CE, XXIV (February, 1963), 396-7.

Ryan, Marjorie, "Katherine Anne Porter: SHIP OF FOOLS,"
Crit, V, ii (Fall, 1962), 94-9.
_____, "Katherine Anne Porter: SHIP OF FOOLS and the
Short Stories," BuR, XII, i (March, 1964), 51-63. Also
in Booth, Wayne, ed. , The Rhetoric of Fiction, Chicago:
Un. of Chicago, 1962, 274-7.
Solotaroff, Theodore, "SHIP OF FOOLS and the Critics,"
Ctary, XXXIV (October, 1962), 277-86.
Thompson, John, in PR, XXIX (Fall, 1962), 608-12.
Walcutt, C.C., Man's Changing Mask, 145-55.
Walton, Gerald, "Katherine Anne Porter's Use of Quakerism
in SHIP OF FOOLS," Criticism, VII (Fall, 1966), 15-23.
Weber, Brom, in MinnR, III (Fall, 1962), 127-30.
Wescott, Glenway, Images of Truth, 25-48 passim; 49-56.
Also (expanded) as "Katherine Anne Porter: The Making
of a Novel," Atlantic, CCIX (April, 1962), 42-9.
West, Ray B. , Jr. , Katherine Anne Porter, 32-43.

BIBLIOGRAPHY

Hartley, L. , and G. Core, eds. , Katherine Anne Porter,
227-36.
Hendrick, G. , Katherine Anne Porter, 161-71.
Waldripp, Louise, and Shirley Ann Bauer, A Bibliography of
the Works of Katherine Anne Porter and A Bibliography of
the Criticism of the Works of Katherine Anne Porter,
Metuchen, N.J.: Scarecrow Pr. , 1969.

POWELL, ANTHONY, 1905-

GENERAL

Brooke, Jocelyn, "From Wauchop to Widmerpol," LonM, VII
(September, 1960), 60-4.
Davis, Douglas M. , "An Interview with Anthony Powell,
Frome, England, June, 1962," CE, XXIV (April, 1963),
533-6.
Lee, James W. , "The Novels of Anthony Powell," DA, XXV
(1965), 5281-82 (Auburn).
Mizener, A. , Sense of Life in the Modern Novel, 79-103.
Morris, R.K. , Novels of Anthony Powell.
Quesenbery, W.D. , Jr. , "Anthony Powell: The Anatomy of
Decay," Crit, VII (Spring, 1964), 5-26.
Radner, Sanford, "Powell's Early Novels: A Study in Point
of View," Ren, XVI (Summer, 1964), 194-200.
Russell, John, "Quintet from the 30's: Anthony Powell," KR,

XXVII (Autumn, 1965), 698-726.
Voorhees, Richard J., "Anthony Powell: The First Phase,"
    PrS, XXVIII (Winter, 1954), 337-44.
Woodward, A. G., "The Novels of Anthony Powell," ESA, X
    (September, 1967), 117-28.

THE ACCEPTANCE WORLD
(See also A DANCE TO THE MUSIC OF TIME)

Hall, James, "The Uses of Polite Surprise," EIC, XII
    (April, 1962), 179-82. Also in Hall, J., Tragic Comedi-
    ans, 141-4.
Morris, R. K., Novels of Anthony Powell, 148-65.

AFTERNOON MEN

Allen, W., Modern Novel, 219-21.
Bergonzi, B., in Bloomfield, P., L. P. Hartley and Anthony
    Powell, 24-6.
Morris, R. K., Novels of Anthony Powell, 13-31.
Russell, John, "Quintet from the Thirties: Anthony Powell,"
    KR, XXVII (Autumn, 1965), 708-11.

AGENTS AND PATIENTS

Morris, R. K., Novels of Anthony Powell, 69-84.

AT LADY MOLLY'S
(See also A DANCE TO THE MUSIC OF TIME)

Hall, J., Tragic Comedians, 141-4.
Morris, R. K., Novels of Anthony Powell, 166-80.

A BUYER'S MARKET
(See also A DANCE TO THE MUSIC OF TIME)

Hall, James, "The Uses of Polite Surpirse: Anthony Powell,"
    EIC, XII (April, 1962), 169-70; 173-7. Also in Hall, J.,
    Tragic Comedians, 135-9.
Morris, R. K., Novels of Anthony Powell, 148-65.

CASANOVA'S CHINESE RESTAURANT
(See also A DANCE TO THE MUSIC OF TIME)

Bliven, Naomi, "Books: The Marriage State," NY, XXXVI
    (December 31, 1960), 53-4.
Hall, J., Tragic Comedians, 144-8.

Kermode, F., Puzzles and Epiphanies, 127-30.
Morris, R. K., Novels of Anthony Powell, 181-99.
Pritchett, V. S., "The Bored Barbarians," NStat, LIX (June
    25, 1960), 947-8.
Waugh, Evelyn, "Marriage à la Mode - 1936," Spectator
    (June 24, 1960), 53-4.

A DANCE TO THE MUSIC OF TIME

Allen, W., Modern Novel, 221-3.
Arnold, Bruce, "Powell: THE MUSIC OF TIME," in Har-
    ward, T. B., European Patterns: Contemporary Patterns
    in European Writing, Chester Springs, Pa.: Dufour,
    1966, 49-52.
Bergonzi, B., in Bloomfield, P., L. P. Hartley and Anthony
    Powell, 28-39.
Glazebrook, Mark, "The Art of Horace Isbister, E. Bos-
    worth Deacon, and Ralph Barnby," LonM, VII (September,
    1967), 76-82.
Hall, James, "The Uses of Polite Surprise: Anthony Powell,"
    EIC, XII (April, 1962), 167-83. Also in Hall, J., Tragic
    Comedians, 129-50.
Herring, Anthony D., "Anthony Powell: A Reaction Against
    Determinism," BSUF, IX (Winter, 1968), 17-21.
Hynes, Sam, "Novelist of Society," Cweal, LXX (July 31,
    1959), 396-7.
Karl, Frederick R., "Anthony Powell's THE MUSIC OF
    TIME," Contemporary English Novel, 238-44.
_____, "Bearers of War and Disaster," NRep, CXLVII
    (September 24, 1962), 21-2.
Lee, James W., "The Novels of Anthony Powell," DA, XXV
    (1965), 5281-2 (Auburn).
McCall, Raymond G., "Anthony Powell's Gallery," CE,
    XXVII (December, 1965), 227-32.
McLaughlin, Richard, "In the Comic Tradition," AmMerc,
    LXXXVII (November, 1958), 154-5.
Mizener, Arthur, "A DANCE TO THE MUSIC OF TIME:
    The Novels of Anthony Powell," KR, XXII (Winter, 1960),
    79-92.
_____, Sense of Life in the Modern Novel, 82-5; 89-103.
Morris, R. K., Novels of Anthony Powell, 1-10; 103-12; 247-
    52.
Pritchett, V. S., "The Bored Barbarians," Living Novel,
    294-303. Also in Pritchett, V. S., Working Novelist, 172-
    80.
Quesenbery, W. D., Jr., "Anthony Powell: The Anatomy of
    Decay," Crit, VII (Spring, 1964), 5-26.

Radner, Sanford, "The World of Anthony Powell," ClareQ,
    X, ii (Winter, 1963), 41-7.
Ruoff, Gene W., "Social Mobility and the Artist in MANHAT-
    TAN TRANSFER and THE MUSIC OF TIME," WSCL, V,
    i (Winter-Spring, 1964), 64-76.
Schlesinger, Arthur L., "Waugh a la Proust," NRep,
    CXXXIX (October 20, 1958), 20-1.
Shapiro, C., "Widmerpol and THE MUSIC OF TIME," Con-
    temporary British Novelists, 81-94.
Vinson, James, "Anthony Powell's MUSIC OF TIME," Per,
    X (Summer-Autumn, 1958), 146-52.
Voorhees, Richard J., "THE MUSIC OF TIME: Themes
    and Variations," DR, XLII (Autumn, 1962), 213-21.
Walcutt, C.C., Man's Changing Mask, 336-9.
Webster, Harvey C., "A Dance of British Eccentrics," New
    Leader, XLII (January 12, 1959), 26-7.
Zegerell, James J., "Anthony Powell's MUSIC OF TIME:
    Chronicle of a Declining Establishment," TCL, XII (Oc-
    tober, 1966), 138-46.

FROM A VIEW TO A DEATH

Morris, R.K., Novels of Anthony Powell, 49-68.
Pritchett, V.S., "The Bored Barbarians," Working Novelist,
    173-5.
Russell, John, "Quintet from the Thirties: Anthony Powell,"
    KR, XXVII (Autumn, 1965), 716-23.

THE KINDLY ONES
(See also A DANCE TO THE MUSIC OF TIME)

Hartley, L.P., "Good Dog, Good Dog," T&T, XLIII (June
    28, 1962), 21-2.
Karl, Frederick R., "Bearers of War and Disaster," NRep,
    CXLVII (September 24, 1962), 21-2.
McDowell, Frederick P.W., " 'The Devious Involutions of
    Human Characters and Emotions': Reflections on Some
    Recent British Novels," WSCL, IV, iii (Autumn, 1963),
    362-5.
Morris, R.K., Novels of Anthony Powell, 200-17.
Symons, J., "A Long Way from Firbank," Critical Occa-
    sions, 74-9.

THE MILITARY PHILOSOPHERS
(See also A DANCE TO THE MUSIC OF TIME)

Anon., in TLS (October 17, 1968). Also in T.L.S.: Essays

and Reviews from The Times Literary Supplement, 1968,
183-5.

THE MUSIC OF TIME
(See A DANCE TO THE MUSIC OF TIME)

A QUESTION OF UPBRINGING
(See also A DANCE TO THE MUSIC OF TIME)

Hall, J., Tragic Comedians, 134-5.
Morris, R. K., Novels of Anthony Powell, 132-47.

THE SOLDIERS ART
(See also A DANCE TO THE MUSIC OF TIME)

Anon., "War Games," TLS (September 15, 1966), 853. Al-
so in T. L. S.: Essays and Reviews from The Times Lit-
erary Supplement, 1966, 74-7.
Grandsen, K. W., "Taste of the Old Time," Encounter,
XXVII (December, 1966), 106-8.
Morris, R. K., Novels of Anthony Powell, 231-46.
Seymour-Smith, Martin, "Jenkins Marches On," Spectator
(September 16, 1966), 353.

THE VALLEY OF BONES
(See also A DANCE TO THE MUSIC OF TIME)

Anon., "Nick Goes to War," TLS (March 5, 1964), 189.
Also in T. L. S.: Essays and Reviews from The Times
Literary Supplement, 1964, 105-7.
Morris, R. K., Novels of Anthony Powell, 218-30.
Radner, Sanford, "Anthony Powell and THE VALLEY OF
BONES," EngR, XV (April, 1965), 8-9.
Spender, Stephen, "Tradition vs Underground Novels," in
Encyclopaedia Britannica. Great Ideas Today, 1965, 190-
2.

VENUSBERG

Morris, R. K., Novels of Anthony Powell, 32-48.
Russell, John, "Quintet from the Thirties: Anthony Powell,"
KR, XXVII (Autumn, 1965), 711-16.

WHAT'S BECOME OF WARING

Morris, R. K., Novels of Anthony Powell, 85-100.
Russell, John, "Quintet from the Thirties: Anthony Powell,"

KR, XXVII (Autumn, 1965), 723-6.

POWERS, (J)AMES (F)ARL, 1917-

GENERAL

Evans, F., ed., J.F. Powers.
Hagopian, J.V., J.F. Powers.
Jacobsen, Josephine, "A Catholic Quintet," ChS, XLVII
(Summer, 1964), 146-9.
Kristin, Sister, "The Catholic and Creativity: J.F. Powers,"
(Interview), ABR, XV (March, 1964), 63-80. Also in
Evans, F., ed., J.F. Powers, 1-22.

MORTE D'URBAN

Boyle, Robert, S.J., "To Look Outside: The Fiction of J.
F. Powers," in Mooney, H.J., Jr., and Staley, T.F.,
eds., Shapeless God, 102-15.
Carruth, Hayden, "Reviving the Age of Satire," NRep,
CXLVII (September 24, 1962), 23-4. Also in Evans, F.,
ed., J.F. Powers, 69-72.
Collignon, Joseph B., "Powers' MORTE D'URBAN: A Lay-
man's Indictment," Ren, XVI (Fall, 1963), 20-1, 51-2.
Curley, Thomas, "J.F. Powers' Long Awaited First Novel,"
Cweal, LXXVII (October 12, 1962), 77-8.
Dupee, F.W., "In the Powers Country," PR, XXX (Spring,
1963), 113-16. Also in Dupee, F.W., King of the Cats,
149-55.
Gass, William H., "Bingo Game at the Foot of the Cross,"
Nation, CXCV (September 29, 1962), 182-3. Also in
Evans, F., ed., J.F. Powers, 73-7.
Gilbert, Sister Mary, S.N.J.M., "MORTE D'URBAN," SR,
LXXI (Autumn, 1963), 673-5.
Green, Martin, "J.F. Powers and Catholic writing," Yeats's
Blessing on von Hügel, 97-121.
Hagopian, John V., "Irony and Involution in J.F. Powers'
MORTE D'URBAN," WSCL, IX (1968), 151-71.
_____, J.F. Powers, 123-51.
Henault, Marie, "The Saving of Father Urban," America,
CVIII (March 2, 1963), 290-2.
Hertzel, Leo J., "Brother Juniper, Father Urban and the
Unworldly Tradition," Ren, XVII (Summer, 1965), 207-10,
215. Also in Evans, F., ed., J.F. Powers, 90-3.
Hinchcliffe, Arnold P., "Nightmare of Grace," Blackfriars,
XLV (February, 1964), 61-9.

Hyman, Stanley E., "The Priest with the Fishnet Hatband,"
  New Leader, XLV (September 17, 1962), 22-3. Also in
  Hyman, S. E., Standards, 95-7.
Hynes, Joseph, "Father Urban's Renewal: J. F. Powers'
  Difficult Precision," MLQ, XXIX (December, 1968), 450-
  66.
Kaufman, Maynard, "J. F. Powers and Secularity," in Scott,
  N. A., Jr., Adversity and Grace, 167-81.
McCorry, Vincent P., "Urban in the Lion's Den," America,
  CVIII (March 2, 1963), 292-4.
Merton, Thomas, "MORTE D'URBAN: Two Celebrations,"
  Worship, XXXVI (November, 1962), 645-50. Also in
  Evans, F., ed., J. F. Powers, 95-100.
Poss, Stanley, "J. F. Powers: The Gin of Irony," TCL,
  XIV (July, 1968), 65-74.
Rowan, Thomas, C. S. S. R., "MORTE D'URBAN: A Novel
  About Priests," HPR, LXIII (January, 1963), 291-4. Al-
  so in Evans, F., ed., J. F. Powers, 101-5.
Sandra, Sister Mary, S. S. A., "The Priest-Hero in Modern
  Fiction," Person, XLVI (October, 1965), 531-5.
Sisk, John P., in Crit, V, iii (Winter, 1962-63), 99-103.
  _____, in Ren, XVI (1963), 101.
Smith, Patrick J., "Typology and Peripety in Four Catholic
  Novels," DA, XXVIII (1967), 2265A (Calif., Davis).
Twombly, Robert G., "Hubris, Health, and Holiness: The
  Despair of J. F. Powers," in Whitbread, T. B., ed.,
  Seven Contemporary Authors, 143-62.
Webster, Harvey C., "Comedy and Darkness," KR, XXV
  (1963), 166-9.

BIBLIOGRAPHY

Evans, F., ed., J. F. Powers, 115-16.
Hagopian, J. V., J. F. Powers, 165-8.

PRICE, REYNOLDS, 1933-

GENERAL

Barnes, Daniel R., "The Names and Faces of Reynolds
  Price," KyR, II, ii (1968), 76-91.
Eichelberger, Clayton L., "Reynolds Price: 'A Banner in
  Defeat'," JPC, I (Spring, 1968), 410-17.
Kaufman, Wallace, "A Conversation with Reynolds Price,"
  Shen, XVII, iv (Summer, 1966), 3-25.

A GENEROUS MAN

Barnes, Daniel R., "The Names and Faces of Reynolds
   Price," KyR, II, ii (1968), 85-90.
Eichelberger, Clayton L., "Reynolds Price: 'A Banner in
   Defeat'," JPC, I (Spring, 1968), 414-16.
Hoffman, F. J., Art of Southern Fiction, 141-3.
Price, Reynolds, "News for the Mineshaft," VQR, XLIV
   (Autumn, 1968), 641-58. Also in McCormack, T., ed.,
   Afterwords, 107-23.
Wain, John, "Mantle of Faulkner?" NRep, CLIV (May 14,
   1966), 31-3.

A LONG AND HAPPY LIFE

Barnes, Daniel R., "The Names and Faces of Reynolds
   Price," KyR, II, ii (1968), 81-5.
Eichelberger, Clayton L., "Reynolds Price: 'A Banner in
   Defeat'," JPC, I (Spring, 1968), 412-14.
Hoffman, F. J., Art of Southern Fiction, 137-9.

PRIESTLEY, (J)OHN (B)OYNTON, 1894-

GENERAL

Braine, John, "Lunch with J. B. Priestley," Encounter, X
   (June, 1958), 8-14.
Brown, I., J. P. Priestley.
Hughes, D., J. B. Priestley.
Lindsay, Jack, "J. B. Priestley," in Baker, D. V., ed.,
   Writers of Today, 72-82.
West, A., Mountain in the Sunlight, 155-83.

ADAM IN MOONSHINE

Hughes, D., J. B. Priestley, 67-74.

ANGEL PAVEMENT

Brown, I., J. B. Priestley, 17-19.
Hughes, D., J. B. Priestley, 104-12.
West, A., Mountain in the Sunlight, 159-68.

BENIGHTED

Hughes, D., J. B. Priestley, 79-83.

BRIGHT DAY

Hughes, D. , J. B. Priestley, 176-82.
West, A. , Mountain in the Sunlight, 177-83.

DAYLIGHT ON SATURDAY

Hughes, D. , J. B. Priestley, 170-2.
West, A. , Mountain in the Sunlight, 168-77.

FARAWAY

Hughes, D. , J. B. Priestley, 112-16.

FESTIVAL AT FARBRIDGE

Hughes, D. , J. B. Priestley, 182-8.

SATURN OVER THE WATER

Deakin, Nicholas, "J. B. Priestley's Anglo-Saxon Attitudes,"
T&T, XLII (July 13, 1961), 1159-61.

THEY WALK THE CITY

Hughes, D. , J. B. Priestley, 118-23.

PROKOSCH, FREDERIC, 1906-

GENERAL

Carpenter, Richard C. , "The Novels of Frederic Prokosch,"
CE, XVIII (February, 1957), 261-7.
Squires, R. , Frederic Prokosch.

AGE OF THUNDER

Hendry, Irene, "Westcott, Prokosch, and Three Others,"
SR, LIII (1945), 492-3.
Squires, R. , Frederic Prokosch, 91-6.

THE ASIATICS

Squires, R. , Frederic Prokosch, 22-5, 48-53.

A BALLAD OF LOVE

Squires, R., Frederic Prokosch, 79-83.

THE CONSPIRATORS

Squires, R., Frederic Prokosch, 87-91.

THE IDOLS OF THE CAVE

Squires, R., Frederic Prokosch, 96-101.

THE NIGHT OF THE POOR

Squires, R., Frederic Prokosch, 102-4.

NINE DAYS TO MUKALLA

Jones, Howard M., "Love and Geography," SatR, XXXVI
(March 21, 1953), 15.
Squires, R., Frederick Prokosch, 61-9.

THE SEVEN SISTERS

Squires, R., Frederic Prokosch, 120-30.

THE SEVEN WHO FLED

Squires, R., Frederick Prokosch, 106-20.
Straumann, H., American Literature in the Twentieth Century, 78-9.

THE SKIES OF EUROPE

Squires, R., Frederic Prokosch, 28-9, 70-9.

STORM AND ECHO

Squires, R., Frederic Prokosch, 54-61.

A TALE FOR MIDNIGHT

Squires, R., Frederic Prokosch, 104-6.

PURDY, JAMES, 1923-

GENERAL

Coffey, Warren, "The Incompleat Novelist," Ctary, XLIV
(September, 1967), 98-103.
Cott, Jonathan, "The Damaged Cosmos," in Kostelanetz, R.,
ed., On Contemporary Literature, 498-505.
Hyman, S. E., Standards, 254-8.
Maloff, Saul, "James Purdy's Fictions: The Quality of De-
spair," Crit, VI, i (Spring, 1963), 106-12.
Pomeranz, Regina, "The Hell of Not Loving: Purdy's Mod-
ern Tragedy," Ren, XVI (Spring, 1964), 149-53.
Schott, Webster, "James Purdy: American Dreams," Nation,
CXCVIII (March 23, 1964), 300-2.
Schwarzschild, B., Not-Right House.

CABOT WRIGHT BEGINS

Boyers, Robert, "Attitudes Toward Sex in American 'High
Culture'," AAAPSS, CCCLXXVI (March, 1968), 49.
French, Warren, Seasons of Promise, Columbus: Un. of
Missouri Pr., 1968, 19-26.
Malin, Irving, "Mélange à Trois," Ramparts, III, vi (March,
1965), 79-80.

EUSTACE CHISHOLM AND THE WORKS

Coffey, Warren, "The Incompleat Novelist," Ctary, XLIV
(September, 1967), 101-3.
Malin, I., in Cweal, LXXXVI (July 28, 1967), 476-7.
Morris, Robert K., "James Purdy and the Works," Nation,
CCV (October 9, 1967), 342-4.
Schwarzschild, B., Not-Right House, 58-65.
Trickett, Rachel, "Recent Novels: Craftmanship in Violence
and Sex," YR, LVII (Spring, 1968), 443-4.

MALCOLM

Cott, Jonathan, "The Damaged Cosmos," in Kostelanetz, R.,
ed., On Contemporary Literature, 501-5.
Daiches, David, "A Preface to James Purdy's MALCOLM,"
AR, XXII (Spring, 1962), 122-30.
Denniston, Constance, "The American Romance-Parody: A
Study of Purdy's MALCOLM and Heller's CATCH-22,"
ESRS, XIV, ii (December, 1965), 42-59, 63-4.
French, Warren, "The Quaking World of James Purdy" in
Langford, R. E., ed., Essays in Modern American Liter-
ature, 112-18.

Herr, Paul, "The Small Sad World of James Purdy," ChiR,
    XIV, iii (Autumn-Winter, 1963), 19-25.   Also in Wald-
    meir, J. J. , ed. , Recent American Fiction, 246-51.
Kolve, Del, "James Purdy: An Assessment," T&T, XLII
    (March 23, 1961), 476-7.
Kostelanetz, Richard, "The New American Fiction," Ram-
    parts, III (January-February, 1965), 60.   Also in Kostel-
    anetz, R. , ed. , New American Arts, 217-18.
Lorch, Thomas M. , "Purdy's MALCOLM: A Unique Vision
    of Radical Emptiness," WSCL, VI (Summer, 1965), 204-
    13.
McNamara, Eugene, "The Post-Modern American Novel,"
    QQ, LXIX (Summer, 1962), 272-4.
Malin, I. , New American Gothic, 46-9.
Schwarzschild, Bettina, "The Forsaken: An Interpretive Es-
    say on James Purdy's MALCOLM," TQ, X, i (Spring,
    1967), 170-7.   Also in Schwarzschild, B. , Not-Right
    House, 23-34.
_____, Not-Right House, 13-23.

THE NEPHEW

Finkelstein, S. , Existentialism and Alienation in American
    Literature, 249-52.
French, Warren, "The Quaking World of James Purdy," in
    Langford, R. E. , ed. , Essays in Modern American Lit-
    erature, 118-22.
Kolve, Del, "James Purdy: An Assessment," T&T, XLII
    (March 23, 1961), 476-7.
Krummel, Regina P. , "Two Quests in Two Societies,"
    EngR, XVIII (April, 1967), 28-32.
Miller, Nolan, "Three of the 'Best'," AR, XXI (Spring,
    1961), 125-8.
Pomeranz, Regina, "The Hell of Not Loving: Purdy's Mod-
    ern Tragedy," Ren, XVI (Spring, 1964), 150-2.
Schwarzschild, Bettina, "Aunt Alma: James Purdy's THE
    NEPHEW," UWR, III, i (Fall, 1967), 80-7.   Also in
    Schwarzschild, B. , Not Right-House, 35-44.
Tornquist, Elizabeth, "The New Parochialism," Ctary,
    XXXI (May, 1961), 449-52.
Weales, Gerald, in Moore, H. T. , ed. , Contemporary Amer-
    ican Novelists, 145-9.

PYNCHON, THOMAS, 1937-

THE CRYING OF LOT 49

Hunt, John W., "Comic Escape and Anti-Vision: The Novels of
   Joseph Heller and Thomas Pynchon," in Scott, N.A., Jr., ed.,
   Adversity and Grace, 107-10.
McNamara, Eugene, "The Absurd Style in Contemporary Litera-
   ture," HAB, XIX (1968), 44-9.
Sklar, Robert, "The New Novel, U.S.A.: Thomas Pynchon,"
   Nation, CCV (September 25, 1967), 277-80.
Young, James D., "The Enigma Variations of Thomas Pynchon,"
   Crit, X, i (1968), 69-77.

V.

Hausdorff, Don, "Thomas Pynchon's Multiple Absurdities,"
   WSCL, VII (Autumn, 1966), 258-69.
Hoffman, Frederick J., "The Questing Comedian: Thomas
   Pynchon's V," Crit, VI, iii (Winter, 1963-64), 174-7.
Hunt, John W., "Comic Escape and Anti-Vision: The Novels
   of Joseph Heller and Thomas Pynchon," in Scott, N.A.,
   Jr., ed., Adversity and Grace, 98-107.
Hyman, Stanley E., "The Goddess and the Schlemiel," New
   Leader, XLVI (March, 18, 1963), 22-3. Also in Kostel-
   anetz, R., ed., On Contemporary Literature, 506-10. Al-
   so in Hyman, S.E., Standards, 138-42.
Kostelanetz, Richard, "The New American Fiction," in Kos-
   telanetz, R., ed., New American Arts, 214-17.
Lewis, R.W.B., "Days of Wrath and Laughter," Trials of
   the World, 228-34.
McNamara, Eugene, "The Absurd Style in Contemporary
   American Literature," HAB, XIX (1968), 44-9.
Sklar, Robert, "The New Novel, U.S.A.: Thomas Pynchon,"
   Nation, CCV (September 25, 1967), 277-8.
Slatoff, Walter, "Thomas Pynchon," Epoch, XII (Spring,
   1963), 255-7.
Young, James D., "The Enigma Variations of Thomas Pyn-
   chon," Crit, X, i (1968), 69-77.

RAPHAEL, FREDERIC, 1931-

GENERAL

McDowell, Frederick P.W., "The Varied Universe of Frederic Raphael's Fiction," Crit, VIII, i (Fall, 1965), 21-50.

THE EARLSDON WAY

McDowell, Frederick P.W., "The Varied Universe of Fred-

eric Raphael's Fiction," Crit, VIII, i (Fall, 1965), 24-8.
Urwin, G.G., ed., Taste for Living, 74-77.

THE GRADUATE WIFE

McDowell, Frederick P.W., "The Varied Universe of Frederic Raphael's Fiction," Crit, VIII, i (Fall, 1965), 39-43.

THE LIMITS OF LOVE

McDowell, Frederick P.W., "The Varied Universe of Frederic Raphael's Fiction," Crit, VIII, i (Fall, 1965), 39-43.
_____, "World Within World: Gerda Charles, Frederick (sic) Raphael, and the Anglo-Jewish Community," Crit, VI, iii (Winter, 1963-64), 147-50.

LINDMANN

McDowell, Frederick P.W., "The Varied Universe of Frederic Raphael's Fiction," Crit, VIII, i (Fall, 1965), 43-5.

OBBLIGATO

McDowell, Frederick P.W., "The Varied Universe of Frederic Raphael's Fiction," Crit, VIII, i (Fall, 1965), 23-4.

THE TROUBLE WITH ENGLAND

McDowell, Frederick P.W., "The Varied Universe of Frederic Raphael's Fiction," Crit, VIII, i (Fall, 1965), 37-9.

A WILD SURMISE

McDowell, Frederick P.W., "The Varied Universe of Frederic Raphael's Fiction," Crit, VIII, i (Fall, 1965), 32-7.

RECHY, JOHN, 1934-

CITY OF NIGHT

Gilman, R., Confusion of Realms, 53-61.
Heifetz, Henry, "The Anti-Social Act of Writing," StL, IV (Spring, 1964), 6-9.
Hoffman, Stanton, "The Cities of Night: John Rechy's CITY OF NIGHT and the American Literature of Homosexuality," ChiR, XVII, ii-iii (1964), 195-206.

Southern, Terry, "Rechy and Gover," in Moore, H. T., ed.,
Contemporary American Novels, 222-7.

RICHLER, MORDECAI, 1931-

GENERAL

Cohen, Nathan, "A Conversation with Mordecai Richler,"
TamR, No. 1 (Winter, 1957), 6-23.
_____, "Heroes of the Richler View," TamR, No. 6
(Winter, 1958), 47-60.
Kattan, Naim, "Mordecai Richler: Craftsman or Artist,"
CanL, No. 21 (Summer, 1964), 46-51.
Pacey, D., Creative Writing in Canada, 264-5.
Scott, Peter, "A Choice of Certainties," TamR, No. 8 (Sum-
mer, 1958), 73-82.

THE ACROBATS

Bowering, George, "And the Sun Goes Down: Richler's
First Novel," CanL, No. 29 (Summer, 1966), 7-17.

THE APPRENTICESHIP OF DUDDY KRAVITZ

New, William, "The Apprenticeship of Discovery," CanL,
No. 29 (1966), 18-33.
Sherman, B., Invention of the Jew, 178-82.
Tallman, Warren, in Canadian Literature. Choice of Critics,
72-6.
_____, "Richler and the Faithless City," CanL, No. 3
(Winter, 1960), 62-4.
_____, "Wolf in the Snow. Part Two: The House Re-
possessed," CanL, No. 6 (Autumn, 1960), 44-8.
Watt, F. W., in UTQ, XXIX (July, 1960), 463-5.

A CHOICE OF ENEMIES

Cohen, Nathan, "Heroes of the Richler View," TamR, No.
6 (Winter, 1958), 47-60.
Scott, Peter, "A Choice of Certainties," TamR, No. 8
(Summer, 1958), 73-83.

STICK OUT YOUR NECK

Kostelanetz, Richard, "The New American Fiction," in Kostelanetz, R., ed., New American Arts, 218-19.

RICHTER, CONRAD, 1890-1968

GENERAL

Barnes, H. J., Conrad Richter.
Carpenter, Frederick I., "Conrad Richter's Pioneers, Real-
ity and Myth," CE, XII (November, 1950), 77-82.
Flanagan, John T., "Conrad Richter, Romance of the South-
west," SWR, XLIII (Summer, 1958), 189-96.
_____, "Folklore in the Novels of Conrad Richter," MF,
II (Spring, 1952), 5-14.
Gaston, E. W., Jr., Conrad Richter.
Kohler, Dayton, "Conrad Richter: Early Americana," CE,
VIII (February, 1947), 221-7.
LaHood, Marvin J., "Richter's Early America," UR, XXX
(June, 1964), 311-16.
_____, "A Study of the Major Themes in the Work of
Conrad Richter, and His Place in the Tradition of the
American Frontier Novel," DA, XXIII (1962), 1365-6
(Notre Dame).
Sutherland, Bruce, "Conrad Richter's Americana," NMQR,
XV (Winter, 1945), 413-22.
Wagenknecht, E., Cavalcade of the American Novel, 436-7.
Young, David L., "The Art of Conrad Richter," DA, XXV
(1965), 4712 (Ohio State).

ALWAYS YOUNG AND FAIR

Gaston, E. W., Jr., Conrad Richter, 121-4.

THE AWAKENING LAND (See OHIO Trilogy)

THE FIELDS (See also OHIO Trilogy)

Gaston, E. W., Jr., Conrad Richter, 103-7.

THE FREE MAN

Gaston, E. W., Jr., Conrad Richter, 117-21.
Sutherland, Bruce, "Conrad Richter's Americana," NMQR,
XV (Winter, 1945), 421-2.

THE GRANDFATHERS

Gaston, E. W., Jr., Conrad Richter, 131-7.

THE LADY

Barnes, R. J., Conrad Richter, 30-6.
Gaston, E. W., Jr., Conrad Richter, 89-94.

THE LIGHT IN THE FOREST

Folsom, J. K., American Western Novel, 159-62.
Gaston, E. W., Jr., Conrad Richter, 125-31.
LaHood, Marvin J., "THE LIGHT IN THE FOREST: History as Fiction," EJ, LV (March, 1966), 298-304.

OHIO Trilogy

Barnard, Kenneth J., "Presentation of the West in Conrad Richter's Trilogy," NOQ, XXIX (Autumn, 1957), 224-34.
Carpenter, Frederick I., "Conrad Richter's Pioneers: Reality and Myth," CE, XII (November, 1950), 79-83.
Edwards, Clifford D., "Conrad Richter's OHIO Trilogy: It's Ideas, Themes, and Relationship to Literary Tradition," DA, XXIV (1963), 1614-15 (Mich.).
Flanagan, John T., "Folklore in the Novels of Conrad Richter," MF, II (Spring, 1952), 5-14.
Prescott, O., In My Opinion, 137-40.

THE SEA OF GRASS

Barnes, R. J., Conrad Richter, 16-25.
Folsom, J. K., American Western Novel, 94-7.
Gaston, E. W., Jr., Conrad Richter, 74-84.
Kohler, Dayton, "Conrad Richter: Early Americana," CE, VIII (February, 1947), 223-4.
Sutherland, Bruce, "Conrad Richter's Americana," NMQR, XV (Winter, 1945), 418-19.

A SIMPLE HONORABLE MAN

Gaston, E. W., Jr., Conrad Richter, 145-51.
LaHood, Marvin J., "Richter's Pennsylvania Trilogy," SUS, VIII (June, 1968), 10-13.

TACY CROMWELL

Barnes, R. J., Conrad Richter, 25-30.
Gaston, E. W., Jr., Conrad Richter, 84-9.
Sutherland, Bruce, "Conrad Richter's Americana," NMQR, XV (Winter, 1945), 420-1.

THE TOWN (See also OHIO Trilogy)

Gaston, E.W., Jr., Conrad Richter, 107-16.
Pearce, T.H., "Conrad Richter," NMQR, XX (Autumn, 1950),
371-3.
Stuckey, W.J., Pulitzer Prize Novels, 154-7.

THE TREES (See also OHIO Trilogy)

Gaston, E.W., Jr., Conrad Richter, 96-103.
Kohler, Dayton, "Conrad Richter: Early Americana," CE,
VIII (February, 1947), 224-5.
Sutherland, Bruce, "Conrad Richter's Americana," NMQR,
XV (Winter, 1945), 419-20.

THE WATERS OF KRONOS

Gaston, E.W., Jr., Conrad Richter, 139-45.
LaHood, Marvin J., "Richter's Pennsylvania Trilogy," SUS,
VIII (June, 1968), 5-10.

ROTH, HENRY, 1906-

CALL IT SLEEP

Allen, Walter, "Afterward," in Roth, H., Call It Sleep,
N.Y.: Avon, 442-7.
_____, Modern Novel, 172-5.
_____, "Two Neglected American Novelists," LonM, II
(May, 1962), 77-84.
_____, Urgent West, 101-2.
Fiedler, Leslie, "The Breakthrough: The American Jewish
Novelist and the Fictional Image of the Jew," Midstream,
IV (Winter, 1958), 23-4. Also in Waldmeir, J.J., ed.,
Recent American Fiction, 94-5.
_____, "Henry Roth's Neglected Masterpiece," Ctary,
XXX (August, 1960), 102-7.
_____, Waiting for the End, 48-9.
Freedman, William, "Henry Roth and the Redemptive Imag-
ination," in French, W., ed., Thirties, 107-14.
Geismar, Maxwell, "A Critical Introduction," in CALL IT
SLEEP, N.Y.: Cooper Square, 1962, xxxvi-xlv.
Knowles, A. Sidney, Jr., "The Fiction of Henry Roth," MFS,
XI (Winter, 1965-66), 393-404.
Ledbetter, Kenneth, "Henry Roth's CALL IT SLEEP: The
Revival of a Proletarian Novel," TCL, XII (October, 1966),

123-30.

Levin, Meyer, "A Personal Appreciation," in CALL IT
  SLEEP, N.Y.: Cooper Square, 1962, xlvi-li.

Nelson, Kenneth M., "A Religious Metaphor," Reconstructionist (N.Y.), XXXI, xv (1965), 7-16.

Ribalow, Harold U., "Henry Roth and His Novel CALL IT
  SLEEP," WSCL, III, iii (Fall, 1962), 5-14.

_____, "The History of Henry Roth and CALL IT SLEEP,"
  in CALL IT SLEEP, N.Y.: Cooper Square, 1962, xi-
  xxxv.

Rideout, W.B., Radical Novel in the U.S., 186-90.

Sherman, B., "CALL IT SLEEP As a Depression Novel,"
  Invention of the Jew, 82-92.

Syrkin, Marie, "Revival of a Classic," Midstream, VII
  (Winter, 1961), 89-93.

ROTH, PHILIP, 1933-

GENERAL

Cheuse, Alan, "A World Without Realists," StL, IV, ii
  (Spring, 1964), 70-6.

Deer, Irving, and Harriet, "Philip Roth and the Crisis in
  American Fiction," MinnR, VI, iv (Winter, 1966), 353-60.

Hochman, Baruch, "Child and Man in Philip Roth," Midstream, XIII (December, 1967), 68-76.

Kramer, Maurice, "The Secular Mode of Jewishness,"
  Works, I (Autumn, 1967), 108, 110.

Landis, Joseph C., "The Sadness of Philip Roth: An Interim Report," MR, III (1962), 259-68.

Malin, I., Jews and Americans.

Meeter, M., Philip Roth and Bernard Malamud.

Mudrick, Marvin, "Who Killed Herzog? or, Three American
  Novelists," UDQ, I, i (Spring, 1966), 61-97.

Roth, Philip, "Writing About Jews," Ctary, XXXVI (December, 1963), 446-52.

_____, "Writing American Fiction," Ctary, XXXI (March,
  1961), 223-33.

GOODBYE, COLUMBUS

Clerk, Charles, "Goodbye to All That: Theme, Character
  and Symbol in GOODBYE, COLUMBUS," in Clerk, Charles,
  and Louis Leiter, eds., Seven Contemporary Short Novels,
  Glenview, Ill.: Scott, Foresman, 1969, 106-33.

Howe, Irving, "The Suburbs of Babylon," NRep, CXL (June

15, 1959), 17-19.

Isaac, Dan, "In Defense of Philip Roth," ChiR, XVII (Summer-Autumn, 1964-65), 84-90.

Kazin, A., Contemporaries, 258-62.

Koch, Eric, "Roth's GOODBYE, COLUMBUS," TamR, No. 13 (1959), 129-32.

Larner, Jeremy, "The Conversion of the Jews," PR, XXVII (Fall, 1960), 760-8.

Leer, Norman, "Escape and Confrontation in the Short Stories of Philip Roth," ChS, XLIX (Summer, 1966), 135-40.

Mann, Meryl, "Goodbye Columbus, Hello Radcliffe," PR, XXVIII (January-February, 1961), 154-7.

Meeter, G., Philip Roth and Bernard Malamud, 30-3.

Raban, J., "Character and Dialogue," Techniques of Modern Fiction, 88-9.

Sherman, B., "GOODBYE, COLUMBUS: A Controversy," Invention of the Jew, 167-75.

Siegel, Ben, "Jewish Fiction and the Affluent Society," NWR, IV (Spring, 1961), 89-96.

Trachtenberg, Stanley, "The Hero in Stasis," Crit, VII, ii (Winter, 1964-65), 5-17.

LETTING GO

Cheuse, Alan, "A World Without Realists," StL, IV, ii (Spring, 1964), 70-5.

Detweiler, R., "Philip Roth and the Test of Dialogic Life," Four Spiritual Crises in Mid-Century American Fiction, 25-35.

Hentoff, Nat. "The Appearance of LETTING GO," Midstream, VIII (December, 1962), 103-6.

Hyman, Stanley E., "A Novelist of Great Promise," New Leader (June 11, 1962). Also in Kostelanetz, R., ed., On Contemporary Literature, 533-6. Also in Hyman, S. E., Standards, 73-7.

Meeter, G., Philip Roth and Bernard Malamud, 39-40.

Podhoretz, Norman, "The Gloom of Philip Roth," Show, II (July, 1962), 92-3. Also in Podhoretz, N., Doings and Undoings, 236-43.

Walcutt, C. C., Man's Changing Mask, 350-2.

White, Robert L., "The English Instructor as Hero... Two Novels by Roth and Malamud," ForumH, IV (Winter, 1963), 16-22.

WHEN SHE WAS GOOD

Alter, Robert, "When He is Bad," Ctary, XLIV (November,

1967), 86-7.
Angoff, Charles, in CJF, XXVI (1968), 151-2.
Gilman, Richard, "Let's Lynch Lucy," NRep, CLVI (June
    24, 1967), 19-21.
Hicks, Granville, "A Bad Little Good Girl," SatR, L (June
    17, 1967), 25-6.
Lehan, Richard, "Fiction 1967," Contemporary Literature,
    IX, iv (Autumn, 1968), 542-3.
Meeter, G., Philip Roth and Bernard Malamud, 43-4.
Thompson, John, "The Professionals," NYRB, VIII (June
    15, 1967), 14-16.

SALINGER, (J)EROME (D)AVID, 1919-

GENERAL

Barr, Donald, "Saints, Pilgrims and Artists," Cweal,
    LXVII (October 25, 1957), 88-90. Also in Kostelanetz,
    R., ed., On Contemporary Literature, 537-43.   Also in
    Simonson, H.P., and P.E. Hager, eds., Salinger's
    CATHER IN THE RYE, 102-6.
Belcher, W.F., and J.W. Lee, eds., J.D. Salinger and the
    Critics.
Bostwick, Sally, "Reality, Compassion and Mysticism,"
    MidR, V (1963), 30-43.
Cecile, Sister Marie, "J.D. Salinger's Circle of Privacy,"
    CathW, CXCIV (February, 1962), 296-301.
Costello, Donald P., "Salinger and His Critics," Cweal,
    LXXIX (October 25, 1963), 132-5.
French, W., J.D. Salinger.
Green, Martin, "Amis and Salinger: The Latitude of Private
    Conscience," ChiR, XI (Winter, 1958), 20-5.
Grunewald, H.A., ed., Salinger.
Gwynn, F.L., and J.L. Blotner, Fiction of J.D. Salinger.
Hamilton, Kenneth, J.D. Salinger.
_____, "J.D. Salinger's Happy Family," QQ, LXXI (Sum-
    mer, 1964), 176-87.
Harper, J.M., Jr., "J.D. Salinger - Through Glasses Dark-
    ly," Desperate Faith, 65-95.
Hassan, Ihab H., "J.D. Salinger: Rare Quixotic Gesture,"
    WR, XXI (Summer, 1957), 261-80.
Haveman, Ernest, "The Search for the Mysterious J.D. Sal-
    inger: The Recluse in the Rye," Life, LI (November 3,
    1961), 129-30+.
Hicks, Granville, "J.D. Salinger: Search for Wisdom,"
    SatR, XLII (July 25, 1959), 13+.

Kennedey, Richard, "The Theme of the Quest," EngR, VIII (1957), 2-17. (Not seen.)

Larner, Jeremy, "Salinger's Audience," PR, XXIX (Fall, 1962), 594-8.

Laser, M., and N. Fruman, eds., Studies in J.D. Salinger.

Levin, Beatrice, "Everybody's Favorite: Concepts of Love in the Works of J.D. Salinger," Motive, No. 22 (October, 1961), 9-11. (Not seen.)

Lorch, Thomas, "J.D. Salinger: the Artist, the Audience, and the Popular Arts," SDR, V (Winter, 1967), 3-22.

Matthews, James F., "J.D. Salinger: An Appraisal," UVM, I (Spring, 1956), 52-60. (Not seen.)

Miller, J.E., Jr., J.D. Salinger.

Mizener, Arthur, "The Love Song of J.D. Salinger," Harpers, CCXVIII (February, 1959), 83-90. Also in Off Campus, I (January, 1963), 18-20, 44, 51, 54, 64.

Noland, Richard W., "The Novel of Personal Formula: J.D. Salinger," UR, XXXIII (October, 1966), 19-24.

Ramamurthy, V., "J.D. Salinger: The Tragi-Comic Vision," Banasthali Patrika (Rajasthan), No. 11 (July, 1968), 37-42. (Not seen.)

Rees, Richard, "The Salinger Situation," in Moore, H.T., ed., Contemporary American Novelists, 95-105.

Ross, Theodore J., "Notes on J.D. Salinger," CJF, XXII (1968), 149-53.

Russell, John, "Salinger's Feat," MFS, XII (Autumn, 1966), 299-311.

Skow, John, and the Editors of Time, "Sonny: An Introduction," Time, LXXVIII (September 15, 1961), 84-90. Also in Belcher, W.F., and J.W. Lee, eds., J.D. Salinger and the Critics, 1-7.

Slabey, Robert M., "Salinger's 'Casino': Wayfarers and Spiritual Acrobats," EngR, XIV, iii (February, 1964), 16-20.

Steiner, George, "The Salinger Industry," Nation, CLXXXIX (November 14, 1959), 360-3. Also in Laser, M., and N. Fruman, eds., Studies in J.D. Salinger, 113-18. Also in Marsden, M.M., ed., If You Really Want to Know, 62-6.

Wiegand, William, "J.D. Salinger: Seventy-Eight Bananas," ChiR, XI (1957), 3-19. Also in Waldmeir, J.J., ed., Recent American Fiction, 252-64.

_____, "The Knighthood of J.D. Salinger," NRep, CXLI (October 19, 1959), 19-21.

THE CATCHER IN THE RYE

Ahrne, Marianne, "Experience and Attitude in THE CATCHER

IN THE RYE and NINE STORIES by J. D. Salinger,"
MSpr, LXI, iii (1967), 242-63.
Aldridge, John, In Search of Heresy, 129-31. Also in Laser,
M., and N. Fruman, eds., Studies in J. D. Salinger, 50-
2. Also in Simonson, H. P., and P. E. Hager, eds.,
Salinger's CATCHER IN THE RYE, 80-1. Also in Mars-
den, M. M., ed., If You Really Want to Know, 126-7.
Allen, W., Modern Novel, 309-13.
Barr, Donald, in Balakian, N., and C. Simmons, eds.,
Creative Present, 53-7.
_____, "Saints, Pilgrims and Artists," Cweal, LXVII
(October 25, 1957), 89. Also in Kostelanetz, R., ed.,
On Contemporary Literature, 538-9. Also in Marsden,
M. M., ed., If You Really Want to Know, 39-40. Also
in Simonson, H. P., and P. E. Hager, eds., Salinger's
CATCHER IN THE RYE, 103-4.
Baumbach, Jonathan, "The Saint as Young Man: A Reap-
praisal of THE CATCHER IN THE RYE," MLQ, XXV
(December, 1964), 461-72. Also in Baumbach, J., Land-
scape of Nightmare, 55-57.
Bhaerman, Robert D., "Rebuttal" to Bernard Oldsey, "The
Movies in the Rye," CE, XXIII (March, 1962), 507-8.
Also in Marsden, M. M., ed., If You Really Want to
Know, 122-3. Also in Simonson, H. P., and P. E. Hager,
eds., Salinger's CATCHER IN THE RYE, 46.
Bonheim, Helmut W., "An Introduction to Salinger's THE
CATCHER IN THE RYE," Exercise Exchange, IV (April,
1957), 8-11.
Bowden, Edwin T., Dungeon of the Heart, 54-65. Also in
Simonson, H. P., and P. E. Hager, eds., Salinger's
CATCHER IN THE RYE, 94-100.
Bowen, Robert O., "The Salinger Syndrome: Charity Against
Whom?" Ramparts, I (May, 1962), 52-60. Also in Sim-
onson, H. P., and P. E. Hager, eds., Salinger's CATCHER
IN THE RYE, 21-30.
Branch, Edgar, "Mark Twain and J. D. Salinger: A Study
in Literary Continuity," AQ, IX (Summer, 1957), 144-58.
Also in Belcher, W. F., and J. W. Lee, eds., J. D. Sal-
inger and the Critics, 20-34. Also in Grunwald, H. A.,
ed., Salinger, 205-17. Also in Laser, M., and N. Fru-
man, eds., Studies in J. D. Salinger, 39-49. Also in
Marsden, M. M., ed., If You Really Want to Know, 132-
44. Also in Simonson, H. P., and P. E. Hager, eds.,
Salinger's CATCHER IN THE RYE, 81-91.
Bungert, Hans, "Salinger's THE CATCHER IN THE RYE:
The Isolated Youth and His Struggle to Communicate," in
Laser, M., and N. Fruman, eds., Studies in J. D. Sal-

inger, 177-85.

Burack, Boris, "Holden the Courageous," CEA, XXVII (May, 1965), 1. (Reply to Warner.)

Cagle, Charles, "THE CATCHER IN THE RYE Revisited," MQ, IV (Summer, 1964), 343-51.

Carpenter, Frederic I., "The Adolescent in American Fiction," EJ, XLVI (September, 1957), 315-16. Also in Laser, M., and N. Fruman, eds., Studies in J. D. Salinger, 69-71. Also in Simonson, H. P., and P. E. Hager, eds., Salinger's CATCHER IN THE RYE, 92-3.

Chugunov, Konstantin, "Soviet Critics on J. D. Salinger's Novel, THE CATCHER IN THE RYE," Soviet Lit, No. 5 (1962), 182-4. Also in Laser, M., and N. Fruman, eds., Studies in J. D. Salinger, 186-9.

Cohen, Hubert I., " 'A Woeful Agony Which Forced Me to Begin My Tale': THE CATCHER IN THE RYE," MFS, XII (Autumn, 1966), 355-66.

Conrad, Robert C., "Two Novels About Outsiders: The Kinship of Salinger's THE CATCHER IN THE RYE with Heinrich Böll's ANSICHTEN EINES CLOWNS," UDR, V, iii (Winter, 1968-69), 23-7.

Corbett, Edward P. J., "Raise High the Barriers, Censors," America, CIV (January 7, 1961), 441-3. Also in Laser, M., and N. Fruman, eds., Studies in J. D. Salinger, 134-41. Also in Marsden, M. M., ed., If You Really Want to Know, 68-73. Also in Simonson, H. P., and P. E. Hager, eds., Salinger's CATCHER IN THE RYE, 5-9.

Costello, Donald P., The Language of THE CATCHER IN THE RYE," AS, XXIV (October, 1959), 172-81. Also in Belcher, W. F., and J. W. Lee, eds., Salinger and the Critics, 45-53. Also in Grunwald, H. A., ed., Salinger, 266-76. Also in Laser, M., and N. Fruman, eds., Studies in J. D. Salinger, 92-104. Also Marsden, M. M., ed., If You Really Want to Know, 87-95. Also in Simonson, H. P., and P. E. Hager, eds., Salinger's CATCHER IN THE RYE, 32-9.

Costello, Patrick, "Salinger and 'Honest Iago'," Ren, XVI (Summer, 1964), 171-4.

Creeger, George R., "Treacherous Desertion: Salinger's THE CATCHER IN THE RYE," in Belcher, W. F., and J. W. Lee, eds., J. D. Salinger and the Critics, 98-104.

D'Avanzo, Mario L., "Gatsby and Holden Caulfield," FitzN, No. 38 (Summer, 1967), 4-6.

Davis, Tom, "J. D. Salinger: 'Some Crazy Cliff' Indeed," WHR, XIV (Winter, 1960), 97-9. Also in Marsden, M. M., ed., If You Really Want to Know, 45-7.

Deer, Irving, and John H. Randall, III, "J. D. Salinger and

the Reality Beyond Words," LHR, No. 6 (1964), 19-29.

Dodge, Stewart, "The Theme of Quest: III In Search of 'The Fat Lady'," EngR, VIII (Winter, 1957), 10-13. Also (condensed) in Marsden, M.M., ed., If You Really Want to Know, 40-2.

Drake, Robert Y., Jr., "Two Old Juveniles," GaR, XIII (Winter, 1959), 443-53.

Ducharme, Edward, "J.D. Sonny, Sunny, and Holden," EngR, XIX, ii (1968), 54-8.

Ely, Sister M. Amanda, "The Adult Image in Three Novels of Adolescence," EJ, LVI (November, 1967), 1130-31.

Erwin, Kenneth J., "An Analysis of the Dramatic and Semantic Use of Altruism in the Writings of J.D. Salinger," DA, XIX (1968), 1535A-36A (Un. of Texas).

Finkelstein, S., Existentialism and Alienation in American Literature, 219-24.

Fogel, Amy, "Where the Ducks Go: THE CATCHER IN THE RYE," BSCTF, III (Spring, 1962), 75-9.

Foran, Donald J., "A Doubletake on Holden Caulfield," EJ, LVII (October, 1968), 977-9.

Fowler, Albert, "Alien in the Rye," ModA, I, No. 2 (Fall, 1957), 193-7. Also in Belcher, W.F., and J.W. Lee, eds., J.D. Salinger and the Critics, 34-40.

French, Warren, "Holden's Fall," MFS, X (Winter, 1964-65), 389.

_____, J.D. Salinger, 64-7, 102-29, 161-5.

_____, "Steinbeck's Winter Tale," MFS, XII (Autumn, 1966), 66-74.

Gale, Robert L., "Redburn and Holden - Half-Brothers One Century Removed," ForumH, III, xii (Winter, 1963), 32-6.

Galloway, D.D., Absurd Hero, 140-5.

Gardiner, Harold C., "Words and Conscience," America, CIV (January 7, 1961), 444.

Geismar, M., American Moderns, 195-9. Also in Belcher, W.F., and J.W. Lee, eds., J.D. Salinger and the Critics, 43-5. Also in Grunwald, H.A., ed., Salinger, 87-91.

Giles, Barbara, "The Lonely War of J.D. Salinger," Mainstream, XII (February, 1959), 2-8+.

Goldstein, Bernice and Sanford, "Zen and Salinger," MFS, XI (Autumn, 1966), 322-3.

Gooder, R.D., "One of Today's Best Little Writers," CamQ, I (Winter, 1965-66), 83-6.

Goodman, Anne L., "Mad About Children," NRep, CXXV (July 16, 1951), 20-1. Also in Simonson, H.P., and P.E. Hager, eds., Salinger's CATCHER IN THE RYE, 3-4.

Green, Martin, "American Rococo: Salinger and Nabokov,"
    Re-Appraisals, 211-29.
_____, "Franny and Zooey," Re-Appraisals, 197-210.
_____, "The Image-Maker," in Grunwald, H. A. , ed. ,
    Salinger, 251-2.
Grunwald, Henry A. , " 'He Touches Something Deep in Us
    ...'," Horizon, IV (May, 1962), 100-7.
Gutwillig, Robert, "Everybody's Caught THE CATCHER IN
    THE RYE," NYTBR Paperback Section (January 15,
    1961). Also in Laser, M. , and N. Fruman, eds. , Stud-
    ies in J. D. Salinger, 1-5.
Gwynn, F. L. , and J. L. Blotner, Fiction of J. D. Salinger,
    28-31. Also in Laser, M. , and N. Fruman, eds. ,
    Studies in J. D. Salinger, 85-7. Also in Marsden, M. M. ,
    ed. , If You Really Want to Know, 45-7. Also in Simon-
    .son, H. P. , and P. E. Hager, eds. , Salinger's CATCHER
    IN THE RYE, 93-4.
Hainsworth, J. D. , "J. D. Salinger," HJ, LXIV (Winter,
    1966), 63-4.
_____, "Maturity in J. D. Salinger's THE CATCHER IN
    THE RYE," ES, XLVIII (October, 1967), 426-31.
Hall, James, Lunatic Giant in the Drawing Room, 75-7.
_____, "Play, the Training Camp, and American Angry
    Comedy," HAB, XV (Spring, 1964), 9-11.
Hamilton, Kenneth, J. D. Salinger, 22-7, 37-9.
_____, "One Way to Use the Bible: The Example of J. D.
    Salinger," ChS, XLVII (Fall, 1964), 244-6.
Harper, H. M. , Jr. , "J. D. Salinger - Through Glasses Dark-
    ly," Desperate Faith, 66-71.
Hassan, Ihab, "Rare Quixotic Gesture: The Fiction of J. D.
    Salinger," WR, XXI (Summer, 1957), 271-4. Also (re-
    vised) in Hassan, I. , Radical Innocence, 272-6. Also in
    Belcher, W. F. , and J. W. Lee, eds. , J. D. Salinger and
    the Critics, 117-20. Also in Grunwald, H. A. , ed. , Sal-
    inger, 148-52. Also in Laser, M. , and N. Fruman, eds. ,
    Studies in J. D. Salinger, 63-7. Also in Marsden, M. M. ,
    ed. , If You Really Want to Know, 30-2.
Hayes, Ann L. , "J. D. Salinger: A Reputation and a Prom-
    ise," in Carnegie Institute of Technology. Lectures on
    Modern Novelists, 15-18.
Heiserman, Arthur, and James E. Miller, Jr. , "J. D. Sal-
    inger: Some Crazy Cliff," WHR, X (Spring, 1956), 129-
    32. Also in Belcher, W. F. , and J. W. Lee, eds. , J. D.
    Salinger and the Critics, 14-17. Also in Grunwald, H. A. ,
    ed. , Salinger, 196-205. Also in Laser, M. , and N. Fru-
    man, eds. , Studies in J. D. Salinger, 23-30. Also in
    Marsden, M. M. , ed. , If You Really Want to Know, 16-22.

Also in Simonson, H. P., and P. E. Hager, eds., Salinger's CATCHER IN THE RYE, 74-80. Also in Miller, J. E., Quests Surd and Absurd, 31-40.

Herndl, George C., "Golding and Salinger: A Clear Choice," WiseR, No. 502 (1964), 309-22.

Howell, John M., "Salinger in the Waste Land," MFS, XII (Autumn, 1966), 367-75.

_____, "The Waste Land Tradition in the American Novel," DA, XXIV (1964), 3337 (Tulane).

Jacobs, Robert G., "J. D. Salinger's THE CATCHER IN THE RYE: Holden Caulfield's 'Goddam Autobiography," IEY (Fall, 1959), 9-14. Also (condensed) in Marsden, M. M., ed., If You Really Want to Know, 55-62.

Johnson, James W., "The Adolescent Hero: A Trend in Modern Fiction," TCL, V (April, 1959), 5.

Jones, Ernest, "Case History of All of Us," Nation, CLXXIII (September 1, 1951), 176. Also in Simonson, H. P., and P. E. Hager, eds., Salinger's CATCHER IN THE RYE, 4-5.

Kaplan, Charles, "Holden and Huck: The Odysseys of Youth," CE, XVIII (November, 1956), 76-80. Also in Laser, M., and N. Fruman, eds., Studies in J. D. Salinger, 31-8. Also in Marsden, M. M., ed., If You Really Want to Know, 127-32.

Kearns, Francis E., "Salinger and Golding: Conflict on the Campus," America, CVIII (January 26, 1963), 136-9. Also in Nelson, W., ed., William Golding's LORD OF THE FLIES, 148-55.

Kegel, Charles H., "Incommunicability in Salinger's THE CATCHER IN THE RYE," WHR, XI (Spring, 1957), 188-90. Also in Belcher, W. F., and J. W. Lee, eds., J. D. Salinger and the Critics, 17-20. Also in Laser, M., and N. Fruman, eds., Studies in J. D. Salinger, 53-6. Also in Marsden, M. M., ed., If You Really Want to Know, 25-7. Also in Simonson, H. P., and P. E. Hager, eds., Salinger's CATCHER IN THE RYE, 63-5.

Kermode, Frank, "Fit Audience," Spectator, CC (May 30, 1958), 705-6. Also in Belcher, W. F., and J. W. Lee, eds., J. D. Salinger and the Critics, 40-3. Also in Kermode, F., Puzzles and Epiphanies, 188-92.

Kinney, Arthur F., "J. D. Salinger and the Search for Love," TSLL, V (1963), 111-14.

_____, "The Theme of Charity in THE CATCHER IN THE RYE," PMASAL, XLVIII (1963), 691-702.

Laser, Marvin, "Character Names in THE CATCHER IN THE RYE," CEJ, I (1965), 29-40.

_____, and N. Fruman, "Salinger: The Early Reviews,"
in Laser, M., and N. Fruman, eds., Studies in J. D.
Salinger, 6-17.

Leitch, David, "The Salinger Myth," TC, CLXVIII (November, 1960), 428-35. Also in Mlle, CCLXIV (August,
1961), 264-5, 73, 88. Also (selection) in Marsden, M.
M., ed., If You Really Want to Know, 66-8.

Lettis, Richard, J. D. Salinger: THE CATCHER IN THE
RYE (Barron's Studies in American Literature), Great
Neck, N. Y.: Barrons Educ. Ser., 1964.

Levine, Paul, "J. D. Salinger: The Development of the Mis-
fit Hero," TCL, IV (October, 1958), 92-9. Also (selection) in Marsden, M. M., ed., If You Really Want to
Know, 47-8.

Light, James F., "Salinger's THE CATCHER IN THE RYE,"
Expl, XVIII (June, 1960), Item 59. Also in Marsden, M.
M., ed., If You Really Want to Know, 98-9. Also in
Simonson, H. P., and P. E. Hager, eds., Salinger's
CATCHER IN THE RYE, 39-40.

Little, Gail B., "Three Novels for Comparative Study in the
Twelfth Grade," EJ, LII (September, 1963), 501-5.

Ludwig, J., Recent American Novelists, 28-30, 33-5.

Lydenberg, John, "American Novelists in Search of a Lost
World," RLV, XXVII, No. 4 (1961), 312-13.

McCarthy, Mary, "J. D. Salinger's Closed Circuit," Harpers,
CCXXV (October, 1962), 46-7. Also (selection) in Marsden, M. M., ed., If You Really Want to Know, 84.

Maclean, Hugh N., "Conservatism in Modern American Fic-
tion," CE, XV (March, 1954), 315-22. Also in Belcher,
W. F., and J. W. Lee, eds., J. D. Salinger and the Crit-
ics, 11-14. Also in (condensed) Marsden, M. M., ed.,
If You Really Want to Know, 14-15. Also in Simonson,
H. P., and P. E. Hager, eds., Salinger's CATCHER IN
THE RYE, 101-2.

McNamara, Eugene, "Holden as Novelist," EJ, LIV (March,
1965), 166-70.

Malin, Irving, "The Gothic Family," Psychoanalysis and
American Fiction, 264-66. Also in Malin, I., New American Gothic, 61-3.

Marcus, Fred, "THE CATCHER IN THE RYE: A Live Circuit," EJ, LII (January, 1963), 1-8.

Margolies, John D., "Salinger's THE CATCHER IN THE
RYE," Expl, XXI (November, 1963), Item 23.

Marks, Barry A., "Rebuttal" to Peter Seng, "The Fallen
Idol: Holden Caulfield," CE, XXIII (March, 1962), 507.
Also (complete letter) in Marsden, M. M., ed., If You
Really Want to Know, 81-2. Also in Simonson, H. P.,

and P. E. Hager, eds., Salinger's CATCHER IN THE
RYE, 71-2.
Marsden, M. M., ed., If You Really Want to Know.
Martin, Augustine, "A Note on J. D. Salinger," Studies,
XLVIII (Autumn, 1959), 336-45.
Martin, Dexter, "Rebuttal" to Bernard S. Oldsey, "The Mov-
ies in the Rye," CE, XXIII (March, 1962), 507-9. Also
(complete letter) in Marsden, M. M., ed., If You Really
Want to Know, 82-3. Also (unpublished portion) in Simon-
son, H. P., and P. E. Hager, eds., Salinger's CATCHER
IN THE RYE, 45-6.
_____, "Rebuttal" to Peter Seng, "The Fallen Idol: Hold-
en Caulfield," CE, XXIII (March, 1962), 507-9. Also in
Simonson, H. P., and P. E. Hager, eds., Salinger's
CATCHER IN THE RYE, 72.
Martin, Hansford, "The American Problem of Direct Ad-
dress," WR, XVI (Winter, 1952), 101-14.
Miller, J. E., Jr., J. D. Salinger, 8-19.
Moore, Robert P., "The World of Holden," EJ, LIV (March,
1965), 159-65. Reply by M. Gilbert Porter, EJ, LIV
(September, 1965), 562.
Noon, William T., "Three Young Men in Rebellion," Thought,
XXXVIII (Winter, 1963), 571-7.
O'Hara, J. D., "No Catcher in the Rye," MFS, IX (Winter,
1963-64), 370-6. Also in Westbrook, M., ed., Modern
American Novel, 211-20.
Oldsey, Bernard S., "The Movies in the Rye," CE, XXIII
(December, 1961), 209-15. Also in Belcher, W. F., and
J. W. Lee, eds., Salinger and the Critics, 68-75. Also
in Marsden, M. M., ed., If You Really Want to Know,
116-22. Also in Simonson, H. P., and P. E. Hager, eds.,
Salinger's CATCHER IN THE RYE, 40-5.
Padovano, A., Estranged God, 139-49.
Parker, Christopher, "Why the Hell Not Smash All the Win-
dows?" in Grunwald, H. A., ed., Salinger, 254-8.
Peavy, Charles D., " 'Did You Ever Have a Sister?' Holden,
Quentin, and Sexual Innocence," FloQ, I, iii (1968), 82-
95.
_____, "Holden's Courage Again," CEA, XXVIII (October,
1965), 1, 6, 9.
Pilkington, John, "About this Madman Stuff," UMSE, VII
(1966), 65-75.
_____, "Mummies and Ducks," UMSE, VI (1965), 15-22.
Pomeranz, Regina E., "The Search for Self in the Adoles-
cent Protagonist in the Contemporary Novel: A Method of
Approach for the College Teacher of Literature," DA,
XXVII (1966), 780A (Columbia).

Rees, Richard, Brave Men: A Study of D. H. Lawrence and Simone Weil, Carbondale: Southern Ill. Un. Pr. , 1959, 178-87; London: Victor Gollancz, 1958.

Reiman, Donald H. , "Rebuttal" to Peter Seng, "The Fallen Idol: Holden Caulfield," CE, XXIII (March, 1962), 507. Also in Marsden, M. M. , ed. , If You Really Want to Know, 82. Also in Simonson, H. P. , and P. E. Hager, eds. , Salinger's CATCHER IN THE RYE, 72-3.

_____, "Salinger's THE CATCHER IN THE RYE," Expl, XXII (March, 1963), Item 58.

Saha, Winifred M. , "J. D. Salinger: The Younger Writer and Society," Master's Thesis, Divinity School, Un. of Chicago, June, 1957. Also (selection) in Marsden, M. M. , ed. , If You Really Want to Know, 28-9.

Schrader, Allen, "Emerson to Salinger to Parker," SatR, XLII (April 11, 1959), 52+. Also in Simonson, H. P. , and P. E. Hager, eds. , Salinger's CATCHER IN THE RYE, 106-8.

Scott, Nathan A. , Jr. , Modern Literature and the Religious Frontier, N. Y.: Harper, 1958, 90-4.

Seng, Peter J. , "The Fallen Idol: The Immature World of Holden Caulfield," CE, XXIII (December, 1961), 203-9. Also in Belcher, W. F. , and J. W. Lee, eds. , J. D. Salinger and the Critics, 60-8. Also in Marsden, M. M. , ed. , If You Really Want to Know, 55-62. Also in Simonson, H. P. , and P. E. Hager, eds. , Salinger's CATCHER IN THE RYE, 65-71.

Sherr, Paul C. , "THE CATCHER IN THE RYE and the Boarding School," ISB, XXVI, ii (1966), 42-54.

Slabey, Robert M. , "THE CATCHER IN THE RYE: Christian Theme and Symbol," CLAJ, VI (March, 1963), 170-83.

_____, "Salinger's 'Casino': Wayfarers and Spiritual Acrobats," EngR, XIV, iii (February, 1964), 16-20 passim.

Smith, Harrison, "Manhattan Ulysses, Junior," SatR, XXXIV (July 14, 1951), 12-13. Also in Simonson, H. P. , and P. E. Hager, eds. , Salinger's CATCHER IN THE RYE, 2-3.

Stevenson, David, "J. D. Salinger: The Mirror of Crisis," Nation, CLXXXIV (March 9, 1957), 216-17. Also in Belcher, W. F. , and J. W. Lee, eds. , Salinger and the Critics, 139-41. Also in Grunwald, H. A. , ed. , Salinger, 39-41. Also in Marsden, M. M. , ed. , If You Really Want to Know, 24-5. Also in Nation (Periodical). View of the Nation, 59-60.

Stone, Edward, "Salinger's Carrousel," MFS, XIII (Winter, 1967-68), 520-3.

Strauch, Carl F., "Kings in the Back Row: Meaning Through Structure - A Reading of J. D. Salinger's THE CATCHER IN THE RYE," WSCL, II (Winter, 1961), 5-30. Also in Belcher, W. F., and J.W. Lee, eds., J. D. Salinger and the Critics, 76-98. Also in Laser, M., and M. Fruman, eds., Studies in J. D. Salinger, 143-71. Also in Marsden, M.M., ed., If You Really Want to Know, 99-116. Also in Simonson, H. P., and P.E. Hager, eds., Salinger's CATCHER IN THE RYE, 46-62.

_____, "Salinger: The Romantic Background," WSCL, IV, i (Winter, 1963), 31-40.

Tanner, T., Reign of Wonder, 341-3.

Tarinya, M., "Salinger: THE CATCHER IN THE RYE," LHY, VII (July, 1966), 49-60.

Tink, Stanley, "Initiation In and Out: The American Novel and the American Dream," Quadrant, V, iii [No. 19] (Winter, 1961), 63-74.

Tirumalai, Canadadai K., "Salinger's THE CATCHER IN THE RYE," Expl, XXII (March, 1964), Item 56.

Travis, Mildred K., "Salinger's THE CATCHER IN THE RYE," Expl, XXI (December, 1962), Item 36.

Trowbridge, Clinton W., "Hamlet and Holden," EJ, LVII (January, 1968), 26-9.

_____, "Salinger's Symbolic Use of Character and Detail in THE CATCHER IN THE RYE," CimR, IV (June, 1968), 5-11.

_____, "The Symbolic Structure of THE CATCHER IN THE RYE," SR, LXXIV (Summer, 1966), 681-93.

Vanderbilt, Kermit, "Symbolic Resolution in THE CATCHER IN THE RYE: The Cap, the Carrousel and the American West," WHR, XVII (Summer, 1963), 271-7.

Wakefield, Dan, "Salinger and the Search for Love," in New World Writing, No. 14, N. Y.: New American Library, 1958, 72-5. Also in Laser, M., and N. Fruman, eds., Studies in J. D. Salinger, 77-84. Also (selection) in Marsden, M.M., ed., If You Really Want to Know, 52-4.

Walcutt, C. C., Man's Changing Mask, 317-26.

Walzer, Michael, "In Place of a Hero," Dissent, VII (Spring, 1960), 156-9.

Warner, Deane M., "Huck and Holden," CEA, XXVII (March, 1965), 4a-4b.

Way, Brian, "FRANNY AND ZOOEY and J. D. Salinger," New Left Rev, (May-June, 1962), 74-82. Also in Laser, M., and N. Fruman, eds., Studies in J. D. Salinger, 190-201.

Weber, Donald, "Narrative Method in A SEPARATE PEACE, SSF, III (Fall, 1965), 63-72.

Wells, Arvin R., "Huck Finn and Holden Caulfield: The
Situation of the Hero," OUR, II (1960), 31-42. Also in
Marsden, M. M., ed., If You Really Want to Know, 144-
51.
Widmer, K., Literary Rebel, 127-8.
Wiegand, William, "J. D. Salinger: Seventy-Eight Bananas,"
ChiR, XI (Winter, 1958), 3-19. Also (condensed) in
Marsden, M. M., ed., If You Really Want to Know, 48-
52.

BIBLIOGRAPHY

Beebe, Maurice, and Jennifer Sperry, "Criticism of J. D.
Salinger: A Selected Checklist," MFS, XII (Autumn,
1966), 377-90.
Fiene, Donald M., "J. D. Salinger: A Bibliography," WSCL,
IV, i (Winter, 1963), 109-49.
Galloway, D. D., Absurd Hero, 234-51.
Simonson, H. P., and P. E. Hager, eds., Salinger's
CATCHER IN THE RYE, 110-11.

SANSOM, WILLIAM, 1912-

GENERAL

Karl, F. R., Contemporary English Novel, 285-7.
Vickery, John B., "William Sansom and Logical Empiri-
cism," Thought, XXXVI (Summer, 1961), 231-45.

THE BODY

Allen, W., Modern Novel, 268-9.

SAROYAN, WILLIAM, 1908-

GENERAL

Fisher, William J., "What Ever Happened to Saroyan?" CE,
XVI (March, 1955), 336-40. Also in EJ, XLIV (March,
1955), 129-34.
Floan, H. R., William Saroyan.
Schulberg, Budd, "Saroyan: Ease and Unease on the Flying
Trapeze," Esquire, LIV, iv (October, 1960), 85-91.
Tsujimoto, Ichiro, "William Saroyan, An Improvisator,"
KAL, No. 2 (May, 1959), 12-16. (Not seen.)

VanGelder, Robert, Writers on Writing, 29-30.

THE ADVENTURES OF WESLEY JACKSON

Floan, H. R. , William Saroyan, 126-9.
Wilson, Edmund, "William Saroyan and His Darling Old
Province," NY, XXII (June 15, 1946), 76-8. Also in
Wilson, E. , Classics and Commercials, 327-30.

THE HUMAN COMEDY

Burgum, Edwin B. , "Lonesome Young Man on the Flying
Trapeze," VQR, XX (Summer, 1944), 392-402. Also in
Burgum, E. B. , Novel and the World's Dilemma, 269-71.
Carpenter, Frederic I. , "The Time of William Saroyan's
Life," PacSp, I (Winter, 1947), 88-96. Also in Carpen-
ter, F. I. , American Literature and the Dream, 176-84.
Floan, H. R. , William Saroyan, 123-6.
Gray, J. , On Second Thought, 114-15.

THE LAUGHING MATTER

Floan, H. R. , William Saroyan, 138-43.

ROCK WAGRAM

Floan, J. R. , William Saroyan, 134-7.
Sarkisian, Levon, "Saroyan's ROCK WAGRAM: A Psycho-
Social Character," Armenian Rev, XI (1959), 61-8.

TRACY'S TIGER

Floan, H. R. , William Saroyan, 137-8.

BIBLIOGRAPHY

Floan, H. R. , William Saroyan, 164-7.

SCHULBERG, BUDD WILSON, 1914-

GENERAL

Eisinger, C. E. , Fiction of the Forties, 103-6.
Van Gelder, Robert, Writers on Writing, 197-200.

THE DISENCHANTED

Connolly, C., Previous Convictions, 299-301.
Farr, Finis, "In a Workmanlike Manner," NatR, VI (April 11, 1959), 656-8.
Robinson, Jean J., "Henry James and Schulberg's THE DIS-ENCHANTED," MLN, LXVII (November, 1952), 472-3.

WHAT MAKES SAMMY RUN?

Sherman, B., Invention of the Jew, 176-8.

SEAGER, ALLAN, 1906-1968

GENERAL

Bloom, Robert, "Allan Seager: Some Versions of Disen-gagement," Crit, V, iii (Winter, 1962-63), 4-26.
Hanna, Allan, "The Muse of History: Allan Seager and the Criticism of Culture," Crit, V, iii (Winter, 1962-63), 37-61.
Kenner, Hugh, "The Insider," Crit, II (Winter, 1959), 3-15.
Lid, R.W., "The Innocent Eye," Crit, V, iii (Winter, 1962-63), 62-74.
Webster, Harvey C., "Allan Seager as Social Novelist," Crit, V, iii (Winter, 1962-63), 27-36.

AMOS BERRY

Barrows, Herbert, in MAQR, LIX (Summer, 1953), 364-6.
Hanna, Allan, "The Muse of History: Allan Seager and the Criticism of Culture," Crit, V, iii (Winter, 1962-63), 40-9, 51-4.
Lid, R.W., "The Innocent Eye," Crit, V, iii (Winter, 1962-63), 62-7.
Miles, George, "Some Tired Businessmen," Cweal, LVII (March 20, 1953), 607-8.
Webster, Harvey C., "Allan Seager as Social Novelist," Crit, V, iii (Winter, 1962-63), 33-4.

DEATH OF ANGER

Bloom, Robert, "Allan Seager: Some Versions of Disen-gagement," Crit, V, iii (Winter, 1962-63), 11-16.

EQUINOX

Bloom, Robert, "Allan Seager: Some Versions of Disen-
gagement," Crit, V, iii (Winter, 1962-63), 4-8.
Lid, R.W., "The Innocent Eye," Crit, V, iii (Winter, 1962-
63), 67-72.
Webster, Harvey C., "Allan Seager as Social Novelist,"
Crit, V, iii (Winter, 1962-63), 30-2.

HILDA MANNING

O'Neill, James C., "Madame Bovary in Michigan?" MAQR,
LXIII (Winter, 1957), 178-9.

THE INHERITANCE

Bloom, Robert, "Allan Seager: Some Versions of Disengage-
ment," Crit, V, iii (Winter, 1962-63), 16-22.
Gehman, Richard B., "The Ogre of a Small Town," SatR,
XXXI (April 24, 1948), 17-18.
Webster, Harvey C., "Allan Seager as Social Novelist,"
Crit, V, iii (Winter, 1962-63), 32-3.
Williams, Mentor L., in MAQR, LIV (Summer, 1948), 371-2.

BIBLIOGRAPHY

Hanna, Allan, "An Allan Seager Bibliography," Crit, V, iii
(Winter, 1962-63), 75-90.

SHAW, IRWIN, 1913-

GENERAL

Evans, Bergen, "Irwin Shaw," EJ, XL (November, 1951),
485-91. Also in CE, XIII (November, 1951), 71-7.
Fiedler, Leslie, "Irwin Shaw: Adultery, the Last Politics,"
Ctary, XXII (July, 1956), 71-4.
Startt, William, "Irwin Shaw: An Extended Talent," MQ, II
(July, 1961), 325-37.

LUCY CROWN

Fiedler, Leslie, "Irwin Shaw: Adultery, the Last Politics,"
Ctary, XXII (July, 1956), 71-4.
Startt, William, "Irwin Shaw: An Extended Talent," MQ,
II (July, 1961), 329-31.

THE TROUBLED AIR

Eisinger, C. E. , Fiction of the Forties, 111-12.
Evans, Bergen, "Irwin Shaw," EJ, XL (November, 1951),
    488-90. Also in CE, XIII (November, 1951), 74-6.
Milne, G. , American Political Novel, 150-1.
Startt, William, "Irwin Shaw: An Extended Talent," MQ, II
    (July, 1961), 328-9.

TWO WEEKS IN ANOTHER TOWN

Startt, William, "Irwin Shaw: An Extended Talent," MQ, II
    (July, 1961), 331-7.

THE YOUNG LIONS

Aldridge, J.W. , After the Lost Generation, 147-56.
Eisinger, C. E. , Fiction of the Forties, 111-12.
Evans, Bergen, "Irwin Shaw," EJ, XL (November, 1951),
    486-8. Also in CE, XIII (November, 1951), 72-4.
Glicksberg, Charles, "Anti-Semitism and the Jewish Novel-
    ist," in Ribalow, H. , ed. , Mid-Century, 346-8.
Healey, Robert C. , in Gardiner, H. C. , ed. , Fifty Years
    of the American Novel, 264-5.
Hoffman, F. J. , Mortal No, 235-7.
Startt, William, "Irwin Shaw: An Extended Talent," MQ, II
    (July, 1961), 326-8.
Waldmeir, J. J. , American Novels of the Second World War,
    92-101, 107-8, 149-52.

SILLITOE, ALAN, 1928-

GENERAL

Aldridge, J.W. , "Alan Sillitoe: The Poor Man's Bore,"
    Time to Murder and Create, 239-44.
Atherton, Stanley S. , "Alan Sillitoe's Battleground," DR,
    XLVIII (Autumn, 1968), 324-31.
Gindin, James, "Alan Sillitoe's Jungle," TSLL, IV (1962),
    35-48. Also in Gindin, J. , Postwar British Fiction, 14-
    33.
Hurrell, John D. , "Alan Sillitoe and the Serious Novel,"
    Crit, IV, i (1961), 3-16.
Karl, F. R. , Contemporary English Novel, 283-4.
Klotz, Gunther, "Alan Sillitoe's Heroes," in Lingner, Erica,
    et al, eds. , Essays in Honor of William Gallacher, Ber-

lin: Humboldt Univ., 1966, 259-63.
Lockwood, Bernard, "Four Contemporary British Working-
  Class Novelists: A Thematic and Critical Approach to
  the Fiction of Raymond Williams, John Braine, David
  Storey and Alan Sillitoe," DA, XXVIII (1967), 1081A
  (Wisc.).
Maloff, Saul, "The Eccentricity of Alan Sillitoe," in Shapiro,
  C., ed., Contemporary British Novelists, 95-113.
Rosselli, John, "A Cry from the Brick Streets," Reporter,
  XXXIII (November 10, 1960), 37, 40, 43.
Shestakov, Dmitri, "Alan Sillitoe from Nottingham," Soviet
  Lit, No. 9 (1963), 176-9.

THE DEATH OF WILLIAM POSTERS

Kermode, Frank, "Rammel," NStat (May 14, 1965), 765-66.
  Also in Kermode, F., Continuities, 227-32.
Penner, Allen R., "The Political Prologue and Two Parts of
  a Trilogy: THE DEATH OF WILLIAM POSTERS and A
  TREE ON FIRE," UR, XXXV (October, 1968), 11-20.

THE GENERAL

Gindin, James, "Allen Sillitoe's Jungle," TSLL, IV (1962),
  35-48. Also in Gindin, J., Postwar British Fiction, 14-
  33.
Rippier, J.S., Some Postwar English Novelists, 200-1.

KEY TO THE DOOR

McDowell, Frederick P.W., "Self and Society: Alan Silli-
  toe's KEY TO THE DOOR," Crit, VI, i (Spring, 1963),
  16-23.
Penner, Allen R., "Dantesque Allegory in Sillitoe's KEY TO
  THE DOOR," Ren, XX (1968), 79-85, 103.
Rippier, J.S., Some Postwar English Novelists, 201-6.
Wiley, Paul, in WSCL, IV, ii (Spring-Summer, 1963), 228-9.

SATURDAY NIGHT AND SUNDAY MORNING

Gindin, James, "Alan Sillitoe's Jungle," TSLL, IV (1962),
  35-48. Also in Gindin, J., Postwar British Fiction, 14-
  33.
Howe, Irving, "The Worker as a Young Tough," NRep,
  CXLI (August 24, 1959), 27-8.
Hurrell, John D., "Alan Sillitoe and the Serious Novel,"
  Crit, IV, i (1961), 9-11, 14-16.

Maloff, Saul, in Shapiro, C. , ed. , Contemporary British
Novelists, 108-13.
Nemerov, H. , Poetry and Fiction, 277-8.
Osgerby, J. R. , "Alan Sillitoe's SATURDAY NIGHT AND
SUNDAY MORNING," in Hibbard, G. R. , ed. , Renaissance
and Modern Essays Presented to Vivian de Sola Pinto in
Celebration of His Seventieth Birthday, London: Rout-
ledge and K. Paul, 1966, 215-30.
Prince, Rod, in New Left Rev, No. 6 (November-December,
1960), 14-17.
Rippier, J. S. , Some Postwar English Novelists, 194-8.
Staples, Hugh B. , "SATURDAY NIGHT AND SUNDAY MORN-
ING: Alan Sillitoe and the White Goddess," MFS, X (Sum-
mer, 1964), 171-81.
Urwin, G. G. , ed. , Taste for Living, 166-9.
West, Anthony, "On the Inside Looking In," NY, XXXV
(September 5, 1959), 103-4.

A TREE ON FIRE

Penner, Allen R. , "The Political Prologue and Two Parts of
a Trilogy: THE DEATH OF WILLIAM POSTERS and A
TREE ON FIRE," UR, XXXV (October, 1968), 11-20.

SINCLAIR, UPTON BEALL, 1878-

GENERAL

Becker, George J. , "Upton Sinclair: Quixote in a Flivver,"
CE, XXI (December, 1959), 133-40.
Blankenship, R. , American Literature, 753-5.
Blinderman, Abraham, "The Social Passions of Upton Sin-
clair," CJF, XXV (Spring, 1967), 203-8.
Cantwell, Robert, in Cowley, M. , ed. , After the Genteel
Tradition, 37-47.
Chalmers, David M. , The Political and Social Ideas of the
Muckrakers, N. Y. : Citadel, 1964, 88-95.
Koerner, J. D. , "The Last of the Muckrake Men," SAQ, LV
(April, 1956), 221-32. Also in Publications in the Hu-
manities, No. 19, Cambridge: MIT Pr. , 1958.
Sinclair, Upton, The Autobiography of Upton Sinclair, N. Y. :
Harcourt, 1962.
_____, My Lifetime in Letters, Columbia: Un. of Mo.
Pr. , 1960.
Straumann, H. , American Literature in the Twentieth Cen-
tury, 11-14.

THE JUNGLE

Brook, Van Wyk, <u>Confident Years,</u> 373-6.
Chalmers, David M. , <u>The Political and Social Ideas of the</u>
  <u>Muckrakers,</u> N. Y.: Citadel, 1964, 93-5.
Downs, Robert B. , "Afterward," THE JUNGLE, N. Y.: New
  American Library, 1960.
Rideout, W. B. , <u>Radical Novel in the U. S.</u> , 30-7.
Swados, Harvey, "THE JUNGLE Revisited," <u>Atlantic,</u> CCVIII
  (December, 1961, 96+. Also in Swados, H. , <u>Radical's</u>
  <u>America,</u> 3-11.

KING COAL

Rideout, W. B. , <u>Radical Novel in the U. S.</u> , 37-8.

LANNY BUDD Series (See WORLD'S END Series)

OIL

Blotner, J. , <u>Modern American Political Novel,</u> 113-17.

WORLD'S END Series

Becker, George J. , "Upton Sinclair: Quixote in a Flivver,"
  <u>CE,</u> XXI (December, 1959), 135-9.
Brooks, Van Wyk, <u>Confident Years,</u> 377-8.
Koerner, J. D. , "The Last of the Muckrake Men," <u>SAQ,</u> LV
  (April, 1956), 227-32. Also in <u>Publications in the Hu-</u>
  <u>manities,</u> No. 19, Cambridge: M. I. T. Pr. , 1958.
Sinclair, Upton, "Farewell to Lanny Budd," <u>SRL,</u> XXXII
  (August 13, 1949), 18-19, 38.
Spitz, Leon, "Upton Sinclair and Nazism," <u>AmHebrew,</u>
  CLVIII (October 22, 1948), 2.

<u>SINGER, ISAAC BASHEVIS, 1904-</u>

GENERAL

Allentuck, M. , ed. , <u>Achievement of Isaac Bashevis Singer.</u>
Blocker, Joel, and Richard Elman, "An Interview With Isaac
  Bashevis Singer," <u>Ctary,</u> XXXVI (November, 1963), 364-
  72. Also in Malin, I. , ed. , <u>Critical Views of Isaac Ba-</u>
  <u>shevis Singer,</u> 3-26.
Bregner, Marshall, and Bob Barnhart, "A Conversation With
  Isaac Bashevis Singer," <u>The Handle</u> (Un. of Penn.), II

(Fall, 1964-Winter, 1965), 9-21. Also in Malin, I., ed.,
Critical Views of Isaac Bashevis Singer, 27-43.
Buchen, Irving H., "The Art and Gifts of Isaac Bashevis
Singer," CJF, XXIV (Summer, 1966), 308-12.
_____, Isaac Bashevis Singer and the Eternal Past.
_____, "Isaac Bashevis Singer and the Eternal Past,"
Crit, VIII, iii (Spring-Summer, 1966), 5-18.
Chametsky, Jules, "History in I. B. Singer's Novels," in
Malin, I., ed., Critical Views of Isaac Bashevis Singer,
169-77.
Eisenberg, J. A., "Isaac Bashevis Singer - Passionate Primi-
tive or Pious Puritan?" Judaism, XI (Fall, 1962), 345-
56.   Also in Malin, I., ed., Critical Views of Isaac Ba-
shevis Singer, 48-67.
Fixler, Michael, "The Redeemers: Themes in the Fiction
of Isaac Bashevis Singer," KR, XXVI (Spring, 1964), 371-
86.   Also in Malin, I., ed., Critical Views of Isaac Ba-
shevis Singer, 68-85.
Flender, Harold, "The Art of Fiction XLII: Isaac Bashevis
Singer," ParisR, IX, No. 44 (1968), 53-73.
Friedman, Melvin J., "Isaac Bashevis Singer: The Appeal
of Numbers," in Malin, I., ed., Critical Views of Isaac
Bashevis Singer, 178-93.
Gass, William H., "The Shut-In," in Allentuck, M., ed.,
Achievement of Isaac Bashevis Singer, 1-13.
Golden, Morris, "Dr. Fischelson's Miracle; Duality and Vision in Singer's Fiction," in Allentuck, M., ed., Achieve-
ment of Isaac Bashevis Singer, 26-43.
Gottlieb, Elaine, "A Talk with Isaac Bashevis Singer," Re-
constructionist, XXV (March 6, 1959), 7-11.
Hemley, Cecil, Dimensions of Midnight: Prose and Poetry,
ed. by Elaine Gottlieb, Athens: Ohio Un. Pr., 1966, 217-
33.
Hernandez, Frances, "Isaac Bashevis Singer: New Impact
of a Medieval Tradition on Modern Fiction," Proceedings
of the Conf. of College Teachers of English, XXXIII (Sep-
tember, 1968), 18-23.   (Not seen.)
Hindus, Milton, in Jewish Heritage, V (Fall, 1962), 44-52.
Also in Jewish Heritage Reader, 242-52.
Hochman, Baruch, "I. B. Singer's Vision of Good and Evil,"
Midstream, XIII (March, 1967), 66-73.   Also in Malin,
I., ed., Critical Views of Isaac Bashevis Singer, 120-34.
Howe, Irving, "I. B. Singer, Encounter, XXVI (March, 1966),
60-70.
_____, "Introduction," Selected Short Stories of Isaac Ba-
shevis Singer, N. Y.: Modern Library, 1966.
Hughes, Ted., "The Genius of Isaac Bashevis Singer,"

NYRB, IV (April 22, 1965), 8-10.
Hyman, Stanley E., "The Yiddish Hawthorne," New Leader,
(July 23, 1962), 20-1. Also in Kostelanetz, R., ed.,
On Contemporary Literature, 586-90. Also in Hyman,
S. E., Standards, 83-7.
Jacobson, Dan, "The Problem of Isaac Bashevis Singer,"
Ctary, XXXIX (February, 1965), 48-52.
Katz, Eli, "Isaac Bashevis Singer and the Classical Yiddish
Tradition," in Allentuck, M., ed., Achievement of Isaac
Bashevis Singer, 14-25.
Madison, C.A., "I. Bashevis Singer: Novelist of Hasidic
Gothicism," Yiddish Literature, 479-99.
Malin, I., ed., Critical Views of Isaac Bashevis Singer.
Malkoff, Karl, "Demonology and Dualism: The Supernatural
in Isaac Singer and Muriel Spark," in Malin, I., ed.,
Critical Views of Isaac Bashevis Singer, 149-68.
Mucke, Edith, "Isaac B. Singer and Hassidic Philosophy,"
MinnR, VII, iii (1967), 214-21.
Newman, Richard A., "Isaac Bashevis Singer: The Faith of
His Devils and Magicians," HJ, LXV (Autumn, 1966), 27-
8.
Novak, Maximillian E., "Moral Grotesque and Decorative
Grotesque in Singer's Fiction," in Allentuck, M., ed.,
Achievement of Isaac Bashevis Singer, 44-63.
Pinsker, Samuel S., "The Schlemiel as Metaphor: Studies in
the Yiddish and American Jewish Novel," DA, XXVIII
(1968), 3679A-80A (Un. of Wash.).
Ribalow, Reena S., "A Visit to Isaac Bashevis Singer," Re-
constructionist, XXX (May 29, 1964), 19-26.
Schulz, Max F., "Isaac Bashevis Singer, Radical Sophistica-
tion, and the Jewish-American Novel," SHR, III (Winter,
1968), 60-6. Also in Schulz, M. F., Radical Sophistica-
tion, 13-22. Also in Malin, I., ed., Critical Views of
Isaac Bashevis Singer, 135-48. (Altered version.)
Siegel, Ben, Isaac Bashevis Singer.
_____, "Sacred and Profane: Isaac Bashevis Singer's
Embattled Spirits," Crit, VI, i (Spring, 1963), 24-47.
Sloman, Judith, "Existentialism in Par Lagerqvist and Isaac
Bashevis Singer," MinnR, V (August-October, 1966), 206-
12.
Sontag, Susan, "Demons and Dreams," PR, XXIX (Summer,
1962), 460-3.
Whitman, Ruth, "Translating with Isaac Bashevis Singer," in
Malin, I., ed., Critical Views of Isaac Bashevis Singer,
44-7.
Wolkenfeld, J.S., "Isaac Bashevis Singer: The Faith of His
Devils and Magicians," Criticism, V (Fall, 1963), 349-59.

Also in Malin, I., ed., Critical Views of Isaac Bashevis
Singer, 48-67.

THE FAMILY MOSKAT

Buchen, I. H., Isaac Bashevis Singer and the Eternal Past,
31-76, 108-9.
Elman, Richard, in Cavalier, XV (August, 1965), 10-12.
Hindus, Milton, in Jewish Heritage Reader, 242-6.
_____, in NYTBR (March 14, 1965), 4, 44-5.
Hughes, Ted, "The Genius of Isaac Bashevis Singer," NYRB,
IV (April 22, 1965), 9-10.
Madison, C. A., Yiddish Literature, 483-7.
Schulz, Max F., "The Family Chronicle as Paradigm of
History; THE BROTHERS ASHKENAZI and THE FAMILY
MOSKAT," in Allentuck, M., ed., Achievement of Isaac
Bashevis Singer, 77-92.
Siegel, Ben, Isaac Bashevis Singer, 11-14.
_____, "Sacred and Profane: Isaac Bashevis Singer's
Embattled Spirits," Crit, VI, i (Spring, 1963), 25-8.

THE MAGICIAN OF LUBLIN

Buchen, I. H., Isaac Bashevis Singer and the Eternal Past,
101-12, 210-11.
Chametsky, Jules, "Stereotypes and Jews: Fagin and the
Magician of Lublin," MR, II (Winter, 1961), 373-5.
Friedman, Melvin J., "Isaac Bashevis Singer: The Appeal
of Numbers," in Malin, I., ed., Critical Views of Isaac
Bashevis Singer, 185-8.
Hemley, Cecil, Dimensions of Midnight: Prose and Poetry,
ed. by Elaine Gottlieb, Athens: Ohio Un. Pr., 1966,
232-3.
Hindus, Milton, in Jewish Heritage Reader, 249-50.
Howe, Irving, "Demonic Fiction of a Yiddish 'Modernist',"
Ctary, XXX (October, 1960), 350-3. Also in Commentary.
Commentary Reader, 589-94. Also in Kostelanetz, R.,
ed., On Contemporary Literature, 579-85.
Madison, C. A., Yiddish Literature, 489-91.
Mercier, Vivian, "Sex, Success and Salvation," HudR, XIII
(Autumn, 1960), 455-6.
Pondrom, Cyrena N., "Conjuring Reality; I. B. Singer's
THE MAGICIAN OF LUBLIN," in Allentuck, M., ed.,
Achievement of Isaac Bashevis Singer, 93-111.
Rubinstein, Annette T., "An Obscurantist Yiddish Novel,"
Jewish Currents, XV (May, 1961), 36-8.
Siegel, Ben, Isaac Bashevis Singer, 21-3.

_____, "Sacred and Profane: Isaac Bashevis Singer's
Embattled Spirits," Crit, VI, i (Spring, 1963), 35-8.
Wolkenfeld, J.S., "Isaac Bashevis Singer: The Faith of His
Devils and Magicians," Criticism, V (Fall, 1963), 355-8.
Also in Malin, I., ed., Critical Views of Isaac Bashevis
Singer, 94-8.

THE MANOR

Buchen, I.H., Isaac Bashevis Singer and the Eternal Past,
173-94.
Chametsky, Jules, "The Old Jew in New Times," Nation,
CCV (October 30, 1967), 436-8.
Ellmann, Mary, "The Piety of Things in THE MANOR," in
Allentuck, M., ed., Achievement of Isaac Bashevis Singer,
124-44.
Hughes, Catharine R., "The Two Worlds of Isaac Singer,"
America, CXVII (November 18, 1967), 611-13.
Jonas, Gerald, "People With a Choice," NYTBR (November
5, 1967), 1, 52.
Madison, C.A., Yiddish Literature, 497-9.
Siegel, Ben, Isaac Bashevis Singer, 36-9.
Toynbee, Philip, "Inside the Pale," NRep, CLVII (November
11, 1967), 39-40.
Wain, John, "Trouble in the Family," NYRB (October 26,
1967), 32-3.
Wincelberg, Shimon, "Probing a Vanished Past," New Lead-
er, LI (February 26, 1968), 26-9.

SATAN IN GORAY

Buchen, Irving H., Isaac Bashevis Singer and the Eternal
Past, 83-97.
_____, "Isaac Bashevis Singer and the Revival of Satan,"
TSLL, IX (Spring, 1967), 129-42.
Friedman, Melvin J., "Isaac Bashevis Singer: The Appeal
of Numbers," in Malin, I., ed., Critical Views of Isaac
Bashevis Singer, 188-90.
Gittleman, Edwin, "Singer's Apocalyptic Town; SATAN IN
GORAY," in Allentuck, M., ed., Achievement of Isaac
Bashevis Singer, 64-76.
Hemley, Cecil, Dimensions of Midnight: Prose and Poetry,
ed. by Elaine Gottlieb, Athens: Ohio Un. Pr., 1966,
223-8.
Hindus, Milton, "The False Messiah," New Leader, XXXVIII
(November 28, 1955), 24-6.
_____, in Jewish Heritage Reader, 247-9.

Howe, Irving, "In the Day of the False Messiah," NRep,
    CXXXIII (October 31, 1955), 20-2.
Hughes, Ted, "The Genius of Isaac Bashevis Singer," NYRB,
    IV (April 22, 1965), 8-9.
Kibel, Alvin C., "The Political Novel," Reconstructionist,
    XXIV (October 31, 1958), 28-31.
Madison, C. A., Yiddish Literature, 480-3.
Malkoff, Karl, "Demonology and Dualism: The Supernatural
    in Isaac Singer and Muriel Spark," in Malin, I., ed.,
    Critical Views of Isaac Bashevis Singer, 188-90.
Siegel, Ben, Isaac Bashevis Singer, 14-16.
_____, "Sacred and Profane: Isaac Bashevis Singer's
    Embattled Spirits," Crit, VI, i (Spring, 1963), 28-30.
Teller, Judd, "Unhistorical Novels," Ctary, XXI (April,
    1956), 393-6.
Wolkenfeld, J. S., "Isaac Bashevis Singer: The Faith of His
    Devils and Magicians," Criticism, V (Fall, 1963), 350-4.
    Also in Malin, I., ed., Critical Views of Isaac Bashevis
    Singer, 88-94.

THE SLAVE

Buchen, Irving H., Isaac Bashevis Singer and the Eternal
    Past, 149-71.
_____, "The Present Revealed Through the Past," (Balti-
    more) Sunday Sun (June 24, 1962), Sec. A, 5.
Fixler, Michael, "The Redeemers: Themes in the Fiction
    of Isaac Bashevis Singer," KR, XXVI (Spring, 1964), 383-
    6. Also in Malin, I., ed., Critical Views of Isaac Ba-
    shevis Singer, 82-5.
Friedman, Melvin J., "Isaac Bashevis Singer: The Appeal
    of Numbers," in Malin, I., ed., Critical Views of Isaac
    Singer, 183-5.
Goodheart, Eugene, "Singer's Moral Novel," Midstream,
    VIII (September, 1962), 99-102.
Hughes, Ted, "The Genius of Isaac Bashevis Singer,"
    NYRB, IV (April 22, 1965), 10.
Hyman, Stanley E., "The Yiddish Hawthorne," New Leader,
    XLV (July 23, 1962), 20-1. Also in Kostelanetz, R.,
    ed., On Contemporary Literature, 586-90. Also in Hy-
    man, S. E., Standards, 83-7.
Karl, Frederick R., "Jacob Reborn, Zion Regained; I. B.
    Singer's THE SLAVE," in Allentuck, M., ed., Achieve-
    ment of Isaac Bashevis Singer, 112-23.
Madison, C. A., Yiddish Literature, 493-5.
Malkoff, Karl, "Demonology and Dualism: The Supernatural
    in Isaac Singer and Muriel Spark," in Malin, I., ed.,

Critical Views of Isaac Bashevis Singer, 161-4.
Siegel, Ben, Isaac Bashevis Singer, 28-30.
_____, "Sacred and Profane: Isaac Bashevis Singer's
    Embattled Spirits," Crit, VI, i (Spring, 1963), 43-7.
Sontag, Susan, "Demons and Dreams," PR, XXIX (Summer,
    1962), 460-3.
Stafford, Jean, "The Works of God, the Ways of Man,"
    NRep, CXLVI (June 18, 1962), 21-2.
Weintroub, in CJF, XXI (Winter, 1962-3), 169-70.

BIBLIOGRAPHY

Bryer, Jackson R., and P. E. Rockwell, "Isaac Bashevis
    Singer in English: A Bibliography," in Malin, I., ed.,
    Critical Views of Isaac Bashevis Singer, 220-65.
Buchen, I. H., Isaac Bashevis Singer and the Eternal Past,
    221-34.
Siegel, Ben, Isaac Bashevis Singer, 45-8.

SNOW, (C)HARLES (P)ERCY, 1905-

GENERAL

Anon., "Interview with C. P. Snow," REL, III, iii (July, 1962),
    91-108.
Bernard, Kenneth, "C. P. Snow and Modern Literature," UR,
    XXXI (March, 1965), 231-33.
Cooper, William, C. P. Snow.
_____, "The World of C. P. Snow," Nation, CLXXXIV
    (February 2, 1957), 104-5.
Davis, Robert G., C. P. Snow (Columbia Essays on Modern
    Writers, No. 8), N.Y.: Columbia Un. Pr., 1965.
Finkelstein, Sidney, "The Art and Science of C. P. Snow,"
    Mainstream, XIV, ix (September, 1961), 31-57.
Fuller, E., "C. P. Snow: Spokesman of Two Communities,"
    Books With the Men Behind Them, 102-34.
Goodwin, Donald F., "The Fiction of C. P. Snow," DA,
    XXVII (1967), 3009A (Iowa).
Graves, Nora C., "The Two Culture Theory in C. P. Snow's
    Novels," DA, XXVIII (1967), 1434A-35A (So. Miss.).
Greacen, Robert, The World of C. P. Snow, London: Scorpi-
    on Pr., 1962; N.Y.: London House & Maxwell, 1963.
_____, "The World of C. P. Snow," TQ, IV, iii (Autumn,
    1961), 266-74.
Hamilton, Kenneth, "C. P. Snow and Political Man," QQ,
    LXIX (Autumn, 1962), 416-27.

Jaffa, Herbert C., "C. P. Snow, Portrait of Man as an
    Adult," Humanist, XXIV (September-October, 1964), 148-
    50.
Johnson, Pamela H., "Three Novelists and the Drawing of
    Character: C. P. Snow, Joyce Cary and Ivy Compton-
    Burnett," in English Association. Essays and Studies,
    1950, 82-9.
Karl, Frederick R., C. P. Snow.
_____, "C. P. Snow: The Unreason of Reason," in Sha-
    piro, C., ed., Contemporary British Novelists, 114-24.
Kermode, Frank, "The House of Fiction. Interviews with
    Seven English Novelists," PR, XXX (Spring, 1963), 74-7.
_____, Puzzles and Epiphanies, 161-3.
Ketals, Violet B., "Shaw, Snow, and the New Men," Person,
    XLVII (Fall, 1966), 520-31.
Leavis, F. R., "Two Cultures? The Significance of C. P.
    Snow," MCR, No. 5 (1962), 90-101. Also in Spectator,
    CCVIII (March 16, 1962), 297-303. Also in book form,
    N. Y.: Pantheon, 1963.
Macdonald, Alastair, "Imagery in C. P. Snow," UR, XXXII
    (June, 1966), 303-6; XXXIII (October, 1966), 33-8.
Mandel, E. W., "Anarchy and Organization," QQ, LXX
    (Spring, 1963), 131-41.
_____, "C. P. Snow's Fantasy of Politics," QQ, LXIX
    (Spring, 1962), 24-37.
Millgate, Michael, "Structure and Style in the Novels of C. P.
    Snow," REL, I, ii (April, 1960), 34-41.
Murray, Byron O., "C. P. Snow: Grounds for Reappraisal,"
    Person, XLVII (January, 1966), 91-101.
Rabinovitz, R., Reaction Against Experiment in the English
    Novel, 128-65.
Shestakov, Dmitri, "What C. P. Snow Means to Us," Soviet
    Lit, No. 1 (1966), 174-9.
Smith, LeRoy W., "C. P. Snow as Novelist: A Delimitation,"
    SAQ, LXIV (Summer, 1965), 316-31.
Stanford, Derek, "C. P. Snow: The Novelist as Fox,"
    Meanjin, XIX (September, 1960), 236-51.
_____, "A Disputed Master: C. P. Snow and His Critics,"
    Month, XXIX (February, 1963), 91-4.
_____, "Sir Charles and the Two Cultures," Critic, XXI
    (October-November, 1962), 17-21.
Stanford, Raney, "The Achievement of C. P. Snow," WHR,
    XVI (Winter, 1962), 43-52.
_____, "Personal Politics in the Novels of C. P. Snow,"
    Crit, II, i (Spring-Summer, 1958), 16-28.
Thale, Jerome, C. P. Snow.
_____, "C. P. Snow: The Art of Worldliness," KR, XXII

(Autumn, 1960), 621-34.
Vogel, Albert W., "The Academic World of C. P. Snow,"
   TCL, IX (October, 1963), 143-52.

THE AFFAIR
(See also STRANGERS AND BROTHERS Series)

Cooper, W., C. P. Snow, 28-9.
Heppenstall, R., Fourfold Tradition, 239-41.
Karl, Frederick R., C. P. Snow, 136-53.
_____, "The Politics of Conscience: The Novels of C. P.
   Snow," Contemporary English Novel, 79-83.
Millgate, Michael, "Strangers and Brothers," Ctary, XXIX
   (July, 1960), 76-9.
Nelson, Bryce E., in Audit, I (March, 1961), 11-15.
Stanford, Raney, "The Achievement of C. P. Snow," WHR,
   XVI (Winter, 1962), 43-52.
Thale, J., C. P. Snow, 56-60.
Turner, Ian, "Above the Snow-Line: The Sociology of C. P.
   Snow," Overland, XVIII (Winter-Spring, 1960), 42-3.

THE CONSCIENCE OF THE RICH
(See also STRANGERS AND BROTHERS Series)

Cooper, W., C. P. Snow, 18-19.
Karl, F. R., C. P. Snow, 4-5, 117-35.
_____, "The Politics of Conscience: The Novels of C. P.
   Snow," Contemporary English Novel, 63-4, 75-9.
Thale, J., C. P. Snow, 64-6.

CORRIDORS OF POWER

Anon., "The Realism of the Worldly," in TLS (November 5,
   1964), 993. Also in T. L. S.: Essays and Reviews from
   The Times Literary Supplement, 1964, 100-3.
Burgess, Anthony, "Powers That Be," Encounter, XXIV
   (January, 1965), 71-6.
Enright, D. J., "Easy Lies the Head," NStat (November 6,
   1964), 698-9. Also in Enright, D. J., Conspirators and
   Poets, 106-10.
Muggeridge, Malcolm, "Oh No, Lord Snow," NRep, CLI
   (November 28, 1964), 27-9.
Shils, Edward, "The Charismatic Centre," Spectator, No.
   7115 (November 6, 1964), 608-9.
Thale, J., C. P. Snow, 20-2.

HOMECOMING (HOMECOMINGS)
(See also STRANGERS AND BROTHERS Series)

Cooper, W., C. P. Snow, 26-8.
Heppenstall, R., Fourfold Tradition, 233-8.
Karl, F. R., C. P. Snow, 101-16.
Thale, J., C. P. Snow, 73-5.

THE LIGHT AND THE DARK
(See also STRANGERS AND BROTHERS Series)

Cooper, W., C. P. Snow, 21-3.
Karl, F. R., C. P. Snow, 52-66.
_____, "The Politics of Conscience: The Novels of C. P.
    Snow," Contemporary English Novel, 68-71.
Thale, J., C. P. Snow, 48-52.

THE MASTERS
(See also STRANGERS AND BROTHERS Series)

Allen, W., Reading a Novel, 46-50.
Cooper, W., C. P. Snow, 26-8.
Karl, F. R., C. P. Snow, 101-16.
_____, "The Politics of Conscience: The Novels of C. P.
    Snow," Contemporary English Novel, 71-5.
Latham, Earl, "The Managerialization of the Campus," Pub-
    lic Administration Review, XIX (Winter, 1959), 48-57
    passim.
Lehan, Richard, "The Divided World: THE MASTERS Ex-
    amined," in Sutherland, W. O. S., ed., Six Contemporary
    Novels, 46-57.
Noon, William T., "Satire, Poison and the Professor,"
    EngR, XI, i (Fall, 1960), 54-5.
Olsen, F. Bruce, in Hagopian, J. V., and M. Dolch, eds.,
    Insight II, 332-6.
Proctor, Mortimer R., English University Novel, Berkeley
    and Los Angeles: Un. of Cal., 1957, 179-80.
Stanford, Raney, "Personal Politics in the Novels of C. P.
    Snow," Crit, II, i (1958), 20-2.
Thale, J., C. P. Snow, 53-6.

NEW LIVES FOR OLD

Thale, J., C. P. Snow, 20-2.

THE NEW MEN
(See also STRANGERS AND BROTHERS Series)

Cooper, W., C. P. Snow, 2-4.
Karl, F. R., C. P. Snow, 83-100.
Ketels, Violet B., "Shaw, Snow, and the New Men," Person,
  XLVII (Fall, 1966), 520-31.
Miner, Earl, "C. P. Snow and the Realistic Novel," Nation,
  CXC (June 25, 1960), 555-6.
Stanford, Raney, "Personal Politics in the Novels of C. P.
  Snow," Crit, II, i (1958), 22-6.
Symons, J., "On Bureaucratic Man," Critical Occasions,
  68-73.
Watson, Kenneth, "C. P. Snow and THE NEW MEN," English, XV (Spring, 1965), 134-9.

THE SEARCH

Karl, F. R., C. P. Snow, 21-3.
Thale, J., C. P. Snow, 22-4.

THE SLEEP OF REASON
(See also STRANGERS AND BROTHERS Series)

Anon., "Monsters at Bay," TLS (October 31, 1968), 1217.
  Also in T. L. S.: Essays and Reviews from The Times
  Literary Supplement, 1968, 175-7.

STRANGERS AND BROTHERS
(See also STRANGERS AND BROTHERS Series)

Cooper, W., C. P. Snow, 28-34.
Karl, F. R., C. P. Snow, 28-34.
Stanford, Raney, "Personal Politics in the Novels of C. P.
  Snow," Crit, II, i (1958), 19-20.
Thale, J., C. P. Snow, 46-8.

STRANGERS AND BROTHERS Series

Adams, Robert, "Pomp and Circumstance: C. P. Snow,"
  Atlantic, CCXIV (November, 1964), 95-8.
Allen, W., Modern Novel, 248-51.
Bergonzi, Bernard, "The World of Lewis Eliot," TC, CLXVII
  (March, 1960), 214-25. (See reply by P. Frison.)
Cooper, W., C. P. Snow, 15-16, 30-4.
Dobree, Bonamy, "The Novels of C. P. Snow," LHY, II (July,
  1961), 28-34.

Fison, Peter, "A Reply to Bernard Bergonzi's 'The World of
Lewis Eliot'," TC, CLXVII (June, 1960), 568-71.

Fraser, G.S., Modern Writer and His World, 161-4.

Gardner, Helen, "The World of C.P. Snow," NStat, LV
(March 29, 1958), 409-10.

Gindin, J., Postwar British Fiction, 207-15.

Halio, Jay L., "C.P. Snow's Literary Limitations," NWR,
V (Winter, 1962), 97-102.

Hall, William F., "The Humanism of C.P. Snow," WSCL,
IV, ii (Spring-Summer, 1963), 199-208.

Heppenstall, R., Fourfold Tradition, 224-46.

Ivasheva, V., "Illusion and Reality (About the Works of C.P.
Snow)," IL, No. 6 (June, 1960), 198-203.

Karl, F.R., C.P. Snow, 3-21, 25-34.

_____, "The Politics of Conscience: The Novels of C.P.
Snow," Contemporary English Novel, 62-84.

Kazin, Alfred, "A Gifted Boy from the Midlands," Reporter,
XX (February 5, 1959), 37-9. Also in Kazin, A., Contemporaries, 171-7.

Mandel, E.W., "C.P. Snow's Fantasy of Politics," QQ,
LXIX (Spring, 1962), 24-37.

Mayne, Richard, "The Club Armchair," Encounter, XXI
(November, 1963), 76-82.

Millgate, Michael, "STRANGERS AND BROTHERS," Ctary,
XXX (July, 1960), 76-9.

Miner, Earl, "C.P. Snow and the Realistic Novel," Nation,
CXC (June 25, 1960), 554-6.

Stanford, Derek, "C.P. Snow: The Novelist as Fox," Meanjin, XIX (September, 1960), 236-51.

Thale, Jerome, C.P. Snow, 76-84, 109-15.

_____, "C.P. Snow: The Art of Worldliness," KR, XXII
(Autumn, 1960), 628-34.

Turner, Ian, "Above the Snow-Line: The Sociology of C.P.
Snow," Overland, XVIII (Spring-Winter, 1960), 37-43.

Wagner, Geoffrey, "Writer in the Welfare State," Cweal,
LXV (October 12, 1956), 49-50.

Wall, Steven, "The Novels of C.P. Snow," LonM, n.s., IV
(April, 1964), 68-74.

Webster, Harvey C., "The Sacrifices of Success," SatR,
XLI (July 12, 1958), 8-10+.

TIME OF HOPE
(See also STRANGERS AND BROTHERS Series)

Cooper, W., C.P. Snow, 19-21.
Karl, F.R., C.P. Snow, 41-51.
Thale, J., C.P. Snow, 70-3.

BIBLIOGRAPHY

Thale, J., <u>C. P. Snow</u>, 154-60.

SONTAG, SUSAN, 1933-

THE BENEFACTOR

Flint, Robert W., in <u>Ctary</u>, XXXVI (December, 1963), 489-90.

Wain, John, "Song of Myself, 1963," <u>NRep</u>, CXLIX (September 21, 1963), 26-7, 30.

DEATH KIT

Lehan, Richard, "Fiction 1967," <u>Contemporary Literature</u>, IX, iv (Autumn, 1968), 551-2.

Solotaroff, Theodore, "Death in Life," <u>Ctary</u>, XLIV (November, 1967), 87-9.

SOUTHERN, TERRY, 1924-

GENERAL

Algren, Nelson, "The Donkeyman by Twilight," <u>Nation</u>, CXCVIII (May 18, 1964), 509-12.

CANDY

Arn, Robert, "Obscenity and Pornography," <u>CamR</u>, LXXXIXA (December 2, 1967), 161-2.

THE MAGIC CHRISTIAN

Scholes, R., <u>Fabulators</u>, 61-6.

SPARK, MURIEL, 1918-

GENERAL

Adler, Renata, in Kostelanetz, R., ed., <u>On Contemporary Literature</u>, 591-6.

Baldanza, Frank, "Muriel Spark and the Occult," <u>WSCL</u>, VI (Summer, 1965), 190-203.

Davison, Peter, "The Miracles of Muriel Spark," Atlantic,
    CCXXII (October, 1968), 139-42.
Greene, George, "A Reading of Muriel Spark," Thought,
    XLIII (Autumn, 1968), 393-407.
Grosskurth, Phyllis, "The World of Muriel Spark: Spirits
    or Spooks?" TamR, No. 39 (Spring, 1966), 62-7.
Hoyt, Charles A., "Muriel Spark: The Surrealist Jane Aus-
    ten," in Shapiro, C., ed., Contemporary British Novel-
    ists, 125-43.
Hynes, Samuel, "The Prime of Muriel Spark," Cweal, LXXV
    (February 23, 1962), 562-8.
Jacobsen, Josephine, "A Catholic Quartet," ChS, XLVII
    (Summer, 1964), 140-3.
Kermode, Frank, "The House of Fiction: Interviews with
    Seven English Novelists," PR, XXX (Spring, 1963), 79-82.
_____, "The Prime of Miss Muriel Spark," NStat, LXVI
    (September 27, 1963), 397-8. Also as "To The Girls of
    Slender Means," in Kermode, F., Continuities, 202-7.
Malkoff, Karl, "Demonology and Dualism: The Supernatural
    in Isaac Singer and Muriel Spark," in Malin, I., ed.,
    Critical Views of Isaac Bashevis Singer, 149-68.
_____, Muriel Spark.
Mayne, Richard, "Fiery Particle: On Muriel Spark," En-
    counter, XXV (December, 1965), 61-8.
Murphy, Carol, "A Spark of the Supernatural," Approach,
    No. 60 (Summer, 1966), 26-30.
Potter, Nancy A.J., "Muriel Spark: Transformer of the
    Commonplace," Ren, XVII (Spring, 1965), 115-20.
Ricks, Christopher, "Extreme Distances," NYRB, XI (De-
    cember 19, 1968), 30-2.
Schneider, Harold W., "A Writer in Her Prime: The Fic-
    tion of Muriel Spark," Crit, V, ii (Fall, 1962), 28-45.
Stanford, Derek, Muriel Spark.
_____, "The Work of Muriel Spark: An Essay on Her
    Fictional Method," Month, XXVIII (August, 1962), 92-9.
Updike, John, "Creatures of the Air," NY, XXXVII (Septem-
    ber 30, 1967), 161-7.
Wildman, John H., "Translated by Muriel Spark," in San-
    ford, D.E., ed., Nine Essays in Modern Literature, 129-
    44.

THE BACHELORS

Malkoff, Karl, "Demonology and Dualism: The Supernatural
    in Isaac Singer and Muriel Spark," in Malin, I., ed.,
    Critical Views of Isaac Bashevis Singer, 164-6.
_____, Muriel Spark, 26-30.

Schneider, Harold W., "A Writer in Her Prime: The Fiction of Muriel Spark," Crit, V, ii (Fall, 1962), 40-2.

THE BALLAD OF PECKHAM RYE

Dierickx, J., "A Devil-figure in a Contemporary Setting: Muriel Spark's THE BALLAD OF PECKHAM RYE," RLV, XXXIII (1967), 576-87.

Lanning, George, "Silver Fish in the Plumbing," KR, XXIII (Winter, 1961), 173-5, 177-8.

Malkoff, Karl, "Demonology and Dualism: The Supernatural in Isaac Singer and Muriel Spark," in Malin, I., ed., Critical Views of Isaac Bashevis Singer, 157-61.

_____, Muriel Spark, 22-6.

Wildman, John H., in Sanford, D. E., ed., Nine Essays in Modern Literature, 133-5.

THE COMFORTERS

Kermode, Frank, "The Prime of Miss Muriel Spark," NStat, LXVI (September 27, 1963), 397. Also as "TO THE GIRLS OF SLENDER MEANS," in Kermode, F., Continuities, 203-4.

Malkoff, K., Muriel Spark, 7-11.

Price, Martin, in YR, XLVII (Autumn, 1957), 148-50.

Schneider, Harold W., "A Writer in Her Prime: The Fiction of Muriel Spark," Crit, V, ii (Fall, 1962), 36-7.

Stanford, D., Muriel Spark, 123-6.

Wildman, John H., in Sanford, D. E., ed., Nine Essays in Modern Literature, 139-40.

THE GIRLS OF SLENDER MEANS

Adler, Renata, in Kostelanetz, R., ed., On Contemporary Literature, 593-6.

Anon., in TLS (September 20, 1963), 701. Also in T. L. S.: Essays and Reviews from The Times Literary Supplement, 1963, 100-2.

Casson, Alan, "Muriel Spark's THE GIRLS OF SLENDER MEANS," Crit, VII, iii (1965), 94-6.

Kermode, Frank, "The Prime of Miss Muriel Spark," NStat, LXVI (September 27, 1963), 398. Also as TO THE GIRLS OF SLENDER MEANS," in Kermode, F., Continuities, 206-7.

Malkoff, K., Muriel Spark, 36-9.

Soule, George, "Must a Novelist Be an Artist?" Carleton Miscellany, V (Spring, 1964), 92-8.

THE MANDELBAUM GATE

Anon., in TLS (October 14, 1965), 913. Also in T.L.S.:
Essays and Reviews from The Times Literary Supplement,
1965, 34-6.
Berthoff, Warner, "Fortunes of the Novel: Muriel Spark
and Iris Murdoch," MR, VIII (Spring, 1967), 304-13.
Cohen, Gerda L., "Tilting the Balance," Midstream, XII
(January, 1966), 68-70.
Grosskurth, Phyllis, "The World of Muriel Spark: Spirits
of Spooks?" TamR, No. 39 (Spring, 1966), 65-7.
Kermode, Frank, "The Novel as Jerusalem: Muriel Spark's
MANDELBAUM GATE," Atlantic, CCXVI (October, 1965),
92-8. Also in Kermode, F., Continuities, 207-16.
Malkoff, K., Muriel Spark, 39-45.

MEMENTO MORI

Gable, Sister Mariella, "Prose Satire and the Modern Chris-
tian Temper," ABR, XI (March-June, 1960), 29-30, 33.
Malkoff, K., Muriel Spark, 17-22.
Schneider, Harold W., "A Writer in Her Prime: The Fic-
tion of Muriel Spark," Crit, V, ii (Fall, 1962), 38-9.
Stanford, D., Muriel Spark, 128-31.
Wildman, John H., in Sanford, D.E., ed., Nine Essays in
Modern Literature, 130-3.

THE PRIME OF MISS JEAN BRODIE

Schneider, Harold W., "A Writer in Her Prime: The Fic-
tion of Muriel Spark," Crit, V, ii (Fall, 1962), 42-4.
Stanford, D., Muriel Spark, 133-7.
Wildman, John H., in Sanford, D.E., ed., Nine Essays in
Modern Literature, 141-2.

THE PUBLIC IMAGE

Anon., "Shallowness Everywhere," TLS (June 13, 1968), 612.
Also in T.L.S.: Essays and Reviews from The Times
Literary Supplement, 1968, 71-3.
Davison, Peter, "The Miracles of Muriel Spark," Atlantic,
CCXXII (October, 1968), 140-2.
Malkoff, K., Muriel Spark, 45-6.

ROBINSON

Malkoff, K., Muriel Spark, 11-16.

Ohmann, Carol B., "Muriel Spark's ROBINSON," <u>Crit,</u> VIII
i (Fall, 1965), 70-84.
Stanford, D., <u>Muriel Spark,</u> 126-8.
Wildman, John H., in Sanford, D. E., ed., <u>Nine Essays on
Modern Literature,</u> 135-9.

BIBLIOGRAPHY

Malkoff, K., <u>Muriel Spark,</u> 47-8.

SPENCER, ELIZABETH, 1921-

GENERAL

Haley, Josephine, "An Interview with Elizabeth Spencer,"
<u>NMW,</u> I, ii (Fall, 1968), 42-53.

FIRE IN THE MORNING

Burger, Nash K., "Elizabeth Spencer's Three Mississippi
Novels," <u>SAQ,</u> LXIII (Summer, 1964), 351-4.

KNIGHTS AND DRAGONS

Kauffmann, Stanley, "Sense and Sensibility," <u>NRep,</u> CLII
(June 26, 1965), 27-8.

LIGHT IN THE PIAZZA

Miller, Nolan, "Three of the 'Best'," <u>AR,</u> XXI (Spring,
1961), 123-5.

THIS CROOKED WAY

Burger, Nash K., "Elizabeth Spencer's Three Mississippi
Novels," <u>SAQ,</u> LXIII (Summer, 1964), 354-7.

THE VOICE AT THE BACK DOOR

Burger, Nash K., "Elizabeth Spencer's Three Mississippi
Novels," <u>SAQ,</u> LXIII (Summer, 1964), 357-62.
Hoffman, F. J., <u>Art of Southern Fiction,</u> 113-14.
Meeker, Richard K., in Simonini, R. C., Jr., ed., <u>Southern
Writers,</u> 175-6.

STAFFORD, JEAN, 1915-

GENERAL

Auchincloss, L., Pioneers and Caretakers, 152-60.
Eisinger, C. E., Fiction of the Forties, 294-306.
Hassan, Ihab, "Jean Stafford: The Expense of Style and the
    Scope of Sensibility," WR, XIX (Spring, 1955), 185-203.
Vickery, Olga W., "Jean Stafford the Ironic Vision," SAQ,
    LXI (Autumn, 1962), 484-91.
_____, "The Novels of Jean Stafford," Crit, V, i (Spring-
    Summer, 1962), 14-26.

BOSTON ADVENTURE

Auchincloss, L., Pioneers and Caretakers, 152-4.
Eisinger, C. E., Fiction of the Forties, 296-8.
Hassan, Ihab, "Jean Stafford: The Expense of Style and the
    Scope of Sensibility," WR, XIX (Spring, 1955), 185-91.
Vickery, Olga W., "The Novels of Jean Stafford," Crit, V,
    i (Spring-Summer, 1962), 14-19.

THE CATHERINE WHEEL

Auchincloss, L., Pioneers and Caretakers, 157-9.
Eisinger, C. E., Fiction of the Forties, 301-6.
Hassan, Ihab, "Jean Stafford: The Expense of Style and the
    Scope of Sensibility," WR, XIX (Spring, 1955), 194-7.
Vickery, Olga W., "The Novels of Jean Stafford," Crit, V,
    i (Spring-Summer, 1962), 23-6.

THE MOUNTAIN LION

Auchincloss, L., Pioneers and Caretakers, 155-7.
Burns, Stuart L., "Counterpoint in Jean Stafford's THE
    MOUNTAIN LION," Crit, IX, ii (1967), 20-32.
Eisinger, C. E., Fiction of the Forties, 298-301.
Hassan, Ihab, "Jean Stafford: The Expense of Style and the
    Scope of Sensibility," WR, XIX (Spring, 1955), 191-4.
Vickery, Olga W., "The Novels of Jean Stafford," Crit, V,
    i (Spring-Summer, 1962), 19-23.

STEAD, CHRISTINA, 1902-

GENERAL

Geering, R. G., "The Achievement of Christina Stead,"
    Southerly, XXII, iv (1962), 193-212.
_____, Christina Stead.
_____, "Christina Stead in the 1960's," Southerly, XXVIII,
    i (1968), 26-36.
Green, H. M., History of Australian Literature, 1070-77.
Hadgraft, C., Australian Literature, 246-8.
Roderick, Colin, "Christina Stead," Southerly, XXVII, i
    (1967), 87-92.
_____, Introduction to Australian Literature, 132-8.
Saxelby, Jean, and Gwen Walker-Smith, "Christina Stead,"
    Biblionews (Book Collectors Soc. of Australia), II (De-
    cember, 1949), 37-43. (Not seen.)
Wilding, Michael, "Christina Stead's Australian Novels,"
    Southerly, XXVII, i (1967), 20-33.

THE BEAUTIES AND THE FURIES

Geering, R. G., Christina Stead, 56-65.

COTTER'S ENGLAND
(See DARK PLACES OF THE HEART)

DARK PLACES OF THE HEART

Geering, R. G., Christina Stead, 156-9.
_____, "Christina Stead in the 1960's," Southerly, XXVIII,
    i (1968), 28-34.
West, Paul, "A Lady in Waiting," NYHTBW (September 11,
    1966), 4, 8.
Yglesias, Jose, "Marking Off a Chunk of England," Nation,
    CCIII (October 24, 1966), 420-1.

FOR LOVE ALONE

Geering, R. D., Christina Stead, 106-20.
Roderick, Colin, "Christina Stead," Southerly, VII, ii
    (1946), 89-91.
_____, Introduction to Australian Literature, 135-7.
Stewart, Douglas, "Glory and Catastrophe," The Flesh and
    the Spirit, Sydney: Angus & Robertson, 1948, 235-8.
Wilding, Michael, "Christina Stead's Australian Novels,"

Southerly, XXVII, i (1967), 27-33.

HOUSE OF ALL NATIONS

Geering, R. G. , Christina Stead, 66-85.

LETTY FOX: HER LUCK

Geering, R. G. , Christina Stead, 122-34.
McCrory, Mary, in NYTBR (October 6, 1946), 24.

THE MAN WHO LOVED CHILDREN

Geering, R. G. , Christina Stead, 86-106.
Hardwick, Elizabeth, "The Novels of Christina Stead," NRep,
    CXXXIII (August 1, 1955), 17-19.   Also in Hardwick, E. ,
    View of My Own, 41-8.
Howarth, R. G. , "Christina Stead," Biblionews (Book Collec-
    tors Soc. of Australia), XI (January, 1958), 1-3.
Jarrell, Randall, "An Unread Book," Introduction to THE
    MAN WHO LOVED CHILDREN, N.Y.: Holt, Rinehart &
    Winston, 1965; London: Secker & Warburg, 1966.
_____, "THE MAN WHO LOVED CHILDREN," Atlantic,
    CCXV (March, 1965), 166-71.
Katz, Alfred A. , "Some Psychological Themes in a Novel by
    Christina Stead," L&P, XV (Fall, 1965), 210-15.
Roderick, C. , Introduction to Australian Literature, 134-5.
Ricks, Christopher, "Domestic Manners," NYRB, IV (June
    17, 1965), 14-15.
Wain, John, in (London) Observer (May 22, 1966).
Yglesias, Jose, "Marx as Muse," Nation, CC (April 5,
    1965), 368-70.

THE PEOPLE WITH DOGS

Geering, R. G. , Christina Stead, 142-51.

SEVEN POOR MEN OF SYDNEY

Geering, R. G. , Christina Stead, 30-45.
_____, "Introduction" to Seven Poor Men of Sydney, Syd-
    ney: Angus & Robertson, 1965, ix-xv.
Green, Dorothy, "Chaos, or a Dancing Star? Christina
    Stead's SEVEN POOR MEN OF SYDNEY," Meanjin,
    XXVII (1968), 150-61.
Green, H. M. , History of Australian Literature, 1071-74.
Miller, Sidney, in Westerly, No. 2 (1968), 61-6.

Roderick, C., Introduction to Australian Literature, 133-4.
Wilding, Michael, "Christina Stead's Australian Novels,"
  Southerly, XXVII, i (1967), 20-7.

BIBLIOGRAPHY

Geering, R. G., Christina Stead, 171-7.

STEGNER, WALLACE EARLE, 1909-

GENERAL

Eisinger, Chester E., Fiction of the Forties, 324-8.
_____, "Twenty Years of Wallace Stegner," CE, XX
  (December, 1958), 110-16.

THE BIG ROCK CANDY MOUNTAIN

Eisinger, Charles E., "Twenty Years of Wallace Stegner,"
  CE, XX (December, 1958), 112-13.

THE PREACHER AND THE SLAVE

Eisinger, Charles E., "Twenty Years of Wallace Stegner,"
  CE, XX (December, 1958), 113-14.

A SHOOTING STAR

Burke, Hatton, "The Ninth Circle," SR, LXX (Winter, 1962),
  172-5.

STEINBECK, JOHN, 1902-1968

GENERAL

Alexander, Stanley G., "Primitivism and Pastoral Form in
  John Steinbeck's Early Fiction," DA, XXVI (1965), 2201-
  02 (Texas).
Beach, Joseph W., "John Steinbeck: Journeyman Artist,"
  American Fiction: 1920-1940, 309-47. Also in Tedlock,
  E. W. Jr., and C. V. Wicker, eds., Steinbeck and His
  Critics, 80-91.
Blake, N. M., Novelist's America, 133-8.
Blankenship, R., American Literature, 745-9.
Bode, Elroy, "The World on Its Own Terms: A Brief for

Steinbeck, Miller, and Simenon," SWR, LIII (1968), 406-16.

Bracher, Frederick, "Steinbeck and the Biological View of Man," PacSp, II (Winter, 1948), 14-29. Also in Tedlock, E. W. , Jr. , and C. V. Wicker, eds. , Steinbeck and His Critics, 183-96.

Brown, Daniel R. , " 'A Monolith of Logic Against Waves of Nonsense,' " Ren, XVI (Fall, 1963), 48-51.

_____, "The Natural Man in John Steinbeck's Non-Teleological Tales, BSUF, VII (Spring, 1966), 47-52.

Burgum, Edwin B. , "The Sensibility of John Steinbeck," S&S, X (1946), 132-47. Also in Burgum, E. B. , Novel and the World's Dilemma, 272-91. Also in Tedlock, E. W. , Jr. , and C. V. Wicker, eds. , Steinbeck and His Critics, 104-18.

Carpenter, Frederic I. , "John Steinbeck: American Dreamer," SWR, XXVI (July, 1941), 454-67. Also in Tedlock, E. W. , Jr. , and C. V. Wicker, eds. , Steinbeck and His Critics, 68-79.

Casimir, Louis J. , Jr. , "Human Emotion and the Early Novels of John Steinbeck," DA, XXVII (1966), 472A (Texas).

Champney, Freeman, "John Steinbeck, Californian," AR, VII (September, 1947), 345-62. Also in Tedlock, E. W. , Jr. , and C. V. Wickers, eds. , Steinbeck and His Critics, 135-51.

Covici, Pascal, Jr. , "John Steinbeck and the Language of Awareness," in French, W. , ed. , Thirties, 47-54.

Ditsky, John M. , "Land-Nostalgia in the Novels of Faulkner, Cather, and Steinbeck," DA, XXVIII (1967), 1072A (N. Y. U.).

Fontenrose, J. , John Steinbeck.

French, Warren G. , in French, W. G. , and W. E. Kidd, eds. , American Winners of the Nobel Literary Prize, 193-223.

_____, John Steinbeck.

Frietzsche, Arthur H. , "Steinbeck as a Western Author," PUASAL, XLII, i (1965), 11-13. (Not seen.)

Frohock, W. M. , "John Steinbeck's Men of Wrath," SWR, XXXI (Spring, 1946), 144-52. Also as "John Steinbeck: The Utility of Wrath," in Frohock, W. M. , Novel of Violence in America, 124-43.

Fukuma, Kin-ichi, " 'Man' in Steinbeck's Works," KAL, No. 7 (1964), 21-30. (Not seen.)

Gannett, Louis, "John Steinbeck: Novelist at Work," Atlantic, CLXXVI (December, 1945), 55-61. Also in Tedlock, E. W. , Jr. , and C. V. Wicker, eds. , Steinbeck and

His Critics, 23-37. Also as "John Steinbeck's Way of
Writing," in The Portable Steinbeck, ed. by Pascal Co-
vici, N. Y.: Viking, 1958, vii-xviii.
Geismar, M., Writers in Crisis, 239-70.
Gurko, Leo, Angry Decade, 212-21.
_____, and Miriam Gurko, "The Steinbeck Temperament,"
Rocky Mountain Rev, IX (Fall, 1944-45), 17-22.
Hamada, Seijiro, "Parabiblical Elements in John Steinbeck,"
Ushione, V (Autumn, 1955), 3-9. (Not seen.)
Higashiyama, Masayoshi, "On Works of John Steinbeck, A
Great Modern Novelist," Kansai Gakuin Times, VII (1957),
15-28. (Not seen.)
Hyman, Stanley E., "John Steinbeck: Of Invertebrates and
Men," The Promised End: Essays and Reviews, 1942-
1962, Cleveland and N. Y.: World, 1963, 17-22.
_____, "Some Notes on John Steinbeck," AR, VII (Sep-
tember, 1947), 185-200. Also in Tedlock, E. W., Jr.,
and C. V. Wickers, eds., Steinbeck and His Critics, 152-
66.
Inoue, Atsuko, "A Study of John Steinbeck: The Group in
His Fiction," Essays and Studies in British and American
Literature (Tokyo Women's Christian College), XI (Winter,
1964), 49-99. (Not seen.)
Irvine, John C., "The Fringes of John Steinbeck," LIT, No.
6 (Spring, 1965), 14-19. (Not seen.)
Jackson, Joseph H., "Preface" to The Short Novels of John
Steinbeck, N. Y.: Viking, 1963, vii-xv.
Kennedy, John S., "John Steinbeck: Life Affirmed and Dis-
solved," in Gardiner, H. C., ed., Fifty Years of the Amer-
ican Novel, 217-36. Also in Tedlock, E. W., Jr., and C. V.
Wicker, eds., Steinbeck and His Critics, 119-34.
Koike, Bobuo, "A Study of John Steinbeck with Special Ref-
erence to the Works in the Thirties," British and Ameri-
can Literature (Kansei Gakuin Univ.), III (April, 1954),
57-90. (Not seen.)
Levant, Howard S., "A Critical Study of the Longer Fiction
of John Steinbeck," DA, XXIII (1962), 633 (Cornell).
Levidova, I., "The Post-War Books of John Steinbeck,"
SovietR, IV Summer, 1963), 3-13.
Lewis, R. W. B., "John Steinbeck: The Fitful Daemon," in
Bode, C., ed., Young Rebel in American Literature, 121-
41. Also in Litz, A. W., ed., Modern American Fiction,
265-77.
Lisca, Peter, "The Art of John Steinbeck: An Analysis and
Interpretation of Its Development," DA, XVI (1956), 965
(Wisc.).
_____, "Steinbeck's Image of Man and His Decline as a

Writer," MFS, XI (Spring, 1965), 3-10.
_____, Wide World of John Steinbeck.
McCormick, B. , "John Steinbeck: An Evaluation," Way,
   XIX (March, 1963), 53-8. (Not seen.)
Magny, Claude-Edmonde, "Steinbeck, or the Limits of the
   Impersonal Novel," in Tedlock, E. W. , Jr. , and C. V.
   Wicker, eds. , Steinbeck and His Critics, 216-27.
Marks, L. J. , Thematic Design in the Novels of John Stein-
   beck.
Mizener, Arthur, "Does a Moral Vision of the Thirties De-
   serve a Nobel Prize?" NYTBR (December 9, 1962), 4,
   43-5. Also in Donohue, A. M. , ed. , Casebook on THE
   GRAPES OF WRATH, 267-72.
_____, "John Steinbeck and His World," in Brown, F. ,
   ed. , Opinions and Perspectives, 181-8.
Moore, H. T. , Novels of John Steinbeck.
Morioka, Sakae, "John Steinbeck's Art," English and Ameri-
   can Language and Literature Studies (Kyusha Univ.), III
   (1953), 51-8. (Not seen.)
Nelson, Harland S. , "Steinbeck's Politics Then and Now,"
   AR, XXVII (Spring, 1967), 118-33.
Nevius, Blake, "Steinbeck: One Aspect," PacSp, III (Sum-
   mer, 1949), 302-10. Also in Tedlock, E. W. , Jr. , and
   C. V. Wicker, eds. , Steinbeck and His Critics, 197-205.
Nichols, Lewis, "Talk with John Steinbeck," NYTBR (Sep-
   tember 28, 1952), 30.
Nosson, Evon, "The Beast-Man Theme in the Work of John
   Steinbeck," BSUF, VII, ii (Spring, 1966), 52-64.
Oliver, H. J. , "John Steinbeck," AusQ, XXIII (June, 1951),
   79-83.
Rao, B. Ramachandra, "John Steinbeck the Novelist," Andh-
   ra Univ. Magazine (Waltair, India), XX (1959-60), 20-6.
   (Not seen.)
Rascoe, Burton, "John Steinbeck," EJ, XXVII (March, 1938),
   205-16. Also in Tedlock, E. W. , Jr. , and C. V. Wicker,
   eds. , Steinbeck and His Critics, 57-67.
Raymund, Bernard, "John Steinbeck," in Baker, D. V. , ed. ,
   Writers of Today, 122-38.
Roane, Margaret C. , "John Steinbeck as a Spokesman for
   the Mentally Retarded," WSCL, V, ii (Summer, 1964),
   127-32.
Ross, Woodburn O. , "John Steinbeck: Earth and Stars," in
   Studies in Honor of A. H. R. Fairchild, Un. of Mo. Studies, XXI, 1946, 179-97. Also in Tedlock, E. W. , Jr. ,
   and C. V. Wicker, eds. , Steinbeck and His Critics, 167-
   82.
_____, "John Steinbeck: Naturalism's Priest," CE, X

(May, 1949), 432-8. Also in Tedlock, E.W., Jr., and
C.V. Wicker, eds., Steinbeck and His Critics, 206-15.
Rundell, Walter, Jr., "Steinbeck's Image of the West,"
American West, I (Spring, 1964), 4-17, 79.
Smith, Donald B., "The Decline in John Steinbeck's Critical
Reputation Since World War II: An Analysis and Evalua-
tion of Recent Critical Practices With a Suggested Revi-
sion," DA, XXVIII (1967), 1449A (N. Mex.).
Snell, G., Shapers of American Fiction, 187-97.
Spiller, R.E., Cycle of American Literature, 289-91.
Taylor, Horace P., Jr., "The Biological Naturalism of John
Steinbeck," DA, XXII (1962), 3674 (La. State).
_____, "The Biological Naturalism of John Steinbeck,"
McNR, XII (Winter, 1960-61), 81-97.
_____, "John Steinbeck - The Quest," McNR, XVI (1965),
33-45.
Tedlock, E.W., Jr., and C.V. Wicker, eds., Steinbeck and
His Critics.
Tuttleton, James W., "Steinbeck in Russia: The Rhetoric of
Praise and Blame," MFS, XI (Spring, 1965), 79-89. Al-
so in Donohue, A.M., ed., Casebook on THE GRAPES
OF WRATH, 245-56.
Wagenknecht, E., Cavalcade of the American Novel, 443-8.
Walcutt, C.C., American Literary Naturalism, 258-69. Al-
so (part) in Donohue, A.M., ed., Casebook on THE
GRAPES OF WRATH, 162-5.
Wallis, Prentiss B., Jr., "John Steinbeck: The Symbolic
Family," DA, XXVII (1966), 1842A-43A (Kan.).
Watt, F.W., Steinbeck.
Wilson, Earl, "The Californians: Storm and Steinbeck,"
NRep, CIII (December 9, 1940), 785-7. Also in Wilson,
E., The Boys in the Back Room, San Francisco: Colt
Pr., 1947, 41-53. Also in Wilson, E., Classics and
Commercials, 35-45. Also in Donohue, A.M., ed.,
Casebook on THE GRAPES OF WRATH, 151-8.
Woodress, James, "John Steinbeck: Hostage to Fortune,"
SAQ, LXIII (Summer, 1964), 385-98. Also in Donohue,
A.M., ed., Casebook on THE GRAPES OF WRATH, 278-
90.

BURNING BRIGHT

Fontenrose, J., John Steinbeck, 115-17.
French, W., John Steinbeck, 148-52.
Geismar, Maxwell, in SatR, XXXIII (October 21, 1950), 4.
Also in Geismar, M., American Moderns, 153-5.
Lisca, P., Wide World of John Steinbeck, 248-60.

Watt, F. W., Steinbeck, 91-3.

CANNERY ROW

Alexander, Stanley, "CANNERY ROW: Steinbeck's Pastoral
    Poem," WAL, II (Winter, 1968), 281-95.
Fontenrose, J., John Steinbeck, 101-8.
French, Warren, in French, W. G., and W. E. Kidd, eds.,
    American Winners of the Nobel Literary Prize, 213-15.
————, John Steinbeck, 120-36.
Gray, J., On Second Thought, 137-9.
Kawamura, Yoneichi, "Steinbeck's Humor and Pathos in
    TORTILLA FLAT and CANNERY ROW," Hokkaido Univ.
    Essays in Foreign Languages and Literature, I (Decem-
    ber, 1953), 24-30.
Levidova, I., "The Post-War Books of John Steinbeck,"
    SovietR, IV (Summer, 1963), 5-6.
Lisca, P., Wide World of John Steinbeck, 197-217.
Marks, L. J., Thematic Design in the Novels of John Stein-
    beck, 92-9.
Moore, Ward, "Cannery Row Revisited: Steinbeck and the
    Sardines," Nation, CLXXIX (October 16, 1954), 325-7.
Prescott, O., In My Opinion, 60-1.
Snell, G., Shapers of American Fiction, 196-7.
Walcutt, C. C., American Literary Naturalism, 265-6.
Watt, F. W., Steinbeck, 79-84.
Weeks, Donald, "Steinbeck Against Steinbeck," PacSp, I
    (Autumn, 1947), 447-57.

CUP OF GOLD

Carpenter, Frederic I., in SWR, XXVI (July, 1941), 456-8.
    Also in Tedlock, E. W., Jr., and C. V. Wicker, eds.,
    Steinbeck and His Critics, 69-71.
Fontenrose, J., John Steinbeck, 7-13.
French, Warren G., in French, W. G., and W. E. Kidd, eds.,
    American Winners of the Nobel Literary Prize, 200-1.
————, John Steinbeck, 31-8.
Geismar, M., Writers in Crisis, 246-8.
Lisca, P., Wide World of John Steinbeck, 26-38.
Marks, L. J., Thematic Design in the Novels of John Stein-
    beck, 27-33.
Moore, H. T., Novels of John Steinbeck, 11-17.
Snell, G., Shapers of American Fiction, 188-9.
Watt, F. W., Steinbeck, 25-8.

EAST OF EDEN

Brashers, H. C., Introduction to American Literature, 154-5.
Fontenrose, J., John Steinbeck, 118-27.
French, W., John Steinbeck, 152-6.
Frohock, W. H., Novel of Violence in America, 141-2.
Gardiner, Harold C., "Novelist to Philosopher," America,
    LXXXVIII (October 4, 1952), 18. Also in Gardiner, H. C.,
    In All Conscience, 136-8.
Geismar, M., American Moderns, 164-7.
Krutch, Joseph W., "John Steinbeck's Dramatic Tale of
    Three Generations," NYHTBR (September 21, 1955), 1.
    Also in Tedlock, E. W., Jr., and C. V. Wicker, eds.,
    Steinbeck and His Critics, 302-5.
Leonard, Frank G., "Cozzens Without Sex: Steinbeck With-
    out Sin," AR, XVIII (Summer, 1958), 209-18.
Levidova, I., "The Post-War Books of John Steinbeck,"
    SovietR, IV (Summer, 1963), 10-11.
Lewis, R. W. B., "John Steinbeck: The Fitful Daemon," in
    Bode, C., ed., Young Rebel in American Literature, 131-
    34 and passim. Also in Litz, A. W., ed., Modern Ameri-
    can Fiction, 271-3 and passim.
Lisca, P., Wide World of John Steinbeck, 261-75.
Magny, Claude-Edmonde, "EAST OF EDEN," PUSA, V (Fall,
    1953), 146-52.
Marks, L. J., Thematic Design in the Novels of John Stein-
    beck, 114-31.
Osborn, Paul, ed., "Dialogue Script: EAST OF EDEN,"
    Study of Current English (Tokyo), X (September, 1955),
    16-32.
Phillips, William, "Male-ism and Moralism," AmMerc,
    LXXV (October, 1952), 93-8.
Sawney, Orlan, "Another Look at EAST OF EDEN," Appa-
    lachian State Teachers College Faculty Publications (1964),
    54-8.
Watt, F. W., Steinbeck, 93-9.
West, Anthony, "California Moonshine," NY, XXVIII (Septem-
    ber 20, 1952), 121-2, 125.

THE GRAPES OF WRATH

Allen, W., Modern Novel, 164-6.
_____, Urgent West, 216-18.
Beach, Joseph W., "John Steinbeck: Art and Propaganda,"
    American Fiction, 1920-1940, 325-47. Also in Tedlock,
    E. W., Jr., and C. V. Wicker, eds., Steinbeck and His
    Critics, 250-65.

Beck, Warren, "On John Steinbeck," in Madden, C. F.,
     Talks With Authors, 57-72.
Blake, N. M., Novelist's America, 139-62.
Bluestone, George, Novels Into Film, Baltimore: Johns
     Hopkins Un. Pr., 1957, 147-69. Also in French, W.,
     ed., Companion to THE GRAPES OF WRATH, 165-89.
Bowden, E. T., "The Commonplace and the Grotesque,"
     Dungeon of the Heart, 138-48. Also in Donohue, A. M.,
     ed., Casebook on THE GRAPES OF WRATH, 195-203.
Bowron, Bernard, "THE GRAPES OF WRATH: A 'wagons
     west' romance," ColQ, III (Summer, 1954), 84-91. Also
     in French, W., ed., Companion to THE GRAPES OF
     WRATH, 208-16.
Browning, Chris, "Grape Symbolism in THE GRAPES OF
     WRATH," Discourse, XI (Winter, 1968), 129-40.
Burgum, Edwin B., "The Sensibility of John Steinbeck,"
     S&S, X (1946), 140-5. Also in Burgum, E. B., Novel and
     the World's Dilemma, 283-8.
Cannon, Gerard, "The Pauline Apostleship of Tom Joad,"
     CE, XXIV (December, 1962), 222-4. Also in Donohue,
     A. M., ed., Casebook on THE GRAPES OF WRATH, 118-
     22.
Carlson, Eric W., "Symbolism in THE GRAPES OF WRATH,"
     CE, XIX (January, 1958), 172-5. Also in Donohue, A. M.,
     ed., Casebook on THE GRAPES OF WRATH, 96-102.
Carpenter, Frederic I., "The Philosophical Joads," CE, II
     (January, 1941), 315-25. Also in Tedlock, E. W., Jr.,
     and C. V. Wicker, eds., Steinbeck and His Critics, 241-
     9. Also in Carpenter, F. I., American Literature and
     the Dream, 167-75. Also in Donohue, A. M., ed., Case-
     book on THE GRAPES OF WRATH, 80-9.
Chametsky, Jules, "The Ambivalent Endings of THE GRAPES
     OF WRATH," MFS, XI, i (Spring, 1965), 33-44. Also in
     Donohue, A. M., ed., Casebook on THE GRAPES OF
     WRATH, 232-44.
Crockett, H. Kelly, "The Bible and THE GRAPES OF
     WRATH," CE, XXIV (December, 1962), 193-9. Also in
     Donohue, A. M., ed., Casebook on THE GRAPES OF
     WRATH, 105-14.
DeSchweinitz, George, "Steinbeck and Christianity," CE,
     XIX (May, 1958), 369. Also in Donohue, A. M., ed.,
     Casebook on THE GRAPES OF WRATH, 103-4.
Detweiler, Robert, "Christ and the Christ Figure in Ameri-
     can Fiction," ChS, XLVII (Summer, 1964), 111-24.
Donohue, Agnes M., ed., Casebook on THE GRAPES OF
     WRATH.
     _____, " 'The Endless Journey to No End': Journey and

Eden Symbolism in Hawthorne and Steinbeck," in Donohue, A. M. , ed. , Casebook on THE GRAPES OF WRATH, 257-66.

Dougherty, Charles T. , "The Christ-Figure in THE GRAPES OF WRATH," CE, XXIV (December, 1962), 224-6. Also in Donohue, A. M. , ed. , Casebook on THE GRAPES OF WRATH, 115-17.

Dunn, Thomas F. , "THE GRAPES OF WRATH," CE, XXIV (April, 1963), 566-7. Also in Donohue, A. M. , ed. , Casebook on THE GRAPES OF WRATH, 123-5.

Eisinger, Charles E. , "Jeffersonian Agrarianism in THE GRAPES OF WRATH," UKCR, XIV (1947), 149-54. Also in Donohue, A. M. , ed. , Casebook on THE GRAPES OF WRATH, 143-50.

Fontenrose, J. , John Steinbeck, 67-83.

French, Warren G. , in French, W. G. , and W. E. Kidd, eds. , American Winners of the Nobel Literary Prize, 210-13.

_____, "Another Look at THE GRAPES OF WRATH," ColQ, III (Winter, 1955), 337-43. Also in French, W. , ed. , Companion to THE GRAPES OF WRATH, 217-24.

_____, ed. , Companion to THE GRAPES OF WRATH.

_____, John Steinbeck, 95-112. Also (part) in Donohue, A. M. , ed. , Casebook on THE GRAPES OF WRATH, 204-8.

_____, Social Novel at the End of An Era, 42-49, and passim.

Frohock, W. M. , "John Steinbeck's Men of Wrath," SWR, XXXI (1946), 146-50. Also in Frohock, W. M. , Novel of Violence in America, 129-34.

Geismar, M. , Writers in Crisis, 239-41, 263-6. Also in Donohue, A. M. , ed. , Casebook on THE GRAPES OF WRATH, 134-42.

Gray, J. , On Second Thought, 133-6.

Griffin, Robert J. , and William A. Freedman, "Machines and Animals: Pervasive Motifs in THE GRAPES OF WRATH," JEGP, LXII (July, 1963), 569-80. Also in Donohue, A. M. , ed. , Casebook on THE GRAPES OF WRATH, 219-31.

Hayashi, Tetsumaro, "THE GRAPES OF WRATH," Modern Review (Calcutta), (March, 1968), 160-2.

_____, "John Steinbeck's THE GRAPES OF WRATH: The Joad Clan and Women," Lumina, IV (1961), 1-4.

_____, "Women and the Principle of Continuity in THE GRAPES OF WRATH," KAL, X (1967), 75-80.

Hunter, J. P. , "Steinbeck's Wine of Affirmation in THE GRAPES OF WRATH," in Langford, R. E. , ed. , Essays in Modern American Literature, 76-89.

Isherwood, Christopher, "The Tragedy of Eldorado," KR, I
(Autumn, 1939), 450-3. Also in Donohue, A.M., ed.,
Casebook on THE GRAPES OF WRATH, 76-9.

Kazumi, Kazushi, "Notes on THE GRAPES OF WRATH,"
English and American Literature Study (Aoyama Gakuin
Univ.), VIII (February, 1962), 1-17.

Klammer, Enno, "THE GRAPES OF WRATH - A Modern
Exodus Account," Cresset, XXV (February, 1962), 8-11.

Lewis, R.W.B., "John Steinbeck: The Fitful Daemon," in
Bode, C., ed., Young Rebel in American Literature,
137-40+. Also in Litz, A.W., ed., Modern American
Fiction, 275-6+.
_____, Picaresque Saint, 183-5.

Lisca, Peter, "THE GRAPES OF WRATH as Fiction,"
PMLA, LXXII (March, 1957), 296-309. Also in West-
brook, M., ed., Modern American Novel, 173-93. Also
in Donohue, A.M., ed., Casebook on THE GRAPES OF
WRATH, 166-81. Also (revised and expanded) in Lisca,
P., Wide World of John Steinbeck, 144-77.

McCarthy, Paul, "House and Shelter as Symbol in THE
GRAPES OF WRATH," SDR, V (Winter, 1967-68), 48-67.

McElderry, B.R., Jr., "THE GRAPES OF WRATH: In the
Light of Modern Critical Theory," CE, V (March, 1944),
308-13. Also in French, W., ed., Companion to THE
GRAPES OF WRATH, 199-208. Also in Donohue, A.M.,
ed., Casebook on THE GRAPES OF WRATH, 126-33.

Marks, L.J., Thematic Design in the Novels of John Steinbeck, 66-82.

Moore, H.T., Novels of John Steinbeck, 53-72.

Morris, L., "Fiery Gospel," Postscript to Yesterday, 166-
71.

Moseley, E.M., "Christ as the Brother of Man: Steinbeck's
THE GRAPES OF WRATH," Pseudonyms of Christ in the
Modern Novel, 163-74. Also in Donohue, A.M., ed.,
Casebook on THE GRAPES OF WRATH, 209-17.

Nakachi, Akira, "THE GRAPES OF WRATH: A Novel of
Mankind," Taira Technical Junior College Reports of
Study, I (1961), 1-15.

Nelson, Harland S., "Steinbeck's Politics Then and Now,"
AR, XXVII (Spring, 1967), 118-33, passim.

Pollock, Theodore, "On the Ending of THE GRAPES OF
WRATH," MFS, IV (Summer, 1958), 177-8. Also in
French, W., ed., Companion to THE GRAPES OF
WRATH, 224-6. Also in Donohue, A.M., ed., Casebook
on THE GRAPES OF WRATH, 182-4.

Poore, Charles, "Introduction" to THE GRAPES OF WRATH,
N.Y.: Harper's Modern Classics, 1951, vii-xv.

Raymund, Bernard, in Baker, D. V., ed., Writers of Today, 128-36.
Rundell, Walter, Jr., "Steinbeck's Image of the West," American West, I (Spring, 1964), 4-8, and passim.
Sanford, Charles L., "Classics of American Reform Literature," AmQ, X (Fall, 1958), 308-11.
Saw, Sally, "Religious Symbols in Steinbeck's GRAPES," The Joad Newsletter, I (January, 1963), 1-2.
Shockley, Martin, "Christian Symbolism in THE GRAPES OF WRATH," CE, XVIII (November, 1956), 87-90. Also in Tedlock, E. W., Jr., and C. V. Wicker, eds., Steinbeck and His Critics, 87-96. Also Donohue, A. M., ed., Casebook on THE GRAPES OF WRATH, 90-5.
_____, "The Reception of THE GRAPES OF WRATH in Oklahoma," AL, XV (January, 1944), 351-61. Also in Tedlock, E. W., Jr., and C. V. Wicker, eds., Steinbeck and His Critics, 231-40.
Slade, Leonard A., Jr., "The Use of Biblical Allusions in THE GRAPES OF WRATH," CLAJ, XI (March, 1968), 241-7.
Slochower, H., No Voice is Wholly Lost, 299-305.
Snell, G., Shapers of American Fiction, 194-6.
Stuckey, W. J., Pulitzer Prize Novels, 119-21.
Taylor, Walter F., "THE GRAPES OF WRATH Reconsidered," Miss Q, XII (Summer, 1959), 136-44. Also in Donohue, A. M., ed., Casebook on THE GRAPES OF WRATH, 185-94.
Thompson, Eric, "Steinbeck's Okies," Status, II (December, 1966), 42-5.
Watt, F. W., Steinbeck, 63-75.
Wright, Celeste T., "Ancient Anologues of an Incident in John Steinbeck," WF, XIV (January, 1955), 50-1. Also in Donohue, A. M., ed., Casebook on THE GRAPES OF WRATH, 159-61.
Yoshida, Hiroshige, "Gender of Animation in John Steinbeck's THE GRAPES OF WRATH," Anglica, II (October, 1956), 106-22.

IN DUBIOUS BATTLE

Allen, W., Modern Novel, 161-2.
Beach, J. W., American Fiction, 328-9.
Burgum, Edwin B., "The Sensibility of John Steinbeck," S&S, X (1946), 136-7. Also in Burgum, E. B., Novel and the World's Dilemma, 277-8.
Dvorak, Wilfred P., "Notes Toward the Education of the Heart," IEY, X (1965), 46-9.

Fontenrose, J., John Steinbeck, 42-53.
French, Warren G., in French, W. G., and W. E. Kidd, eds.,
American Winners of the Nobel Literary Prize, 205-7.
_____, John Steinbeck, 62-71.
Frohock, W. M., "John Steinbeck's Men of Wrath," SWR,
XXXI (Spring, 1946), 150-1. Also in Frohock, W. M.,
Novel of Violence in America, 135-7.
Geismar, M., Writers in Crisis, 259-63.
Hartt, J. N., Lost Image of Man, 74-5.
Levant, Howard, "The Unity of IN DUBIOUS BATTLE: Vio-
lence and Dehumanization," MFS, XI, i (Spring, 1965),
21-33.
Lisca, P., Wide World of John Steinbeck, 108-29.
Marks, L. J., Thematic Structure in the Novels of John
Steinbeck, 47-57, 58-63.
Moore, H. T., Novels of John Steinbeck, 40-7.
Walcutt, C. C., American Literary Naturalism, 260-2.
_____, Man's Changing Mask, 258-65.
Watt, F. W., Steinbeck, 51-8.

THE MOON IS DOWN

Burgum, Edwin B., "The Sensibility of John Steinbeck,"
S&S, X (1946), 145-7. Also in Burgum, E. B., Novel
and the World's Dilemma, 288-91.
Fontenrose, J., John Steinbeck, 98-101.
French, W., John Steinbeck, 113-19.
Frohock, W. M., "John Steinbeck's Men of Wrath," SWR,
XXXI (Spring, 1946), 151-2. Also in Frohock, W. M.,
Novel of Violence in America, 137-9.
Gurko, L., Angry Decade, 219-20.
Lisca, P., Wide World of John Steinbeck, 186-96.
Marks, L. J., Thematic Design in the Novels of John Stein-
beck, 98-105.
Watt, F. W., Steinbeck, 77-9.

OF MICE AND MEN

Allen, W., Modern Novel, 163-4.
Beach, J. W., American Fiction, 322-4.
Burgum, Edwin B., "The Sensibility of John Steinbeck,"
S&S, X (1946), 137-40. Also in Burgum, E. B., Novel
and the World's Dilemma, 278-83.
Fontenrose, J., John Steinbeck, 53-9.
French, Warren G., in French, W. G., and W. E. Kidd,
eds., American Winners of the Nobel Literary Prize,
207-8.
_____, John Steinbeck, 72-9.

Ganapathy, R., "Steinbeck's OF MICE AND MEN: A Study
    of Lyricism Through Primitivism," LCrit, V, iii (1962),
    101-4.
Geismar, M., Writers in Crisis, 256-9.
Gurko, L., Angry Decade, 217-19.
Lisca, Peter, "Motif and Pattern in OF MICE AND MEN,"
    MFS, II (Winter, 1956-57), 228-34. Also (revised and ex-
    panded) in Lisca, P., Wide World of John Steinbeck,
    130-43.
Marks, L. J., Thematic Structure in the Novels of John
    Steinbeck, 58-65.
Moore, H. T., Novels of John Steinbeck, 47-52.
Rascoe, Burton, "John Steinbeck," EJ, XXVII (March, 1938),
    205-16. Also in Tedlock, E. W., Jr., and C. V. Wickers,
    eds., Steinbeck and His Critics, 60-5.
Watt, F. W., Steinbeck, 58-62.

THE PASTURES OF HEAVEN

Carpenter, Frederic I., "John Steinbeck: American Dream-
    er," SWR, XXVI (July, 1941), 458-60. Also in Tedlock,
    E. W., Jr., and C. V. Wicker, eds., Steinbeck and His
    Critics, 71-3.
Fontenrose, J., John Steinbeck, 20-9.
French, W., John Steinbeck, 39-46.
Geismar, M., Writers in Crisis, 242-6.
Moore, H. T., Novels of John Steinbeck, 18-23.
Snell, G., Shapers of American Fiction, 192-3.
Watt, F. W., Steinbeck, 33-8.

THE PEARL

Corin, Fernand, "Steinbeck and Hemingway: A Study in Lit-
    erary Economy," RLV, XXIV (January-February, 1958),
    60-75; (March-April, 1958), 153-63.
Fuller, Edward, and Blanche J. Thompson, eds., Four
    Novels for Appreciation, N. Y.: Harcourt, Brace, 1960,
    256-60.
Geismar, M., in SatR, XXX (November 22, 1947), 14. Al-
    so in Geismar, M., American Moderns, 151-3.
Karsten, Ernest E., Jr., "Thematic Structure in THE
    PEARL," EJ, LIV (January, 1965), 1-7.
Levidova, I., "The Post-War Books of John Steinbeck,"
    SovietR, IV (Summer, 1963), 7-8.
Marks, L. J., Thematic Design in the Novels of John Stein-
    beck, 105-7.
Morris, Harry, "THE PEARL: Realism and Allegory," EJ,

LII (October, 1963), 487-95.

Prescott, O., In My Opinion, 62-4.

Scoville, Samuel, "The Weltanschauung of Steinbeck and Hemingway: An Analysis of Themes, EJ, LVI (January, 1967), 60-3, 66.

Tarr, E. Whitney, "Steinbeck on One Plane," SatR, XXX (December 20, 1947), 20.

Walcutt, C. C., American Literary Naturalism, 267-8.

Watt, F. W., Steinbeck, 84-7.

THE SHORT REIGN OF PIPPIN IV

Fontenrose, J., John Steinbeck, 130-2.

French, W., John Steinbeck, 165-9.

Geismar, M., American Moderns, 155-6.

Johnson, Pamela H., in NStat, LIV (July 13, 1957), 61-2.

Lisca, P., Wide World of John Steinbeck, 285-8.

Watt, F. W., Steinbeck, 101-2.

SWEET THURSDAY

Fontenrose, J., John Steinbeck, 127-30.

French, W., John Steinbeck, 156-60.

Holman, Hugh, "A Narrow-gauge Dickens," NRep, CXXX (June 7, 1954), 18-20.

Levidova, I., "The Post-War Books of John Steinbeck," SovietR, IV (Summer, 1963), 6-7.

Lisca, P., Wide World of John Steinbeck, 276-84.

Metzger, Charles R., "Steinbeck's Version of the Pastoral," MFS, VI (Summer, 1960), 115-24.

Moore, Ward, "Cannery Row Revisited: Steinbeck and the Sardine," Nation, CLXXIX (October 16, 1954), 325-7.

Watt, F. W., Steinbeck, 99-101.

TO A GOD UNKNOWN

Beach, J. W., American Fiction, 315-16.

Carpenter, Frederic I., "John Steinbeck: American Dreamer," SWR, XXVI (July, 1941), 460-1. Also in Tedlock, E. W., Jr., and C. V. Wicker, eds., Steinbeck and His Critics, 73-4.

Fontenrose, J., John Steinbeck, 13-19.

French, W., John Steinbeck, 47-52.

Geismar, M., Writers in Crisis, 248-9.

Lisca, P., Wide World of John Steinbeck, 39-55.

Marks, L. J., Thematic Design in the Novels of John Steinbeck, 34-46.

Moore, H. T. , Novels of John Steinbeck, 23-33.
Shimada, Saburo, "A Study of John Steinbeck's TO A GOD
    UNKNOWN," Beacon Study in English Language and Lit-
    erature, V (1964), 23-5.
Snell, G. , Shapers of American Fiction, 189-90.
Uchida, Shigeharu, "John Steinbeck's Non-Teleogy and TO
    A GOD UNKNOWN," KAL, No. 6 (April, 1963), 13-17.
Watt, F. W. , Steinbeck, 29-33.

TORTILLA FLAT

Alexander, Stanley, "The Conflict of Form in TORTILLA
    FLAT," AL, XL (March, 1968), 58-66.
Beach, Joseph W. , American Fiction, 317-22.   Also (re-
    vised) in Tedlock, E. W. , Jr. , and C. V. Wicker, eds. ,
    Steinbeck and His Critics, 85-90.
Fontenrose, J. , John Steinbeck, 30-41.
French, Warren G. , in French, W. G. , and W. E. Kidd, eds. ,
    American Winners of the Nobel Literary Prize, 204-5.
    _____ , John Steinbeck, 53-61.
Geismar, M. , Writers in Crisis, 252-6.
Kawamura, Yoneichi, "Steinbeck's Humor and Pathos in
    TORTILLA FLAT and CANNERY ROW," Hokkaido Univ.
    Essays in Foreign Languages and Literatures, I (Decem-
    ber, 1953), 24-30.
Kinney, Arthur F. , "The Arthurian Cycle in TORTILLA
    FLAT," MFS, XI, i (Spring, 1965), 11-20.
Lisca, P. , Wide World of John Steinbeck, 72-91.
Moore, H. T. , Novels of John Steinbeck, 35-9.
Raymund, Bernard, in Baker, D. V. , ed. , Writers of Today,
    125-7.
Snell, G. , Shapers of American Fiction, 192-3.
Uchida, Shigeharu, "Sentimental Steinbeck and His TORTILLA
    FLAT," KAL, No. 7 (1964), 8-12.
Walcutt, C. C. , American Literary Naturalism, 259-60.
Watt, F. W. , Steinbeck, 38-42.

THE WAYWARD BUS

Clark, Eleanor, in Nation, CLXIV (March 29, 1947), 370-3.
Cousins, Norman, "Bankrupt Realism," SatR, XXX (March
    8, 1947), 22-3.
Fontenrose, J. , John Steinbeck, 108-11.
French, W. , John Steinbeck, 143-8.
Gardiner, Harold C. , "The Emperor's New (Literary)
    Clothes," America, LXXVI (March 22, 1947), 689-91.
    Also in Gardiner, H. C. , In All Conscience, 131-6.

Levidova, I., "The Post-War Books of John Steinbeck,"
SovietR, IV (Summer, 1963), 8-9.
Lisca, Peter, "THE WAYWARD BUS - A Modern Pilgrim-
age," in Tedlock, W.E., Jr., and C.V. Wicker, eds.,
Steinbeck and His Critics, 281-90.
_____, Wide World of John Steinbeck, 231-47.
Marks, L.J., Thematic Design in the Novels of John Stein-
beck, 107-12.
Prescott, Orville, in YR, XXXVI (Summer, 1947), 765-6.
_____, In My Opinion, 61-2.
Redman, Ben R., "The Case of John Steinbeck," AmMerc,
LXIV (May, 1947), 624-30.
Seixas, Antonia, "John Steinbeck and the Non-Teleological
Bus," in Tedlock, E.W., Jr., and C.V. Wickers, eds.,
Steinbeck and His Critics, 275-80.
Tsunoda, Toshio, "THE WAYWARD BUS, by Steinbeck,"
Yukei-tsushin (Japan), No. 11 (1947).
Walcutt, C.C., American Literary Naturalism, 266-7.
Watt, F.W., Steinbeck, 87-91.
Weeks, Donald, "Steinbeck Against Steinbeck," PacSp, I
(Autumn, 1947), 447-57.

THE WINTER OF OUR DISCONTENT

Fontenrose, J., John Steinbeck, 132-7.
French, Warren, in French, W.G., and W.E. Kidd, eds.,
American Winners of the Nobel Literary Prize, 219-21.
_____, "Steinbeck's Winter Tale," MFS, XI, i (Spring,
1965), 66-74.
Gerstenberger, Donna, "Steinbeck's American Wasteland,"
MFS, XI, i (Spring, 1965), 59-65.
Hartt, J.N., "The Return of the Moral Passion," YR, LI,
No. 2 (Winter, 1962), 305-6.
Hyman, S.E., "John Steinbeck and the Nobel Prize," Stand-
ards, 113-17.
Lemaire, Marcel, "Some Recent American Novels and Es-
says," RLV, XXVIII (1962), 74-5.
Levidova, I., "The Post-War Books of John Steinbeck,"
SovietR, IV (Summer, 1963), 11-13.
Nelson, Harland S., "Steinbeck's Politics Then and Now,"
AR, XXVII (Spring, 1967), 118-33, passim.
Watt, F.W., Steinbeck, 102-3.

BIBLIOGRAPHY

Beebe, Maurice, and Jackson R. Bryer, "Criticism of John
Steinbeck: A Selected Checklist," MFS, XI, i (Spring,

1965), 90-103.
Donohue, A. M. , ed. , Casebook on THE GRAPES OF WRATH,
   196-9.
French, Warren, "Bibliography," Companion to THE
   GRAPES OF WRATH, 229-35.
_____, John Steinbeck, 177-81.
Hayashi, Tetsumaro, "A Brief Survey of John Steinbeck Bib-
   liographies," KAL, No. 9 (1966), 54-61.
_____, "John Steinbeck: A Checklist of Unpublished Ph. D.
   Dissertations (1946-1967)," Serif, V, iv (1968), 30-1.
_____, John Steinbeck: A Concise Bibliography (1930-65).
   Metuchen, N. J. : Scarecrow, 1967.
Steele, Joan, "John Steinbeck: A Checklist of Biographical
   Critical and Bibliographical Material," BB, XXIV (May-
   August, 1965), 149-52, 162-3.

STERN, RICHARD GUSTAVE, 1928-

GENERAL

Raeder, Robert L. , "An Interview with Richard G. Stern,"
   ChiR, XVIII (Autumn-Winter, 1965-66), 170-5.

STOREY, DAVID, 1933-

GENERAL

Gindin, James, "The Fable Begins to Break Down," WSCL,
   VIII (Winter, 1967), 5-8.
Lockwood, Bernard, "Four Contemporary British Working-
   Class Novelists: A Thematic and Critical Approach to
   the Fiction of Raymond Williams, John Braine, David
   Storey and Allan Sillitoe," DA, XXVIII (1967), 1081A
   (Wisc.).
McGuiness, Frank, "The Novels of David Storey," LonM,
   III (March, 1964), 79-93.
Newton, J. M. , in CamQ, I (Summer, 1966), 284-95.
Storey, David, "Writers on Themselves: Journey Through a
   Tunnel," Listener, LXX (August 1, 1963), 159-61.

FLIGHT INTO CAMDEN

Gindin, J. , "Education and Class Structure," Postwar British Fiction, 85-108.
Newton, J. M. , in CamQ, I (Summer, 1966), 290-2.

Raban, J., "Imagery in the Language of Fiction," Technique
   of Modern Fiction, 177-9.
Urwin, G. G., ed., Taste for Living, 124-7.

RADCLIFFE

Anon., "And Hell Up North," TLS (September 20, 1963), 701.
   Also in T. L. S.: Essays and Reviews from The Times Lit-
   erary Supplement, 1963, 102-3.
Gindin, James, "The Fable Begins to Break Down," WSCL,
   VIII (Winter, 1967), 6-8.
Newton, J. M., in CamQ, I (Summer, 1966), 292-5.
Spender, Stephen, "Must There Always Be a Red Brick Eng-
   land?" in Encyclopaedia Britannica. Great Ideas Today,
   1965, 180-1.

THIS SPORTING LIFE

Churchill, Thomas, "Waterhouse, Storey, and Fowles:
   Which Way Out of the Room?" Crit, X, iii (1968), 72-87.
Gindin, J., "Education and Class Structure," Postwar Brit-
   ish Fiction, 85-108.
Newton, J. M., in CamQ, I (Summer, 1966), 285-90.
O'Connor, W. V., "The New Hero and a Shift in Literary
   Convention," New University Wits, 136-8.

STOW, RANDOLPH, 1935-

GENERAL

Burgess, O. N., "On the Novels of Randolph Stow," AusQ,
   XXXVII, ii (March, 1965), 73-81.
Clarke, Donovan, "The Realities of Randolph Stow," Bridge,
   II (February, 1966), 37-42. (Not seen.)
Dutton, Geoffrey, "The Search for Permanence: The Novels
   of Randolph Stow," JCL, No. 1 (September, 1965), 135-
   48.
Heseltine, Harry, in Dutton, G., ed., Literature of Aus-
   tralia, 211-12.
Johnston, G. K. W., "The Art of Randolph Stow," Meanjin,
   XX (July, 1961), 139-43.
Kramer, Leonie, "The Novels of Randolph Stow," Southerly,
   XXIV (1964), 78-91.
Martin, David, "Among the Bones," Meanjin, XVIII (April,
   1959), 52-8.
New, William H., "Outsider Looking Out: The Novels of
   Randolph Stow," Crit, IX, i (1967), 90-9.

Oppen, Alice, "Myth and Reality in Randolph Stow," Southerly, XXVII, ii (1967), 82-94.

THE BYSTANDER

Dutton, Geoffrey, "The Search for Permanence: The Novels
of Randolph Stow," JCL, No. 1 (1965), 141-3.
Newby, P. H. , "The Novels of Randolph Snow," AusL, I
(November, 1957), 50-1.
Oppen, Alice, "Myth and Reality in Randolph Stow," Souther-
ly, XXVII, ii (1967), 85-6.

A HAUNTED LAND

Burgess, O. N. , "The Novels of Randolph Stow," AusQ,
XXXVII (March, 1965), 74-6.
Dutton, Geoffrey, "The Search for Permanence: The Novels
of Randolph Stow," JCL, No. 1 (1965), 137-40.
Martin, David, in Meanjin, XVI (1957), 88-9.
Oppen, Alice, "Myth and Reality in Randolph Stow," Souther-
ly, XXVII, ii (1967), 82-5.

THE MERRY-GO-ROUND IN THE SEA

New, William H. , "Outsider Looking Out: The Novels of
Randolph Stow," Crit, IX, i (1967), 96-9.
Oppen, Alice, "Myth and Reality in Randolph Stow," Souther-
ly, XXVII, ii (1967), 92-4.

TO THE ISLANDS

Buckley, Vincent, "In the Shadow of Patrick White," Mean-
jin, XX (July, 1961), 144-50.
Burgess, O. N. , "The Novels of Randolph Stow," AusQ,
XXXVII (March, 1965), 76-7.
Dutton, Geoffrey, "The Search for Permanence: The Novels
of Randolph Stow," JCL, No. 1 (1965), 143-5.
Martin, David, "Among the Bones," Meanjin, XVIII (April,
1959), 52-8.
Maxwell, D. E. S. , "Landscape and Theme," in Press, John,
ed. , Commonwealth Literature: Unity and Diversity in a
Common Culture, London: Heinemann, 1965, 82-9.
New, William H. , "Outsider Looking Out: The Novels of
Randolph Stow," Crit, IX, i (1967), 93-6.
Oppen, Alice, "Myth and Reality in Randolph Stow," Souther-
ly, XXVII, ii (1967), 86-9.

TOURMALINE

Burgess, O. N., "The Novels of Randolph Stow," AusQ,
    XXXVII (March, 1965), 73-81.
Dutton, Geoffrey, "The Search for Permanence: The Novels
    of Randolph Stow," JCL, No. 1 (1965), 145-6.
Oppen, Alice, "Myth and Reality in Randolph Stow," Souther-
    ly, XXVII, ii (1967), 89-92.

STYRON, WILLIAM, 1925-

GENERAL

Aldridge, J. W., "William Styron and the Derivative Imagina-
    tion," Time To Murder and Create, 30-51.
Bryant, Jerry H., "The Hopeful Stoicism of William Styron,"
    SAQ, LXII (Autumn, 1963), 539-50.
Canzoneri, Robert, and Page Stegner, "An Interview With
    William Styron," Per/Se, I, ii (Summer, 1966), 37-44.
Clarke, John Henrik, William Styron's NAT TURNER: Ten
    Black Writers Respond, Boston: Beacon, 1968.
Davis, Robert G., "Styron and the Students," Crit, III, iii
    (Summer, 1960), 37-46.
Doar, Harriet, "Interview With William Styron," Red Clay
    Reader, No. 1 (1964), 26-30.
Fenton, Charles A., "William Styron and the Age of the
    Slob," SAQ, LIX (Autumn, 1960), 469-76.
Fossum, R. H., William Styron.
Friedman, Melvin J., "William Styron: An Interim Ap-
    praisal," EJ, L (March, 1961), 149-58, 192.
Galloway, David D., "The Absurd Man as a Tragic Hero:
    The Novels of William Styron," TSLL, VI (Winter, 1965),
    512-34. Also in Galloway, D. D., Absurd Hero, 51-81.
Gosset, L. Y., "The Cost of Freedom: William Styron,"
    Violence in Recent Southern Fiction, 117-31.
Hoffman, Frederick J., Art of Southern Fiction, 143-6.
————————, "The Cure of 'Nothing': The Fiction of William
    Styron," in Browne, R. B., and others, eds., Frontiers
    of American Culture, 69-87.
Hux, Samuel H., "American Myth and Existential Vision:
    The Indigenous Existentialism of Mailer, Bellow, Styron
    and Ellison," DA, XXVI (1966), 5437 (Conn.).
Jones, James, and William Styron, "Two Writers Talk It
    Over," Esquire, LX, i (July, 1963), 57-9.
Klotz, Marvin, "The Triumph Over Time: Narrative Form
    in William Faulkner and William Styron," MissQ, XVII

(Winter, 1963-64), 9-20.

Mackin, C. R., William Styron.

McNamara, Eugene, "The Post-Modern Novel, QQ, LXIX (Summer, 1962), 268-70.

Matthiessen, Peter, and George Plimpton, "The Art of Fiction V: William Styron," ParisR, No. 5 (Spring, 1954), 42-57. Also in Writers at Work, 1st ser., 267-82. Also (portion) in Rubin, L. D., Jr., and J. R. Moore, eds., Idea of an American Novel, 368-70.

Mudrick, Marvin, "Mailer and Styron: Guests of the Establishment," HudR, XVII (Autumn, 1964), 346-66.

Nigro, Augustine J., Jr., "William Styron and the Adamic Tradition," DA, XXVI (1966), 3958-59 (Un. of Maryland).

O'Connell, Shaun, "Expense of Spirit: The Vision of William Styron," Crit, VIII, ii (1966), 20-33.

Scott, James B., "The Individual and the Society: Norman Mailer Versus William Styron," DA, XXV (1965), 5942 (Syracuse).

Stevenson, David L., "William Styron and the Fiction of the Fifties," Crit, III, iii (Summer, 1960), 47-58. Also in Waldmeir, J. J., ed., Recent American Fiction, 265-74.

Urang, Gunnar, "The Voices of Tragedy in the Novels of William Styron," in Scott, N. A., Jr., ed., Adversity and Grace, 163-209.

THE CONFESSIONS OF NAT TURNER

Anon., "Unslavish Fidelity: The Confessions of William Styron," TLS (May 9, 1968), 480. Also in T. L. S.: Essays and Reviews from The Times Literary Supplement, 1968, 81-6.

Aptheker, Herbert, "A Note on the History," Nation, CCV (October 16, 1967), 373-4.

_____, "Styron's Turner vs. Nat Turner," New South Student, (May, 1968), 3-7.

_____, and William Styron, "Truth and NAT TURNER," Nation, CCVI (April 22, 1968), 543-4.

Brown, Cecil M., in Negro Digest, XVII (February, 1968), 51-2, 89-91.

Canzeroni, Robert, and Page Stegner, "An Interview With William Styron," Per/Se, I, ii (Summer, 1966), 37-44.

Clarke, John Hendrik, ed., William Styron's Nat Turner: Ten Black Writers Respond, Boston: Beacon, 1968.

Coles, Robert, "Backlash," PR, XXXV (Winter, 1968), 128-33.

_____, "Response to Thelwell (Turner Thesis)," PR, XXV (Summer, 1968), 412-14.

Cooke, Michael, "Nat Turner's Revolt," YR, LVII (Winter, 1968), 273-8.

Core, George, "NAT TURNER and the Final Reckoning of Things," SoR, n. s., IV (July, 1968), 745-51.

————, ed., Southern Fiction Today: Renascence and Beyond, Athens: Un. of Georgia Pr., 1969, 1-5, 42-3, 74-9.

Delaney, Lloyd T., "A Psychologist Looks at THE CONFESSIONS OF NAT TURNER," Psychology Today, I (January, 1968), 11-14.

Driver, Tom F., "Black Consciousness Through a White Scrim," Motive, XXVII (February, 1968), 56-8.

Friedman, Melvin J., "THE CONFESSIONS OF NAT TURNER: The Convergence of 'Nonfiction Novel' and 'Meditation on History'," JPC, I (Fall, 1967), 166-75. Also (abridged) in Univ. of Wisconsin at Milwaukee Magazine (Spring, 1968), 3-7.

Fossum, R. H., William Styron, 34-46.

Gilman, Richard, "Nat Turner Revisited," NRep, CLVIII (April 27, 1968), 23-6, 28-32.

Goodheart, Eugene, "When Slaves Revolt," Mainstream, XIV (January, 1968), 69-72.

Green, Martin, "The Need for a New Liberalism," Month, n. s., XL (September, 1968), 183-6.

Hairstone, Loyle, "William Styron's Dilemma," Freedomways, VIII (Winter, 1968), 7-11.

Harnack, Curtis, "The Quidities of Detail," KR, XXX (Winter, 1968), 125-32.

Kaufman, Walter, "Tragedy vs. History: THE CONFESSIONS OF NAT TURNER," Tragedy and Philosophy, N. Y.: Doubleday, 1968, 347-54.

Kauffmann, Stanley, "Styron's Unwritten Novel," HudR, XX (Winter, 1967-68), 675-9.

Kazin, Alfred, "Instinct for Tragedy: A Message in Black and White," Book World (October 8, 1967), 1, 22.

Lehan, Richard, "Fiction, 1967," Contemporary Literature, IX, iv (Autumn, 1968), 540-2.

Lewis, R. W. B., and C. Vann Woodward, "Slavery in the First Person: An Interview with William Styron," Yale Alumni Mag (November, 1967), 37-9.

McPherson, James L., "America's Slave Revolt," Dissent, XV (January-February, 1968), 86-9.

Mackin, C. R., William Styron, 22-37.

Malin, Irving, "Nat's Confessions," UDQ (Winter, 1968), 94-6.

Miller, William L., "The Meditations of William Styron," Reporter, XXXVII (November 16, 1967), 42-6.

Murray, Albert, "A Troublesome Property," New Leader,
    X (December 4, 1967), 18-20.
Neri, Judith, "On THE CONFESSIONS OF NAT TURNER,"
    Umanesimo, II, i-ii (1968), 135-8.
Newcomb, Horace, "William Styron and the Act of Memory:
    THE CONFESSIONS OF NAT TURNER," ChiR, XX, i
    (1968), 86-94.
O'Connell, Shaun, "Styron's Nat Turner," Nation, CCV (Oc-
    tober 16, 1967), 373-4.
Platt, Gerald M., "A Sociologist Looks at THE CONFES-
    SIONS OF NAT TURNER," Psychology Today, I (January,
    1968), 14-15.
Rahv, Philip, "Through the Midst of Jerusalem," NYRB, IX
    (October 26, 1967), 6-10.
Rubin, Louis D., Jr., "William Styron and Human Bondage:
    THE CONFESSIONS OF NAT TURNER," HC, IV, v (De-
    cember, 1967), 1-12.
Sheed, Wilfred, "The Slave Who Became a Man," NYTBR
    (October 8, 1967), 1-3.
Sitkoff, Harry, and Michael Wreszin, "Who's Nat Turner?:
    William Styron vs. the Black Intellectuals," Midstream,
    XIV (November, 1968), 10-20.
Sokolov, Raymond, "Into the Mind of Nat Turner," News-
    week, LXX (October 16, 1967), 65-9.
Steiner, George, "The Fire Last Time," NY, XLIII (Novem-
    ber 25, 1967), 236-44.
Thelwell, Michael, "Mr. William Styron and The Reverend
    Turner," MR, IX (Winter, 1968), 7-29. Also in Clarke,
    J. H., ed., William Styron's Nat Turner: Ten Black
    Writers Respond, Boston: Beacon, 1968, 79-91.
_____, "The Turner Thesis," PR, XXXV (Summer, 1968),
    403-12.
Thompson, John, "Rise and Slay," Ctary, XLIV (November,
    1967), 81-5.
Turner, Darwin T., "THE CONFESSIONS OF NAT TURNER,
    by William Styron," JNH, LIII (1968), 183-6.
Wells, Anna M., Vincent Harding, Mike Thelwell, and Eu-
    gene D. Genovese, "An Exchange on NAT TURNER,"
    NYRB, XI (November 7, 1968), 31-6.
Woodward, C. Vann, "Confessions of a Rebel: 1831," NRep,
    CLVII (October 7, 1967), 25-8.

LIE DOWN IN DARKNESS

Aldridge, James W., In Search of Heresy, 146-8.
_____, "William Styron and the Derivative Imagination,"
    Time To Murder and Create, 30-42.

Allen, W., Modern Novel, 305-7.

Baumbach, Jonathan, "Paradise Lost: The Novels of William Styron," SAQ, LXIII (Spring, 1964), 207-14. Also in Baumbach, J., Landscape of Nightmare, 123-34.

Bryant, Jerry H., "The Hopeful Stoicism of William Styron," SAQ, LXII (Autumn, 1963), 541-4.

Cowley, Malcolm, "The Faulkner Pattern," NRep, CXXV (October 8, 1951), 19-20.

Davis, Robert G., in Balakian, N., and C. Simmons, eds., Creative Present, 130-4.

_____, "A Grasp of Moral Realities," ASch, XXI (Winter, 1951-52), 114-16.

Finkelstein, S., Existentialism and Alienation in American Literature, 215-16.

Fossum, R. H., William Styron, 8-19.

Friedman, Melvin J., "William Styron: An Interim Appraisal," EJ, L (March, 1961), 150-3.

Galloway, David D., "The Absurd Man as Tragic Hero: The Novels of William Styron," TSLL, VI (Winter, 1965), 513-19. Also in Galloway, D. D., Absurd Hero, 53-61.

Geismar, Maxwell, American Moderns, 239-46.

_____, "Domestic Tragedy in Virginia," SatR, XXXIV (September 15, 1951), 12-13.

Gossett, L. Y., Violence in Recent Southern Fiction, 122-7.

Hartt, J. N., Lost Image of Man, 60-3.

Hassan, Ihab, Radical Innocence, 124-31. Also in Kostelanetz, R., ed., On Contemporary Literature, 597-606.

Hoffman, Frederick J., Art of Southern Fiction, 148-54.

_____, "The Cure of 'Nothing!': The Fiction of William Styron," in Browne, R. B., and others, eds., Frontiers of American Culture, 72-7.

Klotz, Marvin, "The Triumph Over Time: Narrative Form in William Faulkner and William Styron," MissQ, XVII (Winter, 1963-64), 16-18.

Lawson, John H., "Styron: Darkness and Fire in the Modern Novel," Mainstream, XIII (October, 1960), 9-18.

Ludwig, J., Recent American Novelists, 31-2.

Mackin, C. R., William Styron, 4-12.

Meeker, Richard K., in Simonini, R. C., Jr., ed., Southern Writers, 171-3.

O'Connell, Shaun, "Expense of the Spirit: The Vision of William Styron," Crit, VIII, ii (1966), 21-5.

O'Connor, W. V., in Moore, H. T., ed., Contemporary American Novelists, 214-18.

Rubin, Louis D., Jr., Faraway Country, 185-215.

_____, "What to Do About Chaos," Hopkins Rev, V (Fall, 1951), 65-8.

Urang, Gunnar, "The Voices of Tragedy in the Novels of
    William Styron," in Scott, N. A. , Jr. , ed. , Adversity and
    Grace, 185-91+.

THE LONG MARCH

Bandriff, Welles T. , "The Role of Order and Disorder in
    THE LONG MARCH," EJ, LVI (January, 1967), 54-9.
Bryant, Jerry H. , "The Hopeful Stoicism of William Styron,"
    SAQ, LXII (Autumn, 1963), 544-7.
Carver, Wayne, "The Grand Inquisitor's Long March," UDQ,
    I, ii (Summer, 1966), 49-57.
Finkelstein, S. , Existentialism and Alienation in American
    Literature, 216-18.
Fossum, R. H. , William Styron, 20-5.
Galloway, David D. , "The Absurd Man as Tragic Hero: The
    Novels of William Styron," TSLL, VI (Winter, 1965),
    519-22.   Also in Galloway, D. D. , Absurd Hero, 61-4.
Geismar, M. , American Moderns, 246-50.
Gossett, L. Y. , Violence in Recent Southern Fiction, 118-21.
Hays, Peter L. , "The Nature of Rebellion in THE LONG
    MARCH," Crit, VIII, ii (Winter, 1965-66), 70-4.
Hoffman, Frederick J. , Art of Southern Fiction, 146-8.
_____, "The Cure of 'Nothing!': The Fiction of William
    Styron," in Browne, R. B. , and others, eds. , Frontiers
    of American Culture, 71-2.
Mackin, C. R. , William Styron, 12-14.
McNamara, Eugene, "William Styron's LONG MARCH: Ab-
    surdity and Authenticity," WHR, XV (Summer, 1961), 267-
    72.
Meeker, Richard K. , in Simonini, R. C. , Jr. , ed. , Southern
    Writers, 187-8.
Nigro, August, "THE LONG MARCH: The Expansive Hero
    in a Closed World," Crit, IX, iii (1967), 103-12.
O'Connell, Shaun, "Expense of the Spirit: The Vision of
    William Styron," Crit, VIII, ii (1966), 25-7.
Walcutt, C. C. , Man's Changing Mask, 252-7.

SET THIS HOUSE ON FIRE

Aldridge, J. W. , "William Styron and the Derivative Imagina-
    tion," Time To Murder and Create, 42-51.
Baumbach, Jonathan, "Paradise Lost: The Novels of William
    Styron," SAQ, LXIII (Spring, 1964), 214-17.   Also in
    Baumbach, J. , Landscape of Nightmare, 134-7.
Benson, Alice R. , "Techniques in the Twentieth-Century
    Novel for Relating the Particular to the Universal: SET

THIS HOUSE ON FIRE," PMASAL, XLVII (1962), 587-94.
Borklund, Elmer, "The Fiction of Violence and Pain,"
Ctary, XXX (November, 1960), 452-4.
Breit, Harvey, "A Second Novel," PR, XXVIII (Summer,
1960), 561-3.
Bryant, Jerry H., "The Hopeful Stoicism of William Styron,"
SAQ, LXII (Autumn, 1963), 547-50.
Davis, Robert G., in Balakian, N., and C. Simmons, eds.,
Creative Present, 135-41.
Detweiler, R., "William Styron and the Courage to Be,"
Four Crises in Mid-Century American Fiction, 6-13.
Fenton, Charles A., "William Styron and the Age of the
Slob," SAQ, LIX (Autumn, 1960), 469-76.
Finkelstein, S., Existentialism and Alienation in American
Literature, 218-19.
Fossum, R. H., William Styron, 26-34.
Foster, Richard, "An Orgy of Commerce: William Styron's
SET THIS HOUSE ON FIRE," Crit, III, iii (Summer,
1960), 59-70.
Friedman, Melvin J., "William Styron: An Interim Ap-
praisal," EJ, L (March, 1961), 156-8+.
Galloway, David D., "The Absurd Man as Tragic Hero: The
Novels of William Styron," TSLL, VI (Winter, 1965),
522-34. Also in Galloway, D. D., Absurd Hero, 65-81.
Gossett, L. Y., Violence in Recent Southern Fiction, 128-30.
Hoffman, Frederick J., Art of Southern Fiction, 154-61.
_____, "The Cure of 'Nothing!': The Fiction of William
Styron," in Browne, R. B., and others, eds., Frontiers
of American Culture, 78-82.
Klotz, Marvin, "The Triumph Over Time: Narrative Form
in William Faulkner and William Styron," MissQ, XVII
(Winter, 1963-64), 19-20.
Lawson, John H., "Styron: Darkness and Fire in the Mod-
ern Novel," Mainstream, XIII, x (October, 1960), 9-18.
Lawson, Lewis, "Cass Kinsolving: Kierkegaardian Man of
Despair," WSCL, III, iii (Fall, 1962), 54-66.
Lemaire, Marcel, "Some Recent American Novels and Es-
says," RLV, XXVIII (1962), 72-4.
Ludwig, J., Recent American Novelists, 32-3.
Lytle, A., Hero With the Private Parts, 50-2.
Mackin, C. R., William Styron, 14-22.
Moore, L. Hugh, "Robert Penn Warren, William Styron,
and the Use of Greek Myth," Crit, VIII, ii (Winter,
1965-66), 80-7.
Newberry, Mike, "Shock of Recognition," Mainstream,
XIII (September, 1960), 61-3.
O'Connell, Shaun, "Expense of Spirit: The Vision of Wil-

liam Styron," Crit, VIII, ii (Winter, 1965-66), 27-32.

O'Connor, W. V., in Moore, H. T., ed., Contemporary American Novelists, 218-21.

Robb, Kenneth A., "William Styron's Don Juan," Crit, VIII, ii (Winter, 1965-66), 34-46.

Rothberg, Abraham, "Styron's Appointment in Sambuco," New Leader, XLIII (July 4-11, 1960), 24-7.

Rubin, Louis D., Jr., "An Artist in Bonds," SR, LXIX (Winter, 1961), 174-9.

_____, Faraway Country, 215-30.

Stevenson, David L., "Styron and the Fiction of the Fifties," Crit, III, iii (Summer, 1960), 49-53. Also in Waldmeir, J. J., ed., Recent American Fiction, 267-70.

Thompson, Frank, in PrS, XXXVII (Summer, 1963), 183-5.

Urang, Gunnar, "The Broader Vision: William Styron's SET THIS HOUSE ON FIRE," Crit, VIII, ii (Winter, 1965-66), 47-69. Also in Scott, N. A., Jr., ed., Adversity and Grace, 191-209.

Winner, Anthony, "Adjustment, Tragic Humanism and Italy," SA, VII (1961), 338-61.

BIBLIOGRAPHY

Fossum, R. H., William Styron, 47-8.

Galloway, D. D., Absurd Hero, 203-10.

Mackin, C. R., William Styron, 39-43.

Schneider, Harold W., "Two Bibliographies: Saul Bellow, William Styron," Crit, III, iii (Summer, 1960), 71-91.

SWADOS, HARVEY, 1920-

GENERAL

Feinstein, Herbert, "Contemporary American Fiction: Harvey Swados and Leslie Fiedler," WSCL, II, i (Winter, 1961), 79-98.

Shapiro, Charles, "Harvey Swados: Private Stories and Public Fiction, in Moore, H. T., ed., Contemporary American Novelists, 182-92.

FALSE COIN

Gottfried, Alex, and Sue Davidson, "Utopia's Children: An Interpretation of Three Political Novels," Western Pol. Qtly, XV (March, 1962), 27-32.

Mizener, Arthur, "Some Kinds of Modern Novel," SR,

LXIX (Winter, 1961), 155-6.

OUT WENT THE CANDLE

Hassan, I., Radical Innocence, 134-40.
Shapiro, Charles, in Moore, H. T., ed., Contemporary
American Novelists, 184-8.

THE WILL

Siegelman, Ellen, "A Battle of Wills: Swados' New Novel,"
Crit, VII (Spring, 1964), 125-8.

TAYLOR, ELIZABETH, 1912-

GENERAL

Austin, Richard, "The Novels of Elizabeth Taylor," Cweal,
LXII (June 10, 1955), 258-9.
Liddell, Robert, "The Novels of Elizabeth Taylor," REL,
I, ii (April, 1960), 54-61.

AT MRS. LIPPINCOTE'S

Boll, Ernest, "AT MRS. LIPPINCOTE'S and TRISTRAM
SHANDY," MLN, LXV (1950), 119-21.

TAYLOR, PETER HILLSMAN, 1917-

A WOMAN OF MEANS

Brown, Ashley, "The Early Fiction of Peter Taylor," SR,
LXX (Autumn, 1962), 599-602.
Cathey, Kenneth C., "Peter Taylor: An Evaluation," WR,
XVIII (Autumn, 1953), 15-17.
Eisinger, C. E., Fiction of the Forties, 196-8.
Pickrel, Paul, in YR, XXXIX (Summer, 1950), 765-8.
Shattuck, Roger, in WR, XVI (Autumn, 1951), 87-8.
Smith, James P., "Narration and Theme in Taylor's A
WOMAN OF MEANS," Crit, IX, iii (1967), 19-30.
Wilcox, Thomas, "A Novelist of Means," SR, LIX (January-
March, 1951), 151-4.

BIBLIOGRAPHY

Smith, James P. , "A Peter Taylor Checklist," Crit, IX,
iii (1967), 31-6.

THIRKELL, ANGELA, 1890-1961

GENERAL

McIntyre, Clara F. , "Mrs. Thirkell's Barsetshire," CE,
XVII (April, 1956), 398-401.
Pendry, E. D. , New Feminism of English Fiction, 51-4.

THOMAS, HUGH, 1931-

THE WORLD'S GAME

Allsop, K. , Angry Decade, 136-9.
Gindin, J. , "Comedy and Understatement," Postwar British
Fiction, 165-77.

TOLKIEN, (J)OHN (R)ONALD (R)EUEL, 1892-

GENERAL

Bisenieks, Dainis, "Reading and Misreading Tolkien," Man-
kato State College Studies, II (February, 1967), 98-100.
Carter, L. , Tolkien.
Castell, Daphne, "The Realms of Tolkien," New Worlds, L
(November, 1966), 143-54. (Not seen.)
Ellman, May, "Growing Up Hobbitic," in Solotaroff, Theo-
dore, ed. , New American Review #2, N. Y.: New Ameri-
can Library, 1967, 217-29.
Hodgart, Matthew, "Kicking the Hobbit," NYRB, VIII (May
4, 1967), 10-11.
Irwin, W. R. , "There and Back Again: The Romances of
Williams, Lewis, and Tolkien," SR, LXIX (Autumn, 1961),
566-78.
Kilby, Clyde S. , "Tolkien as Scholar and Artist," TJ, III
i (Spring, 1967), 9-11.
Matthewson, Joseph, "The Hobbit Habit," Esquire, LXVI,
(September, 1966), 130-1, 221-2.
Menen, Aubrey, "Learning to Love the Hobbits," Diplomat,
XVIII (October, 1966), 32-4, 37-8. (Not seen.)

Norman, Philip, "The Prevalence of Hobbits," NYTMag
    (January 15, 1967), 30-1, 97, 100, 102.
Ready, William, "The Tolkien Relation," Canadian Library,
    XXV (September, 1968), 128-36.
_____, The Tolkien Relation; A Personal Inquiry, Chi-
    cago: Regnery, 1968.
Reilly, Robert J., "Romantic Religion in the Work of Owen
    Barfield, C. S. Lewis, Charles Williams, and J. R. R. Tol-
    kien," DA, XXI (1961), 3461-2 (Michigan State).
Ryan, J. S., "German Mythology Applied - The Extension of
    the Literary Folk Memory," Folklore (London), LXXVII
    (Spring, 1966), 45-59.
Stein, Ruth M., "The Changing Style in Dragons," Elem Eng,
    XLV (February, 1968), 181-3.
Stevens, Cj., "Sound Systems of the Third Age of Middle
    Earth," QJS, LIV (October, 1968), 232-40.
Stimpson, C. R., J. R. R. Tolkien.
Tolkien, J. R. R., "Tolkien on Tolkien," Diplomat, XVIII
    (October, 1966), 39. (Not seen.)
Trowbridge, Clinton, "The Twentieth Century British Super-
    natural Novel," DA, XVIII (1958), 1800 (Un. of Fla.).
Wojcik, Jan, S. J., "Tolkien and Coleridge: Remaking of the
    'Green Earth'," Ren, XX (Spring, 1968), 134-9, 146.
Wright, Marjorie E., "The Cosmic Kingdom of Myth: A
    Study in the Myth-Philosophy of Charles Williams, C. S.
    Lewis, and J. R. R. Tolkien," DA, XXI (1961), 3464-5
    (Illinois).

THE HOBBIT

Carter, L., Tolkien, 31-42.
Ready, William, The Tolkien Relation; A Personal Inquiry,
    Chicago: Regnery, 1968.
Stimpson, C. R., J. R. R. Tolkien, 30-3.

THE FELLOWSHIP OF THE RING
(See also THE LORD OF THE RINGS Trilogy)

Auden, W. H., "The Hero is a Hobbit," NYTBR (October 31,
    1954), 37.
_____, "A World Imaginary, but Real," Encounter, III
    (November, 1954), 59-62.
Carter, L., Tolkien, 43-54.
Hughes, Richard, "LORD OF THE RINGS," Spectator (Oc-
    tober 1, 1954), 408-9.
Lewis, C. S., "The Gods Return to Earth," T&T, XXXV
    (August 14, 1954), 1082-3.

Mitchison, Naomi, "One Ring to Bind Them," NStat, XLVIII (September 18, 1954), 331.

THE LORD OF THE RINGS Trilogy

Auden, W. H., "Good and Evil in THE LORD OF THE RINGS," CritQ, X (1968), 138-42. Also in TJ, III, i (Spring, 1967), 5-8.
_____, "The Quest Hero," TQ, IV (1962), 81-93. Also in Isaacs, N. D., and R. A. Zimbardo, eds., Tolkien and the Critics, 40-61.
Barber, Dorothy K., "The Meaning of THE LORD OF THE RINGS," Mankato State College Studies, II (February, 1967), 38-50.
_____, "The Structure of THE LORD OF THE RINGS," DA, XXVII (1966), 470A (Michigan).
Beagle, Peter S., "Tolkien's Magic Ring," Holiday, XXXIX (June, 1966), 128, 130, 133-4. Also as "Preface" to The Tolkien Reader, N. Y.: Ballantine, 1966, ix-xvi.
Beatie, Bruce A., "A Folk Tale, Fiction, and Saga in J. R. R. Tolkien's THE LORD OF THE RINGS," Mankato State College Studies, II (February, 1967), 1-17.
_____, "THE LORD OF THE RINGS: Myth, Reality, Relevance," WR, IV (Winter, 1967), 58-9.
Blackmun, Kathryn, "The Development of Runic and Fëanorian Alphabets for the Transliteration of English," Mankato State College Studies, II (February, 1967), 76-83.
_____, "Translations from the Elvish," Mankato State College Studies, II (February, 1967), 95-7.
Blissett, William, "The Despots of the Rings," SAQ, LVIII (Summer, 1959), 448-56.
Bradley, Marion Z., "Men, Halfling and Hero Worship," Niekas, #16 (June 30, 1966), 25-44. Also (abridged) in Isaacs, N. D., and R. A. Zimbardo, eds., Tolkien and the Critics, 109-27.
Carter, L., Tolkien.
Cox, C. B., "The World of the Hobbits," Spectator (December 30, 1966), 844.
Ellwood, Gracis F., Good News from Tolkien's Middle Earth, Grand Rapids: Eerdmans, 1969.
Evans, W. D. Emrys, "THE LORD OF THE RINGS," The School Librarian, XVI (December, 1968), 284-8.
Fifield, Merle, "Fantasy in the Sixties, EJ, LV (October, 1966), 841-4.
Fuller, Edmund, Books with Men Behind Them, 169-96. Also (revised) in Isaacs, N. D., and R. A. Zimbardo, eds., Tolkien and the Critics, 17-39.

Gasque, Thomas J., "Tolkien: The Monsters and the Critics," in Isaacs, N.D., and R.Z. Zimbardo, eds., Tolkien and the Critics, 151-63.

Halle, Louis J., "History Through the Mind's Eye," SatR, XXXIX (January 28, 1956), 11-12.

Hayes, Noreen, and Robert Renshaw, "Of Hobbits: THE LORD OF THE RINGS," Crit, IX, ii (1967), 58-66.

Hope, Francis, "Welcome to Middle Earth," NStat, LXXII (November 11, 1966), 701-2.

Hughes, Daniel, "Pieties and Giant Forms in THE LORD OF THE RINGS," in Hillegas, M.R., ed., Shadows of Imagination, 81-96.

Isaacs, Neil D., "On the Possibilities of Writing Tolkien Criticism," in Isaacs, N.D., and R.A. Zimbardo, eds., Tolkien and the Critics, 1-11.

_____, and R.A. Zimbardo, eds., Tolkien and the Critics.

Johnston, George B., "The Poetry of J.R.R. Tolkien," Mankato State College Studies, II (February, 1967), 63-75.

Keenan, Hugh T., "The Appeal of THE LORD OF THE RINGS," in Isaacs, N.D., and R.A. Zimbardo, eds., Tolkien and the Critics, 62-80.

Kelly, Mary Q., "The Poetry of Fantasy: Verse in THE LORD OF THE RINGS," in Isaacs, N.D., and R.A. Zimbardo, eds., Tolkien and the Critics, 170-200.

Kiley, Clyde S., "Meaning in THE LORD OF THE RINGS," in Hillegas, M.R., ed., Shadows of Imagination, 70-80.

Levitin, Alexis, "The Hero in J.R.R. Tolkien's THE LORD OF THE RINGS," Mankato State College Studies, II (February, 1967), 25-37.

Lewis, C.S., "The Dethronement of Power," T&T, XLIII (October, 1955), 1373-4. Also in Isaacs, N.D., and R.A. Zimbardo, eds., Tolkien and the Critics, 12-16.

Lobdell, James C., "Words That Sound Like Castles," NatR, XIX (September 5, 1967), 972-4.

Matthewson, Joseph, "The Hobbit Habit," Esquire, LXVI (September, 1966), 130-31, 221-2.

Miesel, Sandra L., "Some Motifs and Sources for LORD OF THE RINGS," RQ, III (March, 1968), 125-8.

_____, "Some Religious Aspects of LORD OF THE RINGS," RQ, III (August, 1968), 209-13.

Miller, David M., "The Moral Universe of J.R. Tolkien," Mankato State College Studies, II (February, 1967), 51-62.

Moorman, Charles, " 'Now Entertain Conjecture of a Time' - The Fictive Worlds of C.S. Lewis and J.R.R. Tolkien,"

in Hillegas, M. R. , ed. , Shadows of Imagination, 59-69.
_____, Precincts of Felicity, Gainesville: Un. of Fla.
Pr. , 1966, 86-100. Also in Isaacs, N.D. , and R. A.
Zimbardo, eds. , Tolkien and the Critics, 201-17.
Norwood, W. D. , "Tolkien's Intention in THE LORD OF THE
RINGS," Mankato State College Studies, II (February,
1967), 18-24.
Parker, Douglass, "Hwaet We Holbytla...," HudR, IX
(Winter, 1956-57), 598-609.
Raffel, Burton, "THE LORD OF THE RINGS as Literature,"
in Isaacs, N. D. , and R. A. Zimbardo, eds. , Tolkien and
the Critics, 218-46.
Rang, Jack C. , "Two Servants," Mankato State College Stud-
ies, II (February, 1967), 84-94.
Ratliff, William E. , and Charles G. Flinn, "The Hobbit and
the Hippie," ModA, XII (Spring, 1968), 142-6.
Ready, William, The Tolkien Relation; A Personal Inquiry,
Chicago: Regnery, 1968.
Reilly, R. J. , "Tolkien and the Fairy Story," Thought,
XXXVIII (Spring, 1963), 89-103.
Reinken, Donald L. , "J. R. R. Tolkien's THE LORD OF THE
RINGS: A Christian Refounding of the Political Order,"
ChrPer, (Winter, 1966), 16-23.
Roberts, Mark, "Adventures in English," EIC, VI (October,
1956), 450-9.
Russell, Mariann B. , "The Idea of the City of God," DA,
XXVI (1965), 3350-1 (Columbia).
Sale, Roger, "England's Parnassus: C. S. Lewis, Charles
Williams, and J. R. R. Tolkien," HudR, XVII (1964), 215-
25. Also (revised) as "Tolkien and Frodo Baggins," in
Isaacs, N. D. , and R. A. Zimbardo, eds. , Tolkien and the
Critics, 247-88.
Sklar, Robert, "Tolkien and Hesse: Top of the Pops," Na-
tion, CCIV (May, 1967), 598-601.
Spacks, Patricia M., " 'Ethical Patterns' in THE LORD OF
THE RINGS," Crit, III (Spring-Fall, 1959), 30-42. Also
(revised) in Isaacs, N. D. , and Zimbardo, eds. , Tolkien
and the Critics, 81-99.
Stewart, Douglas J. , "The Hobbit War," Nation, CCV, (Oc-
tober 9, 1967), 332-5.
Stimpson, C. R. , J. R. R. Tolkien, 33-41.
Straight, Michael, "Fantastic World of Professor Tolkien,"
NRep, CXXXIV (January 16, 1956), 24-6.
Taylor, William R. , "Frodo Lives: J. R. Tolkien's THE
LORD OF THE RINGS," EJ, LVI (September, 1967), 818-
21.
Thomson, George H. , "THE LORD OF THE RINGS: The

Novel as Traditional Romance," WSCL, VIII (Winter, 1967), 43-59.
Tinkler, John, "Old English in Rohan," in Isaacs, N. D., and R. A. Zimbardo, eds., Tolkien and the Critics, 164-9.
Torrens, James, "With Tolkien in Middle-Earth," Good Work, XXXI, iv (Winter, 1968), 17-23.
Urang, Gunnar, "Tolkien's Fantasy: The Phenomenology of Hope," in Hillegas, M. R., ed., Shadows of Imagination, 97-110.
Woods, Samuel H., Jr., "J. R. R. Tolkien and the Hobbits," CimR, I (September, 1967), 44-52.
Wilson, C., Strength to Dream, 145-8.
Wilson, Edmund, "Oo Those Awful Orcs!" Nation, CLXXXII (April 14, 1956), 312-14. Also in Wilson, E., The Bit Between My Teeth, N. Y.: Farrar, Straus & Giroux, 1965, 332-6.
Zimbardo, Rose A., "Moral Vision in THE LORD OF THE RINGS," in Isaacs, N. D., and R. A. Zimbardo, eds., Tolkien and the Critics, 100-8.

THE RETURN OF THE KING
(See also THE LORD OF THE RINGS Trilogy)

Auden, W. H., "At the End of the Quest, Victory," NYTBR (January 22, 1956), 5.
Carter, L., Tolkien, 65-78.
Huxley, Francis, "The Endless Worm," NStat, L (November 5, 1955), 587-8.
Traversi, Derek A., "The Realm of Gondor," Month, XV (June, 1956), 370-1.

THE TWO TOWERS
(See also THE LORD OF THE RINGS Trilogy)

Carter, L., Tolkien, 55-64.

BIBLIOGRAPHY

Carter, L., Tolkien, 203-4.
West, Richard C., "An Annotated Bibliography of Tolkien Criticism," Extrapolation, X (1968), 17-45.

TRACY, HONOR, 1915-

GENERAL

Gindin, J. , Postwar British Fiction, 165-77.

TRILLING, LIONEL, 1905-

GENERAL

Frohock, W. M. , "Lionel Trilling and the American Reality,"
SWR, XLV (Summer, 1960), 224-32.

THE MIDDLE OF THE JOURNEY

Allen, W. , Modern Novel, 178-9.
Blotner, J. , Modern American Political Novel, 315-20.
Boyers, Robert, "THE MIDDLE OF THE JOURNEY and Be-
yond: Observations on Modernity and Commitment," Sal-
magundi, I, iv (1967), 8-18.
Eisinger, Charles E. , Fiction of the Forties, 135-44.
_____, "Trilling and the Crises in Our Culture," UKCR,
XXV (October, 1958), 27-35.
Fergusson, Francis "Three Novels," Perspectives USA, No.
6 (Winter, 1954), 30-44.
Freedman, William, "THE MIDDLE OF THE JOURNEY:
Lionel Trilling and the Novel of Ideas," in French, W. ,
ed. , Forties, 239-48.
Frohock, W. M. , "Lionel Trilling and the American Reality,"
SWR, XLV (Summer, 1960), 225-9.
Joost, Nicholas, in Gardiner, H. C. , ed. , Fifty Years of the
American Novel, 288-9.
Kubal, David L. , "Trilling's THE MIDDLE OF THE JOUR-
NEY: An American Dialectic," BuR, XIV (March, 1966),
60-73.
McCormick, J. , Catastrophe and Imagination, 79-84.
Milne, G. , American Political Novel, 139-49.
Montgomery, Marion, "Lionel Trilling's THE MIDDLE OF
THE JOURNEY," Discourse, IV (Autumn, 1961), 263-72.
Zabel, Morton D. , "The Straight Way Lost," Nation, CLXV
(October 18, 1947), 413-16. Also in Zabel, M. D. , Craft and
Character, 312-17.

UPDIKE, JOHN, 1932-

GENERAL

Aldridge, J. W. , "The Private Vice of John Updike," Time
to Murder and Create, 164-70.

Burgess, Anthony, "Language, Myth and Mr. Updike,"
Cweal, LXXXIII (February 11, 1966), 557-8.

Doyle, Paul A. , "Updike's Fiction: Motifs and Techniques,"
CathW, CXCIX (September, 1964), 356-62.

Enright, D. J. , "Updike's Ups and Downs," Holiday, XXXVIII
(November, 1965), 162-6. Also as "The Inadequate American: John Updike's Fiction," in Enright, D. J. , Conspirators and Poets, 134-40.

Fisher, Richard E. , "John Updike: Theme and Form in the
Garden of Epiphanies," MSpr, LVI (Fall, 1962), 255-60.

Galloway, David D. , "The Absurd Man as Saint: The Novels
of John Updike," MFS, XI (Summer, 1964), 111-27. Also in Galloway, D. D. , Absurd Hero, 21-50.

Hainsworth, J. D. , "John Updike," HJ, LXV (Spring, 1967),
115-16.

Hamilton, K. , and A. John Updike.

Hamilton, Kenneth, "John Updike: Chronicler of the Time
of the 'Death of God'," ChC, XXXIV (June 7, 1967), 745-
8.

Harper, H. M. , Jr. , "John Updike: The Intrinsic Problem
of Human Goodness," Desperate Faith, 162-90.

Hicks, Granville, in Balakian, N. , and C. Simmons, eds. ,
Creative Present, 232-7.

La Course, Guerin, "The Innocence of John Updike," Cweal,
LXXVII (February 8, 1963), 512-14.

Muradian, Thaddeus, "The World of Updike," EJ, LIV (October, 1965), 577-84.

Murphy, Richard W. , "John Updike," Horizon, IV (March,
1962), 84-5.

Rupp, Richard H. , "John Updike: Style in Search of a Center," SR, LXXV (Autumn, 1967), 693-709.

Samuels, Charles T. , "The Art of Fiction XLII: John Updike," ParisR, No. 45 (Winter, 1968), 84-117.

_____, John Updike.

Ward, J. A. , "John Updike's Fiction," Crit, V, i (Spring-
Summer, 1962), 27-40.

Wyatt, Bryant N. , "John Updike: The Psychological Novel
in Search Structure," TCL, XIII (July, 1967), 89-96.

Yates, Norris W. , "The Doubt and Faith of John Updike,"
CE, XXVI (March, 1965), 469-74.

THE CENTAUR

Adler, Renata, "Arcadia, Pa.," NY, XXXIX (April 13, 1963), 182-8.

Alley, Alvin D., "THE CENTAUR: Transcendental Imagination and Metamorphic Death," EJ, LVI (October, 1967), 982-5.

Anon., in TLS (September 27, 1963), 728. Also in T.L.S.: Essays and Reviews from The Times Literary Supplement, 1963, 103-5.

Bell, Vivian, "A Study in Frustration," Shen, XIV (Summer, 1963), 69-72.

Curley, Thomas, "Between Heaven and Earth," Cweal, LXXVIII (March 29, 1963), 26-7.

Davenport, Guy, "Novels Without Masks," NatR, XIV (April 9, 1963), 287-8.

Enright, D.D., "Updike's Ups and Downs," Holiday, XXXVIII (November, 1965), 162-4. Also as "The Inadequate American: John Updike's Fiction," in Enright, D.J., Conspirators and Poets, 135-7.

Finkelstein, S., Existentialism and Alienation in American Literature, 246-7.

Galloway, David D., "The Absurd Man as Saint: The Novels of John Updike," MFS, XI (Summer, 1964), 121-7. Also in Galloway, D.D., Absurd Hero, 40-50.

_____, "Clown and Saint: The Hero in Current American Fiction," Crit, VII (Spring-Summer, 1965), 60-1.

Gardiner, Harold C., in America, CVIII (March 9, 1963), 340-1.

Gilman, Richard, "The Youth of an Author," NRep, CXLVIII (April 13, 1963), 25-7. Also in Gilman, R., Confusion of Realms, 62-8.

Guyol, Hazel S., "The Lord Loves a Cheerful Corpse," EJ, LV (October, 1966), 863-6.

Hamilton, K., and A., John Updike, 36-9.

Harper, H.M., Jr., Desperate Faith, 173-82.

Hyman, Stanley E., "Chiron at Olinger High," New Leader, XLVI (February 4, 1963), 20-1. Also in Hyman, S.E., Standards, 128-32.

Kuehn, Robert, in WSCL, V (Winter-Spring, 1964), 77-8.

Levidova, Inna, "John Updike's THE CENTAUR in Russian," Soviet Lit, No. 10 (1965), 188-94.

Malin, Irving, "Occasions for Loving," KR, XXV (Spring, 1963), 348-52.

Miller, Jonathan, "Off-Centaur," NYRB, I, i (1963), 28.

Mizener, A., "The American Hero as High School Boy: Peter Caldwell," Sense of Life in the Modern Novel, 247-66.

O'Connor, W. V. , in Moore, H. T. , ed. , Contemporary
American Novelists, 212-14.
Podhoretz, Norman, "A Dissent on Updike," Show, III (April,
1963), 49-52. Also in Podhoretz, N. , Doings and Undo-
ings, 251-7.
Rupp, Richard H. , "John Updike: Style in Search of a Cen-
ter," SR, LXXV (Autumn, 1967), 703-6.
Samuels, C. T. , John Updike, 15-19.
Tate, Sister Judith M. , "John Updike: Of Rabbits and Cen-
taurs," Critic, XXII (February-March, 1964), 44-51.
Taubman, Robert, "God is Delicate," NStat, LXVI (Septem-
ber 27, 1963), 406.
Walcutt, C. C. , Man's Changing Mask, 326-30.
Ward, J. A. , "John Updike: THE CENTAUR," Crit, VI, ii
(Fall, 1963), 109-14.
Yates, Norris W. , "The Doubt and Faith of John Updike,"
CE, XXVI (March, 1965), 473-4.

COUPLES

Anon. , "Community Feeling," TLS (November 7, 1968), 1245.
Also in T. L. S. : Essays and Reviews from The Times
Literary Supplement, 1968, 180-3.
_____ , "View From the Catacombs," Time, XCI (April
26, 1968), 66-8, 73-5.
Flint, Joyce, "John Updike and COUPLES: The Wasps Di-
lemma," RS, XXXVI (December, 1968), 340-7.
Gordon, David J. , "Some Recent Novelists: Styles of Mar-
tyrdom," YR, LVIII (Autumn, 1968), 117-19.
Hyman, Stanley E. , "Couplings," New Leader, LI (May 20,
1968), 20-1.
Samuels, C. T. , John Updike, 34-7.
Tanner, Tony, "Hello, Olleh," Spectator, No. 7324 (Novem-
ber 8, 1968), 658-9.
Thompson, John, "Updike's COUPLES," Ctary, XLV (May,
1968), 70-3.

OF THE FARM

Aldridge, J. W. , "The Private Vice of John Updike," Time
To Murder and Create, 164-70.
Enright, D. J. , "Updike's Ups and Downs," Holiday, XXXVIII
(November, 1965), 165-6. Also as "The Inadequate Amer-
ican: John Updike's Fiction," in Enright, D. J. , Conspira-
tors and Poets, 138-40.
Hamilton, K. , and A. , John Updike, 43-6.
Harper, H. M. , Jr. , Desperate Faith, 182-6.

Rupp, Richard H., "John Updike: Style in Search of a Center," SR, LXXV (Autumn, 1967), 706-9.
Samuels, C.T., John Updike, 22-7.

THE POORHOUSE FAIR

Balliett, Whitney, "Writer's Writer," NY, XXXIV (February
7, 1959), 138-42.
Buchanan, Leigh, in Epoch, IX (Spring, 1959), 252-4.
Doyle, Paul A., "Updike's Fiction: Motifs and Techniques,"
CathW, CXCIX (September, 1964), 356-8.
Fitelson, David, "Conflict Unresolved," Ctary, XXVII (March,
1959), 275-6.
Galloway, David D., "The Absurd Man as Saint: The Nov-
els of John Updike," MFS, X (Summer, 1964), 111-14.
Also in Galloway, D.D., Absurd Hero, 21-7.
Gilman, Richard, in Cweal, LXIX (February 6, 1959), 499-
500.
Hamilton, K., and A., John Updike, 13-22.
Harper, H.M., Jr., Desperate Faith, 163-5.
Klausler, Alfred P., "Steel Wilderness," ChC, LXXVIII
(February 22, 1961), 245-7.
O'Connor, W.V., in Moore, H.T., ed., Contemporary Amer-
ican Novelists, 207-8.
Samuels, C.T., John Updike, 21-4.
Ward, J.A., "John Updike's Fiction," Crit, V, i (Spring-
Summer, 1962), 30-3.
Yates, Norris W., "The Doubt and Faith of John Updike,"
CE, XXVI (March, 1965), 470-1.

RABBIT, RUN

Alley, Alvin D., and Hugh Agee, "Existential Heroes:
Frank Alpine and Rabbit Angstrom," BSUF, IX (1968),
3-5.
Balliett, Whitney, "Books: The American Expression," NY,
XXXVI (November 5, 1960), 222-4.
Brenner, Gerry, "RABBIT, RUN: John Updike's Criticism
of the 'Return to Nature'," TCL, XII (April, 1966), 3-14.
Detweiler, R., Four Spiritual Crises in Mid-Century Amer-
ican Fiction, 14-24.
Doner, Dean, "Rabbit Angstrom's World," New World Writ-
ing, No. 20, Phila., and N.Y.: Lippincott, 1962, 58-75.
Doyle, Paul A., "Updike's Fiction: Motifs and Techniques,"
CathW, CXIX (September, 1964), 358-9.
Duncan, Graham H., "The Thing Itself in RABBIT, RUN,"
EngR, XIII (April, 1963), 25-8, 36-7.

Falke, Wayne C. , "The Novel of Disentanglement: A The-
matic Study of Lewis's BABBITT, Bromfield's MR. SMITH
and Updike's RABBIT, RUN," DA, XXVIII (1967), 194A
(Mich.).
Finkelstein, S. , Existentialism and Alienation in American
Literature, 244-6.
Galloway, David D. , "The Absurd Man as Saint: The Novels
of John Updike," MFS, X (Summer, 1964), 114-21. Also
in Galloway, D. D. , Absurd Hero, 27-40.
_____, "Clown and Saint: The Hero in Current American
Fiction," Crit, VII (Spring-Summer, 1965), 59-60.
Gilman, Richard, "A Distinguished Image of Precarious
Life," Cweal, LXXIII (October 28, 1960), 128-9.
Hamilton, K. , and A. , John Updike, 31-6.
Harper, H. M. , Jr. , Desperate Faith, 165-73.
Killinger, John, "The Death of God in American Literature,"
SHR, II (Spring, 1968), 167-8.
Klausler, Alfred P. , "Steel Wilderness," ChC, LXXVIII
(February 22, 1961), 245-7.
Lyons, R. , "A High E. Q. ," MinnR, I (Spring, 1961), 385-9.
Miller, Nolan, "Three of the 'Best'," AR, XXI (Spring,
1961), 120-3.
O'Connor, W. V. , in Moore, H. T. , ed. , Contemporary
American Novelists, 209-12.
Rupp, Richard H. , "John Updike: Style in Search of a Cen-
ter," SR, LXXV (Autumn, 1967), 699-703.
Samuels, C. T. , John Updike, 37-43.
Sinclair, Andrew, "See How He Runs," T&T, XLII (Septem-
ber 21, 1961), 1571.
Standley, Fred L. , "RABBIT, RUN: An Image of Life,"
MQ, VIII (July, 1967), 371-86.
Stubbs, John C. , "The Search for Perfection in RABBIT,
RUN," Crit, X, ii (1968), 94-101.
Tate, Sister Judith M. , "John Updike: Of Rabbits and Cen-
taurs," Critic, XXII (February-March, 1964), 44-51.
Thompson, John, "Other People's Affairs," PR, XXVII (Jan-
uary-February, 1961), 120-2.
Walcutt, C. C. , Man's Changing Mask, 330-2.
Ward, J. A. , "John Updike's Fiction," Crit, V, i (Spring-
Summer, 1962), 33-7.
Yates, Norris W. , "The Doubt and Faith of John Updike,"
CE, XXVI (March, 1965), 471-3.

BIBLIOGRAPHY

Galloway, D. D. , Absurd Hero, 198-200.
Hamilton, K. , and A. , John Updike, 47-8.

Samuels, C. T. , John Updike, 44-6.
Taylor, C. Clarke, John Updike: A Bibliography, Kent,
Ohio: Kent State Un. Pr. , 1968.

VIDAL, GORE, 1925-

Aldridge, J. W. , After the Lost Generation, 170-83.
Walter, Eugene, "Conversations With Gore Vidal," Trans-
atlantic Rev, No. 4 (Summer, 1960), 5-17.
White, R. L. , Gore Vidal.

THE CITY AND THE PILLAR

Aldridge, J. W. , After the Lost Generation, 175-8.
Hoffman, Stanton, "The Cities of Night: John Rechy's CITY
OF NIGHT and the American Literature of Homosexuality,"
ChiR, XVII, ii-iii (1964-65), 197-8.
McLaughlin, Richard, "Precarious Status," SatR, XXXI (Jan-
uary 10, 1948), 14-15.
Shrike, J. S. , "Recent Phenomena," HudR, I (Spring, 1948),
136-44.
White, R. L. , Gore Vidal, 49-57.

DARK GREEN, BRIGHT RED

Barr, Donald, "From Patio to Jungle," NYTBR (October 8,
1950), 4, 28.
White, R. L. , Gore Vidal, 71-7.

IN A YELLOW WOOD

Aldridge, J. W. , After the Lost Generation, 173-6.
White, R. L. , Gore Vidal, 44-9.

THE JUDGMENT OF PARIS

Aldridge, John W. , "Three Tempted Him," NYTBR (March
9, 1952), 4, 29.
White, R. L. , Gore Vidal, 84-9.

JULIAN

Allen, Walter, "The Last Pagan," NYRB, III (July 30, 1964),
20-1.
Auchincloss, Louis, "The Best Man, Vintage 361 A. D. ,"
Life, LVIII (June 12, 1964), 19, 21.

Leone Arthur T., in CathW, CXCIX (September, 1964), 381-
4.
White, R. L., Gore Vidal, 111-19.

MESSIAH

White, R. L., Gore Vidal, 89-94.

A SEARCH FOR THE KING

Aldridge, J. W., After the Lost Generation, 181-3.
White, R. L., Gore Vidal, 64-71.

THE SEASON OF COMFORT

Aldridge, James W., After the Lost Generation, 178-81.
_____, "A Boy and His Mom," SatR, XXXII (January 15,
1949), 19-20.
White, R. L., Gore Vidal, 58-64.

WASHINGTON, D. C.

Lehan, Richard, "Fiction, 1967," Contemporary Literature,
IX, iv (Autumn, 1968), 543-4.
Sheed, Wilfred, "Affairs of State," Ctary, XLIV (September,
1967), 93-4.
White, R. L., Gore Vidal, 119-24.

WILLIWAW

Aldridge, J. W., After the Lost Generation, 170-3.
White, R. L., Gore Vidal, 38-44.

BIBLIOGRAPHY

White, R. L., Gore Vidal, 147-52.

VONNEGUT, KURT, 1922-

GENERAL

Bryan, C. D. B., "Kurt Vonnegut on Target," NRep, CLV
(October 8, 1966), 21-6.
Scholes, Robert, " 'Mithridates, he died old': Black Humor
and Kurt Vonnegut, Jr.," HC, III, iv (October, 1966),
1-12.

CAT'S CRADLE

Brien, Alan, "Afterthought," Spectator, CCII (August, 1963), 158-9.
Schickel, Richard, "Black Comedy With Purifying Laughter," Harpers, CCXXXII (May, 1966), 103-4.
Scholes, Robert, Fabulators, 47-55.
_____, " ' Mithridates, he died old': Black Humor and Kurt Vonnegut, Jr.," HC, III, iv (October, 1966), 8-9.

GOD BLESS YOU, MR. ROSEWATER

Bryan, C. D. B., "Kurt Vonnegut on Target," NRep, CLV (October 8, 1966), 24-5.

MOTHER NIGHT

Bryan, C. D. B., "Kurt Vonnegut on Target," NRep, CLV (October 8, 1966), 21-2.
Scholes, Robert, Fabulators, 47-55.
_____, " 'Mithridates, he died old': Black Humor and Kurt Vonnegut, Jr.," HC, III, iv (October, 1966), 9-11.
Smith, William J., in Cweal, LXXXIV (September 16, 1966), 592-4.
Weales, Gerald D., "Whatever Happened to Tugboat Annie?" Reporter, XXXV (December 1, 1966), 50, 52-6.

PLAYER PIANO

Hillegas, Mark R., "Dystopian Science Fiction: New Index to the Human Situation," NMQ, XXXI (Autumn, 1961), 245-7.
Schickel, Richard, "Black Comedy With Purifying Laughter," Harpers, CCXXXII (May, 1966), 103-4.
Walsh, Chad, From Utopia to Nightmare, N.Y.: Harper & Row, 1962, 85-8.

WAGONER, DAVID, 1926-

GENERAL

Schafer, William J., "David Wagoner's Fiction: In the Mills of Satan," Crit, IX, i (1967), 71-89.

THE ESCAPE ARTIST

Schafer, William J., "David Wagoner's Fiction: In the Mills of Satan," Crit, IX, i (1967), 85-9.

THE MAN IN THE MIDDLE

Schafer, William J., "David Wagoner's Fiction: In the Mills of Satan," Crit, IX, i (1967), 72-6.

MONEY MONEY MONEY

Schafer, William J., "David Wagoner's Fiction: In the Mills of Satan," Crit, IX, i (1967), 76-80.

ROCK

Schafer, William J., "David Wagoner's Fiction: In the Mills of Satan," Crit, IX, i (1967), 80-3.

WAIN, JOHN, 1925-

GENERAL

Allsop, K., Angry Decade, 58-68.
Bluestone, George, "John Wain and John Barth: The Angry and the Accurate," MR, I (May, 1960), 582-9.
Cox, C. B., Free Spirit, 155-61.
Gindin, J., "The Moral Center of John Wain's Fiction," Postwar British Fiction, 128-44.
Heppenstall, R., Fourfold Tradition, 213-224.
Kermode, Frank, "The House of Fiction: Interviews With Seven English Novelists," PR, XXX (Spring, 1963), 77-9.
Lehmann, J., "The Wain-Larkin Myth," SR, LXVI (Autumn, 1958), 578-87.
O'Connor, William Van, "John Wain: The Will to Write," WSCL, I, i (Winter, 1960), 35-49.
Walzer, Michael, "John Wain: The Hero in Limbo," Per, X (Summer-Autumn, 1958), 137-45.

BORN IN CAPTIVITY (See HURRY ON DOWN)

THE CONTENDERS

Gindin, J., "The Moral Center of John Wain's Fiction," Postwar British Fiction, 133-4+.

O'Connor, William Van, "John Wain: The Will to Write,"
  WSCL, I, i (Winter, 1960), 46-7.
_____, New University Wits, 48-50.
Rippier, J. S., Some Postwar English Novelists, 165-8.
Walzer, Michael, "John Wain: The Hero in Limbo," Per,
  X (Summer-Autumn, 1958), 143-5.

HURRY ON DOWN
(American title: BORN IN CAPTIVITY)

Cox, C. B., Free Spirit, 158-9.
Gindin, J., "The Moral Center of John Wain's Fiction,"
  Postwar British Fiction, 128-31+.
Karl, F. R., "The Angries: Is There a Protestant in the
  House?" Contemporary English Novel, 224-6.
O'Connor, William Van, "John Wain: The Will to Write,"
  WSCL, I, i (Winter, 1960), 42-4.
_____, New University Wits, 42-6.
Rippier, J. S., Some Postwar English Novelists, 159-65.
Walzer, Michael, "John Wain: The Hero in Limbo," Per,
  X (Summer-Autumn, 1958), 139-41.

LIVING IN THE PRESENT

Gindin, J., "The Moral Center of John Wain's Fiction,"
  Postwar British Fiction, 131-3+.
O'Connor, William Van, "John Wain: The Will to Write,"
  WSCL, I, i (Winter, 1960), 44-6.
_____, New University Wits, 46-8.
Walzer, Michael, "John Wain: The Hero in Limbo," Per,
  X (Summer-Autumn, 1958), 141-3.

STRIKE THE FATHER DEAD

McDowell, Frederick P. W., " 'The Devious Involutions of
  Human Character and Emotions': Reflections on Some Recent British Novels," WSCL, IV, iii (Autumn, 1963), 342-
  4.
Rippier, J. S., Some Postwar English Novelists, 170-3.

A TRAVELLING WOMAN

Gindin, J., "The Moral Center of John Wain's Fiction,"
  Postwar British Fiction, 134-6+.
O'Connor, William Van, "John Wain: The Will to Write,"
  WSCL, I, i (Winter, 1960), 47-8.
_____, New University Wits, 50-2.

Rippier, J.S., Some Postwar English Novelists, 168-70.
Ross, T.J., "A Good Girl is Hard to Find," NRep, CXLI
    (September 21, 1959), 17-19.
Urwin, G.G., ed., Taste for Living, 134-7.

WALLANT, EDWARD LEWIS, 1926-1962

GENERAL

Davis, William V., "Sleep Like the Living: A Study of the
    Novels of Edward Lewis Wallant," DA, XXVIII (1968),
    3177A (Ohio U).
    _____, "A Synthesis in the Contemporary Jewish Novel:
Edward Lewis Wallant," Cresset, XXXI, vii (1968), 8-13,
    45.
Lorch, Thomas M., "The Novels of Edward Lewis Wallant,"
    ChiR, XIX, ii (1967), 78-91.
Ribalow, Harold U., "The Legacy of Edward L. Wallant,"
    CJF, XXII (Summer, 1964), 325-7.
Rovit, Earl, "A Miracle of Moral Animation," Shen, XVI
    (Summer, 1965), 59-62.
Schulz, Max F., "Wallant and Friedman: The Glory and
    Agony of Love," Crit, X, iii (1968), 31-47. Also in
    Schulz, M.F., Radical Sophistication, 173-85.

THE CHILDREN AT THE GATE

Davis, William V., "The Sound of Silence: Edward Lewis
    Wallant's CHILDREN AT THE GATE," Cithara, VIII
    (November, 1968), 3-25.
Galloway, David D., "Clown and Saint: The Hero in Current
    American Fiction," Crit, VII, iii (1965), 58-9.
Lorch, Thomas M., "The Novels of Edward Lewis Wallant,"
    ChiR, XIX, ii (1967), 84-7.
Rovit, Earl, "A Miracle of Moral Animation," Shen, XVI
    (Summer, 1965), 61-2.
Rubin, Louis D., Jr., "Southerners and Jews," SoR, II
    (1966), 703-5. Also in Rubin, L.D., Jr., Curious Death
    of the Novel, 269-71.

THE HUMAN SEASON

Lorch, Thomas M., "The Novels of Edward Lewis Wallant,"
    ChiR, XIX, ii (1967), 79-80.

THE PAWNBROKER

Baumbach, J., "The Illusion of Indifference: THE PAWN-
BROKER," Landscape of Nightmare, 138-46.
Casey, Bill, "Commitment, Compassion, and Cant: The
Quality Fiction Formula," ForumH, IV (Spring-Summer,
1964), 28-30.
Lorch, Thomas M., "The Novels of Edward Lewis Wallant,"
ChiR, XIX, ii (1967), 80-4.
Lyons, Joseph, "THE PAWNBROKER: Flashback in the
Novel and Film," WHR, XX (Summer, 1966), 243-8.
Petrie, Graham, "A Note on the Novel and the Film: Flash-
backs in TRISTAM SHANDY and THE PAWNBROKER,"
WHR, XXI (Spring, 1967), 165-9.

THE TENANTS OF MOONBLOOM

Baumbach, J., Landscape of Nightmare, 146-51.
Galloway, David D., "Clown and Saint: The Hero in Cur-
rent American Fiction," Crit, VII, iii (1965), 54-8.
Lorch, Thomas M., "The Novels of Edward Lewis Wallant,"
ChiR, XIX, ii (1967), 87-90.

WARNER, REX, 1905-

GENERAL

Allen, W., Modern Novel, 240-1.
Atkins, John, "On Rex Warner," in Rajan, B., and A.
Pearse, eds., Focus One, 59-65. Also in McLeod, A.
L., ed., Achievement of Rex Warner, 23-7.
Curry, Elizabeth, "Theme and Method in the Allegorical
Novels of Rex Warner," DA, XXIII (1963), 3370-1 (Wisc.).
DeVitis, Angelo A., "Religious Theme in the Novels of Rex
Warner, Evelyn Waugh, and Graham Greene," SDD-UW,
XV (1955), 605-6.
_____, "Rex Warner and the Cult of Power," TCL, VI,
iii (October, 1960), 107-16.
_____, "Rex Warner and the Cult of Power," in McLeod,
A. L., ed., Achievement of Rex Warner, 50-4.
Drenner, Don V., "Kafka, Warner and the Cult of Power,"
KM (1952), 62-4.
Harrison, Tom, "Rex Warner's Writing," in Rajan, B., and
A. Pearse, eds., Focus One, 39-42.
Maini, Darshan S., "Rex Warner's Political Novels: An Al-
legorical Crusade Against Fascism," Indian Jnl. of Eng-

lish Studies (Calcutta), II (1961), 91-107.   Also in Mc-
Leod, A. L. , ed. , Achievement of Rex Warner, 39-49.
McLeod, A. L. , ed. , Achievement of Rex Warner.
_____, Rex Warner: Writer.
Pritchett, V. S. , "Rex Warner," in Baker, D. V. , ed. , Mod-
ern British Writing, 304-9.   Also in McLeod, A. L. , ed. ,
Achievement of Rex Warner, 35-8.
Rajan, B. , and A. Pearse, eds. , Focus One.
Stonier, G. W. , "The New Allegory," in Rajan, B. , and A.
Pearse, eds. , Focus One, 26-9.
Woodcock, George, "Kafka and Rex Warner," Writer and
Politics, 197-207.   Also in Rajan, B. , and A. Pearse,
eds. , Focus One, 59-65.   Also in McLeod, A. L. , ed. ,
Achievement of Rex Warner, 28-34.

THE AERODROME

Atkins, John, "On Rex Warner," in Rajan, B. , and A.
Pearse, eds. , Focus One, 33-7.   Also in McLeod, A. L. ,
ed. , Achievement of Rex Warner, 32-7.
Churchill, Thomas, "Rex Warner: Homage to Necessity,"
Crit, X, i (1968), 31-40.
Curry, Elizabeth, "Rex Warner and Modern Tragedy: A
Study in Conflict and Conformity," in McLeod, A. L. , ed. ,
Achievement of Rex Warner, 55-68.
Davenport, John, "Re-assessment: The Air Marshall's
Story," Spectator (June 24, 1966), 796.
Fraser, G. S. , Modern Writer and His World, 139-41.
Karl, F. R. , Contemporary English Novel, 265-9.
McLeod, A. L. , Rex Warner: Writer, 22-6.
Pritchett, V. S. , in Baker, D. V. , ed. , Modern British Writ-
ing, 307-8.   Also in McLeod, A. L. , ed. , Achievement
of Rex Warner, 37-8.
Rajan, B. , "Kafka - A Comparison With Rex Warner," in
Rajan, B. , and A. Pearse, eds. , Focus One, 7-14.   Al-
so in McLeod, A. L. , ed. , Achievement of Rex Warner,
16-23.
Stonier, G. W. , "The New Allegory," in Rajan, B. , and A.
Pearse, eds. , Focus One, 26-9.
Woodcock, George, "Kafka and Rex Warner," Writer and
Politics, 202-6.   Also in Rajan, B. , and A. Pearse,
eds. , Focus One, 59-65.   Also in McLeod, A. L. , ed. ,
Achievement of Rex Warner, 28-34.

ESCAPADE: A TALE OF AVERAGE

McLeod, A. L. , Rex Warner: Writer, 32-3.

MEN OF STONES: A MELODRAMA

DeVitis, A. A., "Rex Warner and the Cult of Power," TCL,
VI (October, 1960), 112-16.
McLeod, A. L., Rex Warner: Writer, 30-2.

THE PROFESSOR

Curry, Elizabeth, "Rex Warner and Modern Tragedy: A
Study in Conflict and Conformity," in McLeod, A. L., ed.,
Achievement of Rex Warner, 55-68.
McLeod, A. L., Rex Warner: Writer, 18-22.

RETURN OF THE TRAVELLER
(English title: WHY WAS I KILLED?:
A DRAMATIC DIALOGUE)

McLeod, A. L., Rex Warner: Writer, 26-30.
Nandakumar, Prema, "Rex Warner's WHY WAS I KILLED?"
in McLeod, A. L., ed., Achievement of Rex Warner, 69-
73.

THE WILD GOOSE CHASE

Atkins, John, "On Rex Warner," in Rajan, B., and A.
Pearse, eds., Focus One, 33-7. Also in McLeod, A. L.,
ed., Achievement of Rex Warner, 23-7.
Churchill, Thomas, "Rex Warner: Homage to Necessity,"
Crit, X, i (1968), 40-4.
DeVitis, A. A., "Rex Warner and the Cult of Power," TCL,
VI (October, 1960), 108-9.
Harris, Henry, "The Symbol of the Frontier in the Social Al-
legory of the 'Thirties'," ZAA, XIV (1966), 127-40.
McLeod, A. L., Rex Warner: Writer, 10-18.
Rajan, B., "Kafka - A Comparison With Rex Warner," in
Rajan, B., and A. Pearse, eds., Focus One, 7-14. Al-
so in McLeod, A. L., ed., Achievement of Rex Warner,
23-7.
Woodcock, George, "Kafka and Rex Warner," Writer and
Politics, 202-6. Also in Rajan, B., and A. Pearse, eds.,
Focus One, 59-65. Also in McLeod, A. L., ed.,
Achievement of Rex Warner, 28-34.

WHY WAS I KILLED?: A DRAMATIC DIALOGUE
(See RETURN OF THE TRAVELLER)

WARREN, Robert Penn, 1905-

GENERAL

Allen, Charles A., "Robert Penn Warren: The Psychology
of Self-Knowledge," L&P, VIII (Spring, 1958), 21-5.
Anderson, Charles R., "Violence and Order in the Novels of
Robert Penn Warren," Hopkins Rev, VI (Winter, 1953),
88-105. Also in Rubin, L. D., Jr., and R. D. Jacobs,
eds., Southern Renascence, 207-24. Also in Litz, A. W.,
ed., Modern American Fiction, 278-95.
Beatty, Richmond C., and others, eds., The Literature of
the South, Chicago: Scott, Foresman, 1952, 629-31.
Beatty, Richmond C., "The Poetry and Novels of Robert
Penn Warren," in Beatty, R. C., and others, eds., Van-
derbilt Studies in the Humanities, Vol. I, 142-60.
Bentley, Eric, "The Meaning of Robert Penn Warren's
Novels," KR, X (Summer, 1948), 407-24. Also in O'Con-
nor, W. V., ed., Forms of Modern Fiction, 255-72. Al-
so (revised) in Kostelanetz, R., ed., On Contemporary
Literature, 616-33. Also (portion) in Rubin, L. D., Jr.,
and J. R. Moore, eds., Idea of an American Novel, 364-7.
Bohner, C. H., Robert Penn Warren.
Bradbury, John M., "Robert Penn Warren's Novels: The
Symbolic and Textual Patterns," Accent, XIII (Spring,
1953), 77-89. Also in Longley, J. L., Jr., ed., Robert
Penn Warren, 3-17. Also (revised and enlarged) in Brad-
bury, J. M., Fugitives, 195-230.
Brooks, C., "R. P. Warren: Experience Redeemed in Knowl-
edge," Hidden God, 98-127.
Cargill, Oscar, "Anatomist of Monsters," CE, IX (October,
1947), 1-8. Also in Cargill, O., Toward a Pluralistic
Criticism, Carbondale: So. Ill. Un. Pr., 1965, 141-53.
Carter, Everett, "The 'Little Myth' of Robert Penn Warren,"
MFS, VI (Spring, 1960), 3-12.
Casper, Leonard, Robert Penn Warren.
_____, "Robert Penn Warren: An Assessment," DilimanR,
II (October, 1954), 400-24.
Clark, Marden J., "Religious Implications in the Novels of
Robert Penn Warren," BYUS, IV (Autumn, 1961), 67-79.
_____, "Symbolic Structure in the Novels of Robert Penn
Warren," DA, XVIII (1958), 229-30 (Wash.).
Davis, Joe, "Robert Penn Warren and the Journey to the
West," MFS, VI (Spring, 1960), 73-82.
Douglas, Wallace W., "Drug Store Gothic: The Style of Ro-
bert Penn Warren," CE, XV (February, 1954), 265-72.

Eisinger, C. E., Fiction of the Forties, 198-229.

Ellison, Ralph, and Eugene Walter, "The Art of Fiction XVIII: Robert Penn Warren," ParisR, No. 4 (Spring-Summer, 1957), 112-40. Also in Writers at Work, 1st ser., 183-207. Also in Longley, J. L., Jr., ed., Robert Penn Warren, 18-45.

Flint, F. Cudworth, "Robert Penn Warren," AmOx, XXXIV (April, 1947), 65-79.

Frank, Joseph, "Romanticism and Reality in Robert Penn Warren," The Widening Gyre: Crisis and Mastery in Modern Literature, New Brunswick, N.J.: Rutgers Un. Pr., 1963, 179-200.

Frank, William, "Mr. Warren's Achievement," CE, XIX (May, 1958), 365-6.

Frohock, W. M., "Mr. Warren's Albatross," SWR, XXXVI (Winter, 1951), 48-59. Also in Frohock, W. M., Novel of Violence in America, 86-105.

Gossett, L. Y., "Violence and the Integrity of the Self," Violence in Recent Southern Fiction, 52-75.

Gross, Seymour, "Robert Penn Warren," Critic, XVIII (October-November, 1959), 11-13, 80-2.

Hardy, John E., "Robert Penn Warren's Double Hero," VQR, XXXVI (Autumn, 1960), 583-97.

Havard, William C., "The Burden of the Literary Mind: Some Meditations on Robert Penn Warren as Historian," SAQ, LXII (Autumn, 1963), 516-31. Also in Longley, J. L., Jr., ed., Robert Penn Warren, 178-94.

Hayashi, Nobunyuki, "On the Novels of Robert Penn Warren," Jinbun Gakuho (Tokyo Metropolitan Univ.), No. 28 (March, 1962), 3-24. (Not seen.)

Hendry, Irene, "The Regional Novel: The Example of Robert Penn Warren," SR, LIII (January, 1945), 84-102.

Heseltine, H. P., "The Deep, Twisting Strain of Life: The Novels of Robert Penn Warren," McR, No. 5 (1962), 76-89.

Hoffman, F. J., Art of Southern Fiction, 31-3.

Humboldt, Charles, "The Lost Cause of Robert Penn Warren," M&M, I (July, 1948), 8-23.

Hynes, Sam, "Robert Penn Warren: The Symbolic Journey," UKCR, XVII (Summer, 1951), 279-85.

Jones, Madison, "The Novels of Robert Penn Warren," SAQ, LXII (Autumn, 1963), 488-98.

Joost, Nicholas, "Robert Penn Warren and New Directions in the Novel," in Gardiner, H. C., ed., Fifty Years of the American Novel, 273-84.

Justus, James H., "The Concept of Gesture in the Novels of Robert Penn Warren," DA, XXII (1962), 3201 (Un. of Wash.).

_____, "The Mariner and Robert Penn Warren," TSLL, VIII (Spring, 1966), 117-28.

Kehl, Delmar G., "The Dialectics of Reality in the Fiction of Robert Penn Warren," DA, XXVIII (1968), 4633A (So. Cal.).

Kelvin, Norman, "The Failure of Robert Penn Warren," CE, XVIII (April, 1957), 355-64.

Linenthal, Mark, Jr., "Robert Penn Warren and the Southern Agrarians," DA, XVII (1957), 2611-12 (Stanford).

Longley, John Lewis, Jr., Robert Penn Warren.

_____, ed., Robert Penn Warren.

_____, "Robert Penn Warren: American Man of Letters," A&S (Spring, 1965), 16-22. (Not seen.)

_____, "Robert Penn Warren: The Deeper Rub," SoR, I (Autumn, 1965), 968-73.

Mohrt, Michael, "Robert Penn Warren and the Myth of the Outlaw," YFS, No. 10 (1953), 70-84.

Moore, Littleton H., Jr., "Robert Penn Warren and History: 'The Big Myth We Live'," DA, XXV (1965), 5283-4 (Emory).

_____, "Robert Penn Warren and the Terror of Answered Prayer," MissQ, XXI (Winter, 1968), 29-36.

Ruoff, James E., "Robert Penn Warren's Pursuit of Justice: From Briar Patch to Cosmos," RSSCW, XXVII (March, 1959), 19-38.

Samuels, Charles T., "In the Wilderness," Crit, V (Fall, 1962), 46-57.

Shepherd, Allen G., III, "A Critical Study of the Fiction of Robert Penn Warren," DA, XXVI (1966), 7325-26 (Un. of Penn.).

Stewart, John L., "The Achievement of Robert Penn Warren," SAQ, XLVII (October, 1948), 562-79.

_____, Burden of Time, 486-98, 517-18, 530-42.

_____, "Robert Penn Warren and the Knot of History," ELH, XXVI (March, 1959), 102-36.

Strandberg, Victor, "Warren's Osmosis," Criticism, X (Winter, 1968), 23-40.

Strugnell, John R., "Robert Penn Warren and the Uses of the Past," REL, IV, iv (October, 1963), 93-102.

Thorp, W., American Writing in the Twentieth Century, 252-4.

Wasserstrom, William, Heiress of All the Ages: Sex and Sentiment in the Genteel Tradition, Minneapolis: Un. of Minn. Pr., 1959, 114-22.

_____, "Robert Penn Warren: From Paleface to Redskin," PrS, XXXI (Winter, 1957), 323-33.

West, P., Robert Penn Warren.

Widmer, Kingsley, "The Father-Killers of R. P. Warren,"
    Paunch, XXII (January, 1965), 57-64.
White, Ellington, in Rubin, L. D., Jr., and R. D. Jacobs,
    eds., South, 198-209.
White, Robert, "Robert Penn Warren and the Myth of the
    Garden," Faulkner Studies, III (Winter, 1954), 59-67.

ALL THE KING'S MEN

Allen, Charles, "Robert Penn Warren: The Psychology of
    Self-Knowledge," L&P, VIII (Spring, 1958), 23-5.
Allen, W., Modern Novel, 128-30.
Anderson, Charles R., "Violence and Order in the Novels
    of Robert Penn Warren," Hopkins Rev, VI, ii (Winter,
    1953), 96-100. Also in Rubin, L. D., Jr., and R. D.
    Jacobs, eds., Southern Renascence, 215-19. Also in
    Litz, A. W., ed., Modern American Fiction, 286-90.
Baker, Joseph E., "Irony in Fiction: ALL THE KING'S
    MEN," CE, IX (December, 1947), 122-30. Also in
    Beebe, M., and L. A. Field, eds., Robert Penn Warren's
    ALL THE KING'S MEN, 90-100.
Baumbach, J., "The Metaphysics of Demagoguery: ALL THE
    KING'S MEN," Landscape of Nightmare, 16-34.
Beebe, Keith, "Biblical Motifs in ALL THE KING'S MEN,"
    Jnl of Bible & Religion, XXX (April, 1962), 123-30.
Bentley, Eric, "The Meaning of Robert Penn Warren's Nov-
    els," KR, X (1948), 413-21. Also in O'Connor, W. V.,
    ed., Forms of Modern Fiction, 255-72. Also in Kostel-
    anetz, R., ed., On Contemporary Literature, 621-9.
Blotner, J., Modern American Political Novel, 219-26.
Bohner, C. H., Robert Penn Warren, 82-98.
Bradbury, John M., "Robert Penn Warren's Novels: The
    Symbolic and Textual Patterns," Accent, XIII (Spring,
    1953), 82-4. Also in Longley, J. L., Jr., ed., Robert
    Penn Warren, 9-11. Also (revised) in Bradbury, J. M.,
    Fugitives, 209-12, 229.
Brantley, Frederick, "The Achievement of Robert Penn War-
    ren," in Rajan, B., ed., Modern American Poetry (Focus
    Five), London: Denis Dobson, 1950, 67-72.
Brooks, C., Hidden God, 103-9.
Byrne, Clifford M., "The Philosophical Development in Four
    of Robert Penn Warren's Novels," McNeese Rev, IX
    (Winter, 1957), 63-5.
Cargill, Oscar, "Anatomist of Monsters," CE, IX (October,
    1947), 6-8. Also in Cargill, O., Towards a Pluralistic
    Criticism, Carbondale: So. Ill. Un. Pr., 1965, 148-52.
Carter, Everett, "The 'Little Myth' of Robert Penn Warren,"

MFS, VI (Spring, 1960), 8-10.
Casper, Leonard, "Mirror for Mobs: The Willie Stark Sto-
    ries," Drama Critique, II (November, 1959), 120-4.
_____, Robert Penn Warren, 121-32.
_____, "Robert Penn Warren: Method and Canon," Dili-
    manR, II (July, 1954), 285-8.
Clements, A. L., "Theme and Reality in AT HEAVEN'S
    GATE and ALL THE KING'S MEN," Criticism, V (1963),
    27-44.
Cottrell, Beekman W., "Cass Mastern and the Awful Re-
    sponsibility of Time," in Sochatoff, A. F., and Others,
    ALL THE KING'S MEN: A Symposium, 39-49.
Eisinger, Chester E., "Robert Penn Warren: The Conserva-
    tive Quest for Identity," Fiction of the Forties, 214-23.
    Also in Beebe, M., and L. A. Field, eds., Robert Penn
    Warren's ALL THE KING'S MEN, 149-57.
Fergusson, Francis, "Three Novels," Perspectives USA, No.
    6 (Winter, 1954), 30-44.
Flint, F. Cudworth, "Robert Penn Warren," AmOx, XXXIV
    (April, 1947), 65-73.
Fortin, Marilyn B., "Jack Burden's Search for Identity in
    ALL THE KING'S MEN," Lit, No. 4 (1963), 33-7.
Frank, Joseph, "Romanticism and Reality in Robert Penn
    Warren," HudR, IV (Summer, 1951), 248-50. Also in
    Frank, J., The Widening Gyre: Crisis and Mastery in
    Modern Literature, New Brunswick, N. J.: Rutgers Un. Pr.,
    1963, 183-6. Also in Beebe, M., and L. A. Field, eds.,
    Robert Penn Warren's ALL THE KING'S MEN, 147-9.
Gerhard, George, "ALL THE KING'S MEN: A Symposium,"
    Folio, XV (May, 1950), 4-11.
Girault, Norton R., "The Narrator's Mind as Symbol: An
    Analysis of ALL THE KING'S MEN," Accent, VII (Sum-
    mer, 1947), 220-34. Also in Aldridge, J.W., ed., Crit-
    iques and Essays in Modern Fiction, 200-16. Also in
    Beebe, M., and L. A. Field, eds., Robert Penn Warren's
    ALL THE KING'S MEN, 101-17.
Gross, Harvey, "History as Metaphysical Pathos: Modern
    Literature and the Idea of History," DenverQ, I (Autumn,
    1966), 1-5.
Gross, Seymour L., "The Achievement of Robert Penn War-
    ren," CE, XVIII (April, 1957), 361-5. Also in Beebe,
    M., and L. A. Field, eds., Robert Penn Warren's ALL
    THE KING'S MEN, 133-9.
_____, "Conrad and ALL THE KING'S MEN," TCL, III
    (April, 1957), 27-32.
_____, "Robert Penn Warren," Critic, XVIII (October-
    November, 1959), 11-13, 80-2.

Hall, J., Lunatic Giant in the Drawing Room, 81-110.

Hardy, John E., "Robert Penn Warren's Double-Hero," VQR, XXXVI (Autumn, 1960), 588-97. Also as "Robert Penn Warren: The Dialectic of Self," in Hardy, J. E., Man in the Modern Novel, 194-207. Also in Beebe, M., and L. A. Field, eds., Robert Penn Warren's ALL THE KING'S MEN, 157-67.

Hart, John A., "Some Major Images in ALL THE KING'S MEN," in Sochatoff, A. F., and Others, ALL THE KING'S MEN: A Symposium, 63-74.

Heilman, Robert B., "Melpomene as Wallflower; or, The Reading of Tragedy," SR, LV (Winter, 1947), 154-66. Also in Beebe, M., and L. A. Field, eds., Robert Penn Warren's ALL THE KING'S MEN, 79-89. Also in Longley, J. L., Jr., ed., Robert Penn Warren, 82-95.

Heseltine, H. P., "The Deep, Twisting Strain of Life: The Novels of Robert Penn Warren," MCR, No. 5 (1962), 85-9.

Hoffman, F. J., Art of Southern Fiction, 33-6.

Hudson, Richard B., "ALL THE KING'S MEN: A Symposium," Folio, XV (May, 1950), 11-13.

Humboldt, Charles, "The Lost Cause of Robert Penn Warren," M&M, I (July, 1948), 15-18.

Humphrey, R., Stream of Consciousness in the Modern Novel, 114-16.

Inge, M. Thomas, "An American Novel of Ideas," UCQ, XII, iv (March, 1967), 35-40.

Justus, James H., "All the Burdens of Warren's ALL THE KING'S MEN," in French, W., ed., Forties, 191-201.

Kaplan, Charles, "Jack Burden: Modern Ishmael," CE, XXII (October, 1960), 19-24.

Kelvin, Norman, "The Failure of Robert Penn Warren," CE, XVIII (April, 1957), 58-60. Also in Beebe, M., and L. A. Field, eds., Robert Penn Warren's ALL THE KING'S MEN, 129-32.

Kerr, Dell, "An Exercise on Robert Penn Warren's ALL THE KING'S MEN," Exercise Exchange, V (October, 1957), 8-9.

Kerr, Elizabeth M., "Polarity of Themes in ALL THE KING'S MEN," MFS, VI (Spring, 1960), 25-46. Also in Beebe, M., and L. A. Field, eds., Robert Penn Warren's ALL THE KING'S MEN, 175-95.

King, Roma A., Jr., "Time and Structure in the Early Novels of Robert Penn Warren," SAQ, LVI (Autumn, 1957), 486-93.

Longley, J. L., Jr., Robert Penn Warren, 12-17.

Milne, G., American Political Novel, 153-63.

Mizener, Arthur, "Robert Penn Warren: ALL THE KING'S
MEN," SoR, III (October, 1967), 874-94.

_____, Twelve Great American Novels, 177-98.

Nemerov, Howard, in Furioso, II (Fall, 1946), 69-71.

Noble, D.W., Eternal Adam and the New World Garden, 178-
86.

Payne, Ladell, "Willie Stark and Huey Long: Atmosphere,
Myth or Suggestion," AQ, XX (Fall, 1968), 580-95.

Raben, Joseph, "ALL THE KING'S MEN: A Symposium,"
Folio, XV (May, 1950), 14-18.

Ransom, John Crowe, "ALL THE KING'S MEN: A Symposium," Folio XV (May, 1950), 2-3.

Ray, Robert J., and Ann, "Time in ALL THE KING'S MEN:
A Stylistic Analysis," TSLL, V (Autumn, 1963), 452-7.

Rubin, Louis D., Jr., "All the King's Meanings," GaR, VIII
(Winter, 1954), 422-34. Also in Rubin, L.D., Jr., Curi-
ous Death of the Novel, 222-38. Also in Beebe, M., and
L.A. Field, eds., Robert Penn Warren's ALL THE
KING'S MEN, 28-39.

_____, "Burden's Landing: ALL THE KING'S MEN and
the Modern South," Faraway Country, 105-30.

Ruoff, James, "Humpty Dumpty and ALL THE KING'S MEN:
A Note on Robert Penn Warren's Teleology," TCL, III
(October, 1957), 128-34. Also in Westbrook, M., ed.,
Modern American Novel, 196-208. Also in Beebe, M.,
and L.A. Field, eds., Robert Penn Warren's ALL THE
KING'S MEN, 139-47.

_____, "Robert Penn Warren's Pursuit of Justice,"
RSSCW, XXVII (1959), 25-30.

Sale, Roger, "Having It Both Ways in ALL THE KING'S
MEN," HudR, XIV (Spring, 1961), 68-76. Also in
Beebe, M., and L.A. Field, eds., Robert Penn Warren's
ALL THE KING'S MEN, 168-75.

Satterwhite, Joseph N., "Robert Penn Warren and Emily
Dickinson," MLN, LXXI (May, 1956), 347-9.

Sillars, Malcolm O., "Warren's ALL THE KING'S MEN: A
Study in Populism," AQ, IX (Fall, 1957), 345-53. Also
in Beebe, M., and L.A. Field, eds., Robert Penn Warren's ALL THE KING'S MEN, 117-25.

Slack, Robert C., "The Telemachus Theme," in Sochatoff,
A.F., and Others, ALL THE KING'S MEN: A Symposium, 30-8.

Sochatoff, A. Fred, "Some Treatments of the Huey Long
Theme," in Sochatoff, A.F., and Others, ALL THE
KING'S MEN: A Symposium, 3-15.

Stallknecht, Newton P., "A Study in Nihilism," Folio, XV

(May, 1950), 18-22. Also in Beebe, M., and L. A. Field, eds., Robert Penn Warren's ALL THE KING'S MEN, 125-8.

Steinberg, Erwin R., "The Enigma of Willie Stark," in Sochatoff, A. F., and Others, ALL THE KING'S MEN: A Symposium, 17-28.

Stewart, James T., "Two Uses of Maupassant by R. P. Warren," MLN, LXX (April, 1955), 279-80.

Stewart, John L., Burden of Time, 504-6.

Strugnell, John R., "Robert Penn Warren and the Uses of the Past," REL, IV, iv (October, 1963), 96-8.

Stuckey, W. J., Pulitzer Prize Novels, 132-7.

Trilling, Diana, in Nation, CLXIII (August 24, 1946), 220.

Tyler, Parker, "Novel Into Film: ALL THE KING'S MEN," KR, XII (Spring, 1950), 369-76. Also in Kenyon Review. Kenyon Critics, 225-32.

Wade, John D., in VQR, XXIII (Winter, 1947), 138-41.

Walcutt, C. C., Man's Changing Mask, 298-300.

Warren, Robert Penn, "ALL THE KING'S MEN: The Matrix of Experience," YR, LIII (Winter, 1964), 161-7. Also in Warren, R. P., ALL THE KING'S MEN, "Introduction," Time Reading Program edition, N. Y.: Time-Life, 1964. Also in Beebe, M., and L. A. Field, eds., Robert Penn Warren's ALL THE KING'S MEN, 23-8. Also in Longley, J. L., Jr., ed., Robert Penn Warren, 75-81.

_____, "A Note to ALL THE KING'S MEN," SR, LXI (1953), 476-80.

Weissbuch, Ted N., "Jack Burden: Call Me Carraway," CE, XXII (February, 1961), 361.

West, P., Robert Penn Warren, 28-34.

White, Robert, "Robert Penn Warren and the Myth of the Garden," Faulkner Studies, III (Winter, 1954), 61-4.

Whittington, Curtis, Jr., "The 'Burden' of Narration: Democratic Perspective and First-Person Point of View in the American Novel," SHR, II (Spring, 1968), 236-45.

Wilcox, Earl, "Warren's ALL THE KING'S MEN, Epigraph," Expl, XXVI (December, 1967), Item 29.

Woodruff, Neal, Jr., "The Technique of ALL THE KING'S MEN," in Sochatoff, A. F., and Others, ALL THE KING'S MEN: A Symposium, 51-62.

AT HEAVEN'S GATE

Anderson, Charles R., "Violence and Order in the Novels of Robert Penn Warren," Hopkins Rev, VI, ii (Winter, 1953), 94-6. Also in Rubin, L. D., Jr., and R. D. Jacobs, eds., Southern Renascence, 213-15. Also in Litz,

A.W., ed., <u>Modern American Fiction,</u> 284-6.

Beatty, Richmond C., "The Poetry and Novels of Robert
   Penn Warren," in Beatty, R. C., and Others, eds., <u>Van-
   derbilt Studies in the Humanities,</u> Vol. I, 152-4.

Bentley, Eric, "The Meaning of Robert Penn Warren's Novels," <u>KR,</u> X (1948), 411-13. Also in O'Connor, W. V.,
   ed., <u>Forms of Modern Fiction,</u> 259-61. Also in Kostelanetz, R., ed., <u>On Contemporary Literature,</u> 619-21.

Bohner, C.H., <u>Robert Penn Warren,</u> 70-82.

Bradbury, John M., "Robert Penn Warren's Novels: The
   Symbolic and Textual Patterns," <u>Accent,</u> XIII (Spring,
   1953), 80-2. Also in Longley, J.L., Jr., ed., <u>Robert
   Penn Warren,</u> 6-9. Also (revised) in Bradbury, J.M.,
   <u>Fugitives,</u> 206-9+.

Byrne, Clifford M., "The Philosophical Development in Four
   of Robert Penn Warren's Novels," <u>McNR,</u> IX (Winter,
   1957), 61-3.

Cargill, Oscar, "Anatomist of Monsters," <u>CE,</u> IX (October,
   1947), 4-6. Also in Cargill, O., <u>Towards a Pluralistic
   Criticism,</u> Carbondale: So. Ill. Un. Pr., 1965, 146-8.

Casper, Leonard, <u>Robert Penn Warren,</u> 70-82.

_____, "Robert Penn Warren: Method and Canon," <u>Dili-
   manR,</u> II (July, 1954), 282-3.

Clements, A.L., "Theme and Reality in AT HEAVEN'S
   GATE and ALL THE KING'S MEN," <u>Criticism,</u> V (Winter,
   1963), 27-44.

Eisinger, C.E., <u>Fiction of the Forties,</u> 210-14.

Frank, Joseph, "Romanticism and Reality in Robert Penn
   Warren," <u>The Widening Gyre: Crisis and Mastery in
   Modern Literature,</u> New Brunswick, N.J.: Rutgers Un.
   Pr., 1963, 186-200.

Hardwick, Elizabeth, "Poor Little Rich Girls," PR, XII
   (Summer, 1945), 420-2.

Hendry, Irene, "The Regional Novel: The Example of Robert Penn Warren," <u>SR,</u> LIII (January, 1945), 84-102.

Humboldt, Charles, "The Lost Cause of Robert Penn Warren," <u>M&M,</u> I (July, 1948), 11-15.

King, Roma A., Jr., "Time and Structure in the Early
   Novels of Robert Penn Warren," <u>SAQ,</u> LVI (Autumn,
   1957), 486-93.

Longley, John L., Jr., "AT HEAVEN'S GATE: The Major
   Themes," <u>MFS,</u> VI (Spring, 1960), 13-24. Also (revised)
   in Longley, J.L., Jr., ed., <u>Robert Penn Warren,</u> 60-74.

_____, <u>Robert Penn Warren,</u> 6-12.

Ruoff, James E., "Robert Penn Warren's Pursuit of Justice,"
   <u>RSSCW,</u> XXVII (1959), 24-5.

Stewart, J.L., <u>Burden of Time,</u> 500-4.

Walcutt, Charles C., "The Regional Novel and Its Future,"
    ArQ, I (Summer, 1945), 23-6.
West, P., Robert Penn Warren, 27-8.

BAND OF ANGELS

Bohner, C. H., Robert Penn Warren, 127-35.
Bradbury, J. M., Fugitives, 223-8.
Brown, Ashley, in Shen, VII (Autumn, 1955), 87-91.
Casper, Leonard, "Miscegenation as Symbol: BAND OF
    ANGELS," Audience, VI (Autumn, 1959), 66-74. Also in
    Longley, J. L., Jr., ed., Robert Penn Warren, 140-8.
    Also (revised) in Casper, L., Robert Penn Warren, 148-
    62.
Fiedler, Leslie, Love and Death in the American Novel,
    393-4.
_____, "Romance in the Operatic Manner," NRep,
    CXXXIII (September 26, 1955), 28-30. Also in Fiedler,
    L., No! In Thunder, 131-3.
Flint, F. Cudworth, "Mr. Warren and the Reviewers," SR,
    LXIV (Autumn, 1956), 632-45. Also in Longley, J. L.,
    Jr., ed., Robert Penn Warren, 125-39.
Geismar, Maxwell, "Agile Pen and Dry Mind," Nation,
    CLXXXI (October 1, 1955), 287.
Longley, J. L., Jr., Robert Penn Warren, 24-7.
McDowell, Frederick P. W., in WR, XX (Winter, 1956),
    167-71.
Magmer, James, "Robert Penn Warren's Quest for an An-
    gel," CathW, CLXXXIII (June, 1956), 178-83.
Martin, Terence, "BAND OF ANGELS: The Definition of
    Self-definition," Folio, XXI (Winter, 1955), 31-7.
Mizener, Arthur, "A Nature Divided Against Itself," NYTBR,
    (August 21, 1955), 1, 18.
Ruoff, James E., "Robert Penn Warren's Pursuit of Jus-
    tice," RSSCW, XXVII (1959), 36-7.
Stewart, J. L., Burden of Time, 516-17.
Vidal, Gore, "Book Report," Zero, II (Spring, 1956), 95-8.
Wasserstrom, William, Heiress of All the Ages: Sex and
    Sentiment in the Genteel Tradition, Minneapolis: Un. of
    Minn. Pr., 1959, 118-21.
West, P., Robert Penn Warren, 40-2.

THE CAVE

Abel, Lionel, "Refinement and Vulgarity," Ctary, XXVIII
    (December, 1959), 541-4.
Allen, Charles A., in ArQ, XVI (Summer, 1960), 182-4.

Bohner, C.H., Robert Penn Warren, 146-53.
Casper, Leonard, "Journey to the Interior: THE CAVE,"
    MFS, VI (Spring, 1960), 65-72. Also in Longley, J.L.,
    Jr., ed., Robert Penn Warren, 149-58.
Davison, Richard A., "Robert Penn Warren's 'Dialectical
    Configuration' and THE CAVE," CLAJ, X (1967), 349-57.
DeMott, Benjamin, in HudR, XII (Winter, 1959-60), 621-3.
Glazier, Lyle, "Reconstructed Platonism: Robert Penn War-
    ren's THE CAVE," Litera, VII (1960), 16-26.
Holmes, Theodore, "The Literary Mode," Carleton Miscel-
    lany, IV (Winter, 1963), 124-8.
Justus, James H., "The Uses of Gesture in Warren's THE
    CAVE," MLQ, XXVI (September, 1965), 448-61.
Longley, J.L., Jr., Robert Penn Warren, 27-8.
Malcolm, Donald, "Cavities," NY, XXXV (October 31, 1959),
    198, 201-2.
Nemerov, Howard, in PR, XXVII (Winter, 1960), 176, 178-
    80, 183-4. Also in Nemerov, H., Poetry and Fiction,
    281-3.
Price, Martin, in YR, XLIX (Autumn, 1959), 124-6.
Sandeen, Ernest, "Warren's Latest Novel," Critic, XVIII
    (October-November, 1959), 13, 63.
Symons, J., "Fables for Our Time," Critical Occasions,
    119-25.
West, P., Robert Penn Warren, 42-3.
Widmer, Kingsley, "The Father-Killers of R.P. Warren,"
    Paunch, XXII (January, 1965), 62-3.

                                FLOOD

Hardy, John E., in VQR, XL (Summer, 1964), 485-9.
Longley, John L., Jr., Robert Penn Warren, 30-5.
_____, "Robert Penn Warren: The Deeper Rub," SoR, I
    (Autumn, 1965), 973-80.
_____, "When All Is Said and Done: Warren's FLOOD,"
    in Longley, J.L., Jr., ed., Robert Penn Warren, 169-
    77.
Mizener, Arthur, "The Uncorrupted Consciousness," SR,
    LXXII (Autumn, 1964), 690-8.
Shepherd, Allen, "Character and Theme in R.P. Warren's
    FLOOD," Crit, IX, iii (1967), 95-102.
Stewart, J.L., in YR, LIV (Winter, 1965), 252-8.
Wain, John, in NRep, CL (May 16, 1964), 23-5.
West, Anthony, in NY, XL (September 12, 1964), 204-5.
West, P., Robert Penn Warren, 44-5.

NIGHT RIDER

Allen, Charles A. , "Robert Penn Warren: The Psychology
of Self-Knowledge," L&P, VIII (Spring, 1958), 21-2.
Allen, W. , Modern Novel, 131-2.
Anderson, Charles R. , "Violence and Order in the Novels of
Robert Penn Warren," Hopkins Rev, VI, ii (Winter, 1953),
92-4.   Also in Rubin, L. D. , Jr. , and R. D. Jacobs, eds. ,
Southern Renascence, 211-12.   Also in Litz, A. W. , ed. ,
Modern American Fiction, 282-4.
Bentley, Eric, "The Meaning of Robert Penn Warren's Nov-
els," KR, X (1948), 408-10.   Also in O'Connor, W. V. ,
ed. , Forms of Modern Fiction, 256-8.   Also in Kostelan-
etz, R. , ed. , On Contemporary Literature, 617-19.
Bohner, C. H. , Robert Penn Warren, 61-70.
Bradbury, John M. , "Robert Penn Warren's Novels: The
Symbolic and Textual Patterns," Accent, XIII (Spring,
1953), 78-80.   Also in Longley, J. L. , Jr. , ed. , Robert
Penn Warren, 5-6.   Also (revised) in Bradbury, J. M. ,
Fugitives, 204-6+.
Burke, Kenneth, The Philosophy of Literary Form, 2nd ed. ,
Baton Rouge: La. State Un. Pr. , 1967, 84-6.
Byrne, Clifford M. , "The Philosophical Development in Four
of Robert Penn Warren's Novels," McNR, IX (Winter,
1957, 57-61.
Cargill, Oscar, "Anatomist of Monsters," CE, IX (October,
1947), 2-4.   Also in Cargill, O. , Toward a Pluralistic
Criticism, Carbondale: So. Ill. Un. Pr. , 1965, 143-6.
Casper, Leonard, Robert Penn Warren, 100-7.
_____, "Robert Penn Warren: Method and Canon," Dili-
manR, II (July, 1954), 281-2.
Eisinger, C. E. , Fiction of the Forties, 206-10.
French, W. , Social Novel at the End of An Era, 184-93.
Hendry, Irene, "The Regional Novel: The Example of Ro-
bert Penn Warren," SR, LIII (January, 1945), 84-102.
Heseltine, H. P. , "The Deep, Twisting Strain of Life: The
Novels of Robert Penn Warren," MCR, No. 5 (1962), 77-
80.
Humboldt, Charles, "The Lost Cause of Robert Penn War-
ren," M&M, I (July, 1948), 9-11.
Kelvin, Norman, "The Failure of Robert Penn Warren,"
CE, XVIII (April, 1957), 357-8.
King, Roma A. , Jr. , "Time and Structure in the Early Nov-
els of Robert Penn Warren," SAQ, LVI (Autumn, 1957),
486-93.
Letargeez, J. , "Robert Penn Warren's Views of History,"
RLV, XXII (1956), 533-43.

Longley, J. L. , Jr. , Robert Penn Warren, 5-6.
Ruoff, James E. , "Robert Penn Warren's Pursuit of Just-
    ice," RSSCW, XXVII (1959), 22-4.
Ryan, Alvan S. , "Robert Penn Warren's NIGHT RIDER: The
    Nihilism of the Isolated Temperament," MFS, VII (Winter,
    1961-62), 338-46. Also in Longley, J. L. , Jr. , ed. , Ro-
    bert Penn Warren, 49-59.
Stewart, J. L. , Burden of Time, 469-80.
Strugnell, John R. , "Robert Penn Warren and the Uses of
    the Past," REL, IV, iv (October, 1963), 94-6.
West, P. , Robert Penn Warren, 25-6.
Wilson, Angus, "The Fires of Violence," Encounter, IV
    (May, 1955), 75-8.
Yanagi, Kiichiro, "NIGHT RIDER and Robert Penn Warren's
    Ideas," Bulletin of the Univ. of Osaka Prefecture, Series
    C, IX (1961), 57-72.

WILDERNESS

Casper, Leonard, "Trial By Wilderness: Warren's Exemp-
    lum," WSCL, III, iii (Fall, 1962), 45-53. Also in Long-
    ley, J. L. , Jr. , ed. , Robert Penn Warren, 159-68.
Kleine, Don W. , in Epoch, XI (Winter, 1962), 263-8.
Longley, J. L. , Jr. , Robert Penn Warren, 28-30.
Moore, L. Hugh, Jr. , "Robert Penn Warren and History:
    'The Big Myth We Live'," DA, XXV (1965), 5283-4
    (Emory).
_____, "Robert Penn Warren, William Styron, and the
    Use of Greek Myth," Crit, VIII, ii (1966), 75-80.
Samuels, Charles T. , "In the Wilderness," Crit, V, ii
    (Fall, 1962), 52-7.
West, P. , Robert Penn Warren, 43-4.

WORLD ENOUGH AND TIME

Allen, W. , Modern Novel, 130-1.
Anderson, Charles R. , "Violence and Order in the Novels
    of Robert Penn Warren," Hopkins Rev, VI, ii (Winter,
    1953), 100-5. Also in Rubin, L. D. , Jr. , and R. D.
    Jacobs, eds. , Southern Renascence, 219-24. Also in
    Litz, A. W. , ed. , Modern American Fiction, 290-5.
Baker, Carlos, in VQR, XXVI (Autumn, 1950), 603-5.
Beatty, Richmond C. , "The Poetry and Novels of Robert
    Penn Warren," in Beatty, R. C. , and Others, eds. , Van-
    derbilt Studies in the Humanities, Vol. I, 157-60.
Berner, Robert, "The Required Past: WORLD ENOUGH
    AND TIME," MFS, VI (Spring, 1960), 55-64.

Bohner, C.H., Robert Penn Warren, 106-17.

Bradbury, John M., "Robert Penn Warren's Novels: The Symbolic and Textual Patterns," Accent, XIII (Spring, 1953), 84-6. Also in Longley, J.L., Jr., ed., Robert Penn Warren, 11-14. Also (revised) in Bradbury, J.M., Fugitives, 212-14+.

Byrne, Clifford M., "The Philosophical Development in Four of Robert Penn Warren's Novels," McNR, IX (Winter, 1957), 65-7.

Campbell, Harry M., "Mr. Warren as Philosopher in WORLD ENOUGH AND TIME," Hopkins Rev, VI (Winter, 1953), 106-16. Also in Rubin, L.D., Jr., and R.D. Jacobs, eds., Southern Renascence, 225-35.

Carter, Everett, "The 'Little Myth' of Robert Penn Warren," MFS, VI (Spring, 1960), 6-8.

Casper, Leonard, Robert Penn Warren, 136-48.
_____, "Robert Penn Warren: Method and Canon," Dili-manR, II (July, 1954), 288-92.

Eisinger, C.E., Fiction of the Forties, 224-8.

Fiedler, Leslie, "On Two Frontiers," PR, XVII (September-October, 1950), 739-43.
_____, "Toward Time's Cold Womb," New Leader (July 22, 1950). Also in Fiedler, L., No! In Thunder, 119-26.

Frank, Joseph, "Romanticism and Reality in Robert Penn Warren," HudR, IV (1951), 248-58. Also in Frank, J., Widening Gyre: Crisis and Mastery in Modern Literature, New Brunswick, N.J.: Rutgers Un. Pr., 1963, 186-200.

Guthrie, A.B., "Virtue Plundered in Kentucky," SatR, XXXIII (June 24, 1950), 11-12.

Heilman, Robert B., "Tangled Web," SR, LIX (Winter, 1951), 107-19. Also in Longley, J.L., Jr., ed., Robert Penn Warren, 96-109.

Janeway, Elizabeth, "Man in Conflict," NYTBR (June 25, 1950), 1, 22.

Jones, Ernest, "Through a Glass Darkly," Nation, CLXXI (July, 1950), 42.

Justus, James H., "Warren's WORLD ENOUGH AND TIME and Beauchamp's CONFESSION," AL, XXXIII (January, 1962), 500-11.

Kelvin, Norman, "The Failure of Robert Penn Warren," CE, XVIII (April, 1957), 360-1.

Lane, Calvin W., "Narrative Art and History in Robert Penn Warren's WORLD ENOUGH AND TIME," DA, XVII, (1957), 1340 (Mich.).

Longley, J.L., Jr., Robert Penn Warren, 17-24.

McDowell, Frederick P.W., "The Romantic Tragedy of Self

in WORLD ENOUGH AND TIME," Crit, I, ii (Summer,
1957), 34-48. Also in Longley, J. L. , Jr. , ed. , Robert
Penn Warren, 110-24.
Mizener, Arthur, "Amphibium in Old Kentucky," KR, XII
(Autumn, 1950), 697-701.
O'Connor, W. V. , Grotesque, 14-16.
Rathbun, John W. , "Philosophy, WORLD ENOUGH AND
TIME, and the Art of the Novel," MFS, VI (Spring, 1960),
47-54.
Renguette, Dale T. , "The Gray Pessimism of Robert Penn
Warren," Fresco, I, i (1960), 34-42.
Ridgely, Joseph V. , "Tragedy in Kentucky," Hopkins Rev,
IV (Fall, 1950), 61-3.
Ruoff, James E. , "Robert Penn Warren's Pursuit of Just-
ice," RSSCW, XXVII (1959), 31-3.
Schiller, Andrew, "The World Out of Square," WR, XV
(Spring, 1951), 234-7.
Stewart, J. L. , Burden of Time, 506-10.
Strugnell, John R. , "Robert Penn Warren and the Uses of
the Past," REL, IV, iv (October, 1963), 98-9.
West, P. , Robert Penn Warren, 38-40.
White, Robert, "Robert Penn Warren and the Myth of the
Garden," Faulkner Studies, III (Winter, 1954), 64-7.

BIBLIOGRAPHY

Beebe, Maurice, and Erin Marcus, "Criticism of Robert
Penn Warren: A Selected Checklist," MFS, VI (Spring,
1960), 83-8.
Casper, L. , Robert Penn Warren, 191-208.
Huff, Mary N. , Robert Penn Warren: A Bibliography,
N. Y. : David Lewis, 1968.
Longley, J. L. , Jr. , ed. , Robert Penn Warren, 247-57.

WATERHOUSE, KEITH, 1929-

GENERAL

Corbett, Martyn, "First Person Singular," Delta (Cambridge,
Eng.), No. 35 (Spring, 1965), 9-16.

BILLY LIAR

Churchill, Thomas, "Waterhouse, Story, and Fowles:
Which Way Out of the Room?" Crit, X, iii (1968), 72-87.
Crobett, Martyn, "First Person Singular," Delta (Cam-

bridge, Eng.), No. 35 (Spring, 1965), 10-15.

Gindin, J., "Creeping Americanism," Postwar British Fiction, 109-14.

O'Connor, W. V., "The New Hero and a Shift in Literary Convention," New University Wits, 135-6.

Urwin, G. G., ed., Taste for Living, 56-9.

JUBB

Churchill, Thomas, "Waterhouse, Storey, and Fowles: Which Way Out of the Room?" Crit, X, iii (1968), 72-87.

WAUGH, EVELYN, 1903-1966

GENERAL

Allen, W., Modern Novel, 208-14.

Bannington, T. J., "Mr. Waugh's Pieties," The Bell, XIII (February, 1947), 58-63. (Reply to Donat O'Donnell.)

Beattie, A. M., "Evelyn Waugh," CanF, XXXIII (January, 1954), 226-7.

Benedict, Stewart H., "The Candide Figure in the Novels of Evelyn Waugh," PMASAL, XLVIII (1963), 685-90.

Bergonzi, Bernard, "Evelyn Waugh's Gentlemen," CritQ, V (Spring, 1963), 23-36. Also in Davis, R. M., ed., Evelyn Waugh, 69-88.

Boyle, Alexander, "Evelyn Waugh," IrM, LXXVIII (February, 1950), 75-81.

Boyle, R., "Evelyn Waugh, Master of Satire," Grail, XXXV (November, 1953), 28-32. (Not seen.)

Bradbury, M., Evelyn Waugh.

Brady, C. A., "Evelyn Waugh: Shrove Tuesday Motley and Lenten Sackcloth," Catholic Library World, XVI (March, 1945), 163-77.

Braybrooke, Neville, "Evelyn Waugh," Fortnightly, CLXXI (March, 1952), 197-202.

Burgess, Anthony, "Evelyn Waugh, 1903-1966: The Comedy of Ultimate Truths," Spectator, No. 7190 (April 15, 1966), 462.

Carens, J. F., Satiric Art of Evelyn Waugh.

Churchill, Thomas P., "The House of Waugh: A Critical Study of Evelyn Waugh's Major Novels," DA, XXIV (1964), 2906 (Un. of Wash.).

Corr, Patricia, "Evelyn Waugh: Sanity and Catholicism," Studies, LI (Autumn, 1962), 388-99. Also in Davis, R. M., ed., Evelyn Waugh, 33-49.

Cosman, Max, "The Nature and Work of Evelyn Waugh,"
    ColQ, IV (Spring, 1956), 428-41.
Davis, Robert M. , ed. , Evelyn Waugh.
_____, "Evelyn Waugh on the Art of Fiction," PLL, II
    (Summer, 1966), 243-52.
_____, "Evelyn Waugh's Early Work: The Formation of
    a Method," TSLL, VII (Spring, 1965), 97-108.
_____, "The Mind and Art of Evelyn Waugh," PLL, III
    (Summer, 1967), 270-87. Also in Davis, R. M. , ed. ,
    Evelyn Waugh, 89-110.
De Vitis, Angelo A. , "The Religious Theme in the Novels of
    Rex Warner, Evelyn Waugh, and Graham Greene," SDD-
    UW, XV (1955), 605-6.
_____, Roman Holiday.
Dooley, David, "The Impact of Satire on Fiction: Studies in
    Norman Douglas, Sinclair Lewis, Aldous Huxley, Evelyn
    Waugh and George Orwell," DA, XV (1955), 2203-4 (Iowa).
_____, "Strategy of the Catholic Novelist," CathW,
    CLXXXIX (July, 1959), 300-4. Also in Davis, R. M. ,
    ed. , Evelyn Waugh, 51-6.
_____, "Waugh and Black Humor," EWN, II, ii (Autumn,
    1968), 1-3.
Doyle, Paul A. , "The Church, History and Evelyn Waugh,"
    ABR, IX (Autumn-Winter, 1958-9), 202-8.
_____, Evelyn Waugh.
_____, "The Persecution of Evelyn Waugh," America,
    XCIX (May 3, 1958), 165, 168-9.
Dyson, A. E. , "Evelyn Waugh and the Mysteriously Disap-
    pearing Hero," CritQ, II (Spring, 1960), 72-9. Also in
    Dyson, A. E. , Crazy Fabric, 187-96.
Featherstone, Joseph, "The Ordeal of Evelyn Waugh," NRep,
    CLV (July 16, 1966), 21-3.
Fytton, Francis, "Waugh-fare," CathW, CLXXXI (August,
    1955), 349-55.
Gleason, James, "Evelyn Waugh and the Stylistics of Com-
    mitment," WisSL, II (1965), 70-4.
Grace, William J. , "Evelyn Waugh as a Social Critic," Ren,
    I, ii (Spring, 1949), 28-40.
Green, Martin, "British Comedy and the British Sense of
    Humour: Shaw, Waugh and Amis," TQ, IV, iii (Autumn,
    1961), 220-5.
Greenblatt, S. J. , Three Modern Satirists, 1-33, 105-17.
Greene, George, "Scapegoat with Style: The Status of Eve-
    lyn Waugh," QQ, LXXI (Winter, 1965), 485-93.
Griffiths, Joan, "Waugh's Problem Comedies," Accent, IX
    (Spring, 1949), 165-70.
Hall, James, "The Other Post-War Rebellion: Evelyn Waugh

Twenty-Five Years After," ELH, XXVIII (June, 1961),
187-202. Also in Hall, J. , Tragic Comedians, 43-65.
Hinchcliffe, Peter, "Fathers and Children in the Novels of
Evelyn Waugh," UTQ, XXXV (April, 1966), 293-310.
Hines, Leo, "Waugh and His Critics," Cweal, LXXVI (April
13, 1962), 60-3.
Hollis, C. , Evelyn Waugh.
Howarth, Herbert, "Quelling the Riot: Evelyn Waugh's Pro-
gress," in Mooney, H. J. , Jr. , and T. F. Staley, eds. ,
Shapeless God, 67-89.
Jebb, Julian, "The Art of Fiction XXX: Evelyn Waugh,"
ParisR, No. 30 (Summer-Fall, 1963), 72-85. Also in
Writers at Work, 3rd ser. , 103-14.
Jervis, Steven A. , "The Novels of Evelyn Waugh: A Criti-
cal Study," DA, XXVII (1966), 1058A (Stanford).
Karl, F. R. , "The Word of Evelyn Waugh: The Normally
Sane," Contemporary English Novel, 167-82.
Kenny, H. A. , "Evelyn Waugh and the Novel," Magnificat,
XCII (1953), 278-80. (Not seen.)
Kermode, Frank, "Mr. Waugh's Cities," Encounter, XV
(November, 1960), 63-70. Also in Kermode, F. , Puzzles
and Epiphanies, 164-75.
Kernan, Alvin B. , "The Wall and the Jungle: The Early
Novels of Evelyn Waugh," YR, LIII (Winter, 1964), 199-
220. Also in Davis, R. M. , ed. , Evelyn Waugh, 1-24.
Macaulay, Rose, "The Best and the Worst, II - Evelyn
Waugh," Horizon, XIV (December, 1946), 360-76. Also
in Baker, D. V. , ed. , Writers of Today: 2, 135-52.
McCay, Robert D. , "Idea and Pattern in the Novels of Eve-
lyn Waugh," DA, XIII (1953), 1197 (Iowa).
Marcus, Steven, "Evelyn Waugh and the Art of Entertain-
ment," PR, XXIII (Summer, 1956), 348-57.
Marshall, Bruce, "Graham Greene and Evelyn Waugh,"
Cweal, LI (March 3, 1950), 551-3.
Meyer, Henrich, "Evelyn Waugh (1903-66)," BA, XL (Au-
tumn, 1966), 410-11.
Mikes, George, Eight Humorists, London: Allan Wingate,
1954, 131-46.
Mosely, Nicholas, "A New Puritanism," The European, No.
3 (May, 1953), 35-40. (Answer to A. J. Neame. See
items under BRIDESHEAD REVISITED and MEN AT
ARMS.)
Nichols, James W. , "Romantic and Realistic: The Tone of
Evelyn Waugh's Early Novels," CE, XXIV (October, 1962),
46-56.
O'Donnell, Donat, "The Pieties of Evelyn Waugh," The Bell,
XIII (December, 1946), 38-49. Also in KR, IX (Summer,

1947), 400-11.   Also in O'Donnell, D., <u>Maria Cross</u>, 119-
34.   Also in O'Brien, C. C., <u>Maria Cross</u>, 109-23.   Al-
so in Kenyon Review.   <u>Kenyon Critics</u>, 88-98.
_____, Reply to "Mr. Waugh's Pieties," <u>The Bell</u>, XIII
     (March, 1947), 57-62.   (Answer to T. J. Bannington.)
O'Faolain, S., <u>Vanishing Hero</u>, 23-44.
Pandeya, S. M., "The Satiric Technique of Evelyn Waugh,"
     <u>Criticism and Research</u> (Banaras Hindu Univ.), (1965),
     107-23.   (Not seen.)
Rolo, Charles J., "Evelyn Waugh: the Best and the Worst,"
     <u>Atlantic</u>, CXCIV (October, 1954), 80-6.
Savage, D. S., "The Innocence of Evelyn Waugh," <u>WR</u>, XIV
     (Spring, 1950), 197-206.   Also in Rajan, B., ed., <u>Novel-
     ist as Thinker</u>, 34-46.
Spender, S., "The World of Evelyn Waugh," <u>Creative Ele-
     ment</u>, 159-74.
Stopp, F. J., <u>Evelyn Waugh</u>.
Sykes, Christopher, "A Critique of Waugh," <u>Listener</u>,
     LXXVIII (August 31, 1967), 267-9.
Van Zeller, Dom H., "Evelyn Waugh," <u>Month</u>, XXXVI (1966),
     69-71.
Voorhees, Richard J., "Evelyn Waugh Revisited," <u>SAQ</u>,
     XLVIII (April, 1949), 270-80.
Wilson, C., <u>Strength to Dream</u>, 42-6.
Wilson, Edmund, "Never Apologize, Never Explain," <u>NY</u>,
     XX (March 4, 1944), 68, 70, 72.   Also in Wilson, E.,
     <u>Classics and Commercials</u>, 140-6.
Woodcock, George, "Evelyn Waugh: The Man and His Work,"
     <u>WoR</u>, I (March, 1949), 51-6.
Wooton, Carl W., "Responses to the Modern World: A Study
     of Evelyn Waugh's Novels," <u>DA</u>, XXVIII (1968), 3693A
     (Ore.).

BLACK MISCHIEF

Bradbury, M., <u>Evelyn Waugh</u>, 51-5.
Carens, J. F., <u>Satiric Art of Evelyn Waugh</u>, 77-80, 139-44.
De Vitis, A. A., <u>Roman Holiday</u>, 29-31.
Doyle, P. A., <u>Evelyn Waugh</u>, 16-18.
Greenblatt, S. J., <u>Three Modern Satirists</u>, 16-22, and <u>passim</u>.
Hall, James, "The Other Post-War Rebellion: Evelyn Waugh
     Twenty-Five Years After," <u>ELH</u>, XXVIII (June, 1961),
     195-8.   Also in Hall, J., <u>Tragic Comedians</u>, 53-7.
Hollis, C., <u>Evelyn Waugh</u>, 8-11.
Stopp, F. J., <u>Evelyn Waugh</u>, 77-83.
Tucker, M., <u>Africa in Modern Literature</u>, 141-5.

BRIDESHEAD REVISITED

Allen, W. Gore, "Evelyn Waugh and Graham Greene," IrM,
LVII (January, 1949), 16-22.

Beary, Thomas J., "Religion and the Modern Novel, CathW,
CLXVI (December, 1947), 209-10.

Bergonzi, Bernard, "Evelyn Waugh's Gentlemen," CritQ, V
(Spring, 1963), 35-40. Also in Davis, R. M., ed., Evelyn Waugh, 75-81.

Boyle, Alexander, "Evelyn Waugh," IrM, LXXVIII (February, 1950), 79-81.

Bradbury, M., Evelyn Waugh, 85-93.

Carens, J. F., Satiric Art of Evelyn Waugh, 98-111.

Churchill, Thomas, "The Trouble with BRIDESHEAD RE-
VISITED," MLQ, XXVIII (June, 1967), 213-28.

Cogley, John, "Revisiting Brideshead," Cweal, LXXX (April
17, 1964), 103-6.

Davis, Robert M., "Notes Toward a Variorum BRIDES-
HEAD," EWN, II, iii (1968), 4-6.

Delasanta, Rodney, and Mario L. D'Avanzo, "Truth and
Beauty in BRIDESHEAD REVISITED," MFS, XI (Summer,
1965), 140-52.

De Vitis, A. A., Roman Holiday, 40-53.

Doyle, Paul A., Evelyn Waugh, 24-30.

_____, "Waugh's BRIDESHEAD REVISITED," Expl, XXIV
(March, 1966), Item 57.

Dyson, A. E., "Evelyn Waugh and the Mysteriously Disap-
pearing Hero," CritQ, II (Spring, 1960), 75-8. Also in
Dyson, A. E., Crazy Fabric, 192-4.

Gardiner, H. C., "Nigh Draws the Chase," America, LXXIV
(January 12, 1946), 411. Also in Gardiner, H. C., In
All Conscience, 89-91.

Grace, William J., "Evelyn Waugh as a Social Critic," Ren,
I, ii (Spring, 1949), 35-40.

Hardy, J. E., Man in the Modern Novel, 159-74.

Harty, E. R., "BRIDESHEAD Re-read: A Discussion of Some
of the Themes of Evelyn Waugh's BRIDESHEAD REVISIT-
ED," UES, III (1967), 66-74.

Heilman, Robert, "Sue Bridehead Revisited," Accent, VII
(1947), 123-6.

Hollis, C., Evelyn Waugh, 17-21.

Karl, F. R., "The World of Evelyn Waugh: The Normally
Insane," Contemporary English Novel, 172-5, 177-8.

LaFrance, Marston, "Context and Structure of Evelyn
Waugh's BRIDESHEAD REVISITED," TCL, X (April, 1964),
12-18. Also in Davis, R. M., ed., Evelyn Waugh, 57-68.

Martindale, C. C., "Back Again to BRIDESHEAD," Twentieth

Century (Australia), II (March, 1948), 26-33.
Neame, A. J., "Black and Blue: A Study in the Catholic
    Novel," The European, No. 2 (April, 1953), 30-2.
O'Faolain, S., Vanishing Hero, 34-42.
Prescott, O., In My Opinion, 169-71.
Spender, S., "The World of Evelyn Waugh," Creative Ele-
    ment, 169-74.
Staley, Thomas F., "Waugh the Artist," Cweal, LXXXIV
    (May 27, 1966), 280-2.
Stopp, Frederick J., Evelyn Waugh, 108-23, 150-2.
_____, "Grace in Reins: Reflections on Mr. Waugh's
    BRIDESHEAD and HELENA," Month, X, n. s. (August,
    1953), 69-84.
Vredenburgh, Joseph, "The Character of the Incest Object:
    A Study of Alternation between Narcissism and Object
    Choice," AI, XIV (1957), 45-52.
_____, "Further Contributions to a Study of the Incest Ob-
    ject," AI, XVI (Fall, 1959), 263-8.
Waugh, Evelyn, "BRIDESHEAD REVISITED Revisited,"
    Critic, XX (December, 1961-January, 1962), 35.
Wilson, Edmund, "Splendors and Miseries of Evelyn Waugh,"
    NY, XXI (January 5, 1946), 71+. Also in Wilson, E.,
    Classics and Commercials, 298-302.

DECLINE AND FALL

Bradbury, M., Evelyn Waugh, 34-46.
Carens, J. F., Satiric Art of Evelyn Waugh, 11-12, 16-17,
    26-8, 47-8, 70-4.
De Vitis, A. A., Roman Holiday, 19-24.
Doyle, Paul A., "DECLINE AND FALL: Two Versions,"
    EWN, II (1967), 4-5.
_____, Evelyn Waugh, 5-7.
Dyson, A. E., "Evelyn Waugh and the Mysteriously Disap-
    pearing Hero," CritQ, II (Spring, 1960), 72-5. Also in
    Dyson, A. E., Crazy Fabric, 188-90.
Greenblatt, S. J., Three Modern Satirists, 5-12.
Highet, G., Anatomy of Satire, 193-4.
Kleine, Don W., "The Cosmic Comedies of Evelyn Waugh,"
    SAQ, LXI (Autumn, 1962), 533-9.
Mehoke, James S., "Sartre's Theory of Emotion and Three
    English Novelists: Waugh, Green, Amis," WisSL, No. 3
    (1966), 106-8.
Nichols, James W., "Romantic and Realistic: The Tone of
    Evelyn Waugh's Early Novels," CE, XXIV (October, 1962),
    51-2.
Noon, William T., "Satire, Poison and the Professor,"

EngR, XI, i (July, 1960), 55-6.
Stopp, F. J., Evelyn Waugh, 63-70.
Symons, J., "A Long Way from Firbank," Critical Occasions, 74-9.
Tysdahl, Bjorn, "The Bright Young Things in the Early Novels of Evelyn Waugh," Edda, LXII (1962), 326-34.

END OF THE BATTLE (See UNCONDITIONAL SURRENDER)

A HANDFUL OF DUST

Bergonzi, Bernard, "Evelyn Waugh's Gentleman," CritQ, V (Spring, 1963), 24-7. Also in Davis, R. M., ed., Evelyn Waugh, 70-5.
Bradbury, M., Evelyn Waugh, 55-68.
Brophy, Brigid, in NStat, LXVIII (September, 1964), 450. Also in Brophy, B., Don't Never Forget, 156-9.
Carens, J. F., Satiric Art of Evelyn Waugh, 27-9, 81-6.
De Vitis, A. A., Roman Holiday, 31-3.
Doyle, P. A., Evelyn Waugh, 18-22.
Green, Peter, "Du Côté de Chez Waugh," REL, II, ii (April, 1961), 89-100.
Greenblatt, S. J., Three Modern Satirists, 57-63.
Hall, James, "The Other Post-War Rebellion: Evelyn Waugh Twenty-Five Years After," ELH, XXVIII (June, 1961), 198-201. Also in Hall, J., Tragic Comedians, 57-63.
Kearful, Frank J., "Tony Last and Ike McCaslin: The Loss of a Usable Past," UWR, III, ii (Spring, 1968), 45-52.
Nichols, James W., "Romantic and Realistic: The Tone of Evelyn Waugh's Early Novels," CE, XXIV (October, 1962), 53-6.
Staley, Thomas F., "Waugh the Artist," Cweal, LXXXIV (May 27, 1966), 281-2.
Stopp, F. J., Evelyn Waugh, 90-100.
Wasson, Richard, "A HANDFUL OF DUST: Critique of Victorianism," MFS, VII (Winter, 1961-62), 327-37.
Wilson, C., Strength to Dream, 42-3.

HELENA

Allen, W. Gore, "Evelyn Waugh's HELENA," IrM, LXXIX (February, 1951), 96-7.
Bradbury, M., Evelyn Waugh, 100-3.
Carens, J. F., Satiric Art of Evelyn Waugh, 111-19.
Dever, Joe, "Echoes of Two Waughs," Cweal, LIII (October 27, 1950), 68-70.
De Vitis, A. A., Roman Holiday, 60-7.

Doyle, P. A. , <u>Evelyn Waugh,</u> 33-5.
Hollis, C. , <u>Evelyn Waugh,</u> 25-31.
Joost, Nicholas, "Waugh's HELENA, Chapter VI," <u>Expl,</u> IX
    (April, 1951), Item 43.
Menen, Aubrey, "The Baroque and Mr. Waugh," <u>Month,</u> V
    (April, 1951), 226-37.
Stopp, Frederick J. , <u>Evelyn Waugh,</u> 123-9, 207-9.
_____, "Grace in Reins: Reflections on Mr. Waugh's
    BRIDESHEAD and HELENA," <u>Month,</u> X, n. s. (August,
    1953), 69-84.

LOVE AMONG THE RUINS

Bradbury, M. , <u>Evelyn Waugh,</u> 103-4.
Carens, J. F. , <u>Satiric Art of Evelyn Waugh,</u> 151-6.
Stopp, F. J. , <u>Evelyn Waugh,</u> 152-7, 189-90.

THE LOVED ONE

Bayley, John, "Two Catholic Novelists," <u>NatR,</u> CXXXII
    (1949), 232-5.
Bradbury, M. , <u>Evelyn Waugh,</u> 142-52.
Carens, J. F. , <u>Satiric Art of Evelyn Waugh,</u> 20-2.
Connolly, Cyril, "Introduction to THE LOVED ONE," <u>Hori-
    zon,</u> XVII (February, 1948), 76-7.
De Vitis, A. A. , <u>Roman Holiday,</u> 54-9.
Doyle, P. A. , <u>Evelyn Waugh,</u> 30-3.
Griffiths, Joan, "Waugh's Problem Comedies," <u>Accent,</u> IX
    (Spring, 1949), 165-70.
Hall, J. , <u>Tragic Comedians,</u> 63-4.
Hollis, C. , <u>Evelyn Waugh,</u> 22-4.
Mikes, George, <u>Eight Humorists,</u> London: Allan Wingate,
    1954, 135-8.
Powers, J. F. , "Waugh Out West," <u>Cweal,</u> XLVIII (July 16,
    1948), 326-7.
Ryan, Harold F. , "A vista of diminished truth," <u>America,</u>
    LXXXII (November 12, 1949), 157-8.
Stopp, F. J. , <u>Evelyn Waugh,</u> 142-52.
Wagner, Linda W. , "Satiric Masks: Huxley and Waugh,"
    <u>SNL,</u> III (Spring, 1966), 160-2.
Wecter, Dixon, "On Dying in Southern California," <u>PacSp,</u>
    II (Autumn, 1948), 375-87.
Wilson, E. , "Splendors and Miseries of Evelyn Waugh,"
    <u>Classics and Commercials,</u> 304-5.

MEN AT ARMS   (See also MEN AT ARMS Trilogy)

Braybrooke, Neville, "Evelyn Waugh and Blimp," Black-
friars, XXXVIII (December, 1952), 508-12.
Carens, J. F., Satiric Art of Evelyn Waugh, 41-5.
De Vitis, A. A., Roman Holiday, 68-79.
Hollis, C., Evelyn Waugh, 31-3.
Neame, A. J., "Black and Blue: A Study in the Catholic
Novel," The European, No. 2 (April, 1953), 33-6.
Semple, H. E., "Evelyn Waugh's Modern Crusade," ESA, XI
(March, 1968), 48-52.
Stopp, Frederick J., "The Circle and the Tangent: An In-
terpretation of Mr. Waugh's MEN AT ARMS," Month, XII
n. s. (July, 1954), 18-34.
_____, Evelyn Waugh, 158-69.
Voorhees, Richard J., "Evelyn Waugh's War Novels," QQ,
LXV (Spring, 1958), 53-63.

MEN AT ARMS Trilogy

Anon., in TLS (March 17, 1966), 216. Also in T. L. S.:
Essays and Reviews from The Times Literary Supplement,
1966, 123-7.
Bergonzi, Bernard, "Evelyn Waugh's Gentleman," CritQ, V
(Spring, 1963), 31-6. Also in Davis, R. M., ed., Evelyn
Waugh, 81-8.
_____, "Evelyn Waugh's THE SWORD OF HONOUR,"
Listener, LXXI (1964), 306-7.
Bradbury, M., Evelyn Waugh, 106-15.
Didion, Joan, "Evelyn Waugh: Gentleman in Battle," NatR,
XII (March 27, 1962), 215-17.
Doyle, P. A., Evelyn Waugh, 36-41.
Greene, George, "Scapegoat With Style: The Status of Eve-
lyn Waugh," QQ, LXXI (Winter, 1964-65), 484-93.
Hart, Jeffrey, "The Roots of Honor," NatR, XVIII (Febru-
ary 22, 1966), 168-9.
Kiely, Robert, "The Craft of Despondency - The Traditional
Novelists," Daedalus (Spring, 1963), 223-6, 233-4.
O'Donovan, Patrick, "Evelyn Waugh's Opus of Disgust,"
NRep, CXLVI (February 12, 1962), 21-2.
Parker, Kenneth, "Quantitative Judgments Don't Apply," ESA,
IX (September, 1966), 192-201.
Rutherford, Andrew, "Waugh's SWORD OF HONOUR," in
Mack, Maynard, and Ian Gregor, eds., Imagined Worlds:
Essays on Some English Novels and Novelists in Honour
of John Butt, London: Methuen, 1968, 441-60.
Semple, H. E., "Evelyn Waugh's Modern Crusade," ESA, XI

(March, 1968), 47-59.

OFFICERS AND GENTLEMEN
(See also MEN AT ARMS Trilogy)

Carens, F. J. , Satiric Art of Evelyn Waugh, 160-5.
De Vitis, A. A. , Roman Holiday, 79-81.
Hollis, C. , Evelyn Waugh, 33-4.
Stopp, Frederick J. , Evelyn Waugh, 169-78.
_____, "Waugh: End of an Illusion," Ren, IX (1956), 59-
   67+.
Voorhees, Richard J. , "Evelyn Waugh's War Novels," QQ,
   LXV (Spring, 1958), 53-63.

THE ORDEAL OF GILBERT PINFOLD

Anon. , "Stout Party," NStat (October 20, 1961), 592-4.
Bradbury, M. , Evelyn Waugh, 2-4, 104-6.
Price, Martin, in YR, XLVII (Autumn, 1957), 150-1.
Stopp, Frederick J. , "Apology and Explanation," Ren, X
   (Winter, 1958), 94-7.
_____, Evelyn Waugh, 219-34.

PUT OUT MORE FLAGS

Bradbury, M. , Evelyn Waugh, 80-5.
De Vitis, A. A. , Roman Holiday, 36-9.
Hollis, C. , Evelyn Waugh, 15-17.
Stopp, F. J. , Evelyn Waugh, 130-6.

SCOOP

Bradbury, M. , Evelyn Waugh, 68-74.
Carens, J. F. , Satiric Art of Evelyn Waugh, 144-8.
Davis, Robert M. , "Some Textual Variants in SCOOP,"
   EWN, II (1967), 1-3.
De Vitis, A. A. , Roman Holiday, 33-6.
Hollis, C. , Evelyn Waugh, 11-14.
Stopp, F. J. , Evelyn Waugh, 83-9.
Tucker, M. , Africa in Modern Literature, 141-5, 236-7.

SCOTT-KING'S MODERN EUROPE

Bradbury, M. , Evelyn Waugh, 93-4.
Carens, J. F. , Satiric Art of Evelyn Waugh, 148-51.
Hollis, C. , Evelyn Waugh, 21-2.
Stopp, F. J. , Evelyn Waugh, 136-42.

SWORD OF HONOUR   (See MEN AT ARMS Trilogy)

UNCONDITIONAL SURRENDER
(See also MEN AT ARMS Trilogy)

Amis, Kingsley, "Crouchback's Regress," Spectator, No.
   6957 (October 27, 1961), 581-2.
Burrows, L. R., "Scenes de la Vie Militaire," Westerly, No.
   1 (1962), 3-6.
Carens, J. F., Satiric Art of Evelyn Waugh, 165-73.
O'Donovan, Patrick, "Evelyn Waugh's Opus of Disgust,"
   NRep, CXLVI (February 12, 1962), 21-2.
Pritchett, V. S., "Vanities and Servitudes," NStat (October
   20, 1961), 603-4.

VILE BODIES

Allen, W., Modern Novel, 209-10.
Bradbury, M., Evelyn Waugh, 46-51.
Carens, J. F., Satiric Art of Evelyn Waugh, 17-19, 24-5,
   74-7.
Doyle, P. A., Evelyn Waugh, 14-16.
Greenblatt, S. J., Three Modern Satirists, 12-16.
Hall, James, "The Other Post-War Rebellion: Evelyn Waugh
   Twenty-Five Years After," ELH, XXVIII (June, 1961),
   191-5.   Also in Hall, J., Tragic Comedians, 49-53.
Isaacs, Neil D., "Evelyn Waugh's Restoration Jesuit," SNL,
   II (Spring, 1965), 91-4.
Jervis, Steven A., "Evelyn Waugh, VILE BODIES, and the
   Younger Generation," SAQ, LXVI (Summer, 1967), 440-8.
Kleine, Don W., "The Cosmic Comedies of Evelyn Waugh,"
   SAQ, LXI (Autumn, 1962), 533-9.
Nichols, James W., "Romantic and Realistic: The Tone of
   Evelyn Waugh's Early Novels," CE, XXIV (October, 1962),
   52-3.
Stopp, F. J., Evelyn Waugh, 70-7.
Tysdahl, Bjorn, "The Bright Young Things in the Early Nov-
   els of Evelyn Waugh," Edda, LXII (1962), 326-34.

THE WAR TRILOGY (See MEN AT ARMS Trilogy)

WORK SUSPENDED

Bradbury, M., Evelyn Waugh, 76-80.
Stopp, F. J., Evelyn Waugh, 101-7.

BIBLIOGRAPHY

Bradbury, M. , Evelyn Waugh, 116-20.
Davis, Robert N. , "The Year's Work in Waugh Studies,"
    EWN, II, i (1968), 3-5.
Doyle, Paul A. , Evelyn Waugh, 46-8.
_____, "Evelyn Waugh: A Bibliography," BB, XXII (1957),
    57-62.
English, William A. , "Some Irish and English Waugh Bibli-
    ography," EWN, I, iii (1967), 5; II, ii (1968), 3-4.
Kosok, Heinz, "Evelyn Waugh: A Checklist of Criticism,"
    TCL, XI (January, 1966), 211-15.
_____, "Evelyn Waugh: A Supplementary Checklist of
    Criticism," EWN, II, i (1968), 1-3.
Stopp, F. J. , Evelyn Waugh, 238-40.

WEIDMAN, JEROME, 1913-

THE ENEMY CAMP

Rosenthal, Raymond, "What's In It for Weidman?" Ctary,
    XXVII (February, 1959), 171-3.

I CAN GET IT FOR YOU WHOLESALE

Sherman, B. , Invention of the Jew, 176-8.

WELTY, EUDORA, 1909-

GENERAL

Appel, A. , Jr. , Season of Dreams.
Bryant, J. A. , Jr. , Eudora Welty.
Buswell, Mary C. , "The Love Relationships of Women in the
    Fiction of Eudora Welty," WVUPP, XIII (December, 1961),
    94-106.
Eisinger, C. E. , Fiction of the Forties, 258-62.
Folsom, Gordon R. , "Form and Substance in Eudora Welty,"
    DA, XXI (1960), 621 (Wisconsin).
Gossett, L. Y. , "Violence as Revelation: Eudora Welty,"
    Violence in Recent Southern Fiction, 98-117.
Griffith, Albert J. , Jr. , "Eudora Welty's Fiction," DA, XX
    (1959), 2289-90 (Texas).
Hicks, Granville, "Eudora Welty," CE, XIV (November,
    1952), 69-72. Also in EJ, XLI (November, 1952), 461-8.

Hoffman, F. J. , Art of Southern Fiction, 51-9.
Isaacs, N. , Eudora Welty.
Jones, Alun R. , "The World of Love: The Fiction of Eu-
    dora Welty," in Balakian, N. , and C. Simmons, eds. ,
    Creative Present, 175-92.
Jones, William M. , "Name and Symbol in the Prose of Eu-
    dora Welty," SFQ, XXII (December, 1958), 173-85.
Morris, Harry C. , "Eudora Welty's Use of Myth," Shen, VI
    (Spring, 1955), 34-40.
Rechnitz, Robert M. , "Perception, Identity, and the Gro-
    tesque: A Study of Three Southern Writers," DA, XXVIII
    (1967), 2216A (Colorado).
Rouse, Sarah A. , "Place and People in Eudora Welty's Fic-
    tion: A Portrait of the Deep South," DA, XXIII (1963),
    3901 (Fla. State).
Vande Kieft, R. M. , Eudora Welty.
Van Gelder, R. , Writers on Writing, 287-90.
Welty, Eudora, "How I Write," VQR, XXXI (Spring, 1955),
    240-51. Also in Brooks, Cleanth, and R. P. Warren,
    eds. , Understanding Fiction, N. Y. : Appleton, 1959, 545-
    53.

DELTA WEDDING

Appel, A. , Jr. , Season of Dreams, 199-204.
Bryant, J. A. , Jr. , Eudora Welty, 20-6.
Eisinger, C. E. , Fiction of the Forties, 275-80.
Hardy, J. E. , "DELTA WEDDING as Region and Symbol,"
    SR, LX (Summer, 1952), 397-417. Also in Hardy, J. E. ,
    Man in the Modern Novel, 175-93.
Hoffman, F. J. , Art of Southern Fiction, 59-63.
Isaacs, N. , Eudora Welty, 33-6.
Prescott, Orville, in YR, XXXV (Summer, 1946), 765-6.
Ransom, John Crowe, "Delta Fiction," KR, VIII (Summer,
    1946), 503-7.
Rosenfeld, Isaac, in NRep, CXIV (April 29, 1946), 633-4.
Rouse, Sarah A. , "Place and People in Eudora Welty's Fic-
    tion: A Portrait of the Deep South," DA, XXIII (1963),
    3901 (Fla. State).
Rubin, L. D. , Jr. , Faraway Country, 134-41.
Trilling, Diana, "Fiction in Review," Nation, CLXII (May
    11, 1946), 578.
Vande Kieft, R. M. , Eudora Welty, 20-6.

THE PONDER HEART

Appel, A. , Jr. , Season of Dreams, 51-60.

Bryant, J. A., Jr., <u>Eudora Welty</u>, 33-5.
Daniel, Robert W., "Eudora Welty: The Sense of Place,"
   in Rubin, L. D., Jr., and R. D. Jacobs, eds., <u>South,</u>
   276-7, 285-8.
Drake, Robert Y., Jr., "The Reasons of the Heart," <u>GaR,</u>
   XI (Winter, 1957), 420-6.
Dusenbury, Winifred, "BABY DOLL and THE PONDER
   HEART," <u>MD,</u> III (1961), 393-5.
French, Warren, "A Note on Eudora Welty's THE PONDER
   HEART," <u>CE</u>, XV (May, 1954), 474.
Holland, Robert B., "Dialogue as a Reflection of Place in
   THE PONDER HEART," <u>AL,</u> XXXV (November, 1963),
   352-8.
Isaacs, N., <u>Eudora Welty</u>, 12-14.
Opitz, Kurt, "Eudora Welty: The Order of a Captive Soul,"
   <u>Crit,</u> VII, ii (1965), 86-8.
Rouse, Sarah A., "Place and People in Eudora Welty's Fic-
   tion: A Portrait of the Deep South," <u>DA,</u> XXIII (1963),
   3901 (Fla. State).

THE ROBBER BRIDEGROOM

Appel, A., Jr., <u>Season of Dreams,</u> 69-72, 182-3.
Bishop, J. P., "The Violent Country," <u>NRep,</u> CVII (Novem-
   ber 16, 1942), 646-7. Also in Bishop, J. P., <u>Collected
   Essays,</u> 257-9.
Bryant, J. A., Jr., <u>Eudora Welty</u>, 17-20.
Eisinger, C. E., <u>Fiction of the Forties,</u> 272-5.
Glenn, Eunice, "Fantasy in the Fiction of Eudora Welty," in
   Tate, A., ed., <u>A Southern Vanguard,</u> N. Y.: Prentice
   Hall, 1947, 85-7. Also in Aldridge, J. W., ed., <u>Crit-
   iques and Essays on Modern Fiction,</u> 512-14.
Isaacs, N., <u>Eudora Welty</u>, 16-19.
Rouse, Sarah A., "Place and People in Eudora Welty's Fic-
   tion: A Portrait of the Deep South," <u>DA,</u> XXIII (1963),
   3901 (Fla. State).
Straumann, H., <u>American Literature in the Twentieth Cen-
   tury,</u> 137-8.

BIBLIOGRAPHY

Gross, Seymour L., "Eudora Welty: A Bibliography of
   Criticism and Comment," <u>Secretary's News Sheet,</u> No.
   45 (April, 1960), Bibliog. Soc., Univ. of Va., 1-32.
Jordan, Leona, "Eudora Welty: Selected Criticism," <u>BB,</u>
   XXIII (January-April, 1960), 14-15.
Vande Kieft, R. M., <u>Eudora Welty</u>, 195-9.

WEST, JESSAMYN, 1907-

GENERAL

West, Jessamyn, To See the Dream, N.Y.: Harcourt,
Brace, 1957.

CRESS DELAHANTY

Carpenter, Frederic I., "The Adolescent in American Fiction," EJ, XLVI (September, 1957), 317-18.

THE WITCH DIGGERS

Bergler, Edmund, M.D., "Writers of Half-Talent," AI, XIV
(1957), 159-61.

WEST, REBECCA, 1892-

GENERAL

Allen, W., Modern Novel, 62-4.
Hutchinson, George E., Itinerant Ivory Tower; Scientific and
Literary Essays, New Haven: Yale Un. Pr., 1953, 241-
55.
Orlich, Sister Mary M., C.S.J., "The Novels of Rebecca
West: A Complex Unity," DA, XXVII (1967), 2540A
(Notre Dame).

THE BIRDS FALL DOWN

Ellmann, Mary, "The Russians of Rebecca West," Atlantic,
CCXVIII (December, 1966), 68-71.

WHITE, PATRICK, 1912-

GENERAL

Alexander, J.C., "Vision of Depth - Australian Image, No.
3," Meanjin, XXI (1962), 328-35. (Not seen.)
Argyle, B., Patrick White.
Barnes, John, "A Note on Patrick White's Novels," LCrit,
VI, iii (1964), 93-101. Also in Narasimahaiah, C.D.,
ed., Introduction to Australian Literature, 93-101.

Bradley, David, "Australia Through the Lookingglass,"
    Overland, No. 23 (Autumn, 1962), 41-5.
Brand, Mona, "Another Look at Patrick White," Realist
    Writer (Sydney), No. 12 (August, 1963), 21-2.   (Not seen.)
Brissenden, R. F., Patrick White.
Buckley, Vincent, "In the Shadow of Patrick White," Mean-
    jin, XX (July, 1961), 144-54.
_____, "The Novels of Patrick White," in Dutton, G.,
    Literature of Australia, 413-26.
Davies, Brian, "An Australian Enigma: Conversations with
    Patrick White," Melbourne Univ. Mag, (Spring, 1962),
    69-71.
Donaldson, I., "Return to Abyssinia," EIC, XIV (1964),
    210-14.   (Reply to M. MacKenzie.)
Dutton, Geoffrey, "The Novels of Patrick White," Crit, VI,
    iii (Winter, 1963-64), 7-28.
_____, Patrick White.
Heseltine, H. P., "Patrick White's Style," Quadrant, VII
    (Winter, 1963), 61-74.
Lindsay, Jack, "The Alienated Australian Intellectual,"
    Meanjin, XXII (March, 1963), 56-9.
MacKenzie, Manfred, "Abyssinia Lost and Regained," EIC,
    XIII (1963), 292-300.
_____, "Patrick White's Later Novels: A Generic Read-
    ing," SoRA, I, iii (1965), 5-18.
_____, "Yes, Let's Return to Abyssinia," EIC, XIV
    (1964), 433-5.   (Reply to I. Donaldson.)
McLaren, John, "The Image of Reality in Our Writing (With
    special reference to the work of Patrick White)," Over-
    land, Nos. 27-8 (July–September, 1963), 43-7.   Also in
    Semmler, C., ed., Twentieth Century Australian Literary
    Criticism, 235-44.
Martin, David, "Among the Bones," Meanjin, XVIII, No. 1
    (April, 1959), 52-8.
Potter, Nancy A. J., "Patrick White's Minor Saints," REL,
    V, iv (October, 1964), 9-19.
Stern, James, "Patrick White: The Country of the Mind,"
    LonM, V, vi (June, 1958), 49-56.
Thompson, John, "Australia's White Policy: Analysis of
    White's Critics," AusL, I (April, 1958), 42-5.
Walters, Margaret, "Patrick White," New Left Rev, XVIII
    (January-February, 1963), 37-50.
White, Patrick, "The Prodigal Son," AusL, I (April, 1958),
    37-40.
Wood, Peter, "Moral Complexity in Patrick White's Novels,"
    Meanjin, XXI (March, 1962), 21-8.

THE AUNT'S STORY

Argyle, B., Patrick White, 22-30.
Barnard, Marjorie, "The Four Novels of Patrick White,"
Meanjin, XV (June, 1956), 163-5.
_____, "Theodora Again," Southerly, XX (1959), 51-5.
Barnes, John, "A Note on Patrick White's Novels," LCrit,
VI, iii (1964), 96-7. Also in Narasimahaiah, C. D., ed.,
Introduction to Australian Literature, 96-7.
Brissendon, R. F., Patrick White, 19-24.
Buckley, Vincent, "The Novels of Patrick White," in Dutton,
G., ed., Literature of Australia, 416-18.
Burrows, J. F., " ' Jardin Exotique': The Central Phase of
THE AUNT'S STORY," Southerly, XXVI, iii (1966), 152-
73.
Dutton, Geoffrey, "The Novels of Patrick White," Crit, VI,
iii (Winter, 1963-64), 9-11.
_____, Patrick White, 21-7.
Hadgraft, C., Australian Literature, 241-2.
Herring, T., "Odyssey of a Spinster: A Study of THE
AUNT'S STORY," Southerly, XXV, i (1965), 6-22.
Howarth, R. G., "The Image," Southerly, XI, iv (1950), 209-
10.
McAuley, James, in Quadrant, III, iv (Spring, 1959), 91-3.
MacKenzie, Manfred, "Patrick White's Later Novels: A
Generic Reading," SoRA, I, iii (1965), 5-14.
Potter, Nancy A. J., "Patrick White's Minor Saints," REL,
V, iv (October, 1964), 9-11.
Tanner, G., "The Road to Jerusalem," Nimrod, II, i (1964),
33-9.

HAPPY VALLEY

Argyle, B., Patrick White, 6-11, 13-15.
Barnard, Marjorie, "The Four Novels of Patrick White,"
Meanjin, XV (June, 1956), 157-60.
Brissendon, R. F., Patrick White, 14-17.
Buckley, Vincent, "The Novels of Patrick White," in Dutton,
G., ed., Literature of Australia, 413-14.
Dutton, G., Patrick White, 11-15.
Hadgraft, C., Literature of Australia, 240-1.

THE LIVING AND THE DEAD

Argyle, B., Patrick White, 15-21.
Barnard, Marjorie, "The Four Novels of Patrick White,"
Meanjin, XV (June, 1956), 160-3.

Brissenden, R. F., <u>Patrick White,</u> 17-18.
Buckley, Vincent, "The Novels of Patrick White," in Dutton,
  G., ed., <u>Literature of Australia,</u> 414-15.
Dutton, G., <u>Patrick White,</u> 15-21.
Maes-Jelinek, H., "THE LIVING AND THE DEAD," <u>RLV,</u>
  XXIX (1963), 521-8.

RIDERS IN THE CHARIOT

Anon., "RIDERS IN THE CHARIOT: A Note on the Title,"
  <u>Westerly,</u> Nos. 2 & 3 (1962), 108-10.
Argyle, B., <u>Patrick White,</u> 48-57.
Aughterson, M., "The Way Through Suburbia," <u>Prospect,</u> V
  (1962), 30-1.
Aurousseau, Marcel, "Odi Profanum Vulgus: Patrick White's
  RIDERS IN THE CHARIOT," <u>Meanjin,</u> XXI (March, 1962),
  29-31.
Balliet, W., "Mrs. Jolley and Mrs. Flack," <u>NY,</u> XXXVII
  (December 9, 1961), 244-7.
Barnes, John, "A Note on Patrick White's Novels," <u>LCrit,</u>
  VI, iii (1964), 100-1. Also in Narasimahaiah, C. D., ed.,
  <u>Introduction to Australian Literature,</u> 100-1.
Bradley, D., Australia Through the Looking-Glass; Patrick
  White's Latest Novel," <u>Overland,</u> XXIII (Autumn, 1965),
  41-5.
Brissenden, R. F., <u>Patrick White,</u> 34-8.
Buckley, Vincent, "The Novels of Patrick White," in Dutton,
  G., ed., <u>Literature of Australia,</u> 424-6.
Burgess, O. N., in <u>AusQ,</u> XXXIV (March, 1962), 110-13.
Burrows, J. F., "Archtypes and Stereotypes: RIDERS IN
  THE CHARIOT," <u>Southerly,</u> XXV, i (1965), 46-68.
Dillistone, Frederick W., <u>Patrick White's RIDERS IN THE
  CHARIOT</u> (Religious Dimensions in Literature), N. Y.:
  Seabury, 1967.
Dutton, Geoffrey, "The Novels of Patrick White," <u>Crit,</u> VI,
  iii (Winter, 1963-64), 21-7.
_____, <u>Patrick White,</u> 39-43.
_____, "White's Triumphal Chariot," <u>Australian Book Re-
  view,</u> I (November, 1963), 1-3.
Edwards, Allan, "RIDERS IN THE CHARIOT: A Note on the
  Title," <u>Westerly,</u> Nos. 2 & 3 (1962), 108-10.
Gzell, Sylvia, "Themes and Imagery in VOSS and RIDERS IN
  THE CHARIOT," <u>ALS,</u> I (June, 1964), 180-95. Also in
  Semmler, C., ed., <u>Twentieth Century Australian Criti-
  cism,</u> 252-67.
Heydon, J. D., "Patrick White," <u>OR,</u> No. 1 (1966), 42-6.
Kantor, P. P., "Jews and Jewish Mysticism in Patrick

White's RIDERS IN THE CHARIOT," <u>BB Bulletin</u> (Sydney),
  XI (March, 1963), 14+.
McAuley, James, in <u>Quadrant,</u> VI, ii (1962), 79-81.
MacKenzie, Manfred, "Abyssinia Lost and Regained," <u>EIC,</u>
  XIII (1963), 296-300.
McLaren, John, "Patrick White's Use of Imagery," <u>ALS,</u> II
  (June, 1966), 217-20. Also in Semmler, C., ed., <u>Twen-</u>
  <u>tieth Century Australian Literary Criticism,</u> 268-72.
Martin, David, "A Chariot Between Faith and Despair: On
  Patrick White's RIDERS IN THE CHARIOT," <u>Bridge</u> (Syd-
  ney), I (Autumn, 1964), 7-12.
New, William H., "The Island and the Madman: Recurrent
  Imagery in the Major Novelists of the Fifties," <u>ArQ,</u>
  XXII (Winter, 1966), 332-4.
Phillips, A.A., "Patrick White and the Algebraic Symbol,"
  <u>Meanjin,</u> XXIV (1965), 455-61.
Potter, Nancy A.J., "Patrick White's Minor Saints," <u>REL,</u>
  V, iv (October, 1964), 16-19.
Roderick, Colin, "RIDERS IN THE CHARIOT: An Exposi-
  tion," <u>Southerly,</u> XXII, ii (1962), 62-77.
Walters, Margaret, "Patrick White," <u>New Left Rev,</u> XVIII
  (January-February, 1963), 47-50.

THE SOLID MANDALA

Anon., "Reading the Marbles," <u>TLS</u> (June 9, 1966), 509.
  Also in <u>T.L.S.: Essays and Reviews from The Times</u>
  <u>Literary Supplement, 1966,</u> 23-7.
Argyle, B., <u>Patrick White,</u> 57-65.
Herring, Thelma, "Self and the Shadow: The Quest for
  Totality in THE SOLID MANDALA," <u>Southerly,</u> XXVI, iii
  (1966), 180-9.
_____, "THE SOLID MANDALA: Two Notes," <u>Southerly,</u>
  XXVIII (1968), 216-22.
Phillips, A.A., "THE SOLID MANDALA: Patrick White's
  New Novel," <u>Meanjin,</u> XXV (Autumn, 1966), 31-3.

THE TREE OF MAN

Argyle, B., <u>Patrick White,</u> 30-40.
Barden, Carrett, "Patrick White's THE TREE OF MAN,"
  <u>Studies,</u> LVII (Spring, 1968), 78-85.
Barnard, Marjorie, "The Four Novels of Patrick White,"
  <u>Meanjin,</u> XV (June, 1956), 165-70.
Barnes, John, "A Note on Patrick White's Novels," <u>LCrit,</u>
  VI, iii (1964), 98-100. Also in Narasimahaiah, C.D.,
  ed., <u>Introduction to Australian Literature,</u> 98-100.
Brissenden, R.F., <u>Patrick White,</u> 24-9.

_____, "Patrick White," Meanjin, XVIII (December, 1959), 410-25.

Buckley, Vincent, "The Novels of Patrick White," in Dutton, G., ed., Literature of Australia, 418-22.

_____, "Patrick White and His Epic," TCM, XII (1958), 239-52. Also in Johnston, Grahame, ed., Australian Literary Criticism, Melbourne: Oxford Un. Pr., 1962, 187-97.

Cooperman, S., "An Epic of Australia," Nation, CLXXXI (November 5, 1955), 404-5.

Dutton, Geoffrey, "The Novels of Patrick White," Crit, VI, iii (Winter, 1963-64), 11-16.

_____, Patrick White, 27-32.

Hadgraft, C., Australian Literature, 242-4.

Heydon, J.D., "Patrick White," OR, No. 1 (1966), 33-9.

Krim, Seymour, "Big Little Novel," Cweal, LXIII (December 9, 1955), 265-7.

Mackenzie, Manfred, "Apocalypse in Patrick White's THE TREE OF MAN," Meanjin, XXV (December, 1966), 405-16.

Oliver, H.J., "The Expanding Novel," Southerly, XVII, iii (1956), 168-70.

Potter, Nancy A.J., "Patrick White's Minor Saints," REL, V, iv (October, 1964), 11-14.

Reimer, A.P., "Visions of the Mandala in THE TREE OF MAN," Southerly, XXVII, No. 1 (1967), 3-19.

Rorke, John, "Patrick White and the Critics," Southerly, XX (1959), 66-74.

Thomson, A.K., "Patrick White's THE TREE OF MAN," Meanjin, XXV, (Autumn, 1966), 21-30.

Walters, Margaret, "Patrick White," New Left Rev, XVIII (January-February, 1963), 40-4.

Wilkes, G.A., "Patrick White's THE TREE OF MAN," Southerly, XXV, i (1965), 23-33.

VOSS

Argyle, B., Patrick White, 40-8.

Aurousseau, M., "The Identity of VOSS," Meanjin, XVII (1958), 85-7.

Barnard, Marjorie, in Meanjin, XVII (April, 1958), 96-100.

Brissenden, R.F., Patrick White, 29-34.

_____, "Patrick White," Meanjin, XVIII (December, 1959), 410-25.

Buckley, Vincent, "The Novels of Patrick White," in Dutton, G., ed., Literature of Australia, 422-4.

Burgess, O.N., "Patrick White, His Critics and Laura Trevelyan," AusQ, XXXIII, iv (December, 1961), 49-57.

Burrows, J. F., "VOSS and the Explorers," AUMLA, No. 26 (November, 1966), 234-40.

Cowburn, John, "The Metaphysics of VOSS," TCM, XVIII (Winter, 1964), 352-61.

Dutton, Geoffrey, "The Novels of Patrick White," Crit, VI, iii (Winter, 1963-64), 16-21.

_____, Patrick White, 32-9.

Fraser, E., in TCM, CLXIII (March, 1958), 277-8.

Fry, Robert, in AusL, I (April, 1958), 40-1.

Gzell, Sylvia, "Themes and Imagery in VOSS and RIDERS IN THE CHARIOT," ALS, I (June, 1964), 180-95. Also in Semmler, C., ed., Twentieth Century Australian Criticism, 252-67.

Heydon, J. D., "Patrick White," OR, No. 1 (1966), 39-42.

Hughes, Ted, "Patrick White's VOSS," Listener, LXXI (February 6, 1964), 229-30.

McAuley, James, "The Gothic Splendours of Patrick White's VOSS," Southerly, XXV, i (1965), 34-44.

_____, in Quadrant, II, viii (1958), 4-5.

_____, in Quadrant, III, iv (Spring, 1959), 91-3.

McLaren, John, "Patrick White's Use of Imagery," ALS, II (June, 1966), 217-20. Also in Semmler, C., ed., Twentieth Century Australian Criticism, 268-72.

Mather, Rodney, "VOSS," Melbourne Critical Rev, VI (1963), 93-101.

Oliver, H. J., "Patrick White's Significant Journey," Southerly, XIX (1958), 46-9.

Phillips, A. A., "Patrick White and the Algebraic Symbol," Meanjin, XXIV (1965), 455-61.

Potter, Nancy A. J., "Patrick White's Minor Saints," REL, V, iv (October, 1964), 14-16.

Shrubb, Peter, "Patrick White: Chaos Accepted," Quadrant, XII, iii (No. 53) (May-June, 1968), 7-19.

Stern, James, "Patrick White: The Country of the Mind," LonM, V, vi (June, 1958), 53-6.

Turner, I., "The Parable of VOSS," Overland, XII (Winter, 1958), 36-7.

Walters, Margaret, "Patrick White," New Left Rev, XVIII (January-February, 1963), 44-7.

Wilkes, G. A., "A Reading of Patrick White's VOSS," Southerly, XXVII, No. 3 (1968), 159-73.

WILDER, THORNTON NIVEN, 1897-

Burbank, R., Thornton Wilder.

Cowie, Alexander, "The Bridge of Thornton Wilder," in
    Gohdes, G., ed., Essays on American Literature, 307-
    28.
Cowley, Malcolm, "The Man Who Abolished Time," SatR,
    XXXIX (October 6, 1956), 13-14, 50-2. Also (slightly
    abridged) as "Introduction" to A Thornton Wilder Trio,
    N.Y.: Criterion Books, 1956.
Drew, Fraser, "Thornton Wilder: His 'Grand Theme' and
    the Pinch of Time," Trace, No. 33 (August-September,
    1959), 23-6.
Edgell, David P., "Thornton Wilder Revisited," CaiSE
    (1960), 47-59.
Firebaugh, Joseph, "The Humanism of Thornton Wilder,"
    PacSp, IV (Autumn, 1950), 426-38.
Fuller, Edmund, "Thornton Wilder: The Notation of the
    Heart," ASch, XXVIII (Spring, 1959), 210-17. Also in
    American Scholar. American Scholar Reader, N.Y.:
    Atheneum, 1960, 476-89. Also in Fuller, E., Books
    With the Men Behind Them, 36-62.
Four Quarters, XVI, iv (May, 1967) Thornton Wilder Num-
    ber.
Germer, Rudolf, and John Stambaugh, "Modern Writers:
    Thornton Wilder," Praxis des neusprachlichen Unterrichts,
    IX (1962), 200-6. (Not seen.)
Goldstein, M., Art of Thornton Wilder.
Goldstone, Richard H., "The Art of Fiction XVI: Thornton
    Wilder," ParisR, No. 15 (1957), 37-57. Also in Writers
    at Work, 1st ser., 99-118.
Grebanier, B., Thornton Wilder.
Greene, George, "The World of Thornton Wilder," Thought,
    XXXVII (Winter, 1962), 563-84.
Loyd, Allen D., "The Shudder of Awe: A Study of the Nov-
    els of Thornton Wilder," DA, XIX (1968), 1541A-42A
    (Peabody).
Morgan, H., Wayne, "The Early Thornton Wilder," SWR,
    XLIII (Summer, 1958), 248-53.
Papajewski, H., Thornton Wilder.
Singh, Ram Sewak, "Thornton Wilder: The Chronicler of
    Civilization," Banasthali Patrika (Rajasthan), No. 11 (July,
    1968), 53-62. (Not seen.)
Wagenknecht, E., Cavalcade of the American Novel, 405-8.
Wescott, Glenway, "Conversations with Thornton Wilder,"
    Images of Truth, 242-308.

THE BRIDGE OF SAN LUIS REY

Burbank, R., Thornton Wilder, 44-56.

Cowie, Alexander, "The Bridge of Thornton Wilder," in
    Gohdes, C., ed., Essays on American Literature, 310-11.
Fuller, Emund, "Thornton Wilder: The Notation of the
    Heart," ASch, XXVIII (Spring, 1959), 210-11+. Also in
    American Scholar. American Scholar Reader, N.Y.:
    Atheneum, 1960, 477-8+. Also in Fuller, E., Books
    With the Men Behind Them, 37-9, 45-8.
Friedman, Paul, "The Bridge: A Study in Symbolism,"
    Psychoanalytic Quart., XXXI (1952), 49-80. Also in
    Yearbook of Psychoanalysis (1953), 257-82.
Goldstein, M., Art of Thornton Wilder, 49-62.
Grebanier, B., Thornton Wilder, 15-20.
Papajewski, H., Thornton Wilder, 16-36.
Stuckey, W.J., Pulitzer Prize Novels, 74-8.
Wilson, Edmond, "Thornton Wilder: Influence of Proust,"
    NRep, LV (August 8, 1928), 303-5. Also in Wilson, E.,
    Shores of Light, 384-91.

THE CABALA

Allen, W., Modern Novel, 103-4.
_____, Urgent West, 187-8.
Burbank, R., Thornton Wilder, 35-44.
Cowie, Alexander, "The Bridge of Thornton Wilder," in
    Gohdes, C., ed., Essays on American Literature, 308-
    10.
Goldstein, M., Art of Thornton Wilder, 34-48.
Grebanier, B., Thornton Wilder, 12-15.
Papajewski, H., Thornton Wilder, 1-15.
Wilson, Edmund, "Thornton Wilder: Influence of Proust,"
    NRep, LV (August 8, 1928), 303-5. Also in Wilson, E.,
    Shores of Light, 384-91.

THE EIGHTH DAY

Goldstone, Richard, "Wilder, Studying and Studied," AR,
    XXVII (Summer, 1967), 264-8.
Oliver, Edith, "The Summing Up," NY, XLIII (May 27, 1967),
    146-8.

HEAVEN'S MY DESTINATION

Allen, W., Modern Novel, 104-5.
Burbank, R., Thornton Wilder, 72-81.
Cowie, Alexander, "The Bridge of Thornton Wilder," in
    Gohdes, C., ed., Essays on American Literature, 313-
    17.

Goldstein, M., <u>Art of Thornton Wilder</u>, 82-94.
Grebanier, B., <u>Thornton Wilder,</u> 26-9.
Greene, George, "The World of Thornton Wilder," <u>Thought</u>,
    XXXVII (Winter, 1962), 570-4.
Haberman, Donald, "The Americanization of Thornton
    Wilder," <u>FQ</u>, XVI (May, 1967), 18-27.
Papajewski, H., <u>Thornton Wilder,</u> 51-61.
Wilson, Edmund, "Mr. Wilder in the Middle West," in
    <u>NRep</u>, LXXI (January 16, 1934), 282-3.   Also in Wilson,
    E., <u>Shores of Light</u>, 587-92.

THE IDES OF MARCH

Burbank, R., <u>Thornton Wilder</u>, 112-22.
Cowie, Alexander, "The Bridge of Thornton Wilder," in
    Gohdes, C., ed., <u>Essays on American Literature</u>, 317-
    18.
Davis, Elmer, "Caesar's Last Months," <u>SatR</u>, XXXI (Febru-
    ary 21, 1948), 11-12.
Goldstein, M., <u>Art of Thornton Wilder,</u> 131-45.
Grebanier, B., <u>Thornton Wilder,</u> 38-42.
Papajewski, H., <u>Thornton Wilder,</u> 62-90.
Wescott, G., <u>Images of Truth,</u> 256-62.

THE WOMAN OF ANDROS

Burbank, R., <u>Thornton Wilder,</u> 56-62.
Cowie, Alexander, "The Bridge of Thornton Wilder," in
    Gohdes, C., ed., <u>Essays on American Literature</u>, 312-
    13.
Goldstein, M., <u>Art of Thornton Wilder,</u> 63-71.
Grebanier, B., <u>Thornton Wilder,</u> 20-4.
Papajewski, H., <u>Thornton Wilder,</u> 37-50.
Wilson, Edmund, "Dahlberg, Dos Passos and Wilder," <u>NRep</u>,
    LXII (March 26, 1930), 156-7.   Also in Wilson, E.,
    <u>Shores of Light</u>, 442-5.

BIBLIOGRAPHY

Bryer, Jackson, "Thornton Wilder and the Reviewers,"
    <u>PBSA</u>, LVIII (1964), 35-49.
Kosok, Heinz, "Thornton Wilder: A Bibliography of Criti-
    cism," <u>TCL</u>, IX (1963), 93-100.

WILLIAMS, TENNESSEE, 1914-

THE ROMAN SPRING OF MRS. STONE

Falk, Signi L., _Tennessee Williams_ (TUSAS, 10), N.Y.:
Twayne, 1961, 144-9.
Gerard, Albert, "The Eagle and the Star, Symbol Motifs in
THE ROMAN SPRING OF MRS. STONE," _ES_, XXXIV
(August, 1955), 145-53.
Nelson, Benjamin, _Tennessee Williams: The Man and His
Work_, N.Y.: Obolensky, 1961, 165-71.
Tischler, Nancy M., _Tennessee Williams: Rebellious Puri-
tan_, N.Y.: Citadel, 1961, 177-8.

WILLINGHAM, CALDER, 1922-

ETERNAL FIRE

Walcutt, C.C., _Man's Changing Mask_, 217-28.

WILSON, ANGUS, 1913-

GENERAL

Cox, C.B., "Angus Wilson: Studies in Depression," _Free
Spirit_, 117-53.
Drescher, Horst, "Angus Wilson: An Interview," _NS_, XVII
(July, 1968), 351-6.
Edelstein, Arthur, in Shapiro, C., ed., _Contemporary Brit-
ish Novelists_, 144-61.
Fraser, G.S., _Modern Writer and His World_, 152-5.
Gransden, K.W., _Angus Wilson._
Halio, Jay L., _Angus Wilson._
_____, "The Novels of Angus Wilson," _MFS_, VIII (Sum-
mer, 1962), 171-81.
Katona, Anna, "Angus Wilson's Fiction and Its Relation to
the English Tradition," _ALitASH_, X (1968), 111-27.
Kermode, Frank, "The House of Fiction: Interviews with
Seven English Novelists," _PR_, XXX (Spring, 1963), 68-71.
Millgate, Michael, "Angus Wilson," _ParisR_, No. 17 (1958),
89-105. Also in _Writers at Work_, 1st ser., 251-66.
Poston, Lawrence, III., "A Conversation with Angus Wilson,"
_BA_, XL (Winter, 1966), 29-31.
Rabinovitz, R., _Reaction Against Experiment in the English_

Novel, 64-96.
Rippier, J.S., Some Postwar English Novelists, 19-44.
Scott-Kilvert, Ian, "Angus Wilson," REL, I, ii (April, 1960),
   42-53.
Smith, William J., "Angus Wilson's England," Cweal,
   LXXXII (March 26, 1965), 18-21.
Zimmerman, Muriel, "The Fiction of Angus Wilson," DA,
   XXVIII (1968), 4195A-96A (Temple).

ANGLO-SAXON ATTITUDES

Allen, W., Modern Novel, 272-3.
Cox, C.B., Free Spirit, 138-43.
Edelstein, Arthur, in Shapiro, C., ed., Contemporary Brit-
   ish Novelists, 156-9.
Gable, Sister Mariella, "Prose Satire and the Modern Chris-
   tian Temper," ABR, XI (March-June, 1960), 30-1.
Gindin, J., "Angus Wilson's Nationalism," Postwar British
   Fiction, 152-6.
Gransden, K.W., Angus Wilson, 19-22.
Halio, Jay L., Angus Wilson, 39-49.
_____, "The Novels of Angus Wilson," MFS, VIII (Sum-
   mer, 1962), 175-80.
Karl, F.R., "A Question of Morality: Angus Wilson," Con-
   temporary English Novel, 244-7.
Raban, J., "Narrative: Point of View," Technique of Mod-
   ern Fiction, 41-4.
Rippier, J.S., Some Postwar English Novelists, 27-32.
Scott- Kilvert, Ian, "Angus Wilson," REL, I, ii (April,
   1960), 50-2.

HEMLOCK AND AFTER

Allen, W., Modern Novel, 270-1.
Cockshut, A.O.J., "Favored Sons; The Moral World of Ang-
   us Wilson," EIC, IX (January, 1959), 50-60.
Cox, C.B., Free Spirit, 125-38.
_____, "The Humanism of Angus Wilson: A Study of
   HEMLOCK AND AFTER," CritQ, III (Autumn, 1961), 227-
   37.
Fraser, G.S., Modern Writer and His World, 153-5.
Gindin, J., "Angus Wilson's Nationalism," Postwar British
   Fiction, 150-2.
Gransden, K.W., Angus Wilson, 17-19.
Halio, Jay L., Angus Wilson, 27-38.
_____, "The Novels of Angus Wilson," MFS, VIII (Sum-
   mer, 1962), 171-4.

Kerr, Walter, "Cold Eye on the Best People," Cweal, LVII
    (October 24, 1952), 72-3.
Rippier, J. S., Some Postwar English Novelists, 21-6.
Scott-Kilvert, Ian, "Angus Wilson," REL, I, ii (April, 1960),
    45-8.

LATE CALL

Anon., "Not Painted--But Made Up," TLS (November 5,
    1964), 1013.   Also in T. L. S.: Essays and Reviews from
    The Times Literary Supplement, 1964, 103-5.
Burgess, Anthony, "Powers That Be," Encounter, XXIV
    (January, 1965), 71-6.
Edelstein, Arthur, in Shapiro, C., ed., Contemporary Brit-
    ish Novelists, 144-53.
Gindin, James, "The Fable Breaks Down," WSCL, VIII
    (Winter, 1967), 10-17.
Gransden, K. W., Angus Wilson, 25-7.
Spender, Stephen, "Must There Always be a Red Brick Eng-
    land?" in Encyclopaedia Britannica.   Great Ideas Today,
    1965, 177-80.

THE MIDDLE AGE OF MRS. ELIOT

Allen, W., Modern Novel, 273-4.
Cox, C. B., Free Spirit, 143-53.
Edelstein, Arthur, in Shapiro, C., ed., Contemporary Brit-
    ish Novelists, 154-6.
Gindin, J., "Angus Wilson's Nationalism," Postwar British
    Fiction, 156-9.
Gransden, K. W., Angus Wilson, 22-3.
Halio, Jay L., Angus Wilson, 50-61.
_____, "The Novels of Angus Wilson," MFS, VIII (Sum-
    mer, 1962), 175-80.
Karl, F. R., "A Question of Morality," Contemporary Eng-
    lish Novel, 247-9.
Kermode, Frank, "Mr. Wilson's People," Spectator (No-
    vember 21, 1958), 705-6.   Also in Kermode, F., Puz-
    zles and Epiphanies, 193-7.
Raymond, John, "Meg Eliot Surprised," Doge of Dover, 170-
    8.
Rippier, J. S., Some Postwar English Novelists, 32-7.
Scott-Kilvert, Ian, "Angus Wilson," REL, I, ii (April, 1960),
    50-2.

NO LAUGHING MATTER

Gransden, K.W., Angus Wilson, 27-9.
Parrinder, Patrick, "Pastiche and After," CamR, LXXXIXA, No. 2156 (November 4, 1967), 66-7.
Trickett, Rachel, "Recent Novels: Craftmanship in Violence and Sex," YR, LVII (Spring, 1968), 446-8.

THE OLD MEN AT THE ZOO

Cox, C.B., Free Spirit, 155-7.
Gindin, James, "Angus Wilson's Nationalism," Postwar British Fiction, 159-64.
_____, "The Fable Breaks Down," WSCL, VIII (Winter, 1967), 8-10.
Gransden, K.W., Angus Wilson, 23-5.
Halio, Jay L., Angus Wilson, 84-92.
_____, in Crit, V, i (Spring-Summer, 1962), 77-82.
McDowell, Frederick P.W., " 'The Devious Involutions of Human Character and Emotions': Reflections on Some Recent British Novels," WSCL, IV, iii (Autumn, 1963), 359-62.
Pritchett, V.S., "Bad-Hearted Britain," NStat (September 29, 1961), 429-30.
Rippier, J.S., Some Postwar English Novelists, 37-42.

BIBLIOGRAPHY

Halio, J.L., Angus Wilson, 117-20.

WILSON, COLIN, 1931-

GENERAL

Campion, S., World of Colin Wilson.
Dillard, R.H., "Toward an Existential Realism: The Novels of Colin Wilson," HC, IV, iv (October, 1967), 1-12.

ADRIFT IN SOHO

Gindin, J., Postwar British Fiction, 222-5.

RITUAL IN THE DARK

Campion, S., World of Colin Wilson, 178-86.
Gindin, J., Postwar British Fiction, 222-25.

THE VIOLENT WORLD OF HUGH GREENE

Campion, S., World of Colin Wilson, 237-8.
Urwin, G.G., ed., Taste for Living, 25-8.

THE WORLD OF VIOLENCE
(See THE VIOLENT WORLD OF HUGH GREENE)

WOLFERT, IRA, 1908-

GENERAL

Aldridge, J.W., "Ira Wolfert: The Failure of a Form," In
Search of Heresy, 177-85.

MARRIED MEN

Aldridge, J.W., "Ira Wolfert: The Failure of Form," In
Search of Heresy, 179-85.

TUCKER'S PEOPLE

Eisinger, Chester E., in Madden, D., ed., Proletarian
Writers of the Thirties, 177-82.

WOUK, HERMAN, 1915-

GENERAL

Aldridge, J.W., In Search of Heresy, 123-4.
Carpenter, Frederic I., "Herman Wouk," CE, XVII (January,
1956), 211-15. Also in EJ, XLV (1956), 1-6+.
Geismar, Maxwell, "The Age of Wouk," Nation, CLXXXI (November 5, 1955), 399-400. Also in Nation (Periodical).
View of the Nation, 37-40. Also in Geismar, M., American Moderns, 41-5.
McElderry, B.R., Jr., "The Conservative as Novelist: Herman Wouk," ArQ, XV (Summer, 1959), 128-36.

THE CAINE MUTINY

Bierstadt, Robert, "The Tergiversation of Herman Wouk (THE
CAINE MUTINY)," in MacIver, R.M., ed., Great Moral
Dilemmas in Literature Past and Present, N.Y.: Institute
for Religious and Social Studies, 1956, 1-14.

Browne, James R., "Distortion in THE CAINE MUTINY,"
    CE, XVII (January, 1956), 216-18.
Carpenter, Frederic I., "Herman Wouk," CE, XVII (Janu-
    ary, 1956), 212-14. Also in EJ, XLV (1956), 3-5.
Eisinger, C. E., Fiction of the Forties, 46-7.
Frankel, Theodore, "The Anatomy of a Bestseller: Second
    Thoughts on THE CAINE MUTINY," WHR, IX (Autumn,
    1955), 333-9.
Fuller, Edmund, Man in Modern Fiction; Some Minority
    Opinions on Contemporary American Writing, N.Y.: Ran-
    dom House, 1958, 134-46.
Hoffman, F. J., Mortal No, 242-4.
McCormick, J., Catastrophe and Imagination, 222-26.
McElderry, B. R., Jr., "The Conservative as Novelist:
    Herman Wouk," ArQ, XV (Summer, 1959), 128-32.
Métrauz, Rhoda, "THE CAINE MUTINY," Explor., No. 5
    (1956), 36-55.
Prescott, O., In My Opinion, 163-4.
Stuckey, W. J., Pulitzer Prize Novels, 158-64.
Swados, Harvey, "THE CAINE MUTINY," in Brossard,
    Chandler, ed., The Scene Before You, N.Y.: Rinehart,
    1955, 138-46.
_____, "Popular Taste and THE CAINE MUTINY," PR, XX
    (March-April, 1953), 248-56. Also in Swados, H.,
    Radical's America, 235-44.
Whipple, William, "Justice - the Phantom of the Literary
    Trail," BSTCF, II (Winter, 1961-62), 35-7.
Whyte, William, The Organization Man, N.Y.: Simon &
    Schuster, 1956, 243-8.
Waldmeir, J. J., American Novels of the Second World War,
    124-30.

MARJORIE MORNINGSTAR

Carpenter, Frederic I., "Herman Wouk," CE, XVII (Janu-
    ary, 1956), 214-15. Also in EJ, XLV (January, 1956),
    5-6.
Cohen, Joseph, "Wouk's Morningstar and Hemingway's Sun,"
    SAQ, LVIII (Spring, 1959), 213-24.
Fiedler, L., Love and Death in the American Novel, 248-53.
Fitch, Robert E., "The Bourgeois and the Bohemian," AR,
    XVI (1956), 131-45.
Geismar, Maxwell, "The Age of Wouk," Nation, CLXXXI
    (November 5, 1955), 399-400. Also in Nation (Periodi-
    cal). View of the Nation, 37-40. Also in Geismar, M.,
    American Moderns, 41-5.
_____, in NYTBR (September 4, 1955), 1. Also in Geis-

mar, M., American Moderns, 38-40.

Hofstadter, Beatrice K., "Popular Culture and the Romantic Heroine," ASch, XXX (Winter, 1960-61), 114-16.

McElderry, B. R., Jr., "The Conservative as Novelist: Herman Wouk," ArQ, XV (Summer, 1959), 132-5.

Rosenfeld Isaac, "For God and Suburbs," PR, XXII (Fall, 1955), 565-9. Also in Rosenfeld, I., Age of Enormity, 309-14.

YOUNGBLOOD HAWKE

Hyman, S. E., "Some Questions About Herman Wouk," Standards, 68-72.

WRIGHT, RICHARD, 1908-1960

GENERAL

Baldwin, James, "Richard Wright," Encounter, XVI (April, 1961), 58-60.

Blake, N. M., Novelist's America, 226-34.

Bone, R., Richard Wright.

Bontemps, Arna, in Griffin, W., ed., Literature in the Modern World, 115-19.

Brignano, Russell C., "Richard Wright: The Major Themes, Ideas, and Attitudes in His Works," DA, XXVIII (1967), 666A-7A (Wis.).

Britt, David, "The Image of the White Man in the Fiction of Langston Hughes, Richard Wright, James Baldwin and Ralph Ellison," DA, XIX (1968), 1532A (Emory).

Brown, Cecil, "Richard Wright's Complexes and Black Writing Today," Negro Digest, XVIII (December, 1968), 45-50, 78-82.

Charney, Maurice, "James Baldwin's Quarrel with Richard Wright," AQ, XV (Spring, 1963), 65-75.

Delpech, Jeanine, "An Interview with Native Son," Crisis, CVII (November, 1950), 625-6, 678.

Ellison, Ralph, "The World and the Jug," New Leader, XLVI (December 9, 1963), 22-6. (Rejoinder to Howe, I., "Black Boys and Native Sons.") Expanded in Ellison, R., Shadow and Act, N.Y.: Random House, 1964, 107-43.

Ford, Nick A., "Four Popular Negro Novelists," Phylon, XV (1954), 29-32.

――――, "The Ordeal of Richard Wright," CE, XV (November, 1953), 87-94.

――――, "Richard Wright, a Profile," CJF, XXI (Fall,

1962), 26-30.

French, Warren, "The Lost Potential of Richard Wright," in Bigsby, C. W. E., ed., Black American Writer, Vol. I, 125-42.

Gayle, Addison, Jr., "Beyond Nihilism," Negro Digest, XVIII (December, 1968), 4-10.

Gray, Yohma, "An American Metaphor: The Novels of Richard Wright," DA, XXVIII (1968), 4175A (Yale).

Hand, Clifford, "The Struggle to Create Life in the Fiction of Richard Wright," in French, W., ed., Thirties, 81-7.

Hill, Herbert, ed., "Reflections on Richard Wright: A Symposium on an Exiled Native Son," Anger and Beyond: The Negro Writer in the United States, N. Y.: Harper & Row, 1966, 196-212.

Howe, Irving, "Black Boys and Native Sons," Dissent, X (Autumn, 1963), 353-68. Also in Howe, I., World More Attractive, 98-122.

_____, "A Reply to Ralph Ellison," New Leader, XLVII (February 3, 1964), 12-14.

Isaacs, Harold R., "Five Writers and Their African Ancestors," Phylon, XXI (Fall, 1960), 254-65.

Jarrett, Thomas D., "Recent Fiction by Negroes," CE, XVI (November, 1954), 85-7.

Littlejohn, D., Black on White, 102-10.

McCall, D., Example of Richard Wright.

Margolies, E., Art of Richard Wright.

Reilly, John M., "Insight and Protest in the Works of Richard Wright," DA, XXVIII (1968), 4185A-86A (Wash. Un.).

Sanders, Ronald, "Richard Wright and the Sixties," Midstream, XIV (August/September, 1968), 28-40.

_____, "Richard Wright Then and Now," Negro Digest, XVIII (December, 1968), 83-98.

Scott, Nathan A., Jr., "The Dark and Haunted Tower of Richard Wright," Comment (Wayne State Un.), VII (July, 1964), 93-9.

_____, "A Search for Beliefs: Fiction of Richard Wright," UKCR, XXIII (Autumn, 1956), 19-24.

Webb, Constance, Richard Wright.

_____, "What Next for Richard Wright?" Phylon, X, 2nd quar., (1949), 161-6.

Winslow, Henry F., "Richard Nathaniel Wright: Destroyer and Preserver (1908-1960)," Crisis, LXIX (March, 1962), 149-63, 187.

Zeitlow, Edward R., "Wright to Hansberry: The Evolution of Outlook in Four Negro Writers," DA, XXVIII (1967), 701A (Un. of Wash.).

LAWD TODAY

Ford, Nick A., in CLAJ, VII (March, 1964), 269-70.
French, W., Social Novel at the End of An Era, 171-3.
McCall, D., Example of Richard Wright, 18-23.
Margolies, E., Art of Richard Wright, 90-103.

THE LONG DREAM

Hicks, Granville, "The Power of Richard Wright," SatR,
    XLI (October 18, 1958), 13, 65.
McCall, D., Example of Richard Wright, 155-61.
Margolies, E., Art of Richard Wright, 121-38.
Poster, William S., "Black Man's Burden," New Leader,
    XLII (August 31, 1959), 23-4.
Redding, J. Saunders, "The Way It Was," NYTBR (October
    26, 1958), 4, 38.
Webb, C., Richard Wright, 306-14.

NATIVE SON

Allen, W., Modern Novel, 155-8.
Baldwin, James, "Everybody's Protest Novel," PR, XVI
    (June, 1949), 584-5. Also in Baldwin J., Notes of a
    Native Son, Boston: Beacon Pr., 1955, 21-3.
    _____, "Many Thousands Gone," PR, XVII (November-
    December, 1951), 665-80. Also in Baldwin, J., Notes
    of a Native Son, Boston: Beacon Pr., 1955, 24-45. Al-
    so in Gross, S.L., and J.E. Hardy, eds., Images of the
    Negro in American Literature, 233-48.
Bayliss, John F., "NATIVE SON: Protest or Psychological
    Study?" NALF, I (Fall, 1967), 4-5.
Blake, N.M., Novelist's America, 234-53.
Bone, R.A., Negro Novel in America, 140-52.
    _____, Richard Wright, 20-5.
Britt, David, "NATIVE SON: Watershed of Negro Protest
    Literature," NALF, I (Fall, 1967), 4-5.
Burgum, Edwin B., "The Promise of Democracy in the Fic-
    tion of Richard Wright," S&S, VII (September, 1943),
    338-52. Also in Burgum, E.B., Novel and the World's
    Dilemma, 223-40.
Cowley, Malcolm, "Richard Wright: The Case of Bigger
    Thomas," NRep, CII (March 18, 1940), 382-3. Also in
    Cowley, M., Think Back on Us, 355-7.
Davis, Robert G., "Art and Anxiety," PR, XII (1945), 315-
    17.
Eisinger, C.E., Fiction of the Forties, 68-70.

Emanuel, James A., "Fever and Feeling: Notes on the
Imagery in NATIVE SON," Negro Digest, XVIII (December, 1968), 16-24.

Ford, Nick A., "The Ordeal of Richard Wright," CE, XV
(November, 1953), 87-94.

French, W., Social Novel at the End of An Era, 173-9.

Glicksberg, Charles I., "The Furies in Negro Fiction," WR,
XIII (Winter, 1949), 109-10.

_____, "Negro Fiction in America," SAQ, XLV (October,
1946), 481-8.

Gloster, Hugh M., Negro Voices in American Literature,
Chapel Hill: Un. of No. Carolina, 1948, 228-34. Reprinted, N.Y.: Russell and Russell, 1965.

Hand, Clifford, in French, W., ed., Thirties, 84-6.

Howe, Irving, "Black Boys and Native Sons," Dissent, X
(Autumn, 1963), 354-7. Also in Howe, I., World More
Attractive, 100-10.

Hughes, Carl M., The Negro Novelist, N.Y.: Citadel, 1953,
41-68, 198-206.

Jackson, Blyden, "The Negro's Image of the Universe as
Reflected in His Fiction," CLAJ, IV (September, 1960),
22-31 passim.

Jackson, Esther M., "The American Negro and the Image of
the Absurd," Phylon, XXIII (4th quarter, Winter, 1962),
264-8.

Littlejohn, D., Black on White, 106-7.

McCall, D., Example of Richard Wright, 64-102.

Margolies, E., Art of Richard Wright, 104-20.

_____, "Richard Wright: NATIVE SON and Three Kinds
of Revolution," Native Sons, 65-86.

Owens, William A., "Introduction," NATIVE SON, N.Y.:
Harper, 1957, vii-xii.

Sanders, Ronald, "Richard Wright Then and Now," Negro
Digest, XVIII (December, 1968), 83-98.

Scott, Nathan A., Jr., "The Dark and Haunted Tower of
Richard Wright," Comment (Wayne State Un.), VII (July,
1964), 93-5.

_____, "Judgment Marked by a Cellar: The American
Negro Writer and the Dialectic of Despair," UDQ, II, ii
(1967). Also in Mooney, H.J., and T.F. Staley, eds.,
Shapeless God, 154-6.

_____, "Search for Beliefs: Fiction of Richard Wright,"
UKCR, XXIII (Winter, 1956), 131-5.

Sillen, Samuel, "The Meaning of Bigger Thomas," New
Masses, XXXV (1960), 13-21.

Slochower, H., No Voice is Wholly Lost, 87-92.

Webb, Constance, Richard Wright, 169-75.

_____, "What Next for Richard Wright?" Phylon, X (2nd quarter, 1949), 161-6.
Wertham, Frederic, "An Unconscious Determinant in NATIVE SON," Jnl of Clinical Psychology, VI (1944-45), 111-15. Also in Ruitenbeck, Hendrik M. , ed. , Psychoanalysis and Literature, N.Y.: Dutton, 1964, 321-5.

THE OUTSIDER

Adams, Phoebe, "The Wrong Road," Atlantic, CLXLI (May, 1953), 77-8.
Bone, R. , Richard Wright, 38-43.
Bontemps, Arna, in Griffin, W. , ed. , Literature in the Modern World, 116-19.
Davis, Arthur P. , "THE OUTSIDER as a Novel of Race," MJ, VII (Winter, 1955-56), 320-6.
Ford, Nick A. , "The Ordeal of Richard Wright," CE, XV (November, 1953), 90-4.
Glicksberg, Charles I. , "Existentialism in THE OUTSIDER," FQ, VII (January, 1958), 17-26.
_____, "The God of Fiction," ColQ, VII (Autumn, 1958), 217-19.
Knox, George, "The Negro Novelist's Sensibility and the Outsider Theme," WHR, XI (Spring, 1957), 137-48.
Lehan, Richard, "Existentialism in Recent American Fiction," TSLL, I (Summer, 1959), 192-5, 199.
McCall, D. , Example of Richard Wright, 149-55.
Marcus, Steven, "The American Negro in Search of Identity: Three Novelists: Richard Wright, Ralph Ellison, James Baldwin," Ctary, XVI (May, 1953), 457-8.
Margolies, E. , Art of Richard Wright, 121-38.
Scott, Nathan A. , Jr. , "The Dark and Haunted Tower of Richard Wright," Comment (Wayne State Un.), VII (July, 1964), 96-7.
_____, "Judgment Marked by a Cellar: The American Negro Writer and the Dialectic of Despair," UDQ, II, ii (1967), 22-4. Also in Mooney, H. J. , and T.F. Staley, eds. , Shapeless God, 156-8.
_____, "Search for Beliefs: Fiction of Richard Wright," UKCR, XXIII (Winter, 1956), 135-8.
Webb, C. , Richard Wright, 306-14.
Widmer, Kingsley, "The Existential Darkness: Richard Wright's THE OUTSIDER," WSCL, I, iii (Fall, 1960), 13-21.

SAVAGE HOLIDAY

Margolies, E., Art of Richard Wright, 138-48.
Webb, C., Richard Wright, 314-17.

BIBLIOGRAPHY

Bryer, Jackson, "Richard Wright: A Selected Check List of Criticism," WSCL, I, iii (Fall, 1960), 22-33.

Adams, Richard P., Faulkner: Myth and Motion, Princeton, N.J.: Princeton Un. Pr., 1968.

Aiken, Conrad P., A Reviewer's ABC; Collected Criticism of Conrad Aiken, from 1916 to the Present, N.Y.: Meridian Books, 1958.

Aldridge, John W., After the Lost Generation, N.Y.: McGraw-Hill, 1951.

_____, ed., Critiques and Essays on Modern Fiction: 1920-1951, N.Y.: Ronald Pr., 1952.

_____, In Search of Heresy: American Literature in an Age of Conformity, N.Y.: McGraw-Hill, 1956.

_____, A Time to Murder and Create; The Contemporary Novel in Crisis, N.Y.: David McKay, 1966.

Alldritt, Keith, The Making of George Orwell; An Essay in Literary History, N.Y.: St. Martin's Pr., 1969.

Allen, Walter, Joyce Cary (Writers and Their Work, No. 41), London; N.Y.: Longmans, Green, Rev. ed., 1954.

_____, The Modern Novel in Britain and the United States, N.Y.: Dutton, 1964. Printed in England as Tradition and Dream, Harmondsworth, Penguin, 1965.

_____, Reading a Novel, London: Phoenix House, Rev. ed., 1963.

_____, The Urgent West; the American Dream and Modern Man, N.Y.: Dutton, 1969.

Allentuck, Marcia, ed., The Achievement of Isaac Bashevis Singer, Carbondale: So. Illinois Un. Pr., 1969.

Allott, Kenneth, and Miriam Farris (Allott), The Art of Graham Greene, London: Hamish Hamilton, 1951; N.Y.: Russell & Russell, 1963.

Allsop, Kenneth, The Angry Decade: A Survey of the Cultural Revolt of the Nineteen-fifties, London: P. Owen, 1958; N.Y.: British Book Centre, 1958.

Alter, Robert, After the Tradition: Modern Jewish Writing, N.Y.: Dutton, 1969.

_____, Rogue's Progress; Studies in the Picaresque Novel, Cambridge: Harvard Un. Pr., 1964.

Appel, Alfred, Jr., A Season of Dreams: The Fiction of Eudora Welty, Baton Rouge: La. State Un. Pr., 1965.

585

Argyle, Barry, Patrick White (Writers and Critics), Edin-
burgh and London: Oliver & Boyd, 1967.
Atkins, John, The Art of Ernest Hemingway; His Work and
Personality, London: Spring Books, 1952.
_____, Arthur Koestler, N.Y.: Roy, 1957.
_____, George Orwell: A Literary and Biographical
Study, N.Y.: Ungar, 1954.
_____, Graham Greene, London: Calder and Boyars,
New Rev. Ed., 1966.
Auchincloss, Louis, Pioneers and Caretakers; a Study of
Nine American Women Novelists, Minneapolis: Un. of
Minn. Pr., 1965.
Axthelm, Peter M., The Modern Confessional Novel, New
Haven and London: Yale Un. Pr., 1967.

Backman, Melvin, Faulkner: The Major Years; A Critical
Study, Bloomington: Indiana Un. Pr., 1966.
Baker, Carlos, ed., Ernest Hemingway: Critiques of Four
Major Novels, N.Y.: Scribner's, 1962.
_____, ed., Hemingway and His Critics: An Internation-
al Anthology, N.Y.: Hill and Wang, 1961.
_____, Hemingway: The Writer as Artist, Princeton,
N.J.: Princeton Un. Pr., 3rd ed., 1963.
Baker, Denys Val, ed., Modern British Writing, N.Y.:
Vanguard, 1947.
_____, ed., Writers of Today, London: Sidgwick & Jack-
son, 1946.
_____, ed., Writers of Today: 2, London: Sidgwick &
Jackson, 1948.
Baker, James R., William Golding: A Critical Study,
N.Y.: St. Martin's, 1965.
_____, and A.P. Ziegler, Jr., eds., Casebook Edition
of William Golding's LORD OF THE FLIES: Text, Notes
and Criticism, N.Y.: Putnam's, 1964.
Baker, Sheridan, Ernest Hemingway; An Introduction and In-
terpretation, N.Y.: Holt, 1967.
_____, ed., Paton's CRY, THE BELOVED COUNTRY:
The Novel, The Critics, The Setting (Scribner Research
Anthologies), N.Y.: Charles Scribner's Sons, 1968.
Balakian, Nona, and Charles Simmons, eds., The Creative
Present: Notes on Contemporary American Fiction,
N.Y.: Doubleday, 1963.
Baldanza, Frank, Ivy Compton-Burnett (TEAS, No. 11),
N.Y.: Twayne, 1964.
Barnes, Robert J., Conrad Richter (Southwest Writers Se-
ries, No. 14), Austin: Steck-Vaughn, 1968.

Baumbach, Jonathan, The Landscape of Nightmare: Studies in the Contemporary American Novel, N.Y.: New York Un. Pr., 1965.

Baxter, Annette K., Henry Miller, Expatriate (Critical Essays in English and American Literature, No. 5), Pittsburgh: Un. of Pittsburgh Pr., 1961.

Beach, Joseph Warren, American Fiction, 1920-1940, N.Y.: Russell and Russell, 1960.

Beatty, Richmond C., and others, eds., Vanderbilt Studies in the Humanities, Vol. I, Nashville: Vanderbilt Un. Pr., 1951.

Beck, Warren, Man in Motion: Faulkner's Trilogy, Madison: Un. of Wisconsin Pr., 1961.

Beebe, Maurice, and Leslie A. Field, eds., Robert Penn Warren's ALL THE KING'S MEN: A Critical Handbook, Belmont, Calif.: Wadsworth, 1966.

Belcher, William F., and J.W. Lee, eds., J.D. Salinger and the Critics, Belmont, Calif.: Wadsworth, 1962.

Benson, Jackson J., Hemingway: The Writer's Art of Self-Defense, Minneapolis: Un. of Minn. Pr., 1969.

Bien, Peter, L.P. Hartley, University Park: Penn. State Un. Pr., 1963.

Bigsby, C.W.E., ed., The Black American Writer, Vol. I: Fiction, De Land, Fla.: Everett/Edwards, Inc., 1969.

Bishop, John Peale, Collected Essays of John Peale Bishop, ed., with an introd. by Edmund Wilson, N.Y.: Charles Scribner's Sons, 1948.

Blake, Nelson Manfred, Novelist's America: Fiction as History, 1910-1940, Syracuse, N.Y.: Syracuse Un. Pr., 1969.

Blankenship, Russell, American Literature as an Expression of the National Mind, Rev. ed., N.Y.: Holt, Rinehart & Winston, 1958.

Bloom, Robert, The Indeterminate World: A Study of the Novels of Joyce Cary, Philadelphia: Un. of Pa. Pr., 1962.

Bloomfield, Paul, L.P. Hartley and Anthony Powell, by Bernard Bergonzi (Writers and Their Work, 144), London; N.Y.: Longmans, Green, 1962.

Blotner, Joseph, The Modern American Political Novel, Austin: Un. of Texas Pr., 1966.

Bode, Carl E., ed., The Young Rebel in American Literature, London: William Heinemann, 1959; N.Y.: Praeger, 1960.

Bohner, Charles H., Robert Penn Warren, N.Y.: Twayne, 1964.

Bone, Robert A., The Negro Novel in America, Rev. ed.,

New Haven and London: Yale Un. Pr., 1965.
_____, Richard Wright (UMPAW, No. 74), Minneapolis:
Un. of Minn. Pr., 1969.
Bowden, Edwin T., The Dungeon of the Heart: Human Iso-
lation and the American Novel, N.Y.: Macmillan, 1961.
Bowen, Elizabeth, Seven Winters; Memories of a Dublin
Childhood & Afterthoughts; Pieces on Writing, N.Y.:
Knopf, 1962.
Bowering, Peter, Aldous Huxley: a Study of the Major Nov-
els, N.Y.: Oxford, 1969.
Bracher, Frederick, The Novels of James Gould Cozzens,
N.Y.: Harcourt, 1959.
Bradbury, John M., The Fugitives: A Critical Account,
Chapel Hill: Un. of North Carolina Pr., 1958.
Bradbury, Malcolm, Evelyn Waugh (Writers and Critics),
Edinburgh & London: Oliver & Boyd, 1964.
Branch, Edgar M., James T. Farrell (UMPAW, 29), Minne-
apolis: Un. of Minn. Pr., 1963.
Brander, Lawrence, George Orwell, London: Longmans,
Green, 1954.
Brantley, John D., The Fiction of John Dos Passos, The
Hague, The Netherlands: Mouton, 1968.
Brashers, Howard C., An Introduction to American Litera-
ture, Stockholm: Svenska Borkförlaget, 1964.
Brewster, Dorothy, Doris Lessing (TEAS, 21), N.Y.:
Twayne, 1965.
Brissenden, R. F., Patrick White (Writers and Their Work,
No. 190), London: Longmans, Green, 1966.
Broes, Arthur T., and Others, Lectures on Modern Novel-
ists (Carnegie Series in English, 7), Pittsburgh: Dept. of
Eng., Carnegie Institute of Technology.
Brooke, Jocelyn, Aldous Huxley (Writers and Their Work,
No. 55), Rev. ed., London: Longmans, Green, 1963.
_____, Elizabeth Bowen, London: Longmans, Green,
1952.
Brooks, Cleanth, The Hidden God: Studies in Hemingway,
Faulkner, Yeats, Eliot, and Warren, New Haven and Lon-
don: Yale Un. Pr., 1963.
_____, William Faulkner: The Yoknapatawpha Country,
New Haven, Conn.: Yale Un. Pr., 1963.
Brooks, Van Wyk, The Confident Years: 1885-1915, N.Y.:
Dutton (Everyman's Library), 1952.
Brophy, Brigid, Don't Never Forget; Collected Views and
Re-reviews, N.Y.: Holt, 1967.
Brown, Francis, ed., Opinions and Perspectives from the
New York Times Book Review, Boston: Houghton-Mifflin,
1964.

Brown, Ivor, J.B. Priestley (Writers and Their Work, No. 84), London: Longmans, Green, 1957.
Browne, Ray B., and Others, eds., Frontiers of American Culture, Lafayette: Purdue Un. Pr., 1968.
Bryant, J.A., Jr., Eudora Welty (UMPAW, 66), Minneapolis: Un. of Minn. Pr., 1968.
Brylowski, Walter, Faulkner's Olympian Laugh: Myth in the Novels, Detroit: Wayne State Un. Pr., 1968.
Buchen, Irving H., Isaac Bashevis Singer and the Eternal Past, N.Y.: New York Un. Pr., 1968; London: Un. of London Pr., 1968.
Burbank, Rex, Thornton Wilder, N.Y.: Twayne, 1961.
Burgess, Anthony, Urgent Copy; Literary Studies, N.Y.: Norton, 1968.
Burgum, Edwin Berry, The Novel and the World's Dilemma, N.Y.: Oxford Un. Pr., 1947. Reprinted, N.Y.: Russell & Russell, 1963.
Burkhart, Charles, I. Compton-Burnett, London: V. Gollancz, 1965.
Byatt, A.S., Degrees of Freedom: The Novels of Iris Murdoch, N.Y.: Barnes and Noble, 1965.

Calder, Jenni, Chronicles of Conscience: A Study of George Orwell and Arthur Koestler, London: Secker and Warburg, 1968; Pittsburgh: Un. of Pittsburgh, 1969.
Callan, Edward, Alan Paton (TWAS 40), N.Y.: Twayne, 1968.
Campbell, Harry Modean, and Ruel E. Foster, William Faulkner, A Critical Appraisal, Norman: Un. of Okla. Pr., 1951.
Campion, Sidney R., The World of Colin Wilson: A Biographical Study, London: Frederick Muller Ltd., 1962.
Canadian Literature. A Choice of Critics: Selections from CANADIAN LITERATURE, ed. by George Woodcock, Toronto: Oxford Un. Pr., 1966.
Carens, James F., The Satiric Art of Evelyn Waugh, Seattle: Un. of Washington Pr., 1966.
Cargas, Harry J., ed., Graham Greene (Christian Critic Series), St. Louis, Mo.: B. Herder, 1969.
Carnegie Institute of Technology. Lectures on Modern Novelists (Carnegie Series in English, No. 7), Pittsburgh: Dept. of English, Carnegie Institute of Technology, 1963.
Carpenter, Frederic I., American Literature and the Dream, N.Y.: Philosophical Library, 1955.
Carson, Edward R., The Fiction of John O'Hara (Critical Essays in English and American Literature, No. 7),

Pittsburgh: Un. of Pittsburgh Pr., 1961.

Carter, Lin, Tolkien: A Look Behind THE LORD OF THE RINGS, N.Y.: Ballantine Books, 1969.

Casper, Leonard, Robert Penn Warren: The Dark and Bloody Ground, Seattle: Un. of Washington Pr., 1960.

Chase, Richard, The American Novel and Its Tradition, Garden City, N.Y.: Doubleday Anchor, 1957.

Church, Margaret A., Time and Reality: Studies in Contemporary Fiction, Chapel Hill: Un. of North Carolina Pr., 1963.

Clayton, John Jacob, Saul Bellow: In Defense of Man, Bloomington: Indiana Un. Pr., 1968.

Coe, Richard N., Beckett (Writers and Critics), Edinburgh: Oliver & Boyd, 1964; N.Y.: Grove, 1964.

Cohn, Ruby, Samuel Beckett: The Comic Gamut, New Brunswick, N.J.: Rutgers Un. Pr., 1962.

Commentary. The Commentary Reader; Two Decades of Articles and Stories; ed. by Norman Podhoretz, with an Introd. by Alfred Kazin, N.Y.: Atheneum, 1966.

Connolly, Cyril, Previous Convictions, N.Y. and Evanston: Harper & Row, 1963.

Conron, Brandon, Morley Callaghan, N.Y.: Twayne, 1966.

Cooper, William, C.P. Snow, Rev. ed., London: Longmans, Green, 1962.

Cooperman, Stanley, World War I and the American Novel, Baltimore: Johns Hopkins Pr., 1967.

Cowan, Michael H., ed., Twentieth Century Interpretations of THE SOUND AND THE FURY: A Collection of Critical Essays, Englewood Cliffs, N.J.: Prentice-Hall, 1968.

Cowley, Malcolm, ed., After the Genteel Tradition: American Writers, 1910-1930, Rev. & enl., Carbondale: So. Illinois Un. Pr., 1964.

_____, Think Back on Us... A Contemporary Chronicle of the 1930's; ed., with an introd. by Henry Dan Piper, Carbondale: So. Illinois Un. Pr., 1967.

Cox, C.B., The Free Spirit: A Study of Liberal Humanism in the Novels of George Eliot, Henry James, E.M. Forster, Virginia Woolf, and Angus Wilson, London: Oxford, 1963.

Cruickshank, John, ed., The Novelist as Philosopher: Studies in French Fiction, 1935-1960, London: Oxford, 1962.

Davies, Horton, A Mirror of the Ministry in Modern Novels, N.Y.: Oxford Un. Pr., 1959.

Davies, Robertson, The Voice from the Attic, N.Y.: Knopf, 1960.

Davis, Robert G. , John Dos Passos (UMPAW, No. 20),
Minneapolis: Un. of Minn. Pr. , 1962.
Davis, Robert M. , ed. , Evelyn Waugh (The Christian Critic
Series), St. Louis: B. Herder, 1969.
Dembo, L. S. , ed. , Nabokov: The Man and His Work, Mad-
ison: Un. of Wisconsin, 1967.
Detweiler, Robert, Four Spiritual Crises in Mid-Century
American Fiction (Un. of Fla. Monographs: Humanities,
No. 14, Fall, 1963), Gainesville: Un. of Florida Pr. ,
1964.
DeVitis, A. A. , Graham Greene (TEAS, 3), N. Y.: Twayne,
1964.
_____, Roman Holiday: The Catholic Novels of Evelyn
Waugh, N. Y.: Bookman Associates, 1956.
Dick, Bernard F. , William Golding (TEAS, 57), N. Y.:
Twayne, 1967.
Doàn-Cao-Lý, The Image of the Chinese Family in Pearl
Buck's Novels, Dúc-Sinh, Saigon, 1964. Dissertation (St.
John's), 1964.
Donohue, Agnes McNeill, A Casebook on THE GRAPES OF
WRATH, N. Y.: T. Y. Crowell, 1968.
Donohue, H. E. F. , Conversations with Nelson Algren, N. Y.:
Hill & Wang, 1964.
Dooley, D. J. , The Art of Sinclair Lewis, Lincoln: Un. of
Nebraska Pr. , 1967.
Doyle, Paul A. , Evelyn Waugh; A Critical Essay (CWCP),
Grand Rapids, Mich.: Eerdmans, 1969.
_____, Pearl S. Buck, N. Y.: Twayne, 1965.
Drake, Robert, Flannery O'Connor (CWCP), Grand Rapids,
Mich.: Eerdmans, 1966.
Duffin, Henry Charles, The Novels and Plays of Charles
Morgan, London: Bowes and Bowes, 1959.
Dupee, Frederick Wilcox, The King of the Cats and Other
Remarks on Writers and Writing, N. Y.: Farrar, Straus
& Giroux, 1965.
Dutton, Geoffrey, ed. , The Literature of Australia, Balti-
more: Penguin, 1965.
_____, Patrick White, Melbourne, Australia: Lansdowne
Press, 3rd ed. rev. , 1963.
Dyson, Anthony E. , The Crazy Fabric; Essays in Irony,
London: Macmillan, 1965; N. Y.: St. Martin's Pr. , 1965.

Edel, Leon, The Psychological Novel, 1900-1950, N. Y. and
Philadelphia: 1955. Same as Edel, Leon, Modern Psy-
chological Novel, Rev. & enl. , N. Y.: Grosset & Dunlap, 1964.
Edmonds, Dale, Carson McCullers (Southern Writers Series,
No. 6), Austin: Steck-Vaughn, 1969.

Eisinger, Chester E., Fiction of the Forties, Chicago and
London: Un. of Chicago Pr., 1963.
Elmen, Paul, William Golding; a Critical Essay (CWCP),
Grand Rapids, Mich.: Eerdmans, 1967.
Encyclopaedia Britannica. Great Ideas Today, 1965, N.Y.:
Atheneum, 1965.
English Association. Essays and Studies, 1950, London:
John Murray, 1950.
_____. Essays and Studies, 1966, ed. by R.M. Wilson,
N.Y.: Humanities, 1966.
English Institute Essays, 1952, ed. by Alan S. Downer,
N.Y.: Columbia Un. Pr., 1954. Reprinted N.Y.: AMS,
1965.
Enright, Dennis Joseph, Conspirators and Poets, Chester
Springs, Pa.: Dufour, 1966.
Epstein, Perle S., The Private Labyrinth of Malcolm Lowry:
UNDER THE VOLCANO and the CABBALA, N.Y.: Holt, 1969.
Esslin, Martin, ed., Samuel Beckett: A Collection of Criti-
cal Essays, Englewood Cliffs, N.J.: Prentice-Hall, 1965.
Evans, Fallon, ed., J.F. Powers, St. Louis, Mo.: B.
Herder, 1968.
Evans, Oliver, The Ballad of Carson McCullers, A Biogra-
phy, N.Y.: Coward-McCann, 1966. Published in
England as Carson McCullers, Her Life and Work, Lon-
don: Owen, 1965.
Evans, Robert O., ed., Graham Greene: Some Critical Con-
siderations, Lexington: Un. of Kentucky Pr., 1963.
Everett, Walter K., Faulkner's Art and Characters, Wood-
bury, N.Y.: Barron's, 1969.

Fadiman, Clifton, Party of One; the Selected Writings of
Clifton Fadiman, N.Y.: World, 1955.
Federman, Raymond, Journey to Chaos: Samuel Beckett's
Early Fiction, Berkeley: Un. of California Pr., 1965.
Feied, Frederick, No Pie in the Sky: The Hobo as Ameri-
can Cultural Hero in the Works of Jack London, John Dos
Passos, and Jack Kerouac, N.Y.: Citadel, 1964.
Feidelson, Charles, Jr., and Paul Brodtkorb, Jr., eds.,
Interpretations of American Literature, N.Y.: Oxford
Un. Pr., 1959.
Fiedler, Leslie, Love and Death in the American Novel,
N.Y.: Criterion, 1960.
_____, No! In Thunder: Essays on Myth and Literature,
Boston: Beacon Pr., 1960.
_____, Waiting for the End, N.Y.: Stein and Day, 1964.
Field, Andrew, Nabokov: His Life in Art, Boston: Little,
Brown, 1967.

Finkelstein, Sidney, Existentialism and Alienation in American Literature, N.Y.: International Pubs., 1965.
Fletcher, John, The Novels of Samuel Beckett, N.Y.: Barnes & Noble, 1964.
Floan, Howard R., William Saroyan, N.Y.: Twayne, 1966.
Flora, Joseph M., Vardis Fisher, (TUSAS, 76), N.Y.: Twayne, 1965.
Folsom, James K., The American Western Novel, New Haven: College and University Pr., 1966.
Fontenrose, John, John Steinbeck: An Introduction and Interpretation, N.Y.: Barnes & Noble, 1963.
Ford, Thomas W., A.B. Guthrie, Jr. (Southwest Writers Series, 15), Austin: Steck-Vaughn, 1968.
Fossum, Robert H., William Styron: A Critical Essay (CWCP), Grand Rapids, Mich.: Eerdmans, 1968.
Foster, Malcolm, Joyce Cary: A Biography, Boston: Houghton, 1968.
Foster, Richard, Norman Mailer (UMPAW, 73), Minneapolis: Un. of Minnesota Pr., 1968.
Fraser, G.S., Lawrence Durrell; A Critical Study, N.Y.: Dutton, 1968.
_____, The Modern Writer and His World; Continuity and Innovation in Twentieth Century English Literature, N.Y.: Praeger, 1964.
French, Warren, and Walter E. Kidd, eds., American Winners of the Nobel Literary Prize, Norman: Un. of Oklahoma Pr., 1968.
French, Warren, ed., A Companion to THE GRAPES OF WRATH, N.Y.: Viking, 1963.
_____, ed., The Forties: Fiction, Poetry, Drama, DeLand, Fla.: Everett/Edwards, 1969.
_____, J.D. Salinger, N.Y.: Twayne, 1963.
_____, John Steinbeck (TUSAS, 2), N.Y.: Twayne, 1961.
_____, The Social Novel at the End of an Era, Carbondale: So. Illinois Un. Pr., 1966.
_____, ed., The Thirties: Fiction, Poetry, Drama, DeLand, Fla.: Everett/Edwards, 1967.
Friedman, Melvin J., and Lewis A. Lawson, eds., The Added Dimension: The Art and Mind of Flannery O'Connor, N.Y.: Fordham Un. Pr., 1966.
Friedman, Melvin J., Stream of Consciousness: A Study in Literary Method, New Haven: Yale Un. Pr., 1955.
Frohock, Wilbur M., The Novel of Violence in America, 2nd ed., rev. and enl., Dallas: Southern Methodist Un. Pr., 1957; Boston: Beacon Pr., 1964.
_____, Strangers to This Ground: Cultural Diversity in Contemporary American Writing, Dallas: Southern Meth-

odist Un. Pr., 1961.

Fuller, Edmund, Books With the Men Behind Them, N.Y.: Random House, 1962.

Galloway, David D., The Absurd Hero in American Fiction: Updike, Styron, Bellow, Salinger, Austin: Un. of Texas Pr., 1966.

Gardiner, Harold C., ed., Fifty Years of the American Novel: A Christian Appraisal, N.Y. and London: Scribner's 1951.

_____, In All Conscience: Reflections on Books and Culture, N.Y.: Hanover House, 1959.

Gaston, Edwin W., Jr., Conrad Richter, N.Y.: Twayne, 1965.

Geismar, Maxwell, American Moderns: From Rebellion to Conformity, N.Y.: Hill and Wang, 1958.

_____, The Last of the Provincials; The American Novel, 1915-1925, Boston: Houghton-Mifflin, 1947.

_____, Writers in Crisis; The American Novel, 1925-1940, Boston: Houghton-Mifflin, 1947; rev., 1961.

Gelfant, Blanche Housman, The American City Novel, Norman: Un. of Oklahoma Pr., 1954.

Ghose, Sisirkumar, Aldous Huxley: A Cynical Salvationist, N.Y.: Asia Pub. House, 1962.

Gilman, Richard, The Confusion of Realms, N.Y.: Random House, 1969.

Gindin, James, Postwar British Fiction: New Attitudes and Accents, Berkeley and Los Angeles: Un. of California Pr., 1962.

Glicksberg, Charles I., The Self in Modern Literature, University Park: Pa. State Un. Pr., 1963.

Ghodes, Clarence, ed., Essays on American Literature in Honor of Jay B. Hubbell, Durham: Duke Un. Pr., 1967.

Gold, Joseph, William Faulkner: A Study in Humanism From Metaphor to Discourse, Norman: Un. of Oklahoma Pr., 1966.

Goldstein, Malcolm, The Art of Thornton Wilder, Lincoln: Un. of Nebraska Pr., 1965.

Gordon, William A., The Mind and Art of Henry Miller, Baton Rouge: La. State Un. Pr., 1967.

_____, Writer and Critic: A Correspondence with Henry Miller, Baton Rouge: La. State Un. Pr., 1968.

Gossett, Louise Y., Violence in Recent Southern Fiction, Durham: Duke Un. Pr., 1965.

Graef, Hilda, Modern Gloom and Christian Hope, Chicago: Regnery, 1959.

Gransden, K. W. , <u>Angus Wilson</u> (Writers and Their Work, No. 208), London: Longmans, Green, 1969.

Graver, Lawrence, <u>Carson McCullers</u> (UMPAW, 84), Minneapolis: Un. of Minn. Pr. , 1969.

Gray, James, <u>On Second Thought,</u> Minneapolis: Un. of Minn. Pr. , 1946.

Greacen, Robert, <u>The World of C. P. Snow,</u> London: Scorpion Pr. , 1962; N. Y. : London House & Maxwell, 1963.

Grebanier, Bernard, <u>Thornton Wilder</u> (UMPAW, 34), Minneapolis: Un. of Minn. Pr. , 1964.

Grebstein, Sheldon Norman, <u>John O'Hara</u>, N. Y. : Twayne, 1966.

_____, <u>Sinclair Lewis</u> (TUSAS, 14), N. Y.: Twayne, 1962.

Green, H. M. , <u>A History of Australian Literature, Pure and Applied,</u> Vol. II, <u>1923-1950</u>, Sydney: Angus and Robertson, 1961.

Green, Martin, <u>Re-Appraisals: Some commonsense readings in American Literature,</u> N. Y. : Norton, 1965.

_____, <u>Yeats's Blessing on von Hügel: Essays on Literature and Religion</u>, London: Longmans, Green, 1967.

Greenblatt, Stephan Jay, <u>Three Modern Satirists: Waugh, Orwell, and Huxley</u> (Yale College Series, 3), New Haven: Yale Un. Pr. , 1965.

Griffin, Robert J. , ed. , <u>Twentieth Century Interpretations of ARROWSMITH: A Collection of Critical Essays,</u> Englewood Cliffs, N. J. : Prentice-Hall, 1968.

Griffin, William, ed. , <u>Literature in the Modern World; Lectures Delivered at George Peabody College for Teachers, 1951-1954</u>, Nashville: George Peabody College for Teachers, 1954.

Gross, John J. , <u>John P. Marquand</u> (TUSAS, 33), N. Y. : Twayne, 1963.

Gross, Seymour L. , and John Edward Hardy, eds. , <u>Images of the Negro in American Literature</u>, Chicago and London: Un. of Chicago Pr. , 1966.

Grosshans, Henry, ed. , <u>To Find Something New: Studies in Contemporary Literature,</u> Pullman: Washington State Un. Pr. , 1969.

Grumbach, Doris, <u>The Company She Kept</u>, N.Y. : Coward-McCann, 1967.

Grunwald, Henry A. , ed. , <u>Salinger: A Critical and Personal Portrait</u>, N. Y. : Harper, 1962.

Gurko, Leo, <u>Ernest Hemingway and the Pursuit of Heroism,</u> N. Y. : Crowell, 1968.

_____, <u>Angry Decade,</u> N. Y. : Dodd, Mead, 1947; Reprinted, N. Y. : Harper and Row, 1968.

Gwynn, Frederick L. , and Joseph L. Blotner, eds. , <u>Faulk-</u>

ner in the University: Class Conferences at the University of Virginia, 1957-1958, Charlottesville: Un. of Va. Pr. , 1959.
_____, The Fiction of J. D. Salinger, Pittsburgh: Un. of Pittsburgh Pr. , 1958.

Hadgraft, Cecil, Australian Literature, London: Wm. Heinemann, 1962.
Hagopian, John V. , and Martin Dolch, Insight II: Analyses of Modern British Literature, Frankfurt am Main: Hirschgraben-Verlag, 1965.
Hagopian, John V. , J. F. Powers (TUSAS, 130), N. Y.: Twayne, 1968.
Halio, Jay L. , Angus Wilson (Writers and Critics), Edinburgh: Oliver & Boyd, 1964.
Hall, James, The Lunatic Giant in the Drawing Room: The British and American Novel Since 1930, Bloomington: Indiana Un. Pr. , 1968.
_____, The Tragic Comedians: Seven Modern British Novelists, Bloomington: Indiana Un. Pr. , 1963.
Hamilton, Kenneth, J. D. Salinger: A Critical Essay (CWCP), Grand Rapids, Mich.: Eerdmans, 1967.
_____, and Alice, John Updike: A Critical Essay (CWCP), Grand Rapids, Mich.: Eerdmans, 1967.
Hardwick, Elizabeth, A View of My Own: Essays in Literature and Society, N. Y.: Farrar, Straus & Cudahy, 1962.
Hardy, John Edward, Man in the Modern Novel, Seattle: Un. of Washington Pr. , 1964.
Harper, Howard M. , Jr. , Desperate Faith: A Study of Bellow, Salinger, Mailer, Baldwin and Updike, Chapel Hill: Un. of No. Carolina Pr. , 1967.
Hartley, Lodwick, and George Core, eds. , Katherine Anne Porter: A Critical Symposium, Athens: Un. of Georgia Pr. , 1969.
Hartt, Julian N. , The Lost Image of Man, Baton Rouge: La. State Un. Pr. , 1963.
Hassan, Ihab, The Literature of Silence: Henry Miller and Samuel Beckett, N. Y.: Knopf, 1967.
_____, Radical Innocence: Studies in the Contemporary American Novel, Princeton, N. J.: Princeton Un. Pr. , 1961.
Heath, William, Elizabeth Bowen: An Introduction to Her Novels, Madison: Un. of Wisconsin Pr. , 1961.
Hendrick, George, Katherine Ann Porter (TUSAS, 90), N. Y.: Twayne, 1965.
Heppenstall, Rayner, The Fourfold Tradition, London: Bar-

rie and Rockliff, 1961; N.Y.: New Directions, 1961.

Hicks, Granville, James Gould Cozzens (UMPAW, 58), Minneapolis: Un. of Minn. Pr., 1966.

Highet, Gilbert, The Anatomy of Satire, Princeton, N.J.: Princeton Un. Pr., 1962.

Hilfer, Anthony Channel, The Revolt from the Village, 1915-1930, Chapel Hill: Un. of North Carolina, 1969.

Hillegas, Mark R., ed., Shadows of the Imagination: The Fantasies of C.S. Lewis, J.R.R. Tolkien, and Charles Williams, Carbondale and Edwardsville: So. Illinois Un. Pr., 1969.

Hines, Bede, The Social World of Aldous Huxley, 3rd ed., Loretto, Pa.: Mariale Pr., 1962.

Hodson, Leighton, Golding, Edinburgh: Oliver and Boyd, 1969.

Hoffman, Frederick J., The Art of Southern Fiction: A Study of Some Modern Novelists, Carbondale: So. Illinois Un. Pr., 1967.

_____, The Mortal No: Death and the Modern Imagination, Princeton, N.J.: Princeton Un. Pr., 1964.

_____, Samuel Beckett: The Language of Self, Carbondale: So. Illinois Un. Pr., 1962.

_____, The Twenties: American Writing in the Post War Decade, N.Y.: Viking, 1955.

_____, William Faulkner, 2nd ed., (TUSAS, 1), N.Y.: Twayne, 1966.

_____, and Olga W. Vickery, eds., William Faulkner: Three Decades of Criticism, East Lansing: Michigan State Un. Pr., 1960. NOTE: References in the text to Hoffman, F.J., and O.W. Vickery, eds., William Faulkner, are to the above.

_____, William Faulkner: Two Decades of Criticism, East Lansing: Michigan State Coll. Pr., 1951.

Hoffmann, Charles G., Joyce Cary: The Comedy of Freedom (Critical Essays in Modern Literature), Pittsburgh: Un. of Pittsburgh Pr., 1964.

Hollis, Christopher, Evelyn Waugh (Writers and Their Work, No. 46), Rev. ed., London: Longmans, Green, 1958.

_____, A Study of George Orwell; The Man and His Works, N.Y.: Regnery, 1956; London: Hollis and Carter, 1956.

Holman, C. Hugh, Three Modes of Modern Southern Fiction: Ellen Glasgow, William Faulkner, Thomas Wolfe (Mercer University Lamar Memorial Lectures, No. 9), Athens: Un. of Georgia Pr., 1966.

Hopkinson, Tom, George Orwell (Writers and Their Work, No. 39), Rev. ed., London: Longmans, Green, 1965.

597

Hovey, Richard B., Hemingway: The Inward Terrain, Seattle: Un. of Washington Pr., 1968.
Howard, Leon, Wright Morris (UMPAW, 69), Minneapolis: Un. of Minn. Pr., 1968.
Howe, Irving, ed., Orwell's NINETEEN EIGHTY-FOUR: Text, Sources, Criticism (Harbrace Sourcebooks), N.Y.: Harcourt, Brace, 1963.
_____, Politics and the Novel, N.Y.: Horizon Pr.; Meridian Books, 1957.
_____, William Faulkner: A Critical Study, 2nd rev. ed., N.Y.: Vintage, 1962.
_____, A World More Attractive; A View of Modern Literature and Politics, N.Y.: Horizon Pr., 1963.
Hughes, David, J.B. Priestley: An Informal Study of his Work, London: R. Hart-Davis, 1958.
Humphrey, Robert, Stream of Consciousness in the Modern Novel, Berkeley and Los Angeles: Un. of California Pr., 1954.
Hunt, John W., William Faulkner: Art in Theological Tension, Syracuse, N.Y.: Syracuse Un. Pr., 1965.
Hyman, Stanley Edgar, Flannery O'Connor (UMPAW, 54), Minneapolis: Un. of Minn. Pr., 1966.
_____, Standards: A Chronicle of Books for Our Time, N.Y.: Horizon Pr., 1966.
Hynes, Samuel, William Golding (CEMW, 2), N.Y.: Columbia Un. Pr., 1964.

International Literary Annual, No. 2, ed. by John Wain, N.Y.: Criterion Books, 1959.
International Literary Annual, No. 3, ed. by Arthur Boyars and Pamela Lyon, London: John Calder, 1961.
Isaacs, Neil, Eudora Welty (Southern Writers Series, No. 8), Austin: Steck-Vaughn, 1969.
_____, and Rose A. Zimbardo, eds., Tolkien and the Critics: Essays on J.R.R. Tolkien's THE LORD OF THE RINGS, Notre Dame, Ind.: Un. of Notre Dame, 1968.
Isabelle, Julanne, Hemingway's Religious Experience, N.Y.: Vantage Pr., 1964.

Jacobsen, Josephine, and William R. Mueller, The Testament of Samuel Beckett, N.Y.: Hill and Wang, 1964; London: Faber, 1966.
Jellema, Roderick, Peter De Vries: A Critical Essay (CWCP), Grand Rapids, Mich.: Eerdmans, 1966.
Jewish Heritage Reader; selected, with an Introduction by

Morris Adler, N.Y.: Taplinger, 1965.

Jobes, Katharine T., ed., Twentieth Century Interpretations of THE OLD MAN AND THE SEA, Englewood Cliffs, N.J.: Prentice-Hall, 1968.

Jog, D.V., Aldous Huxley; The Novelist, Bombay, India: Book Centre Private, Ltd., n.d.

Johnson, Pamela Hansford, I. Compton-Burnett, London: Longmans, 1951.

Kaplan, Harold, The Passive Voice: An Approach to Modern Fiction, Athens: Ohio Un. Pr., 1966.

Karl, Frederick R., The Contemporary English Novel, N.Y.: Farrar, Straus, 1962.

_____. C. P. Snow: The Politics of Conscience (Crosscurrents: Modern Critiques), Carbondale: So. Illinois Un. Pr., 1963.

_____, and Marvin Magalaner, A Reader's Guide to Great Twentieth Century Novels, N.Y.: Noonday Pr., 1959.

Kaufmann, Donald L., Norman Mailer: The Countdown (The First Twenty Years), Carbondale: So. Illinois Un. Pr., 1969.

Kazin, Alfred, Contemporaries, Boston: Little, Brown, 1962.

Kenyon Review. The Kenyon Critics: Studies in Modern Literature from THE KENYON REVIEW, ed. by John Crowe Ransom, N.Y.: World, 1951. Reprinted, Port Washington, N.Y.: Kennikat Pr., 1967.

Kermode, Frank, Continuities, N.Y.: Random House, 1968.

_____. Puzzles and Epiphanies: Essays and Reviews, 1958-1961, N.Y.: Chilmark Pr., 1962.

Kettle, Arnold, An Introduction to the English Novel, Vol. II: Henry James to the Present Day, London: Hutchinson, 1953.

Kinkead-Weekes, Mark, and Ian Gregor, William Golding: A Critical Study, London: Faber, 1967; N.Y.: Harcourt, 1968.

Klein, Marcus, After Alienation: American Novels in Mid-Century, Cleveland: World, 1962; Meridian, 1965.

Kohn, Lynette, Graham Greene: The Major Novels (Stanford Honors Essays in Humanities, No. 4), Stanford, Calif.: Stanford Un. Pr., 1961.

Korges, James, Erskine Caldwell (UMPAW, 78), Minneapolis: Un. of Minnesota Pr., 1969.

Kostelanetz, Richard, ed., The New American Arts, N.Y.: Horizon, 1965.

_____, ed., On Contemporary Literature, N.Y.: Avon, 1964.

Krause, Sydney J., ed., Essays on Determinism in American Literature (Kent Studies in English, No. 1), Kent, Ohio: Kent State Un. Pr., 1964.

Kunkel, Frances L., The Labyrinthine Ways of Graham Greene, N.Y.: Sheed and Ward, 1959.

Langford, Richard E., ed., Essays in Modern American Literature, DeLand, Fla.: Stetson Un. Pr., 1963.

————, and William E. Taylor, eds., The Twenties, Poetry and Prose: 20 Critical Essays, DeLand, Fla.: Everett Edwards Pr., 1966.

Lanzinger, Klaus, ed., Americana-Austriaca: Fetschrift des Amerika-Instituts der Universität Innsbruck anglässlich seines zehnjährigen Besthens (Beiträge zur Amerikakunde, Band 1), Wein, Stuttgart: W. Braumüller Univ.-Verl., 1966.

Larsen, Golden L., The Dark Descent: Social Change and Moral Responsibility in the Novels of Joyce Cary, N.Y.: Roy, 1966.

Laser, Marvin, and Norman Fruman, eds., Studies in J.D. Salinger: Reviews, Essays, and Critiques of THE CATCHER IN THE RYE and Other Fiction, N.Y.: Odyssey, 1963.

Lee, James W., John Braine (TEAS. 62), N.Y.: Twayne, 1968.

————, William Humphrey (Southwest Writers Series, 7), Austin: Steck-Vaughn, 1967.

Lee, Robert A., Orwell's Fiction, Notre Dame, Ind.: Un. of Notre Dame Pr., 1969.

Leeds, Barry H., The Structured Vision of Norman Mailer, N.Y.: New York Un. Pr., 1969.

LeStourgeon, Diana E., Rosamond Lehmann (TEAS), N.Y.: Twayne, 1965.

Levi, Albert W., Literature, Philosophy, and the Imagination, Bloomington: Indiana Un. Pr., 1962.

Lewis, R.W.B., The Picaresque Saint: Representative Figures in Contemporary Fiction, Philadelphia: Lippincott, 1959.

————, Trials of the Word: Essays in American Literature and the Humanistic Tradition, New Haven and London: Yale Un. Pr., 1965.

Lewis, Robert W., Jr., Hemingway on Love, Austin: Un. of Texas Pr., 1965.

Lewis, Sinclair, The Man from Main Street: A Sinclair Lewis Reader; Selected Essays and Other Writings, 1904-1950; ed. by Harry E. Maule and Melville H. Cane, N.Y.: Random House, 1953.

Leyburn, Ellen Douglass, <u>Satiric Allegory: Mirror of Man</u> (Yale Studies in English, Vol. 130), New Haven: Yale Un. Pr., 1956.

Lief, Ruth Ann, <u>Homage to Oceania: The Prophetic Vision of George Orwell</u>, Columbus: Ohio State Un. Pr., 1969.

Lisca, Peter, <u>The Wide World of John Steinbeck</u>, New Brunswick, N.J.: Rutgers Un. Pr., 1958.

Littlejohn, David, <u>Black on White; A Critical Survey of Writing by American Negroes</u>, N.Y.: Grossman, 1966.

Litz, A. Walton, <u>Modern American Fiction: Essays in Criticism</u>, N.Y.: Oxford Un. Pr., 1963.

Lodge, David, <u>Graham Greene</u> (CEMW, 17), N.Y.: Columbia Un. Pr., 1966.

Longley, John Lewis, Jr., ed., <u>Robert Penn Warren: A Collection of Critical Essays</u>, N.Y.: New York Un. Pr., 1965.

_____, <u>Robert Penn Warren</u> (Southern Writers Series, No. 2), Austin: Steck-Vaughn, 1969.

_____, <u>The Tragic Mask: A Study of Faulkner's Heroes</u>, Chapel Hill: Un. of North Carolina, 1963.

Ludwig, Jack, <u>Recent American Novelists</u> (UMPAW, 22), Minneapolis: Un. of Minn. Pr., 1962.

Lyons, John O., <u>The College Novel in America</u>, Carbondale: So. Illinois Un. Pr., 1962.

Lytle, Andrew, <u>The Hero with the Private Parts</u>, Baton Rouge: La. State Un. Pr., 1966.

McCaffery, John K.M., ed., <u>Ernest Hemingway: The Man and His Work</u>, Cleveland: World, 1950.

McCall, Dan, <u>The Example of Richard Wright</u>, N.Y.: Harcourt, 1969.

McCormack, Thomas, ed., <u>Afterwords: Novelists on Their Novels</u>, N.Y.: Harper, 1968.

McCormick, John, <u>Catastrophe and Imagination; An Interpretation of the Recent English and American Novel</u>, London: Longmans, Green, 1957.

McDowell, Frederick P.W., <u>Caroline Gordon</u> (UMPAW, 59), Minneapolis: Un. of Minn. Pr., 1966.

McKenzie, Barbara, <u>Mary McCarthy</u> (TUSAS, 108), N.Y.: Twayne, 1966.

Mackin, Cooper R., <u>William Styron</u> (Southern Writers Series, No. 7), Austin: Steck-Vaughn, 1969.

McLeod, Alan Lindsey, ed., <u>The Achievement of Rex Warner</u>, Sydney: Wentworth Pr., 1965.

_____, <u>Rex Warner: Writer</u>, Sydney: Wentworth Pr., 1960.

McNeir, Waldo, and Leo B. Levy, eds., Studies in American Literature (La. State Un. Studies. Humanities Series, No. 8), Baton Rouge: La. State Un. Pr., 1960.

Madden, Charles F., ed., Talks with Authors, Carbondale and Edwardsville: So. Illinois Un. Pr., 1968.

Madden, David, ed., Proletarian Writers of the Thirties, Carbondale and Edwardsville: So. Illinois Un. Pr., 1968.

_____, ed., Tough Guy Writers of the Thirties, Carbondale and Edwardsville: So. Illinois Un. Pr., 1968.

_____, Wright Morris (TUSAS, 71), N.Y.: Twayne, 1964.

Madison, Charles A., Yiddish Literature; Its Scope and Major Writers, N.Y.: Ungar, 1968.

Mahood, M.M., Joyce Cary's Africa, London: Methuen; Boston: Houghton-Mifflin, 1965.

Malin, Irving, ed., Critical Views of Isaac Bashevis Singer, N.Y.: New York Un. Pr., 1969.

_____, Jews and Americans (Crosscurrents), Carbondale and Edwardsville: So. Illinois Un. Pr., 1965.

_____, New American Gothic, Carbondale: So. Illinois Un. Pr., 1962.

_____, ed., Psychoanalysis and American Fiction, N.Y.: Dutton, 1965.

_____, ed., Saul Bellow and the Critics, N.Y.: New York Un. Pr., 1967.

_____, Saul Bellow's Fiction, Carbondale: So. Illinois Un. Pr., 1969; London: Feffer and Simons, 1969.

_____, ed., Truman Capote's IN COLD BLOOD: A Critical Handbook, Belmont, Calif.: Wadsworth, 1968.

Malkoff, Karl, Muriel Spark (CEMW, No. 36), N.Y.: Columbia Un. Pr., 1968.

Manheim, Leonard and Eleanor, Hidden Patterns: Studies in Psychoanalytic Literary Criticism, N.Y.: Macmillan, 1966.

Margolies, Edward, The Art of Richard Wright, Carbondale: So. Illinois Un. Pr., 1969.

_____, Native Sons: A Critical Study of Twentieth-Century Negro-American Authors, Phila. and N.Y.: Lippincott, 1968.

Marks, Lester J., Thematic Design in the Novels of John Steinbeck, N.Y.: Humanities, 1969.

Marsden, Malcolm M., ed., If You Really Want to Know: A CATCHER Casebook, Chicago: Scott, Foresman, 1963.

Martin, Carter W., The True Country: Themes in the Fiction of Flannery O'Connor, Nashville: Vanderbilt Un. Pr., 1968.

Matthews, Honor, The Hard Journey; The Myth of Man's Rebirth, N.Y.: Barnes & Noble, 1968.

Mauriac, Claude, The New Literature, N.Y.: Braziller, 1959.

Maurois, André, Points of View from Kipling to Graham Greene, N.Y.: Ungar, 1968.

Maxwell, D. E. S., American Fiction: The Intellectual Background, N.Y.: Columbia Un. Pr.; London: Routledge and Kegan Paul, 1963.

_____, Cozzens, Edinburgh: Oliver and Boyd, 1964.

Meckier, Jerome, Aldous Huxley: Satire and Structure, N.Y.: Barnes & Noble, 1969.

Meeter, Glenn, Bernard Malamud and Philip Roth; a Critical Essay (CWCP), Grand Rapids, Mich.: Eerdmans, 1968.

Meinke, Peter, Howard Nemerov (UMPAW, 70), Minneapolis: Un. of Minn. Pr., 1968.

Mesnet, Marie-Béatrice, Graham Greene and the heart of the matter, London: Cresset, 1954.

Miller, James E., Jr., J. D. Salinger (UMPAW, 51), Minneapolis: Un. of Minn. Pr., 1965.

_____, Quests Surd and Absurd: Essays in American Literature, Chicago and London: Un. of Chicago Pr., 1967.

Millgate, Michael, The Achievement of William Faulkner, London: Constable, 1966; N.Y.: Random House, 1966.

_____, American Social Fiction: James to Cozzens, N.Y.: Barnes & Noble, 1965; Edinburgh and London: Oliver and Boyd, 1964.

_____, William Faulkner, Edinburgh: Oliver and Boyd, 1961; N.Y.: Barnes & Noble, 1965.

Milne, Gordon, The American Political Novel, Norman: Un. of Oklahoma Pr., 1966.

Miner, Ward L., The World of William Faulkner, Durham, N.C.: Duke Un. Pr., 1952.

Mizener, Arthur, The Sense of Life in the Modern Novel, Boston: Houghton-Mifflin, 1964.

_____, Twelve Great American Novels, N.Y.: New American Library, 1967.

Mooney, Harry J., Jr., The Fiction and Criticism of Katherine Anne Porter, Rev. ed. (Critical Essays in English and American Literature, No. 2), Pittsburgh: Un. of Pittsburgh Pr., 1962.

_____, James Gould Cozzens: Novelist of Intellect, Pittsburgh: Un. of Pittsburgh Pr., 1963.

_____, and Thomas F. Staley, eds., The Shapeless God: Essays on Modern Fiction, Pittsburgh: Un. of Pittsburgh Pr., 1968.

Moore, Harry T., ed., Contemporary American Novelists,

Carbondale: So. Illinois Un. Pr., 1964.

_____, The Novels of John Steinbeck: A First Critical Study, 2nd ed., Port Washington, N.Y.: Kennikat, 1968.

_____, ed., The World of Lawrence Durrell (Crosscurrents: Modern Critiques), Carbondale: So. Illinois Un. Pr., 1962.

Morris, Lloyd, Postscript to Yesterday; America: The Last Fifty Years, N.Y.: Random House, 1947.

Morris, Robert K., The Novels of Anthony Powell (Critical Essays in Modern Literature), Pittsburgh: Un. of Pittsburgh Pr., 1968.

Morris, Wright, The Territory Ahead, N.Y.: Harcourt, 1958.

Moseley, Edwin M., Pseudonyms of Christ in the Modern Novel: Motifs and Methods, Pittsburgh: Un. of Pittsburgh Pr., 1962.

Mueller, William R., The Prophetic Voice in Modern Fiction, N.Y.: Association Pr., 1959.

Narasimhaiah, C.D., ed., An Introduction to Australian Literature, Brisbane: Jacaranda Pr., 1965.

Nance, William L., Katherine Anne Porter and the Art of Rejection, Chapel Hill: Un. of North Carolina Pr., 1964.

The Nation. A View of the Nation; an Anthology, 1955-1959, ed. by Henry M. Christman, N.Y.: Grove, 1960.

Nelson, William, William Golding's LORD OF THE FLIES: A Source Book, N.Y.: Odyssey Pr., 1963.

Nemerov, Howard, Poetry and Fiction: Essays, New Brunswick, N.J.: Rutgers Un. Pr., 1963.

New World Writing (13th Mentor Selection), N.Y.: New American Library, 1958.

Nilon, Charles H., Faulkner and the Negro, N.Y.: Citadel, 1965.

Noble, David W., The Eternal Adam and the New World Garden; The Central Myth in the American Novel Since 1830, N.Y.: Braziller, 1968.

O'Brien, Conor Cruise, Maria Cross: Imaginative Patterns in a Group of Modern Catholic Writers, New Edition. London: Burns and Oates, 1963; Fresno, Calif.: Academy Guild Pr., 1963.

O'Connor, William Van, ed., Forms of Modern Fiction; Essays Collected in Honor of Joseph Warren Beach, Bloomington: Un. of Indiana Pr. (Midland edition), 1959. Originally published by Un. of Minn., 1948.

_____, The Grotesque: An American Genre and Other Essays, Carbondale: So. Illinois Un. Pr., 1962.
_____, Joyce Cary (CEMW, 16), N.Y.: Columbia Un. Pr., 1966.
_____, The New University Wits and the End of Modernism (Crosscurrents/Modern Critiques), Carbondale: So. Illinois Un. Pr., 1963.
_____, ed., Seven Modern American Novelists; An Introduction, Minneapolis: Un. of Minn. Pr., 1964.
_____, The Tangled Fire of William Faulkner, Minneapolis: Un. of Minn. Pr., 1954.
_____, William Faulkner (UMPAW, 3), Minneapolis: Un. of Minn. Pr., 1959.
O'Donnell, Donat, Maria Cross: Imaginative Patterns in a Group of Modern Catholic Writers, N.Y.: Oxford Un. Pr., 1952.
O'Faolain, Sean, The Vanishing Hero: Studies in Novelists of the Twenties, Boston: Little, Brown, 1956.
Ohlin, Peter H., Agee, N.Y.: Obolensky, 1966.
Oldsey, Bernard S., and Stanley Weintraub, The Art of William Golding, N.Y.: Harcourt, 1965.
Opdahl, Keith M., The Novels of Saul Bellow: An Introduction, University Park: Penn. State Un. Pr., 1967.
Orwell, George, Such, Such Were the Joys, N.Y.: Harcourt, 1953.
Oxley, B.T., George Orwell (Literature in Perspective), London: Evans Bros., 1967; (Arco Literary Critiques), N.Y.: Arco, 1969.

Pacey, Desmond, Creative Writing in Canada: a Short History of English-Canadian Literature, Rev. ed., Toronto: Ryerson Pr., 1961.
Padovano, Anthony T., The Estranged God: Modern Man's Search for Belief, N.Y.: Sheed and Ward, 1966.
Panichas, George A., ed., Mansions of the Spirit; Essays in Religion and Literature, N.Y.: Hawthorn, 1967.
Papajewski, Helmut, Thornton Wilder, Franfurt am Main: Athenäum, 1961; N.Y.: Ungar, 1968 (Transl. by John Conway).
Parkinson, Thomas, ed., A Casebook on the Beat, N.Y.: Thomas Y. Crowell, 1961.
Pemberton, Clive, William Golding (Writers and Their Work, 210), London: Longmans, Green, 1969.
Pendry, E.D., The New Feminism of English Fiction, Tokyo: Kenkyusha, 1956.
Phelps, Arthur L., Canadian Writers, Toronto: McClelland

and Stewart, 1951.

Podhoretz, Norman, Doings and Undoings; the Fifties and After in American Writing, N.Y.: Farrar, Straus & Giroux, 1964.

Prescott, Orville, In My Opinion; An Inquiry into the Contemporary Novel, Indianapolis: Bobbs-Merrill, 1952.

Pritchett, Victor Sawdon, Books in General, N.Y.: Harcourt, 1953.

_____, The Living Novel and Later Appreciations, N.Y.: Random House, 1964.

_____, The Working Novelist, London: Chatto and Windus, 1965.

Pryce-Jones, David, Graham Greene, N.Y.: Barnes and Noble, 1967; Edinburgh: Oliver and Boyd, 1963.

Quigly, Isabel, Pamela Hansford Johnson (Writers and Their Work, 203), London: Longmans, Green, 1968.

Raban, Jonathan, The Technique of Modern Fiction: Essays in Practical Criticism, Notre Dame, Ind.: Un. of Notre Dame Pr., 1968.

Rabinovitz, Rubin, Iris Murdoch (CEMW, 34), N.Y.: Columbia Un. Pr., 1968.

_____, The Reaction Against Experiment in the English Novel, 1950-1960, N.Y. and London: Columbia Un. Pr., 1967.

Rahv, Philip, Image and Idea: Twenty Essays on Literary Themes, Rev. and enl., Norwalk, Conn.: New Directions, 1957.

_____, Literature and the Sixth Sense, Boston: Houghton-Mifflin, 1969.

_____, ed., Literature in America, N.Y.: Meridian, 1957.

_____, The Myth and the Powerhouse, N.Y.: Farrar, 1965.

Rajan, B., and A. Pearce, eds., Focus One, London: Denis Dobson, 1945.

Rajan, B., ed., The Novelist as Thinker (Focus Four), London: Denis Dobson, 1947.

Raymond, John, The Doge of Dover and Other Essays, London: Macgibbon and Kee, 1960.

Rees, Richard, George Orwell: Fugitive from the Camp of Victory, London: Secker and Warburg, 1961; Carbondale: So. Illinois Un. Pr., 1962.

Reiter, Robert E., ed., Flannery O'Connor (The Christian

Critic Series), St. Louis: Herder, 1968.

Ribalow, Harold U. , ed. , Mid-Century: An Anthology of Jewish Life and Culture in Our Times, N.Y.: Beechhurst Pr. , 1955.

Richardson, H. Edward, William Faulkner: The Journey to Self-Discovery, Columbia: Un. of Missouri Pr. , 1969.

Richardson, Kenneth E. , Force and Faith in the Novels of William Faulkner, The Hague, The Netherlands: Mouton, 1967.

Richman, Sidney, Bernard Malamud (TUSAS, 109), N.Y.: Twayne, 1966.

Rideout, Walter B. , The Radical Novel in the United States, 1900-1955; Some Interrelations of Literature and Society, Cambridge: Harvard Un. Pr. , 1956.

Rippier, Joseph S. , Some Postwar English Novelists, Frankfurt am Main: Verlag Moritz Diesterweg, 1965.

Roderick, Colin, An Introduction to Australian Fiction, Sydney: Angus and Robertson, 1950.

Rosenfeld, Isaac, An Age of Enormity: Life and Writing in the Forties and Fifties, Cleveland and N.Y.: World, 1962.

Rovit, Earl, Ernest Hemingway (TUSAS, 41), N.Y.: Twayne, 1963.

_____, Saul Bellow (UMPAW, 65), Minneapolis: Un. of Minn. Pr. , 1967.

Rubin, Louis D. , Jr. , The Curious Death of the Novel; Essays in American Literature, Baton Rouge: La. State Un. Pr. , 1967.

_____, The Faraway Country: Writers of the Modern South, Seattle: Un. of Washington Pr. , 1963.

_____, and Robert D. Jacobs, eds. , South: Modern Southern Literature in Its Cultural Setting, N.Y.: Doubleday (Dolphin Books), 1961.

_____, and Robert D. Jacobs, eds. , Southern Renascence: The Literature of the Modern South, Baltimore: Johns Hopkins Pr. , 1953.

_____, and John Rees Moore, eds. , The Idea of an American Novel, N.Y.: T.Y. Crowell, 1961.

Russell, John, Henry Green: Nine Novels and an Unpacked Bag, New Brunswick, N.J.: Rutgers Un. Pr. , 1960.

Ryf, Robert S. , Henry Green (CEMW, 29), N.Y.: Columbia Un. Pr. , 1967.

Samuels, Charles T. , John Updike, Minneapolis: Un. of Minn. Pr. , 1969.

Sandelin, Clarence K. , Robert Nathan (TUSAS, 147), N.Y.:

Twayne, 1968.

Sanders, David, John Hersey (TUSAS, 112), N.Y.: Twayne, 1967.

Sanderson, Stewart F., Ernest Hemingway, Edinburgh: Oliver and Boyd, 1961; N.Y.: Grove, 1961.

Sartre, Jean-Paul, Literary and Philosophical Essays, N.Y.: Criterion Books, 1955.

Savage, D.S., The Withered Branch: Six Studies in the Modern Novel, N.Y.: Pellegrini & Cudahy, 1952.

Scholes, Robert, The Fabulators, N.Y.: Oxford Un. Pr., 1967.

Schorer, Mark, Sinclair Lewis (UMPAW, 27), Minneapolis: Un. of Minn. Pr., 1963.

_____, ed., Sinclair Lewis: A Collection of Critical Essays, Englewood Cliffs, N.J.: Prentice-Hall, 1962.

_____, Sinclair Lewis: An American Life, N.Y.: McGraw, 1961.

_____, The World We Imagine: Selected Essays, N.Y.: Farrar, 1968.

Schulz, Max F., Radical Sophistication: Studies in Contemporary Jewish-American Novelists, Athens: Ohio Un. Pr., 1969.

Schwarzschild, Bettina, The Not-Right House: Essays on James Purdy, (Missouri Literary Frontiers Series Number 5), Columbia: Un. of Missouri Pr., 1968.

Scott, Nathan A., Jr., Adversity and Grace: Studies in Recent American Literature (Essays in Divinity, Vol. IV), Chicago and London: Un. of Chicago Pr., 1968.

_____, Craters of the Spirit: Studies in the Modern Novel, Washington, D.C.: Corpus Books, 1968.

_____, Ernest Hemingway: A Critical Essay (CWCP), Grand Rapids, Mich.: Eerdmans, 1966.

_____, Samuel Beckett, London: Bowes, 1965; Toronto: Queenswood, 1965; N.Y.: Hillary House, 1965.

Seib, Kenneth, James Agee: Promise and Fulfillment, Pittsburgh: Un. of Pittsburgh Pr., 1968.

Semmler, Clement, ed., Twentieth Century Australian Literary Criticism, Melbourne: Oxford Un. Pr., 1967.

Shannon, William V., The American Irish, Rev. ed., N.Y.: Macmillan, 1966.

Shapiro, Charles, Contemporary British Novelists (Crosscurrents), Carbondale and Edwardsville: So. Illinois Un. Pr., 1965.

_____, ed., Twelve Original Essays on Great American Novels, Detroit: Wayne State Un. Pr., 1958.

Sherman, Bernard, The Invention of the Jew; Jewish-American Education Novels (1916-1964), N.Y.: Thomas Yoseloff, 1969.

Siegel, Ben, Isaac Bashevis Singer (UMPAW, 86), Minneapolis: Un. of Minn. Pr., 1969.

Simonini, R.C., Jr., Southern Writers; Appraisals in Our Time, Charlottesville: Un. of Virginia Pr., 1964.

Simonson, Harold P., and Philip E. Hager, eds., Salinger's CATCHER IN THE RYE: Clamor vs. Criticism, Boston: Heath, 1963.

Slatoff, Walter J., Quest for Failure: A Study of William Faulkner, Ithaca, N.Y.: Cornell Un. Pr., 1960.

Slochower, Harry, No Voice is Wholly Lost...Writers and Thinkers in War and Peace, N.Y.: Creative Age Pr., 1945.

Smart, George K., Religious Elements in Faulkner's Early Novels: A Selective Concordance (UMPEAL, No. 8), Coral Gables, Fla.: Un. of Miami Pr., 1965.

Smith, Arthur James Marshall, ed., Masks of Fiction: Candian Critics on Canadian Prose, Toronto: McClelland and Stewart, 1961.

Snell, George, The Shapers of American Fiction, 1798-1947, N.Y.: Dutton, 1947. Reprinted, N.Y.: Cooper Square, 1961.

Sochatoff, A. Fred, and Others, ALL THE KING'S MEN: A Symposium, (CaSE No. 3), Pittsburgh: Carnegie Institute of Technology, 1957.

Spender, Stephen, The Creative Element; A Study of Vision, Despair and Orthodoxy among some Modern Writers, N.Y.: British Book Centre, 1954.

Spiller, Robert E., Cycle of American Literature; an Essay in Historical Criticism, N.Y.: Macmillan, 1955.

Squires, Radcliffe, Frederic Prokosch (TUSAS, 61), N.Y.: Twayne, 1964.

Stanford, Derek, Muriel Spark: A Biographical and Critical Study, Fontwell, England: Centaur Pr., 1963.

Stanford, Donald E., ed., Nine Essays in Modern Literature (La. State Un. Studies; Humanities Series, No. 15), Baton Rouge: La State Un. Pr., 1965.

Stegner, Page, Escape Into Aesthetics: The Art of Vladimir Nabokov, N.Y.: Dial, 1966.

Stegner, Wallace, ed., The American Novel; From James Fenimore Cooper to William Faulkner, N.Y.: Basic Books, 1965.

Stevens, Joan, The New Zealand Novel, 1860-1960, Wellington, N.Z.: A.H. and A.W. Reed, 1961.

Stewart, Douglas, The Ark of God; Studies in Five Modern Novelists, London: Carey Kingsgate Pr., 1961.

Stewart, John L., The Burden of Time: The Fugitives and Agrarians, Princeton, N.J.: Princeton Un. Pr., 1965.

Stimpson, Catharine R., J. R. R. Tolkien (CEMW, 41), N. Y.: Columbia Un. Pr., 1969.

Stock, Irvin, Mary McCarthy (UMPAW, 72), Minneapolis: Un. of Minn. Pr., 1968.

Stokes, Edward, The Novels of James Hanley, Melbourne: F. W. Cheshire, 1964.

Stopp, Frederick J., Evelyn Waugh: Portrait of an Artist, London: Chapman, Hall, 1958; Boston: Little, Brown, 1958.

Strachey, John, The Strangled Cry, and Other Unparliamentary Papers, N. Y.: Sloane, 1962.

Stratford, Philip, Faith and Fiction: Creative Process in Greene and Mauriac, Notre Dame, Ind.: Un. of Notre Dame Pr., 1964.

Straumann, Heinrich, American Literature in the Twentieth Century, Third rev. ed., N. Y.: Harper & Row, 1965.

Stuckey, W. J., The Pulitzer Prize Novels; A Critical Backward Look, Norman: Un. of Oklahoma Pr., 1966.

Sutherland, William O. S., ed., Six Contemporary Novels: Six Introductory Essays in Modern Fiction, Austin: Un. of Texas Dept. of English, 1962.

Swados, Harvey, A Radical's America, Boston: Little, Brown, 1962.

Swiggart, Peter, The Art of Faulkner's Novels, Austin: Un. of Texas Pr., 1962.

Symons, Julian, Critical Occasions, London: Hamish Hamilton, 1966.

T. L. S.: Essays and Reviews from The Times Literary Supplement, 1963, Vol. 2, London: Oxford Un. Pr., 1964.

T. L. S.: Essays and Reviews from The Times Literary Supplement, 1964, Vol. 3, London: Oxford Un. Pr., 1965.

T. L. S.: Essays and Reviews from the Times Literary Supplement, 1965, Vol. 4, London: Oxford Un. Pr., 1966.

T. L. S.: Essays and Reviews from The Times Literary Supplement, 1966, Vol. 5, London: Oxford Un. Pr., 1967.

T. L. S.: Essays and Reviews from The Times Literary Supplement, 1968, Vol. 7, London: Oxford Un. Pr., 1969.

Tanner, Tony, The Reign of Wonder: Naïvety and Reality in American Literature, Cambridge, England: Cambridge Un. Pr., 1965.

_____, Saul Bellow, Edinburgh: Oliver and Boyd, 1965; N. Y.: Barnes and Noble, 1965.

Tedlock, E. W., Jr., and C. V. Wicker, eds., Steinbeck and His Critics: A Record of Twenty-Five Years, Albuquerque: Un. of New Mexico Pr., 1957.

Thale, Jerome, C. P. Snow (Writers and Critics), Edinburgh
and London: Oliver and Boyd, 1965; N.Y.: Scirbner's
1965.
Thomas, Edward M., Orwell (Writers and Critics), Edin-
burgh and London: Oliver and Boyd, 1965; N.Y.:
Barnes & Noble, 1967.
Thompson, Lawrance, William Faulkner: An Introduction
and Interpretation, 2nd ed., N.Y.: Barnes & Noble,
1967.
Thorp, Willard, American Writing in the Twentieth Century
(Library of Congress Series in American Civilization),
Cambridge: Harvard Un. Pr., 1960.
Tindall, William York, The Literary Symbol, Bloomington:
Indiana Un. Pr., 1955.
_____, Samuel Beckett (CEMW, 4), N.Y.: Columbia Un.
Pr., 1964.
Trilling, Diana, Claremont Essays, N.Y.: Harcourt, 1964.
Tuck, Dorothy, Crowell's Handbook of Faulkner, N.Y.:
Crowell, 1964.
Tucker, Martin, Africa in Modern Literature: A Survey of
Contemporary Writing in English, N.Y.: Ungar, 1967.
Turnell, Martin, Graham Greene; a Critical Essay (CWCP),
Grand Rapids, Mich.: Eerdmans, 1967.

Unterecker, John, Lawrence Durrell (CEMW, 6), N.Y.:
Columbia Un. Pr., 1964.
Urwin, G. G., ed., A Taste for Living; Young People in the
Modern Novel, London: Faber and Faber, 1967.

Vande Kieft, Ruth M., Eudora Welty (TUSAS, 15), N.Y.:
Twayne, 1962.
Van Gelder, Robert, Writers on Writing, N.Y.: Scribner's
1946.
Van Nostrand, A. D., Everyman His Own Poet; Romantic
Gospels in American Literature, N.Y.: McGraw-Hill,
1968.
Vickery, Olga W., The Novels of William Faulkner; A Criti-
cal Interpretation, Rev. ed., Baton Rouge: La. State Un.
Pr., 1964.
Volpe, Edmond L., A Reader's Guide to William Faulkner,
N.Y.: Farrar, Straus, 1964.
Voorhees, Richard J., The Paradox of George Orwell (Pur-
due Univ. Studies: Humanities Ser.), Lafayette, Ind.:
Purdue Research Foundation, 1961.

611

Wagenknecht, Edward, Cavalcade of the American Novel; from the Birth of the Nation to the Middle of the Twentieth Century, N.Y.: Holt, 1952.

Waggoner, Hyatt H., William Faulkner: From Jefferson to the World, Lexington: Un. of Kentucky Pr., 1959.

Walcutt, Charles Child, American Literary Naturalism, a Divided Stream, Minneapolis: Un. of Minn. Pr., 1956.

_____, John O'Hara (UMPAW, 80), Minneapolis: Un. of Minn. Pr., 1969.

_____, Man's Changing Mask: Modes and Methods of Characterization in Fiction, Minneapolis: Un. of Minn. Pr., 1966.

Waldmeir, Joseph J., American Novels of the Second World War (Studies in American Literature, Vol. 22), The Hague, The Netherlands: Mouton, 1968.

Walker, William E., and Robert L. Welker, eds., Reality and Myth: Essays in American Literature in Memory of Richmond Croom Beatty, Nashville: Vanderbilt Un. Pr., 1964.

Warren, Robert Penn, ed., Faulkner: A Collection of Critical Essays, Englewood Cliffs, N.J.: Prentice-Hall, 1966.

_____, Selected Essays, N.Y.: Random House, 1958.

Watt, F.W., Steinbeck, Edinburgh: Oliver and Boyd; N.Y.: Grove, 1962.

Watts, Harold H., Aldous Huxley (TEAS, 79), N.Y.: Twayne, 1969.

Weatherhead, A. Kingsley, A Reading of Henry Green, Seattle: Un. of Washington Pr., 1961.

Webb, Constance, Richard Wright; A Biography, N.Y.: Putnam's, 1968.

Weeks, Robert P., ed., Hemingway: A Collection of Critical Essays, Englewood Cliffs, N.J.: Prentice-Hall, 1962.

Weigel, John A., Lawrence Durrell (TEAS, 29), N.Y.: Twayne, 1965.

Weintraub, Stanley, The Last Great Cause: The Intellectuals and the Spanish Civil War, N.Y.: Weybright & Talley, 1968.

Wescott, Glenway, Images of Truth: Remembrances and Criticism, N.Y. and Evanston: Harper and Row, 1962.

West, Alick, Mountain in the Sunlight: Studies in Conflict and Unity, London: Lawrence and Wishart, 1958.

West, Anthony, Principles and Persuasions; The Literary Essays of Anthony West, N.Y.: Harcourt, Brace, 1957.

West, Paul, Robert Penn Warren (UMPAW, 44), Minneapolis: Un. of Minn. Pr., 1964.

West, Ray B., Jr., Katherine Anne Porter (UMPAW, 28), Minneapolis: Un. of Minn. Pr., 1963.

_____, The Writer in the Room: Selected Essays, East Lansing: Michigan State Un. Pr., 1968.

West, Thomas Reed, Flesh of Steel: Literature and the Machine in American Culture, Nashville: Vanderbilt Un. Pr., 1967.

Westbrook, Max, ed., The Modern American Novel: Essays in Criticism, N.Y.: Random House, 1966.

Whitbread, Thomas B., ed., Seven Contemporary Authors: Essays on Cozzens, Miller, West, Golding, Heller, Albee and Powers, Austin: Un. of Texas Pr., 1966.

White, Ray Lewis, Gore Vidal (TUSAS, 135), N.Y.: Twayne, 1968.

White, William, comp., The Merrill Studies in THE SUN ALSO RISES, Columbus, Ohio: Merrill, 1969.

Wickes, George, Henry Miller (UMPAW, 56), Minneapolis: Un. of Minn. Pr., 1966.

_____, ed., Henry Miller and the Critics, Carbondale: So. Illinois Un. Pr., 1963.

Widmer, Kingsley, Henry Miller (TUSAS, 44), N.Y.: Twayne, 1963.

_____, The Literary Rebel (Crosscurrents/Modern Critiques), Carbondale: So. Illinois Un. Pr., 1965.

Wilson, Colin, The Strength to Dream; Literature and the Imagination, Boston: Houghton-Mifflin, 1962.

Wilson, Edmund, Classics and Commercials: A Literary Chronicle of the Forties, N.Y.: Farrar, Straus, 1950.

_____, O Canada; An American's Notes on Canadian Culture, N.Y.: Farrar, Straus, 1965.

_____, The Shores of Light: A Literary Chronicle of the 1920's and 1930's, N.Y.: Farrar, Straus, 1952.

Wolfe, Peter, The Disciplined Heart: Iris Murdoch and Her Novels, Columbia: Un. of Missouri, 1966.

Wolkenfeld, Jack, Joyce Cary: The Developing Style, N.Y.: New York Un. Pr., 1968.

Woodcock, George, The Crystal Spirit; A Study of George Orwell, Boston: Little, Brown, 1966.

_____, The Writer and Politics, London: Porcupine Pr., 1948.

Woodruff, Neal, Jr., and Others, eds., Studies in Faulkner (CaSE, Vol. 6), Pittsburgh: Carnegie Institute of Technology, 1961.

Wrenn, John H., John Dos Passos (TUSAS, 9), N.Y.: Twayne, 1961.

Wright, Andrew, Joyce Cary: A Preface to His Novels, London: Chatto and Windus; N.Y.: Harper, 1958.

Writers at Work: The Paris Review Interviews, 1st series, ed. by Malcolm Cowley, N.Y.: Viking Pr., 1958.

Writers at Work: The Paris Review Interviews, 2nd series, ed. by George Plimpton, N.Y.: Viking Pr., 1963.

Writers at Work: The Paris Review Interviews, 3rd series, ed. by George Plimpton, N.Y.: Viking Pr., 1967.

Wylder, Delbert E., Hemingway's Heroes, Albuquerque: Un. of New Mexico Pr., 1969.

Wyndham, Francis, Graham Greene (Writers and Their Work, No. 67), Rev. ed., London: Longmans, Green, 1958.

Young, Philip, Ernest Hemingway (UMPAW, 1), Minneapolis: Un. of Minn. Pr., 1959.

_____, Ernest Hemingway; A Reconsideration, University Park: Penn. State Un. Pr., 1966.

Zabel, Morton Dauwen, Craft and Character in Modern Fiction, N.Y.: Viking, 1957.

_____, ed., Literary Opinion in America; Essays Illustrating the Status, Methods, and Problems of Criticism in the United States in the Twentieth Century, Rev. ed., N.Y.: Harper, 1951.